Contributions to Political Science

More information about this series at http://www.springer.com/series/11829

Thomas Bickl

The Border Dispute Between Croatia and Slovenia

The Stages of a Protracted Conflict and Its Implications for EU Enlargement

Springer

Thomas Bickl
Brussels, Belgium

ISSN 2198-7289 ISSN 2198-7297 (electronic)
Contributions to Political Science
ISBN 978-3-030-53332-8 ISBN 978-3-030-53333-5 (eBook)
https://doi.org/10.1007/978-3-030-53333-5

This Springer imprint is published by the registered company Springer Nature Switzerland AG
The registered company address is: Gewerbestrasse 11, 6330 Cham, Switzerland

For Albin Zupanc and Karl Bickl who have proven that friendship can outdo war.

Preface

In mid-June 1991, Slovenia started to build checkpoints along the future international border with Croatia. A row over the location of one of the border posts could be solved by telephone diplomacy on the eve of both countries' declarations of independence. Almost 30 years on, the lifespan of one generation after the dismemberment of Yugoslavia, the two countries were most recently involved in a lawsuit at the EU Court of Justice over whether the territorial application of EU law required the implementation of the arbitration award from 2017 in the first place. How could it come to this? What has made the current situation so intractable? Why is it that two countries that have never been at war apparently find it so difficult to solve a minor territorial issue bilaterally and by diplomatic means?

Some may be inclined to assume a "conflict mindset" in the region for historical reasons, as some Western and other diplomats tend to do. Or is it that good-neighbourly relations that are commonplace on a local level are virtually impossible to achieve at the political level when nobody can afford to be unpatriotic?

If one is inclined to look at the wider picture of the region, an incident from early December 2016 may be worth contemplating. The President of Croatia was visiting war veterans at a Dubrovnik kindergarten to mark the 25th anniversary of the city's shelling by the Yugoslav Army (JNA) when she handed out chocolate bars along with a signed photograph of herself. The children happily ate the chocolate only to find out that an angry parent complained about the origin of the chocolate—made in Serbia—on social media. The President felt obliged to publicly apologise, promising to send Croatian products to the parents whose children had received the Serbian chocolates. The event sparked a fair amount of teasing and mockery on social media. Is "Chocolategate" perhaps more than a communication mishap?

Meanwhile, Slovenian winemakers have heavily protested at the use of "Teran", a local grape from Slovenian Istria and its Karst region, by producers from Croatian Istria. In September 2017, the Slovenian government sued the European Commission for allowing Teran to be used on the labels of Croatian winemakers, a derogation that the Commission had endorsed a few months earlier (the EU Court of Justice dismissed the Slovenian claim in September 2020). Have we witnessed a trade war between Slovenia and Croatia over a grape variety which has been part of the geographical region of Istria for more than 600 years irrespective of political borders?

Many Slovenes go on holiday in Croatia during the summer, and many citizens on both sides of the border are uncomfortable with the border dispute over what they see as a trivial question. Politicians, on the other hand, have used the border dispute in election campaigns, both in Slovenia and Croatia, and there is a lot of patriotic language to go with it.

However, what is at times purely nationalist rhetoric seems largely incomprehensible to many locals and observers alike. Croatia and Slovenia were together in the same political unit for 70 years: during the Habsburg era, during the period in which Yugoslavia was ruled by a monarchy and during the period when Yugoslavia was communist. Nevertheless, Slovenia and Croatia are relatively young States and this is perhaps why borders matter. However, both countries are now members of the European Union, where borders could be seen as administrative-territorial rather than political. After all, contemporary Europe strives for a close union between its peoples where internal borders have until recently become more symbolic rather than functional despite the major disruption to the status quo during the migration and coronavirus crises.

This book re-constructs the development of the bilateral border conflict between Croatia and Slovenia. The aim is to reveal the processes at work, the historical and contemporary circumstances, what the actors in the conflict did, at what moment they did it, and why they did it. In addition, this piece of research aims to highlight the role of the European Union and of judicial third parties in the management of the conflict. Lastly, the book will look at the precedent-setting value of the Slovenian–Croatian conflict, the attempts at resolving it and what this means for ongoing and prospective EU enlargement in South-East Europe.

In the scorching heat of late July 2015, this author would go on early morning runs from Savudrija on the Croatian mouth of Piran Bay to Sečovlje by the salt pans on the Slovenian side. Stops had to be made, passing the border checkpoints back and forth at one of the most stunning sections along the former Parenzana railway path from Trieste to Poreč. As it happened, the arbitration procedure between Croatia and Slovenia to settle the common State border imploded the very same week. And this was the moment the idea for this book was born.

Brussels, Belgium Thomas Bickl

Acknowledgements

This book would not have come into being without the considerable amount of support provided by a number of individuals. From an academic perspective, I am highly indebted to Profs. Susanne Pickel and Michael Kaeding at Duisburg-Essen University for the supervision of my doctoral research. Susanne and Michael's availability, expert guidance, and particularly helpful suggestions were outstanding. I wish to thank my fellow postgraduates at Susanne's seminar, in particular Toralf Stark and Wiebke Breustedt, for their clever reflections, and Jutta Wergen for her support. Special thanks go to Prof. Dejan Jović at Zagreb University for the inspirational chats on domestic politics, EU issues and the legacy left by the former Yugoslavia in the region. For early academic inspiration on European Union issues, I am particularly grateful to Isabelle Canu and Thomas Fischer. I would like to thank Johannes Glaeser and Irene Barrios-Kežić at Springer for their helpful suggestions and impressive availability throughout the entire publication process. My appreciation also goes to Julian Hale and my brother Martin for reading my manuscript.

The numerous interviews I had the privilege to conduct were extremely fruitful, and everyone proved remarkably open, keen, and supportive. I am highly indebted to all interviewees (listed at the end of each chapter) for their readiness to talk to me and for providing both specialist expertise and invaluable anecdotal and documentary evidence. Many civil servants, who must remain anonymous according to the rules of the game, have given me a great deal of enlightening insight into the secret workings of national, intergovernmental, and supranational diplomacy behind the scenes, which I greatly appreciate. It has been enormously rewarding and a true privilege to be on this process-tracing journey, meeting so many gifted and passionate people with strong views on what they do or did.

I have benefitted immensely from experiencing the wonderful support and inspiration from Damir Arnaut, Shakuntala Banerjee, Filip Boras, Elmar Brok, Daniel Brössler, Helene Bubrowski, Božena Bulum, Agata Byczewska, Giuseppe Cataldi, Hannelore Crolly, Andrea Čović-Vidović, Vladmir-Đuro Degan, Moritz Dütemeyer, Florian Eder, Uroš Esih, Tanja Fajon, Detlef Fechtner, Jean-Luc Feixa,

Damir Fras, Angela Franz-Balsen, Tina Freyburg, Theo Georgitsopoulos, Markus Grabitz, Mitja Grbec, Oliver Grimm, Marek Hannibal, Per Heister, Frank Hoffmeister, Helge Holleck, Stephan Israel, Marion Jeanne, Nataša Jovović, Lada Jurica, Matías Kambič, Thomas Kirchner, Milica Kotur, Thomas Krings, Ana Laća, Ulrich Ladurner, Stefan Leifert, Felix Leinemann, Stephan Löwenstein, Alen Legović, Janez Lenarčič, Pedro Lopez, Marko Makovec, Bianca Matković, David McAllister, Andreja Metelko-Zgombić, Ana Milošević, Tanja Miščević, Alexander Mühlauer, Werner Mussler, Niklaus Nuspliger, Alex Oude-Elferink, Marta Osojnik, Doris Pack, Adriana Vincenca Padovan, Augustin Palokaj, Jasna Paro, Alojz Peterle, Antonija Petričušić, Ana Polak Petrič, Bernd Posselt, Margherita Paola Poto, Boštjan Pucelj, Sebastian Ramspeck, Filip Raunić, Olli Rehn, Peter Riesbeck, Eugen Sandu, Goran Šaravanja, Mario Sestito, Christoph Schiltz, Leo Šešerko, Katarina Sinadinovska, Mojca Širok, Tina Štrafela, Lina Stenlund, Mateja Štrumelj Piškur, Jure Tanko, Nina Tavčar, Antti Timonen, Aleksandra Tomasić, Katharina von Tschurtschenthaler, Sandra Veljković, Delia Vlase, Boris Vlašić, Marko Vrevc, Slavko Vukadin, Petra von Wüllerstorf, Aleš Weingerl, Michael Weiss, Irena Zagajšek, Peter Žerjavič, and the two policemen I happened to meet at probably the best and definitely the most inspiring Istrian restaurant (just off Kaldanija). My appreciation also goes to Ivo Brekalo and Stipe Knezović for their fantastic "food for thought" (quite literally) along the way. I am highly indebted to all of you.

I gratefully acknowledge the permission given by the International Boundaries Research Unit (IBRU), Durham University, UK, to reprint the maps entitled "The Free Territory of Trieste" and "United Nations Protected Areas in Croatia 1992–1995" in Chap. 2, given by the University of Chicago Press to reprint the map entitled "The Julian Region and border changes between 1866 and 1954" in Chap. 2, given by the Permanent Court of Arbitration to reprint the map entitled "IMO Traffic Separation Scheme 2004 with designated sea lanes to and from Koper" in Chap. 6 and to reprint the two originals of the 2009 Arbitration Agreement in Appendix A, and given by the *Camera dei deputati* of the Italian Parliament to reprint the map "Fisheries Zone Italy-Yugoslavia" in the same Chapter. Further, I am grateful for the permission given by the Ministry of Foreign and European Affairs of the Republic of Croatia to reprint *note verbale* 55/2016 in Appendix B, and by the Ministry of Foreign Affairs of the Republic of Slovenia to reprint the English translation and the initialled Slovenian original of the draft bilateral agreement from 2001 (Appendices C and D).

Above all, I would like to thank my parents and my brother for their unlimited faith in my abilities, and Mila, Lorenz, and Karla, who have had to cope with me living in a parallel universe for a number of years.

Brussels
September 2020

Thomas Bickl

Contents

About the Author

Thomas Bickl Ph.D. has studied political science and international law and is passionate about conflict and EU integration in the post-Yugoslav sphere.

He researches territorial and other bilateral issues in the Western Balkans. His latest scientific paper "Bridge over Troubled Waters: The Pelješac Project, China, and the Implications for Good-neighbourly Relations and the EU" appeared in *Croatian Political Science Review*.

Abbreviations

ASI	Agreement on Succession Issues
AVNOJ	Anti-Fascist Council for the National Liberation of Yugoslavia
BiH	Bosnia and Herzegovina
BIS	Bank for International Settlements
CEE	Central and Eastern European States
CIA	Central Intelligence Agency
CIS	Community of Independent States
CJEU	Court of Justice of the European Union
COELA	Council Working Group on Enlargement
COREPER	Comité des Représentants Permanents (EU Ambassadors)
CP	Common Position
CS	Continental Shelf
CSCE	Conference on Security and Cooperation in Europe
ČSFR	Czech and Slovak Federative Republic
DCP	Draft Common Position
EC	European Community
ECJ	European Court of Justice
EEC	European Economic Community
EU	European Union
FPRY	Federal Peoples Republic of Yugoslavia
FRY	Federal Republic of Yugoslavia
FTT	Free Territory of Trieste
FYROM	Former Yugoslav Republic of Macedonia
HDZ	Hrvatska Demokratska Zajednica (Croatian Democratic Union)
HSLS	Hrvatska Socijalno-Liberalna Stranka (Croatian Social Liberal Party)
ICJ	International Court of Justice
ICTY	International Criminal Tribunal for the former Yugoslavia
IGC	Intergovernmental Conference
ITLOS	International Tribunal of the Law of the Sea

JNA	Yugoslav People's Army
LCY	League of Communists of Yugoslavia
NATO	North Atlantic Treaty Organisation
OBAR	Opening Benchmark Assessment Report
OSCE	Organisation for Security and Cooperation in Europe
PCA	Permanent Court of Arbitration
PCIJ	Permanent Court of International Justice
SDP	Socijaldemokratska Partija Hrvatske (Social Democratic Party of Croatia)
SDS	Slovenska Demokratska Stranka (Slovenian Democratic Party)
SEE	South-Eastern European States
SFRY	Socialist Federal Republic of Yugoslavia
TFEU	Treaty on the Functioning of the European Union
TO	Territorial Defence
UK	United Kingdom of Great Britain and Northern Ireland
UNCLOS	United Nations Convention on the Law of the Sea
UNPROFOR	United Nations Protection Force
US	United States of America
USSR	Union of Soviet Socialist Republics

List of Figures

List of Tables

Chapter 1
Introduction to the Border Dispute Between Croatia and Slovenia

Abstract This Chapter aims to familiarise the reader with the distinctive features of the Croatia–Slovenia border dispute, the unique context of an asymmetric power relationship during EU accession negotiations, and an awareness of the peculiarities of a bilateral dispute in the post-Yugoslav space. The introduction conceptualises the research gap that this book aims to fill in the context of bilateral conflict and EU enlargement. To achieve this, the analytical framework comprises conflict resolution and third-party-role theory strands and draws on EU enlargement approaches. It makes plain that, for Candidate Countries, there are both rationality and legitimacy considerations when it comes to fulfilling EU conditionality, and that the latter tend to play a vital role in the Western Balkans region. The research design outlines the process-tracing method that this study is based on and the crucial role of the collection of empirical data through qualitative interviews with actors, and draft or undisclosed documents. Lastly, this introductory Chapter provides a map of the book. Interviewees include a senior Croatian and a senior Slovenian civil servant.

Keywords Croatia · Slovenia · Conflict resolution · EU enlargement · Conditionality · Identity

1.1 Main Argument of This Book

The border dispute between Croatia and Slovenia as an inter-State conflict over territory has been frozen at a critical stage. It appears fair to say that the EU has in fact imported a bilateral conflict. Croatia does not recognise the arbitration award handed down in June 2017, and, in January 2020, the European Court of Justice (CJEU) ruled that it had no jurisdiction to hear the Slovenian claim that Croatia was not fulfilling its obligation in relation to the territorial application of EU law. This comes irrespective of the fact that, as the Court noted, there is, under international law, an obligation for both parties to implement the arbitration award.

T. Bickl, *The Border Dispute Between Croatia and Slovenia*, Contributions to Political Science,
https://doi.org/10.1007/978-3-030-53333-5_1

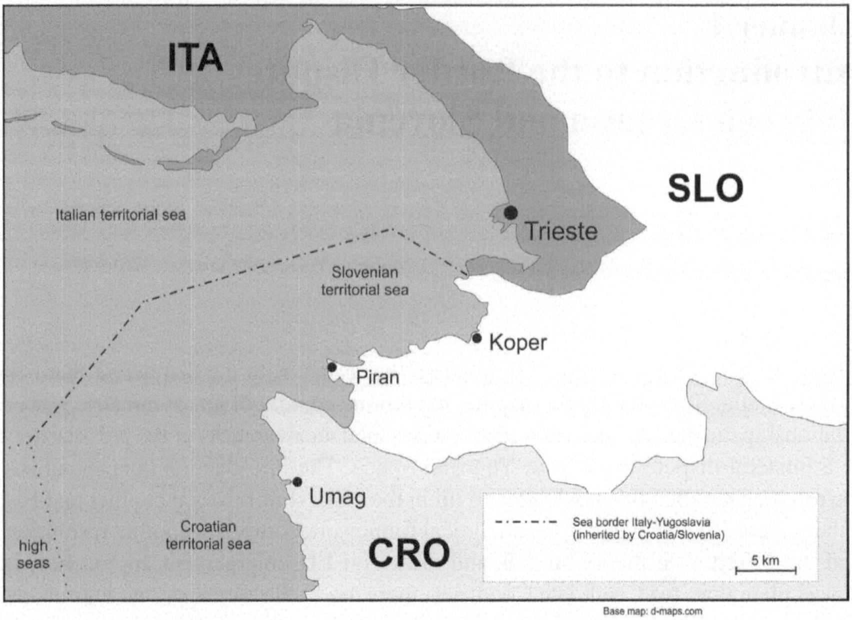

Fig. 1.1 Maritime delimitation in the Gulf of Trieste after the independence of Croatia and Slovenia in 1991 (schematic view; *Source* Author; base map: d-maps.com)

The current state of play also is a result of the dissolution of Yugoslavia in 1991. As a matter of fact, the boundaries of the Republics of the Socialist Federal Republic of Yugoslavia (SFRY) were not clearly determined or lacked determination altogether. This has led to a remarkably rock solid conflict between Croatia and Slovenia, two of Yugoslavia's successor States, almost 30 years on. It must be noted that the boundaries of the SFRY Republics have never been established expressly. There have been no such legal acts, neither by the federal parliament nor by the parliaments of the Republics (Dragićević et al. 2013: 10; Milenkoski and Talevski 2001: 93; Radan 2000: 7). The land boundary was de facto governed by the limits of the cadastral units of the municipalities or districts in the border areas of the SFRY Republics. This "cadastral delimitation", or "administrative border", became the international border after the declarations of independence of both countries in June 1991. At various spots, however, the cadastral records do overlap. As for the sea boundary, the territorial SFRY waters were fully integrated, meaning that there was no internal allocation of territorial waters by Republics. As a result, the question of maritime delimitation between Slovenia and Croatia at the time of independence was fully open (interview senior Croatian civil servant, 19-08-2016; interview senior Slovenian civil servant, 17-10-2016; see also PCA Final Award 2017: 10–11, paras 37–42; 113; see Fig. 1.1).[1]

[1] As was the case with maritime delimitation between Croatia and Bosnia-Herzegovina and between Croatia and the FR Yugoslavia (later between Croatia and Montenegro).

The border dispute between Croatia and Slovenia was a purely bilateral issue in the initial stages of the relations of the two newly independent countries after 1991. As from the mid-2000s, however, the conflict turned into a power struggle between Slovenia as an EU Member and Croatia as a Candidate Country, in particular during Croatia's EU accession negotiations in 2008/09. In a major diplomatic exercise involving the two States, the European Commission and the EU Council Presidency, the settlement of the conflict was finally externalised to a third-party arbitration tribunal. After the Croatian withdrawal from the arbitration procedure in the summer of 2015 following a major disruption due to a leaked intelligence recording of conversations between a Slovenian government representative and the Tribunal member appointed by Slovenia (*ex parte* communication), both the Tribunal's Partial and Final Awards were not recognised by the respective governments in Zagreb. At the beginning of 2020, the CJEU ruled that it has no jurisdiction under EU law with regard to its territorial application.

As a result, the real-life situation at the time of writing is such that two EU Member States continue to be in a territorial conflict over their common State border, both at land and at sea—an unparalleled situation in the history of European integration. This is all the more so, as the matter was the first-ever Art. 259 TFEU Member-State-against-Member-State case on a territorial issue that was brought before the CJEU (by Slovenia in July 2018). In fact, such a manifest territorial conflict within the EU constitutes a serious political burden for the internal political cohesion of the European Union but not just that. On an operational level, vital cross-border issues, such as fisheries or the Schengen border, which are core EU value-added elements on the ground, are hampered or blocked altogether.

This book will attempt to deliver an in-depth analysis into how this deadlock materialised. The two macro-research questions[2] centre around the *causal mechanisms* for the conflict to become ever more intractable:

- What are the specific circumstances and causal mechanisms of a bilateral conflict between an EU Member State and a Candidate Country—Slovenia and Croatia—with regard to conflict resolution?
- What are the conclusions that can be drawn from the Croatia–Slovenia case with regard to other latent or upcoming cases of bilateral conflict and its management in an EU context under very similar circumstances?

The aim is to trace back "the unfolding of events and situations over time" (Collier 2011: 824). To achieve this, one has to examine, first, the actions and behaviour of the agents and institutions of both Slovenia and Croatia as parties to the conflict, second, the third parties involved in the management of the conflict *within* the EU framework, such as the European Commission and the respective EU Council Presidencies, and third, both the externalised arbitral proceedings and the procedure before the EU Court of Justice.

Looking ahead, this book will present recommendations with regard to:

[2]The analytical framework micro-research questions are outlined in Sect. 1.3.3.

(i) A sustainable implementation of the common State border between Croatia and Slovenia including the need to take into account existing agreements and the interests of third States;
(ii) means to strengthen dispute resolution both in terms of an EU framework and concerning reform of international arbitration;
(iii) pressing bilateral issues in the ongoing and prospective accession negotiations with the Candidate Countries from the post-Yugoslav space;
(iv) increasing the credibility and predictability of the EU accession negotiation process, in particular the EU's responsiveness to positive and negative performance with regard to the Candidate Countries.

1.2 Research Gap and Contribution to the Debate

Much has been written about EU enlargement and how conditionality on the part of the EU has been perceived by the Candidate Country, and to what degree the EU requirements have been met (see, e.g., Bojinović Fenko and Urlić 2015; Böhmelt and Freyburg 2015; Grabbe 2014; Jović 2011). Generally, the causal mechanisms of and effects on processes of compliance, for both *acquis* and political criteria, have been subject to solid research. It has been demonstrated that domestic costs weighed up against the EU incentives (the rationalist perspective; see, e.g., Moravcsik 1993; Zhelyazkova et al. 2019; Schimmelfennig and Sedelmeier 2004, 2005; Schimmelfennig 2008; Vachudova 2005; Ladrech 1994), and considerations of the interdependence between human agents and the institutional structure (the constructivist perspective; see, e.g., Checkel 1998; Wendt 1999; Diez and Wiener 2009; Miošić-Lisjak 2006) of the Candidate Country actors play a vital role as to the sustainability and pace of EU accession negotiations.[3]

The research gap in this context is about how bilateral issues feed into ongoing accession negotiations and are, as a matter of fact, able to stall the process, and about whether it is possible to resolve these bilateral issues during accession negotiations. The border dispute between Slovenia and Croatia is a prototype research case. A national veto raised during accession negotiations vis-à-vis a Candidate Country is a new matter. The Croatia–Slovenia case 2008/2009 is the first of its kind. What renders it an item worth analysing in greater detail is the particular salience of the issue in question: conflict over territory. It is useful to note that this piece of territorial conflict is a legacy of the dissolution of Yugoslavia, a country whose successor States all have EU prospects. Slovenia and Croatia have already joined the EU by now, most notably in the context of the present study, however, *not* at the same time. In fact, the remaining SFRY successor States plus Albania already have the status of EU Candidate Country (except for Bosnia-Herzegovina and Kosovo) and EU accession negotiations have been underway with Serbia and with Montenegro, most recently also with North Macedonia and Albania.

[3]For the analytical framework on EU enlargement and the issue of conditionality, see Sect. 1.3.2.

To that end, and in view of the implications for the post-Yugoslav space in relation to the EU, an insight into how bilateral conflict between an EU Member State and a Candidate Country has been handled is urgently needed. The recent so-called Western Balkans Strategies of the European Commission from 2012, 2018, and 2020 have confirmed the *merit-based* approach, meaning that each Candidate Country will join the EU when it fully complies with EU conditionality individually and irrespective of the progress of other Candidate Countries. That merit-based approach, which also includes a re-prioritisation of Chapters (*fundamentals first*), is a sea change in the history of the EU's enlargement policy which, up until 2007 when Bulgaria and Rumania joined together, was based on the so-called convoy approach if there was more than one applicant country.[4] It follows from the current merit-based approach that it appears highly unlikely that the remaining SFRY successor States and Albania will be able to join at the same time. With that in mind, every time a Candidate Country joins the EU, it acquires the Member State veto power vis-à-vis remaining Candidate Countries, so conflict over bilateral issues between Member States and Candidate Countries may become self-energising.

The Croatia–Slovenia case has produced novel ways and unique efforts of conflict management, whereas this process is far from being completed. This book will analyse the roles of processes and the interplay between (i) the bilateral-level Slovenia–Croatia, (ii) the (rotating) EU Council Presidency, (iii) the European Commission, (iv) the Arbitral Tribunal as the third party entrusted with the final substantive decision, (v) the derailment of the arbitration process leading to the conflict on the common State border becoming ever more protracted, and (vi) the CJEU's ruling of non-jurisdiction in terms of EU law.

The conclusions from the analysis of the border dispute between Slovenia and Croatia are of particular and immediate salience to all Candidate Countries of the Western Balkans region. The ongoing accession negotiations between the EU and Serbia have already demonstrated that what is at stake as for bilateral conflict between the EU and prospective members is no less than (i) unresolved territorial issues from the times of Yugoslavia and (ii) the legacy of the Homeland War. Whilst the first issue relates to border delimitation at land and at sea,[5] the latter touches on very straightforward and sensitive national identity issues in the aftermath of the violent break-up of the SFRY and the very painful experience of State-building in the 1990s, such as (regional/universal) war crime jurisdiction, missing persons, or minority rights, to name but a few.

Looking ahead from the angle of EU enlargement in Southeast Europe, no research has been conducted yet as to the need to define a *new operational framework* for the resolution of bilateral disputes (i.e. institutionalised procedures, such as early-warning mechanisms or dispute resolution units in the EU enlargement process), or

---

[4]For the development of the approaches and the operational level of EU accession negotiations, see Sect. 4.2.1.

[5]Unresolved border issues include Croatia versus Serbia (along the Danube in the Baranja/Bačka region; see Sect. 6.3.2), Croatia versus Montenegro (final settlement of the provisional agreement on the sea border around Prevlaka/Outer Herceg Novi Bay; see Sect. 6.3.1), and Croatia versus Bosnia-Herzegovina (maritime access to Neum; see Sect. 6.3.5).

novel approaches to the substantive issues at dispute (such as maritime and territorial delimitation issues between the SFRY successor States). The Croatia–Slovenia case constitutes a precedent in dispute resolution in general and in handling particular circumstances and sensitivities of the post-Yugoslav region. When all is said and done, all current and prospective Candidate Countries (Turkey aside, for fairly obvious reasons of moving away from the EU) are located in the Western Balkans region. And it is the countries from this region which are closest to the EU in both a geographical and a time dimension.

The need to resolve bilateral disputes ahead of EU accession has been the mantra of the European Commission and the Member States for many years. Yet, *how* this can be achieved has remained highly obscure. This study will want to shed light on the efforts in that regard in the border conflict between Croatia and Slovenia, and on the way ahead by concluding with practitioner-proof recommendations.

1.3 Analytical Framework: Conflict Resolution and EU Enlargement

This section will outline several theory approaches on (i) conflict analysis and dispute resolution, and (ii) EU enlargement in order to develop the analytical framework with its research questions. This tool kit will inform the process-tracing[6] in this study. It is important to note that the approaches are not clear-cut "alternatives" to one another. Neither should they be seen as mutually exclusive. Yet, they do highlight distinctive features of conflict analysis and resolution, which is why we look at them individually before merging them into an appropriate analytical framework.

1.3.1 Conflict Resolution

The major theory strands outlined below can be grouped into (i) conflict origins based on *needs* and the *third-party role* in dispute resolution, (ii) conflict based on *rational* or strategic considerations, (iii) the *dynamic* aspect of conflict,[7] and (iv) *judicial* conflict resolution.

1.3.1.1 Human Needs and Third-Party Role in Conflict Resolution

The human needs theory on the ontological needs of human beings (Azar 1990; Burton 1990) first of all posits that "individuals strive to fulfil their developmental

[6]For the process-tracing method, see the research design in Sect. 1.4.

[7]The typology (i)–(iii) is taken from Wallensteen (2015), albeit in an individual fashion as for the order of the strands, and the choice of scholars' works representing them.

human needs through the formation of identity groups". In the group aspect of conflict, Azar follows early writers such as Coser (1964), an American sociologist, and differentiates between three types of ontological needs: *security, access,* and *acceptance needs* (Azar 1990: 7–8).

A crucial point on *protracted social conflict* (*PSC*) appears to be that results of such conflicts (e.g. military victories or negotiated agreements) that do *not* satisfy basic needs "contain latent conflicts which cause further [...] manifest conflict, often involving a shift or spill-over in issues and actors". He diagnoses that the intensification of conflict in developing countries "proved to be devastating in terms of physical, psychological, political and economic costs" (Azar 1990: 13).

Further on the context of needs, Burton distinguishes between *needs, values*, and *interests. Needs* are "non-negotiable" and "universal in the human species". When the needs are not met, the individual's behaviour will inevitably lead to what is "outside the norms of the society". *Values* are "ideas, habits, customs and beliefs that are a characteristic of particular social communities" leading to the formation of "identity groups through which the individual operates in the pursuit of [...] security and cultural identity". He contends that it is the very values which have divided Northern Ireland and other multi-ethnic societies. *Interests*, according to Burton, "are negotiable" [sic], and it is very well "possible to trade an individual interest for a social gain", for example through taxation (Burton 1990: 36–38).

It is the denial of human needs, such as ethnic or cultural identity, that lies at the heart of ethnic conflicts "where boundaries have been drawn as a result of colonialism or conquest". Fundamentally, "majority rule and power sharing" is something the individual has been "coerced to accept" as an "ideological misinterpretation of the notion of democracy" which became "a source of protracted conflict in many multi-ethnic societies" (Burton 1990: 39).

"The distinction between the concepts of needs, values and interests seeks to be analytical, revealing the underlying sources of conflict rather than merely negotiating from fixed positions of relative power" (Burton 1990: 39). Notably, this view is in stark contrast to neo-realist perceptions of international relations which are power-based and where peace tends to be equated with military power (e.g. Morgenthau 1962; see also Kriesberg 1992: 6).

Third-party role in conflict resolution

The concept of "*problem-solving* conflict resolution" abandons traditional forms of conflict management. This can be seen as a new paradigm in how behaviour and conflict are explored (Ramsbotham et al. 2015: 51–52; emphasis added). Irrespective of whether one challenges traditional forms of third-party involvement, the need for a skilled third party is acknowledged.

There is a distinction between conflict *management* and conflict *resolution*—the first being the "traditional" way of invoking containment by means of third-party coercive power, the latter "truly" overcoming the conflict by analysing its causes through the needs-based angle. This translates into the following three-component model:

- *Participation* by the parties;
- *Communication* between the parties; and
- *Third-party involvement* in terms of decision-making power (Burton 1990: 188–9).

Traditional forms of third-party involvement include several standard types.

Direct conflict:

Participation:	---------------
Communication:	-------
Third Party:	-

Full participation being obvious, communication translates into high verbal or physical interaction, and third-party involvement can be assumed at zero.

Direct negotiations:

Participation:	---------------
Communication:	--------
Third Party:	-

Here, the same component degrees are assumed as with direct conflict. The process and the outcome reflect the relative power of the parties and tend to be short-lived due to a static power relationship.

Court settlement:

Participation:	---
Communication:	-
Third Party:	--------------

With the actual participation of the parties at a low level, there is virtually no communication between the parties and the full authoritative power lies with the court with the arguments being based on legal norms and principles rather than an analysis of the values and needs of the parties.

Arbitration represents the following component degrees:

Participation:	-------
Communication:	-
Third Party:	--------------

The measured degrees as for communication and third-party power stay the same, but the participation degree is somewhat higher as the parties have a say in nominating the members of the arbitration tribunal (Burton 1990: 189–192).

The essentially new avenue here is to strive for outcomes which are positive for all (Burton 1990: 196). The differences between *coercive* and *problem-solving* approaches are demonstrated in Fig. 1.2.

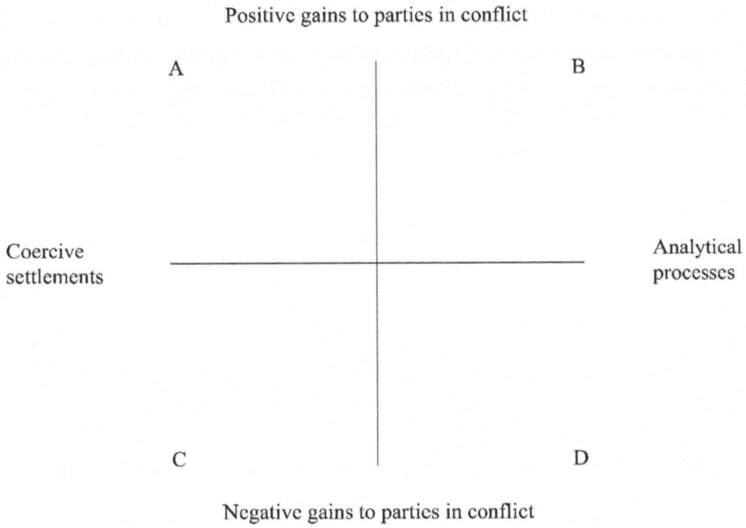

Fig. 1.2 Coercive and problem-solving approaches (*Source* Author; modelled after Burton 1990: 197)

Segment A contains imposed settlements supposed to be favourable to the parties to the conflict, for example the Dayton Peace Accord for Bosnia-Herzegovina in 1995.[8] Segment D represents a win-lose scenario where the rules are accepted. Burton provides the change of government after elections as an example. Segment C stands for "classical" authoritative-power settlements, and area B is the prototype result of the problem-solving approach (Burton 1990: 196–7).

1.3.1.2 Principled Negotiation

Principled negotiation as a rational calculation approach assumes that the parties and the third party have their individual rationality, judgements, decisions, and strategies.

> It is to decide issues on their merits rather than through a haggling process focused on what each side says it will and won't do. It suggests that you look for mutual gains whenever possible, and that where your interests conflict, you should insist that the result be based on some fair standards independent of the will of either side. The method of principled negotiation is hard on the merits, soft on the people. It employs no tricks and no posturing. Principled negotiation shows you how to obtain what you are entitled to and still be decent. It enables you to be fair while protecting you against those who take advantage of your fairness. (Fischer et al. 2012: xxvi)

[8]This author concedes that it is indeed questionable whether the Dayton Accord has in reality been favourable to the statehood of Bosnia-Herzegovina as such. For a critical view on the dilemma between unworkable institutions created by Dayton and the agreement's establishing of sustainable peace, see Chivvis (2010).

Positional bargaining associates with the major problem of "traditional" negotiating. Arguing over positions is assumed to produce unwise outcomes, and the main difficulty is that the more one defends one's position against attack, the more committed one becomes to it. In turn, the more one tries to convince the other side that it is impossible to change one's position, the more difficult it becomes to do exactly that. The result is an interest in saving face, so that it becomes ever less likely that any agreement will be able to reconcile the parties' original interests (Fischer et al. 2012: xxvi).

An enlightening example is the breakdown of the talks about a ban on nuclear testing in 1961. One of the questions was how many on-site inspections per year should the USA and the USSR be allowed to carry out on the other party's territory. Whilst the Soviet Union favoured three, the USA insisted on no less than ten. The talks actually broke down over this disagreement, whilst the nature of the "inspection" had never been discussed, so that it was not at all clear whether there would be one person inspecting for one day or hundred people for one month. In fact, little attempt had been made to reconcile verification with the mutual aim of minimal intrusion.

Besides, positional bargaining tends to be time-consuming and mostly inefficient. Starting out at maximum positions, it takes an awful lot of single steps to make concessions in order to keep the negotiating process open. Assuming extreme opening positions and small steps in terms of concessions (including mutual efforts to deceive the other party as to one's own real intentions), it will be very difficult to assess whether an agreement is feasible at all. Tactics such as threatening to walk out or stone-walling will increase the time and costs of reaching agreement as well as the risk of no deal.

Further, positional bargaining renders the whole process ever more confrontational, for example through trying to force the other side to change its position. Such behaviour tends to create anger and resentment when one side sees itself bending to the rigid will of the other whilst its own legitimate concerns go unaddressed. Positional bargaining can sometimes even shatter the relationship between the parties, and neighbours may stop speaking to each other (Fischer et al. 2012: 5–7).

Instead, principled negotiation is an alternative method beyond positional bargaining. The major aim of this method is to produce wise outcomes in an efficient and amicable manner.

These are the four guideline elements of principled negotiation:

- *People*: Separate people from the problem.
- *Interests*: Focus on interests, not positions.
- *Options*: Invent multiple options looking for mutual gains.
- *Criteria*: Insist that the result be based on objective standards.

1.3.1.3 Timing of Conflict Management Initiatives

Whilst principled negotiation focuses on the role of the negotiators themselves as parties to the negotiations, little is said about the actual role of a facilitating or mediating third party. This is where the concept of the timing of mediation initiatives comes in.

> If it is to succeed, a mediation initiative cannot be launched at just any time; the conflict must be ripe for the initiation of negotiation. Parties resolve their conflict only when they have to do so - when each party's efforts to achieve a unilaterally satisfactory result are blocked and the parties feel trapped in an uncomfortable and costly predicament. (Zartman and de Soto 2010: 5)

Ripeness can be traced and has two main elements. First, the conflicting parties must *perceive* a stalemate. Whilst perception generally is based on subjective factors, it should still be related to objective conditions that are supposed to be brought to the attention of the conflicting parties by a mediator. Second and equally based on perception, the conflicting parties must have a sense of a solution through negotiations. Ripeness can be detected by action based on research and intelligence in order to filter indicators of ripeness, such as pain, the inability to bear the political or social costs of further escalation, casualties, material costs, and expressions of a sense of a way out (Zartman and de Soto 2010: 6–7).

The "mediator's toolkit" comprises five steps:

- 1: Assess the existence and perception of a stalemate.
- 2: Assess the existence and perception of a way out.
- 3: Induce recognition of the stalemate and a way out.
- 4: Ripen the stalemate and a way out.
- 5: Position oneself as a future mediator.

Assessing the stalemate: The crucial question is whether there is a solid stalemate yet. South Africa in 1990, for instance, is a case in point where the newly elected National Party chairperson de Klerk realised that he was no longer able to protect the white minority and "control" the black majority. Besides, the legitimacy of his regime and its acceptance by the international community had been in decline. In the same vein, in the final stages of the second Iran–Iraq War in 1998, Iraq had repeatedly invaded Iran and then withdrew, calling on the neighbouring country to end the war in order to negotiate and to end warfare, which actually happened.

Assessing the way out: Objective and subjective factors are closer to one another and require sharp observation skills on the part of the (prospective) mediator. Government statements or actions that indicate directly or indirectly a readiness to talks are to be detected. In early 2006, after winning the Palestinian Legislative Council (PLC) elections, Hamas declared its intention to initiate a unilateral ceasefire vis-à-vis Israel and also offered to include Fateh in a PLC unity government. Likewise, in February 2009, the Algerian prime minister spelt out a few conditions to Morocco for the opening of the joint border, *not* mentioning, for the first time, the Western Sahara conflict.

Inducing recognition of the stalemate and the way out: The task of the mediator is to persuade the parties that a painful stalemate and the possibility of a way out—the subjective perception of both facts by the parties being absent—do exist. The idea is to divert the parties from thinking about the conflict to move to future opportunities and positive scenarios, leaving the painful stalemate behind. An example from the ground: The President of the constitutional court of Benin, Robert Doussou, persuaded the country's dictator, Mathieu Kerekou, to conclude an agreement with NGOs who had been calling for constitutional reform. Kerekou is reported to have been impressed by TV reporting on the fate of the former Romanian dictator Ceausescu when he would not give in to similar popular pressure. Persuading the parties about the possibility of the existence of an attainable goal and a way out that is worth working towards, the mediator has to devise forward-looking solutions using all the creative imagination that he or she has to promote the attainment of the post-conflict stage.

Ripening the stalemate and a way out: At this stage, the mediator has to play a more intrusive role as they must change the conditions and create a situation where neither side feels too weak to enter into negotiations with the other conflicting side. This requires a powerful mediator. Suitable tools include threats and warnings, such as hinting at positive prospects if mediation is accepted, and negative outlooks if it is turned down. For example, France summoned the conflicting parties of Ivory Coast to Paris in 2003 and they did turn up as they feared relations with France would otherwise deteriorate. Further, economic measures, positive and negative, can be powerful means to an end in that respect. The participation of Slobodan Milošević in the Dayton negotiations and the agreement over Bosnia-Herzegovina in 1995, for instance, was, according to Zartman and de Soto, only possible through the use of sanctions and even military measures.

To increase the appetite for negotiations, the conflict must be reframed, for example in turning its management into a process, starting off with a truce followed by a roadmap for talks. UN resolution 435 served as a roadmap for the independence of Namibia, which brought the parties to negotiations and an agreement in 1987. A constant floating of ideas and suggestions on the part of the mediator helps, not least to assure the parties to the conflict that the negotiations are carried out in manageable proportions.

Positioning oneself as a future mediator: This is a fallback option in case negotiations do not kick off within a short time frame. The mediator should remind the conflicting parties on a regular basis that he or she is at their disposal, that the stalemate is already there, and that it has become impossible to win the conflict anyway. When meeting the Secretary General of the Organization of American States, UN Secretary General Pérez de Cuéllar positioned himself as a prospective mediator of the El Salvador conflict as early as two-and-a-half years before he was actually given the green light by the UN Security Council in 1989 (Zartman and de Soto 2010: 11–44).

1.3.1.4 Dynamics of Conflict and Types of Intervention

More often than not, conflict is a *dynamic* process where parties to the conflict act and react to one another, and where it is indeed possible (and desirable) to influence the dynamics of a conflict and to overcome it, either the parties to it themselves, or by means of a third party.

> Human history is the history of contradictions that crystallize into conflicts, are acted out, resolved in various ways thereby transforming social reality; in this new reality new contradictions start building up, crystallize into conflicts that in turn are acted out, and so on and so forth. The process goes from infinity to infinity, it has no beginning and no end [...] But the condition for this to happen is that actors act [...]. (Galtung 1978: 7)

A conflict has its own life cycle. It can escalate, reach a violent climax in a verbal or physical meaning, and disappear and reappear.

This notion of conflict is best illustrated through the so-called conflict triangle. Conflict may thus be seen as a triangle with Contradiction (C), Attitude (A), and Behaviour (B) at its vertices (see Fig. 1.3). There is a distinction between *manifest* conflict where all three elements (Contradiction, Attitude, and Behaviour) have to be present, and *latent* conflict where Contradiction and Attitude are present, but not Behaviour. As a result, not every conflict is necessarily a manifest or full conflict (Galtung 1996: 73).

Dynamic flows can be traced in all segments of the triangle. It is important to note that a conflict can hardly be fully "solved" in terms of resolution or dissolution. "Solutions" tend not to be final resolutions or dissolutions, but only more or less stable stages in the life cycle of a conflict. One can look at the treatment of a conflict in terms of transformation. Indeed, conflicts can be transformed by means of *simplification* and *complexification*, as examples from international relations demonstrate.

Simplification: During the 1974 UN Conference on the Law of the Sea (UNCLOS), around 5000 delegates from around 150 countries were debating 150 issues or so. As nobody would have been able to handle complexity of that magnitude, some simplification was necessary—and the way to do it was through grouping actors (countries) and themes (issues). Three groups of countries emerged: landlocked (no coast), coastal countries (with coastlines), and islands (coasts only). The issues were grouped along territorial limits and rights, seabed and below, and military issues (see also Sects. 3.2 and 3.2.1).

Complexification: The preparatory meetings leading to the Conference on Security and Cooperation in Europe, CSCE (today the OSCE), in Helsinki, 1975, were handled in a remarkable way. First, to soften the adversarial stance of Cold War East–West confrontation, the third group of Non-Aligned (NA) countries was introduced (regardless of the actual varying degree of alignment). Second, the issues were divided up into three baskets: military–political (including borders), economic (including joint ventures), and other (including human rights). The outcome of the CSCE conference was such that the Cold War was thawing to some degree in that

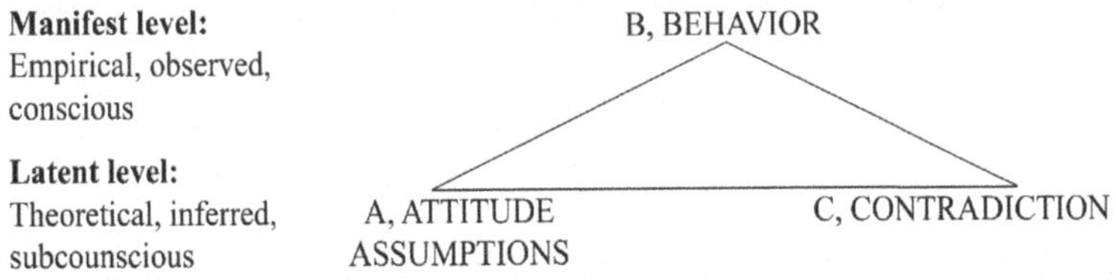

Fig. 1.3 Conflict triangle (*Source* Author; modelled after Galtung 1996: 72)

Table 1.1 Typology for conflict intervention

A	***No communication with outside parties***
Type 0	Parties keep separate, no communication with anyone
Type 1	Parties communicate with each other
B	***Asymmetric communication to outside parties***
Type 2	Outside parties provide the neutral meeting ground
Type 3	Outside parties are present encouraging the dialogue
C	***Symmetric dialogue communication with outside parties***
Type 4	Outside parties enter dialogue on conflict diagnosis
Type 5	Like 4, but + conflict prognosis
Type 6	Like 5, but + conflict therapy
D	***Asymmetric imposed communication from outside parties***
Type 7	Mediation: outside parties listen and propose solutions
Type 8	Arbitration: like 7, but + commitment of parties to accept
Type 9	Rule of law: like 8, but + procedural rules and enforceability
Type 10	Rule of man: conflict dictator imposes solution

Source Author; modelled after Galtung (1996: 104–105)

borders were confirmed, economic cooperation across blocs came into being, and the human rights process was started. In conflict triangle terms, A and B were blunted (Galtung 1996: 89–93).

Types of conflict intervention

A useful typology of conflict interventions highlights how conflict resolution works operationally and can be narrowed down to four categories (see Table 1.1):

- A: conflicting parties communicating only with each other;
- B: minimal involvement of an outside party[9];
- C: active communication involvement of an outside party;
- D: imposed conflict "solution" by means of mediation or arbitration (Galtung 1996: 103–148).

1.3.1.5 Judicial Conflict Resolution

International judicial bodies have become an ever more popular means of dispute settlement. The following approach provides a typology of explanatory variables to assess the nature of delegating the management of a conflict to a third-party judicial body. *Independence* describes the degree of autonomy of the judicial body, *access*

[9]The parties coming from outside the parties to the conflict he labels "outside parties" rather than "third parties", simply to allow for the application of his model also to multiparty conflicts instead of being tied to just two-party conflicts.

Level of independence	Selection method and tenure	International court or tribunal
Low	Direct representatives, perhaps with singe-country veto	UN Security Council
Moderate	Disputants control ad hoc selection of third-party judges	PCA
	Groups of states control selection of third-party judges	ICJ, GATT, WTO
High	Individual governments appoint judges with long tenure	CJEU
	Groups of states select judges with long tenure	ECHR, IACHR

Fig. 1.4 Independence continuum (*Source* Author; modelled after Keohane et al. 2000: 461)

measures what hurdles there are for the submission of a dispute, and *embeddedness* marks the degree of enforcement power.

Independence

This first variable looks at who is in charge of adjudication, i.e. the extent to which a judicial body and its members can carry out their reasoning and reach a judgement independently from national governments. There are two main categories. The first category deals with independent selection and tenure. The continuum ranges from direct representatives of governments to fully independent experts from a specific area in international law. What also deserves some attention is whether the future career of a judge nominated depends on a national government or whether they belong to a group of legal academics. The rules for selection and tenure do vary considerably. At the World Trade Organization (WTO), for example, there is a stable of experts preselected by groups of States. The experts to sit on a particular panel will then be nominated on demand on a case-by-case basis. Generally, the more independent the judges, the longer the tenure. In *ad-hoc* international arbitration, as in the case between Slovenia and Croatia, the selection of the tribunal members is in the hands of the parties to the dispute (Keohane et al. 2000: 459–461). The spectrum of independence as for selection and tenure is shown in Fig. 1.4.

For legal discretion, the second category, the contents of the mandate submitted by the parties to the dispute to the judicial body, is the decisive element. Very few legal bodies, such as the European Court of Justice (CJEU/ECJ[10]) or the European Court of Human Rights (ECHR), have virtually no restrictions by a mandate at all, whereas arbitral tribunals do face mandates where the legal norms and other requirements tend to be precisely fixed. It is important to note that the fiercest kind of inter-State bargaining usually ensues over the terms of the mandate for the tribunal's establishment (Keohane et al. 2000: 459–470).

Access

The second variable relates to the actors who have the legal right to approach a judicial body, i.e. whether the possibility to submit a dispute is restricted to governments or

[10]The Court is now officially referred to as the Court of Justice of the European Union (CJEU) since the entry into force of the Lisbon Treaty on 01 December 2009. Previously, it was the European Court of Justice (ECJ).

Level of access	Who has standig	International court or tribunal
Low	Both states must agree	PCA
		ICJ*, ITLOS*
Moderate	Only a single state can file suit	
	Single states files, influenced by social actors	WTO, GATT
High	Access through national courts	CJEU
	Direct individual (and sometimes group) access if domestic remedies have been exhausted	ECHR, IACHR

*unilateral or bilateral submission

Fig. 1.5 Access continuum (*Source* Author; base chart: Keohane et al. 2000: 464)

whether it is also open to individuals. Access is particularly crucial with regard to dispute resolution bodies as they are "passive" institutions that cannot initiate the treatment of a dispute themselves. The differences between the various judicial bodies in relation to access are enormous, as can be seen in Fig. 1.5.

At the high end of access, every individual citizen from a Member States of the Council of Europe can file a suit with the ECHR. The system of the Inter-American Commission on Human Rights (IACHR) is on an equal level.[11] The CJEU is of a more restricted nature as access is only possible through national courts, or by the EU institutions or by individual Member States. However, an individual may be present before the CJEU during the hearing of their case. At the lower access end, the submission of a dispute to the PCA or the ICJ is restricted to States meaning that only State governments are entitled to take legal action against one another. As for the PCA, both States need to agree on the terms (the mandate) of the dispute resolution that the judicial body is going to be entrusted with.[12] It follows that, with regard to issues that are *not* regulated by means of a treaty that the two conflicting States are party to, either State, as a matter of fact, enjoys the right of a veto (Keohane et al. 2000: 462–464).

Legal Embeddedness

This variable denotes the crucial role of the *enforcement* of judgements and the question of whether a judicial body depends on international or domestic actors for the implementation of a judgement. Keohane et al. (2000: 466) posit that issues of

[11]The IACHR is an autonomous organ of the Organization of American States (OAS) to which all 35 States of the Americas are members. The IACHR's main activity is the *Petition and Case System* open to individuals who perceive themselves as having been subject to a human rights violation. The Commission investigates the situation and can make recommendations to the Member State responsible to restore the enjoyment of human rights. For full details on the IACHR, see https://www.oas.org/en/iachr/mandate/petitions.asp.

[12]Disputes can be brought before the ICJ, a United Nations organ, either (i) through an agreement (mandate) of the two parties to the conflict, or (ii) by means of a unilateral application of one State filing suit against another State in relation to a treaty the two States are party to. That treaty must be subject to the jurisdiction of the ICJ. For a full account of the workings of the ICJ, see https://www.icj-cij.org/court/index.php?p1=1&p2=6.

Level of embeddedness	Who enforces	International court or tribunal
Low	Individual governments can veto implementation of legal judgement	GATT, arbitration
Moderate	No veto, but no domestic legal enforcement; most human rights systems	WTO, ICJ, ITLOS
High	International norms enforced by domestic courts	EU, incorporated human rights norms under ECHR, national systems in which treaties are self-executing or given direct effect

Fig. 1.6 Embeddedness continuum (*Source* Author; base chart: Keohane et al. 2000: 467)

implementation and compliance are much more problematic in international disputes than they are in well-functioning domestic legal systems.

The spectrum, again, is very wide-ranging from strong to weak control. At the low end of enforcement power is the right of member countries to an *ex-post* veto, as used to be the case with the old General Agreement on Trade and Tariffs (GATT) (now WTO) system. Rulings of GATT dispute resolution panels were subject to subsequent consensus of the parties to the conflict. The current WTO system is more advanced in this respect and has no *ex-post* veto. The only way a WTO panel decision can be reversed is by unanimous vote of all WTO members—a rather distant possibility.

On the enforcement side of affairs however, there is no domestic enforcement for WTO panel decisions. In the same vein, judgements of the ICJ do not enjoy domestic enforcement either. Yet, ICJ decisions may be actively enforced by the UN Security Council, which only happens very rarely (Scott 2014: 27–8). At the high end of the legal embeddedness spectrum are the quasi-self-enforcing judgements of the CJEU. The most striking example is indeed the legal system of the EU where national governments are considered fully bound by CJEU judgements that can, according to Keohane et al., be enforced by independent national domestic courts[13] (see Fig. 1.6). In cases where there is no possibility of domestic implementation, there is still a possibility that governments refusing the implementation of an international legal judgement may face some pressure by domestic actors and/or the public sphere as non-implementation may damage the legitimacy of a domestic government (Keohane et al. 2000: 466–467).

[13]This notion, however, is somewhat over-deterministic. Whilst it is true that all national (EU domestic) courts can be expected to accept rulings of the CJEU as the domestic courts *perceive* them as binding, there is no semi-automatism of enforcement. Most cases are brought before the CJEU through the so-called preliminary ruling procedure whereby a national court asks the CJEU to interpret CJEU legislation. The CJEU delivers its judgement, which is subsequently considered and reflected in the domestic court's final judgement.

1.3.2 EU Enlargement

This strand of research examines under which circumstances Candidate Countries are able or ready to meet the EU's political or legislative (*acquis*) requirements and how the interplay between domestic actors and the EU unfolds. Rationalist models have solidly served to explain the enlargement round of the Central and Eastern European States (CEE) in terms of compliance, whilst identity issues tend to be grasped best by a constructivist angle. To assess the compliance record for *Southeast* European (SEE) States, in particular the successor States of Yugoslavia, a combined rationalist–constructivist view appears appropriate.

1.3.2.1 EU Conditionality Model

A rationalist approach related to Liberal Intergovernmentalism[14] and concerned with EU rule transfer to Central and Eastern European countries is the *membership conditionality* or *external incentive* model. Candidate Countries are assumed to comply with conditionality if EU membership is seen by the domestic actors as a credible incentive which compensates the compliance costs borne by the incumbents. The EU is widely seen as having successfully transformed EU candidates, also referred to as democratic change or *Europeanisation*[15] (e.g. Zhelyazkova et al. 2019; Schimmelfennig and Sedelmeier 2004; Vachudova 2005; Ladrech 1994). By and large, EU enlargement is perceived as the most successful "external relation tool" (Giandomenico 2015; Phinnemore 2006).

[14]Liberal Intergovernmentalism (LI) as a rationalist model rests on a two-stage model of (i) preference formation and (ii) intergovernmental bargaining. It combines a liberal theory of preference formation with an intergovernmental approach of States engaging in power-based bargaining. States are seen as rationalist self-interest actors. In the first stage, national governments aggregate the interests of their constituencies and their own interests and spell them out as domestic preferences vis-à-vis European integration. In the second stage, the governments bring these interests to the EU negotiating table (Pollack 2001: 225; Caporaso 1998: 9). Liberal theories of international relations mean individuals and voluntary associations having autonomous interests and constituting the most fundamental actors in politics. The relationship between society and the government is one of principal and agent, and the main interest of the government is to remain in power (Moravcsik 1993: 483). Eising et al. (2017), in their empirical study on interest representation in the EU multi-level system with regard to 20 EU draft directives, have found that interest groups apply different interest representation routines and address national governments and/or the EU level depending, *inter alia*, on whether they need to mobilise opposition against or support a European Commission proposal. The authors conducted their research on interest groups from five EU Member States: Germany, the Netherlands, Slovenia, Sweden, and the UK.

[15]According to Ladrech, "Europeanization is an incremental process reorienting the direction and shape of [domestic] politics to the degree that [the] political and economic dynamics [of the EU] become part of the organisational logic of national politics and policy-making" (Ladrech 1994: 69). Ladrech used this definition—way before the accession negotiations with the CEE countries—as early as in his analysis of the 1992 referendum campaign in France over the Maastricht Treaty. Only later on did the term Europeanisation become key terminology in enlargement literature.

The constituent logic of EU conditionality is a negotiating strategy of reinforcement by reward. The EU provides external incentives for the government of a Candidate Country to comply with the EU conditions. The rule transfer can happen in two ways: first, during the process of political and economic transformation, a Candidate Country government might consider EU rules as solutions to domestic policy goals, such as the opening up of markets, and therefore adopt these rules irrespective of EU conditionality and the will to join the club. Second, the EU may provide membership and financial support as incentives for the adoption of its rules. Still, the way the countries adopt these rules relates to persuasion and learning. These processes, however, are based on EU actors socialising Candidate Countries actors rather than forcing them (Schimmelfennig and Sedelmeier 2004: 662; for the external incentives and social learning aspects, see also Zhelyazkova et al. 2019: 20–1).

There would be cases where the domestic costs of complying with EU conditionality are too high for the incumbent (authoritarian) governments in terms of *democratic* conditionality, threatening the existence of those very governments. Examples from the 1990s include Slovakia under the Mečiar government, Croatia under Tuđman, and Serbia under Milošević where democratic conditionality proved insufficient for successful rule transfer. It only became possible through a change of government (Schimmelfennig and Sedelmeier 2004: 670). Such change could also be brought about through domestic pressure by the societies in the respective countries when the threat of exclusion from the EU was felt by the domestic electorate mobilising a momentum bringing reform-minded parties to power (Vachudova 2003), such as the Račan and Đinđić governments, respectively, in Croatia and Serbia in 2000.

As for *acquis* conditionality, the CEE countries' record for EU rule adoption has been comprehensive and consistent with regard to compliance with the legal–technical adoption and implementation of hard-and-fast EU legislation. This is because the incentives of the EU were particularly credible since EU membership as such constituted the driving factor in domestic cost-benefit calculations and became the top priority with domestic policies. Domestic opposition to *acquis* rule adoption at best affected its timing, but not the implementation as such. After all, it was obvious that the European Commission and the Member States would monitor the *acquis* implementation strictly (Zhelyazkova et al. 2019: 19–23; Schimmelfennig and Sedelmeier 2004: 671–6).[16]

However, with regard to *rule-of-law* conditionality vis-à-vis the contemporary Candidate Countries from the former Yugoslavia, the record appears to be a lot less sound. Looking at judiciary reform in North Macedonia and media freedom in Serbia,

[16] In a non-enlargement context, Kaeding and Mastenbroek (2006) dismiss the hypothesis of "Goodness of Fit" (stipulating that adaptation to prospective EU legislation or implementation of agreed EU legislation is only possible if it fits the existing domestic policies and institutions). Kaeding and Mastenbroek advocate that empirical evidence suggests that it is not the primary interest of domestic actors to maintain the status quo (i.e. EU legislation is only accepted or implemented when it fits the domestic regulatory framework). Rather, the main driving factors are domestic preferences and beliefs on the part of the actors. These—the beliefs and the actors—can and do change, for instance with regard to the opening up of gas or electricity markets after a change of government.

there is considerable obstructionist action by gatekeeper elites and legacies of the past domestically. Nevertheless, there is also a lack of clarity and credibility on the part of EU conditionality. When every allowance is made that it is indeed difficult to quantify the level of achievement as for political criteria, the EU has predominantly engaged in technical issues or financial support. Yet, the main obstacles to rule-of-law reform in the region are "not technical or financial, but rather political". To that end, the EU should stop (i) ignoring some of the evident shortcomings in the Candidate Countries and (ii) refraining from a name-and-shame approach vis-à-vis the politicians responsible for obstructing democracy. For one must fear that, if rule-of-law progress remains low or non-existent, "democracy in the region will remain an empty shell despite the ongoing EU accession process" (Kmezić 2019: 96–106).

1.3.2.2 National Identity Filter Model

The most significant impact of Social Constructivism[17] on European integration theory appears to be on EU enlargement. In analysing the enlargement round of 2004 of the CEE States, the readiness of EU Member States to embrace a new intake can be explained to some degree through the notion of "collective identity" of the existing club. Heads of States and Government and Foreign Ministers, by means of rhetorical speeches, had been preaching about the reunification of the European continent for many years. As a result, they were bound not to oppose enlargement despite the fact that certain Member States may have had other domestic preferences in the first place, especially for the (justified) fear of having to downsize their slice of the EU's financial cake. Then again, the actual negotiations with the Candidate Countries were going about in a rather tight-fisted manner on the part of the Member States. On balance, the concept of collective EU identity serves to explain the general readiness to welcome newcomers, whereas the EU's conduct in the accession negotiations as such proved a rather different affair (Risse 2009: 157).

[17]The main assumption of Social Constructivism is that there is an interdependence between human agents and the institutional structure they are involved in, and that there are norms and identities arising from working and collaborating in those very structures (e.g. Checkel 1998; Wendt 1999; Diez and Wiener 2009: 10). In EU terms, the fact that Member States' representatives work with one another, together with supranational European Commission officials, and—if it is about legislation—with Members of the European Parliament, all actors adhering to the formal and informal "rules of the game", does create common "intersubjective understandings" (Pollack 2001: 234). Likewise, this creates some form of identity beyond given domestic preferences (e.g. Sandholtz 1996; Checkel 1999; Miošić-Lisjak 2006: 102). In other words, Social Constructivism posits that there are "institutional effects on social identities and fundamental interests of actors". Thus, constructivists would not be able to explain the coming about of EU institutional reform (such as the treaties of Maastricht, Amsterdam, Nice, or Lisbon) "without taking the feedback effects of previous institutional [reform] on the identities and interests of the Member States' governments and societies into account" (Risse 2009: 146). As a result, EU institutions not only shape the behaviour and identities of actors, but also influence their *preferences*—an effect which rational-choice approaches would hardly be able to grasp (Pollack 2001: 234). In short, "membership matters" (Sandholtz 1996).

The CEE enlargement can be explained fairly consistently with the rationalist conditionality model of LI (see Sect. 1.3.2.1), where compliance with the EU requirements can be expected as long as the domestic costs for the Candidate Country government do not exceed the credible incentives of EU membership. There is broad acceptance amongst scholars that democratic change has successfully been brought about with this model (e.g. Zhelyazkova et al. 2019; Schimmelfennig and Sedelemeier 2004, 2005; Schimmelfennig 2008; Vachudova 2005).

However, the tide turns when we look at the *Southeast* European (SEE) States, including the successor States of the former Yugoslavia (with the exception of Slovenia which already joined in 2004 with the CEE wave). In most of the remaining Candidate Countries of the region, governments have increasingly shown some substantial reluctance to comply with democratic conditionality. In order to explain the lack of compliance with democracy promotion, one has to go beyond entirely rationalist reasoning and introduce a constructivist variable: *national identity*.

Drawing on a concept by March and Olsen (1998), the basic concept is that national identity works as a *filter* distinguishing between whether a government follows a cost-benefit calculation (consequentialism) or acts in line with socially constructed norms and identities (appropriateness). Referring to rationalist considerations when looking at the compliance record of political membership criteria may be insufficient. Rather, there is a clear need to employ the constructivist concept of national identity as a decisive factor as to whether an issue is subsequently put to pure cost-benefit calculations (Freyburg and Richter 2010: 264).

The reasoning behind this bridge-building approach is that rationalist and constructivist explanatory factors are not contradictory. Rather, they must be seen as complementary to help explain the effectiveness of EU conditionality. National identity is regarded as a cognitive model defining the way in which actors see their interests and to what degree they are legitimate and appropriate to fit a given national identity. If an EU requirement proves partly or fully at odds with the national identity, compliance will follow the appropriateness reasoning. In turn, if a requirement is filtered as non-problematic, its further consideration can go down the consequentialist cost-benefit path. It is vital to note that either way can lead to non-compliance. It is the *reasoning* that is different (Freyburg and Richter 2010: 265–6; see Fig. 1.7).

Croatia empirically serves to illustrate the above argument. During the 1990s, Zagreb was not able to tune into EU membership conditionality as it was bound by

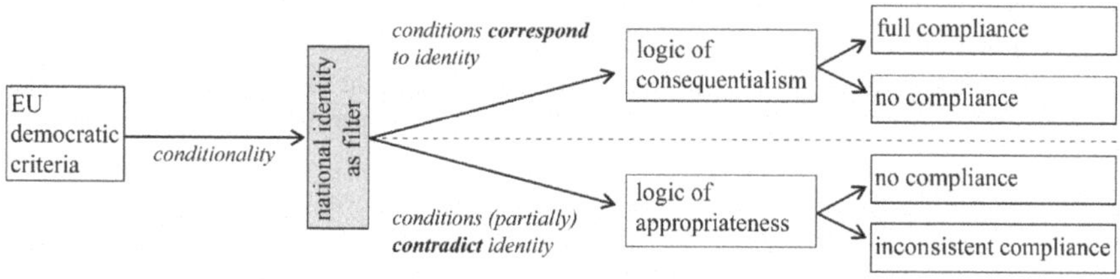

Fig. 1.7 Filter model for conditionality compliance (*Source* Author; modelled after Freyburg and Richter 2010: 266)

the war with Serbia.[18] As war tends to foster authoritarian ways of governance due to the state of emergency, the country could be regarded as a semi-authoritarian, semi-presidential system during Franjo Tuđman's term with a questionable democratic and human rights record in the 1990s. The environment for compliance with external EU conditionality did, however, substantially improve after the death of Tuđman. In 2000, a Social Democrat government under reform-minded Ivo Račan took over. His successor, Ivo Sanader who had in the meantime reformed the HDZ, strengthened and sustained the reform path directed at EU membership after winning the 2003 and the subsequent 2007 elections (Dolenec 2013: 133–4, 146; Sedelius 2006: 89; Rasza and Lindstrom 2004: 629).

The credible membership perspective on the part of the EU existed, albeit it was clear that on top of the Copenhagen criteria there would have to be full co-operation with the International Criminal Tribunal for the former Yugoslavia (ICTY). However, Croatia was facing a twofold identity: the prospect of joining a privileged group such as the EU ran in parallel with the notion of a heroic and innocent nation that fought a defensive war against Serbia (Freyburg and Richter 2010: 269). One the one hand, winning this war (without support from the EU) had strengthened nationalism in Croatia to such a degree that any conditionality approach from the EU had a hard time to achieve compliance. On the other hand, a new narrative emerged in 2000, presenting EU membership as the final step in the transition of Croatia to an independent and sovereign State (Jović 2011: 38–40).[19] EU accession was also linked to the narrative of a debalkanised Croatia returning to Europe (Subotić 2011: 315).

The EU was portrayed as a friend greatly supporting Croatia, not least through early recognition of the newly independent State in early 1992. In other words, identity convergence between the EU and Croatia was at work, a process that was started by Račan and Mesić, later to be driven forward and completed by Sanader, following the indictment of the Croatian Army generals Ademi and Gotovina by the ICTY in July 2001 (Subotić 2011: 317–8).

As for national identity as a filter, the prosecution of war criminals is highly sensitive in Croatia (as it is in Serbia and Bosnia-Herzegovina). It is important to note that the perception of the war against Serbia was subject to a declaration of the Croatian Parliament in October 2000 where it was described as "[…] a legal, legitimate, defensive, liberatory armed conflict in which Croatia defended its internationally recognized borders" (Official Gazette Croatia 102/2000, Sabor declaration 13 October 2000; see Sect. 2.5.2).

In a first phase, it proved extremely difficult for the Croatian governments to fully co-operate with the ICTY and, as a result, to extradite General Ante Gotovina, a *conditio sine qua non* for the opening of accession negotiations with Croatia by

[18]For the Homeland War 1991–1995, see Sect. 2.5.2.

[19]The sovereignty of Croatia since its independence 1991 was infringed in a number of ways. A part of its territory was for some time under de facto control of Serbia, followed by UN peacekeeping forces in the areas of Krajina and Eastern Slavonia. Through the pressure of the ICTY and the related EU conditionality, Croatia's political and justice system was affected, too (Jović 2011: 40).

mid-March 2005, the date that EU leaders had set at its Summit in December 2004. ICTY chief prosecutor Carla del Ponte had repeatedly claimed during 2003 and 2004 that the government would know the whereabouts of Gotovina but not take action, so there must have been tough cost-benefit calculations by the government in Zagreb as to whether to extradite Gotovina and still remain in power (Dolenec 2013: 152). As no extradition had taken place, EU leaders postponed the start of the accession negotiations. The Croatian government has shown *non-compliance* since the prevailing national identity, mainly nurtured by the perception of the Homeland War and the popular support of the "heroes" who helped defend the country in the war (Roter and Bojinović 2005: 451), rendered the extradition of war criminals inappropriate. On balance, national identity can be justifiably seen to be the crucial factor for *non-compliance* in this case (Freyburg and Richter 2010: 273).

In a second phase, after the EU leaders' postponing of the accession negotiations, the Sanader government increased its efforts by setting up an action plan for ICTY cooperation. By October 2005, del Ponte had declared full co-operation on the part of Croatia, so that the European Council was able to decide in favour of beginning accession talks in December 2005. Gotovina was subsequently arrested in Spain in December—subject to a decisive hint on the part of the Croatian government, according to del Ponte. The move behind the arrest of Gotovina can, according to Freyburg and Richter, be best explained in constructivist terms. Confronted with the two conflicting identities of Croatia as the innocent, heroic nation on the one hand and the desire to join the "in-group" EU, Sanader was facing a dilemma. A "face-saving" solution, however, was on offer through Gotovina's arrest in Spain, thus avoiding a humiliating extradition from Croatia (Freyburg and Richter 2010: 274–5). Still, bringing Gotovina before the ICTY was the toughest decision for Sanader as Prime Minister (interview Ivo Sanader, 19-05-2016). Ante Gotovina was convicted to 24 years in prison in April 2011 by the ICTY, but was found not guilty by the court of appeal a year-and-a-half later.[20]

1.3.2.3 Compliance Behaviour Model

A further conceptual model looks at the compliance patterns of (existing and prospective) EU Candidate Countries—Bosnia-Herzegovina, Bulgaria, Serbia–Montenegro (2002–2006), and Kosovo (2002–2008)—with equal consideration of rational and constructivist approaches. The new aspects in this model are EU socialisation and legal coercion. Socialisation works in two ways: first, the EU has an interest in shaping the normative orientations, interests, and identities of the political elite in the (existing or prospective) Candidate Countries for these interests and identities to become sustainable and long term. Second, the EU needs to teach the Candidate Countries the "rules of the game" as, once the new members sit at the table, they will take a full part in the decision- and policy-making. In a nutshell, existing EU members want reliable partners who are accustomed to the code of conduct through

[20] ICTY judgement 15 April 2011 (IT-06-90-T), decision of appeal 16 November 2012 (IT-06-90-A).

Rationality \ Legitimacy	High	Low
Benefits > Costs	**Genuine compliance**	**Rationality-based compliance**
Costs > Benefits	**Legitimacy-based compliance**	**Non-compliance**

Fig. 1.8 Compliance behaviour of EU candidate countries (*Source* Author; modelled after Noutcheva 2012: 29)

social learning. As for legal coercion, Bosnia-Herzegovina and Kosovo account for the extraordinary powers that the EU has/had in those countries. However, it has not been easy for the EU to insist on the domestic ownership of the reforms whilst at the same time maintaining the threat of legal coercion (Noutcheva 2012: 24–27).

The compliance patterns in accession countries unfold as follows: the basic assumption is that compliance depends on rational calculations and/or normative considerations of the domestic actors in power driving the compliance behaviour of governments vis-à vis EU conditionality (see Fig. 1.8).

When rationality and legitimacy contradict one another, the difference is obvious. If an actor complies in a case against their interests, i.e. costs exceeding benefits, but the perceived level of legitimacy is high, then legitimacy can be regarded as having triggered compliance. In a way, "belief change" is there ahead of policy change, which is to follow later. So, *legitimacy-based* compliance can be seen as substantial. In the same vein, if actors see their interests in line with the EU demands for reform, e.g. benefits exceeding costs, but are not convinced by the persuasive nature of the argument, the response can be seen as *rationality-based* compliance. The problem with this type of compliance is that once the material benefits have arrived, the (only selectively implemented) changes may be reversed at some point. Further, such cases may increase the heterogeneity of EU membership and the organisation as such altogether.

Lastly, when the benefits exceed the costs and EU conditionality is perceived as appropriate, high, and legitimate, there is *genuine compliance.* Political actors will carry out reforms quickly and in a sustainable way. A high level of trust in the appropriateness of measures is likely to boost norm-binding State behaviour. Conversely, when the rational cost-benefit ratio for compliance is very high whilst at the same time the level of legitimacy is very low, we are going to see *non-compliance*, which is a distinct possibility in cases of popular issues of national identity (Noutcheva 2012: 28–34). Looking at the legitimacy of EU norms through the eyes of the actors at the receiving end makes us realise that, whatever EU conditionality there is, it may not automatically be seen as a given, but rather be subject to contestation (Križić 2012: 64).

Putting things into perspective, both the *filter* model and the *compliance behaviour* model are able to combine different explanatory modes as inclusive approaches. This is good news as it helps overcome the often artificial distinction between rationalist and constructivist perspectives. The main and most vital benefit appears to be to bring theoretical frameworks closer to reality.

1.3.3 Research Questions

The research project before us has two sets of analysis: first, the causal mechanisms of the development of the border dispute between Croatia and Slovenia, and second, the implications or policy recommendations for existing or upcoming cases in the context of EU enlargement. Therefore, we have two research questions, each of which supplemented by a set of process-tracing micro-questions informed by the analytical framework discussed above.

1.3.3.1 Macro-research Questions

For the single-case study Slovenia–Croatia:

- What are the specific circumstances and causal mechanisms of a bilateral conflict between an EU Member State and a Candidate Country—Slovenia and Croatia—with regard to conflict resolution?

For the implications on EU enlargement and the related policy recommendations:

- What are the conclusions that can be drawn from the Croatia–Slovenia case with regard to other latent or upcoming cases of bilateral conflict and its management in an EU context under very similar circumstances?

On the analytical process-tracing *micro*-level, how then can one venture into reconstructing the causal mechanisms of the border conflict between Croatia and Slovenia? As a reminder, the conflict under scrutiny is a territorial dispute between two independent States, there is no use of arms, and the political power resources are not equally distributed. By the time the Arbitration Agreement was signed (4 November 2009), Croatia was not yet an EU member, but a Candidate Country. However, Slovenia was able to use its veto power as an EU member bearing in mind the Member States' unanimity requirement for enlargement issues. The fact that there was an arbitration procedure reflects the asymmetric bilateral power distribution that existed in the time span between Slovenian accession to the EU on 1 January 2004 and Croatian accession on 1 July 2013. Further, an international organisation (EU)—in its supranational (EU Commission) and intergovernmental (Member States) fashion—and judicial third parties (the Arbitral Tribunal and the EU Court of Justice) are involved.[21]

1.3.3.2 Analytical Framework Micro-questions

In view of the conflict theory strands and EU enlargement approaches discussed above, it appears useful to employ the following theory-informed micro-research questions:

Conflict issues

It is indeed vital—both for the parties to the conflict and for third parties involved—to investigate the real issues at stake. Too often, parties are not on the same wavelength when talking to one another as the *interests* have not been clearly spelt out. Sometimes, they are not put on the table in a straightforward way, which can lead to positional bargaining rather than real negotiations based on those underlying interests (Fischer et al. 2012).

It appears equally worthwhile to explore whether those interests may even represent basic human *needs*, some of which are hardly negotiable (Azar 1990; Burton 1990). Thus, the questions to follow relating to conflict issues are:

- What are the origins of the conflict?
- What are the issues at stake in the conflict?
- Have the real interests of the parties been put on the table?

Conflict dynamics

Virtually no conflict is a lock-in of the parties' positions/interests right from the beginning. Most of the time, the conflict is not static. Rather, it has been moving, from latent to manifest, and has probably taken in new issues.

There may be periods of protraction or relaxation, or even transformation in the life cycle of a conflict, where there often is no clear beginning or end (Galtung 1996). Therefore, the causal mechanisms to trace are:

- How has the conflict been moving *en route* and has it perhaps transformed?
- What can be regarded as the different stages of the conflict?
- How did deadlocks or face-saving opportunities arise?

Conflict management

Conflicts very rarely dissolve "out of the blue". To be contained or resolved, they require some form of management. On an operational level of the Croatia–Slovenia case, the choice of a third-party and subsequently their decisions as for the timing of their initiatives/involvement may play a significant role (Zartman and de Soto

[21] For an outline of the conflict line-up, see Sect. 1.1.

2010). Further, the choice of the judicial resolution body may entail a first-hand power struggle over the mandate for the arbitral tribunal (Keohane et al. 2000) or the question of the kind of judicial body most suitable for implementation from an EU law perspective. The roles of the EU Commission, the Council Presidency, and the EU Court of Justice also need to be assessed. It appears, therefore, that the following issues need to be traced:

- Under which conditions did third parties get involved?
- What third parties did get involved, why and in what role?
- What were the causal mechanisms for the timing for third-party involvement?

Actors in the conflict

There may be salient issues of a large number for potential and real conflict. It takes people, however, to make them open conflicts, to choose which issues to actively pursue or not in a real-life context. This is why we need to take a close look at the *actors* in a conflict on the ground. This entails intra-State actors, governments, the EU institutions, and judicial bodies.

After all, it is the actors who shape the conflict, move it, manage it and may overcome it, or fail to do so. The relevant causal mechanisms to address in this context appear to be:

- Who ran, escalated, or dampened the conflict and by what means?
- What was the behavioural conduct of the parties and the third parties?
- Who initiated the bilateral and the third-party involvement phases?

EU power issues

The border conflict between Croatia and Slovenia was very much in evidence during Croatia's accession negotiations with the EU. Such negotiations usually entail commonplace political and *acquis* conditionality issues (Schimmelfennig and Sedelmeier 2004). Yet, it is always an asymmetric and delicate power relationship between the EU as a whole and the Candidate Country.

This is all the more so when EU accession negotiations, which require unanimity on the part of the Member States to open and close negotiating Chapters, are loaded with a vital national interest or identity issue of the Candidate Country (Freyburg and Richter 2010; Noutcheva 2012). Thus, the following issues that need to be researched are:

- What were or have been the voluntary and coercive aspects in the conflict resolution efforts?
- What were the issues sensitive to national identity or legitimacy concerns?
- In what way did the conflict turn into a piece of *de facto* add-on EU conditionality?

1.4 Research Design

Fundamentally, there is no "case" as such. Rather, every case is constructed and defined by the researcher (e.g. Lauth et al. 2014: 35–6; Gerring 2011: 15; Peters 1998: 146).

1.4.1 Case Selection

The dependent variable of this single-case or "within-case" study (Bennett 2010: 207; Collier 2011: 823) constitutes the development of the territorial conflict between Croatia and Slovenia. The spatial boundaries are defined by the two countries' territory and their common State border area (i) at land, land-bound from Piran Bay in Istria along the hinterland up to the tripoint with Hungary, and (ii) at sea in Piran Bay and in the Gulf of Trieste.

The time period covered ranges from the independence of Croatia and Slovenia in 1991 to the Final Award of the Arbitral Tribunal at the Permanent Court of Arbitration (PCA) in June 2017 and up until the EU Court of Justice (CJEU) judgement on (in)admissibility in January 2020. The starting date can be considered an obvious choice as there were no sovereignty issues between the SFRY Republics prior to the independence declarations of Slovenia and Croatia on 25 June 1991 (and of other Republics a little later). The internal borders between the SFRY Republics were not so much of a territorial but rather of an administrative and political nature. The chosen end-date of this study reflects the unpredictability of the future dynamics of a bilateral implementation of the arbitration award or any other form of bilateral settlement. It is worth recalling that the genesis of the Arbitration Agreement and the unfolding of the arbitration procedure and the CJEU proceedings are the major focus of this study.

The independent variables are the conduct of the actors at (i) the national, bilateral government level in Slovenia and Croatia after 1991, (ii) the EU level in terms of the role of the EU Commission, the EU Council Presidencies, and other Member States between 2008 and 2020, and (iii) the level of the third-party judicial bodies, the Arbitral Tribunal 2012–2017 and the CJEU 2018–2020. In terms of (i) national bilateral governance, actors include the political level (prime ministers and foreign ministers) and the technical level (prime minister's office and foreign ministry civil servants of Croatia and Slovenia). The (ii) EU political level is represented by the Commissioner for Enlargement 2004–2009 and the Swedish EU Council Presidency. The technical level comprises the Commission services involved in drafting the Arbitration Agreement, the French EU Council Presidency staff at the Permanent Representation to the EU and Member State civil servants working in the Council Working Group on Enlargement (COELA), and the foreign ministries. The (iii) Arbitral Tribunal was composed of the three members appointed jointly and two party-appointed members (end of January 2012 to end of July 2015), and of five members of the reconstituted

Tribunal (the two party-appointed members that resigned were replaced by ordinary members) as from late September 2015.

The particular salience of this case, also referred to as the research gap (see Sect. 1.3) is the hitherto non-existent situation of two EU Member States facing an unresolved conflict over territory, here a so-called mixed dispute (maritime and land). This single-case study reconstructs the bilateral conflict over territory and its management covering the period from the end of Yugoslavia (SFRY) to the most recent stage of the lawsuit before the CJEU, with a focus on the events of 2008 to 2020. Prior to Croatia's EU accession on 1 July 2013, the border dispute had led to a blockade by Slovenia of the accession negotiations on the grounds that documents submitted by Croatia prejudiced the definition of the disputed border. In other words, Slovenia, as an EU Member, blocked the other party to the conflict, Croatia, which was not (yet) an EU Member. The inherent feature is that an issue of national interest was pursued by means of a Member State's veto power. That leverage is indeed at hand not least when bilateral attempts have failed. As a result, the power asymmetry between the two countries at the time produced some coercive momentum to resolve the *territorial* conflict or to initiate efforts to resolve it, *during* Croatia's accession negotiations. These features are unique in the history of EU enlargement.[22]

This research gap must be filled in view of the fact that we are going to see more of the same with regard to the remaining Candidate Countries of the former Yugoslavia. It must be noted that the State's dissolution has left some substantial conflictual heritage in a number of areas, not least due to the violent break-up of the country along some of its former internal borders. In fact, a very similar pattern of a bilateral issue being introduced into accession negotiations appeared to emerge in the ongoing negotiations between the EU and Serbia. In the first half of 2016, Croatia vetoed the opening of Chaps. 23 (Judiciary and fundamental rights) and 24 (Justice, freedom and security) in the EU accession negotiations with Serbia for a few months. Croatia had reservations on the grounds that the Serbian law on regional/universal war crime jurisdiction (ZORZ) interfered with the sovereignty of other States. Zagreb's veto materialised also vis-à-vis the non-implementation of a guaranteed seat for the Croatian minority in the Serbian Parliament and with regard to Serbia's co-operation with the ICTY. The veto lasted from April to July 2016.[23]

There are further open bilateral issues between Croatia and Serbia, such as missing persons (from the 1991–95 war), and it is no secret that Croatia appears determined to insist on them being solved ahead of Serbia's EU accession (see, e.g., interview

---

[22]It may be argued that Greece used the Member State leverage to (successfully) press for Cyprus's EU accession as early as during the 2004 enlargement round. It must be noted, however, that the Cyprus issue is not about a bilateral matter between a Member State and a Candidate Country on an unresolved conflict, but one where another *de facto* entity, the so-called Turkish Republic of Northern Cyprus, existed on the territory of the Candidate Country. What matters here, too, is that there were no diplomatic relations between Greece and the *de facto* entity of Northern Cyprus, and between the Republic of Cyprus and the entity in the North; i.e. there was an unresolved (territorial) conflict *within* the Candidate Country. For the EU-Cyprus issue, see, e.g., Demetriou (2008) and Rumelili (2008).

[23]For the war crime jurisdiction issue, see Sect. 6.3.3.

Kolinda Grabar-Kitarović with N1 TV, 27-01-2019). As for territorial issues, Croatia has open ones not only with Serbia, but also with Bosnia-Herzegovina and with Montenegro. The recommendations in Chap. 6 are going to address these issues, providing the link in the light of the findings from the Croatia–Slovenia case.

1.4.2 Method and Data Collection

To analyse a rather pluri-causal phenomenon such as the border dispute between Slovenia and Croatia in the context of EU enlargement, it is appropriate to opt for an *inductive* approach. This is to say that the present qualitative within-case study is going to aim at hypothesis-*generating* theory building (as opposed to *testing* of an existing theory which is usually referred to as a *deductive* approach). For the purpose of this study, the protracted conflict between Croatia and Slovenia is examined to establish the *causal mechanisms*, or causal pathways, leading to the present situation (see e.g. Gerring 2011: 10; Bennett 2010: 207–8; Muno 2016: 81).

1.4.2.1 Method

The method employed in this study is *process-tracing*. It appears to be a suitable method as, first, this book is a single-case study, and the task is to distil meaningful context from a dense layer of information related to several micro-issues. Second, the case examined is a development over time, so naturally there are processes unfolding. The availability of both (i) actors for interviews and (ii) documents from these processes renders process-tracing a suitable method.

In view of the fact that the scope of definitions for process-tracing has considerably broadened over time with some of them becoming increasingly detached from real research (Trampusch and Palier 2016: 2), process-tracing shall be understood as

> "the systematic examination of diagnostic evidence selected and analysed in light of research questions and hypotheses posed by the investigator" (Collier 2011: 823), and the discovery of "who knew what, when, and what they did in response" (Bennett 2010: 209) in a diachronic way (Gerring 2011: 7).

Process-tracing is distinctive by means of three features:

- *Causal-process observations* (*CPOs*) as the results of a *qualitative* research method corresponding to the activity of process-tracing per se are in contrast to *quantitative* research such as data set observations (DSOs; Collier 2011: 823–4).
- *Descriptive inference* is an indispensable component of process-tracing. What matters here is a comprehensive and thorough description,[24] i.e. "taking good

[24]The concept of "thick description" (Geertz 1973), in much the same vein, entails a detailed perception of a case including apt interpretations of the observations made and a familiarity with the codes of communication (Lauth et al. 2014: 55).

snapshots at a series of specific moments" to account for the unfolding of events over time, precisely "why it occurred, when it did, and in the way it did" (Gerring 2011: 18).

- *Diagnostic evidence* gained through holistic process-tracing requires prior knowledge. It does so in two ways: (i) some solid and fine-grained knowledge of the case including its history is indispensable (e.g. Trampusch and Palier 2016: 14); (ii) a conceptual framework is needed "to know in advance where to look for causal mechanisms" (Trampusch and Palier 2016: 6), and to secure the comparative merit (e.g. Muno 2016: 88).[25]

It is important to note that *qualitative* research, such as process-tracing, must be informed by theory in order to be able to look for causal mechanisms (Trampusch and Palier 2016: 6). Without a theory-based approach, an analysis remains purely descriptive (Muno 2016: 84; Faletti 2006) and may be reduced to "lazy story-telling" (Hedström and Ylikoski 2010: 10).

1.4.2.2 Data Collection

It follows from the process-tracing method outlined above that the qualitative approach applies to the two main data collection pillars of this study, interviews and documents.

Interviews

The most apt tool for a relatively small sample of respondents with highly specific expertise is qualitative interviewing. Accordingly, there are specific issues that the researcher will want to cover with individual interviewees. This is because hardly any of the interviewees plays the same role in the conflict development process of the Croatia–Slovenia border dispute as anyone else from the sample group involved in the process. Therefore, the best type of interview is the *semi-structured interview*. There are two reasons for this: first, a standardised interview obviously makes no sense since not only the individual role in the process differs (as already mentioned above). Second, one has to bear in mind the individual background of the members of the sample group and the fact that some of the questions address sensitive issues (Barribal and While 1994: 330). Further, completely unstructured interviews are off the mark, either, as they would run the risk of not capturing the research questions under consideration. Rather, the researcher will want to explore specific topics and listen to the stories of the interviewees. Personal views and anecdotal evidence are of great interest, can open up further research issues and lead to unexpected and revealing findings (Rabionet 2011: 564).

Elite interviews carried out as "in-depth interviews" with a relatively small sample of respondents (Gerring 2011: 15) play a central role in process-tracing and are at the heart of this study as elite actors are vital sources of information. They can help

[25] A single-case study is indeed comparative in itself if the applicable method includes an analytical framework that is measured against the selected case.

reconstruct an event and the causal mechanisms between events. Often, these elite actors are the only source of first-hand testimony from people directly involved in the events in question. Interviewees, provided that they were/have been central to the event, have got a strong memory, are able to produce an impartial recollection of events, also referred to as "oral history" (Grele 1996), and are instruments of utmost importance in a process tracer's toolbox (Tansey 2007). It is vital to recall, however, that expert interviews ought to be conducted in an objective-critical spirit towards both the subject matter and the expert. To that end, the interviewer–researcher must possess "co-expert" knowledge to be able to appropriately put the interview content into perspective, become aware of the interviewee's personal opinion or bias, and identify the issues of particular relevance (Pickel and Pickel 2003: 304–306; 313).

With regard to the appropriate and pertinent group of interviewees, it would include all major actors on the political and technical level in the period between 1991 and 2020. The crucial feature is involvement in the border issue. Target actors include (i) the national level of the parties to the conflict and (ii) the European level. With regard to the judicial third-party level, no interviewees have been available for this study simply due to the fact that the deliberations at the Arbitral Tribunal and at the European Court of Justice are confidential. Yet, another category of interviewees is of interest here: (iii) scholars who have a profound insight into political, historical, or legal developments related to the subject matter or the region.

On the (i) national level in Croatia and Slovenia, the interviewees were former and sitting prime ministers or foreign ministers who were directly involved in the various phases of the border dispute. They can deliver a high-level account of events, not least from the *têtes-à-têtes* with their counterparts and informal communication outside official meetings. As the tenure of government office is limited, senior civil servants who have worked on the file play an equally crucial role for the researcher. They tend to be able to provide expertise across government terms and independent of the personal or sometimes party-political lens of the actors at the political level. Further, civil servants have a profound insight into the technical details and how they have evolved over a longer period of time (i.e. covering more than one phase of the border conflict) at the working level. This is a vital point for the process tracer: bilateral relations at the technical-administrative level tend to be very robust and sustainably good-neighbourly independent of phases of clouding or brightening at the political level. After all, diplomacy is the established channel of communication in the community of States worldwide. It is important to note, in terms of traceability, that, whilst political-level actors speak on a personal account, civil servants need to stay anonymous according to the unwritten rules of diplomacy.

On the (ii) European level, interviewees from the supranational level include the Commissioner for Enlargement 2004–2009 on the political level and civil servants from the European Commission who have worked in the Commission services involved in enlargement tasks and areas in a wider sense, such as screening, benchmarking, and the operational conduct of accession negotiations, but also the areas of the judiciary, fisheries, or regional development. Members of the European Parliament were chosen on the grounds of Committee or Delegation chairpersonship or rapporteurship relevant to countries or subject matters of this study. On the intergovernmental level of the Council, the author has spoken to Member State civil servants working in the Council Working Group on Enlargement (COELA), the body where the individual Candidate Country's accession negotiation Chapters are debated and decided by unanimity[26] once accession negotiations have started.

With regard to (iii) scholars/experts, the author was able to interview experts from the field of the international law of the sea, and of international relations with particular expertise in the post-Yugoslav space.

Altogether, I conducted 76 qualitative, semi-structured interviews. A relatively small sample of respondents together with the individual specialist knowledge of the interviewees requires tailor-made questions related to the individual area of expertise. Divided up by the above categories, I interviewed 31 actors from the political level, 33 civil servants, and seven scholars/experts. Further, I conducted interviews with two journalists. Two civil servants whom I have interviewed wished to remain fully incognito and are therefore not included in the figures or the list. Some interviewees I talked to on more than one occasion. Interviewees are listed at the end of each Chapter.

As for arranging and conducting the actual interviews, I felt it was helpful to explain the background of my study and to narrow down my issues of interest as much as possible beforehand. Also, it is important to inquire as to the amount of time that the interviewee is going to be able to set aside. At the beginning of the interview, it is vital to agree, first, whether it can be attributed *ad personam* or if the respondent is going to stay anonymous, but attributed to a category (such as "civil servant"), and second, whether it may be useful to distinguish between "on the record" and "off the record". The latter issue tends to naturally unfold as the interview progresses.

With regard to the means of keeping records, I have decided not to record the interviews live, but to take notes instead. The huge advantage of this mode is that there is no focus on how something is being phrased, but rather on the contents of what is at issue. Further, this allows for an open conversation where also anecdotal evidence or lighter points can be raised and discussed. The disadvantage is that the researcher is under considerable pressure to take notes very quickly and to grasp the essential points on the spot. In addition, the interview notes should be transcribed as soon as possible after the interview when the notes can be combined with the interviewer's memory as to what the full wording of the interviewee was on any of the points taken down.

Documents

Documents are the second pillar of the data collection that this study is based on. In fact, documents are a first-hand primary source and an equally crucial instrument alongside interviews in the process tracer's toolbox. The various units of a case under scrutiny tend to spend most of their lifetime outside the public domain and

[26]For the institutional line-up and decision-making procedure of EU accession negotiations, see Sect. 4.2.1.2. On unanimity in accession negotiations, see Sect. 6.4.2.

thus resemble an iceberg. The tip of the iceberg is the final and official document. The much bigger part that is most vital to the process tracer consists of draft documents or internal documents, the invisible rest of the iceberg. The draft and internal side of documents, i.e. the genesis of documents and the relationship between internal and official documents, are obviously most helpful for detecting causal mechanisms (Trampusch and Palier 2016: 6).

To that end, the author analysed (i) documents from the public domain, and (ii) draft or unpublished documents. The particular relevance of (i) official or published documents with regard to a bilateral conflict is that they constitute either a unilateral piece of communication, such as an oral or written statement, a bilateral agreement on the disputed issue, or a mandate for dispute resolution by a third party, or pleas of law before the EU Court of Justice. Further, an official document can also constitute a decision of a third-party judicial body or a piece of communication of any third party on the conflict issue. Such documents tend to mark a particular stage of the conflict. Sometimes, they are also a good reference when compared to actions or declarations of the political level to see whether these actions/declarations fully or partly correspond to or contradict the actual document.

The particular value of (ii) draft or unpublished documents is that they, first, highlight the dynamics of a process over time compared to the final official or non-official document, especially if there is a series of drafts ahead of the final document or if there is no final document altogether. Second, draft or unpublished documents provide additional information to achieve both a maximum of precision and accuracy in the process-tracing as such, as well as novel and cutting-edge or investigative research findings.

Draft or non-official documents analysed in this study include individual pieces of national diplomatic communication, European Commission drafts, or internal drafts, submissions, or notes from the government domain in Slovenia and Croatia and the relevant EU Council Presidencies. Of particular interest here, to mention but a few, were the bilateral Initialled Draft Agreement from 2001 and the internal drafts of both Slovenia and Croatia for the submission of the dispute to the International Court of Justice (ICJ) in the aftermath of the Bled Agreement 2007. Further, the French EU Council Presidency's draft letter on the non-prejudging nature of the Croatian accession negotiation documents was crucial from the late-2008 stage of Slovenia's veto of the Croatian EU accession negotiations. The major bulk of documents relates to the period of the drafting stage of the later Arbitration Agreement (January–November 2009), such as the many non-public drafts and internal notes from the European Commission as the third-party mediator and the non-public submissions or notes of the governments of Croatia or Slovenia. In addition, pieces of internal communication from the European Commission or between the Swedish EU Council Presidency and the European Commission add to the very useful file. From the stage of the arbitral proceedings (2013–2017), letters, and *notes verbales* from Slovenia or Croatia, any communication between the Tribunal and the parties, and submissions from the parties (as far as they were made available to the author by the parties) constitute useful material. The Tribunal's (public) Partial Award and Final Award, as well as both the Opinion of the CJEU Advocate General and the Court's Judgement, are also a vital data source as they neatly reveal *ex post* some of the submissions of the parties. With regard to the implications of the bilateral dispute for EU enlargement, internal notes from the government domains of Croatia, Serbia, Montenegro, Kosovo, and the USA were of substantial analytical value.

It must be noted that, in the context of data collection, the interplay between, on the one hand, the data from the interviews conducted with the persons involved in the drafting of or negotiations on the documents and, on the other hand, the data from the actual documents was of enormous value for the analysis of the processes. Only when actors and the related documents can be brought together can a maximum of causal mechanisms and inference be traced and reconstructed.

1.5 Map of the Book

This introductory chapter contains the book's main argument and the research gap it aims to fill, the analytical framework and the research design. The analytical framework consists of several angles of conflict analysis and resolution: basic human needs and the role of third-party mediators, rational calculations (such as the distinction between negotiating positions and real interests), the dynamics of conflict (arguing that there can be phases of relaxation or protraction), and finally judicial dispute resolution (categorising legal bodies as to their independence or the enforceability of their judgements and the influence of the parties to the conflict on the work of such bodies). With regard to EU enlargement theory, rationalist and constructivist approaches are synthesised so that EU conditionality towards Candidate Countries is complemented by national identity and compliance behaviour considerations. The research design touches on the case selection, the applicable research method of process-tracing, and the means of data collection. Interviews and documents are, as the main data pillars, at the heart of this study.

Chapter 2 will deal with a condensed outline of the history of territorial, political, and violent conflict in the post-SFRY neighbourhood from the late days of the Venice Empire to the dissolution process of Yugoslavia. To that end, this Chapter highlights the role of the EU in the matter of the recognition of the successor States of Yugoslavia. Further, there is an outline of the history of the border dispute between Slovenia and Croatia, and to what extent the matter is historically loaded irrespective of EU enlargement considerations.

Chapter 3 will outline maritime delimitation issues looking at the complex geographical situation in the Northern Adriatic and the legal bases for various methods of delimitation related to the United Nations Convention of the Law of the Sea (UNCLOS). In this respect, the "lawfare" between Croatia and Slovenia (and the EU Commission) over maritime zones ahead of the 2008 deadlock at the EU accession stage is a vital prerequisite to the later analysis of the development of the border dispute at the EU stage (which is why that Chapter needs to precede

Chap. 4). Further, Chap. 3 sheds light on the methodologies used in maritime delimitation. Lastly, there is a brief outline of the rich body of jurisprudence by international courts and tribunals on maritime delimitation issues.

Chapter 4 is the focal point of the evolution and the containment efforts of the bilateral territorial conflict between Croatia and Slovenia and its causal mechanisms. The process is divided into four phases, the first one dealing with the bilateral efforts to overcome the conflict. The establishment of the Joint Diplomatic Commission between the two countries in 1993 marked the beginning of a phase which saw a Draft Agreement on the common State border in 2001, which stopped short of ratification, and a bilateral summit in 2007 declaring the will to submit the issue to a judicial body whilst no agreement could be reached subsequently over the exact terms. The second phase marked the escalation of the conflict during the accession negotiations of Croatia with the EU in 2008/2009 when a Slovenian veto on the grounds that Croatian accession documents prejudged the common State border triggered the need for mediation. The process of drafting the later Arbitration Agreement in a trilateral set-up (the EU Commission and the two States) followed by a predominantly bilateral finalising of the Agreement is the focus of tracing there. The third phase deals with the workings of the arbitral tribunal entrusted with a final verdict on the matter. From a smooth start with the selection of judges by the two parties, to the Croatian withdrawal from the arbitration procedure following a leaked conversation of Slovenia with their party-appointed arbitrator, to the Tribunal's Partial and Final Awards lacking the recognition of Croatia, and the follow-up period up until the Slovenian submission of the lawsuit before the EU Court of Justice (CJEU), the conflict became long and drawn out. The last phase analyses the CJEU judgement in January 2020, ruling that it had no jurisdiction to entertain the case, returning the conflict (which is now one about the implementation obligations stemming from the Final Award under international law) to the bilateral level.

Chapter 5, the first of two concluding chapters, discusses the repercussions of the empirical findings on the analytical framework theory strands (such as the dynamics of a conflict in terms of stages of protraction or relaxation, the interplay of bilateral and third-party conflict management modes, positions vs. interests, or new aspects of EU conditionality including national identity and legitimacy considerations).

Chapter 6 offers policy recommendations that cover four main areas. Firstly, they pinpoint matters of urgency with regard to implementation issues of the Croatian–Slovenian border including aspects of involvement of third countries. Secondly, the recommendations aim at strengthening dispute settlement, both in an EU context and with regard to reform of international arbitration. Thirdly, they address several pressing bilateral issues of immediate relevance to the prospective EU enlargement with a view to a clear risk of negotiations being held up vis-à-vis the Candidates Countries from the former Yugoslavia. And lastly, the recommendations should like to help increase the credibility and predictability of the EU accession negotiation process, in particular the EU's responsiveness to positive and negative performance with regard to the Candidate Countries.

Interviews

Senior Croatian civil servant. Zagreb, 19 August 2016.
Senior Slovenian civil servant. Brnik, 17 October 2016.
Sanader, Dr. Ivo. Prime Minister of Croatia 2003–2009. Deputy Foreign Minister 1993–2000. Velika Gorica, 19 May 2016.

References

Azar, E. (1990). *The management of protracted social conflict: Theory and cases*. Aldershot: Gower Publications.

Barribal, L., & While, A. (1994). Collecting data using a semi-structured interview: A discussion paper. *Journal of Advanced Nursing, 19*(2), 328–335.

Bennett, A. (2010). Process-tracing and causal interference. In H. Brady & D. Collier (Eds.), *Rethinking social inquiry* (pp. 207–220). Plymouth: Rowman and Littlefield Publishers.

Böhmelt, T., & Freyburg, T. (2015). Diffusion of compliance in the 'race towards Brussels'? A spatial approach to EU accession conditionality. *West European Politics, 38*(3), 601–626.

Bojinović Fenko, A., & Urlić, A. (2015). Political criteria vs. political conditionality: Comparative analysis of Slovenian and Croatian European Union accession processes. *Croatian International Relations Review, 21*(72), 107–137.

Burton, J. (1990). *Conflict: Human needs theory*. Houndmills and London: Macmillan Press.

Caporaso, J. (1998). Regional integration theory: Understanding our past and anticipating our future. *Journal of European Public Policy, 5*(1), 1–16.

Checkel, J. (1999). Norms, Institutions, and National Identity in Contemporary Europe. *International Studies Quarterly, 43*(1), 83–114.

Checkel, J. (1998). The constructive turn in international relations theory. *World Politics, 50*(2), 324–348.

Chivvis, C. (2010). The Dayton Dilemma. *Survival—Global Politics and Strategy, 52*(5), 47–74.

Collier, D. (2011). Understanding process-tracing. *Political Science and Politics, 44*(4), 823–830.

Coser, L. (1964). *The functions of social conflicts*. New York: Free Press.

Demetriou, O. (2008). Catalysis, catachresis: The EU's impact on the Cyprus conflict. In T. Diez, M. Albert, & S. Stetter (Eds.), *The European Union and border conflicts* (pp. 64–93). New York: Cambridge University Press.

Diez, T., & Wiener, A. (Eds.). (2009). *European integration theory*. Oxford: Oxford University Press.

Dolenec, D. (2013). *Democratic institutions and authoritarian rule in southeast Europe*. Colchester: ECPR Press.

Dragićević, S., Tošič, R., Stepić, M., Živković, N., & Novković, I. (2013). Consequences of the river bank erosion in the southern part of the Pannonian Basin: Case study—Serbia and the Republic of Srpska. *Forum Geografic, XI, I*(1), 5–15.

Eising, R., Rasch, D., Rozbicka, P., Fink-Hafner, D., Hafner-Fink, M., & Novak, M. (2017). Who says what to whom? Alignments and arguments in EU policy-making. *West European Politics, 40*(5), 957–980.

Faletti, T. (2006). *Theory-guided process-tracing in comparative politics: Something old, something new*. https://www.polisci.upenn.edu/~falleti/Falleti-CP-APSANewsletter06-TGPT.pdf. Accessed December 3, 2017.

Fischer, R., Ury, W., & Patton, B. (2012). *Getting to yes: Negotiating an agreement without giving in*. London: Random House.

Freyburg, T., & Richter, S. (2010). National identity matters: The limited impact of EU political conditionality in the Western Balkans. *Journal of European Public Policy, 17*(2), 263–281.

Galtung, J. (1978). *The theory of conflict and the concept of probability*. Oslo: University of Oslo.
Galtung, J. (1996). *Peace by peaceful means*. International Peace Research Institute Oslo: SAGE Publications. https://legacy.earlham.edu/~chriss/ConflictRes/pdf%20files/GaltungPeaceByPeacefulMeans_p70_114.pdf. Accessed December 3, 2017.
Geertz, C. (1973). *The Interpretation of Cultures*. New York: Basic Books.
Gerring, J. (2011). The case study: What it is and what it does. In R. Goodin (Ed.), *The Oxford handbook of political science* (pp. 1–43). Oxford: Oxford University Press.
Giandomenico, J. (2015). *Transformative power challenged: EU membership conditionality in the Western Balkans Revisited* (Ph.D. thesis). Acta Universitatis Upsaliensis, Uppsala.
Grabbe, H. (2014). Six lessons of enlargement ten years on: The EU's transformative power in retrospect and prospect. *Journal of Common Market Studies, 52*(S1), 40–56.
Grele, R. (1996). Oral history: Method and theory. *Radical History Review, 65*(1), 131–135.
Hedström, P., & Ylikoski, P. (2010). Causal mechanisms in the social sciences. *Annual Review of Sociology, 36*(1), 49–67.
International Criminal Tribunal for the Former Yugoslavia. (2012, November 16). *Prosecutor v. Ante Gotovina, Mladen Markač*. Appeals Chamber Judgement. https://www.icty.org/x/cases/gotovina/acjug/en/121116_judgement.pdf. Accessed May 4, 2020.
Jović, D. (2011). Turning nationalists into EU supporters: The case of Croatia. In J. Rupnik (Ed.), *The Western Balkans and the EU: 'The hour of Europe'* (pp. 33–45). Chaillot Paper 126. Paris: European Union Institute for Security Studies (EUISS).
Kaeding, M., & Mastenbroek, E. (2006). Europeanization beyond the goodness of fit: Domestic politics in the forefront. *Comparative European Politics, 4*(4), 331–354.
Keohane, R., Moravcsik, A., & Slaughter, A. M. (2000). Legalized dispute resolution: Interstate and transnational. *International Organization, 54*(3), 457–488.
Kmezić, M. (2019). EU rule of law conditionality: Democracy or 'Stabilitocracy' promotion in the Western Balkans? In J. Džankić, S. Keil, & M. Kmezić (Eds.), *The Europeanisation of the Western Balkans: A failure of EU conditionality?* (pp. 87–110). Cham: Springer Nature.
Křižić, I. (2012). Gergana Noutcheva: European foreign policy and the challenges of Balkan accession: Conditionality, legitimacy and compliance (book review). *Contemporary Issues, 5*(1), 61–65.
Kriesberg, L. (1992). *International conflict resolution: The US-USSR and Middle East cases*. New Haven: Yale University Press.
Ladrech, R. (1994). Europeanization of domestic politics and institutions: The case of France. *Journal of Common Market Studies, 32*(1), 69–88.
Lauth, H. J., Pickel, G., & Pickel, S. (2014). *Vergleich politischer Systeme*. Paderborn: Schöningh.
March, J., & Olsen, J. (1998). The institutional dynamics of international political orders. *International Organisation, 52*(4), 943–969.
Milenkoski, M., & Talevski, J. (2001). Delineation of the state border between the Republic of Macedonia and the Federal Republic of Yugoslavia. *IBRU Boundary and Security Bulletin Summer, 2001*, 93–98.
Miošić-Lisjak, N. (2006). Croatia and the European Union: A social constructivist perspective. *Policy Studies, 27*(2), 101–114.
Moravcsik, A. (1993). Preferences and power in the European Community: A liberal intergovernmentalist approach. *Journal of Common Market Studies, 31*(4), 473–524.
Morgenthau, H. (1962). A political theory of foreign aid. *The American Political Science Review, 56*(2), 301–309.
Muno, W. (2016). Fallstudien und process-tracing in der Vergleichenden Politikwissenschaft. In H. J. Lauth, G. Pickel, & S. Pickel (Eds.), *Handbuch der Vergleichenden Politikwissenschaft* (pp. 79–90). Paderborn: Schöningh.
N1 Zagreb. (2019, January 27). Grabar Kitarović: Vučić ništa nije uradio po pitanju nestalih, razočarana sam. https://rs.n1info.com/Region/a455303/Grabar-Kitarovic-Vucic-nista-nije-uradio-po-pitanju-nestalih.html. Accessed May 16, 2020.

Noutcheva, G. (2012). *European foreign policy and the challenges of Balkan accession.* London and New York: Routledge.
Permanent Court of Arbitration. (2017, June 29). *Croatia v Slovenia.* PCA Case No. 2012-04. Final Award. https://pcacases.com/web/sendAttach/2172. Accessed May 4, 2020.
Peters, G. (1998). *Comparative politics. Theory and methods.* New York: NYU Press.
Phinnemore, D. (2006). Beyond 25—The changing face of EU enlargement: Commitment, conditionality and the Constitutional Treaty. *Journal of Southern Europe and the Balkans, 8*(1), 7–26.
Pickel, G., & Pickel, S. (2003). Einige Notizen zu qualitativen Interviews als Verfahren der vergleichenden Methode der Politikwissenschaft. In S. Pickel, G. Pickel, H. J. Lauth, & D. Jahn (Eds.), *Vergleichende politikwissenschaftliche Methoden* (pp. 289–315). Wiesbaden: VS Verlag für Sozialwissenschaften.
Pollack, M. (2001). International relations theory and European integration. *Journal of Common Market Studies, 39*(2), 221–244.
Rabionet, S. (2011). How I learned to design and conduct semi-structured interviews: An ongoing and continuous journey. *Qualitative Report, 16*(2), 563–566.
Radan, P. (2000). Post-secession international borders: A critical analysis of the opinions of the Badinter Arbitration Commission. *Melbourne University Law Review, 24*(1), 50–75.
Ramsbotham, O., Woodhouse, T., & Miall, H. (2015). *Contemporary Conflict Resolution.* Cambridge: Polity Press.
Rasza, M., & Lindstrom, N. (2004). Balkan is beautiful: Balkanism in the political discourse of Tudman's Croatia. *East European Politics and Societies and Cultures, 18*(4), 628–650.
Risse, T. (2009). Social constructivism and european integration. In T. Diez & A. Wiener (Eds.), *European integration theory* (pp. 144–162). Oxford: Oxford University Press.
Roter, P., & Bojinović, A. (2005). Croatia and the European Union: A troubled relationship. *Mediterranean Politics, 10*(3), 447–454.
Rumelili, B. (2008). Transforming the Greek-Turkish conflicts: The EU and 'What We Make of It'. In T. Diez, M. Albert, & S. Stetter (Eds.), *The European Union and border conflicts* (pp. 94–128). New York: Cambridge University Press.
Sandholtz, W. (1996). Membership matters: Limits of the functional approach to European institutions. *Journal of Common Market Studies, 34*(3), 403–429.
Schimmelfennig, F. (2008). EU political accession conditionality after the 2004 enlargement: Consistency and effectiveness. *Journal of European Public Policy, 15*(6), 918–937.
Schimmelfennig, F., & Sedelmeier, U. (2004). Governance by conditionality: EU rule transfer to the candidate countries of Central and Eastern Europe. *Journal of European Public Policy, 11*(4), 661–679.
Schimmelfennig, F., & Sedelmeier, U. (Eds.). (2005). *The politics of European Union enlargement: Theoretical approaches.* London and New York: Routledge.
Scott, S. (2014). Litigation versus dispute resolution through political processes. In N. Klein (Ed.), *Litigating international law disputes: Weighing the options* (pp. 24–41). Cambridge: Cambridge University Press.
Sedelius, T. (2006). *The Tug-of-War between presidents and prime ministers. Semi-presidentialism in Central and Eastern Europe* (Ph.D. thesis). Örebro University, Örebro.
Subotić, J. (2011). Europe is a state of mind: Identity and Europeanization in the Balkans. *International Studies Quarterly, 55*(2), 309–330.
Tansey, O. (2007). Process-tracing and elite interviewing: A case for non-probability sampling. *Political Science and Politics, 40*(4), 1–23.
Trampusch, C., & Palier, B. (2016). Between X and Y: How process-tracing contributes to opening the black box of causality. *New Political Economy, 21*(5), 1–18.
Vachudova, M. (2005). Strategies for democratization and European integration in the Balkans. In M. Cremona (Ed.), *The enlargement of the European Union. Collected courses of the Academy for European Law* (pp. 141–160). Oxford: Oxford University Press.

Vachudova, M. (2003). Strategies for Democratization and European Integration in the Balkans. In: M. Cremona (Ed.), *The Enlargement of the European Union. Collected courses of the Academy for European Law* (pp. 141–160). Oxford: Oxford University Press.

Wallensteen, P. (2015). *Understanding conflict resolution*. London, Thousand Oakes, New Delhi, Singapore: SAGE Publications.

Wendt, A. (1999). *Social theory of international politics*. Cambridge: Cambridge University Press.

Zartman, W., & de Soto, A. (2010). *Timing mediation initiatives: The peacemaker's toolkit*. Washington, D.C.: United States Institute of Peace.

Zhelyazkova, A., Damjanovski, I., Nechev, Z., & Schimmelfennig, F. (2019). European Union conditionality in the Western Balkans: External incentives and Europeanisation. In J. Džankić, S. Keil, & M. Kmezić (Eds.), *The Europeanisation of the Western Balkans: A failure of EU conditionality?* (pp. 15–38). Cham: Springer Nature.

Chapter 2
History of Territorial, Political, and Violent Conflict in the Region

Abstract The aim of this Chapter is to provide an insight into why territorial and other issues have been a source of conflict throughout the more recent times of the region. A brief outline of the history of the North-Eastern Adriatic, and both the birth and the dismemberment of Yugoslavia, including the role of the then European Community (EC), may help shed light on a few root causes pertaining to territorial conflict and frontier-making in Southeast-Central and Southeast Europe. In view of the fact that Slovenia and Croatia have not been independent entities for most of their history during the contemporary international system after 1648, there is a need to review the joint history of Yugoslavia where appropriate to trace convergent or divergent processes and conflictual issues in relation to the joint statehood between 1918 and 1991. Another emphasis rests on the dissolution of the Socialist Federal Republic of Yugoslavia (SFRY, or "Yugoslavia II") and issues of violent conflict around the independence of Slovenia and Croatia (and the other Yugoslav Republics).

Keywords Yugoslavia · Croatia · Slovenia · State recognition · Dissolution · State succession

2.1 Border Changes Between the Republic of Venice and World War I

The "disputed and changing frontier" (Lederer 1963: ix) has been a salient issue in Southeast-Central and Southeast Europe for a long time in recent history.[1] In looking at past events, we must bear in mind that territorial conflict is the most serious issue

[1] This author follows Ramet's (2006) labels: "Yugoslavia I" for the interwar kingdom 1918–1941 (referred to as "Yugoslavia" only after 1929, initially "Kingdom of Serbs, Croats, and Slovenes"), "Yugoslavia II" for the communist federal republic 1945–1991, since 1974 known as the Socialist Federal Republic of Yugoslavia SFRY, and "Yugoslavia III" for the rump Yugoslav State 1992–2003 consisting of Serbia and of Montenegro labelled Federal Republic of Yugoslavia (FRY). The country was subsequently rebranded "Serbia and Montenegro" before it split into "Serbia" and "Montenegro" in 2006 following the independence referendum in Montenegro.

T. Bickl, *The Border Dispute Between Croatia and Slovenia*, Contributions to Political Science,
https://doi.org/10.1007/978-3-030-53333-5_2

over which governments or States can be at odds with (Gibler 2012: 9; Huth and Allee 2002: 32).

There is hardly a region in Europe that has experienced as many territorial conflicts and subsequent border changes in the nineteenth and twentieth centuries as the Julian Region[2] (see Fig. 2.1). Almost all boundary changes followed armed conflicts in what were outright wars. This Chapter's outline focuses on what can be considered relevant periods and events over time. The goal is to raise the awareness for political and territorial conflict, and frontier-making, and how these processes were driven by or may have affected political entities, State actors, and citizens' lives. Still, it is beyond the scope of this study to give a full account of the region's history.

For the purposes of this book, issues of particular relevance are the processes of

(i) Changing territorial sovereignty and political conflict before and during Yugoslav times;
(ii) Conflict management efforts by the EC/EU during the dissolution of the SFRY;
(iii) The establishing of international borders between the successor States, and the new borders' effects on violent conflict;
(iv) The successor States of Yugoslavia negotiating and implementing a plurilateral treaty on succession issues (e.g. assets and liabilities, State property, or pensions).

For the following brief sketch of the history of the Julian Region in the North-Eastern Adriatic, the end of the Venice Empire (1797) appears a reasonable starting point.[3] For two reasons: First, the Peace of Westphalia in 1648 is widely considered the beginning of the contemporary international system with territory-bound sovereign States (e.g. Hobson 2013). This system was already up and running in the Venice Empire's phase of decline after 1669 (McNeill 1974). Second, the Venice Empire has had the most lasting civilisation impact on the Northern Adriatic still visible today. Third, frontier-making as an exercise for diplomacy craftsmanship through treaties following (armed) conflicts was established in the region around that time.

[2] *Julian Region* is the most suitable term as all other designations have a particular national and emotional connotation, such as *Venezia Giulia* or *Julijska Krajina* (Julian March). Julian Region is used as a purely *geographical* term along the North-Eastern Adriatic ranging from *Grado* west of *Trieste/Trst* to *Rijeka/Fiume* covering the coastal areas and the hinterland karst region including the peninsula of Istria. All place names reflect the present-day language regime unless specified otherwise.

[3] Substantial surveys on the pre-nineteenth-century history of the Julian Region can *inter alia* be found in Duroselle (1966: 52–69), Moodie (1945: 46–96), and Rojnić (1945: 75–115). For the developments of the historical units of the later Yugoslav State from early settlements to the Balkan Wars 1912/13, see Hondius (1968: 30–76).

Fig. 2.1 Julian Region and border changes between 1866 and 1954 (Novak 1970: 261). ©University of Chicago Press

2.1.1 *Late Venice Empire and Napoleon's Interregnum*

The Venice Empire came to an end through the Treaty of Campo Formio in 1797 when the Republic had to cede its eastern Adriatic territories to Austria and France (Lederer 1963: 9). During the foregone centuries, Venice, as a hegemonic power in the Adriatic with her naval and merchant fleets, had ruled over most of the eastern Adriatic coast and its surrounding hinterland, such as Dalmatia and what is today the coastal area of Croatian and Slovenian Istria. The city of Trieste, however, had remained under Habsburg rule. The Venetian–Mediterranean civilisation had been the predominant culture along the eastern coast of the Adriatic for a few centuries, had also affected Trieste to some degree, but was very different to the form of civilisation in the inland settlements of the other parts of the (Habsburg-ruled) Julian Region (Prunk 1996: 32–3). Today, the impact of Venice in the eastern Adriatic is still very much visible in the distinctive architecture of the old towns of Kotor (Montenegro), Dubrovnik, Split, and Rovinj (Croatia), or Piran and Koper (Slovenia), to name but a few.

Venetian rule in Istria was perceived by the local Slavic population in two ways. On the one hand, the comparably refined administration of Venice was widely appreciated. On the other hand, there was a strong sense of exploitation of both human power and raw material for the Venice fleet. Deforestation in Istria and on the islands of the Kvarner region was substantial (Krebs 1907: 137; Rojnić 1945: 108–112), and its long-term effects are still noticeable today on the islands of Krk, Cres, Rab, and Pag, and in the karst hinterland on both sides of the land border between present-day Croatia and Slovenia.

Following Napoleon's victory over Venice,[4] Austria, through the Treaty of Campo Formio 1797, was granted the territory of Istria. Beating Austria and Russia in the Battle of Austerlitz in 1805, Napoleon subsequently took over in Istria—with the exception of Trieste which he gained only in 1809 through the Schönbrunn Treaty (Duroselle 1966: 58; Rojnić 1945: 114).

Napoleon included the Istrian peninsula and Slovenia in his so-called Ilyric Provinces. The cultural gains of the French administration were noticeable. The free use of the native language, also in schools and for the Italian population in the coastal towns, was introduced for the first time in the area (Moodie 1945: 94–95; Prunk 1996: 72–73), and the French administration was trying to get rid of the Habsburg-style privileges of the church and the aristocracy (Rojnić 1945: 115). It is worth noting that Trieste and Fiume (Rijeka), for the very first time, were granted control of their hinterland regions enabling them to fully function as port cities (Moodie 1945: 98).

[4] Venice's alleged and mythical decadence as portrayed in the contemporary British and French press at the time contrasts sharply with the necessity of Venice having to give in to French military determination, as was contended in informed diplomatic circles back then (Laven 2011).

2.1.2 *Return of Habsburg Rule*

Following the Battle of Leipzig in 1813 Austrian rule returned to Istria and Slovenia, a fact confirmed by the Vienna Congress in 1815. Subsequently, Austria rolled back the French administrative reform and reintroduced their previous system (Prunk 1996: 73). Moodie argues that, through destroying the Venetian Republic, Napoleon had strengthened Italian unity in its early stages. The Austro-Hungarian role in the Upper Adriatic had indirectly also been consolidated. As a result, "the stage was set for the Austro-Italian struggle in and around the Julian Region which was to have important effects on later boundary disputes" (Moodie 1945: 95). Further, the dualistic set-up of a re-enforced Austria and the dominance of large parts of the Balkans peninsula by the Ottoman Empire resulted in barriers to the independence of the Southern Slavs altogether (Hösch 2011: 30–1). A contemporary leftover of the Ottoman Empire, Bosnia-Herzegovina's access to the Adriatic, the so-called Neum corridor (see Sect. 6.3.5), is a result of the 1699 Treaty of Sremski Karlovci and the 1718 Treaty of Požarevac where Venice ceded two buffer areas that separated it from the Republic of Ragusa (today Dubrovnik) to the Ottoman Empire (Fuerst-Bjeliš and Zupanc 2007: 43). In particular, establishing an independent Slovenia or Croatia proved virtually impossible as the newly acquired taste of many Croats and Slovenes for the French ideas of Enlightenment and autonomous government clashed with the views in Vienna (Moodie 1945, 95–6) who would not compromise on the concept of centralist rule (Rojnić 1945: 116; Prunk 1996: 73–4).

The frequency of *boundary changes* in the Julian Region between the Campo Formio Treaty in 1797 and the Vienna Congress in 1815 is substantial and highlights the borderland character of the area at the time. After the defeat of Venice, Austria took over Istria and Dalmatia (in addition to the domestic Venice "homeland" area). Eight years later, when the Kingdom of Italy was founded, Austria had to hand over its newly acquired territories. In 1809, after a successful French military campaign, Austria had to cede Trieste, Fiume (Rijeka), and Dalmatia to Napoleon. Further, between 1811 and 1814, internal boundaries were rearranged following military-administrative considerations. After the lands had come back to Austria, the region termed Illyrian Kingdom—to be rebranded "Küstenland" (Littoral) in 1849—remained largely intact until after the end of World War I in 1919. In 1866, however, Austria had to cede so-called Venetian Slovenia in the north-west to Italy as a result of the defeat in the war against Prussia and Italy (Novak 1970: 15; Prunk 1996: 87–8). Whilst the Ljubljana plain had been of strategic importance for Napoleon looking to the north-east, facing Austria as the main rival, the comeback Austrian rulers in the Julian Region now shifted their focus towards the Adriatic coast with Pola (Pula) on the southern tip of Istria becoming the naval base for the Habsburg fleet (Moodie 1945: 96–9; Duroselle 1966: 59).

2.1.3 Treaty of London

By the end of 1914, World War I had become a stalemate and the Triple Entente (Great Britain, France, and Russia), in their fight against imperial Germany and its ally Austria-Hungary, was trying hard to gain momentum (Djokić 2010: 40; Lederer 1963: 5). Italy which had stayed neutral was, in the view of the Entente, to be persuaded to join the war, or, in the view of Austria-Hungary, to stay neutral. This put Italy in a strong bargaining position (Novak 1970: 23). At the end of the day, the Entente Powers managed to gain Italy's support through the secret Treaty of London. As a result, Italy entered the war joining the Entente in May 1915 after six weeks of negotiations (Djokić 2010: 41). The Treaty of London from the same year promised Rome key territories in the eastern Adriatic by the time the war was over (Moodie 1945: 140–2; Novak 1970: 23–4; Von Reiswitz 1954: 69).

The territories assigned to Italy by the Treaty of London were:

(i) Trentino, South Tyrol, Trieste, the counties of Gorizia and Gradisca; (ii) the whole of Istria including Trieste[5]; (iii) the Quarnero (Kvarner) Bay including Volosko (Opatija) and the Kvarner islands of Cherso (Cres) and Lussino (Lošinj; all under Article 4); and (iv) the Province of Dalmatia (Article 5).[6]

The remainder of the eastern Adriatic territory including the coast and Fiume/Rijeka[7] was assigned to Croatia, Serbia, Montenegro, and Albania, respectively (Articles 5 and 7). Serbia, notably, had not been informed about the treaty as the odds were that it would never have accepted Dalmatia (which was considered South Slav land[8]) to go to Italy. The Serb leaders were, however, not able to persuade Russia to block the treaty (Djokić 2010: 41–2).

Putting things into perspective, it could be argued that Italy, by means of the Treaty of London, seemed enabled to re-establish the earlier hegemony of the Republic of Venice in the Adriatic (Moodie 1945: 136) or at least strengthen its leading role in Southeast Europe (Lederer 1963: 9).

To sum up, the phase between the end of the Venice Empire 1797 and the end of World War I saw an unparalleled time of near-constant violent conflict in the Upper Adriatic. Slovenes and Croats were under foreign rule, and many thousands of them lost their lives in the battles fought for the occupying rulers. Besides, the Croats and Slovenes themselves had no say on the heavy frequency of boundary changes the local population had to come to terms with. On top of the alterations of territorial sovereignty came the varying degrees of appreciation of cultural autonomy. For the first time, the Napoleonic administration allowed for the use of the native language (Slovenian, Croatian, and Italian) in schools. Whilst not cutting back on language

---

[5]Fiume/Rijeka, however, was not assigned to Italy, but to Yugoslavia (see Sect. 2.2.2).

[6]Place names in brackets are added by the author to reflect current place names.

[7]The port city became a thorny issue during the Paris Peace Conference only to be settled later on; see Sect. 2.2.2.

[8]According to Lederer (1963: 9), Dalmatia had become "the cradle of Yugoslav nationalism, the center of the Illyrian Movement, and subsequently the fountainhead of Serbo-Croat cooperation" in the nineteenth century.

autonomy, the comeback of Habsburg equated the return of centralist rule. These processes may suggest that the appetite for shaking off heteronomy has constantly grown for the South Slav people over that period.

2.2 Yugoslavia I

During World War I, preparations had been underway for the eventual founding of a South Slav, i.e. Yugoslav, State. Major efforts on the diplomatic front had to be made in order to achieve this goal. Nevertheless, the views within the Southern Slav communities on the future State's disposition and constitution differed substantially (Newman 2015: 15–6; Hondius 1968: 92–94). Yet, the common aim prevailed to live in a joint State of some kind and to emancipate from foreign rule (such as Habsburg, Italy, or the Ottoman Empire), aggression, the massive loss of lives,[9] and exploitation (Newman 2015: 14; Calic 2014: 74–78; Sekulić 2004: 465).

2.2.1 Founding a New State

Many political leaders from the Slovene, Croat, and Serb community, respectively, left their home regions after the start of World War I. In May 1915, they founded the South Slav or Yugoslav Committee (*Jugoslovanski odbor*) in London organised by the Croats Frano Supilo and Ante Trumbić (Novak 1970: 25; Calic 2014: 78–9; Djokić 2010: 37). What the Yugoslav Committee founders had in mind was a Yugoslav State as an equal partnership of Serbs, Croats, and Slovenes (Lederer 1963: 5). By 1917, there were three in-exile groups of actors determined to shape the stakes of a future Yugoslav State. Apart from (i) the *Yugoslav Committee* in London, there was the (ii) *Serbian government-in-exile* on Corfu[10] headed by Nikola Pašić. His approach was the liberation and unification of Serbs, Croats, and Slovenes into one State, but within a Serbian national framework (Lederer 1963: 5; Djokić 2010: 20; Ramet 2006: 42). The third strand of South Slav unification was represented by the (iii) *Yugoslav Club* under the chairmanship of Anton Korošec of Slovenia, with a Croat and Serb Vice-President respectively. The Yugoslav Club explored ways of uniting the areas of Slovenes, Croats, and Serbs within the realm of Austria-Hungary (Calic 2014: 79; Djokić 2010: 53; Ramet 2006: 40).

[9]During World War I, according to Calic (2014: 76), Serbia lost 1.2 million lives (soldiers and civilians). 300,000 Slovene, Croat and Bosnian soldiers fighting for Austria-Hungary were killed on the Isonzo/Soča front in the battles against Italian troops in the north-west. Serbia lost a fifth of its population on the battleground, due to disease and starvation during the war (Newman 2015: 14).

[10]The Serbian government had retreated from the temporary capital Niš through the mountains of Montenegro and Albania to Corfu in late 1915 (Djokić 2010: 47).

The initially competing camps of (i) the Yugoslav Committee and (ii) the Serbian government-in-exile finally joined forces. What might have united them was the view that a future Yugoslavia was the best means of protection against Italian expansion and German aggression (Djokić 2010: 46). The details of the Treaty of London (which had become public knowledge in the meantime) on Istria and Dalmatia—and with it some 500,000 South Slavs[11] going to Italy—did play a role. The joint Corfu Declaration of both exile bodies from July 1917 stated the plan of setting up a *Kingdom of the Serbs, Croats, and Slovenes* under the Karađorđević dynasty after the end of the war (Calic 2014: 79; Von Reiswitz 1954: 70). Pašić and Trumbić, however, had not reached agreement on whether the State should be decentralised or not.[12] In October 1918, the Yugoslav Club founded the Zagreb-based *National Council* which was to be in charge of the South Slavs in what still was Austria-Hungary. The National Council announced the founding of a State of Slovenes, Croats, and Serbs (Djokić 2010: 49–53) as an independent entity within the Habsburg jurisdiction (Newman 2015: 127–9; Lederer 1963: 25).

Notwithstanding the failure of a joint meeting of the Serbian government, the main Serbian opposition parties, the Yugoslav Committee, and the National Council on the terms of Yugoslav unification in Geneva in early November 1918,[13] Prince Regent Alexander of Serbia proclaimed the *Kingdom of Serbs, Croats, and Slovenes*[14] on 1 December 1918 (Djokić 2010: 54–55; Calic 2014: 81; Newman 2015: 129). It has to be noted that such unilateral pre-determination of the constitutional nature of the common State did not go down well with Croats and Slovenes (Calic 2014: 86; Ramet 2006: 44). Yet, Serbia naturally played a strong role in practice, not least because it had been an independent State since 1878 (as opposed to the other two entities) and had a victorious recent past in the 1912–18 Balkan Wars with Prince Regent Alexander Karađorđević as the perceived peoples' liberator (Newman 2015: 16–7). During the debate in the Constituent Assembly, alternative structures for the State were discussed. Korošec of the Yugoslav Club presented a model of six provinces determined by political–historical criteria, i.e. three Catholic and three Orthodox provinces. Trumbić introduced a federal province-based devolution of legislation away from the central parliament. In the final vote on the draft constitution on 28 June 1921, however, the parliamentary-monarchy model, the so-called *Vidovan Constitution*, was adopted by 223 votes in favour, 35 votes against, and 152 abstentions (Hondius 1968: 96–7). The subsequent introduction of the *oblast* system in 1922, i.e. new administrative territorial units thus rejecting the former regional entities

[11]The figures slightly differ. Moodie (1945: 149–150) posits "477,000 Yugoslavs". This figure is substantiated by Calic's (2014: 84) "almost half a million Slovenes and Croats". Čermelj (1945: 245) accounts for "600,000 Croats and Slovenes". Cresciani (2004: 4) reports 325,000 Slovenes.

[12]Trumbić was against a centralised State, but would also reject federalism since it was too complex. Pašić favoured centralism. The compromise solution was to leave the issue open (Djokić 2010: 49–52).

[13]Serbian troops liberated Belgrade and the entire Serbian State by 3 November 1918 (Djokić 2010: 53; Lederer 1963: 46).

[14]Notwithstanding the fact that the *Kingdom* was renamed *Yugoslavia* only in 1929, the author uses *Yugoslavia* for reasons of clarity and coherence.

from Austrian-Hungarian times, could indeed be seen as a centralist move meant to discourage disunity and separatism. The 33 *oblasti* constituted a large number of relatively small units that had nothing to do with former historical or cultural borders (Radan 1999: 138–9; Jović 2009: 48).

The young State had lately been under heavy territorial pressure. Following the armistice of the Allied Powers with Austria-Hungary and Germany on 31 October 1918, Italy was entitled to occupy the former Austrian-Hungarian territory up to the 1915 Treaty-of-London line (see Sect. 2.1.3). As a matter of fact, however, the Italian navy and army went further taking over Trieste, Pula, the whole of Istria, Fiume/Rijeka,[15] Zara/Zadar, and large parts of Dalmatia including its respective hinterlands within days. Almost the entire Austro-Hungarian naval fleet was finally under the control of Italy (Novak 1970: 27; Lederer 1963: 54–59).

2.2.2 *Paris Peace Conference and Treaty of Rapallo*

The first Yugoslav State was facing a tough struggle for recognition,[16] not least at the Paris Peace Conference commencing in January 1919.[17] The Paris Conference marked the first of two phases of efforts to settle the borders in the Julian Region after the end of World War I. The second phase constituted direct negotiations between Yugoslavia and Italy between March 1920 and January 1924 (Moodie 1945: 166).

The USA who had entered World War I only in April 1918 attempted to broker compromise at the Paris Conference. President Wilson, whose 14 Points[18] stipulated the principle of self-determination, had become a pivotal factor for the post-war political order in East-Central and Southeast Europe (Calic 2014: 83). He tabled a number of detailed proposals,[19] but neither the Yugoslav nor the Italian delegation was ready to accept them, so the delimitation of the Italo-Yugoslav border had to be left to a future agreement (Novak 1970: 29–30). What had further complicated the talks at Paris was the fact that the Yugoslav delegation led by Nikola Pašić with Ante Trumbić as deputy chair was not united and had no common approach to (i) self-determination and (ii) the Yugoslav territorial claims at the beginning of the

[15]Fiume was expressly not part of the 1915 Treaty of London, but had recently become a demand by Italian nationalists no Italian government could ignore (Novak 1970: 29–30).

[16]The USA recognised Yugoslavia in February 1919, and Britain and France did so only in early June followed by Italy at the end of that month (Lederer 1963: 205; Hondius 1968: 91).

[17]Representatives of the new State were formally accredited as the delegation of the "Kingdom of Serbia", despite the fact that such state politically no longer existed. The delegation members themselves would always refer to "Kingdom of Serbs, Croats, and Slovenes" (Djokić 2010: 53). On the question of whether the Serb–Croat–Slovene delegation was indeed a new State, there were many different views (Hondius 1968: 91).

[18]The Wilson Points are reprinted in Djokić (2010: 50–51).

[19]For an analysis of the sophisticated US boundary proposal, the so-called Wilson line, see Moodie (1945: 168–184). Lederer gives an insight into Wilson's handling of the delicate boundary issue (1963: 184–217).

conference (Djokić 2010: 74–80). In the end, the Yugoslav claims in the eastern Adriatic vis-à-vis Italy turned out to include the Province of Dalmatia (with around 600,000 inhabitants, predominantly Yugoslav, and a mere three per cent Italians), the town of Rijeka (Fiume) with 50,000 inhabitants (Yugoslavs and Italians), and Istria including Trieste and Gorica (780,000 inhabitants) with 55% Yugoslavs and 37% Italians (Djokić 2010: 82).

As mentioned above, the future of the Italo-Yugoslav frontier was still open when the Paris Conference ended in June 1919. By November 1920, the Yugoslavs accepted an Italian invitation to a bilateral conference to settle what was termed the Adriatic question. The Yugoslav delegation went to Rapallo under fairly unfortunate conditions: US President Wilson, who had been sympathetic to the Yugoslav cause,[20] reached the end of his term, and a Republican was to succeed him. As a result, any interest in the Yugoslav destiny on the part of the USA was gone for the time being. In mid-October 1920, the Klagenfurt plebiscite resulted in the Klagenfurt Basin being assigned to Austria despite its substantially Slovene character.[21] That event was a bitter blow to the Yugoslav prestige weakening the country's claims to Slovene territories. Further, citizens in Yugoslavia and Italy had, by and large, become annoyed by the endless conferences on border issues (Moodie 1945: 186–188). On the diplomatic front, Italy had acted skilfully in retreating from Albania, thus doing away with the "Italian threat" on Yugoslavia's southern border. Equally unfavourably for the South Slavs, Britain and France had become increasingly reluctant with Yugoslavia (Lederer 1963: 300–1).

With no allies at hand, foreign minister Trumbić had to accept a deal which had largely and secretly been prepared between the two capitals over the preceding months. Italy's military strength had certainly played its role, too. The Yugoslav government, however, instructed the negotiating delegation for Rapallo with far-reaching goals, and, remarkably, *arbitration* [sic] under the auspices of Britain, France, and the USA was to be the option in the case of non-agreement (Lederer 1963: 301–2).

The Rapallo conference was to last for only four days, from 8 to 12 November 1920. The main results as for the Adriatic were:

(i) Istria including Trieste went to Italy; (ii) Yugoslavia retained Dalmatia except for Zara/Zadar; (iii) Fiume/Rijeka was to become an independent State with a small corridor to Italian-held Istria; (iv) the Kvarner islands of Cres/Cherso and Lošinj/Lussino went to Italy. Krk/Veglia was assigned to Yugoslavia (e.g. Hondius 1968: 92).

Italy gained considerably more than it could have expected. The territorial gains in the north-east of the Julian Region, which cannot be covered here in detail, were substantial and exceeded those promised by the Allies in the Treaty of London. All railway traffic to and from the two Adriatic ports of Trieste and Fiume/Rijeka

[20]Wilson has acted as a strong champion of self-determination and rejected secret treaties, such as the Treaty of London (Djokić 2010: 110).

[21]The Yugoslav Army occupied the plebiscite zone but had to humiliatingly retreat within two days after a joint Franco-British-Italian ultimatum (Lederer 1963: 296–7).

came under the control of Italy[22] meaning that transport outlets for most Yugoslav exports did depend on Italian non-interference. Road links between Fiume/Rijeka and Ljubljana also came under Italian control (Moodie 1945: 191–193; Novak 1970: 31–2).

The status of Fiume/Rijeka, the second largest port in the Upper Adriatic after Trieste, was a special case in point. According to the Rapallo agreement, the city was to be an independent State linked by a tiny strip of coastal land to Italian-controlled Istria. In 1924, following internal power struggles between local Italian nationalists in Fiume and the government in Rome, and after Mussolini had come to power in the meantime, Fiume became Italian by means of the Treaty of Rome (Hondius 1968: 92). Notably, Sušak, the eastern suburb of Fiume across the River Eneo/Rejčina, was assigned to Yugoslavia, including Baroš pier[23] (Novak 1970: 33–4; Calic 2014: 84). As a result, the River Eneo/Rečina became an international boundary between two parts of a conurbation that had for centuries been one single settlement and functionally coherent. Frontier permits (*cartes frontalières*) and temporary permits (*cartes de passage*) were supplied to dampen inconveniences for Yugoslavs from Sušak and its hinterland commuting into Fiume or visiting relatives there. Still, the new arrangement seriously hampered the day-to-day activities of tens of thousands of Yugoslavs, creating a feeling of bitterness and anger (Moodie 1945: 207–8).

Overall, the Rapallo and Rome provisions may be seen as a major boost to Italian claims at the expense of Yugoslav territory. Whilst the Allies were relieved that the struggle over the Adriatic was finally over, the government in Rome was in a triumphant mood. The opposite spirit prevailed in Belgrade, although there was also some sense of relief (Moodie 1945: 208; Lederer 1963: 307). Novak (1970: 34) argues that, in terms of the moral of the story, "to gain a territory one must occupy it by force. A *de facto* occupation is better security than awaiting settlement at a peace conference". The cost of the Italian territorial expansion, however, was the poisoning of the future relations between the two countries. It appears fair to say that the territorial settlements in the Julian Region after World War I resulted in the birth of Yugoslav irredentism (Moodie 1945: 212; Lederer 1963: 307; Novak 1970: 42–3).

2.2.3 *Italian Rule in Istria*

As a consequence of the massive territorial shifts in favour of Italy,[24] around 500,000 Slovenes and Croats came under Italian rule in Istria. The following years marked a policy of systematic neglect of minority rights on the part of the Italian authorities in

[22] Except for the Fiume/Rijeka–Karlovac–Zagreb line.

[23] Yugoslav access to the Baroš port facilities had been secured already at Rapallo, albeit not in the treaty provisions proper, but in a secret exchange of letters (Lederer 1963: 306).

[24] Moodie cites two studies (an Italian one from 1920 and an American one from 1937) which account for 9000 km^2 having been annexed to Italy (Moodie 1945: 191, 211–2).

Istria. The new rulers operated a policy of assimilation or so-called ethnic homogenisation (*bonifica etnica*) towards or "colonisation" of the Slavic population (Wörsdörfer 2004: 221–223; 241). Other scholars speak of "persecution", "denationalisation" (Novak 1970: 34–37), or "occupation" and "cultural subjugation" (Cresciani 2004: 3).

The Italian policy of forced assimilation proved particularly heavy in the fields of schooling, education, and language use, not least because the Treaty of Rapallo did not entail any provisions on minority rights for the newly acquired Italian territory in Istria and the Julian Region, whereas the Italian minority in Dalmatia was to enjoy minority protection (Slovene–Italian Report[25] 2004: 14). Many Croat and Slovene institutions were shut down in the first ten years after Italian expansion; 488 primary schools were closed alongside some 400 cultural, social, or professional organisations. Equally, 31 newspapers were banned between 1918 and 1928. The use of Slovene and Croatian was prohibited in public, in all State institutions, and in churches (Cresciani 2004: 4; Novak 1970: 37). By the beginning of the 1923/24 school year, Italian was the only language in all primary schools in Istria (Čermelj 1945: 261). By 1928, the Italian Regime forced Croats and Slovenes in Istria to "Italianise" their names and surnames (Cresciani 2004: 4; Novak 1970: 37; Čermelj 1945: 265–268).[26]

As a result, the ethnic relations in the peninsula deteriorated drastically and the traditional "borders" between the towns and the countryside were fortified. Istrian cities became more or less completely italianised, whereas the Croatian and Slovenian political and cultural life in Istria was pushed to the small villages in the countryside (D'Alessio 2006: 26). Still, the Croat and Slovene population would show an interest in the Italian language and literature, many people being bilingual,[27] whereas the Italian speakers' interest in the language of the local population was virtually zero (Schiffrer 1946: 22; Slovene–Italian Report 2004: 17).

Despite the fact that a good 100,000 Slovenes and Croats left the newly acquired Italian territories in the Julian Region, the Kvarner and Dalmatia between the two World Wars (Slovene–Italian Report 2004: 16), the relative demographic strength of the Croats and Slovenes would not change, but even slightly increase (D'Alessio 2006: 26–7).

---

[25]A joint bilateral Historical and Cultural Commission was established in October 1993 by the foreign ministers of Italy and Slovenia. The Commission worked for seven years and produced the remarkably frank report "Slovene–Italian Relations 1880–1956" in July 2000. The report was meant to be included in the secondary-school curricula of both countries. To that end, the curricula in Slovenia are being amended (information obtained from the Slovenian Ministry of Education, 07-01-2019). Schools in Italy have a high level of autonomy since the reform in 2000, so that the decision on the selection of curricula items is a matter for the individual schools at local level (information obtained from the Italian Ministry for Education, 18-01-2019).

[26]In the Province of Trieste, the surnames and names of 60,000 people were Italianised (Cresciani 2004: 4). In Pola/Pula, 100,000 people had to change their surname (Čermelj 1945: 265).

[27]In Fiume/Rijeka, for example, the first bilingual classes started as early as 1521 (Kobler 1896 [sic]: 185).

The Italian fascist assimilation policy, often carried out in a merciless manner, "sowed [...] the seeds of hatred and a yearning of revenge" (Cresciani 2004: 11) fostering the spread of an anti-fascist spirit and subsequent action—peaceful, violent, and sometimes terrorist. Such action, in turn, provoked severe repression on the part of the Italian authorities, including prison sentences and even executions.[28] The Italian Communist Party came to realise only step by step that the Yugoslav irredentist movement was an ally, despite differing notions of what self-determination meant in practice. In 1936, an Action Pact between the Communist Party of Italy and the National Revolutionary Movement of Slovenes and Croatians (TIGR[29]) materialised leading to a robust anti-fascist movement (Slovene–Italian Report 2004: 17–8) on the eve of the heavy impact of World War II on Yugoslavia.

In a nutshell, the birth of the first Yugoslav State was a delicate and difficult task for the South Slav leaders. There was nothing much to gain on the negotiating table at the end of World War I. On the contrary, the secret territorial concessions given to Italy by the Entente Powers already *during* the war meant the humiliating loss of the Istrian territories for the newly founded Yugoslavia and a source of future irredentism. Domestically, the constitutional nature of the common State was disputed between centralists and federalists, and the "compromise" was to simply continue the pre-existing Serbian parliamentary-monarchy model as a three-named kingdom. A weak State and the external threat of the fascist movement appear to have paved the way for a more unifying political force not least determined to regain territorial sovereignty over the lost territories in Istria.

2.3 Yugoslavia and World War II

The Kingdom of Yugoslavia collapsed with the unconditional surrender on 17 April 1941 following the German air raids on Belgrade on Easter Sunday 1941,[30] and the subsequent German–Italian invasion of Macedonia, Serbia, Slovenia, and Croatia, respectively, from 7 to 15 April 1941 (Calic 2014: 136; Matl 1954: 101).

2.3.1 Partition of Yugoslavia

Hitler and Mussolini tore Yugoslavia apart. On 3 May 1941, in a move breaking international law banning the annexation of territory before a peace treaty has been

---

[28]The Special Tribunal for the Protection of the [Italian] State "passed fourteen death sentences, ten of which were executed" (Slovene–Italian Report 2004: 17).

[29]Representing the initials of Trieste, Istria, Gorizia, Rijeka (Cresciani 2004: 4).

[30]The city was bombed on 6 April 1941 without prior notice (Pirjevec 2018: 62); 3,000 people lost their lives exceeding the total casualties of the World War II bombings of Warsaw, Rotterdam, and Coventry (Calic 2014: 136).

signed, Italy raked in the Province of Ljubljana with more than 5000 km^2 of Slovenia including around 350,000 people. In addition, Dalmatia including the islands of Arbe (Rab) and Veglia (Krk) was incorporated into Italy accounting for another 5000 km^2 and 380,000 inhabitants of whom 280,000 were Croat, 90,000 Serbs, and 5000 Italians. The Italian territorial "enlargement" accounted for a total of around 700,000 Slovenes, almost half of the Slovene nation (Cresciani 2004: 5; Slovene–Italian Report 2004: 19; Calic 2014: 137).

Germany equally unlawfully annexed Lower Styria and Upper Carniola from Slovenia including Maribor and Bled (Ramet 2006: 113). Croatia without Istria, Dalmatia (except for the islands of Brač and Korčula), and the Kvarner islands became the semi-autonomous, so-called Independent State of Croatia (NDH), led by Ante Pavelić, incorporating Croat lands (safe for the coastal territories held by Italy) and including Bosnia-Herzegovina, under the *de facto* control of the Axis powers (Newman 2015: 245; Calic 2014: 137–8; Ramet 2006: 113–4, 128–9; Matl 1954: 103–5).[31] Serbia was stripped off most of its recent territorial gains and, after a brief period of German direct rule, was run by the pro-Axis government of Milan Nedić, albeit with very little domestic support (Newman 2015: 245–9).

By means of the Vienna agreement from 22 April 1941 drawn up between the foreign ministers of Germany and Italy—including treaties with Hungary, Bulgaria, and Albania—the whole of what was the Kingdom of Yugoslavia ended up as a sphere of interest divided up between Germany and Italy (Novak 1970: 46; Wörsdörfer 2004: 350–2)[32] for around two-and-a-half years. Whereas Mussolini considered Southeast Europe as Italy's natural sphere of interest and *spazio vitale*, Hitler was driven by the desire to destroy the post-World-War-I order, secure transport corridors and economic resources relevant for warfare, and prevent an Allied landing in the region (Calic 2014: 137–8; Ramet 2006: 128).

2.3.2 *Resistance Movement*

Whilst the Yugoslav surrender marked the peak of German and Italian power and territorial expansion in the region, it may also be considered as the starting point for a strong and sustainable Yugoslav resistance movement against fascist occupation. In short, two resistance organisations emerged: the royalist *Chetniks* and the communist *Partisans*.

The Chetniks under the leadership of Draža Mihajlović, a former colonel of the (royal) Yugoslav Army, consisted of former army officers who recruited volunteers after they had retreated into the mountains as from mid-April 1941. Mihajlović also

[31]On the rise of the fascist *Ustaše* movement in Croatia, see Newman (2015: 176–183).

[32]Hungary (following Bulgaria and Romania) had, in March 1941, become party to the German–Italian–Japanese Triple Pact of 1940 and was assigned the south-west of Slovenia (Prekmurje), the western part of Vojvodina and Baranja (along the Danube). Bulgaria was authorised to rake in Macedonia (Calic 2014: 136; Ramet 2006: 113; Novak 1970: 50). For the situation in the various occupation zones, see Ramet (2006: 129–142).

became war minister in the Yugoslav government-in-exile resident in London, whilst he stayed on the ground, largely in the Chetnik headquarters in Ravna Gora, Serbia. The Chetniks would avoid open warfare with the occupant powers (Newman 2015: 249–50; Novak 1970: 47–8; Ramet 2006: 142; Calic 2014: 145–6).

The Partisans, the armed units of the National Liberation Movement, fought for a new and communist order in Yugoslavia. Their leader was Josip Broz, known as Tito. The Partisans organised a network of regional Liberation Committees with the Anti-Fascist Council for the National Liberation of Yugoslavia (*AVNOJ*) becoming the supreme body for the whole country acting as a quasi-federal government by 1943 (Pirjevec 2018: 89–93, 111–115; Đilas[33] 1985: 27; Novak 1970: 48–49; Calic 2014: 147). The Partisans, like the Chetniks, would gather in the mountains, in an attacking rather than an attentive conduct (Newman 2015: 259–60; Wörsdörfer 2004: 336–8; Calic 2014: 147).

After some initial joint Chetnik–Partisan action, the irreconcilable ideological–political differences between the two camps lead to an atrocious "civil war" (Pirjevec 2018: 78; Novak 1970: 44) following a Chetnik attack on the Partisans headquarter in Užice in western Serbia in early November 1941 (Ramet 2006: 144). Subsequently, the Partisans became the leading resistance force for broadly three reasons: (i) the Chetnik movement depended on orders from the government-in-exile, whilst the Partisans had a local command; (ii) the Partisan units had been built up rapidly by experienced veterans from the Spanish civil war and by former Yugoslav Army officers, and the units were run efficiently; (iii) the Partisans were able to win the support of the Western Allied Powers, notably Britain and the USA (Pirjevec 2018: 78–89; Calic 2014: 147–8; Matl 1954: 115–7; Ramet 2006: 152).

The atrocities and massacres committed during and immediately after World War II, including ethnic cleansing, cannot be described but as ruthless and enormous. They occurred between the rivalling Partisan and Chetnik forces of the resistance movement, were committed by the German and Italian troops against the resistance movement and the local population,[34] and happened between pro-fascist forces and the resistance movement, not least in Slovenia and with regard to the *Ustaše* in NDH Croatia, a pseudo-independent puppet State on behalf of the German occupiers. The cruelties clearly exceed the scope of this study.[35]

---

[33]Milovan Đilas was one of the closest aides to Tito during World War II and the early years of the second Yugoslavia. He was Tito's special envoy to inform Stalin about Yugoslavia's breakaway from the Kremlin in 1948. Đilas later became increasingly critical towards his own Communist Party. Turning into a dissident in 1954, he was put on trial and sentenced to prison several times (see Schmemann 1995).

[34]For example, the killing of 2,300 Serb civilians by the *Wehrmacht* in October 1941 in Kragujevac as a revenge for Partisan and Chetnik sabotage, see Pirjevec (2018: 79–80).

[35]A general survey for Yugoslavia as a whole can be found in Calic (2014: 157–166, 169–70). Ramet touches on the activities of Chetniks and Partisans, the activities of Ustaše, the role of the Catholic Church in Croatia (2006: 114–129), and the massacres at Bleiburg and Kočevje (160–2). Novak gives an account of the events with particular regard to Slovenia (1970: 50–69). Cresciani provides an insight into the Yugoslav "rollback", including the *foibe* in Istria, and the events in Zara and Fiume (2004: 6–10). Wörsdörfer delivers an Italo-Yugoslav national-sentiment angle to

It must be borne in mind, however, that many of the atrocities occurring during World War II in Yugoslavia have led to bilateral relations of the successor States being historically burdened. When political leaders abused and instrumentalised national(ist) sentiments, they greatly resurfaced during and immediately after the dissolution of Yugoslavia II. This is particularly evident for the relations between Croatia and Serbia (see Sects. 2.5 and 2.5.2).

2.3.3 Liberation of Yugoslavia

After Italy's unconditional surrender to the Allied Powers and the Soviet Union on 8 September 1943, the German army took over the Adriatic Littoral ("Operationszone Adriatisches Küstenland"—OZAK). The Germans on their part had a special interest in the ports of Trieste, Fiume/Rijeka, and Pula. In addition, Hitler issued a direct order to ruthlessly extinguish Communist resistance in Istria (Wörsdörfer 2004: 429). For a few days, the Partisans had managed to occupy the area of Italian retreat safe for the cities of Trieste, Pula, and Rijeka, but had to retreat themselves deep into the forests and mountains by the time the Germans arrived. However, large amounts of weapons and ammunition of the Italian army had fallen into the Partisans' hands (Novak 1970: 70–1, 80–1; Calic 2014: 153–4).[36] By and large, Italian surrender had strengthened Tito's army all over the place.[37]

The positive momentum for the Partisans was further advanced by the events on the international diplomatic stage. The Teheran Conference in December 1943 produced an agreement on Yugoslavia between Churchill and Stalin. US President Roosevelt was in the loop, but not a party to the deal. The Partisans were declared the only underground organisation to receive British military support. The Chetniks were asked to join forces with Tito's troops, and both parties were ordered to form a coalition to act as a provisional caretaker government[38] (Pirjevec 2018: 126–31, 140–44; Đilas 1985: 25–8; Novak 1970: 89–92).

After a heavy attack of German troops (who were on the retreat from Greece) on the Partisan headquarters in Drvar, Tito was evacuated to the island of Vis in early

---

the Partisan movement (2004: 332–349). For a bilaterally agreed Italian–Slovene account, see the seminal report of the joint expert group (Slovene–Italian Report 2004: 21–24).

[36]Tito's Partisan army accounted for 300,000 men and women by late 1943. The Germans had to deploy 250,000 troops to fight the growing resistance (Calic 2014: 153).

[37]Bosnia-Herzegovina with the Partisan headquarters at Bihać remained a Partisan stronghold. Tito's troops also had a firm grip on Slovenia and Macedonia. Serbia's underground forces, however, remained in the hands of Mihajlović's Chetniks (Novak 1970: 89).

[38]In November 1943, the second session of AVNOJ had declared the establishment of a nine-member National Committee of Liberation as the supreme legislative and executive body of a federal Yugoslavia. This body constituted a *de facto* provisional government (Prunk 1996: 134–5; Ramet 2006: 157; Calic 2014: 154). The coalition agreement the Allies had called for between Tito's AVNOJ and the government-in-exile was signed in June 1944 on the island of Vis (Matl 1954: 118; Novak 1970: 92; Prunk 1996: 134).

June 1944 (Pirjevec 2018: 435),[39] where he had his new headquarters protected by the British navy[40] and still managed to go on a secret trip to Moscow to see Stalin.[41] By September 1944, Tito had become the sole *de facto* leader of Yugoslavia, also in full command of the armed forces (Newman 2015: 259–260; Novak 1970: 92–93; Matl 1954: 118).

Partisan and Soviet[42] troops liberated Belgrade on 20 October 1944[43] where Tito's headquarters subsequently moved to. The liberation of Belgrade may also be seen as a major boost for Tito's popularity marking "the final, crowning step toward personal, autocratic power" (Đilas 1985: 12). The Partisan army had further increased by then, and with a massive 800,000 troops[44] the liberation of the rest of the country was only a question of time. On 6 April 1945, the Partisans gained control over Sarajevo, and on 9 May 1945, Tito's troops took over Zagreb and Ljubljana. At the end of the day, Yugoslavia was able to do away with the occupation without much help of the allies (Calic 2014: 172; Pirjevec 2018: 135–140). Tito went even further moving across the northern border into the Klagenfurt/Celovec area in Austrian Carinthia with the aim of "bringing home" the Slovenian community there, but had to retreat following Allied pressure (Ramet 2006: 159, 172; Prunk 1996: 136).

2.3.4 *Founding of Yugoslavia II*

After the election for the constitution-forming body on 11 November 1945,[45] the Constituent Assembly declared Yugoslavia a republic, and King Petar was banned from the country on the grounds of collaboration with Chetnik forces. On 31 January 1946, the regime adopted a new constitution, the Federal People's Republic of Yugoslavia (FPRY) consisting of a federation of equal nations, the six Republics Serbia, Croatia, Slovenia, Bosnia-Herzegovina, Macedonia, and Montenegro with

---

[39] For Operation "Rösselsprung" during which Tito and his staff were in the end evacuated to Bari by a Russian plane, see Pirjevec (2018: 122–6). The British subsequently flew Tito from Bari to Vis (Pirjevec 2018: 127).

[40] Remarkably, Tito managed to achieve the retreat of two British battalions who had already landed in Kotor Bay, Montenegro (Matl 1954: 118).

[41] Russian planes stationed in Bari, Southern Italy, were officially practising incognito nocturnal landings without signalling on Vis. In a top-secret operation co-ordinated beforehand, Tito together with his dog (sic) managed to board a Russian C-47 on the runway without the Brits noticing and took off to Craiova on 19 September 1944 at 3 a.m. early in the morning. The following day he flew to Moscow (Pirjevec 2018: 133–4).

[42] In a clandestine visit to Moscow from Vis (unnoticed by the British), Tito had convinced Stalin to send Soviet troops (Ramet 2006: 158; Novak 1970: 94).

[43] 15,000 German troops and 3,000 Partisan soldiers lost their lives in that very fierce battle (Calic 2014: 171).

[44] Vis-à-vis 400,000 German and 15,000 NDH soldiers (Ramet 2006: 159).

[45] The communist-controlled Popular Front received 81.5% of the vote (Ramet 2006: 169).

Fig. 2.2 Socialist Federal Republic of Yugoslavia—SFRY (*Source* Author; base map: d-maps.com)

Serbia entailing the autonomous provinces of Vojvodina and Kosovo (Ramet 2006: 169; Jović 2009: 57; Hondius 1968: 135–7); see Fig. 2.2.

It is worth noting that none of the six Republics had existed in this shape before, and that there were now three official languages (Serbo-Croatian, Slovenian, and Macedonian) and many minority languages,[46] three religious denominations (Catholic, Orthodox, and Muslim), and two alphabets (Latin and Cyrillic) in the new Yugoslavia of "brotherhood and unity"[47] (Hondius 1968: 140; Accetto 2007: 193). Fundamentally, for Tito and Kardelj, the social revolution and the national question were clearly linked, and the national question was the main point of departure for the new Yugoslavia and the answer to the Great Serbian Bourgeoisie Kingdom since 1918. In Tito's words:

> The […] national liberation struggle would be nothing but words […] if they did not have […] a specifically national meaning for each people individually, if they did not mean, together with the liberation of Yugoslavia, the liberation at the same time, too, of Croats, Slovenes, Serbs, Macedonians […], Muslims, and the rest; […] if the national liberation struggle did not contain the substance of effective freedom, equality, and brotherhood for all peoples of

[46] Albanian, Hungarian, Italian, Slovak, Bulgarian, and Romanian (Jončić 1967: 216).

[47] Wachtel and Bennett hold that "brotherhood and unity" actually is an oxymoron referring to separate and at the least potentially contradictory notions. Whereas "unity" stood for full agreement, "brotherhood" implied some substantial level of difference irrespective of the will for closeness (2009: 17).

> Yugoslavia. This is the real essence of the national liberation struggle. (Tito 1942: 3; cited in Jović 2009: 56–7)

The constitution combined elements of direct democracy, notably to replace the parliamentary multi-party system (a crucial point in Kardelj's concept; see Pirjevec 2018: 395–6), and local rule with the leading role of the Communist Party of Yugoslavia in virtually all areas of life (Calic 2014: 176; Ramet 2006: 169; Zellweger 1954: 126; Jović 2009: 58–61). The most distinctive feature of the 1946 constitution was the concept of the *unity of power* rejecting the classical *separation of power* familiar to contemporary rule-of-law democracies since Montesquieu times (see Accetto 2007: 207–8; 228–9), thus transplanting "Soviet rules of operation onto the Yugoslav scene" (Hondius 1968: 152). A full assessment of Yugoslavia II (1946–1991) as a polity is beyond the scope of this book (for the SFRY's dissolution, see Sect. 2.5).

Nevertheless, it appears fair not to assess the Yugoslav experience merely as "a failed attempt at federalism, but primarily as a unique way of constructing a federal polity" (Accetto 2007: 196).[48] Neither was Yugoslavia about preventing the various ethnic groups from fighting one another. Sekulić et al. have tested the causal link between intolerance and ethnic conflict ahead, during and after the dissolution of Yugoslavia. They have demonstrated that (i) ethnic intolerance in post-World-War-II Yugoslavia was low, (ii) it was even slightly in decline towards the end of the SFRY and after the wars of secession, (iii) outright ethnic conflict amongst individuals was absent, but (iv) elite manipulation[49] was a substantial contributor to a rise in ethnic intolerance (Sekulić et al. 2006; see also Milošević and Touquet 2018).[50] These findings appear to disconfirm a widespread popular myth that the break-up of Yugoslavia was inevitable anyway because of built-in ethnic conflict.

In summary, the German–Italian invasion of Yugoslavia strengthened Tito's resistance movement. Profiting from Italian surrender in 1943, the resistance movement increased its military power and subsequently received active British and Soviet recognition and support. These processes put Tito in an allied role and secured him the return of the Istrian territories which had been under Italian rule since 1918. Domestically, the military victory over the fascist occupation, branded the "liberation war", put him in a position to replace the monarchy by a republic. A quasi-federal constitution with communist one-party rule was supposed to secure both the country's unity and some degree of its constituent nations' relative autonomy. The role of the inter-republican borders appears to have been mainly administrative-territorial rather than ethnic–political.

---

[48] Accetto (2007) provides a profound analysis of the interplay between law and politics in Yugoslavia II.

[49] Meaning persuasion of citizens *by* the political elite.

[50] For a survey on the post-Yugoslav sociologists' reflection of the SFRY dissolution processes, see Flere (2014).

2.4 Free Territory of Trieste (FTT)

The Trieste crisis deserves particular attention. To start with, it constituted the first larger-scale confrontation between the East and the West around the end of World War II. Second, it was the first piece of Allied governance in a bilateral territorial conflict on the southern fringe of the Yalta line. Third, the Trieste issue involved substantial border changes.

2.4.1 Liberation of Trieste

During the last weeks of the war, Tito, in a clever move to secure maximum territorial claims (most importantly the return of the entire Julian Region to Yugoslavia), had his troops move into Trieste and the remaining parts of Istria (Duroselle 1966: 442; Calic 2014: 178). By April 1945, the struggle was on between British–American Allied troops and the Yugoslav Army over who would first occupy the Julian Region. Tito was determined to conquer the territory disputed by Italians and South Slavs since 1870 (Calic 2014: 178) to put a *fait accompli* before the Allies (Pirjevec 2018: 156; Novak 1970: 125; Hildebrandt 1954: 158).[51]

Between the Yalta Conference in February 1945 (partitioning Europe into a Western and Eastern sphere of interest) and mid-April of that year, Yugoslavia had become a part of the Eastern bloc, not least through the Treaty of Friendship between Tito and Stalin. Churchill and Roosevelt had agreed that the Julian Region needed to be under Allied control to have a clear picture of the advancement of the Eastern bloc (Novak 1970: 132). The Yugoslav Army, coming from the south-east, arrived in the centre of Trieste on 1 May 1945, one day before the British troops entered the town from the west.[52] By mid-May, tensions between the Yugoslav troops and the Anglo-American armed forces had climaxed. The British–American combined chiefs of staff had, in late April, instructed the troops on the ground to occupy the entire Julian Region including Trieste, Rijeka, and the Kvarner islands, and to establish an *Allied Military Government* (AMG), whereas Tito's forces would not retreat by a single inch (Novak 1970: 161–196). However, Yugoslav full "possession" of Trieste lasted for only forty days. On 12 June, Tito's troops had to retreat from the city after heavy diplomatic pressure from Britain and the USA,[53] and the absence

[51]The USA and Britain had made it clear to Tito that Yugoslavia should, after the end of the war, claim the Julian Region at the peace conference, which would then put a verdict on just demands (Novak 1970: 130).

[52]The importance of Trieste for Tito may be highlighted by the following facts: the Partisans had proclaimed the annexation of Trieste as early as November 1943 during the second AVNOJ session (Ramet 2006: 172). Operationally, the Partisans liberated Ljubljana and Zagreb only on 9 May 1945, one week after occupying Trieste (Novak 1970: 156, 169).

[53]The tough American–British stance may also be related to a feeling of anger towards the Soviet–Yugoslav Treaty of Friendship which had been signed earlier in the year (Capano 2016: 55; Prunk 1996: 136).

of Soviet support. The latter fact Tito would complain about bitterly (Pirjevec 2018: 157[54]; Wörsdörfer 2004: 522; Cresciani 2004: 8).

2.4.2 Workings of the Free Territory of Trieste (FTT)

Following the Belgrade agreement of 9 June 1945 between Generals Morgan and Jovanović, the *Free Territory of Trieste* (FTT) was established, consisting of Zone A (Trieste and its suburbs, a tiny strip of hinterland including a link to the new Italian border, and Pula) under direct Allied military administration, and Zone B (the coastal strip south of Trieste including the Slovenian district of Koper, Piran Bay, and the Croatian district of Buje) under Yugoslav military administration (Novak 1970: 199; Pirjevec 2018: 157); see Fig. 2.3.[55]

The FTT entered into force in September 1947 as a component of the Paris Peace Treaty with Italy.[56] The provisions entailed an FTT governor appointed by the UN Security Council. However, it proved impossible for the Great Powers to agree on a governor. As a result, the FTT as such "only existed on paper" (Rutar 2010: 249), and what was supposed to be a very short period of temporary military administration lasted for quite a few years (Novak 1970: 275–280) and was seen as an "interim trusteeship over the area" (CIA Report 1948: 3).

In March 1948, Britain, France, and the USA proposed to give the *entire* Zone A to Italy. Yet, this move was fiercely opposed by Yugoslavia and the Soviets. The reasoning behind the Western Allies' move is seen to have been to secure an anti-Communist victory in the upcoming Italian general election and to prepare for Italian accession to NATO (Capano 2016: 54; Hildebrandt 1954: 158; Novak 1970: 281).

In late June 1948, Tito and the Communist Party of Yugoslavia were expelled from the Cominform (the Moscow-led communist league) for "breaking with the Marxist theory" and for an "unfriendly policy toward the Soviet Union" (Džalto 2018b: 17). It was not before September 1949, however, that the Soviet Union and its satellite States' governments in East-Central Europe cancelled the Soviet–Yugoslav Treaty of Friendship (Novak 1970: 299–300, 314–5).[57]

---

[54]Stalin was not ready to risk a World War III over Trieste and therefore demanded the immediate withdrawal of the Yugoslav troops, although he was of the opinion that the Yugoslavs did deserve Trieste (Pirjevec 2018: 157).

[55]The Julian Region as a whole was also divided up into an US-UK Zone A and a Yugoslav Zone B along the so-called Morgan line (Novak 1978: 5–6; Capano 2016: 54).

[56]The zones A and B of the Julian Region (*not* of the FTT) expired by the time the area was assigned to Italy and Yugoslavia, respectively, by the Peace Treaty with Italy in 1947.

[57]Tito had given a speech full of anger towards the Soviet Union in Ljubljana at the end of May 1945 saying that "we are not going to allow ourselves to become entangled in political spheres of interest [and] we will not be dependent on anyone ever again" (Ramet 2006: 176).

Fig. 2.3 Free Territory of Trieste (Blake and Topalović 1996: 22). ©IBRU, Durham University, UK

As a result, Yugoslavia received military and financial and foodstuff support from the West as from 1951 (Hildebrandt 1954: 169; Pirjevec 2018: 220) and considerable military support from the USA, such as two hundred F-84 fighter jets including a training of Yugoslav pilots at their home air bases (Pirjevec 2018: 216).

The London Memorandum of Understanding of 1954 finally settled the FTT issue assigning Zone A to Italy and Zone B to Yugoslavia.[58] This settlement can be regarded as favourable to Yugoslavia as it was able to acquire most of the territory claimed in the first place, in particular the whole of Istria including Fiume/Rijeka, the Kvarner islands of Cherso/Cres and Lussino/Lošinj, and Dalmatia including Zara/Zadar (Cresciani 2004: 8; Slovene–Italian Report 2004: 26). Tito was satisfied with the London Memorandum, although sacrifices in terms of the loss of Trieste had to be made (Novak 1970: 461, 1978: 6–8). Yet, Tito secured the port of Koper/Capodistria which Italy had heavily claimed. There were secret trilateral talks between Yugoslavia, Britain, and the USA between February and September 1954 how to achieve a renouncement of Rome's claims (Pirjevec 2018: 219–221).

It must be noted that the Slovene notion of the "unjust border" which cuts off the Trieste area and its surroundings with a majority Slovene population has lived on to the present day (interview Alojz Peterle,[59] 15-06-2016; interview Ivo Vajgl,[60] 29-09-2015; see also Slovene–Italian Report 2004: 26). Conversely, it could be argued that the present-day Slovenian–Italian border has lost its divisive nature since it constitutes an intra-Schengen border with no controls and thus *de facto* freedom of movement in a truly European cross-border space (interview Tanja Fajon,[61] 22-11-2016).

The return to Yugoslavia of the inter-war Italian territories in Istria, Kvarner, and Dalmatia can be seen as the most relevant changes to Yugoslavia's international boundaries after World War II (Radan 1999: 138). The loss of the Italian territories led to a mass emigration of around 200,000 to 300,000 Italians from the area (Wörsdörfer 2004: 522–560; Cresciani 2004: 8–9), mainly because of oppression by the Yugoslav regime, and for fear of eventually living on the wrong side of the Iron Curtain (Slovene–Italian Report 2004: 30–1).

---

[58] According to Capano (2016: 55), a secret agreement between the US/UK and Tito on the definite partition had been reached as early as 6 October 1953. Pirjevec (2018: 217–8), however, contends that the USA and the UK took the decision themselves before notifying Tito and the Italian Prime Minister Pella. The Memorandum was in the end signed on 5 October 1954 at the Foreign Office in London following heavy diplomatic activity of the USA persuading Tito to accept the partition of the FTT decided by the USA and Britain. As a reward, Yugoslavia received an additional 450,000 tons of wheat from the USA on top of the 400,000 tons already granted plus loans from the International Bank for Reconstruction and Development—IBRD (Pirjevec 2018: 220).

[59] Alojz Peterle was an MEP 2004–2019, Prime Minister of Slovenia 1991–92, and Foreign Minister 1993/94 and 2000.

[60] Ivo Vajgl was an MEP 2009–2019, Foreign Minister of Slovenia in 2004 and Slovenian Ambassador to Germany, Austria, the OSCE, Sweden, and the Nordic and Baltic States.

[61] Tanja Fajon MEP is Chair of the inter-parliamentary delegation with Serbia and was Rapporteur for the EU visa liberalisation for Serbia, Bosnia-Herzegovina, Montenegro, North Macedonia, Albania, and Kosovo 2014–2019.

2.4.3 Osimo Treaty 1975

The 1954 London Memorandum was not a legally binding agreement, notwithstanding its *de facto* nature (Pirjevec 2018: 219). It was initialled, not signed (Rutar 2010: 251),[62] so neither Italy nor Yugoslavia renounced their claims to what had ceased to be the FTT (Novak 1970: 460). Yet, it took another 20 years before a final settlement between Yugoslavia and Italy could be agreed on. The Osimo Treaty of 1975 not only put an end to the "Adriatic Question" between the two countries in delimitating the maritime border in the Gulf of Trieste by means of the equidistance line (Cataldi 2013: 257). The continental shelf boundary agreement between the two States had been concluded in 1968 (Klemenčić and Topalović 2009: 313; Blake and Topalović 1996: 15–17) commencing full delimitation.[63] Osimo also settled the open land border question resulting from the FTT period discussed above (see Sect. 2.4.2).

Trieste had long remained a contentious issue, despite an increasing willingness to phase-out the territorial claims and to look into the benefits of "Adriatic friendship". Both the Italian and the Yugoslav governments had come to accept the mutually beneficial effects of a final settlement on geopolitical stability and economic cooperation (Capano 2016: 58–60; Vlašić 2014). The potential benefits of closer cooperation between Yugoslavia and the European Economic Community (EEC) also played a strong role advanced in particular by the Yugoslav Republics of Croatia and Slovenia, and Rome had become Belgrade's privileged Western European partner after the signing of a bilateral economic agreement in 1964 (Zaccaria 2019: 4–5).[64] The Osimo agreement, which was applauded by international public opinion, did confirm the return of the FTT zones A to Italy and B to Yugoslavia, respectively, as for the land border. As for the maritime border in the Upper Adriatic, the delimitation of the territorial waters was carried out in such fashion that larger freight vessels could approach Trieste through Italian waters and Koper through Yugoslav waters (Vukas 1976: 80).[65]

The Osimo accord marked the first international treaty between States incorporating the principles of the preamble of the newly adopted CSCE Helsinki Final Act

---

[62] Generally, memoranda—as opposed to treaties—are not legally enforceable.

[63] The 1968 agreement between Italy and Yugoslavia was the first-ever continental shelf maritime delimitation treaty in the Adriatic. The boundary runs over 353 nautical miles and reflects the equidistance line (Klemenčić and Topalović 2009: 313). For an introduction to maritime delimitation terminology, see Sect. 3.1.

[64] The development of relations with Yugoslavia was a priority for the new centre-left government of Aldo Moro. This coincided with the souring of relations between the Federal Republic of Germany (FRG) and Yugoslavia after 1957 when Belgrade had recognised the German Democratic Republic (GDR). For the *rapprochement* between the EEC and Yugoslavia in the 1960s and 1970s, see Zaccaria (2016).

[65] The present-day Traffic Separation Scheme of the International Maritime Organization (IMO) which has been operational since 1 December 2004 has incoming vessels to both Trieste and Koper go through Croatian and Slovenian waters, i.e. the former Yugoslav side of the Osimo delimitation line, and outgoing vessels through Italian waters (Vidas 2009: 33–4); see also Sects. 3.1.3.1 and 6.1.1.1.

(Vukas 1976: 76)[66] and eventually made the Italian–Yugoslav border a new bridge rather than a wall between the two countries (Capano 2016: 58).

To sum up, the Trieste crisis marked a major territorial conflict between the British–American Allied troops and the Yugoslav Army just a few months into the new East–West division of Europe decided on at the Yalta Conference in February 1945. The establishment of the Free Territory of Trieste (FTT) as the result of direct negotiations between the two camps on the ground may be seen as an example of pragmatic *ad-hoc* partition. The foreseen FTT governor, however, was never appointed because of a lack of agreement between the Great Powers in the UN Security Council. Despite the fact that the FTT was divided up between Italy and Yugoslavia *de facto* in 1954, it took another 20 years to conclude a final bilateral agreement on the common Italo-Yugoslav State border.

2.5 Dissolution of Yugoslavia

Much has been written on the fall of Yugoslavia and the political, historical, economic, and cultural–societal reasons. Nevertheless, there is no single straightforward way of recapitulating the manifold causal mechanisms that lead to the end of the SFRY,[67] not least because a clear starting point of the country's demise would not be easily identified.[68] As for analyses of the dissolution of Yugoslavia, Bieber (2014: 2) provides a crucial point: any research runs "the risk of reading history backwards", implying that "the knowledge of the State's eventual failure and dissolution interprets developments and events during Socialist Yugoslavia as evidence of its path towards dissolution". That approach is likely to produce a deterministic view that Yugoslavia as an "artificial" State "was doomed to fail" anyway. Further, the benefit of hindsight tends to prevent the researcher from observing and capturing the "evolution of the ongoing process" and it renders us "less able to grasp the atmosphere and context of the decisions taken at the time" (Bieber 2014: 3).

---

[66] The Osimo agreement not only successfully delimitated the common State border, but also set foot to considerable economic cooperation in the fields of transport, energy, and the fight against maritime pollution. The agreement even included a zone for local cross-border traffic with freedom of movement for individuals and workers (Italy and Yugoslavia, Agreement on the development of economic cooperation, 1975).

[67] For a recent account of the state of play of the debate in political science quarters, see e.g. Bieber et al. (2014); on the interplay of law and politics in post-World-War-II Yugoslavia, see Accetto (2007); a comprehensive historian's account can be found in Calic (2014: 264–344).

[68] The break-up of the SFR Yugoslavia generally tends to be associated with the declarations of independence of Slovenia and Croatia on 25 June 1991. However, the process of disintegration started earlier. Historically, and depending on the scope and type of factors taken into account, a possible starting date for the dismemberment of the SFRY can be seen in Slobodan Milošević's coming to power in Serbia 1987 or in Tito's death in 1980 (Ramet 2014: 39; Wachtel and Bennett 2009: 28–9). The effective end of Yugoslavia as a State was there in August 1990 when the League of Communists of Yugoslavia (LCY), the Communist Party, ceased to exist in all Republics, and new political parties had taken shape (Jović 2009: 361).

In respect of the established political historiography of post-World-War-II Yugoslavia, it is worth taking a brief look at Wachtel and Bennett's (2009: 13) stock-taking of the broad consensus amongst scholars. This consensus which, at the popular level, is perhaps not necessarily shared to the same degree in some of the successor States portrays the demise of Yugoslavia as a "multiple organ failure" starting in the late 1980s. Wachtel and Bennet's reconstruction centres around three domestic areas and their respective long-term problems:

(i) The political arena with the perceived illegitimacy and inefficiency of the central State, and the growing disparities of the competing regional power centres: By the mid-1970s, Yugoslavia had changed from a country of relative unity and socialist cooperation to one where the Yugoslav Republics to a great extent behaved like quasi-independent entities. The decentralising effect of the 1974 federal constitution of the SFRY had considerably weakened the federal level. The increasing republicanisation coincided with a more self-centred following of interests other than those of the common central State.
(ii) The economic decline in terms of the inability of the Communist system to generate growth and sufficient prosperity for the citizens: Yugoslavia's economy could only be upheld through international loans and foreign help. Domestically, economic modernisation was increasingly discussed in terms of the "non-motivated South" (Bosnia-Herzegovina, Macedonia, Montenegro) being financially supplied by the "hard-working North" (Croatia and Slovenia) with "Belgrade" being the distribution machine.
(iii) The cultural sphere where the State failed to create a sufficient level of shared identity in terms of a unified multinational Yugoslavia,[69] and where competing separate national narratives gained ground instead: There was no federal education system after 1948. As a result, crucial issues with regard to history and culture were interpreted and taught in a different way in the respective Republics leading to national narratives, such as victimisation (Croatia and Serbia) or exploitation (Slovenia), for example.

On top of the above domestic spheres, two external factors also merit a mention. First, the dissolution of the USSR played its role in so far, as the need for a large Yugoslav State with military power providing security for its citizens was no longer given. After the rift between Tito and Stalin in 1948, fear of the Soviet Union was considered a crucial unifying factor for a common State. Second, the European Community had enlarged by small States such as Ireland (1973), Greece (1981) or Portugal (1986). This meant that there were promising prospects in terms of potential prosperity and political security as members of a larger block, even for small countries with a low GDP per capita (Wachtel and Bennett 2009: 14–28).

With regard to *European integration*, Yugoslavia did play both a prominent and delicate role in the formative decades of the European Economic Community (EEC),

[69] "The nations of Yugoslavia […] have, together with nationalities with which they live, united in a federal republic of free and equal nations and nationalities" (SFRY constitution of 1974, Introductory Part, Basic Principles, I, p. 13).

later the European Community (EC) in the 1960s and 1970s. The EEC/EC[70] was well aware of Yugoslavia's hybrid position between the European blocks in the Cold War. The European Commission and the Member States felt that Yugoslavia's international autonomy was closely linked to its economic prosperity. Therefore, the EC followed a policy of *rapprochement* through the mutual interest in trade (Yugoslavia increasingly felt the negative effects of the Common Agricultural Policy with import tariffs on meat introduced in 1968). This resulted in the first-ever EC accord with a third country under the Common Commercial Policy, the 1970 Trade Agreement with Yugoslavia.[71]

Back to the analysis of the dissolution of Yugoslavia, there is one crucial aspect, however, which many scholars may have underestimated. Jović (2009) argues that it is the issue of the *actors* of the political elite and that one has to reconstruct their ideas, concepts, and perceptions. His approach is that the beliefs, intentions, and explanations of the actors must be taken seriously. This implies that events need to be analysed *as they happened in their context*, and not with the benefit of hindsight (see also Bieber 2014: 2). Jović's main research question is this:

> Why did political actors act as they did? Why did their actions make sense to them? What were their rationales, their motives for action, and their intentions? If we really want to understand the rationale behind the actions of the Yugoslav Communists, we need to take their beliefs seriously. What is relevant here is not whether these actions make sense to us, but whether they made sense to *them*, to those whose actions we analyse and to the relevant segment of the political body on whose approval the existence and stability of the regime depended. It is not the aim [...] to judge the actions taken by the Yugoslav elite in either favourable or unfavourable terms, but to explain them by understanding the reasons the actors had for them. (Jović 2009: 34; emphasis added)

Jović argues that Yugoslavia was primarily destroyed from inside and that the political leaders played the decisive role in the disintegration of the country. His findings include that the ideological consensus of the political elite was originally made up of Kardelj's interpretation of the Marxist concept of self-management—meaning the emancipation from both Stalinist Soviet strong-State Socialism and interwar Yugoslav unitarism (and thus the application of the concept of the withering

[70]At the time consisting of Belgium, France, the Federal Republic of Germany, Italy, the Netherlands, and Luxemburg. Denmark, Ireland, and the UK joined in 1973.

[71]The predominantly economic focus was broadened to political cooperation by the 1976 Declaration explicitly highlighting Yugoslavia's role in the Non-Aligned Movement (NAM) taking into consideration the re-emergence of the East–West confrontation in Europe after several years of superpower *détente*. The threat of the end of Tito's era and the rapid evaporation of *détente* motivated the EC to conclude a more comprehensive agreement in 1980. All in all, the EC-Yugoslavia relationship appeared to be one of *realpolitik* where the Community had to accept that it could neither influence the development of the NAM, nor the relations between the Yugoslav Republics, nor the role of the USSR. Still, it seems that the EC managed to keep Belgrade as close as possible to Brussels (Zaccaria 2016: 47–169; Boeckh 2014: 32–35). Zaccaria is the first scholar to analyse EC-Yugoslav relations on the basis of archive material from the European Commission, the Member States, and the federal government in Belgrade.

away of the State)—and of international non-alignment. Indeed, the Socialist self-management federation consisting of Republics as the real power centres[72] and a weak federal level,[73] the status of the economically most advanced socialist State, and the powerful international role of Yugoslavia through the policy of non-alignment—a successful third-way approach in an antagonist Cold War set-up—provided for a notion shared by the leading SFRY actors in the 1970s and most of the 1980s.

That consensus had started to evaporate even before the death of Tito and left the State (that had indeed already withered away to some degree[74]) so vulnerable that the break-up of the country was unstoppable. As Yugoslavia had based its unity on ideology to a great degree, it was more vulnerable to a collapse of that very identity-creating and identity-sustaining ideology. With regard to classical arguments explaining the dissolution of the SFRY, Jović (2009: 3–5) demonstrates that many of the arguments, albeit helpful in an *ex-post* analysis of the country's down-fall, appear to offer no single satisfying explanation of developments in their context.

According to Jović (2009: 15–28), looking at the (i) economic argument, the last federal government under market-oriented prime minister Marković who came into power in January 1989 achieved a remarkably sharp decrease of inflation, the convertibility of the dinar, and a substantial increase of industry production. That huge economic progress could not stop the dissolution, however. The (ii) ancient ethnic hatred argument, according to Jović, can be dismissed entirely as ethnic hatred was only constructed by political leaders as the country was already disintegrating, and used in order to replace former class enemies within the country or former enemies from the East or West. The (iii) nationalism argument has insufficient explanatory power, too, because the number of self-declared ethnic Yugoslavs (as opposed to Croats, Serbs, Slovenes, and others) had risen significantly in censuses between 1971 and 1981. In addition, a weak State and high uncertainty were nurturing nationalism towards the very end of the country, but outright nationalism had not been latent from the very beginning of post-World-War-II Yugoslavia. Rather, the federation was indeed able to accommodate the regional identities as opposed to the interwar

[72]It is useful to note that parliaments in terms of a representative democracy Kardelj saw as the preservation of class power, a product of the bourgeoisie, and therefore unsuitable for the purpose of radically changing reality. The old parliamentary structure was replaced by new so-called delegate assemblies. They were composed of representatives who were made to vote as instructed by their social group. The Communist Party had a leading role, notwithstanding the fact that it was renamed League of Communists of Yugoslavia—LCY (Jović 2009: 76–7).

[73]Despite the exclusive competence of the federal level for foreign policy and defence, the Republics were granted the right to set-up regional territorial defence units (Ramet 2002: 6). To that end, control over the territorial defence (TO) units proved crucial for Slovenia to fight off the JNA in early July 1991. Despite organised JNA confiscation of weaponry, Slovenia managed to hold on to around 30% of TO weapons, whereas in Croatia there was no organised resistance towards JNA confiscation, so the Yugoslav Army was able to disarm the TOs in Croatia within a few days after the election of Tuđman and his HDZ in April 1990 (Ramet 2006: 371).

[74]For Kardelj (and Tito), the aim of socialism was not to "create a State-sponsored democracy, but rather to socialize State functions and to promote self-management and self-managing democracy [and once this is achieved] the State apparatus will turn into a specialised public service of the self-managing society" (Quoted in Jović 2009: 77–8).

Yugoslavia or the unitarist State after 1918. The (iv) international politics argument, advancing the view that Yugoslavia could not survive the breakdown of the bipolar East–West structure, also falls short of a valid explanation. Rather, according to Jović, the collapse of Soviet-style communism was seen as a recognition of the distinct Yugoslav avenue to socialism. As to the West, there was firm support for the unity of the country from both the US and the European Community at the moment of disintegration. Only after the Ten Days War in Slovenia in July 1991 did the EC and the USA change their policy.

The following analysis of the dissolution of Yugoslavia is confined to the period *after* the independence declarations of Slovenia and Croatia around (i) the activities of the EC/EU up until 1993, (ii) the role of the post-secession war between Croatia and Serbia,[75] and (iii) the Agreement on Succession Issues between all SFRY successor States in 2001.

Joint independence of Slovenia and Croatia

It is impossible to skip a very brief sketch of the major political events in 1991. Croatia and Slovenia both declared their independence on 25 June 1991. The timing and the content of the independence proceedings had been secretly agreed on between the new leaders in Ljubljana and Zagreb (interview Ivo Sanader,[76] 19-05-2016; interview Alojz Peterle, 15-06-2016; see also e.g. Ramet 2006: 392). This deal also included a "defence pact" providing for mutual assistance in case of a military offensive on the part of the Yugoslav Army in either of the two newly independent entities (interview Alojz Peterle, 15-06-2016; interview Ivo Vajgl, 29-09-2015). Politically, the initial point of break-up or meltdown of Yugoslavia may be seen in the event during the League of Communists of Yugoslavia (LCY)'s Congress in January 1990 where the Croatian delegation kind of walked out together with the Slovenian delegation in an act of solidarity (see Ramet 2014: 42; Wachtel and Bennett 2009: 35; Pusić 1997: 97). In fact, after the Slovenian delegation leader Ciril Ribičič had announced the Slovenian walkout, the head of the Croatian delegation, Ivica Račan, hastened to call for an immediate break-off of the Congress which a majority of the delegates endorsed (Meier 1995: 246).

A fact that is often overlooked is that the actual question put to vote in the referenda in Slovenia (13 December 1990) and Croatia (19 May 1991) was not outright independence cutting all ties to the SFRY. Rather, what was on the table in the case of Croatia, was the option of an independent Croatia potentially entering into a "federation of

---

[75] For the wars in Bosnia-Herzegovina (where the death toll amounts to 215,000 people) and Kosovo (12,000 casualties), see Ramet (2006: 414–494; 537–552). Owen (1995) provides a comprehensive personal mediator's account of the EU/UN peace efforts in Bosnia-Herzegovina. Webb et al. (1996) argue that the real-world situation on the ground with an often localised war made mediation efforts an extremely complex affair. For an evaluation of the conflict-reducing effects of UN peacekeeping operations generally see Hegre et al. (2015).

[76] Ivo Sanader was Prime Minister of Croatia 2003–2009, Minister for Science and Research in 1992, and Deputy Foreign Minister in 1993–2003 involved in bilateral relations with Slovenia.

sovereign States"[77] with the other SFRY Republics (interview Vesna Pusić,[78] 24-02-2017). Similarly, the referendum question in Slovenia included an option to enter into a confederation of Yugoslav States (Wachtel and Bennett 2009: 38). Each new State would retain an independent army, but the former Republics would be parties to a defence pact. In economic terms, federal elements such as a common market and even freedom of movement were foreseen (Iglar 1992: 235–7). The referendum questions may also be seen in the light of the joint Croato-Slovene proposal from October 1990 for a confederation of independent Yugoslav Republics. Jović (2008: 251), however, demonstrates that the confederation proposal was a tactical move and "a genuine attempt to achieve first a *de facto* and then a de jure independence without violence".

Two days after the declaration of independence, on 27 June 1991, the Yugoslav Army (JNA) started to attack or occupy infrastructure installations and border crossings to Austria and Italy (Baker 2015: 51; Nešović and Prunk 1994: 251) in what is often labelled the "Ten Days War" in Slovenia (e.g. Džalto 2018a: 53; Bojinović Fenko and Šabič 2014: 49). It ended with the withdrawal of the JNA from Slovenia by 7 July (Türk 1993: 67). There had been a secret understanding between the Slovenian leadership and the Milošević government of Serbia for Slovenia to leave Yugoslavia "without too much resistance from the Serbian side" (Pusić 1997: 96). Peterle, however, insists that his government was not involved in such talks (interview 15-06-2016). Nonetheless, the agreement, if it existed, may help explain the very short duration of JNA activities in Slovenia. In addition, defence preparations in Slovenia had been carried out at an early stage—unlike in Croatia where the JNA barracks were not placed under siege (Ramet 2014: 43; Meier 1995: 267, 273). For the events in Croatia, where a full-blown war broke out in the second half of July 1991, mainly over the areas with a considerable Serbian population in Eastern Slavonia, the Krajina, and Northern Dalmatia, see Sect. 2.5.2.

Role of the European Community

The immediate response of both the EC and the USA around the co-ordinated joint declaration of independence of Croatia and Slovenia was to take a cautious approach, not least in the face of the nuclear superpower USSR being in a process of dissolution,[79] and to support Yugoslav unity for the time being (e.g. Hannum 1993: 59; Rich

[77]The full referendum question read "Are you in favour that the Republic of Croatia, as a sovereign and independent State, which guarantees the cultural autonomy and all civil rights of Serbs and members of other nationalities in Croatia, may enter into a federation of sovereign States with the other republics […]?"; cited in Vukas (2011: 19).

[78]Vesna Pusić MP was Foreign Minister of Croatia in 2011–2015 and Chair of the European Integration Committee of the Croatian Parliament (Sabor) in 2008–2011.

[79]It was unpredictable by the spring and the summer of 1991 whether the Soviet Union would dissolve peacefully. Yet, the independence of the three Baltic States that had been declared on 21 August 1991 was recognised by Moscow on 4 September. The remaining USSR Republics signed the Declaration of Alma Ata on 21 December 1991 mutually agreeing that the Soviet Union ceased to exist, and subsequently founded the Community of Independent States (CIS) on 26 December 1991 (Rich 1993: 37–8; 44–47).

1993: 40).[80] As early as late May 1991, the US State Department had declared that "Yugoslavia's external or internal borders should not be changed unless by peaceful consensual means".[81]

In a first mediation initiative on the part of the EC, Slovenia and Croatia agreed on a three-month moratorium on the implementation of their independence declarations at a meeting on Brioni on 7 July 1991, so that they would only take effect as from 8 October 1991 during which time an agreement between all Yugoslav Republics was supposed to be reached. All Yugoslav Republics were present at the Brioni meeting. The foreseen talks, however, never started over the following weeks (Šelo Šabić 2014: 72; Vukas 2011: 22; Rich 1993: 39),[82] and the full independence of Croatia and Slovenia was implemented following the expiry of the memorandum on 8 October 1991 (e.g. Šelo Šabić 2014: 71; Craven 1996: 141).

At a special meeting of the EC Foreign Affairs Council held in Brussels on 27 August 1991, ministers agreed on a joint declaration expressing their determination "not to recognise changes of borders by force" and to set up a "peace conference" and an "arbitration procedure" (EC Bulletin, Vol. 7/8, 24/1991b: 115–6) which became known as the *Conference on Peace in Yugoslavia* and the *Arbitration Commission*. Prior to the meeting of 27 August, the Dutch EC Presidency had, in a letter to fellow EC Member States dated 13 July, proposed to look into the possibility of a voluntary redrawing of the internal borders of the Yugoslav Republics to reduce the number of national minorities in the respective Republics. This proposal was, however, rejected by the other eleven Member States on the grounds that ethnic borders were out of date and that it was technically impossible to redraw borders without leaving minority "pockets" geographically unconnected (Owen 1995: 33).[83]

2.5.1 Badinter Commission

It is worth quoting the provisions on the arbitration procedure because of their remarkable brevity and the lack of procedural provisions:

[80] On a stopover visit to Belgrade five days before the declarations of independence on the part of Slovenia and Croatia, US Secretary of State James Baker declared that his country would under no circumstances recognise Croatia and Slovenia (Wachtel and Bennett 2009: 42).

[81] State Department Press Release, 24 May 1991, quoted in Hannum (1993: 59).

[82] Further provisions entailed a monitoring mission under the CSCE of 30–50 (sic) staff operating in "Slovenia, and possibly Croatia" (Brioni Declaration, Annex II; reprinted in STA News, 8 July 1991).

[83] The EC Presidency letter is reprinted in Owen (1995: 31–3). Member State diplomats probably perceived the letter as too indecisive in both the spirit and the wording, as there was talk of new borders being the result of "a peaceful process [...] based on general agreement".

> The arbitration procedure in the framework of this peace conference will be established as follows. The relevant authorities will submit their differences to an Arbitration Commission of five members chosen from the Presidents of Constitutional Courts existing in the Community countries. The composition of the Arbitration Commission will be:
>
> (i) two members appointed unanimously by the Federal Presidency [of the SFRY];
>
> (ii) three members appointed by the Community and its Member States.
>
> In the absence of an agreement on the members to be appointed by the Federal Presidency, they will be designated by the three members appointed by the Community.
>
> This Arbitration Commission will [decide] within two months. (EC Bulletin Vol. 7/8, 24/1991b: 116)

Every allowance must be made for the unprecedented and emergency circumstances of the EC meeting of 27 August 1991 when hostilities in Croatia were already in full swing. Still, it is worth noting that the above mandate for the Arbitration Commission does not contain any provisions on "relevant authorities" (would the scope of this term include the warring SFRY Republics, the formally still existing SFRY Federal Presidency, or perhaps also the EC?[84]), the type of submissions to the Arbitration Committee, the EC-internal appointment procedure (i.e. the selection of candidates or the voting procedure), or a reference on the rules of procedure for the Arbitration Commission, to name but a few.

The EC designated the President of the French Constitutional Court, Robert Badinter, the President of the German Federal Constitutional Court, Roman Herzog, and the President of the Italian Constitutional Court, Aldo Corasaniti. As the SFRY Federal Presidency proved unable to unanimously nominate their two candidates, the remaining vacancies were filled according to the above provisions of the declaration by a decision of the other three members of the Arbitration Commission already designated. The further members were the President of the Spanish Constitutional Court, Francisco Tomas y Valiente, and the President of the Belgian *Cours d'Arbitrage*, Irène Petry. Robert Badinter was appointed President and the Commission, hereafter "*Badinter Commission*", adopted rules of procedure which were not made public (Craven 1996: 336). Pellet describes the rules of procedure as foreseeing majority voting for the adoption of opinions. In practice, however, the Opinions of the Badinter Commission were adopted by consensus (Pellet 1992: 332).

2.5.1.1 Opinions of the Badinter Commission

The Arbitration Commission issued 15 Opinions altogether, the first ten Opinions were issued between December 1991 and July 1992. The Commission was reconstituted in January 1993 and delivered a further five Opinions until August 1993 (Craven

[84] The Badinter Commission was in fact called upon by the President of the Conference on Yugoslavia (Opinions 1 and 8–10) and by its later Co-Chairmen respectively (Opinions 11–15), by the Republic of Serbia (Opinions 2 and 3), and the EC Member States (Opinions 4–7) (Pellet 1992: 178; Craven 1996: 333–4).

1996: 333–4). All Opinions[85] will be briefly touched on. Those treating most fundamental issues and/or having met a mixed scholarly response will be discussed in somewhat more detail.

Secession or Dissolution? (Opinions 1 and 8)

The first legal question was put to the Committee by the Chairman of the Conference on Yugoslavia, Lord Carrington, on 20 November 1991. He inquired whether (i) the SFRY Republics are in the process of secession (in which case the SFRY would continue to exist) or (ii) the SFRY was in a process of dissolution (in which case all former SFRY republics would become successor entities to the SFRY which would cease to exist).

In Opinion 1 of 11 January 1992, the Committee found that the SFRY no longer met the criteria of a State under international law, because its State organs were virtually powerless due to a lack of participation of the Republics in the federal organs and due to armed conflict between elements of the federation. As a result, Yugoslavia was in a process of dissolution (I.L.M. 1992: 1494–7).

In Opinion 8 of 4 July 1992, the Committee answered another question from the Conference Chair from 18 May 1992, on whether the dissolution assumed in Opinion 1 could now be regarded as complete. The Committee found that in the light of the fact that no federal body had functioned since the issuance of Opinion 1, the FRY (Serbia and Montenegro) was "a new State", the former SFRY territory and population were now "entirely under the sovereign authority of the new States", and the dissolution was "now complete and that the SFRY no longer exists" (I.L.M. 1992: 1521–3).

Craven (1996: 366–368) posits that as for the assessment of the facts, Opinion 1 was accurate. However, the assumption that the effective control by a State depended on the system of government was too strict for federal States. What was not acceptable, according to Craven, is that a State ceased to exist simply because of a "lack of [...] participation in government itself" which equalled a notion that federal States were more fragile than unitary States. Subsequent evidence, however, as expressed in Opinion 8, did confirm the dismemberment of the SFRY. Türk (1993: 69), somewhat in contrast, approves of the Commission's emphasis on effectiveness as "duly recognised" in Opinions 1 and 8. Agreeing with Türk in substance, Pellet (1992: 179) yet attributes "little originality" to the Commission's findings. Hannum dismisses the concept of dissolution as "*secession* was precisely what was occurring in Yugoslavia" (1993: 62; emphasis added). It is the view of this author that one may well argue that secession has led to dissolution or dismemberment and that it tends to be difficult to say exactly when one ends and the other one starts.

[85]The Opinions are taken from International Legal Materials (I.L.M.) as reproduced primary legal documents.

Self-determination and Internal Borders as International Ones (Opinions 2 and 3)

On 20 November 1991, the Chairman of the Conference put another two question to the Committee which he had received by the Republic of Serbia. The first one asked whether the Serbian population in Croatia and Bosnia-Herzegovina had the right to self-determination.

The Committee, in its Opinion 2 from 11 January 1992, found that international law at the time did not make reference to all implications of self-determination, but that such self-determination had to avoid changing existing borders at the time of independence (*uti possidetis juris*) unless the States concerned did agree otherwise. Further, all ethnic, religious, or language groups within a State had the right to "recognition of their identity" and minority rights for the Serbian population in Bosnia-Herzegovina and Croatia had to be ensured on the part of the State, including the right to choose their nationality (I.L.M. 1992: 1497–9).

The second question by the Republic of Serbia inquired whether "the internal boundaries between Croatia and Serbia and between Bosnia-Herzegovina and Serbia [can] be regarded as frontiers in terms of public international law" (I.L.M. 1992: 1499).

In its Opinion 3 from 11 January 1992, the most far-reaching of the Badinter Opinions, the Committee found that, first, all external frontiers were to be respected following the UN Charter and the Helsinki Final Act. Second, the borders between Croatia and Serbia, and between Bosnia-Herzegovina and Serbia may not be altered unless mutually agreed otherwise. Third and foremost, the former (internal) boundaries were to become international boundaries protected by international law. The Commission invoked the principle of *uti possidetis* stating that this principle "although initially applied in settling decolonisation issues in America and Africa, is today recognised as a general principle". The Committee referred to a judgement of the International Court of Justice (ICJ) of 1986 in the *Burkina Faso v Republic of Mali* case referring to the *uti possidetis* principle as applicable to independence wherever it occurs (I.L.M. 1992: 1499–1500).

Opinion 3 has received a strong scholarly response. Sorel and Mehdi (1994: 18) approve of the Committee's finding and assert that "l'*uti possidetis* s'applique donc sur tous les continents et sur tous les espaces et apparait comme le principe incontournable de toute mutation territoriale à l'époque contemporaine". Pellet (1992: 180) lauds the promotion of *uti possidetis* on the part of the Committee, as the principle ensured the territorial integrity of States, "that great principle of peace, indispensable to international stability", and Europeans were wise not to dispense it, not least because the principle provided for considerable flexibility for adjustment by mutual agreement.

Whilst approving of *uti possidetis* as such, Craven critiques that the Committee appeared not to have grasped the spirit of the ICJ's judgement which was indeed confined to issues of decolonisation. In addition, two different processes had been at work in each case, namely (i) the identification of units of statehood and (ii) the determination of borders "within which those entities are to be confined". However, the original meaning of *uti possidetis* only applied to the second issue. Yet, the Committee used it for the first purpose and established the presumptive statehood of entities from the dismemberment of the SFRY denying the autonomous Serbian provinces the benefit of that presumption (Craven 1996: 388–9).

Radan (1999: 147–151) opposes Opinion 3. He argues that the *uti possidetis* principle was inappropriate mainly since historically Yugoslavia's various internal borders after 1918 were at no point in time foreseen to become international borders, let alone for entities seceding the State.[86] In his view, the post-SFRY "secessionist wars" were in essence wars about borders, and therefore the Badinter Principle did prolong violent conflict. Owen (1995: 34–5) quotes a conversation with Milovan Đilas (a Tito aide who was in charge of designing the boundaries of the post-World-War-II Yugoslav Republics) in which Đilas confirmed to him that the inter-Republican boundaries "were never intended to be international boundaries".

State Recognition (Opinions 4–7)

Before turning to the Badinter Opinions on recognition, it is worth recalling a second special meeting of the EC Foreign Ministers on 16 December 1991. Gathering in Brussels, the ministers where facing the delicate task of formulating the requirements for the recognition of no less than 20 States emerging from the former USSR and the former Yugoslavia.

Whilst several pro-Yugoslav observers generally argue that Germany in particular was pressing for early recognition of Croatia and Slovenia (e.g. Chomsky 2018: 64–6, 201; Džalto 2018a: 58; Hannum 1993: 65), some myths or inaccuracies (have) exist(ed) about the 16 December 1991 meeting. Thus, it may be useful to note that there has been no unilateral recognition of any State by any of the EC Member States (e.g. Major[87] 1995: 533–4). Rather, the EC Foreign Ministers adopted "Guidelines on the Recognition of New States in Eastern Europe and in the Soviet Union". The Foreign Ministers reached

> [...] a common position on the process of recognition of these new States, which requires:

---

[86]Radan (1999: 137–143) demonstrates that the structure of the internal administrative units of Yugoslavia was "a matter of considerable controversy and change". During the *oblast* system (1921–29), 33 *oblasti* replaced the much larger units of the Habsburg Empire in order to discourage disunity and separatism in the new Yugoslav State. The *Banovina* system (1929–39) consisted of 9 *banovine* (provinces) completely ignoring historical and cultural borders. The *Sporazum* system (1939–41) introduced a "quasi-federal system". However, it could neither overcome the divergence of interests between the Serbs and the Croats, nor was it applied to the rest of the country anyway. The socialist republic and its province system (1946–1991) were largely based on older historical borders from the Austro-Hungarian and Ottoman empires. It was important to note that the post-1946 borders were never subject to any legislative or constitutional acts.

[87]According to John Major, UK Prime Minister from 1992 to 1997, UK Foreign Secretary Douglas Hurd phoned him in the evening of 16 December 1991 informing him that all other 11 Member States were ready to recognise Croatia and Slovenia. After the provisions on minority rights were secured, all ministers did agree.

(i) respect for the provisions of the Charter of the United Nations and the commitments subscribed to in the Final Act of Helsinki and in the Charter of Paris, especially with regard to the rule of law, democracy and human rights;

(ii) guarantees for the rights of ethnic and national groups and minorities in accordance with the commitments subscribed to in the framework of the CSCE;

(iii) respect for the inviolability of all frontiers which can only be changed by peaceful means and by common agreement;

(iv) acceptance of all relevant commitments with regard to disarmament and nuclear non-proliferation as well as to security and regional stability;

(v) commitment to settle by agreement, including where appropriate by recourse to arbitration, all questions concerning State succession and regional disputes.

The Community and its Member States will not recognise entities which are the result of aggression. They would take account of the effects of recognition on neighbouring States […]. (EC Bulletin Vol. 12, 24/1991a: 119).

In a separate "Declaration on Yugoslavia", the EC Foreign Ministers offered *conditional* recognition to all five SFRY successor States by 15 January 1992

[…] inviting all Yugoslav Republics to state by 23 December [1991] whether:

(i) they wish to be recognised as independent States;

(ii) they accept the commitments contained in the above-mentioned Guidelines;

(iii) they accept the provisions laid down in the draft Convention - especially those in Chapter II on human rights and rights of national or ethnic groups - under Consideration by the Conference on Yugoslavia;

(iv) they continue to support (a) the efforts of the Secretary General and the Security Council of the United Nations, and (b) the continuation of the Conference on Yugoslavia.

The applications of those Republics which reply positively will be submitted through the Chair of the Conference to the Arbitration Commission for advice before the implementation date […]. (EC Bulletin Vol. 12, 24/1991a: 119–120).

Rich (1993: 43–44) argues that the EC, in view of the increasing need to take action in both the Soviet and the Yugoslav crises, would have to do more than to just stick to traditional criteria for statehood. Adding additional requirements, the process of recognition had become "more difficult". The new method of requiring an application for recognition examined by an arbitral body was unprecedented in recognition practice. Vukas (2011: 30–34) critiques the "long and very complicated process of achieving international recognition" as the EC was only inconsistently respecting the criteria for statehood governed by the doctrine and the practice of international law.

In Opinion 4 from 11 January 1992, the Badinter Committee assessed the request for recognition submitted by *Bosnia-Herzegovina* on 20 December 1991. The verdict was that in view of the diverging development on the ground, in particular the establishment of the "Serbian Republic of Bosnia-Herzegovina", the "will of the peoples of Bosnia-Herzegovina to constitute the Republic of Bosnia-Herzegovina as a sovereign and independent State cannot be held to have been fully established" (I.L.M. 1992: 1503).

In Opinion 5 from the same day on the recognition request of *Croatia* from 19 December 1991, the Committee found that Croatia did fulfil the criteria of the

Guidelines safe for the country's Constitutional Act which had not fully incorporated the minority rights specifications. The Committee asked the government to supplement the Constitutional Act accordingly.[88] The President of Croatia assured the Committee in a reply on the same day that the provisions would be incorporated into the Constitutional Act (I.L.M. 1992: 1518).

In Opinion 6 also from the same day on the request for recognition by the Republic of *Macedonia* from 20 December 1991, the Committee took the view that Macedonia fulfilled the requirements of the Guidelines. Further, the country "had renounced all territorial claims of any kind" and that therefore "the name 'Macedonia' [could not] imply any territorial claim against another State" (I.L.M. 1992: 1511).

In Opinion 7 from 11 January 1992 on *Slovenia*'s request for recognition from December 1991, the Committee found that the country satisfied the requirements.

The FRY (Serbia and Montenegro) declined the offer of recognition. Serbia claimed that it had acquired internationally recognised statehood as early as at the Berlin Congress 1878. Montenegro replied it acquired independence and sovereignty likewise at the Berlin Congress, and that such international legal personality did not cease to exist (Rich 1993: 47).

The EC extended recognition to Croatia and Slovenia on 15 January 1992. Bosnia-Herzegovina was recognised on 7 April 1992. Yet, Greece blocked the EC's recognition of Macedonia for some time over the State name (Rich 1993: 53; Türk 1993: 69; Mrak 1998: 9). The country became a member of the UN on 8 April 1993 under its provisional name Former Yugoslav Republic of Macedonia—FYROM (Craven 1996: 377). Only in 2018 was an agreement reached between Athens and Skopje on North Macedonia being the eventual State name (see Sect. 6.4.1).

State Succession (Opinions 9–15)

In Opinion 9 from 4 July 1992, answering the question from the Chairman of the Conference for Peace in Yugoslavia which he had posed himself, as to the basis and means of settling succession issues between the States emerging from the SFRY, the Committee found that the successor States had to "settle all aspects of the succession by agreement" including SFRY assets and liabilities, and SFRY State property in third countries.[89] Further, none of the SFRY successor States was entitled to claim the membership rights of the SFRY in international organisations (I.L.M. 1992: 1523–5).[90] Opinion 10 issued on the same day answering another question put to it by the Conference's Chair made it clear that the FRY could *not* be considered the sole successor to the SFRY (I.L.M. 1992: 1526).

[88]In a comment from 4 July 1992 on the prior amendment of the Croatian Constitutional Act of 8 May 1992, the Committee found the provisions to be finally satisfying the requirements (I.L.M. 1992: 1505–7).

[89]The subsequent Agreement on Succession Issues was only signed on 29 May 2001; see Sect. 2.5.3.

[90]UN Security Council Resolution 757 dated 30 May 1992 had decided *not* to grant the FRY (Serbia and Montenegro) the automatic succession of the SFRY's UN membership (see Mrak 1998: 10).

Opinions 11 to 13 dated 13 July 1993, and 14–15 dated 13 August 1993, submitted by the Co-Chairmen of the Steering Committee of the International Conference on the Former Yugoslavia (ICFY),[91] dealt with a series of questions on (i) the actual dates of secession of the former SFRY Republics, (ii) the type of assets and liabilities to be divided up between the successor States, and on (iii) the legal principles to apply to the division of State property and archives. Further, the question was raised as to (iv) whether war damages were quantifiable in relation to the above division of State property. Subsequently, (v) the relationship between the National Bank of Yugoslavia and the National Banks of the successor States was addressed as to the competence with regard to rights and obligations vis-à-vis State succession. Finally, (vi) the question of protective measures vis-à-vis the free disposal of State property was posed.

The Committee found that

(i) The dates of secession from the SFRY were 8 October 1991 for Croatia and Slovenia, 17 November 1991 for Macedonia/FYROM, 6 March 1992 for Bosnia and Hercegovina, and 27 April 1992 as for the FRY (Serbia and Montenegro; I.L.M. 1993: 1587–9).
(ii) The States concerned were free to conclude agreements on succession issues, but that third countries on whose territories SFRY State property was situated would not be bound by such agreements (I.L.M. 1993: 1589–91).
(iii) The *overall* outcome of the division of assets and liabilities had to be equitable, but not necessarily the individual issue components.
(iv) It was possible to set off war damages against assets/liabilities (I.L.M. 1993: 1591–2).
(v) Rights and obligations in relation to the National Bank of Yugoslavia were subject to an agreement to be concluded between the SFRY successor States (I.L.M. 1993: 1595–8).
(vi) Third countries were entitled to block the free disposal of SFRY State property in accordance with internal law (I.L.M. 1993: 1590–1).

The successor States of Yugoslavia have addressed most, albeit not all of the above issues during the quarrelsome and lengthy process (which is still ongoing) following the Agreement on Succession Issues of 2001 (see Sect. 2.5.3).

---

[91] The ICFY followed the Conference on Peace in Yugoslavia (convened by means of the EC Foreign Ministers meeting's Declaration on Yugoslavia on 27 August 1991, and subsequently chaired by Lord Carrington, a former UK Foreign Secretary (1979–82) and NATO Secretary General (1984–88); Pellet 1992: 178). As of 27 August 1992, the ICFY took over as a joint UN-EC venture the Co-Chairs being Lord Owen, a former UK Foreign Secretary 1977–9, and Cyrus Vance, US Foreign Secretary 1977–80. The latter handed over to Thorvald Stoltenberg on 3 May 1993 (Owen 1995: 1; 20–4; 148).

2.5.2 Homeland War in Croatia

The first years of Croatian independence and State-building must be seen as heavily affected by the armed conflict of what is officially known as the Homeland War. As from late July 1991, the Yugoslav Army (JNA), having aligned with the Serbian community in Croatia,[92] managed to occupy almost a third of the country by the end of the year (Lamont 2015: 73). The move came after the sensitivities of the 580,000 Serbs[93] in Croatia[94] had not been taken into account by the Croatian government, let alone properly reflected in the Croatian constitution (Stojanović[95] 1995: 345). Zgonjanin (2018: 193–5) holds that Tuđman's refusal to assign the Serbs of an independent Croatia the status of constituent people, and his actual downgrading of the Serbian citizens to a minority by amending the Croatian constitution to that end in December 1990 has caused the secessionist move of the Serbs in the Krajina.[96]

Several months of bitter fighting made the country suffer tremendous losses and hardship, but experience a very high level of unity (Pusić 1997: 102). The town of Vukovar in Eastern Slavonia symbolises the war waged against Croatia by the JNA. Vukovar had been shelled during a "three-months pulverising" (Owen 1995: 3) before it fell in late November 1991 (Baker 2015: 51). During the night from 20 to 21 November, more than 200 civilians and Croatian soldiers were massacred in Ovčara, a farm outside Vukovar, by Serbian forces. It is widely considered "the largest slaughter of individuals committed during the 1990s war in Croatia" (Banjeglav 2012: 12–3). Zgonjanin (2018: 50), in his meticulous account of the Ovčara events based on the ICTY archives, speaks of Vukovar as "a disastrous beginning of the handling of war crimes which boded ill for the subsequent years of the war".[97]

---

[92]Media reports in Serbia had, as from mid-1988, increasingly claimed that the Serbs in Croatia were threatened by a policy of "assimilation and national subordination" (Pauković 2012: 186). Slobodan Milošević's 1989 Gazimestan speech at the occasion of the 600th anniversary of the 1389 Kosovo battle "became the incarnation of the ethno-nationalism that had been gaining momentum" (Milošević and Touquet 2018: 386).

[93]The figure is given in Jović (2011: 37) based on the 1991 census.

[94]According to the 1991 census, the Serbian minority in Croatia accounted for 12.2% of the population at the time (Ramet 2014: 45; Pusić 1997: 99).

[95]Svetozar Stojanović was an advisor to the first president of the Federal Republic of Yugoslavia (FRY), Dobrica Ćosić, 1992–1993.

[96]The concept of constituent peoples goes back to the AVNOJ principles of November 1943 where equality and equal opportunities for the constituent peoples of a future federal Yugoslavia after World War II were established (see Sect. 2.3.2). That principle also held at the level of the Republics, so that the Serbs were granted the status of the second constituent people in the Yugoslav Republics of Croatia and of Bosnia-Herzegovina.

[97]The mass grave was only detected in October 1992 by a Western forensic expert (Zgonjanin 2018: 49). Most of the victims of the atrocities at Ovčara were patients at Vukovar hospital, mainly Croatian soldiers. Three of the JNA officers involved faced a trial before the ICTY. Mile Mrkšić was sentenced to 20 years, and Veselin Šljivančanin to five years. Miroslav Radić, however, was cleared of all charges (Banjeglav 2012: 13–5).

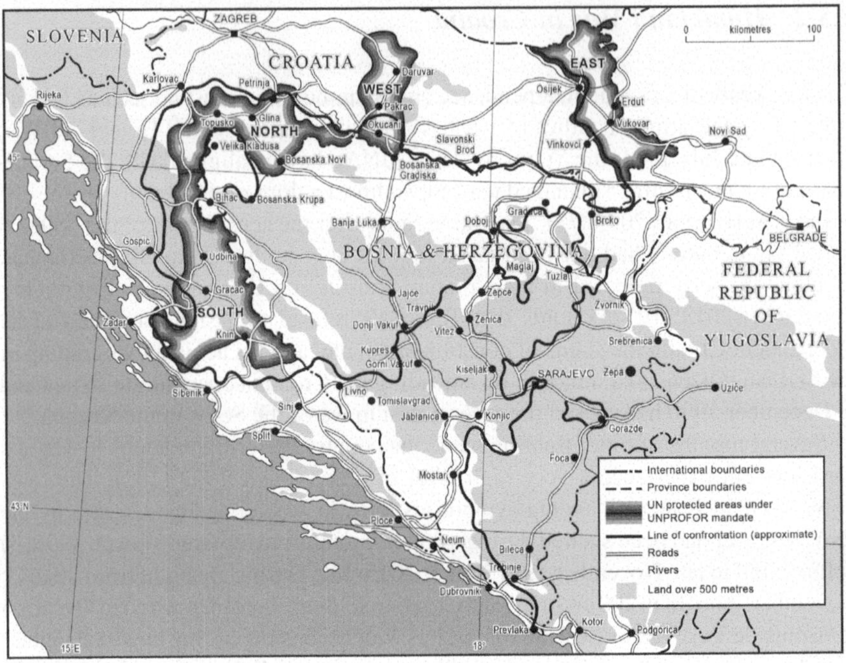

Fig. 2.4 United Nations Protected Areas in Croatia, 1992–1995 (Klemenčić and Schofield 2001: 27). ©IBRU, Durham University, UK

By late 1991, President Tuđman had to realise that winning was not on the cards for the time being, and he accepted a ceasefire and the deployment of an UN peace-keeping force instead (Hague 1995: 3–4), a situation which proved, diplomatically speaking, "an uneasy truce" (Owen 1995: 2). The UNPROFOR forces were deployed in the spring of 1992 in the areas where Serbs were the majority or a significant minority. The so-called UN Protected Areas (UNPA) were divided into four sectors (Klemenčić 1993: 54); see Fig. 2.4.

According to the 1991 census, the Serbs constituted the majority in the sectors North and South. The Croats accounted for 35% (North) and 21% (South), respectively. In sector West, Serbs and Croats made up roughly equal shares of the population, whereas Croats were the majority in sector East (Klemenčić 1993: 54).

After a subsequent, relatively long period of sporadic isolated fighting, and the building up of a Croatian Army, the latter launched two major operations 1–3 May 1995 ("Bljesak"/Flash in Western Slavonia) and 4–7 August 1995 ("Oluja"/Storm in the Krajina)[98] to regain the occupied territories (Lamont 2015: 73; Pusić 1997: 102–3). Despite the military victory, it took almost another two-and-a-half years for the full return of Eastern Slavonia into the constitutional–administrative legal order

[98]Croatia's diplomats worked hard in foreign capitals to gain approval for the operations (Šelo Šabić 2014: 73).

of Croatia to be implemented (Dolenec 2013: 131). The peaceful re-integration was implemented by a transitional administration (UNTAES) set-up by the UN Security Council which, after two extensions of the timeline, expired only on 15 January 1998 (Šelo Šabić 2014: 73–74).[99] Serb civilians had been killed by the Croatian Army during three months after Operation Storm (August 1995), a fact that was somewhat downplayed by the ruling elite after 2001 not least on the grounds that there had been no legal order yet in the respective areas (Banjeglav 2012: 19–21; Renner and Horelt 2008: 17–20). The Croatian Helsinki Committee for Human Rights report (2001: 135) accounts for 600 Serb civilian casualties, and the Serbian NGO Veritas claims 1078 Serb civilian victims.[100]

Declaration of the Croatian Parliament, October 2000

The Homeland War where around 15,000 (Granić 2005; cited in Dolenec 2013: 131; interview Ivo Sanader, 19-05-2016) to 20,000 people (Jović 2011: 37) lost their lives, amongst them 3,000 civilians (Brkić et al. 1997: 49), has become a vital part of the Croatian "self" as a sovereign and independent nation State. The memory of the war lives on to the present day, not least because there are still more than 1,500 people missing (Jurčević and Urlić 2002: 234)[101] after more than 2,000 bodies had been found in mass graves.[102] The overall human toll of the dissolution of Yugoslavia is at around 140,000 casualties and four million displaced persons on the territory of the former SFRY (McConnell 2018: 1). The number of Serbs in Croatia has, as a result of the war, decreased from 580,000 (12.2%) in the 1991 census to 200,000 (4.5%) in the 2001 census. Most of them had become refugees in neighbouring Serbia and Bosnia-Herzegovina (Jović 2011: 4). A substantial number of land mines from the Homeland War remain to be defused, and the process appears yet to be completed at the time of writing.

As a result, post-1995 Croatia largely sees itself as having (i) emancipated from Yugoslavia, (ii) liberated the territories occupied by the Croatian Serbs (supported by Serbia proper), and (iii) acted in a defensive war against the Serbs' attacks. These pillars of Croatian national identity are part of the Croatian Parliament's Declaration on the Homeland War adopted on 13 October 2000 (Lamont 2015: 74; Banjeglav 2012: 11). The declaration stated that Croatia

[99]Croatia and the Serb authorities signed an agreement on 12 November 1995 asking the UN Security Council to set up a transitional administration. By the time the agreement was signed, Eastern Slavonia (UNPA Sector East, see Fig. 2.4) was still under Serbian control (Banjeglav 2012: 13).

[100]Figure from 2014; see https://www.veritas.org.rs/srpske-zrtve-rata-i-poraca-na-podrucju-hrvatske-i-bivse-rsk-1990-1998-godine/zrtve-akcije-oluja-na-srpskoj-strani-2014/.

[101]The figure appears not to have changed. According to the deputy speaker of the Sabor, Milijan Brkić, there are 1544 missing persons (conference "Missing soldiers and civilians", European Parliament, 21 March 2017).

[102]Figure given by the Croatian Red Cross representative Branimir Tomić at the above conference.

> led a just and legitimate, defensive and liberating, and not an aggressive and conquering war […] in which it defended its territory from greater-Serbian aggression within internationally recognized borders.

Further to the above narrative, the Declaration provides for a straightforward and defining interpretation of the Homeland War:

> The fundamental values of the Homeland War are unambiguously accepted by the entire Croatian people and all Croatian citizens. (Official Gazette 2000/102).

The yearly commemorations of the Homeland War in Croatia and Serbia, including the events in Vukovar, have repeatedly led to tensions in the relations between Zagreb and Belgrade since (Banjeglav 2012: 24–5; author's field notes 5-08-2018[103]). Moreover, the repercussions of the Homeland War have had a direct impact on the EU's accession negotiations with Serbia where Croatia submitted reservations vis-à-vis the opening of negotiation chapters in the first half of 2016, not least on the grounds of the war crime jurisdiction in Serbia (see Sect. 6.3.3).

Impact of the International Criminal Tribunal for the Former Yugoslavia (ICTY)

When it was founded by the UN Security Council Resolution 827 in 1993[104] (see also Baker 2015: 98–101), the ICTY was to address what constitute the most atrocious war crimes in Europe since World War II. The ICTY was indeed the first international criminal tribunal since the trials of Nuremberg and Tokio (Zgonjanin 2018: 18). The ICTY sat for almost a quarter of a century, and when it finished on 31 December 2017, a number of essential functions, such as appeal cases, were transferred to the International Residual Mechanism for Criminal Tribunals (MICT).[105] Originally, all trials were supposed to be completed by 2010, and all appeal cases by 2011 (Dragović-Soso and Gordy 2011: 194).

Orentlicher (2018: 6), in her seminal account of the ICTY's impact in Serbia and in Bosnia-Herzegovina, highlights a crucial issue in that context: not only did the ICTY manage do indict and sentence many perpetrators. In addition, a great dividend of the Tribunal's work was its profound "role in catalysing domestic war crime prosecution, a function no one anticipated when the [Tribunal] was launched". In fact, domestic war crime prosecution had been scarce in the 1990s, and the capacity of Bosnia-Herzegovina, Croatia, and Serbia for war crime prosecution was only boosted after 2000. The first special prosecutor for war crimes in Serbia was established in 2003, whilst a special war crime chamber started its work in Croatia in 2005, and in Bosnia-Herzegovina in the same year (Dragović-Soso and Gordy 2011: 198).

With regard to the *impact* of wartime mass atrocities and of war crime tribunals' work on societies, a quick insight into a few issues from social psychology may be justified here. According to Orentlicher (2018: 226–235), the first issue is the

[103]The 2018 Oluja commemorations were held in Knin including a military parade of the Croatian Airforce.

[104]Resolution 827 is available at https://unscr.com/en/resolutions/doc/827.

[105]The MICT also took over functions from the International Criminal Tribunal for Ruanda (ICTR).

impact of official narratives in terms of *heuristics* and *framing*. Whilst heuristics is about cognitive shortcuts during an assessment of whether the contents of a piece of information are true, i.e. a rule of thumb used by the individual in their reckoning, framing is about the availability of stored information to the individual for their evaluation. The information most readily accessible will prevail. To that end, exposure to communication is central. Politicians tend to strive for that framing effect, for instance by creating a notion of victimisation, a popular course of action not only in Serbia, Bosnia-Herzegovina, or Croatia. Second, *motivated reasoning* and *social identity*: Motivation has a central role in shaping beliefs, and the unconscious part of the processing of information leads to a bias in the actual reasoning. The membership of a social group is crucial for social identity. Members of a group will want to maintain a positive self-image and a positive image of the group. This can lead to denialism if, for instance, a member of the group is said to be involved in mass atrocities. Third, *dissonance*, similarly, is about one's personal views conflicting with the conduct of another member of the same social group. The result is either the dismissal of official narratives (of victimhood, for example), or it can create denialism if, for instance, family ties are valued paramount and make you believe that your brother or uncle cannot possibly be responsible for wartime atrocities. The last issue concerns *belief perseverance*. The central argument here is that once you have a belief, any new evidence or arguments coming along will be subject to a confirmation bias. In other words, new pieces of information tend to be interpreted as evidence of your own established views.

2.5.3 Agreement on Succession Issues (ASI)

After prolonged negotiations lasting almost ten years, Bosnia-Herzegovina, Croatia, the Federal Republic of Yugoslavia (Serbia and Montenegro[106]), Macedonia/FYROM, and Slovenia, "being in sovereign equality the five successor States to the former Socialist Federal Republic of Yugoslavia [...]" (Agreement 2001: 1),[107] signed the Agreement on Succession Issues (ASI) on 29 June 2001 in Vienna. The Agreement entered into force on 2 June 2004.

With regard to pluri-lateral treaties of State succession, Oeter (1995) distinguishes between (i) a fully consensual solution as in the case of the Czechoslovak Federation, (ii) a peaceful solution with conflicts about the redistribution of assets and liabilities

[106] Montenegro became independent in 2006. The agreement with Serbia on the ASI items was that Montenegro receives 5.88% of the Serbian assets once the ASI process is completed. In addition, Serbia has rendered some of its gold reserves to Montenegro. Podgorica was also granted observer status for the ASI meetings. The country stopped taking part at a later stage (interview Vladimir Radulović, 20-04-2018).

[107] The FRY further disintegrated after the ASI's conclusion, Montenegro seceding in 2006 and Kosovo seceding in 2008. There are no legal consequences on the remaining parties to the ASI, however, as issues arising from the disintegration of the FRY are a matter solely for the former FRY's three States (see above footnote).

at the break-up of the Soviet Union, and (iii) conflicts on the distribution of liabilities in the case of Yugoslavia.

The SFRY's dissolution was non-consensual and not peaceful. Negotiations over succession issues had begun in 1992 (Hasani 2007: 112),[108] but the Agreement on Succession Issues would only be concluded many years later. This is mainly due to the FRY taking the view for a long time that only itself constituted the successor State of the SFRY (Dumberry 2006: 429; Hasani 2007: 113; Mrak 1998: 9–10), whereas Bosnia and Herzegovina, Croatia, Macedonia/FYROM, and Slovenia had seceded unconstitutionally. In practice, this meant that Serbia and Montenegro were the sole owner of all State property of the former federation. The FRY only gave up its claim of continued legal personality after Milošević was ousted in October 2000 (Škrk et al. 2015: 214; Stahn 2002: 379–80; Stanič 2001: 753). It was only then that the previous conflict on what type of State break-up the SFRY had actually undergone could finally be resolved unanimously amongst the five successor States.

A special negotiator, Sir Arthur Watts, was appointed in 1996 by the High Representative for the civilian implementation of the Dayton Peace Accord (Škrk et al. 2015: 218; Hasani 2007: 127).[109] Watts' "skilled guidance" (Škrk et al. 2015: 214) is widely seen as a major positive factor for establishing a final settlement (Stanič 2001: 752).

The Agreement of 2001 consists of two parts. The basic text, an umbrella agreement which is relatively short, addresses the major issues of the Yugoslav succession and establishes a Standing Joint Committee (SJC) of representatives of each successor State (Article 4), a dispute resolution mechanism (Article 5), and a reference to the Annexes as an integral part of the Agreement (Article 6). The Annexes as the second part cover the rights and obligations of the SFRY successor States for implementation within the below issue components (Article 3):

A: Movable and Immovable Property;
B: Diplomatic and Consular Properties;
C: Financial Assets and Liabilities;
D: Archives;
E: Pensions;
F: Other Rights, Interests, and Liabilities;
G: Private Property and Acquired Rights.

Pursuant to Article 5 of the Agreement, differences over the interpretation or implementation of the Agreement are to be resolved through discussion amongst the States concerned. If they fail to reach an agreement, they can refer the matter to an independent person of their (unanimous) choice who may deliver a binding decision, or to the Standing Joint Committee (SJC). Further, and with regard to *practical* aspects of implementation, the disputing States can aim at binding expert

[108] The International Conference on the former Yugoslavia (ICFY) established various Working Groups. One of them was the Working Group on State succession (Stanič 2001: 752).

[109] The Dayton Accord had set up the Peace Implementation Council which subsequently charged the High Representative with the issue of State succession (Hasani 2007: 112; Stanič 2001: 752).

solution provided they agree on the expert. If they do not agree, the President of the Court of Conciliation and Arbitration within the OSCE shall make the appointment. However, the following issues are not eligible for externalised expert solution: the distribution of BIS assets, the diplomatic and consular properties already allocated in the Agreement proper, the definition of financial assets from the Agreement proper, and the common heritage part of State archives.

There has been some criticism of the powers of the SJC, the steering body for the implementation of the Agreement, and with regard to the dispute settlement mechanism. Hasani (2007: 127) argues that the non-binding nature of the SGJ's recommendations to the governments is "a serious drawback of this body". Škrk et al. (2015: 251–252) critique the insufficient dispute settlement mechanism which was the reason why the most sensitive or complex issues, such as the "old" foreign currency deposits,[110] or the allocation of tangible military property, remain unresolved to the present day.

On a positive note, the Agreement "closed, once and for all, the problem of State succession to the former Yugoslavia" as it followed the stance of the Badinter Commission (Hasani 2007: 112). The Agreement clearly stipulated that, in legal terms, the obligations of the predecessor State towards third countries did not simply disappear, but were transferred upon the successor States (Dumberry 2006: 431).[111] In a more recent study, Dumberry (2015: 30) argues that there is a clear trend of newly independent States continuing, by express or tacit agreement, bilateral treaties entered into by the predecessor State, although the newly independent States are not automatically bound to do so.

A major achievement triggered by the Agreement was the crucial role of the international financial organisations in dividing up the outstanding debts and assets (Stahn 2002: 397).[112] Table 2.1 illustrates the current state of play by the most prominent issues.

It may be posited that, politically, the Agreement is a unique treaty beyond other treaties as it reflects the minimum consensus of five successor States after the violent break-up of a country, and that, in a way, the Agreement could be regarded as a "tiny constitution" for the region despite the slow implementation (Drenik 2013: 96).

The Agreement as such, notably, has settled a few of the outstanding issues *ad hoc*, but the bulk of work arises through the respective Annexes and the Joint Committees (JCs) established in them. A few main issues have been settled. Progress in other

---

[110]For the state of affairs (at the time of writing) on the *Ljubljanska Banka* issue as for the reimbursement of foreign depositors, a highly conflictual and loaded matter not least for Slovenia and Croatia, see Sect. 4.1.4.

[111]Dumberry (2006) provides a comprehensive discussion of *State succession to international responsibility* looking at (i) the integration of the GDR into the Federal Republic of Germany (FRG) in 1990, (ii) the dissolution of Czechoslovakia 1992, (iii) the dissolution of Yugoslavia 1991–2, and (iv) the break-up of the USSR 1991.

[112]The apportionment of the outstanding SFRY debt to the five successor States was indeed carried out with reference to the International Monetary Fund (IMF) key as follows: Bosnia-Herzegovina 13.2%, Croatia 28.49%, Macedonia 5.4%, Slovenia 16.39%, and FRY (Serbia and Montenegro) 36.52%. The IMF key is mirrored in the Appendix to the Agreement.

Table 2.1 State of play implementation of Agreement on Succession Issues[a]

Annex	Settled issues	Open issues	Status
A. Movable and Immovable Property	Cultural heritage property	Military property	Negotiations yet to start; no prospects as most equipment war-related and worn out
		Works of art	Negotiations ongoing
B. Diplomatic and Consular Property	Major property items from Agreement proper (London, Paris, Washington D.C., New York Residence, Tokyo, Bonn); ±80% of property from annexed list	Remaining property (±20%), e.g. New York Mission, Berne, Delhi, Moscow, plus OSCE countries, Asia and Africa	Sale ongoing
C. Financial Assets and Liabilities	All successor States have settled apportioned SFRY[b] debt with creditors[c] bilaterally; BIS assets apportioned	Old foreign currency deposits; unpaid SFRY contributions to UN	Negotiations on currency deposits ongoing at BIS; Slovenia has a compensation scheme in place[d]
D. Archives	Joint letter of intent to digitalise common archival heritage	Full access to archives of NBY[e], defence, and security documents	Digitalisation of available documents ongoing
E. Pensions	All successor States have concluded bilateral agreements respectively	–	–
F. Other Rights, Interests, and Liabilities	–	E.g. State responsibility for unlawful acts	Negotiations ongoing (anything-or-nothing approach)
G. Private Property and Acquired Rights	Individual persons' claims	War damages and ownership rights	Individuals' issues to be settled before courts

Source Author

[a]As of September 2020. Selected and condensed

[b]At the end of 1991, the outstanding SFRY foreign currency debt was at 15.1 billion dollar of which 3.14 billion belonged to the Federation and 5.4 billion to the FRY, i.e. Serbia and Montenegro (Höltschi, 22 September 1992)

[c]International financial institutions (such as the IMF, the World Bank, or the European Bank for Reconstruction and Development), State creditors ("Paris Club"), and private banks ("London Club")

[d]Following the Ališić judgement of the European Court of Human Rights (see Sect. 4.1.4)

[e]National Bank of Yugoslavia

areas, however, has been very slow, and some issues seem to have *de facto* been postponed *sine diem* (interview Ana Polak Petrič, 08-05-2017; interview Andreja Metelko-Zgombić, 01-11-2017; interview Vladimir Radulović, 20-04-2018). Nevertheless, the implementation of the ASI is an ongoing process and the most recent meeting (at the time of writing) of the Senior Representatives for Succession Issues (the Standing Joint Committee SJC) took place on 13 November 2019 in Zagreb, five years after the last such meeting in November 2015 in Sarajevo.

To give an example for the pace of the process: the latest property sale[113] at the time of writing is the former SFRY embassy in Bonn which was sold in November 2019 for 3.7 million Euro (Ministry of Foreign Affairs of the Republic of Slovenia news, 19 November 2019). Earlier in the year, the former Yugoslav embassy and the ambassador's residence in Tokyo were sold on 31 January 2019. Of the total revenue of 14.7 million Euro, Serbia received 5.8 million Euro and Bosnia-Herzegovina 2.2 million Euro according to the ASI apportionment key (N1 info, 18 February 2019; Sarajevo Times, 22 February 2019). The New York Residence of the former Yugoslav UN ambassador, also known as "Tito's apartment", was sold on 31 May 2018. With joint sales, representatives of all five successor States of Yugoslavia who are parties to the ASI have to sign jointly.[114] The New York Residence had been unoccupied since 1992. Of the revenue of 12.1 million US dollar, Croatia obtained 2.08 million, and Serbia 3.48 million. No information is available as for the other States (HINA News, 2 June 2018). The former SFRY Permanent Mission to the UN at Fifth Avenue in New York, rated the most valuable and prestigious property of all, currently used by Serbia, has been put on sale. The former Yugoslav embassy and residence in Berne, Switzerland, have also been placed on the market. The sale of the two real estate properties has been pending at the time of writing, and there have been offers (information provided by the Ministry of Foreign Affairs of the Republic of Slovenia, 9 March 2020). As for the *distribution* of former SFRY diplomatic real estate property, the latest distribution at the time of writing took place at a meeting in Belgrade in July 2019.[115]

---

[113] In November 2016, Bosnia-Herzegovina, Croatia, (North) Macedonia, Serbia, and Slovenia—as the successor States to the SFRY and parties to the ASI—started the sale of the remaining major property items: (i) the Residence of the SFRY Permanent Representative to the UN in New York, (ii) the SFRY Mission to the UN in New York, (iii) the SFRY Residence and Embassy in Tokyo, (iv) the SFRY Embassy in Bonn, and (v) the SFRY Embassy and Residence in Berne (see invitation to tender for the provision of real estate sales services for the sale of diplomatic real estate, 7 November 2016). The invitation to tender was also advertised in The Financial Times and The Economist (Ministry of the Foreign and European Affairs of the Republic of Croatia News, 4 November 2016).

[114] All representatives need to be present at the same time the moment the sale contract is signed. The notary act on 31 May 2018 lasted for three hours (Veljković, 2 June 2018).

[115] Bosnia-Herzegovina was awarded the former SFRY embassy/residence in Montevideo (Uruguay), and Croatia received the embassy in Stockholm and, together with North Macedonia, the embassy in Brussels. North Macedonia, apart from the embassy in Brussels together with Croatia, was awarded the residence in Harare (Zimbabwe). Serbia received the Permanent Mission to the UN at Geneva, the consulate general in Frankfurt and the residence in Harare, and a residence in Conakry (Guinea). Slovenia was awarded the embassy in Georgetown (Guyana). The decision from July 2019 was only the third one taken altogether after the initial decision on property distribution

In a nutshell, the process of the dissolution of Yugoslavia has apparently had the most immediate conflictual impact on the successor States and their bilateral and pluri-lateral relations. The independence of Croatia and Slovenia lead to the outbreak of an atrocious war over the Serb population in Croatia. The subsequent EC crisis management helped shape a new landscape of successor States, whereas hardly anything could be achieved to stop the warfare on the ground. The process of pluri-lateral negotiations of the SFRY's succession issues after 2001 has proven difficult, as some of it still relates to the violent break-up of the country, whilst many financial and property issues have been solved pragmatically. Nevertheless, at the time of writing, the sale or distribution of former SFRY real estate property is still ongoing almost 30 years after the country's dissolution.

2.6 Conclusion

This Chapter has highlighted the processes of political, territorial, and violent conflict in the North-Eastern Adriatic and in parts of the area of the former Yugoslavia in the period between the end of the Venetian Empire and the dismemberment of the Socialist Federal Republic of Yugoslavia (SFRY) including its aftermath. For an analysis of the present-day conflicts between SFRY successor States in general and between Croatia and Slovenia in particular, the following findings appear relevant:

- Changes in territorial sovereignty in the region in the contemporary international system before 1918 have been frequent and considerable. Since the end of the Venetian Empire, people in the region have had to adapt to Napoleonic, Habsburg, and Italian rule without being able to establish independent entities themselves—except for Serbia and for Montenegro at a relatively late stage after the Berlin Congress of 1878. The founding of Yugoslavia in 1918—a historic opportunity to shake off foreign rule—did not take place in the most fortunate circumstances at the Paris Peace Conference, where it was difficult for the new State to fight for international recognition at the negotiating table. In addition, it proved virtually impossible for the new State to secure its territorial claims. Instead, large parts of (present-day) Slovenia and Croatia came under Italian rule during the interwar period. As for the Kingdom of Serbs, Croats, and Slovenes, internal conflict over the constitutional nature of the new State persisted.

The invasion and partition of Yugoslavia by German and Italian troops during World War II strengthened the Partisan movement and, as a result, laid the foundations of the establishment of a quasi-federal State with communist one-party rule. The violent War of Liberation, in which hundreds of thousands of lives were lost, included a bitter fight over the territories in Istria (over which Yugoslavia finally

taken in 2002 and a second one taken in 2012 (press statement, Ministry of Foreign Affairs of the Republic of Serbia, 7 July 2019; information provided by the Ministry of Foreign Affairs of the Republic of Slovenia, 9 March 2020).

gained sovereignty, except for Trieste) and led to the first Cold War military zone governed by the Allies, the Free Territory of Trieste, which lasted until 1954. Only in 1975 was the Yugoslav–Italian boundary finally settled through bilateral negotiations and the Treaty of Osimo.

The second Yugoslavia, despite its leading role in the non-alignment movement in the Cold War world and its status of the most developed socialist country, suffered from the domestic perception that the central State was increasingly becoming illegitimate, from the quasi-independent behaviour of the Republics (which was strengthened by the decentralising 1974 constitution), from temporary economic decline, from increasing domestic conflict over financial resources, and, perhaps most decisive, from the Republics growing apart by developing their own separate national narratives about history, culture, and identity following a withering away of the consensus about the ideological core of the Yugoslav project.

- The European Community took on the delicate role of a third-party mediator in the process of the formal dissolution of Yugoslavia in 1991/92. Despite the sobering fact that very little could be done to stop the warfare on the ground, standards were set through an *ad-hoc* arbitration body, the Badinter Commission, whose Opinions on crucial issues, such as State succession, State recognition, and the transition of internal borders into international ones, were considered binding. Further, the Badinter Opinions have gained considerable weight in international law jurisprudence, since they applied the principle of *uti possidetis* in a post-colonial context and provided for a definition of a State in dissolution, to name but two issues.

Whilst the question of whether the joint EC action has increased or decreased hostilities on the ground will always remain a chicken and egg one, the EC managed to develop and exercise substantial conflict management power on the diplomatic front. This must be seen against the very complex political background of a State being in the process of non-consensual and violent dismemberment or dissolution. Furthermore, the EC had to come to terms with the dissolution of the USSR as a superpower at the same time.

The move by the Slovenian and the Croatian delegations to jointly leave the Communist Party of Yugoslavia's Congress in January 1990 appears to be the beginning of the visible process of the country's dissolution in terms of the end of the workings of the federal institutions. Regardless of the fact that this process proved irreversible, the independence referenda in Croatia and Slovenia did initially foresee confederal elements as opposed to the idea of breaking all ties between the former co-Republics. Thus, it is important to bear in mind that a spirit of good-neighbourly cooperation was not completely lost.

- The "Badinter borders principle", which provides for the recognition of the inter-republican borders as international borders (*uti possidetis*) must be seen as a milestone in terms of post-colonial State recognition and self-determination under international law. Despite the fact that the Badinter principle has been critiqued for being somewhat random on the historical nature of the internal borders, it provided for some degree of stability. Admittedly, the application of *uti possidetis* also reopened the potential for national conflict in Yugoslavia, which had been contained somewhat successfully in the early years of the second Yugoslavia, with its five Republics and multinational approach.

The Homeland War in Croatia (1991–1995) may be contemplated in this context. Amidst the dissolution of Yugoslavia, it marked the first serious outbreak of violent conflict over territories where a substantial or majority share of an ethnic group was living, i.e. the Serbs in Croatia. What did not matter a lot in Yugoslavia, where the multinational approach had assigned the inter-republican borders mainly an administrative, at best territorial role, fundamentally changed with the independence of the successor States. Some ethnic groups became *de facto* expatriated from the "parent" State. During the Homeland War, despite UN peacekeeping as a non-enforcing means of conflict management, the operational control of the escalating or de-escalating aspects of warfare on the ground clearly remained with the parties to the conflict. To this end, the effectiveness of the mediating role of the international community was, for a number of reasons, rather limited.

- The Agreement on Succession Issues concluded by all five successor States in 2001 established the only forum where conflictual issues can be discussed, contained, or settled directly amongst the countries. Whereas the Agreement as such was reached with the assistance of a mediator nominated by the UN, the actual process of *implementation* has since been subject to pluri-lateral negotiations. Whilst rather non-conflictual issues, such as the distribution of the SFRY debt or State pensions, were settled in a pragmatic and timely manner, questions of national interest are far more difficult to resolve.

Although the Agreement has been in force for more than 15 years, its implementation naturally very much depends on the good will and good faith of all successor States. Many issues representing the leftover "conflictual heritage" of Yugoslavia continue to remain unresolved or pending. It appears that the level of the sense of good-neighbourly relations and the spirit of collaboration of all the parties will determine whether the succession issues will be resolved or whether some issues will remain pending *sine diem.*

Interviews

Fajon, Tanja. MEP. Chair European Parliament Delegation with Serbia. Rapporteur for EU visa liberalisation with Serbia, Bosnia-Herzegovina, Montenegro, North Macedonia, Albania, and Kosovo 2014–2019. Strasburg, 22 November 2016.

Metelko-Zgombić, Andreja. State Secretary for European Affairs and High Representative on Succesion Issues for the Republic of Croatia. Zagreb, 01 November 2017.

Peterle, Alojz. MEP 2004–2019. Prime Minister of Slovenia 1990–1992, Foreign Minister of Slovenia 1993–1994 and 2000. Brussels, 15 June 2016.

Polak Petrič, Dr. Ana. High Representative on Succesion Issues for the Republic of Slovenia 2014–2017. Phone interview, 08 May 2017.
Pusić, Dr. Vesna. MP. Minister for Foreign and European Affairs of Croatia 2011–2016. Chair of the European Integration Committee of the Sabor 2008–2011. Zagreb, 24 February 2017.
Radulović, Vladimir. Ambassador of Montenegro to the Benelux States. Brussels, 20 April 2018.
Sanader, Dr. Ivo. Prime Minister of Croatia 2003–2009. Deputy Foreign Minister 1993–2000. Velika Gorica, 19 May 2016.
Vajgl, Ivo. MEP 2009–2019. Foreign Minister of Slovenia in 2004. Slovenian Ambassador to Germany, Austria, the OSCE, Sweden and the Nordic and Baltic States. Brussels, 29 September 2015.

References

Accetto, M. (2007). On law and politics in the Federal Balance: Lessons from Yugoslavia. *Review of Central and East European Law, 32*(2), 191–231.
American Society of International Law. (1992). *Conference on Yugoslavia Arbitration Commission: Opinions on questions arising from the dissolution of Yugoslavia* (pp. 1494–1526). International Legal Materials (I.L.M.).
American Society of International Law. (1993). *Conference on Yugoslavia Arbitration Commission: Opinions on questions arising from the dissolution of Yugoslavia* (pp. 1587–1598). International Legal Materials (I.L.M.).
Baker, C. (2015). *The Yugoslav wars of the 1990s*. London: Palgrave Macmillan.
Banjeglav, T. (2012). *Memory of war or war over memory? The official politics of remembering in 1990s Croatia*. https://www.iwm.at/publications/5-junior-visiting-fellows-conferences/vol-xxxii/memory-of-war-or-war-over-memory/. Accessed February 05, 2019.
Bieber, F. (2014). Introduction. In F. Bieber, A. Galijaš, & R. Archer (Eds.), *Debating the end of Yugoslavia* (pp. 1–7). Farnham: Ashgate Publishing.
Bieber, F., Galijaš, A., Archer, R. (Eds.) (2014). *Debating the End of Yugoslavia*. Farnham: Ashgate Publishing.
Blake, G., & Topalović, D. (1996). *The maritime boundaries of the Adriatic Sea. Maritime Briefing* 1(8). Durham: IBRU Durham University.
Boeckh, K. (2014). Allies are forever (until they are no more): Yugoslavia's multivectoral foreign policy during titoism. In S. Keil & B. Stahl (Eds.), *The foreign policies of post-Yugoslav states* (pp. 18–46). Basingstoke: Palgrave Macmillan.
Bojinović Fenko, A., & Šabič, Z. (2014). From the Balkans to Central Europe and back: The foreign policy of Slovenia. In S. Keil & B. Stahl (Eds.), *The foreign policies of post-Yugoslav states* (pp. 47–68). Basingstoke: Palgrave Macmillan.
Brkić, H., Strinović, D., Skavić, J., Zečević, D., Šlaus, M., & Miličević, M. (1997). Dental identification of war victims from Petrinja in Croatia. *International Journal for Legal Medicine, 110*(2), 47–51.
Bulletin of the European Community. (1991a). No. 12, Vol. 24.
Bulletin of the European Community. (1991b). No. 7/8, Vol. 24.
Calic, M. J. (2014). *Geschichte Jugoslawiens im 20. Jahrhundert*. München: C.H. Beck.
Capano, F. (2016). *Cold-war Trieste: Metamorphosing ideas of Italian nationhood, 1945–1975*. Cambridge: Cambridge University Press.
Cataldi, G. (2013). Prospects for the judicial settlement of the dispute between Croatia and Slovenia over Piran Bay. In N. Boschiero, T. Scovazzi, C. Pitea, & C. Ragni (Eds.), *International courts and the development of international law* (pp. 257–268). The Hague: T.M.C. Asser Press.
Central Intelligence Agency. (1948, April 15). *The current situation in the Free Territory of Trieste*. Washington: US Government Printing Office.

Čermelj, L. (1945). Les promesses et les actes italiens. In J. Roglić, M. Rojnić, R. Maixner, I. Mihovilović, A. Iveša, & L. Čermelj (Eds.), *La Marche Julienne. Étude de Géographie Politique* (pp. 245–288). Sušak: Institut Adriatique.

Chomsky, N. (2018). USA, Germany, and the faith of Yugoslavia. In D. Džalto (Ed.), *Yugoslavia: Peace, war and dissolution* (pp. 63–68). Oakland: PM Press.

Craven, M. (1996). The European community arbitration commission on Yugoslavia. *British Yearbook of International Law, 66*(1), 333–413.

Cresciani, G. (2004). A clash of civilisations? The Slovene and Italian minorities and the problem of Trieste from Borovnica to Bonegilla. *Italian Historical Society Journal, 12*(2), 2–15.

Croatian Helsinki Committee for Human Rights. (2001). *Military operation storm*. Zagreb: HHO. https://snv.hr/oluja-u-haagu/media/sg1/sg1-04-vojna-operacija-oluja-en.pdf. Accessed March 07, 2020.

D'Alessio, V. (2006). Istrians, identifications and the Habsburg Legacy. Perspectives on identities in Istria. *Acta Histriae, 14*(1), 15–39.

Đilas, M. (1985). *Rise and fall*. San Diego: Harcourt Brace Jovanovich.

Djokić, D. (2010). *Pašić and Trumbić. The Kingdom of Serbs, Croats and Slovenes*. London: Haus Publishing.

Dolenec, D. (2013). *Democratic institutions and authoritarian rule in southeast Europe*. Colchester: ECPR Press.

Dragović-Soso, J., & Gordy, E. (2011). Coming to terms with the past: Transitional justice and reconciliation in the post-Yugoslav lands. In D. Djokić & J. Ker-Lindsay (Eds.), *New perspectives on Yugoslavia: Key issues and controversies* (pp. 193–212). London: Routledge.

Drenik, S. (2013). Mednarodne pogodbe v pravnem redu Repubublike Slovenije. In A. Petrič Polak, I. Jager Aegius, & Z. Andraž (Eds.), *Pravo mednarodnih pogodb–Priročnik, strokovni prispevki in dokumenti* (pp. 33–105). Ljubljana: Fakulteta za družbene vede, Založba in Ministrstvo za zunanje zadeve.

Dumberry, P. (2006). The controversial issue of state succession to international responsibility revisited in light of recent state practice. *German Yearbook of International Law, 49*, 414–447.

Dumberry, P. (2015). State succession to bilateral treaties: A few observations on the incoherent and unjustifiable solution adopted for secession and dissolution of states under the 1978 Vienna Convention. *Leiden Journal of International Law, 28*(1), 13–30.

Duroselle, J. B. (1966). *Le Conflit de Trieste*. Bruxelles: Institut de Sociologie de l'Université Libre de Bruxelles.

Džalto, D. (2018a). Solutions and dissolutions. In D. Džalto (Ed.), *Yugoslavia: Peace, war and dissolution* (pp. 50–62). Oakland: PM Press.

Džalto, D. (2018b). Yugoslavia: Dreams and realities. In D. Džalto (Ed.), *Yugoslavia: Peace, war and dissolution* (pp. 6–34). Oakland: PM Press.

Embassy of the Republic of Croatia in the Republic of Kosovo. (2016, November 4). *Public invitation to tender for the provision of real estate sale services*. https://ks.mvep.hr/en/news/public-invitation-to-tender-for-the-provision-of-real-estate-sales-services,39858.html. Accessed March 07, 2020.

Embassy of the Republic of Slovenia New Delhi. (2016, November 7). *Invitation to tender for the provision of real estate sale services for the sale of diplomatic real estate in New York (United States of America), Tokyo (Japan), Bonn (Germany) and Berne (Switzerland)*. https://www.newdelhi.embassy.si/index.php?id=851&L=1&tx_ttnews%5Btt_news%5D=28717&cHash=31dac3c9323eacc28c1ed937844e5c77. Accessed March 07, 2020.

Flere, S. (2014). The dissolution of Yugoslavia as reflected upon by post-Yugoslav sociologists. In F. Bieber, A. Galijaš, & R. Archer (Eds.), *Debating the end of Yugoslavia* (pp. 81–96). Farnham: Ashgate Publishing.

Fuerst-Bjeliš, B., & Zupanc, I. (2007). New 18th century venetian border in Croatia and its spatial and demographic implications. *Hrvatski Geografski Glasnik, 69*(2), 41–52.

Gibler, D. (2012). *The territorial peace: Borders, state development and international conflict*. Cambridge: Cambridge University Press.

Hague, K. (1995). *UNPROFOR: A perspective from the field*. US Army War College. https://apps.dtic.mil/dtic/tr/fulltext/u2/a295010.pdf. Accessed March 07, 2019.

Hannum, H. (1993). Self-determination, Yugoslavia, and Europe: Old wine in new bottles? *Transnational Law and Contemporary Problems, 3*(1), 57–70.

Hasani, E. (2007). The evolution of the succession process in former Yugoslavia. *Thomas Jefferson Law Review, 29*(1), 111–150.

Hegre, H., Hultman, L., & Nygård, H. (2015). *Peacekeeping works: An assessment of the effectiveness of UN peacekeeping operations*. Prio Policy Brief. https://www.prio.org/utility/DownloadFile.ashx?id=96&type=publicationfile. Accessed March 07, 2019.

Hildebrandt, W. (1954). Die außenpolitischen Beziehungen der FVRJ. In W. Markert (Ed.), *Osteuropa-Handbuch Jugoslawien* (pp. 157–172). Köln and Graz: Böhlau.

HINA News. (2018, June 3). *Former Yugoslavia's joint residence in New York sold*.

Hobson, J. (2013). The other side of the Westphalian frontier. In S. Seth (Ed.), *Postcolonial theory and international relations* (pp. 32–48). London and New York: Routledge.

Höltschi, R. (1992, September 22). Finanzprobleme der 'Bundesrepublik Jugoslawien'. *Neue Zürcher Zeitung*, p. 12.

Hondius, F. (1968). *The Yugoslav community of nations*. The Hague and Paris: Mouton.

Hösch, E. (2011). *Geschichte des Balkan*. München: C.H. Beck.

Huth, P., & Allee, T. (2002). *The democratic peace and territorial conflict in the twentieth century*. Cambridge: Cambridge University Press.

Iglar, R. (1992). The constitutional crisis in Yugoslavia and the international law of self-determination: Slovenia's and Croatia's right to secede. *Boston College International and Comparative Law Review, 15*(1), 213–240.

Jončić, K. (1967). *The relations between nationalities in Yugoslavia*. Belgrade: Medunarodna stampa Interpress.

Jović, D. (2008). The Slovenian-Croatian confederation proposal in 1991: A tactical move or an ultimate solution? In L. Cohen & J. Dragović-Soso (Eds.), *State collapse in South-Eastern Europe: New perspectives on Yugoslavia's disintegration* (pp. 249–280). West Lafayette: Purdue University Press.

Jović, D. (2009). *Yugoslavia: A state that withered away*. West Lafazette: Purdue University Press.

Jović, D. (2011). Turning nationalists into EU supporters: The case of Croatia. In J. Rupnik (Ed.), *The Western Balkans and the EU: 'The hour of Europe'* (pp. 33–45). Chaillot Paper 126. Paris: European Union Institute for Security Studies (EUISS).

Jurčević, S., & Urlić, I. (2002). Linking objects in the process of mourning for sons disappeared in war: Croatia 2001. *Croatian Medical Journal, 43*(2), 234–239.

Klemenčić, M. (1993). Boundary issues and solutions following the breakdown of Yugoslavia. In *IBRU boundary and security bulletin* (pp. 49–56). Durham: Durham University.

Klemenčić, M., & Schofield, C. (2001). War and Peace on the Danube: The evolution of the Croatia-Serbia boundary. *International Boundaries Research Unit (IBRU)*. Durham: Durham University.

Klemenčić, M., & Topalović, D. (2009). The maritime boundaries of the Adriatic Sea. *Geoadria, 14*(2), 311–324.

Kobler, G. (1896). *Memorie Per La Storia Della Liburnica Città Di Fiume*. Fiume: Stabilimento Tipo-litografico Fiumano di E. Mohovich.

Krebs, N. (1907). *Die Halbinsel Istrien. Landeskundliche Studie*. Leipzig: Teubner.

Lamont, C. (2015). Contested histories of Croatia's homeland war. *Groniek, 45*(194), 69–80.

Laven, D. (2011). The fall of Venice. *Acta Histriae, 19*(3), 341–358.

Lederer, I. (1963). *Yugoslavia at the Paris Peace Conference: A study in frontier-making*. New Haven: Yale University Press.

Major, J. (1995). *The autobiography*. London: Harper Collins.

Matl, J. (1954). Jugoslawien im Zweiten Weltkrieg. In W. Markert (Ed.), *Osteuropa-Handbuch Jugoslawien* (pp. 99–121). Köln and Graz: Böhlau.

McConnell, T. (2018). Memory abuse, violence and the dissolution of Yugoslavia: A theoretical framework for understanding memory in conflict. *Innovation: The European Journal of*

Social Science Research, 1–13. https://www.tandfonline.com/doi/pdf/10.1080/13511610.2018.1508334?needAccess=true. Accessed March 04, 2019.

McNeill, W. (1974). *Venice: The hinge of Europe*. Chicago: The University of Chicago Press.

Meier, V. (1995). *Wie Jugoslawien verspielt wurde*. München: C.H. Beck.

Milošević, A., & Touquet, H. (2018). Unintended consequences: The EU memory framework and the politics of memory in Serbia and Croatia. *Southeast European and Black Sea Studies, 18*(3), 381–399.

Ministry of Foreign Affairs of the Republic of Serbia. (2019, July 7). A meeting of the joint committee for succession of diplomatic and consular properties of the former SFRY held in Belgrade. https://www.mfa.gov.rs/en/press-service/statements/18841-a-meeting-of-the-joint-committee-for-succession-of-diplomatic-and-consular-properties-of-the-former-sfry-held-in-belgrade-. Accessed March 10, 2020.

Ministry of Foreign Affairs of the Republic of Slovenia. (2019, September 19). Slovenia receives more than EUR 0.5 million from the sale of SFRY embassy premises in Bonn. https://www.gov.si/en/news/sloveniji-vec-kot-05-mio-eur-od-prodaje-diplomatskega-predstavnistva-nekdanje-sfrj-v-bonnu/. Accessed April 26, 2020.

Moodie, A. (1945). *The Italo-Yugoslav boundary. A study in political geography*. London: George Philip & Son.

Mrak, M. (1998). Apportionment and succession of external debts: The case of the SFR Yugoslavia. https://webv3ef.ef.uni-lj.si/_documents/wp/mrak1.doc. Accessed February 06, 2019.

N1 info. (2019, February 2018). Serbia get millions from sale of Yugoslav embassy in Japan. https://rs.n1info.com/English/NEWS/a461339/Serbia-get-millions-from-sale-of-Yugoslav-embassy-in-Japan.html. Accessed March 08, 2020.

Nešović, B., & Prunk, J. (1994). 20. stoletje. Zgodovina za 8. razred osnovne šole. Ljubljana: DZS.

Newman, J. (2015). *Yugoslavia in the shadow of war*. Cambridge: Cambridge University Press.

Novak, B. (1970). *Trieste 1941–1954: The ethnic, political and ideological struggle*. Chicago: The University of Chicago Press.

Novak, B. (1978). American policy toward the Slovenes in Trieste. In R. Susel (Ed.), *Papers in Slovene studies 1977* (pp. 1–25). New York: Society for Slovene Studies.

Oeter, S. (1995). State succession and the struggle over equity: Some observations on the laws of state succession with respect to state property and debts in cases of separation and dissolution of states. *German Yearbook of International Law, 38*(1), 73–102.

Official Gazette of the Republic of Croatia. (2000). Sabor Declaration on the Homeland War. No. 102/2000.

Orentlicher, D. (2018). *Some kind of justice: The ICTY's impact in Bosnia and Serbia*. New York: Oxford University Press.

Owen, D. (1995). *Balkan Odyssey*. New York, San Diego and London: Harcourt Brace.

Pauković, D. (2012). The role of history in legitimizing politics in the transition period in Croatia. In D. Pauković, V. Pavlaković, & V. Raos (Eds.), *Confronting the past: European experiences* (pp. 186–219). Zagreb: Political Science Research Center.

Pellet, A. (1992). The opinions of the Badinter Arbitration Committee. A second breath for the self-determination of peoples. *European Journal of International Law, 3*(1), 178–185.

Pirjevec, J. (2018). *Tito and his comrades*. Madison: The University of Wisconsin Press.

Prunk, J. (1996). *Slowenien: Ein Abriss seiner Geschichte*. Ljubljana: Založba Grad.

Pusić, V. (1997). Croatia's struggle for democracy. *Revija za Sociologiju, 28*(1–2), 95–110.

Radan, P. (1999). Yugoslavia's internal borders as international borders: A question of appropriateness. *East European Quarterly, 28*(2), 137–155.

Ramet, S. (2002). Views from inside: memoirs concerning the Yugoslav breakup and war. *Slavic Review, 61*(3), 558–580.

Ramet, S. (2006). *The three Yugoslavias: State building and legitimation 1918–2005*. Bloomington: Indiana University Press.

Ramet, S. (2014). Disputes about the dissolution of Yugoslavia and its wake. In F. Bieber, A. Galijaš, & R. Archer (Eds.), *Debating the end of Yugoslavia* (pp. 39–45). Farnham: Ashgate Publishing.

Renner, J., & Horelt, M. A. (2008). *'Of Heroes and Villains'—Competing identity constructions in post-war Croatia*. Munich Working Papers in IR. No. 1. Munich: Ludwig-Maximilian University, Geschwister-Scholl Institut.

Rich, R. (1993). Recognition of states: The collapse of Yugoslavia and the Soviet Union. *European Journal of International Law, 19*(1), 36–65.

Rojnić, M. (1945). La Civilisation Slave. In J. Roglić, M. Rojnić, R. Maixner, I. Mihovilović, A. Ivesa, & L. Čermelj (Eds.), *La Marche Julienne. Étude de Géographie Politique* (pp. 75–164) Sušak: Institut Adriatique.

Rutar, S. (2010). Labor and communism in Yugoslavia and Italy. Trieste and the northeastern Adriatic during the cold war (1945–1975). A contribution to the renewal of workers' history. *Acta Histriae, 18*(1–2), 247–274.

Sarajevo Times. (2019, February 23). Former Yugoslavia Embassy in Tokio is being sold, how much will BiH get? https://www.sarajevotimes.com/former-yugoslavia-embassy-in-tokio-is-being-sold-how-much-will-bih-get/. Accessed March 08, 2020.

Schiffrer, P. (1946). *Historic glance at the relations between Italians and Slaves in Venezia Giulia*. Trieste: Instituto di Storia dell'Università di Trieste.

Schmemann, S. (1995, April 21). Milovan Djilas, Yugoslav critic of communism, dies at 83. *New York Times*, p. 12.

Sekulić, D. (2004). Civic and ethnic identity: The case of Croatia. *Ethnic and Racial Studies, 27*(3), 455–483.

Sekulić, D., Massey, G., & Hodson, R. (2006). Ethnic intolerance and ethnic conflict in the dissolution of Yugoslavia. *Ethnic and Racial Studies, 29*(5), 797–827.

Šelo Šabić, S. (2014). Croatia's fast-forward foreign policy: From Yugoslavia to the EU. In S. Keil & B. Stahl (Eds.), *The foreign policies of post-Yugoslav states* (pp. 69–96). Basingstoke: Palgrave Macmillan.

Škrk, M., Petrič Polak, A., & Rakovec, M. (2015). The agreement on succession issues and some dilemmas regarding its implementation. *Zbornik Znanstvenih Razprav, 75*(1), 213–261.

Slovene-Italian Historical and Cultural Commission. (2004). Report on Slovene-Italian relations 1880–1956. Trst/Trieste: Premik. https://www.kozina.com/premik/poreng_enastran.htm. Accessed April 23, 2020.

Sorel, J. M., & Mehdi, R. (1994). L'uti possidetis entre la consécration juridique et la pratique: Essai de réactualisation. *Annuaire Français de droit International, 40*(1), 11–40.

Stahn, C. (2002). The agreement on succession issues of the former socialist Federal Republic of Yugoslavia. *American Journal of International Law, 96*(2), 379–397.

Stanič, A. (2001). Financial aspects of state succession: The case of Yugoslavia. *European Journal of International Law, 12*(4), 751–779.

Stojanović, S. (1995). The destruction of Yugoslavia. *Fordham International Law Journal, 19*(2), 337–362.

Türk, D. (1993). Recognition of states: A comment. *European Journal of International Law, 4*(1), 66–71.

United Nations Treaty Series. (1996). *Italy and Yugoslavia, agreement on the development of economic co-operation, 1975* (Vol. 1466, pp. 134–145). https://treaties.un.org/doc/Publication/UNTS/Volume%201466/v1466.pdf. Accessed March 06, 2020.

United Nations Treaty Series. (2005). *Agreement on succession issues, 2001* (Vol. 2262, pp. 251–338). https://treaties.un.org/doc/Publication/UNTS/Volume%202262/v2262.pdf. Accessed March 07, 2020.

Veljković, S. (2018, June 2). 'Titov stan' u New Yorku prodan za 12 milijuna dolara, kupio ga vijetnamski financijer. *Večernji list*, p. 6.

Vidas, D. (2009). The UN convention on the law of the sea, the European Union and the rule of law: What is going on in the Adriatic Sea? *The International Journal of Marine and Coastal Law, 24*(1), 1–66.

Vlašić, A. (2014). *With time comes change? The evolution of the Yugoslav public opinion towards the Trieste crisis from 1945 to 1975*. Conference paper.

Von Reiswitz, J. (1954). Die politische Entwicklung Jugoslawiens zwischen den Weltkriegen. In W. Markert (Ed.), *Osteuropa-Handbuch Jugoslawien* (pp. 67–98). Köln and Graz: Böhlau.

Vukas, B. (1976). Solution définitive de la question de Trieste par la conclusion des accords entre l'Italie et la Yougoslavie à Osimo (Ancona) le 10 novembre 1975. *Annuaire Français de droit International, 22*, 77–95.

Vukas, B. (2011). The process of the establishment of the independence of the Republic of Croatia from the perspective of International Law. *Review of Croatian History, VII*(1), 11–35.

Wachtel, A., & Bennett, C. (2009). The dissolution of Yugoslavia. https://docs.lib.purdue.edu/cgi/viewcontent.cgi?filename=2&article=1027&context=purduepress_ebooks&type=additional. Accessed February 04, 2019.

Webb, K., Koutrakou, V., & Walters, M. (1996). The Yugoslavian conflict, European Mediation, and the contingency model: A critical perspective. In J. Bercovitch (Ed.), *Resolving international conflicts. The theory and practice of mediation* (pp. 171–190). Boulder and London: Lynne Rienner.

Wörsdörfer, R. (2004). *Krisenherd Adria 1915–1955*. Paderborn: Schöningh.

Zaccaria, B. (2016). *The EEC's Yugoslav policy in cold war Europe, 1968–1980*. Cham: Springer Nature.

Zaccaria, B. (2019). Yugoslavia, Italy, and European integration: Was Osimo 1975 a Pyrrhic victory? *Cold War History*. https://doi.org/10.1080/14682745.2019.1657094. Accessed April 25, 2020.

Zellweger, E. (1954). Staatsaufbau und Gesetzgebung der föderativen Volksrepublik Jugoslawien 1945–1948. In W. Markert (Ed.), *Osteuropa-Handbuch Jugoslawien* (pp. 122–136). Köln and Graz: Böhlau.

Zgonjanin, A. (2018). *Der Umgang mit Kriegsverbrechen im ehemaligen Jugoslawien 1991–1999*. Wien: Promedian.

Chapter 3
Marine Spaces and Maritime Delimitation

Abstract This Chapter outlines the legal foundations related to marine spaces and the identification of maritime borders. The toolbox of maritime law and the legal–political developments in the Adriatic with regard to Slovenia and Croatia prior to 2008 are salient issues. The outline will familiarise the reader with various maritime zones and the main provisions of the United Nations Convention on the Law of the Sea (UNCLOS), the quasi-constitution for the oceans entailing the principles of freedom of navigation, territorial sovereignty, and common heritage of mankind. There is a special focus on the Mediterranean in general and the Adriatic in particular. The "lawfare" between Croatia and Slovenia (and the EU level) over maritime zones ahead of the 2008/2009 deadlock during the EU accession negotiations phase is a prerequisite for the subsequent stages of the border dispute. This chapter also sheds light on the methodologies used in maritime delimitation and rounds off with a brief survey of maritime case law developed by international courts and tribunals.

Keywords UNCLOS · Adriatic Sea · Maritime delimitation · Pluri-State bays · Croatia · Slovenia

3.1 Marine Spaces

It is useful to bear in mind that many of the contemporary territorial conflicts are about space at sea rather than on land. This is all the more relevant if one looks at the size of the overlapping claims most of which triggered by assumed or asserted oil and gas reserves, wind fields, fishing grounds, or, most importantly both in terms of world trade and security and defence, the freedom of navigation. The so-called South China Sea where overlapping claims to the Spratly Islands (to name but one spot) and neighbouring islands involve China, Taiwan, Vietnam, the Philippines, Malaysia, and Brunei, undoubtedly is the most prominent current such example in world affairs (see e.g. Cronin and Neuhard 2020; Ekman 2019; Bateman 2017; Keyuan 2012; Buga 2012: 85–6). In 2016, the Tribunal in the *South China Sea* (Philippines/China)

T. Bickl, *The Border Dispute Between Croatia and Slovenia*, Contributions to Political Science,
https://doi.org/10.1007/978-3-030-53333-5_3

arbitration[1] ruled that China had no historic rights in the area, was in violation of the Philippines' sovereign rights in its exclusive zone by constructing artificial islands, and harmed the fragile ecosystem in the area (PCA Final Award 2016: 471–7, paras 1202–3). In May 2018, China landed bomber aircraft on its Spratly runways and deployed surface-to-air-missiles on the Paracels for the first time (Asia Maritime Transparency Initiative News, 18 and 24 May 2018a, b). The UK, France, and Australia have subsequently asserted their rights of passage in the region, and the US Navy has been conducting freedom-of-navigation operations (FONOPs) in the South China Sea on a regular basis (see e.g. The Japan Times, 28 January 2020; Reuters News, 1 October 2018), as they have been doing in many oceans worldwide since 1979 (see Heritage and Lee 2020: 118–125).

The Adriatic Sea, a subsea of the Mediterranean, as a semi-enclosed sea previously accounted for three riparian States: Albania, Italy, and Yugoslavia. Now there are six of them as the dissolution of the SFRY has led to the establishment of four new littoral States: Croatia, Bosnia-Herzegovina, Montenegro, and Slovenia (Grbec 2015: 11–12; Blake and Topalović 1996: 2–3). Generally, the Adriatic's ecosystem is particularly vulnerable as its waters are shallow and the exchange or renewal of waters with the Ionian Sea through the relatively narrow Strait of Otranto is limited (Vidas 2013: 353; Blake and Topalović 1996: 4). There is a major oil transportation route to the Northern Adriatic ports of Trieste, Venice, Omišalj, and Koper (Vidas 2006: 358–60). Major container ports are Koper, Trieste, Venezia, Ravenna, and Rijeka (Twirdy and Batista 2014; Tomaševic et al. 2011); see Fig. 3.1.

Coming back to the Croatia–Slovenia border, its disputed sections on *land* are relatively tiny strips on what generally is an agreed border following the pre-1991 (administrative–internal) boundary between the former SFRY Republics (see Sect. 1.1).[2] In contrast, the *sea* border was subject to delimitation *de novo* as there were no boundaries in the integrated SFRY sea. Piran Bay, for a start, had the status of internal waters.[3] Croatia and Slovenia have, by their independence in 1991, inherited Yugoslavia's territorial sea border with Italy originally agreed on in 1975 (see Sects. 1.1 and 2.4.3). However, at the time of writing, only one of the bilateral sea borders between the four SFRY successor States with maritime access has been finally delimitated and implemented. The bilateral treaty between Croatia and Bosnia-Herzegovina from 1999 has not been ratified yet, however. Implementation

[1]The Philippines initiated proceedings against China in January 2013. China, however, refused to take part in the arbitration and to accept the award holding that the Tribunal lacked jurisdiction and that the request for proceedings was inadmissible (PCA Final Award 2016: 3–5). It must be noted, however, that non-appearance of one of the parties cannot stall the proceedings and that the judgement is binding also on the non-appearing party (see e.g. Tanaka 2018b: 115).

[2]The Croatia–Slovenia land border issue will be touched on in Sects. 4.1.2.2, 4.1.4, and 4.3.5.1. For the disputed land border between Croatia and Serbia along the Danube, see Sect. 6.3.2.

[3]Piran Bay was closed by a straight baseline in 1965 and is thus a juridical bay (Blake and Topalović 1996: 12; Klemenčić and Schofield 1995: 75; see also PCA Final Award 2017: 272, para 881–885). For straight baselines see Sect. 3.1.1.1.

Fig. 3.1 Riparian States and main ports in the Adriatic (*Source* Author; base map: d-maps.com)

of the 2017 Final Award for the Croatian–Slovenian border is pending,[4] and there is a provisional agreement between Croatia and Montenegro from 2002 (see Sect. 6.3.1).

To obtain a sufficient grasp of the delimitation issues and processes at stake, the sections below will want to explore (i) the types and definitions of marine spaces under national jurisdiction and beyond, (ii) the rules and principles of maritime delimitation governed by the UN Convention of the Law of the Sea (UNCLOS), and, paying tribute to the crucial role of the jurisprudence of international courts and tribunals, (iii) the development of case law.

The following survey of definitions is confined to the marine spaces relevant to the Adriatic. To start with, a principle distinction must be made between areas of

[4]The 2017 Final Award on the Croatia–Slovenia border as a binding decision under international law has yet to be implemented. Croatia, however, objects to this view (see, e.g. Sects. 4.3.6 and 4.4).

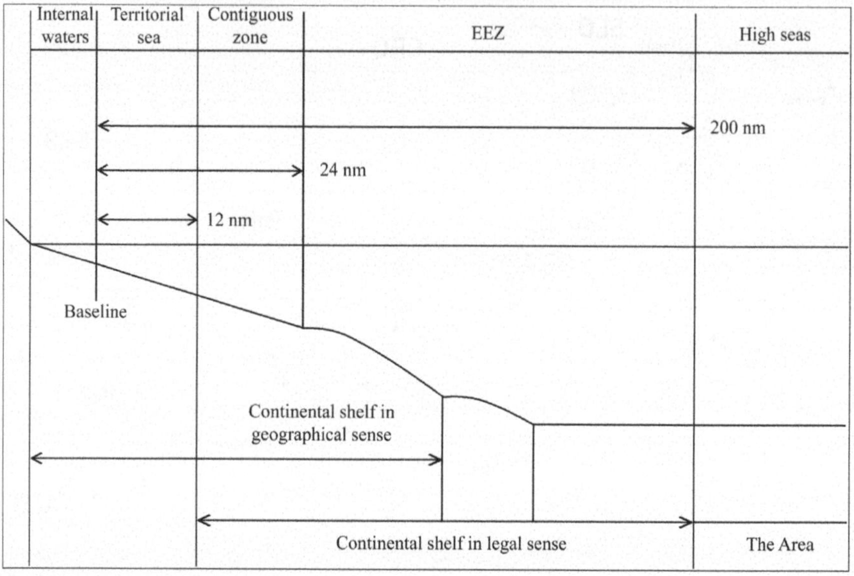

Fig. 3.2 Marine zones (*Source* Author; modelled after Tanaka 2015: 8)

(i) *territorial sovereignty* where a State has full jurisdiction, both legislative and enforcement, over all matters and persons on its territory (complete spatial jurisdiction), and those of
(ii) *sovereign rights* where the State's jurisdiction is limited to matters defined by international law (limited spatial jurisdiction; Tanaka 2015: 6–9).

Thus, marine spaces under *complete spatial jurisdiction* include internal waters and the territorial sea.[5] Marine areas under *limited spatial jurisdiction* include the EEZ, and the continental shelf. Figure 3.2 illustrates the marine spaces.

There is a continuity of marine areas in the international law of the sea, i.e. the spaces are connected to one another through the ocean worldwide and at constant sea level (Gidel 1981: 40–42; Churchill and Lowe 1999: 60). It follows that rivers and lakes (e.g. the Caspian Sea), but also artificial canals (such as Panama or Suez Canal) are considered terrestrial waters and therefore do not fall within the scope of the international law of the sea (Rothwell and Stephens 2016: 56).

UNCLOS is the tool box for the global governance and use of the oceans. On a universal note, it may be said that the Convention

> reconciles radically divergent, civil as well as military, State interests. Building on a significant strategic compromise, its concept and underpinnings make a remarkable geopolitical contribution to international peace and security, by promoting the peaceful coexistence of various uses of the oceans and seas. (Fife 2019: 44)

[5] International straits and archipelagic waters are neglected here.

Technically, the international law of the sea is about "access to and ownership of the oceans" (Rothwell and Stephens 2016: 3). There are three principles governing the international law of the sea: (i) the principle of *freedom*, (ii) the principle of *sovereignty*, and the principle of (iii) *common heritage of mankind* (UNCLOS Preamble[6]; Evans 2010: 651–3; see also Tanaka 2015: 38). The principle of freedom historically was about the freedom of navigation for overseas trade for colonial purposes around the beginning of the seventeenth century (see, e.g. Wirth 2019: 480–482; Agyebeng 2006: 376–7).[7] Today, it means the freedom of various uses of the seas, such as navigation, fishing, overflight, laying pipelines and submarine cables, or the construction of offshore installations/artificial islands. Conversely, the principle of sovereignty aims at advancing the interests of the coastal States.

Historically, the concept of extending national jurisdiction onto offshore spaces goes back to the mid-eighteenth century[8] and mainly served the purposes of security, fisheries, and revenue from customs, a notion already fairly close to the contemporary law of the sea where the distinction between the territorial sea and other areas of national jurisdiction and the high seas is a result of the dichotomy between the principles of freedom and sovereignty. The principle of the common heritage of mankind, however, was only introduced as of relatively late in April 1982 with the adoption of the United Nations Convention of the Law of the Sea (UNCLOS) entering into force on 16 November 1994. This principle, which one may well consider a purely ethical one, is about safeguarding the interests of all humans on this planet and the generations to come (see, e.g. Taylor 2018).

3.1.1 *Baselines, Bays, and Islands*

The baseline is the starting point of the assignment of maritime spaces. It is the point from which the outer limit of national jurisdiction of the coastal State is measured, thus determining the shape of the coastal front in legal terms. At the same time, the baseline distinguishes the land-bound area of internal waters from the sea-bound space of the territorial sea. It is important to note that, unlike in territorial waters, the right of innocent passage does not apply to internal waters (see also Sect. 3.1.2). In addition, baselines matter when it comes to delimitating the maritime border between two States with overlapping zones or claims.

---

[6]"Recognising the desirability of establishing through this Convention, with due regard for the sovereignty of all States, a legal order for the seas and oceans, the equitable and efficient utilisation of their resources, the conservation of their living resources, and the study, protection and preservation of the marine environment."

[7]Reference is to be made here to the works of the Dutch scholar Hugo Grotius. His *Mare Liberum* from 1608 may be considered the nucleus of the freedom-of-the-seas movement and momentum. For an English translation of the Latin original and an introduction to the background of the Dutch East India Company, see Feenstra (2009).

[8]Emmerich de Vattel, in his 1758 book *Le droits des gens*, outlines the concept that in coastal waters, the same jurisdiction may apply as on land. For an English translation, see De Vattel (2003).

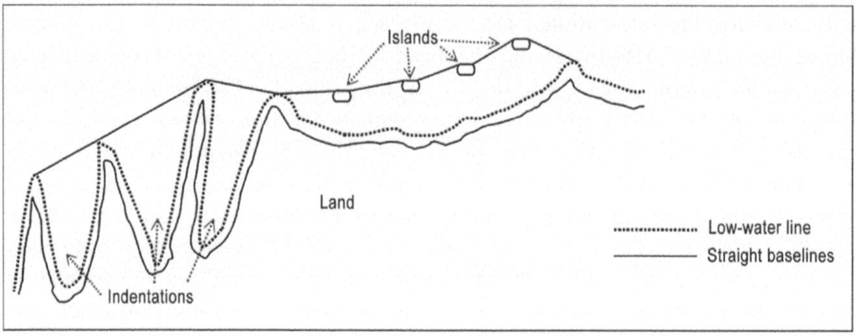

Fig. 3.3 Straight baselines and the low-water line (*Source* Author; modelled after Tanaka 2015: 47)

3.1.1.1 Normal Baselines and Straight Baselines

The normal baseline is the low-water line drawn along the coast. It is the basis every maritime claim is related to. Yet, as coastal configurations tend to be rather irregular including fringe islands, there was a need for devising rules to overcome a somewhat impractical set-up of normal baselines. The result was the application of *straight baselines* the main feature of which is the possibility to draw lines joining specific points along the coast to level off innumerable indentations. As a result, straight baselines are drawn across water rather than along the coast (Rothwell and Stephens 2016: 33–35, 44–5; Tanaka 2015: 44–51); see Fig. 3.3.

Article 7 UNCLOS specifies the conditions for the drawing of baselines in (i) excluding the possibility to draw straight baselines to and from low-tide elevations (unless equipped with a lighthouse or a similar navigational installation), and, (ii) ruling out the drawing of straight baselines in a way that they cut off the territorial waters of another State from the high seas. The latter provision is to deal with exceptional situations where a particularly small territorial unit is quasi-embedded in a larger one, or where small islands of one State are very close to the coast of another State. Three such configurations can be found in the Mediterranean. The former configuration applies to Monaco in France and to the corridor of Bosnia-Herzegovina on the Croatian coast,[9] the latter configuration is represented by the Greek islands along the coast of Turkey (Tanaka 2015: 52–54; Arnaut 2014: 165–7; Churchill and Lowe 1999: 37).

It is important to note that the drawing of baselines is a unilateral act with great diversity in State practice and that some of the claims clearly appear excessive. Nevertheless, international courts or tribunals will only be able to consider the legitimacy of claims once cases are brought before them (Rothwell and Stephens 2016: 53). The

[9]Croatia took over the system of straight baselines from the SFRY. The baseline section between the islands of Korčula and Hvar, however, appears to cut off Bosnia-Herzegovina, a successor State to the SFRY like Croatia, from its access to the high seas; see also Sect. 3.1.2. The matter is discussed in more detail in Sect. 6.3.5.

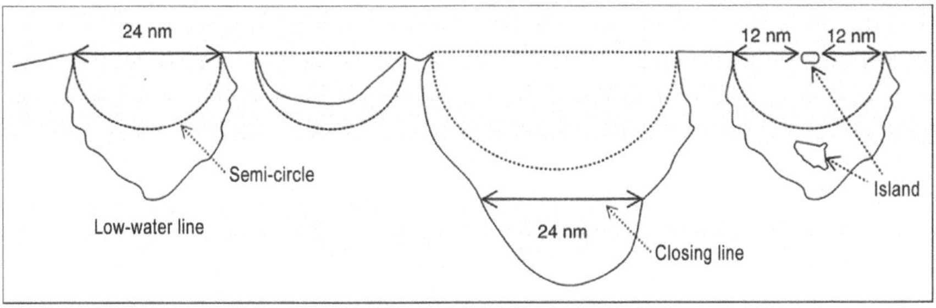

Fig. 3.4 Juridical bay with closing line, (failed) semi-circle test, closing line within bay, and closing line with island at bay's mouth (*Source* Author; modelled after Tanaka 2015: 56)

first-ever judgement on straight baselines was handed down in 1951 when the UK had questioned the legality of the groundbreaking Norwegian straight baselines,[10] and the ICJ endorsed them considering geographic, economic, and historic factors (Scovazzi 2018: 120–2). Judicial bodies have subsequently assessed and modified straight baselines in a number of cases, and it may be said that judicial examination contributes to containing excessive straight baselines (see Tanaka 2015: 214–5).

3.1.1.2 Juridical Bays

Bays play a paramount role for coastal States due to their distinctive connection with land and their more intimate character compared to the open coast. Thus, the concept of bays in a legal sense (juridical bay) emerged as early as in the late nineteenth century, and a special regime applies in the contemporary law of the sea (Tanaka 2015: 54–5; Evans 2010: 655–6).

To qualify as a juridical bay, its features must include "a well-marked indentation [...] contain[ing] land-locked waters constitut[ing] more than a mere curvature of the coast. An indentation shall not, however, be regarded as a bay unless its area is as large as, or larger than, that of the semi-circle whose diameter is a line drawn across the mouth of that indentation" (UNCLOS, Art. 10(2)). Where islands create more than one mouth of the bay, the semicircle will be drawn along the total length of the lines across the various mouths (UNCLOS, Art. 10(3)). If a bay fulfils the above criteria, and is less than 24 nautical miles (nm) across its natural entrance points, a closing line may be drawn between the two low-water lines at its entrance points. If a bay is larger than 24 nm, a closing line of 24 nm may be drawn inside the bay. The so enclosed waters constitute internal waters (UNCLOS, Arts. 10(4) and 10(5)); see Fig. 3.4. It is useful to note that the above provisions hold for bays belonging to a single State, and that pluri-State bays do not fall within the scope of UNCLOS Article 10 (Rothwell and Stephens 2016: 48–9). However, if the pluri-State status of

[10]The Norwegian straight baseline system established in 1935 was unparalleled incorporating 47 segments covering more than 1.500 km with base points chosen from extreme points on the coast, on islands, and rocks out at sea (Scovazzi 2018: 121; Tanaka 2015: 48).

a former juridical bay is the result of State succession, as is the case with Piran Bay, Croatia, and Slovenia being successor States to the SFRY, the status of juridical bay does not change (PCA Final Award 2017: 272, para 885). A similar situation can be found at Prevlaka/Outer Herceg Novi Bay where Croatia and Montenegro are the present-day riparian States (see Sect. 6.3.1).

The concept of a historic bay is not part of UNCLOS, but has developed as a feature of customary international law and State practice (Symmons 2019: 104–110; see also Insolia 2019: 230). Nevertheless, a study of the United Nations Secretariat has identified three main requirements for the title to a historic bay: First, a State claiming a historic bay must exercise authority over the area, second, there must be a continuity of authority exercised, and third, there must be no opposition by third States (Study UN Secretariat 1962: 1–16, paras 80–133). Notably, historic bays can lead to serious conflict. In October 1973, Libya declared the Gulf of Sidra a historic bay drawing a 300 nm [sic] closing line across the Gulf. A considerable number of States, such as the EC Member States, the USA, Australia, and Norway, contested the Libyan claim. In August 1981, the US Navy held military manoeuvres in the area. During an armed conflict that emerged, two Libyan fighter planes were shot down. In August 1986, during another US Navy operation, 25 persons were killed (Symmons 2019: 112–119; Tanaka 2015: 60).

3.1.1.3 Border Bays

Bays which are bordered by more than one State are outside the special regime of Article 10 UNCLOS. With regard to delimitation issues, there are the options of a mutual agreement *sui generis* on the part of the States bordering the bay, or of international court or tribunal decisions (e.g. Insolia 2019: 229). Two different approaches may be distinguished generally: (i) a closing line across the bay and the subsequent apportionment of the internal waters (as is the case in the present Tribunal decision on Piran Bay; see PCA Final Award 2017: 279, paras 912–913),[11] and (ii) the application of normal baselines and an apportionment of the respective territorial sea inside the bay. The latter concept considers a closing line and the establishment of *joint* internal waters of more than one State (*condominium*) a contradiction to the exclusive nature of territorial sovereignty (Tanaka 2015: 60–61).[12]

[11]Tanzania and Mozambique concluded a bilateral agreement in 1988 drawing a closing line over Ruvuma Bay and apportioning the internal waters following the median or equidistance line (Mlimuka 1994: 399–402). Iran and Pakistan have, in several steps, identified and closed certain sections of Gwatar Bay subsequently agreeing on a delimitation of the internal waters (Insolia 2019: 229).

[12]See also the dissenting opinion of judge Oda in the 1992 *Land, Island and Maritime Frontier Dispute* (Gulf of Fonseca) ICJ judgement stipulating that the Gulf was a historic bay with El Salvador, Honduras, and Nicaragua continuing *condominium* sovereignty (co-ownership) over the Bay safe for a three nautical mile belt of national sovereignty internal waters along the respective coasts. Judge Oda argued that there was no such thing in international law as joint internal waters, as internal waters exclusively belonged to *one* State, and that a pluri-State bay did not exist either in

3.1.1.4 Islands

There is a huge amount of island formations in the world, and they are extremely diverse. Still, islands play a crucial part in the delimitation of marine zones since they generate a marine space.[13] UNCLOS provisions stipulate that islands have to be natural formations "surrounded by water", and "above water at high tide", i.e. they must constitute an area of land (UNCLOS, Art. 121(1)). Islands not only create a territorial sea, but also an Exclusive Economic Zone (EEZ) and a continental shelf (for EEZ and continental shelf see Sects. 3.1.4 and 3.1.5). However, rocks "which cannot sustain human habitation or economic life of their own" cannot create an EEZ or continental shelf, but only a territorial sea (UNCLOS, Art. 121(3)). This is of considerable relevance as an EEZ/continental shelf claim can extend up to 200 nautical miles and beyond (Buga 2012: 83–4: Tanaka 2015: 63–68).

3.1.2 Internal Waters

With the recognition of the system of straight baselines in the second half of the twentieth century (for the ICJ landmark decision from 1951 see Sect. 3.1.1.1), the concept of internal waters became increasingly relevant. Therefore, the area enclosed as internal waters has considerably expanded as most coastal States have interpreted the straight baselines provisions liberally.

The distinctive feature of internal waters is that the coastal State enjoys unlimited sovereignty over these waters including a substantial degree of criminal jurisdiction vis-à-vis foreign vessels, and that there generally is no right to innocent passage, i.e. foreign marine vessels need to ask for clearance before entering internal waters (e.g. Evans 2010: 658). There are, however, two exceptions to that general rule. First, access to ports can be considered open to merchant vessels and is governed by specific consular conventions notwithstanding the fact that coastal States do have the jurisdiction to deny access. To that end, some States fully block access of nuclear-powered ships (New Zealand) or whaling vessels (Australia), for example. Second, where internal waters are newly created, the right to innocent passage is considered ongoing when it already existed previously (Rothwell and Stephens 2016: 53–59; Tanaka 2015: 80–2). The latter provision potentially appears to apply in the case of the passage of marine vessels from the territorial waters of Bosnia-Herzegovina through the internal waters of Croatia on their way to the high seas and vice versa (Grbec 2015: 155–7; 160–2; Arnaut 2014: 165–7; Vukas 2008: 187–8; the issue is discussed in Sect. 6.3.5).

---

international law (Dissenting Opinion Judge Oda, Gulf of Fonseca judgement 1992: 745–7, paras 23–26).

[13]The delicate question is, to what extent. Historically, there is a group of island States (such as Fiji, Western Samoa, or Greece) in favour of maximum claims for island-related marine zones. Conversely, other States (such as African States or Turkey) seek to limit the maritime claims related to islands (Van Overbeek 1989: 258–61).

3.1.3 Territorial Sea

The territorial sea is under the territorial sovereignty of a coastal State and extends to a maximum of 12 nautical miles measured from the baselines. It may be regarded the most crucial marine space for a coastal State as the territorial sea accounts for the maximum degree of sovereignty and jurisdiction off the coast. Usually, the highest level of marine activity takes place in that area due to its proximity to the coast.

The main features of the territorial sea include the coastal State's sovereignty over the waters, the seabed, its subsoil, and the airspace, and complete legislative and enforcement jurisdiction over all activities unless international law provides otherwise (Tanaka 2015: 84–6; Rothwell and Stephens 2016: 60–62; Evans 2010: 659).

3.1.3.1 Innocent Passage

The sovereignty of the coastal State over its territorial sea is limited, however, due to the paramount importance of the freedom of navigation (e.g. Hebbar 2020; Evans 2010: 660; Agyebeng 2006: 372). Thus, any vessel enjoys the right of innocent passage in the territorial sea of any State (UNCLOS, Art. 17). Yet, passage must be continuous, and stopping other than in ports or at roadsteads is only allowed for reasons of *force majeure*, or distress, or for the purpose of assisting other vessels or persons in distress (UNCLOS, Art. 18). Warships are also supposed to enjoy innocent passage; submarines, however, need to navigate on the surface and show their flag (UNCLOS, Art. 20).

It is useful to note that there is still "considerable controversy" around innocent passage (Evans 2010: 661), and that several States operate a notification or authorisation policy vis-à-vis warships. In the Adriatic, Croatia, Montenegro, and Albania require prior notification for warships entering the territorial sea.[14] State practice is not uniform on this issue, and a number of States, such as Germany, Italy, the Netherlands, and the UK, consider prior notification and authorisation requirements as being in contradiction to the concept of innocent passage. The USA, although not a party to UNCLOS, equally reject restrictions of innocent passage for warships and so does Russia (Rothwell and Stephens 2016: 289–92; Tanaka 2015: 90–1). Generally, it may be suggested that naval powers are in favour of innocent passage for warships, whereas smaller States or States in a sensitive location are against (Evans 2010: 662).

---

[14] Croatia and Montenegro submitted a declaration to that end at the time of ratification, see Declarations and Statements regarding the application of UNCLOS at https://www.un.org/depts/los/convention_agreements/convention_declarations.htm; Albania has not submitted a declaration, but is operating the notification requirement (see US Department of Defence Freedom of Navigation Report 2018). Other States requiring prior notification for warships include Bangladesh, Denmark, Egypt, Estonia, India, Malta, and South Korea. Prior authorisation is required by States such as Brazil, China, Iran, Pakistan, the Philippines, Poland, the United Arab Emirates, and Vietnam (see Declarations UN website above).

Nuclear-powered ships and vessels carrying hazardous substances may in practice also be subject to restrictions of innocent passage. Countries such as Bangladesh, China, Egypt, Iran, Malaysia, or Oman require prior authorisation for nuclear-powered ships and vessels with dangerous substances when seeking to enter the territorial sea (Rothwell and Stephens 2016: 78). Whilst notification may be seen in accordance with UNCLOS, authorisation policies in relation to innocent passage remain contested. To that end, the UN General Assembly pointed out that States should engage in dialogue and confidence building in collaboration with the International Atomic Energy Agency (IAEA) and the International Maritime Organisation (IMO) in order to address the concerns of small islands and other States in a spirit of mutual understanding (Tanaka 2015: 94).

Coastal States have the legislative and enforcement authority over a number of areas with regard to innocent passage, such as the protection of living resources, the prevention of infringements of fisheries laws, the protection of the environment, and the prevention, reduction or control of pollution (UNCLOS, Art. 21). Clearly, vessels undertaking innocent passage are bound to comply with such coastal State legislation. Innocent passage may also be subject to traffic separation schemes, i.e. foreign (and domestic) vessels cannot navigate freely, but must use designated sea lanes (UNCLOS, Art. 22). Such traffic separation schemes are operational in areas with dense traffic, such as the English Channel, the Strait of Gibraltar, or the Strait of Hormuz, to name but a few, and notably also in the Gulf of Trieste in the Northern Adriatic and the Strait of Otranto in the Southern Adriatic.[15] Lastly, coastal States can exercise criminal jurisdiction vis-à-vis vessels in innocent passage as long as a crime does not concern the internal discipline of a ship, but affects the coastal State's public or territorial sea's order, or in the event of drug trafficking, for instance (UNCLOS, Art. 27).

The obligations of coastal States as regards innocent passage relate to (i) not hampering passage and not discriminating against any vessel or State, (ii) the publication of any dangers to navigation (UNCLOS, Art. 24), such as sandbanks, low-tide elevations, or rocks, and (iii) the free-of-charge passage through the territorial sea (UNCLOS, Art. 26).

3.1.4 Exclusive Economic Zone (EEZ)

The EEZ and the contiguous zone are marine areas subject to a coastal State's sovereign rights or limited jurisdiction (as opposed to territorial sovereignty or complete jurisdiction in internal waters and the territorial sea; see Sects. 3.1.2 and 3.1.3).

[15] Albania, Croatia, Italy, Slovenia, and Serbia and Montenegro concluded an agreement under the International Maritime Organisation (IMO) on designated sea lanes in the Adriatic on 23 March 2003. The IMO's Maritime Safety Committee has subsequently adopted a traffic separation scheme for, *inter alia*, the Gulf of Trieste and the Channel of Otranto (IMO, COLREG.2/Circ.54, Annex III, 28 May 2004).

3.1.4.1 Contiguous Zone

The contiguous zone is an area adjacent to the territorial sea where the coastal State may exercise its authority to prevent or punish infringements of its customs, fiscal, immigration, or sanitary laws in place in its territorial sea or on its territory. The maximum breath of the contiguous zone is 24 nautical miles (UNCLOS, Art. 33).

The contiguous zone may be seen as not a very popular zone. Only some 90 UNCLOS State parties have claimed one, and none of the Adriatic's riparian States, not even Italy which also has considerable territorial maritime jurisdiction in the Ionian, Tyrrhenian, and Ligurian Sea.[16] The reason as for the Adriatic appears obvious since its long and narrow shape leaves not much room for additional maritime zones adjacent to the territorial sea. The prevention or punishment of infringements in fact plays a minor role as most of the passage can be assumed to be lateral rather than high-seas bound.

3.1.4.2 Exclusive Economic Zone

The Exclusive Economic Zone (EEZ), a relatively recent innovation, is neither an area of sovereignty, nor it is a part of the high seas. Rather, it accounts for a division of State competences and the coexistence of rights, jurisdiction, and of obligations (Fife 2019: 44). The idea of the EEZ in functional terms is to make use of the natural resources of the sea, the seabed, and the subsoil beyond the territorial sea of coastal States in order to boost the economies and raise the standard of living of their peoples. Natural resources would be placed under the costal States' jurisdiction whilst the freedom of navigation and overflight would be guaranteed. Iceland claimed a small economic zone in the late 1940s, by which time the US Truman Proclamation from 1945 was already there generally asserting a claim over economic resources off the coast (Rothwell and Stephens 2016: 86). The Andean and Central American States were the first ones to claim a 200 nautical miles EEZ in the late 1940s followed by a few African States in the early 1970s (Tanaka 2015: 127–9). Throughout the 1970s and 1980s, many coastal States around the world claimed an EEZ, so its concept and application can be seen as well-established before UNCLOS entered into force in 1994 (Rothwell and Stephens 2016: 87).

The seaward limit of the EEZ is at a maximum 200 nautical miles measured from the baseline of the territorial sea, i.e. it extends to a maximum of 188 nautical miles from the outer limit of the territorial sea (UNCLOS, Art. 57). In the EEZ, the coastal State enjoys

- Sovereign rights for the exploration and exploitation of living and non-living natural resources of the waters, the seabed, and its subsoil and also for the production of energy from water, current, and wind;

---

[16]See UN, Table of Claims to Maritime Jurisdiction, https://www.un.org/depts/los/LEGISLATIONANDTREATIES/PDFFILES/table_summary_of_claims.pdf.

- Jurisdiction for the establishment and use of artificial islands and installations, marine research, and the protection of the marine environment (UNCLOS, Art. 56).

Notably, (i) the above competencies must be distinguished from territorial sovereignty (as in the territorial sea). However, (ii) the sovereign rights of an EEZ are exclusive, i.e. no other States can exercise them without the consent of the costal State. Further, (iii) the material scope of the jurisdiction is limited to the above matters, i.e. foreign vessels may not engage in fishing or oil drilling, for instance, but do enjoy complete freedom of navigation, overflight, or the lying of submarine cables or pipelines, major components of the so-called high-seas freedoms (UNCLOS, Art. 58; Fife 2019: 44–46). In an EEZ, three of the six high-seas freedoms are under the control of the coastal State (Evans 2010: 674; see also Sect. 3.1.6).

3.1.4.3 Situation in the Mediterranean

Whilst claims to an EEZ have become a huge source of contention and conflict over potential oil and gas resources in the seabed and subsoil, in particular in the South China Sea (SCS) where China, Taiwan, the Philippines, and Vietnam face overlapping claims with China's claims being by far the most far-reaching (and most excessive) with its outermost point of the so-called Nine-Dash Line at almost 800 nm [sic] from China's coast (see, e.g. Kingdon 2015; Schofield et al. 2014: 2; see also PCA Final Award 2016: 471–7, paras 1202–1203), the EEZ had played a relatively minor role in the Mediterranean. More recently, however, EEZs have become politically relevant and contentious in the Mediterranean.

Riparian States had for a long time refrained from claiming an EEZ in the Mediterranean altogether.[17] The "unwritten agreement" not to claim an EEZ in the Mediterranean only came to an end in 1997 when Spain proclaimed an "EEZ light", followed by a similar "EEZ light" agreement between France, Italy, and Monaco in 1999 covering the marine area between Corsica (France), Liguria (Italy) and Provence (Monaco), and France who claimed a quasi-EEZ in 2004 which became a full EEZ in 2012. It is worth noting that the "EEZs light" focused on the protection of the marine living resources,[18] rather than economic exploitation of natural resources in the seabed or subsoil, or the production of energy (Grbec 2015: 75–87).

---

[17] Spain and France only proclaimed an EEZ along their non-Mediterranean, i.e. North Sea or Atlantic coasts, in 1976 and 1977, respectively, whilst a few Northern African States have claimed modest EEZs, albeit without implementing legislation and without affecting the interests of neighbouring States (see Grbec 2015: 74–5).

[18] It is useful to note that the following fishing rights apply within the framework of the EU Fisheries Policy (CFP): In waters under territorial sovereignty or jurisdiction of the Member States, in principle any fishing vessel from any Member State is allowed to fish within 200 nm (EEZ), except in coastal waters (12 nm) where Member States may decide to restrict the access to other fishing vessels who traditionally fish in those waters. Such restrictions are without prejudice to the existing arrangements as laid down in Annex I of EU Regulation 1380/2013 (information obtained from the legal unit of European Commission DG MARE, 18 July 2018; see also Schatz 2019).

Italy, clearly referring to the French EEZ and the danger that environmentally unsafe vessels not accepted in the French EEZ may navigate through the high seas just off the Italian territorial waters in the Ligurian and Tyrrhenian Sea (Grbec 2015: 94), adopted its law on Ecological Protection Zones (ZEP) on 8 February 2006 (LOS Bulletin, UN, No. 61/2006: 98). The Italian ZEP in the Ligurian and Tyrrhenian Sea became operational through an implementing decree from 27 October 2011. It must be noted in this context that Italy has not proclaimed any ZEP or EEZ for the Adriatic to date.[19]

The situation in the Eastern Mediterranean is dominated by the search of hydrocarbon energy resources. Cyprus declared an EEZ in 2004 (subsequently delimitated with Egypt, Lebanon and Israel following the equidistance line; see Yiallourides 2020, August 25). There are, however, severely conflicting maritime claims between Turkey and both Greece and Cyprus. Turkey has an EEZ agreement with the northern entity of Cyprus and, as of late, with Lybia infringing the maritime zones of the Greek islands of Rhodes and Crete. Turkey who, notably, is not part of UNCLOS, has operated drill vessels in the EEZ of Cyprus since November 2019 arguing the maritime area is a part of Turkey's continental shelf (Reuters news 2020, September 12). This conflict in fact originates from the yet unresolved dispute between Greece and Turkey over the continental shelf in the Agean and the maritime zones of islands (see e.g. Leanza 1993: 392–4).

3.1.4.4 Developments in the Adriatic

Croatia declared an Ecological and Fisheries Protection Zone (EFPZ) in October 2003 (LOS Bulletin, UN, No. 53/2004: 68–9; see also Cataldi 2013: 2). Its purpose as set out in Paragraph 1 is the exploitation, conservation, and management of marine living resources, marine scientific research, and the protection of the marine environment. Then again, reference is made in Paragraph 2 to the right to proclaim "other elements" in accordance with UNCLOS which renders it a quasi-EEZ. Vidas (2009: 12–13) notes that any reference to "exclusive" was avoided due to pressure from the European Commission to the extent that anything "exclusive" was not in the European spirit for a country that had just filed its application for EU membership. The spatial ambit of the Croatian EFPZ is described in Paragraph 6 as the area up to the continental shelf delimitation line from the 1968 agreement (of Yugoslavia) with Italy (see also Sect. 3.1.5) and the preliminary delimitation agreement with Serbia and Montenegro (FRY) from 2002 in the South. No delimitation vis-à-vis Slovenia

[19]However, Italy and Greece are reported to have signed an agreement on 9 June 2020 on a respective EEZ in the Southern Adriatic/Ionian Sea in fact extending the bilateral 1977 continental shelf delimitation to the water column. A further agreement apparently seeks to provide Italian fishing vessels access to Greek territorial waters (IBNA News, 09-06-2020). The two parties have notified the European Commission to that end with a view to the EU Fisheries Regulation 2013/1380 (information obtained by the European Commission Directorate General MARE, 16-06-2020) regulating mutual access to the territorial waters. Nevertheless, amendments to this regulation are subject to agreement by the co-legislators EU Member States and European Parliament.

is mentioned. The latter fact appears to be the case simply because no agreement with Slovenia on maritime delimitation had been reached yet.

Slovenia, in a *note verbale* to the Croatian embassy, protested the Croatian decision on the very day of its publication stating that Croatia, by means of unilaterally proclaiming an EFPZ, frustrated "a consensual solution to the issue of the maritime boundary between the two countries and encroached on the area where [...] Slovenia exercises its sovereignty and sovereign rights" (LOS Bulletin, UN, No. 53/2004: 71).

Italy also protested the Croatian decision, albeit for a different reason. In a note from the Italian Permanent Mission to the UN Secretary General dated 16 April 2004, critiquing a general lack of cooperation on the part of Croatia as for agreeing the limits of new zones of jurisdiction in a narrow sea such as the Adriatic, Italy points out that the Yugoslav–Italian agreement on the continental shelf did not contain superjacent waters, i.e. the water column above the seabed (see also Sect. 3.1.5). Further, "the 1968 delimitation was agreed in a moment in which the notion of the exclusive economic zone was not well defined in the international law of the sea" (LOS Bulletin, UN, No. 54/2004: 129). In other words, "you cannot use the [1968] continental shelf agreement for a completely different purpose". Even if Italy was to accept the Croatian EFPZ, it would have to be shifted eastward taking into account the Italian straight baselines established after 1968 (interview Giuseppe Cataldi, 18-07-2018).

Croatian scientists and experts had for years been presenting alarming findings about depleting fish stocks and a need for more marine environmental protection (Vidas 2009: 9). Further, as early as during the UNCLOS III conference (1973–82), experts in the Yugoslav delegation[20] brought these concerns to the attention of the federal Yugoslav government pressing for an introduction of an EEZ, but to no avail. The 2003 decision to declare a Croatian EFPZ, however, may also have been inspired by the preceding Spanish and French EEZ moves (Grbec 2015: 87).

After a series of trilateral meetings of Croatia, Italy, and Slovenia, at a later stage facilitated by the European Commission, in the first half of 2004, a common understanding was reached on 4 June 2004 in Brussels to the extent that vessels from EU Member States ought to be temporarily exempt from the application of the Croatian EFPZ until an agreement on fisheries was reached (Iborra Martin 2009: 8; see also Sancin 2010: 97–8). This exemption of vessels flying the flag of an EU Member State from the application of the Croatian EFPZ is still in operation to date whilst the EFPZ applies to non-EU vessels (interview senior Croatian civil servant, 25-01-2017), a solution which, whilst not ideal, may just about be regarded as "of a practical nature" (Grbec 2015: 94).

It must be mentioned in that context that the exemption for EU vessels—after it was renewed by the Croatian Parliament (Sabor) in 2006—expired on 1 January 2008, but was reintroduced by the Sabor on 13 March 2008. The move came following a

[20] Yugoslavia played a solid role during UNCLOS III. When the site for the proposed Tribunal of the Law of the Sea (ITLOS) was voted in 1981, no candidate received an absolute majority in the first ballot. The result in the second ballot was Federal Republic of Germany 78, Yugoslavia 61. The Seabed Authority went to Jamaica (76 votes) ahead of Malta with 66 votes (Oxman 1982: 14).

blockade of the opening of the Fisheries Chapter in the Croatian accession negotiations by Slovenia since September 2006 (Iborra Martin 2009: 9), and a threat by the Slovenian Foreign Minister Rupel in December 2007 to potentially block five to six other Chapters should Croatia not discontinue the application of its EFPZ to EU vessels. The European Commission also made it clear that this was a matter of urgency in order not to derail Croatia's EU accession, not least through a visit of Commissioner Rehn to Zagreb (Vidas 2009: 58–9). However, a secret meeting between Prime Minister Sanader and European Commission President Barroso in Brussels at the beginning of March 2008 may have played a crucial role, too. The agreement was that Croatia would prolong the exemption of EU vessels from the EFPZ until further notice in return for an assurance that Croatia's accession negotiations could be concluded (on a technical level) by the end of 2009. This date was supposed to feature in the European Commission Progress report for Croatia in November 2008 (Sanader 2017: 109–11; Martens 2008: 206–7), which it did (European Commission Progress Report Croatia 2008: 5).

Slovenia proclaimed its Ecological Protection Zone and Continental Shelf (EPZCSA) on 22 October 2005. Containing also a reference to the Croatian (Adriatic) EFPZ and the Italian (Ligurian and Tyrrhenian) ZEP, the draft version of the later Slovenian law particularly pointed out the need to protect the marine environment and biodiversity in the vulnerable Northern Adriatic with its narrow and shallow waters (Grbec 2015: 101–2; see also Cataldi 2013: 2). The actual law is remarkable in the sense that it starts out by asserting the continental shelf in Paragraph 2 which is to extend "beyond [Slovenia's] territorial sea".[21] Only in the following paragraph is the purpose of the ecological protection zone mentioned. Paragraph 4 maps the (provisional) outer limits. The 1968 continental shelf agreement with Italy is referred to as for the limit in the West, and as for the South, i.e. the delimitation with Croatia, the southern limit of the joint fishing zone established in the bilateral SOPS agreement from 1997[22] is stated (LOS Bulletin, UN, No. 60/2005: 56–7). As a result, the Slovenian EPZCSA considerably overlaps with the Croatian EFPZ in the area of the Croatian territorial sea. Croatia, not unexpectedly, in a *note verbale* to the UN Secretary General dated 31 May 2007, critiqued the Slovenian ZEP as "in utter disregard of the International Law of the Sea" protesting "resolutely" as a country with no access to the high seas was not able to claim any continental shelf (LOS Bulletin, No. 64/2007: 40).

[21] Slovenia has outlined its continental shelf claim in detail only during the arbitral proceedings in 2013/2014. The Tribunal, however, found that Slovenia is *not* entitled to a CS (see PCA Final Award 2017: 348–354, paras 1085–1103).

[22] For the SOPS fishing zone limits, see Sect. 4.1.3 and PCA Final Award (2017: 23, para 79).

3.1.5 *Continental Shelf*

The concept of the continental shelf, historically, is attached to the notion of the use of existing or presumed natural resources in the seabed or its subsoil. The Truman proclamation from 1945 can be seen as a prototype assertion in that regard (see also Sect. 2.1.4.2). The continental shelf (CS) thus "comprises the seabed and the subsoil of the submarine areas [...] beyond the territorial sea" (UNCLOS, Art. 76(1)). The limit of the CS extends up to 200 nm in a juridical sense. Coastal States may claim a geological CS up to 350 nm, however. The full set of criteria for the various definitions of the CS is beyond the scope of this study.[23] Nevertheless, it must be noted that islands also create a CS, i.e. coastal and island States may enjoy a CS to the same extent, and that submarine elevations can also play a role.

To avoid excessive claims, those exceeding 200 nm are subject to scrutiny and a recommendation by the Commission on the Limits of the Continental Shelf (CLCS) which are considered "final and binding" once a State bases its proclamation on the prior CLCS recommendation (UNCLOS, Art. 76(8)). The CLCS has, as of 3 September 2020, received 91 submissions[24] since it became operational in 2001. CS claims are of enormous economic and political importance as they constitute quasi-territorial claims and tend to be based on presumed natural resources, such as oil and gas reserves, and potentially also on geostrategic considerations. The CLCS is not entitled to consider a submission from any State subject to a maritime or land dispute, i.e. overlapping claims, unless all States party to the dispute has given their prior consent (CLCS rules of procedure CLCS/40/rev.1, 2009: 22).

The rights of the coastal State over its continental shelf are as follows:

- Exploration and exploitation of the CS' natural resources;
- The above rights are exclusive, i.e. no other State can consume the natural resources without the agreement of the coastal State (UNCLOS, Art. 77);
- The water column above the seabed (superjacent waters) and the airspace above are *not* within the scope of the CS; and
- The navigational rights and high-sea freedoms of other States—including fishing (Tanaka 2015: 149)—must not be interfered with (UNCLOS, Art. 78).

3.1.5.1 Relationship Between Continental Shelf and EEZ

With the emergence of the EEZ, the CS with a limit of 200 nm can be seen as a well-established fact of customary law (Tanaka 2015: 139). As a result, 36% of the oceans' seabed are under the jurisdiction of coastal or island States (Churchill and Lowe 1999: 148). The ICJ noted in the *Libya/Malta* case that "there can be a continental shelf where there is no exclusive economic zone, [but] there cannot be

[23] For an illustrated discussion of the criteria, see Tanaka (2015: 139–42).

[24] For the submissions to the CLCS, see https://www.un.org/depts/los/clcs_new/commission_submissions.htm.

an exclusive economic zone without a corresponding continental shelf." (ICJ 1985: 24, para 34).

As for the substantive regime, (i) the CS, as opposed to the EEZ, exists *ipso facto et ab initio*, i.e. it does not need to be claimed but simply exists geographical circumstances permitting (see also Grbec 2015: 69), whereas an EEZ must be expressly asserted; (ii) the EEZ is supposed to promote the conservation or management of fisheries, whilst the CS provisions contain no conservation aspect. Rather, its focus is primarily on the exploitation of the non-living resources (Rothwell and Stephens 2016: 125).

3.1.5.2 Situation in the Mediterranean and the Adriatic

The CS has been a field of very modest State activity in the Mediterranean. This is mainly for three reasons: (i) there is no area in the Mediterranean where the coasts of two States would be more than 400 nm apart, i.e. no riparian State to the Mediterranean can extend their jurisdiction up to the maximum provided for by the UNCLOS (such as 200 nm for the EEZ or the CS); (ii) were a coastal State to increase its jurisdiction considerably beyond its territorial sea, the interests of more than one State would be affected due to the general proximity, and there has therefore been some considerable sense of caution (Grbec 2015: 9); the fact that most of the Mediterranean is fairly deep exceeding 1000 m has made the exploration of natural resources somewhat theoretical anyway (Grbec 2015: 68), whilst conservation, environmental, and navigational safety concerns prevail (Vidas 2009: 6–9).

The jurisdictional continental shelf landscape in the Mediterranean includes agreements between Italy and the former SFRY (Yugoslavia), Albania, Greece, Tunisia, and Spain (Grbec 2015: 71). France has delimited its CR (and territorial sea) with Monaco (Arnaut 2002: 50). Further, Libya concluded agreements with Tunisia and Malta, Cyprus with Lebanon and Israel, and Albania with Greece (Grbec 2015: 72).

3.1.6 High Seas

Generally, the high seas comprises any area of the water column or the seabed other than areas under national jurisdiction (e.g. internal waters, territorial sea, EEZ, continental shelf). The *principle of freedom* is a crucial one on the high seas. The high-seas freedoms include

- Freedom of navigation;
- Freedom of overflight;
- Freedom to lay submarine cables and pipelines;
- Freedom to construct artificial islands and installations;
- Freedom of fishing; and
- Freedom of scientific research (UNCLOS, Art. 87(1)).

Yet, the above high-seas freedoms are not unlimited. Rather, they are supposed to be consumed in such a way as to respect "the interests of [all] *other* States in their exercise of the freedom of the high seas" (UNCLOS, Art. 87(2); emphasis added).

The *freedom of navigation* may be seen as iconic since the navigational freedom of a particular vessel as such may not be restricted on the high seas safe for fighting piracy and illicit trafficking in drugs (Rothwell and Stephens 2016: 164–5). The freedom of overflight holds for commercial, government, and military aircraft, and would also hold for spacecraft during take-off, re-entry, or overflight. With regard to the installations of submarine cables or pipelines, the course of the pipelines is subject to the consent of the coastal State on its continental shelf, whereas on the high seas it is not, as long as the interests of other users are taken into account. Artificial islands and other installations may be constructed and installed, but they must not interfere with sea lanes or traffic separation schemes, and abandoned structures must be removed. The freedom of fishing is another cardinal freedom. Still, it may be limited through specific preservation conventions for certain parts of the oceans, or through general provisions for the living resources in the UNCLOS (Rothwell and Stephens 2016: 165–167; Evans 2010: 665–6).

The second core principle on the high seas is the one of *flag State jurisdiction*, i.e. the State which has granted the vessel the right to navigate under its flag has exclusive jurisdiction (UNCLOS, Art. 94(1)), so there is by no means a lack of legal order on the high seas. Flag State jurisdiction relates to both legislative and enforcement jurisdiction regardless of the nationalities of the people on board of a flag State ship (Tanaka 2015: 156). It ought to be mentioned that so-called flags of convenience or open registry States (where foreign ship owners have relatively little connection with the flag State with the latter usually providing for zero-taxation and zero-qualification requirements for the ship crews in return for a registration or annual fee) have given rise to grave concern, not least with regard to compliance with safety and navigational rules, and also illegal fishing (Ford and Wilcox 2019).

3.2 Maritime Delimitation

Whilst land boundaries tend to be well established and stable, the same cannot be said about maritime boundaries. As a result, the map of the maritime world is far less clear than its terrestrial counterpart, and only half of all potential maritime borders have been delimited (Schofield et al. 2014: 1–2). The task of delimiting maritime zones between States with overlapping claims is complex and contentious. This very issue has attracted more cases before international courts and tribunals than any other single subject (Evans 2010: 677).

The difficulties arising with the effort of establishing maritime borders, first, trace back to the need for consensus at the UNCLOS III conference. As a result, some of the UNCLOS provisions on delimitation are ambiguous as they were meant to bridge disagreement between UNCLOS signatories (Heritage and Lee 2020: 115–6; Shearer 2014: 52) and are thus subject to different interpretation. Second, the ever-increasing number of maritime claims has created a clear need for delimitation methods applicable to a wide range of delimitation issues (Rothwell and Stephens 2016: 412).

On a general note, a system for maritime delimitation must be based on the ability to reconcile predictability and flexibility, a classical dilemma in legal affairs altogether, but in particular with maritime delimitation. Further, aspects of both change and continuity may be observed in the practice of international courts and tribunals when interpreting the codified law of the sea (see Sect. 3.2.2). As Rothwell and Stephens (2016: 412) point out, the need for maritime delimitation generally occurs when

(i) Adjacent States share a boundary that terminates at one point on the coast, and/or
(ii) Opposite States face one another in a maritime space.

Both features apply to the maritime dispute between Croatia and Slovenia. As has become clear from the above distinction, maritime delimitation is not a unilateral act, but must obviously be carried out jointly by the States concerned, as also noted by the ICJ in the *Gulf of Maine* case (ICJ 1984: 299–300, para 112). In the words of Natalie Klein,

> [t]he high stakes involved in maritime boundary disputes may prevent easy or prompt delimitation of the maritime areas in question. Maritime entitlements are inherently connected to a [S]tate's sovereignty and that [S]tate's exercise of rights and duties in respect of diverse ocean activities. As such, the national interests involved in dividing up those entitlements may trigger the most assertive claim possible. These potentially excessive claims to exclusivity may well clash with the claims of other [S]tates to either exclusive or inclusive use of the same ocean space. The disputes that result may prove complex, or even intractable. (Klein 2018: 117)

3.2.1 Delimitation Provisions of UNCLOS

The provisions on delimitation of marine spaces set out in UNCLOS concern

- Delimitation of the territorial sea (UNCLOS, Art. 15);
- Delimitation of the EEZ (UNCLOS, Art. 74), and
- Delimitation of the continental shelf (UNCLOS, Art. 83).

As for the delimitation of the *territorial sea*, Article 15 of UNCLOS provides:

> Where the coasts of two States are opposite or adjacent to each other, neither of the two States is entitled, failing agreement between them to the contrary, to extend its territorial sea to the median line every point of which is *equidistant* from the nearest points on the baselines from which the breadth of the territorial seas of each of the two States is measured. The above provision does not apply, however, where it is necessary by reason of historic title or other *special circumstances* to delimit the territorial seas of the two States in a way which is at variant therewith. (emphasis added)

With regard to special circumstances, scholarly opinion appears to agree that there is some considerable discretionary power, albeit there is an emphasis on geographical features (e.g. Rothwell and Stephens 2016: 432–435). The configuration of the coast in particular plays a vital role (Tanaka 2015: 225). Whereas special circumstances are limited in scope, their rather general definition is open to broad interpretation including special coastal configurations or islands in the proximity of the coast (Evans 2018: 226).

The role of equity

With regard to the delimitation of the *EEZ* (UNCLOS, Art. 74) and the *continental shelf* (UNCLOS, Art. 83), it must be noted that there is no reference to a particular delimitation method. Rather, the provisions on both the EEZ and the continental shelf invoke the aim of an "equitable solution". To that end, a brief illumination of the concept of *equity*, a contentious term amongst scholars and practitioners of the international law of the sea alike, appears useful.

> Equity in many legal systems may play a moderating role in the sense that when the rigorous application of accepted rules of law leads to a result which appears unjust, equity may step in to adjust the outcome. (Thirlway 2010: 11)

It is vital to note, however, that the concept of equity can be used in two ways: (i) *infra legem* (within the law) and (ii) *praeter legem* (outside of the law) or "autonomous equity" (Delabie 2018: 152) also known as *ex aequo et bono*. The historical trend in the use of equity for the purposes of maritime delimitation in case law can be described as one of rationalisation meaning to move away from extra-legal considerations and to contemplate equity as an aim to achieve a fair and just solution, but by no means as a method of delimitation. In practice, equity *infra legem* tends to be used as an adjustment tool at the level of the second stage of the contemporary three-stage method of delimitation (see Sect. 3.2.2.3), alongside equity at the level of the general aim to achieve in the process of delimitation (Delabie 2018: 154–162).

Coming back to the delimitation provisions of UNCLOS, convincing as the concept of equity may appear *prima facie*, the reference to an equitable solution renders UNCLOS Articles 74 and 83 less clear than Article 15 (on the territorial sea; see Rothwell and Stephens 2016: 422). The references to equity, however, steer clear of particular definitions such as equidistance, equitable principles, and special or relevant circumstances. Therefore, it may be said that the aim of an equitable solution is difficult to grasp and has very little substantive content (Evans 2010: 678). Generally, the aim of equitable solution in international law may be seen as "highly obscure" (Tanaka 2015: 201).

However, it is useful to note that the above provisions were a compromise formula reached in the late days of the UNCLOS III conference in August 1981 (leading to the adoption of UNCLOS in September 1982). There was an urgent need to bridge the gap between the supporters of the more rigid "equidistance/special circumstances" approach and the more moderating "equitable principles/relevant circumstances" method (Tanaka 2015: 200–1; Evans 2010: 678).[25]

[25] The actual compromise proposal had been secretly worked out by Ireland and Spain representing the two adversarial schools of thought (Oxman 1982: 14–5).

3.2.1.1 Dispute Settlement

As many UNCLOS provisions are compromise formulae due to the unanimity requirement at the UNCLOS III conference, there naturally is room for differing interpretations. This is why UNCLOS contains in-built procedures for dispute settlement to make sure that parties comply with the Convention (Tanaka 2015: 417–8). The UNCLOS dispute settlement procedures are remarkable in public international law in the sense that they are comprehensive and compulsory with very few exceptions. Generally, if disputes cannot be successfully settled bilaterally, or if the parties cannot agree on the terms of submission to dispute settlement, one party can invoke compulsory dispute settlement, i.e. bring the matter before an international court or arbitral tribunal (Rothwell and Stephens 2016: 473).

Broadly, both proceedings initiated by one party and submissions by mutual agreement of the parties have constituted State practice. Looking at the more recent cases, there appears to be a trend towards proceedings triggered by one party to the dispute (see Table 3.1 in Sect. 3.2.2.3).

Voluntary Dispute Settlement

Section 3.1 of part XV of UNCLOS provides for voluntary dispute settlement emphasising conflict resolution by peaceful means. The parties are encouraged to settle a dispute between them without recourse to the settlement provisions (UNCLOS, Art. 280), or at least to agree on how to proceed with the settlement of the dispute (UNCLOS, Art. 283).

It must be noted in this context that Croatia and Slovenia have spent the lion share of their joint settlement efforts since 1991 on bilateral negotiations outside the UNCLOS dispute settlement procedures (see Chap. 4). Serdy (2005: 715) argues that States tend to avoid external dispute settlement and prefer bilateral negotiations for two reasons: (i) they find it difficult to hand over the final say in a dispute to a body over which they have no control, and (ii) externalising dispute settlement equals outright failure of State diplomacy. One could add (iii) a potential lack of democratic legitimacy and accountability of the dispute settlement body.

Compulsory Dispute Settlement

Part XV of UNCLOS contains provisions on "*compulsory* proceedings entailing binding decisions" (Sect. 3.2; emphasis added). In fact,

> any dispute [can] be submitted at the request of any party to the dispute to the court or tribunal having jurisdiction [...]. (UNCLOS, Art. 286)

Art. 287 UNCLOS lists the options available in Paragraph 1:

> When signing, ratifying or acceding to this Convention or at any time thereafter, a State shall be free to choose [...] one or more of the following means for the settlement of disputes concerning the interpretation or application of this Convention:
>
> (a) the International Tribunal for the Law of the Sea [ITLOS[26]];
>
> (b) the International Court of Justice;
>
> (c) an arbitral tribunal [...];
>
> (d) a special arbitral tribunal [...].

To that end, it is useful to note that Croatia (in November 1999) opted for ITLOS[27] and ICJ (in order of preference), and Slovenia (in October 2001) declared its preference for arbitration—safe for delimitation issues.[28] "We believe the UNCLOS provisions do not cover all the specificities to be taken into account in the case of the Slovenia-Croatia delimitation issue. In particular, this issue is not only about maritime delimitation: there are a number of land border sections that are also disputed, including the last land border section right on the coast. And land borders cannot possibly be subject to any arbitration under UNCLOS. Thus, with [our] declaration [...] we simply wanted to avoid any attempt at [a] piece-meal solution of the border issue" (interview senior Slovenian civil servant, 13-06-2017).

3.2.2 Development of Case Law

It is an indispensable fact that the existing common or case law on maritime delimitation has been developed by international courts and tribunals. As a result, their jurisprudence has played a dominant role in the field (Rothwell and Stephens 2016: 422–3; Tanaka 2015: 201).

The following brief survey is to outline several major judgements of international courts and arbitral tribunals with regard to the development of jurisprudence as such and the method of delimitation. An assessment of all decisions is out of place in this study. Whilst every case clearly is *sui generis*, it is suggested here that one may still trace certain stages in the development of case law.

---

[26]ITLOS was newly created by UNCLOS and became operational in 1996. It took some time to establish itself as an alternative to the ICJ or arbitration. As the first ITLOS President would jokingly tell to visitor groups: "The judges would meet once a week for breakfast then going to the letter box together to see whether a case has arrived".

[27]Prof. Budislav Vukas, a Croatian national, was an ITLOS founding-member judge 1996–2005, https://www.itlos.org/the-tribunal/members-of-the-tribunal-since-1996/. In the Croatia–Slovenia arbitration, Vukas served as arbitrator appointed by Croatia until July 2015 (see also PCA Final Award 2017: 47, para 147).

[28]United Nations, Division for Ocean Affairs and the Law of the Sea, Declarations and statements, https://www.un.org/depts/los/convention_agreements/convention_declarations.htm.

3.2.2.1 Result-Oriented Equity Approach (1969–1992)

The "result-oriented equity approach" is an analytical concept and is defined as follows:

> This approach allows international courts [and tribunals] to decide, case by case, on the equitable results to be achieved without being bound by any method of maritime delimitation. Thus, the result-oriented equity approach emphasises maximum *flexibility* of the law of maritime delimitation. (Tanaka 2015: 202; emphasis added)

The first major case in the field of contemporary jurisprudence of maritime delimitation is the 1969 *North Sea Continental Shelf* (Federal Republic of Germany/Denmark; Federal Republic of Germany/Netherlands) judgement[29] where the Court found that "delimitation must be the object of agreement between the States concerned, and that such agreement must be arrived at in accordance with *equitable principles*" (ICJ 1969: 47, para 85; emphasis added). Equitable principles were thus established as customary law in maritime delimitation (Rothwell and Stephens 2016: 425; Tanaka 2015: 202) creating the result-oriented equity approach.

In the 1977 *Anglo-French Continental Shelf* case,[30] the Tribunal did recognise equitable principles as customary law, but only in taking them into account in applying the method of equidistance/special circumstances (Reports of International Arbitral Awards, vol. XVIII, 1977: 45–6). Equidistance was the starting point for equity to come in later as a corrective element, so one could speak of the "corrective-equity approach" (Tanaka 2015: 203). In the *Gulf of Maine* (Canada/USA) case[31] in 1984, however, the ICJ further substantiated the result-oriented equity approach in noting that "delimitation is to be effected by the application of equitable criteria and by the use of practical methods capable of ensuring, with regard to the geographic configuration of the area [...], an equitable result" (ICJ 1984: 300, para 112(2)).

The *Libya/Malta* continental shelf case[32] of 1985 again pronounced the result-oriented equity approach. The ICJ observed that "it is [...] the goal - an equitable result - and not the means used to achieve it, that must be the primary element [in

---

[29]The parties asked the Court to decide on the delimitation of the continental shelf. The Court did not produce a ruling as such as the FRG had not yet ratified the Geneva Convention (a predecessor to UNCLOS), but indicated certain factors for consideration when deciding on the natural prolongation of the land territory under the sea (ICJ, North Sea Continental Shelf, Overview of the Case, https://www.icj-cij.org/en/case/52).

[30]The Tribunal was asked by the parties to delimit the continental shelf boundary in the English Channel/La Manche west of the Greenwich Meridian Line. The main issues were the effect of the Channel Islands and of the Scilly Isles for the Atlantic region (see Arts. 1 and 2 of the Arbitration Agreement, Reports of International Arbitral Awards, vol. XVIII: 5).

[31]Canada and the USA tasked the Court with the delimitation of the continental shelf and fisheries zone in the Gulf with adjacent and opposite coasts. The Court produced a line referring to geographical factors (ICJ, Gulf of Maine, Overview of the Case, https://www.icj-cij.org/en/case/67).

[32]Malta and Libya asked the Court to determine the continental shelf boundary. The opposite coasts of both States are less than 400 nm apart. Although Libya was not party to the Geneva Convention on the Continental Shelf, both parties indicated to the Court that they would respect its provisions and also those of the UNCLOS which had not entered into force yet (ICJ, Continental Shelf, Overview of the Case, https://www.icj-cij.org/en/case/68).

assessing whether a result is equitable]" (ICJ 1985: 38–9, para 45). Similarly, the Tribunal in the 1992 *St. Pierre and Miquelon* (Canada/France) arbitration[33] noted it was carrying out a delimitation "conformément à des principes équitables, ou à des critères équitables, en tenant compte des toutes circonstances pertinentes, afin de parvenir à un resultat équitable [...] sur la prémisse [que] toute méthode obligatoire est réjetée [...]" (Reports of International Arbitral Awards, vol. XXI, 1992: 282).

3.2.2.2 Corrective-Equity Approach (1993–2009)

The "corrective-equity approach", the subsequent analytical strand, operates as follows:

> [T]he equidistance method is applied at the first stage of delimitation and, at the second stage, a shift of the equidistance line may be envisaged if relevant circumstances warrant it. Equidistance is the only predictable method for ensuring predictability of results in the sense that once the base points are fixed, the determination line is mathematically determined. The corrective-equity approach thus highlights *predictability* in the law on maritime delimitation. (Tanaka 2015: 203; emphasis added)

A landmark case with regard to the full recognition of the corrective-equity approach was the 1993 *Greenland/Jan Mayen* (Denmark/Norway) judgement.[34] The Court noted that "it [...] appears that, both for the continental shelf and for the fisheries zones in this case, it is proper to begin the process of delimitation by a median line provisionally drawn" (ICJ 1993: 61–2, para 53). Tanaka (2015: 205) posits that the ICJ, for the first time, "incorporated the equidistance method into the domain of customary law". Churchill (1994: 16–7), however, in this respect, critiques the Court's lack of supporting evidence or arguments for its proposition of having identified customary law.

The corrective-equity approach was subsequently adopted by the arbitral tribunal in the 1999 *Eritrea/Yemen* (Second Phase) case[35] where a provisional equidistance line was drawn to determine the continental shelf and EEZ boundary. The ICJ substantiated the corrective-equity approach as customary law in the 2001 *Qatar/Bahrein*

---

[33]Canada and France tasked the Tribunal with delimiting the sea border between Canada and St. Pierre and Miquelon, a French overseas collectivity some 16 nm off the Canadian coast of south-eastern Newfoundland (Reports of International Arbitral Awards, vol. XXI, 1992: 271–4).

[34]Denmark had instituted proceedings against Norway for the Court to delimit both countries' fishing zones and continental shelf between the east coast of Greenland and the Norwegian island of Jan Mayen. Both parties had overlapping 200 nm claims for an area comprising some 72.000 km^2 (ICJ, Maritime Delimitation between Greenland and Jan Mayen, Overview of the Case, https://www.icj-cij.org/en/case/78).

[35]Eritrea and Yemen asked the Tribunal to determine the maritime boundaries between the two States. The identification of the respective territorial sovereignty over the islands had constituted the First Phase (Reports of International Arbitral Awards, vol. XXII, 1999: 336–7).

case[36] as for territorial sea issues. In the 2002 *Cameroon/Nigeria* case,[37] the ICJ took on the corrective-equity approach for the delimitation of the continental shelf and the EEZ. The observation of the Court reads:

> The Court has on various occasions made it clear what the applicable criteria, principles and rules of delimitation are when a line covering several zones of coincident jurisdiction is to be determined. They are expressed in the so-called equitable principles/relevant circumstances method. This method, which is very similar to the equidistance/special circumstances method applicable in delimitation of the territorial sea, involves first drawing an equidistance line, then considering whether there are factors calling for the adjustment or shifting of that line in order to achieve an 'equitable result' (ICJ 2002: 441, para 288).

In view of the deliberate omission of any reference to a delimitation method at the time of drafting UNCLOS Articles 74 and 83, the above quote may be said to represent "a creative interpretation of the Court" (Tanaka 2015: 205). Yet, "[a]fter 35 years of hesitation, the ICJ finally accepted what it had rejected in the *North Sea* cases, that the equidistance/special circumstances approach reflects customary international law", and that it was "subsequently confirmed that this is the case [...] for the delimitation of the continental shelf, EEZ [2007 *Guyana/Suriname* case[38]], or when drawing a single delimitation line [2009 *Romania/Ukraine* case[39]]" (Evans 2010: 679).

3.2.2.3 Three-Stage Approach (2009–)

The 2009 *Romania/Ukraine* case marks the beginning of the most recent phase of maritime delimitation methodology, the so-called three-stage approach (e.g. Evans 2018: 321; Rothwell and Stephens 2016: 429; Tanaka 2015: 206, 2018a: 304–306)[40] which, strictly speaking, is a refined corrective-equity approach. The ICJ's definition of the method:

---

[36]Qatar initiated proceedings against Bahrein for the Court to determine territorial sovereignty over an island, sovereign rights over two shoals, and the maritime boundary between the two States (ICJ, Maritime Delimitation and Territorial Questions between Qatar and Bahrein, Overview of the Case, https://www.icj-cij.org/en/case/87).

[37]Cameroon instituted proceedings against Nigeria with regard to sovereignty over the Bakassi Peninsula (a part of which was occupied by Nigeria), the delimitation of the joint maritime border, and the terrestrial border at Lake Tschad (ICJ, Land and Maritime Boundary between Cameroon and Nigeria, Overview of the Case, https://www.icj-cij.org/en/case/94).

[38]Guyana initiated arbitral proceedings against Suriname concerning the maritime boundary and the alleged disrespect of the maritime territorial sovereignty of Guyana on the part of Suriname (Reports of International Arbitral Awards, vol. XXX, 2007: 12).

[39]Romania instituted proceedings against the Ukraine with regard to the delimitation of a single maritime boundary in the Black Sea including the continental shelf and the EEZ (ICJ, Maritime Delimitation in the Black Sea, Overview of the Case, https://www.icj-cij.org/en/case/132).

[40]The third stage of the delimitation process, however, appears to have become operational as early as in the *Gulf of Maine* case in 1984 (see Sect. 3.2.2.1) when the Court also "checked for the equitableness of the designated boundary" in terms of avoiding any negative environmental or economic repercussions for the population of the two countries (Ioannides 2020: footnote 8).

> First, the Court will establish a provisional delimitation line, [in the case of adjacent coasts] an equidistance line will be drawn unless there are compelling reasons that make this unfeasible in the particular case [...]. [As for opposite coasts], the provisional delimitation line will consist of a median line between the two coasts [...] The Court will at the next, second stage consider whether there are factors calling for the adjustment or shifting of the provisional equidistance line in order to achieve an equitable result [...]. Finally, and at a third stage, the Court will verify that the line [provisional, or adjusted according to relevant circumstances], does not, as it stands, lead to an inequitable result by reason of any marked disproportion between the ratio of the respective coastal lengths and the ratio between the relevant maritime area of each State by reference to the delimitation line. (ICJ 2009: 44–6, paras 116–122)

In other words, the three-stage approach consists of the two stages of the equidistance/relevant circumstances method or corrective-equity approach, plus a third stage of applying a proportionality test (Solomou 2017: 4; see also Marques Antunes and Becker-Weinberg 2018: 73–77; Delabie 2018: 158–164).[41] Generally, the three-stage approach "has been a way for the judiciary to progressively ensure more objectivity" (Delabie 2018: 158). It must be noted, however, that the three-stage approach introduced by *Romania v. Ukraine* applies to the delimitation of the EEZ and the continental shelf and is different from the delimitation method for the territorial sea (Lando 2017: 1188–1189).

With regard to the third stage and the issue of proportionality, it is useful to note that "the determination of the *relevant area* is crucial for the application of *proportionality*", so that a court or tribunal will have to determine the relevant area under consideration at the very *beginning* of a delimitation process (Rothwell and Stephens 2016: 429; emphasis added). Yet, there generally remains some obscurity of the evaluation criteria for the proportionality between coastal lengths and maritime areas (Tanaka 2009: 422–4): It can be observed that any objective criteria for the determination of both the relevant coastal length and maritime area have been absent in jurisprudence to date. Further, there are no objective criteria as to what constitutes a *significant* disproportionality between coastal lengths and the maritime areas apportioned. In addition, and strikingly, the (dis)proportionality test employed by the courts and tribunals at the third stage is always met, so that the test as such may be seen as purely formalistic.[42]

On the whole, it may be observed that the disproportionality test is in need of enhancing its objectiveness (Tanaka 2018a: 316–318). With regard to *relevant coasts/areas* in particular, Oude Elferink demonstrates that whilst generally two case law approaches may be distinguished: (i) the concept of "seaward extension" and (ii) the "reference to the delimitation method selected" (2018: 178–9), there are virtually no cases where courts or tribunals would provide any *criteria/explanation* for determining or identifying the relevant coasts/areas (Oude Elferink 2018: 181–190).

---

[41] Lathrop (2018: 221) posits that the construction of the provisional equidistance line as the starting point of the three-stage approach merits particular attention. He observes that the provisional equidistance line must be "a solid foundation from which to consider [...] the effect of coastal irregularities and other features".

[42] Evans (2018: 233) talks of "the formalism of the three-stage approach" with regard to the role of relevant circumstances at stages two and three of that approach.

As a result, the case law on relevant coasts/areas could "neither be characterised as wholly predictable nor wholly consistent" (Oude Elferink 2018: 199).

Table 3.1 Major maritime delimitation cases

Year	Case	Body	Mode	Boundary	Configuration	Approach
1969	*North Sea Continental Shelf*	ICJ	A	CS	AC	RE
1977	*Anglo-French Continental Shelf*	AR	A	CS	AC/OC	RE/CE
1984	*Gulf of Maine*	ICJ	A	SMB	AC/OC	RE
1985	*Libya/Malta*	ICJ	A	CS	OC	RE
1992	*St. Pierre and Miquelon*	AR	A	SMB	AC	RE
1993	*Greenland/Jan Mayen*	ICJ	U	CS/F	OC	CE
1999	*Eritrea/Yemen*	AR	A	SMB	OC	CE
2001	*Qatar/Bahrein*	ICJ	U	TS/SMB	AC/OC	CE
2002	*Cameroon/Nigeria*	ICJ	U	TS/SMB	AC	CE
2007	*Guyana/Suriname*	AR	U	TS/SMB	AC	CE
2009	*Romania/Ukraine*	ICJ	U	SMB	AC/OC	3-stage
2012	*Bangladesh/Myanmar*	ITLOS	U	TS/SMB/CS	AC	3-stage
2012	*Nicaragua/Colombia*	ICJ	U	TS/SMB	OC	3-stage
2014	*Peru/Chile*	ICJ	U	TS/SMB	AC	3-stage
2016	*Philippines/China*[a]	AR	U	F/EEZ	OC	–
2017	*Croatia/Slovenia*	AR	A[b]	IW/TS/J[c]	AC/OC	2-stage
2017	*Ghana/Côte d'Ivoire*	ITLOS	U/A	SMB	AC	3-stage
2018	*Costa Rica/Nicaragua*	ICJ	U	TS/EEZ/CS	AC	3-stage[d]

Selected; base charts from Rothwell and Stephens (2016: 424), and Tanaka (2015: 208); enhanced and updated by this author

AR arbitration, *A* submission by mutual agreement of the parties, *U* proceedings initiated by one party, *CS* continental shelf, *SMB* single maritime boundary, *TS* territorial sea, *IW* internal waters, *F* fisheries jurisdiction, *EEZ* exclusive economic zone, *AC* adjacent coast, *OC* opposite coast, *RE* result-oriented equity approach, *CE* corrective-equity approach

[a]The Philippines initiated proceedings against China's EEZ excessive claim over almost the entire South China Sea ("Nine-Dash-Line"). China refused to take part in the arbitral proceedings on the grounds that the Tribunal lacked jurisdiction and did, thus, not recognize the Award either

[b]Induced by Slovenian veto during Croatia's EU accession negotiations

[c]Junction to high seas

[d]2-stage for the territorial sea (no *relevant areas* were needed for the delimitation purposes)

N.B.: *Nicaragua/Columbia*, *Croatia/Slovenia* and *Costa Rica/Nicaragua* are mixed disputes, i.e. sections of the land border were also determined alongside delimiting the maritime spaces

The three-stage approach was subsequently used by ITLOS in the 2012 *Bay of Bengal* (Bangladesh/Myanmar) case,[43] by the ICJ in the 2012 *Nicaragua/Colombia* case,[44] and in the 2014 *Peru/Chile* case[45] (see also Solomou 2017: 4). The 2017 *Ghana/Côte d'Ivoire* ITLOS case[46] and the 2018 *Costa Rica/Nicaragua* ICJ case[47] constitute the most recent three-stage approach judgements at the time of writing.

In the 2017 *Croatia/Slovenia* arbitration under particular scrutiny in this book, the Tribunal noted that the ICJ had developed a well-established jurisprudence with regard to the interpretation of the UNCLOS provisions, and quoted the three-stage approach from the *Peru/Chile* and *Cameroon/Nigeria* cases. Nevertheless, the Arbitral Tribunal in *Croatia/Slovenia* did carry out the classical *two*-stage approach in the delimitation of the territorial sea in first drawing a provisional equidistance line, then shifting it in favour of Slovenia in view of the differing projections of the relevant coastlines (see "Territorial Sea Boundary" in Sect. 4.3.5.2). Table 3.1 illustrates the distinct features of the cases selected above.

3.3 Conclusion

This Chapter has outlined the fundamental legal issues relating to the distribution and delimitation of marine spaces. Furthermore, it has highlighted the underlying legal–political strands and particular features of the conflict dynamics of the dispute between Croatia and Slovenia over the sea border. Ahead of looking at the genesis of the Arbitration Agreement in the context of Croatia's EU accession negotiations in 2008/2009 (see Chap. 4), it is well worth recalling the following:

- The Convention of the Law of the Sea is a product of an enormous and laborious United Nations treaty conference lasting for nearly ten years (UNCLOS III, 1973–1982). As a quasi-constitution of the oceans, the adoption of UNCLOS was subject to unanimity and followed the package-deal principle. All signatories had to agree on the final text. Thus, many provisions of the Convention were only possible after

[43] Bangladesh instituted proceedings against Myanmar for the Tribunal to delimit the maritime boundary with regard to the territorial sea, the EEZ, and the continental shelf (ITLOS 2012: 9–10, paras 1–4).

[44] Nicaragua filed proceedings against Colombia concerning territorial sovereignty and maritime delimitation mainly around the San Andrés Archipelago (ICJ, Territorial and Maritime Dispute, Overview of the Case, https://www.icj-cij.org/en/case/124).

[45] Peru initiated proceedings against Chile seeking the delimitation of the territorial sea and the EEZ (ICJ, Maritime Dispute, Overview of the Case, https://www.icj-cij.org/en/case/137).

[46] Ghana and Côte d'Ivoire, at the initiative of Ghana, submitted a joint request to ITLOS to determine their single maritime boundary (territorial sea, EEZ and continental shelf) in the Atlantic (Special Agreement, https://www.itlos.org/fileadmin/itlos/documents/cases/case_no.23_merits/X001_special_agreement.pdf).

[47] Costa Rica instituted proceedings against Nicaragua asking for the delimitation of the single maritime boundary (territorial sea, EEZ, continental shelf) in the Caribbean, Maritime, and Land Boundary delimitation, Overview of the Case, https://www.icj-cij.org/en/case/157).

fine-tuned compromise formulae had been painstakingly carved out. As a result, the agreed texts are subject to different interpretations.

Against this background, the UNCLOS dispute settlement system is remarkable both from the point of view of its integrity and its ability to manage conflict. With the benefit of hindsight, one cannot overestimate the built-in procedures for settling disputes over the interpretation and implementation of UNCLOS for the purpose of preserving the Convention as a whole. A *binding* settlement procedure is another striking feature of UNCLOS. Even where no joint agreement of the parties is feasible on the submission of a dispute, one party can unilaterally initiate proceedings for which the outcome is binding on both parties. This was truly a novelty in international law and the conduct of international relations.

The process of case law developed by international courts and tribunals has refined the delimitation methodology both in technical terms and in terms of predictability. Parties subject to a maritime dispute can nowadays expect a high and structured level of legal reasoning. There is, however, still room for improvement with regard to the transparency of the delimitation method, in particular as far as the (dis)proportionality test in the three-stage approach is concerned. In terms of effectiveness, the parties' level of compliance has, on the whole, been very solid, which highlights the legitimacy and the general effectiveness of the UNCLOS dispute settlement system.

- The dispute between Croatia and Slovenia over the maritime part of the border became an EU issue immediately after Croatia's application for EU membership in 2003. Croatia's proclamation of a *de facto* economic zone (EFPZ) in the narrow Adriatic later that year triggered a fierce response not only from Slovenia, but also some criticism on the part of Italy and was largely seen as at odds with the "European spirit".

Croatia's EU accession process was facing a particularly rocky road with regard to fisheries. It took some substantial effort from the European Commission acting as a mediator as early as in the spring of 2004 to somewhat defuse the conflict in securing a temporary non-application of the Croatian EFPZ to EU vessels. In late 2006, the actual accession negotiations on the Fisheries Chapter were temporarily blocked by Slovenia in view of the scheduled expiry of the exemption for EU vessels from the EFPZ regime.

- Croatia and Slovenia have acted in an adversarial manner cultivating their political struggle by legal means through their maritime claims in the Adriatic, a pretty narrow playing field for maritime zones anyway. To that end, the Slovenian EPZCSA declaration in 2005—including an overambitious claim to a continental shelf—may be seen as no less confrontational than the Croatian EFPZ declaration from 2003.

The respective maritime claims, on paper predominantly of an ecological preservation nature, escalated the conflict level of the unresolved border dispute, whilst virtually no mention of the underlying territorial conflict as such was made. Any move on maritime claims from either side must have been, and indeed was, perceived as lawfare. Such tit-for-tat diplomatic strikes made the bilateral border dispute a sustainable, as it were, and constant line of conflict in the political domain and served to harden the stance of both parties way ahead of the events in 2008/2009.

Interviews

Cataldi, Dr. Giuseppe. Professor for International Law, Naples University. President of the International Association of the Law of the Sea. Phone interview, 18 July 2018.
Senior Croatian civil servant. Zagreb, 25 January 2017.
Senior Slovenian civil servant. E-mail interview, 13 June 2017.

References

Agyebeng, W. (2006). Theory in search of practice: The right of innocent passage in the territorial sea. *Cornell International Law Journal, 39*(2), 371–399.

Arnaut, D. (2002). Stormy waters on the way to the high seas: The case of the territorial sea delimitation between Croatia and Slovenia. *Ocean and Coastal Law Journal, 8*(1), 21–70.

Arnaut, D. (2014). Adriatic Blues: Delimiting the former Yugoslavia's final frontier. In C. Schofield, S. Lee, & M. S. Kwon (Eds.), *The limits of maritime jurisdiction* (pp. 145–173). Leiden and Boston: Martinus Nijhoff.

Asia Maritime Transparency Initiative News. (2018a, May 18). China lands first bomber on South China Sea Island. https://amti.csis.org/china-lands-first-bomber-south-china-sea-island/. Accessed March 20, 2020.

Asia Maritime Transparency Initiative News. (2018b, May 24). Exercises bring new weapons to the Paracels. https://amti.csis.org/exercises-bring-new-weapons-paracels/. Accessed March 20, 2020.

Bateman, S. (2017). New tensions in the South China Sea: Whose sovereignty over Paracels? In R. Yang (Ed.), *The South China Sea disputes: Flashpoints, turning points and trajectories* (pp. 181–184). Singapore: World Scientific.

Blake, G., & Topalović, D. (1996). *The maritime boundaries of the Adriatic Sea. Maritime Briefing* 1(8). Durham: IBRU Durham University.

Buga, I. (2012). Territorial sovereignty issues in maritime disputes: A jurisdictional dilemma for Law of the Sea tribunals. *The International Journal of Marine and Coastal Law, 27*(1), 59–95.

Cataldi, G. (2013). Prospects for the judicial settlement of the dispute between Croatia and Slovenia over Piran Bay. In N. Boschiero, T. Scovazzi, C. Pitea, & C. Ragni (Eds.), *International courts and the development of international law* (pp. 257–268). The Hague: T.M.C. Asser Press.

Churchill, R. (1994). The Greenland-Jan Mayen case and its significance for the international law of maritime boundary delimitation. *International Journal of Marine and Coastal Law, 9*(1), 1–29.

Churchill, R., & Lowe, V. (1999). *The law of the sea.* Manchester: Manchester University Press.

Cronin, P., & Neuhard, R. (2020). Total competition. China's challenge in the South China Sea. Center for a New American Security CNAS. https://www.cnas.org/publications/reports/total-competition. Accessed March 19, 2020.

Delabie, L. (2018). The role of equity, equitable principles, and the equitable solution in maritime delimitation. In A. Oude Elferink, T. Henriksen, & S. Busch (Eds.), *Maritime boundary delimitation: The case law. Is it consistent and predictable?* (pp. 145–172). Cambridge: Cambridge University Press.

De Vattel, E. (2003). The law of nations or the principles of natural law in four books (1758). Lonang Institute. https://dl4a.org/uploads/pdf/LawofNationsVattel.pdf. Accessed March 07, 2019.

Ekman, A. (2019). US-China competition: Europe as a responsible stabiliser? In: R. Huisken, K. Brett, A. Milner, R. Smith, P. Vermonte, & J. Wanandi (Eds.), *CSCAP regional security outlook 2020* (pp. 27–29). Council for Security Cooperation in the Asia Pacific. https://www.jstor.org/stable/resrep22261. Accessed March 19, 2020.

Evans, M. (2010). The law of the sea. In M. Evans (Ed.), *International law* (pp. 651–686). Oxford: Oxford University Press.

Evans, M. (2018). Relevant circumstances. In A. Oude Elferink, T. Henriksen, S. Busch (Eds.), *Maritime boundary delimitation: The case law. Is it consistent and predictable?* (pp. 222–261). Cambridge: Cambridge University Press.

European Commission. (2008, November 8). *Staff working document.* Croatia 2008 Progress Report. https://ec.europa.eu/neighbourhood-enlargement/sites/near/files/pdf/press_corner/key-documents/reports_nov_2008/croatia_progress_report_en.pdf. Accessed March 21, 2020.

Feenstra, R. (Ed.). (2009). *Hugo Grotius. Mare liberum. 1609–2009.* Leiden: Brill.

Fife, R. E. (2019). Obligations of 'Due Regard' in the exclusive economic zone: Their context, purpose and state practice. *The International Journal of Marine and Coastal Law, 34*(1), 43–55.

Ford, J., & Wilcox, C. (2019). Shedding light on the dark side of maritime trade—A new approach for identifying countries as flags of convenience. *Marine Policy, 99*(1), 298–303.

Gidel, G. (1981). *Le droit international public de la mer*. Vaduz: Topos.

Grbec, M. (2015). *Extension of coastal state jurisdiction in enclosed and semi-enclosed seas—A Mediterranean and Adriatic perspective.* London and New York: Routledge.

Hebbar, A. (2020). Innocent passage under UNCLOS: An exploration of the tenets, trials, and tribulations. In P. Mukherjee, M. Mejia, Jr., & J. Xu (Eds.), *Maritime law in motion* (pp. 227–256). Cham: Springer.

Heritage, A., & Lee, P. (2020). *Order, Contestation and Ontological Security-Seeking in the South China Sea.* Cham: Palgrave/Springer.

IBNA News. (2020, June 9). Greece-Italy sign agreement on demarcation of EEZ. https://balkaneu.com/greece-italy-sign-demarcation-of-eez/. Accessed June 21, 2020.

Iborra Martin, J. (2009). *The common fisheries policy. A practical guide.* Brussels: European Parliament. Policy Department B. https://www.europarl.europa.eu/document/activities/cont/200907/20090720ATT58547/20090720ATT58547EN.pdf. Accessed February 08, 2019.

Insolia, A. (2019). The Law of Maritime Delimitation in the Croatia/Slovenia Final Award, In A. Del Vecchio, & R. Virzo (Eds.), *Interpretations of the United Nations Convention on the Law of the Sea by International Courts and Tribunals* (pp. 225–265). Cham: Springer.

International Court of Justice. (1969, February 20). *North Sea continental shelf* (Federal Republic of Germany/Denmark; Federal Republic of Germany/Netherlands). Judgements. https://www.icj-cij.org/files/case-related/51/051-19690220-JUD-01-00-EN.pdf; https://www.icj-cij.org/files/case-related/52/052-19690220-JUD-01-00-EN.pdf. Accessed March 21, 2020.

International Court of Justice. (1984, October 12). *Gulf of Maine* (Canada/United States of America). Judgement. https://www.icj-cij.org/files/case-related/67/067-19841012-JUD-01-00-EN.pdf. Accessed March 21, 2020.

International Court of Justice. (1985, June 3). *Libya/Malta continental shelf*. Judgement. https://www.icj-cij.org/files/case-related/68/068-19850603-JUD-01-00-EN.pdf. Accessed March 21, 2020.

International Court of Justice (1993, June 14). *Greenland/Jan Mayen.* Judgement. https://www.icj-cij.org/files/case-related/78/078-19930614-JUD-01-00-EN.pdf. Accessed September 12, 2020.

International Court of Justice. (2001, March 15). *Qatar/Bahrein.* Judgement. https://www.icj-cij.org/files/case-related/87/087-20010316-JUD-01-00-EN.pdf. Accessed March 21, 2020.

International Court of Justice. (2002, October 10). *Cameroon/Nigeria*. Judgement. https://www.icj-cij.org/files/case-related/94/094-20021010-JUD-01-00-EN.pdf. Accessed March 21, 2020.

International Court of Justice. (2009, February 3). *Romania/Ukraine*. Judgement. https://www.icj-cij.org/files/case-related/132/132-20090203-JUD-01-00-EN.pdf. Accessed March 21, 2020.

International Court of Justice. (2012, November 19). *Nicaragua/Colombia*. Judgement. https://www.icj-cij.org/files/case-related/124/124-20121119-JUD-01-00-EN.pdf. Accessed March 21, 2020.

International Court of Justice. (2014, January 27). *Peru/Chile*. Judgement. https://www.icj-cij.org/files/case-related/137/137-20140127-JUD-01-00-EN.pdf. Accessed March 20, 2020.

International Court of Justice. (2018, February 2). *Costa Rica/Nicaragua*. Judgement. https://www.icj-cij.org/files/case-related/150/150-20180202-JUD-01-00-EN.pdf. Accessed March 21, 2020.

International Maritime Organisation. (2004, May 28). Traffic separation scheme Northern Adriatic. COLREG.2/Circ.54, Annex III.

International Tribunal for the Law of the Sea (2012, March 14). *Bay of Bengal* (Bangladesh/Myanmar). Judgement. https://www.itlos.org/fileadmin/itlos/documents/cases/case_no_16/C16_Judgement_14_03_2012_rev.pdf. Accessed March 21, 2020.

International Tribunal for the Law of the Sea. (2017, September 23). *Ghana/Côte d'Ivoire*. Judgement. https://www.itlos.org/fileadmin/itlos/documents/cases/case_no.23_merits/C23_Judgement_23.09.2017_corr.pdf. Accessed March 20, 2020.

Ioannides, N. A. (2020). The "Predominant Interest" concept in maritime boundary delimitation. *Ocean Development and International Law*. https://www.tandfonline.com/doi/full/10.1080/00908320.2020.1757215. Accessed May 06, 2020.

Keyuan, Z. (2012). China's U-shaped line in the South China Sea revisited. *Ocean Development and International Law, 43*(1), 18–34.

Kingdon, E. (2015). A case for arbitration: The Philippines' solution for the South China Sea dispute. *Boston International and Comparative Law Review, 38*(1), 129–158.

Klein, N. (2018). Provisional measures and provisional arrangements. In A. Oude Elferink, T. Henriksen, & S. Busch (Eds.), *Maritime boundary delimitation: The case law. Is it consistent and predictable?* (pp. 117–144). Cambridge: Cambridge University Press.

Lando, M. (2017). The Croatia/Slovenia arbitral award of 29 June 2017: Is there a common method for delimiting all maritime zones under international law? *Rivista di diritto internazionale, 100*(4), 1184–1190.

Lathrop, C. (2018). The provisional equidistance line: Charting a course between objectivity and subjectivity? In A. Oude Elferink, T. Henriksen, & S. Busch (Eds.), *Maritime boundary delimitation: The case law. Is it consistent and predictable?* (pp. 200–221). Cambridge: Cambridge University Press.

Leanza, U. (1993). The Delimitation of the Continental Shelf of the Mediterranean Sea. *International Journal of Marine and Coastal Law, 8*(3), 373–396.

Marques Antunes, N., & Becker-Weinberg, V. (2018). Entitlement to maritime zones and their delimitation. In A. Oude Elferink, T. Henriksen, & S. Busch (Eds.), *Maritime boundary delimitation: The case law. Is it consistent and predictable?* (pp. 62–91). Cambridge: Cambridge University Press.

Martens, W. (2008). *Europe, I struggle, I overcome*. Brussels: Centre for European Studies.

Mlimuka, A. (1994). Mozambique and Tanzania. Current legal developments. *International Marine and Coastal Law Journal, 9*(3), 399–407.

Oude Elferink, A. (2018). Relevant coast and relevant area. In A. Oude Elferink, T. Henriksen, & S. Busch (Eds.), *Maritime boundary delimitation: The case law. Is it consistent and predictable?* (pp. 173–199). Cambridge: Cambridge University Press.

Oxman, B. (1982). The third United Nations conference on the law of the sea: The tenth session (1981). *American Journal of International Law, 76*(1), 1–23.

Permanent Court of Arbitration. (2017, June 29). *Croatia v Slovenia*. PCA Case No. 2012-04. Final Award. https://pcacases.com/web/sendAttach/2172. Accessed March 20, 2020.

Permanent Court of Arbitration (2016, July 12). *Philippines v China*. PCA Case No. 2013-19. Final Award. https://docs.pca-cpa.org/2016/07/PH-CN-20160712-Award.pdf. Accessed September 12, 2020

Regulation (EU). (2013, December 11). No 1380/2013 of the European Parliament and of the council on the Common Fisheries Policy. https://eur-lex.europa.eu/legal-content/EN/TXT/?uri=CELEX%3A32013R1380. Accessed March 21, 2020.

Reports of International Arbitral Awards. (2007). *Guyana v Suriname*. Award. http://legal.un.org/riaa/cases/vol_XXX/1-144.pdf. Accessed September 12, 2020.

Reuters News. (2018, October 1). Pentagon chief not expecting ties with China to worsen even as tensions rise.

Reuters News. (2020, September 12). Pompeo says U.S. 'deeply concerned' over Turkey actions in east Med.

Rothwell, D., & Stephens, T. (2016). *The international law of the sea*. Oxford and Portland: Hart Publishing.

Sanader, I. (2017). *Doba politike. Detuđmanizacija*. Zagreb: Večernji list.

Sancin, V. (2010). Slovenia-Croatia border dispute: From 'Drnovšek-Račan' to 'Pahor-Kosor' agreement. *European Perspectives, 2*(2), 93–111.

Schatz, V. (2019). Access to fisheries in the United Kingdom's territorial sea after its withdrawal from the European Union: A European and international law perspective. *Goettingen Journal of International Law, 9*(3), 457–500. https://gojil.eu/issues/93/93_article_schatz.pdf. Accessed March 22, 2020.

Schofield, C., Lee, S., & Kwon, M. S. (Eds.). (2014). *The limits of maritime jurisdiction*. Leiden and Boston: Martinus Nijhoff.

Scovazzi, T. (2018). The contribution of the tribunal to the progressive development of international law. In International Tribunal for the Law of the Sea (Ed.), *The contribution of the international tribunal for the law of the sea to the rule of law: 1996–2016* (pp. 118–160). Leiden: Brill.

Serdy, A. (2005). The paradoxical success of UNCLOS part XV: A half-hearted reply to Rosemary Rayfuse. *Victoria University of Wellington Law Review, 36*(4), 713–721.

Shearer, I. (2014). The limits of maritime jurisdiction. In C. Schofield, S. Lee, & M. S. Kwon (Eds.), *The limits of maritime jurisdiction* (pp. 51–64). Leiden and Boston: Martinus Nijhoff.

Solomou, A. (2017). A commentary on the maritime delimitation issues in the Croatia v. Slovenia final award. EJIL Blog. https://www.ejiltalk.org/a-commentary-on-the-maritime-delimitation-issues-in-the-croatia-v-slovenia-final-award/. Accessed February 08, 2019.

Symmons, C. (2019). *Historic waters and historic rights in the law of the sea*. Leiden: Brill Nijhoff.

Tanaka, Y. (2009). Reflections on maritime delimitation in the Romania/Ukraine case before the international court of justice. *Netherlands International Law Review, 56*(3), 397–427.

Tanaka, Y. (2015). *The international law of the sea*. Cambridge: Cambridge University Press.

Tanaka, Y. (2018a). The disproportionality test in the law of maritime delimitation. In A. Oude Elferink, T. Henriksen, & S. Busch (Eds.), *Maritime boundary delimitation: The case law. Is it consistent and predictable?* (pp. 291–318). Cambridge: Cambridge University Press.

Tanaka, Y. (2018b). *The peaceful settlement of international disputes*. Cambridge: Cambridge University Press.

Taylor, P. (2018). The common heritage of mankind: Expanding the oceanic circle. In International Ocean Institute Canada (Ed.), *The future of ocean governance and capacity development* (pp. 141–150). Leiden: Brill Nijhoff.

The Japan Times. (2020, January 28). US Navy sails warship near disputed islands in South China Sea for first time in 2020. https://www.japantimes.co.jp/news/2020/01/28/asia-pacific/us-navy-warship-disputed-islands-south-china-sea-first-2020/#.XnPK4NLsbIV. Accessed March 28, 2020.

Thirlway, H. (2010). The international court of justice. In M. Evans (Ed.), *International law* (pp. 586–614). Oxford: Oxford University Press.

Tomaševic, M., Jadrijević, N., & Dundović, Č. (2011). Analysis of the container traffic movement in the port of Rijeka compared to the container traffic in the port of Koper. *Scientific Journal of Maritime Research, 25*(2), 469–485.
Twirdy, E., & Batista, M. (2014). Competition between container ports in the Northern Adriatic. *International Journal for Traffic and Transport Engineering, 4*(4), 363–371.
United Nations. (1982, December 10). *United Nations convention on the law of the sea*. https://www.un.org/Depts/los/convention_agreements/texts/unclos/unclos_e.pdf. Accessed April 15, 2020.
United Nations. (2004a). Law of the Sea Bulletin (LOS). No. 54/2004.
United Nations. (2004b). Law of the Sea Bulletin (LOS). No. 53/2004.
United Nations. (2005). Law of the Sea Bulletin (LOS). No. 60/2005.
United Nations. (2006a). Law of the Sea Bulletin (LOS). No. 61/2006.
United Nations. (2006b). *Reports of international arbitral awards* (Vol. XVIII, pp. 3–413). Delimitation of the Continental Shelf between the United Kingdom of Great, Britain and Northern Ireland, and the French Republic (UK, France). https://legal.un.org/riaa/cases/vol_XVIII/3-413.pdf. Accessed March 21, 2020.
United Nations. (2006c). *Reports of international arbitral awards* (Vol. XXI, pp. 265–341). Delimitation of maritime areas between Canada and France. https://legal.un.org/riaa/cases/vol_XXI/265-341.pdf. Accessed March 21, 2020.
United Nations. (2006d). *Reports of international arbitral awards* (Vol. XXII, pp. 335–410). Second stage of the proceedings between Eritrea and Yemen (Maritime Delimitation). https://legal.un.org/riaa/cases/vol_XXII/335-410.pdf. Accessed March 21, 2020.
United Nations. (2007). Law of the Sea Bulletin (LOS). No. 64/2007.
United Nations. (2009, April 8). Rules of procedure of the commission on the limits of the continental shelf. CLCS/40/rev.1. https://www.un.org/Depts/los/clcs_new/commission_rules.htm. Accessed March 21, 2020.
United Nations. (2011, July 15). Division of ocean affairs and the law of the sea. Table of claims to maritime jurisdiction. https://www.un.org/depts/los/LEGISLATIONANDTREATIES/PDFFILES/table_summary_of_claims.pdf. Accessed March 21, 2020.
United Nations. (2019, December 12). Submissions to the commission on the limits of the continental shelf. https://www.un.org/Depts/los/clcs_new/commission_submissions.htm. Accessed March 21, 2020.
United Nations. (2020, February 12). Division of ocean affairs and the law of the sea. Declarations and Statements. https://www.un.org/depts/los/convention_agreements/convention_declarations.htm. Accessed March 21, 2020.
United Nations Secretariat. (1962). Juridical regime of historic waters including historic bays. In *Yearbook of the international law commission* (Vol. II, pp. 1–16). https://legal.un.org/docs/?path=../ilc/publications/yearbooks/english/ilc_1962_v2.pdf&lang=EFS. Accessed March 21, 2020.
US Department of Defence. (2018, December 31). *Freedom of navigation report 2018*. https://policy.defense.gov/Portals/11/Documents/FY18%20DoD%20Annual%20FON%20Report%20(final).pdf?ver=2019-03-19-103517-010. Accessed March 21, 2020.
Van Overbeek, W. (1989). Article 121(3) UNCLOS in Mexican state practice in the Pacific. *International Journal for Estuarine and Coastal Law, 4*(4), 252–282.
Vidas, D. (2006). Particularly sensitive sea areas: The need for regional cooperation in the Adriatic Sea. In Institute of Public Finance & Friedrich-Ebert-Foundation (Eds.), *Croatian accession to the European Union. The challenges of participation* (Vol. 4). Zagreb. https://www.ssoar.info/ssoar/handle/document/6136. Accessed February 08, 2019.
Vidas, D. (2009). The UN convention on the law of the sea, the European Union and the rule of law: What is going on in the Adriatic Sea? *The International Journal of Marine and Coastal Law, 24*(1), 1–66.
Vidas, D. (2013). Subregional marine governance: The case of the Adriatic Sea. In H. Schreiber & J. H. Paik (Eds.), *Regions, institutions, and law of the sea* (pp. 337–355). Leiden: Brill Nijhoff.

Vukas, B. (2008). Pomorski zakonik Republike Hrvatske i međunarodno pravo mora. *Zbornik Pravnog fakulteta u Zagrebu, 58*(1–2), 181–204.

Wirth, C. (2019). Whose 'Freedom of Navigation'? Australia, China, the United States and the making of order in the 'Indo-Pacific'. *The Pacific Review, 32*(4), 475–504. https://doi.org/10.1080/09512748.2018.1515788. Accessed March 21, 2020.

Yiallourides, C. (2020, August 25). Part I: Some Observations on the Agreement between Greece and Egypt on the Delimitation of the Exclusive Economic Zone. *EJIL Talk*. https://www.ejiltalk.org/18969-2/. Accessed September 14, 2020.

Chapter 4
The Four Development Phases of the Croatia-Slovenia Border Dispute

Abstract The current Chapter is at the heart of attempts to resolve the Croatian-Slovenian border dispute. The aim is to trace the processes in the resolution efforts with regard to issues, actors, and conflict dynamics. The management process of the border dispute is grouped into four stages: (i) the bilateral phase (1992–2007) when both countries were negotiating with each other, but were unable to produce a binding settlement, although a bilateral treaty had been successfully negotiated at the highest political level in 2001; (ii) Croatia's EU accession negotiations (2008/2009) when the dispute triggered a veto by Slovenia and subsequently involved third parties in the form of the European Commission and the EU Council Presidency; (iii) the arbitral proceedings (2012–2017)—the result of externalising the resolution of the substantive dispute to third-party judicial dispute resolution—which imploded due to illegal communication and yet produced a binding settlement under international law; and (iv) the infringement proceedings against Croatia brought before the EU Court of Justice by Slovenia on the grounds that the non-implementation of the Final Award by Croatia constituted a breach of the territorial application of EU law, a plea for which the Court found it had no jurisdiction (2018–2020). Interviewees include Miro Cerar, Alojz Peterle, Andrej Plenković, Vesna Pusić, Olli Rehn, and Ivo Sanader.

Keywords Arbitration · Mediation · CJEU · Croatia · Slovenia · EU accession negotiations

4.1 Bilateral Phase (1992–2007)

The common State border did not play much of a role around the independence declarations and implementation by Croatia and Slovenia in the summer and autumn of 1991. Nevertheless, there is one early incident worth mentioning: In mid-June 1991, Slovenia began with construction work for the Slovenian checkpoint of the future Sečovlje-Plovanija border-crossing *south* of the Dragonja (Opassi 23 June 1991).

T. Bickl, *The Border Dispute Between Croatia and Slovenia*, Contributions to Political Science,
https://doi.org/10.1007/978-3-030-53333-5_4

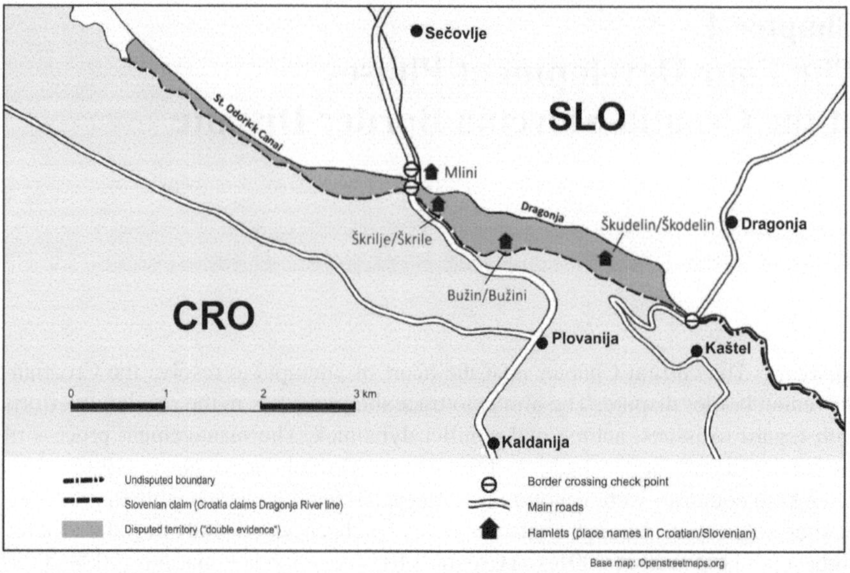

Fig. 4.1 Dragonja strip and Three Hamlets—situation after 1991 (*Source* Author; base map: openstreetmaps.org)

Croatia protested about the works on 21 June, four days before the joint independence declarations,[1] on the grounds that Slovenia was building the checkpoint on Croatian territory (see e.g. Ministry of Foreign Affairs Croatia press release, 12 May 2006). After a few hours of telephone diplomacy, Slovenia withdrew its workers and started constructing a temporary Sečovlje checkpoint north of the Dragonja next to the Mlini hamlet instead (interview Alojz Peterle, 16-09-2015). The reasoning behind that move was that an open conflict at the Slovenian–Croatian border may have been a pretext for the Yugoslav army (JNA) to step in (Ministry of Foreign Affairs Slovenia White Paper on the border between Slovenia and Croatia 2006: 23–24). Ironically, Croatia later completed the works on what was originally a Slovenian checkpoint south of the river and made it the Croatian Plovanija checkpoint. Slovenia repeatedly protested about Croatia operating that crossing point south of the river (Ministry of Foreign Affairs Slovenia White Paper 2006: 26; see also Sect. 4.2.2.1 on the Slovenian blockade in October 2008, and Fig. 4.1). Nevertheless, both checkpoints became permanent ones over time.[2]

[1]Meier (1995: 311) posits that Tuđman considered the independence declarations merely a declaratory act and was therefore not amused that the Slovenes were actually constructing border-crossing points.

[2]There are 57 land border crossing points between Slovenia and Croatia today. 32 are for international traffic, 25 are reserved for local traffic and EU citizens. Some of the local border crossings were temporarily closed in the spring of 2020 due to the coronavirus pandemic (for the list of border crossings, see Slovenian Ministry of the Interior: https://www.policija.si/eng/areas-of-work/border-matters-and-foreigners/border-crossings).

In the first two years after independence, the border with Slovenia played virtually no role in Croatia since the focus of attention to territorial issues was on the Homeland War 1991–1995 in the Krajina, Northern Dalmatia, and in Eastern Slavonia (interview Vesna Pusić, 24-02-2017; interview Ivo Sanader, 19-05-2016; for the Homeland War see Sect. 2.5.2).

4.1.1 Expert Groups and Joint/Mixed Diplomatic Commission

A number of joint bodies were set up in 1992 and 1993 on the political and technical level. On 30 July 1993, the Agreement on the Establishment of Joint Bodies for the Establishment and Identification/Demarcation of the State Border was signed which set up the Joint/Mixed Diplomatic Commission on the political level, and the Joint/Mixed Commission for Border Demarcation, Maintenance and Renewal at the technical level, the latter comprising several subsidiary Joint Expert Groups, such as the Group for the Comparison of the Cadastral Boundaries, the Group for Demarcation, and the Group for the Geodetic Basis (interview senior Slovenian civil servant, 17-10-2016; interview senior Croatian civil servant, 19-08-2016; see also PCA Partial Award 2016: 2, para 9; Sancin 2010: 96).

A first technical-level bilateral meeting of surveying and mapping experts was held on 26 May 1992 where it was agreed that the definition of the cadastral boundaries would be the starting point for the delimitation of the *land* border. After another meeting on 15 March 1993 where an understanding was reached to identify diverging interpretations of the cadastral border, the final report of the surveying and mapping experts was adopted on 2 June 1994 (Crvtila 1993: 40; PCA Final Award 2017: 14–15, paras 51–56). The report, based on 244 sheets of topographic maps at a scale of 1:50.000, noted that

- 77%, i.e. approximately 510 km, of the common land border were aligned;
- 10%, i.e. approximately 70 km, showed a mismatch of up to 2 cm on the maps;
- 13%, i.e. 80 km of the joint border overlapped significantly (more than 2 cm) in the areas along the Mura and Drava river, at the confluence of the Sotla, Sava, and Bregana rivers, and in the following spots: along the Čabranka river, at Snežnik, in the Topolec area, and along the lower reaches of the Dragonja between the Raven/Sečovlje municipalities on the Slovenian side and the Kaštel municipality on the Croatian side up to the mouth of the river (Joint Report 1994; cited in PCA Final Award 2017: 15–16, para 56).

The Expert Group report was fed into the Group for the Comparison of the Cadastral Boundaries (interview senior Slovenian civil servant, 17-10-2016).

The last official Expert Group Report was signed and issued on 20 December 1996 when there was talk of nine per cent or 60 km of the land boundary being unaligned in the sense of cadastral district boundaries diverging by more than 50 m on the ground (PCA Final Award 2017: 70, para 226). In the Parties' submissions during the arbitration procedure starting in 2012, however, it emerged that Slovenia takes the view that the Report did not screen the cadastral records of the *entire* land border and that the Report was of a mere technical nature, whereas Croatia noted that the disputed areas were addressed and that this had indeed been the task of the Expert Group (PCA Final Award 2017: 21–22, paras 73–74).

4.1.2 First Stand-Off Over Piran Bay and the Dragonja Strip 1993–94

An early moment of dissenting views on the *sea* border emerged at a meeting of the joint expert group for establishing and marking the boundary on 16 March 1993 where Piran Bay (and the peak of Sveta Gera/Trdinov Vrh) became an issue. As for the *sea* border to be delimitated *de novo*, Slovenia favoured sovereignty over the entire Bay whilst Croatia opted for a partition of the Bay in terms of equal shares by way of the equidistance line (Cvrtila 1993: 41; see also PCA Final Award 2017: 71–72, paras 227–230; 76, paras 245–246).

4.1.2.1 Piran Bay and the Maritime Border

The Slovenian view soon became official through a Foreign Affairs Committee resolution of 7 April 1993 stating that, with regard to *Piran Bay*

> [t]he Republic of Slovenia advocated the *maintenance of the integrity of the Bay of Piran under its sovereignty and jurisdiction* and the *exit to the high seas* on the basis of admissible criteria of international law and taking into consideration the specific situation of the Republic of Slovenia.
>
> The Republic of Slovenia holds a view that the Bay of Piran is a case sui generis which dictates exclusive regard of the *historic title* and other special circumstances. Slovenia, therefore, resolutely rejects the application of the criterion of the median line, which would - in the case of the Bay of Piran - represent an unjust and impractical solution for the Republic of Slovenia, entirely contrary to the historical and actual state in the Bay of Piran. One should consider the fact that the Republic of Slovenia was executing jurisdiction and power over the Bay of Piran in the former SFRY and that such also was the existing state of affairs at the time of the proclamation of independence of both States [...] on 25 June 1991. (Memorandum on the Bay of Piran, 7 April 1993: 3; emphasis added)

In respect of the maritime border in the territorial sea and *access to the high seas*, the Memorandum states:

> As to the maritime boundary [...] outside the Bay of Piran [...] considering the specific situation, the principle of *equity* - implying also the so-called *special circumstances* [UNCLOS, Art. 15] - also has to be taken into consideration. The Republic of Slovenia undoubtedly meets the requirements for the application of this [provision], since it belongs to the group of the so-called geographically disadvantaged States which, due to their geographic position, cannot declare their exclusive economic zone. The vital question of acquisition of sufficient

> quantities of national resources for the survival of the Slovene nation is also raised here. Therefore, the Republic of Slovenia is of the opinion that it is necessary, in accordance with the principle of equity and considering the [provision] of special circumstances, to draw the maritime boundary with the Republic of Croatia in such a way as to ensure that the *territorial waters of the Republic of Slovenia would*, at least at a narrow section, *join the high seas* of the Adriatic. (Memorandum on the Bay of Piran, 7 April 1993: 5; emphasis added)

In response to the Slovenian Memorandum, Croatia, in the Sabor resolution from 18 November 1993, insisted that

> [the] *equidistance method* is to be applied in Piran Bay, i.e. each point of the borderline should be equally distant from the Croatian and Slovenian coasts [...]; in the Dragonja river area the borderline runs along the St. Odorik channel by which [the] Dragonja flows into the sea as of 25 June 1991 [...]. (Sabor resolution regarding the Determination of the State Border in Piran Bay and the Dragonja River Area, 18 November 1993: 2; emphasis added)

This marked the fully developed conflict between the two parties on the border issue in the Bay. Whilst the different positions were officially noted in an Expert Group Report in December 1996, the political-level Joint/Mixed Diplomatic Commission admitted in March 1997 that the discrepancies along the border could not be overcome by geodetic alignment and that a solution had to be found at the political level. A meeting of the Foreign Affairs ministers in October 1997 in Zagreb did not yield any results, and the Diplomatic Commission met one last time in July 1998, and subsequently negotiations moved to the political level (Sancin 2010: 96; see also PCA Final Award 2017: 21–22).

4.1.2.2 Three Hamlets

The Three Hamlets may be seen as a prototype case of the *land* border territorial dispute between Croatia and Slovenia. In late 1994, by means of a new law on the municipalities and their territory, Slovenia included the three settlements south of the Dragonja (Škudelin/Škodelin, Bužin/Bužini, and Škrilje/Škrile; place names in Croatian/Slovenian), the so-called Three Hamlets, a disputed strip of land of around 110 ha and a length of approximately 6.2 km (PCA Final Award 2017: 229, para 739) along the lower reaches of the river with overlapping claims, in the municipality of Piran (Pipan 2008: 341; Klemenčić and Schofield 1995: 72; Official Gazette Republic of Slovenia, No. 60/1994); see Fig. 4.1.

After a fierce rejection by a Declaration of the Croatian parliament (Klemenčić and Schofield 1995: 72; Official Gazette Republic of Croatia, No. 71/1994) and a request by the Slovenian Constitutional Court, 15 days after the adoption of the original law, Slovenia suspended the application of the new law for the Three Hamlets on the grounds that they were territorially disputed (Pipan 2008: 342; Klemenčić and Schofield 1995: 72; Official Gazette Republic of Slovenia, No. 69/1994). In the 6 December 1994 local elections, only citizens resident in Mlini, on the right bank of the Dragonja, participated (Klemenčić and Schofield 1995: 73).[3]

[3] The Three Hamlets are a remarkable case. In Yugoslav times, the 53 inhabitants of the 17 households (according to the 1991 census; see Klemenčić and Schofield 1995: 76) were essentially under

From a Croatian point of view, the initial Slovenian law may be seen as an attempt to annex territory under *de facto* control[4] of Croatia. Conversely, a Slovenian viewpoint would underline the Slovenian claim[5] over the Three Hamlets to strengthen its bargaining position in the negotiations with Croatia (Klemenčić and Schofield 1995: 72; see also Pipan 2008: 342).

As for the bilateral negotiations in the 1990s, the Joint Diplomatic Commission finished its work after the last unsuccessful meeting in July 1998. In 1999, the parties agreed to attempt third-party mediation seeking the good offices of William Perry, a former US Secretary of Defence. However, a joint meeting in Washington on 5 May 1999, and visits to Lubljana and Zagreb in June 1999 did not produce any results (interview senior Croatian civil servant, 19-08-2016; interview senior Slovenian civil servant, 17-10-2016; see also PCA Final Award 2017: 26, para 91). On balance, there was apparently little more common ground shared by the parties other than the mutual respect for the status quo on 25 June 1991 (Sancin 2010: 96).

4.1.3 Agreement on Local Border Traffic and Cooperation (SOPS) 1997

Despite the solidly protracted border conflict as such, Slovenia and Croatia successfully concluded a pragmatic accord on 25 April 1997, the Agreement on Local Border Traffic and Cooperation (SOPS).[6] It entered into force on 5 September 2001. SOPS is supposed to "improve living conditions of the population in the border areas" along the common border and to enable "free economic cooperation [...] being aware that the border local communities are the foundations of good cooperation between

---

Croatian administration, had Croatian ID cards, their Yugoslav passports were issued in Croatia, and the people from Škudelin, Bužin, and Škrilje who all have Croatian and Slovenian citizenship today were included in the census and electoral register of Croatia. However, during the first years after independence, they were connected to the Slovenian power grid and had Slovenian phone lines. Up until 1984, they had their mail delivered by the Sečovlje post office (subsequently the hamlets inhabitants had to collect their mail at the actual post office in Sečovlje). The Croatian post today delivers to the hamlets, but the inhabitants can still pick up mail across the (factual) border in Sečovlje. Škudelin was connected to the Croatian phone network in 1995, notably with a special local tariff for calls to Slovenia. That tariff, however, expired in 2000 (Pipan 2008: 342).

[4]Croatia, in essence, refers to an accord from July/August 1955 between the Executive Councils of the (Yugoslav) Republics of Croatia and Slovenia according to which mutual consent emerged as to the Dragonja being the border. Both Parties, according to Croatia, "acknowledged and respected the Dragonja River as a boundary between them up until the critical date [25 June 1991]" (PCA Final Award 2017: 230–1, paras 742–3).

[5]Slovenia holds that the inhabitants of Mlini and Bužini have refused to be included in the Croatian district of Buje, and that a 1953 survey established the border of the Sečovlje municipality "including three villages on the left bank of the Dragonja" and that the situation was confirmed by the 1964 Act defining the districts and municipalities of the [Yugoslav] Republic of Slovenia (PCA Final Award 2017: 235–6, para 755).

[6]Agreement between the Republic of Slovenia and the Republic of Croatia on Border Traffic and Cooperation.

neighbouring countries" (SOPS, Preamble). The agreement represents a number of practical arrangements for (i) local traffic along the land border, and (ii) a joint fishing zone in the respective territorial seas[7] covering approximately 1,200 km^2. 1,015 km^2 form part of the Croatian territorial sea, and 169 km^2 are located in the Slovenian territorial sea (if measured based on the median line in Piran Bay; interview Croatian senior civil servant, 25-01-2017). It is worth noting, however, that the joint fishing zone has no implications on the delimitation of the common State border (Art. 59 SOPS).

In the EU context, the joint fishing zone under Article 4 of SOPS has made it into the Fisheries Regulation 1380/2013[8] with regard to the access to the territorial waters of Croatia and Slovenia respectively (points 8 and 10 of Annex I of the Regulation). It is crucial to note, however, that the application of the above provisions of the EU Fisheries Policy is subject to the full implementation of the arbitration award (see Sect. 4.4.2).

Whilst some of its provisions have become obsolete with the EU accession of Croatia (1 July 2013), SOPS has not expired, not least because the border between Croatia and Slovenia remains an external Schengen border. At the time of writing, the last meeting of the Standing Mixed Commission under SOPS took place in Zagreb in December 2016 agreeing on practical measures, such as facilitation of the unhindered cross-border movement of the local population, and repair work on a bridge. The issuance and mutual validation of border-crossing permits at any point of the land border for owners or tenants of cross-border agricultural land appears to continue pragmatically even in the midst of the coronavirus crisis. Although there have been no meetings of the Standing Mixed Commission for more than three years, outstanding issues are resolved through diplomatic channels. However, no agreements have been possible on the repair or reconstruction of cross-border infrastructure, such as a cross-border bridge over the river Kamenica that collapsed during a flooding as early as 2015 (interview senior Slovenian civil servant, 17-04-2020).

4.1.4 Initialled Draft Agreement 2001

What in retrospect turned out to be the most substantial exercise of bilateral diplomacy before 2009 is certainly the Initialled Draft Agreement reached in July 2001. It had been negotiated between the then Prime Ministers Janez Drnovšek (Slovenia) and Ivica Račan (Croatia). The negotiations did not come out of the blue, however. They did build on the previous talks at expert and political level in the 1990s. In addition, the then recent European Commission progress report for Slovenia had

[7] North of the line 45° 10′ N parallel latitude to the coast of Istria at Cape Grgatov Funtana (Art. 1(3) SOPS).

[8] On the conservation and sustainable exploitation of fish-stocks in terms of preservation measures for demersal and small pelagic species including sardine and anchovy. For the Regulation see https://eur-lex.europa.eu/LexUriServ/LexUriServ.do?uri=OJ:L:2013:354:0022:0061:EN:PDF.

mentioned a settlement over the common State border as an outstanding issue (European Commission Progress Report Slovenia 2000: 75),[9] and the Croatian side seemed aware that Slovenia was located on the road from Croatia to Europe (Arnaut 2002: 44). More widely, "a lasting partnership on a common Euro-Atlantic path" was part of Račan's motivation (interview Tonino Picula[10] in telegram.hr, 12-01-2018). In addition, a successful deal on the State border was seen as positively influencing the two separate issues of the joint nuclear power station at Krško (the temporary cut-off from electricity supply to Croatia on the part of Slovenia) and Ljubljanska Banka (the reimbursement of foreign currency depositors from SFRY times[11]; interview senior Croatian civil servant, 19-08-2016; interview Tonino Picula in telegram.hr, 12-01-2018).[12]

It is important to note from a negotiation point of view that, in early 2001, the two Prime Ministers who knew each other from the late days of the Yugoslav Federal State Presidency decided to push away the foreign ministers—notwithstanding the preparatory efforts undertaken by them already in 2000 (interview Alojz Peterle, 28-06-2017)—and tackle the matter personally. The conduct of the negotiations was remarkable as the two Prime Ministers were negotiating over the text and the maps face to face and alone in the room with feedbacks given to their delegations only every couple of hours (interview senior Slovenian civil servant from the then Slovenian negotiating team, 02-12-2016).[13]

On substance, the Drnovšek-Račan[14] Draft Agreement of 17 July 2001[15] "considering that the two States have no territorial claims towards each other" (Preamble)

[9]The 2000 European Commission Report on Slovenia can be found at https://www.esiweb.org/pdf/slovenia_EC-Slovenia%20regular%20report-2000_en.pdf.

[10]Tonino Picula MEP was Foreign Minister of Croatia 2000–2003.

[11]Many citizens' private foreign-currency deposits were illegally used by the Yugoslav State to cover its demand for foreign-currency reserves. For the SFRY banking system and its need for foreign currency reserves see e.g. Hojnik and Mevel (2016: 10–11).

[12]The financial compensation aspect of the Krško dispute was solved in December 2015 by means of investor-State arbitration, see Arbitral Award ARB/05/24 HEP vs. Slovenia (http://icsidfiles.worldbank.org/icsid/ICSIDBLOBS/OnlineAwards/C69/DC7132_En.pdf). The Ljubljanska Banka case was to some extent, solved through the Ališič judgement (http://www.vlada.si/fileadmin/dokumenti/si/projekti/2015/Varcevalci/Grand_Chamber_judgment_Alisic_and_Others__Old_foreign_currency_savings_deposited_in_SFRY__2___1_.pdf) of the European Court of Human Rights of July 2014 ordering Slovenia to take care of the compensation. The issue of burden-sharing *between* the SFRY successor States, however, is subject to voluntary pluri-lateral negotiations (interview senior Slovenian civil servant, 2-12-2016).

[13]A semi-comparable bilateral line-up, from a purely negotiations-technique point of view, was perhaps the one between Vaclav Klaus and Vladimir Mečiar when they were negotiating the terms of the dissolution/separation of the ČSFR into the Czech Republic and the Slovak Republic in the late summer of 1992 (interview Tomáš Prouza, State Secretary in the Foreign Ministry of the Czech Republic in charge of EU affairs 2014–2017, 18-09-2017; interview Eduard Kukan MEP, Foreign Minister of Slovakia 1998–2006, 03-10-2017).

[14]In alphabetical order. In Croatia, the Draft Agreement is usually referred to as Račan-Drnovšek.

[15]English translation by the Slovenian Foreign Ministry of the text initialled by the two heads of the negotiating delegations. For a copy of the initialled Slovenian original see Appendix D.

represents a fully negotiated settlement and a solution *sui generis* with a number of striking features:

As for (i) the delimitation at *Piran Bay* and in the *Gulf of Trieste*, the lateral border goes from the outfall of the Dragonja River (St. Odorick's Canal) to the point (on the former SFRY closing line of the Bay; PCA Final Award 2017: 272, para 880) which is one fourth of the distance between Cape Savudrija (the Croatian entrance to the Bay) and Cape Madona (the Slovenian entrance at Piran). As a result, roughly four fifths of the Bay go to Slovenia and one fifth goes to Croatia [Article 3(1)]. Remarkably, the Final Award of the later arbitration procedure took up this very delimitation line inside the Bay on the basis of the fishing management and factual police patrolling during the period up until 25 June 1991 (PCA Final Award 2017: 279, paras 912–3; see "The Bay" in Sect. 4.3.5.2).

From the above point at the mouth of the Bay, the border turns south and runs in an east–west parallel line up to the former Yugoslav-Italian sea border from 1975[16] except for the tiny strip foreseen for the junction to the high seas [Article 3(1)]. Article 3 is silent on the nature of the respective waters inside the Bay. However, as the line over the mouth of the bay is not expressly referred to as the closing line, it appears that the status of the waters inside the Bay is considered the respective territorial sea (as opposed to internal waters).[17]

In respect of (ii) *access to the high seas* for Slovenia, a novel approach was agreed on: a "junction" between the territorial sea of Slovenia and the high seas via a high-seas corridor through the Croatian territorial sea [Article 4(1)]. The width of the junction is 2.3 nm (Article 4(2); see also PCA Final Award 2017: 340, para 1060). As a by-product, the corridor created a triangular enclave of Croatian territorial sea maintaining the country's sea border with Italy (Article 5). It must be noted that no sovereign rights were accorded to either State as for the corridor's water column, its seabed and its subsoil [Article 4(5)]. In terms of the international law of the sea, a corridor between the territorial sea of a State and the high seas historically only emerged twice before (in a pluri-lateral treaty on free passage through The Sound/Øresund, one of the Danish straits, in 1857,[18] and in an agreement between France and Monaco in 1984; for the latter see Arnaut 2002: 50), and a quasi-extraterritorial triangle strip of territorial sea certainly was unheard of at the time and still is today (see Fig. 4.2).

---

[16]Treaty of Osimo 1975 delimitating the territorial waters of Italy and Yugoslavia. Both Slovenia and Croatia have declared to inherit the respective sea border strip of Yugoslavia. Italy did not object (Cataldi 2013: 1; Klemenčić and Topalović 2009: 313–4). For the Osimo Treaty see Sect. 2.4.3.

[17]It is important to note that, unlike in the territorial sea, there is no right to innocent passage for foreign vessels in internal waters (see Tanaka 2015: 78–81; Rothwell and Stephens 2016: 55–9).

[18]The pluri-lateral treaty was concluded between Denmark and Austria, Belgium, France, Great Britain, Hanover, the Hanse Towns, Mecklenburg-Schwerin, the Netherlands, Oldenburg, Prussia, and Sweden-Norway. A second bilateral treaty was concluded between Denmark and the United States. Strictly speaking, the provisions only apply to the signatories, but Danish State practice has rendered the provisions a quasi-universal regime (see Bangert 1997: 105–7).

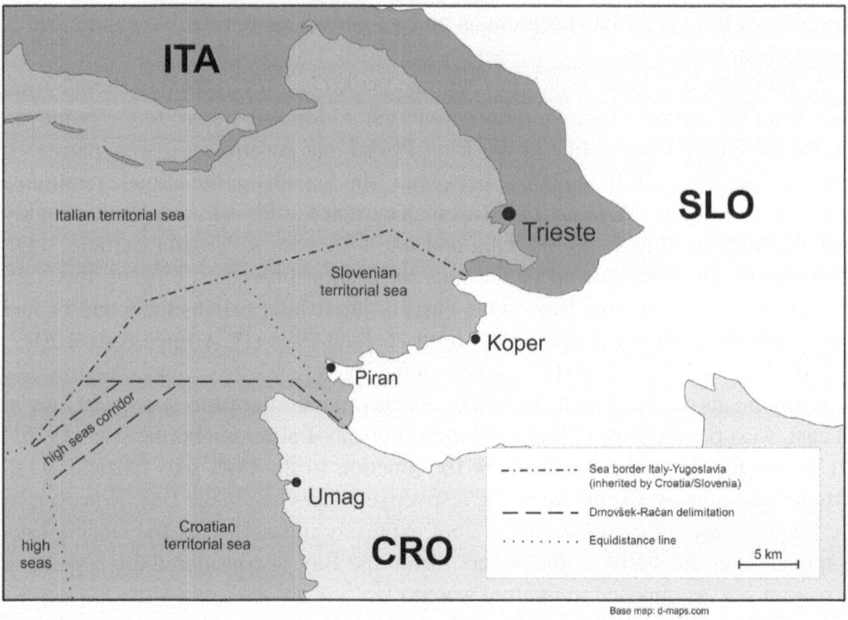

Fig. 4.2 Delimitation in Piran Bay, territorial sea border and high-seas corridor according to the 2001 Initialled Draft Agreement (schematic view; *Source* Author; base map: d-maps.com)

As for (iii) the *land border*, the Three Hamlets south of the Dragonja were finally accorded to Croatia, to name one prominent example.[19] All other disputed spots along the border, such as Trdinov Vrh/Sveta Gera, or the Hotiza-Sveti Martin area along the Mura River, were resolved, too. Annex II of the Draft Agreement contains a verbal description of the border linking 85 points from the tripoint at the border to Hungary to the outfall of the Dragonja into Piran Bay (see Appendix C).

One peculiarity of the Draft Agreement is worth mentioning from a point of view of its authenticity. In the provisions on both the land border and the sea border, reference is made to the verbal description in Annex II prevailing over the maps and coordinates respectively [Articles 3(3) and 4(4)]. Usually, maps and coordinates take precedent over verbal descriptions in the application of a treaty.

It is vital to note that the Initialled Draft Agreement never entered into force. The Foreign Affairs Committee of the Croatian Parliament rejected the text, so it never underwent ratification in the Sabor (PCA Final Award 2017: 27, para 92; letter from Račan to Drnovšek, 3 September 2002).

In retrospect, several reasons may be identified for the failure of the Drnovšek-Račan Draft Agreement:

[19]Trading the Dragonja strip in last-minute to secure the approval of the Croatian delegation has sparked some fierce criticism and opposition in Slovenia (interview Alojz Peterle, 30-11-2015).

(i) The agreement may, on its substantive provisions, have been too innovative, and there were legal doubts as to whether a Croatian triangle enclave disjointed from the rest of the Croatian territorial sea, an unprecedented solution *sui generis*, would be recognized by Italy (Arnaut 2014: 149; see also Grbec 2015: 176);
(ii) Virtually the entire Croatian legal expert establishment was against the text, not least because they had all favoured a delimitation line approximating the equidistance line as for the delimitation in the Bay. What is more, it appears that none of the law-of-the-sea experts in Croatia were consulted ahead or during the secret negotiations (interview Vladimir-Đuro Degan, 21-11-2019). Then again, one could argue that the likelihood of reaching any kind of agreement at all would have been virtually at zero "had there been a greater audience" (interview Vesna Pusić, 24-02-2017);
(iii) Drnovšek, having secured the support of the opposition (mainly Janša's SDS) on his part, had overestimated the command of domestic support for the deal on the part of Račan (interview senior Slovenian civil servant from the then Slovenian negotiating team, 02-12-2016). Račan had indeed failed to persuade all coalition parties, most notably Budiša's HSLS (interview Vesna Pusić, 24-02-2017), and the major opposition party HDZ (interview Ivo Sanader, 19-05-2016).[20] It must be noted in this context that the then government comprised no less than six parties, the first-ever coalition government in Croatia after three consecutive HDZ majority governments, and that by summer 2001, Račan's decision to extradite generals Gotovina and Ademi to the ICTY had provoked the resignation of the HSLS ministers and a subsequent vote of confidence (Dolenec 2013: 150–1)[21];
(iv) The traumatic experience on Croatia's other borders with Serbia and Bosnia-Herzegovina between 1991 and 1995, together with the territorial shape of Croatia, had created a solid sensitivity towards territorial issues (interview Dejan Jović, 02-11-2017; see also Klemenčić and Schofield 1995: 71–2), in particular with regard to the Homeland War (see Koska and Matan 2017: 129–131; Lamont 2015: 72–74) during which Croatia lost around 20,000 lives (all told, military and civilian deaths; Jović 2011: 36). The repercussions of the Homeland War led to the Sabor Declaration from October 2000 stating that the country "led a just and legitimate, defensive and liberating, and not an aggressive and conquering war [...] in which it defended its territory [...]", and that therefore "[t]he fundamental values of the Homeland War are unambiguously accepted by the entire Croatian people and all Croatian citizens" (Official Gazette of the Republic of Croatia, No. 102/2000); see Sect. 2.5.2.

[20] Račan called Sanader on 29 July 2001, 12 days after the initialling of the Draft Agreement, when the HDZ chair was already on summer vacation with his family on Lopud island. The two spoke for three quarters of an hour.

[21] What aggravated the problem of the diversity within the six-party coalition was the fact that HSLS chair Budiša and HSS (Croatian Peasant Party) chair Tomčić were not serving as government ministers which required additional coordination efforts outside the government structures.

In September 2002, Račan sent a passionately gloomy letter to Drnovšek in which he summed up the spirit of the preceding months:

> […] I am certain that you hold that the friendly relations and cooperation between our countries are the strategic interest of both our countries and peoples, and that for democratic forces there cannot be an alternative. However, things are not going in that direction.
>
> Arguments and forces of conflict are gaining momentum on both sides of the joint border and are using open and unsettled issues between our countries, making them bigger and bigger and ever harder to settle. We are facing the risk of unreasonable extension of the problems and conflicts between our countries to our relations where such problems did not previously exist. It would be absurd if today Slovenia and Croatia 'balkanized' their relations and State policy, considering that such a way to 'settle' problems is losing ground throughout Southeast Europe […].
>
> As a failed attempt, the initialled Draft Agreement cannot be a basis for settling the problem […] It was an attempt without legal effects […]. We can, and therefore we must, reconsider what to do under the circumstances. It appears that, concerning the border, we cannot reach a solution amicably and of our own accord […]. The most reasonable solution that remains is, therefore, arbitration. I am prepared to talk with you about binding arbitration, after I obtain support from the Croatian Parliament. (Letter from Račan to Drnovšek, 3 September 2002)

After 2001, a bilaterally negotiated agreement clearly seemed out of reach (see also Petrič 2017: 364). Indeed, no efforts to solve the outstanding border issue were indeed made over the next five years.

4.1.5 Bled Agreement 2007

Only in the summer of 2007 was a new attempt at a solution made. The Slovenian Prime Minister Janez Janša and his Croatian counterpart Ivo Sanader met in Bled on 26 August and agreed to submit the dispute to the International Court of Justice (ICJ). Janša, on his part, had not consulted anyone prior to his decision to move away from the Draft Agreement of 2001 (which was the result of intensive bilateral negotiations) and refer the matter of dispute to an international court instead (interview senior Slovenian civil servant from the 2001 Slovenian negotiating team, 02-12-2016). Some indeed saw the Bled Agreement as a pragmatic, but forward-looking "back-pedalling exercise" in respect of the bilateral Drnovšek-Račan deal (interview Davor Stier, 23-09-2015).

The Bled Agreement tasked a joint team of legal experts with the drafting of the mandate for the Court. That mandate was supposed to be discussed in both parliaments in a cross-party spirit and ready for submission to the ICJ by the end of 2007 (Office of the Prime Minister of Slovenia's tape-recording transcript of the Janša statement at the press conference, 26 August 2007: 1). The joint understanding was such that the mandate for the ICJ was also to be *ratified* by both parliaments (interview Ivo Sanader, 02-11-2017). It is worth noting that, unlike Drnovšek-Račan in 2001, there was no intended link to the other two issues Krško and Ljubljanska Banka. Rather, "the very fact that we have decided to involve a third party in settling the border issue, and to continue to solve other issues bilaterally, shows that we are not dealing with packages" (Janša tape-recording transcript, 26 August 2007: 2).

However, the above timetable proved too ambitious as the *travaux préparatoires* for the mandate for the ICJ turned out to be a rocky road. Drafts were exchanged following a joint meeting of the expert groups in June 2008.[22] Somewhat unexpectedly, the disagreement over which judicial body exactly the dispute was supposed to be submitted to re-surfaced. This is evident from a Slovenian draft of the Special Agreement, the mandate for the judicial body, where reference is made to three options ("International Court of Justice in The Hague/Permanent Court of Arbitration/*Ad-hoc* Arbitration") in virtually any of the draft articles (Special Agreement, September 2008). Articles 1 and 2 shall suffice as an example:

> Article 1
>
> Submission of a dispute
>
> Option 1:
>
> 1. The Parties agree to submit the dispute to the *International Court of Justice* in The Hague […].
>
> 2. The Parties agree to submit the dispute to a Chamber of the Court, composed of five judges […].
>
> Option 2:
>
> The Parties agree to submit the dispute to the *Permanent Court of Arbitration.*
>
> Option 3:
>
> The Parties agree to submit the dispute to *Ad-hoc Arbitration.*
>
> Article 2
>
> Subject of the Litigation
>
> The Parties authorize the *Court/Permanent Court of Arbitration/Ad-hoc Arbitration* to adjudicate on the substantive elements of the dispute regarding the determination of the lateral boundary between the maritime belts of the two Parties and a more precise delimitation of the land border […]. (Special Agreement, September 2008; emphasis added)

Conversely, a Croatian draft solely referred to the ICJ (Special Agreement between the government of the Republic of Croatia and the government of the Republic of Slovenia on the submission of the boundary dispute between the two States to the International Court of Justice, September 2008) as becomes clear in the respective first two articles:

> Article I
>
> The parties agree to submit the dispute to the International Court of Justice […].
>
> Article II
>
> 1. The Court is requested to determine, in accordance with the principles and rules of international law (as applicable in the matter between the Parties) […]. (Special Agreement between the government of the Republic of Croatia and the government of the Republic of Slovenia, September 2008)

---

[22]The initial deadline of December 2007 had proved unattainable. In the context of the entry into force of the Croatian ZERP (see Sect. 3.1.4.4) in early March 2008, Janša and Sanader agreed to intensify the work on the mandate and to refrain from provocations in Piran Bay (interview Ivo Sanader, 02-11-2017).

There were three meetings altogether, and by early 2009, the positions had not changed. Slovenia withdrew its members from the expert groups in March 2009 (interview senior Slovenian civil servant, 17-10-2016; see also PCA Final Award 2017: 31, para 103). Slovenia holds that "the mandates of the negotiating delegations were obviously very different" (interview senior Slovenian civil servant, 17-10-2016). It must not be overlooked in this context, however, that the EU accession negotiations of Croatia had already been heavily affected by the Slovenian "reservations",[23] and that the initial European Commission initiative to forge a deal on mediation or arbitration was already in full swing (see Sect. 4.2.2). In the same vein, the legal–political dispute over the Croatian Ecological and Fisheries Protection Zone (EFPZ/ZERP) and the Slovenian Ecological Protection Zone and Continental Shelf (EPZCSA) between 2003 and 2008 had seriously added to the bilateral tensions over the sea border (see Sect. 3.1.4.4).

The disagreement on substantive issues of the mandate for judicial adjudication is exemplary for the loaded task of negotiating the mandate. The failure of the Bled Agreement is a case in point. As Keohane et al. note, the legal norms and requirements as the core issues of a mandate tend to be precisely fixed. Thus, the fiercest kind of bargaining usually ensues over the terms of a prospective settlement by a third-party judicial body (Keohane et al. 2000: 461–2; 470).

4.2 Croatia's EU Accession Negotiations 2008–09

At this point, it is worth looking at the operational design of the workings of the European Union accession negotiations, the bodies involved, their roles, and the relevant procedural steps.

4.2.1 EU Accession Negotiations

Generally, any EU enlargement process starts with the application for membership of the potential Candidate Country. The application is assessed by the European Commission which drafts an opinion for the European Council (EU Heads of State and Government). The European Council unanimously takes the decision and, in the case of approval, gives the applicant country the status of *Candidate Country*.[24]

[23] The Slovenian government took the decision to use the veto as early as in June 2008 (see Sect. 4.2.2.1).

[24] Croatia applied for EU membership on 21 February 2003. The European Commission recommended Croatia to become a Candidate Country on 1 April 2004, and the European Council approved the candidate status on 1 June 2004. On 1 December 2004, the European Council set the tentative date of 17 March 2005 for the start of the accession negotiations subject to full co-operation of Croatia with the International Criminal Tribunal for the former Yugoslavia (ICTY). The start of the accession negotiations was put on hold by the EU Foreign Ministers on 16 March 2005 (see

The European Council subsequently adopts a *negotiating framework*. The following stage marks the beginning of the operational accession negotiations starting with the *screening* of the Candidate Country's legislation in each policy field (Chapter) to see whether the Candidate Country is sufficiently in compliance with existing EU *acquis*, i.e. existing EU legislation and international agreements concluded by the EU. It is important to note, that the EU *acquis* is constantly evolving. There are currently 35 negotiating Chapters.[25]

4.2.1.1 Dynamics of Rules Governing the Accession Process

As a general rule, the pace of accession is linked to the pace of goal attainment (mostly meaning reforms) on the part of the Candidate Country. It is worth contemplating, however, that the applicable methodology for the operational accession negotiations has changed considerably over time, reflecting developments both inside the EU and in Candidate Countries.

(i) The fundamental conditions for EU accession after the accession of Austria, Finland, and Sweden in 1995[26] are laid down in the so-called Copenhagen Criteria set out in 1993:

- *Political criteria*: stability of institutions guaranteeing democracy, the rule of law, human rights and the respect for and the protection of minorities;

Council of the EU press release 16 March 2005, https://europa.eu/rapid/press-release_PRES-05-44_en.htm?locale=en). Nevertheless, they adopted the negotiating framework, and on 20 October 2005, the screening stage of the accession negotiations began. The first negotiating Chapter with Croatia was opened at an Intergovernmental Conference (IGC) on 12 June 2006 (for the stages of Croatia's EU accession process see European Commission website European Neighbourhood Policy and Enlargement Negotiations, Croatia, https://ec.europa.eu/neighbourhood-enlargement/countries/detailed-country-information/croatia_en).

[25]The Chapters are: (1) Free movement of goods, (2) Freedom of movement for workers, (3) Right of establishment and freedom to provide services, (4) Free movement of capital, (5) Public procurement, (6) Company law, (7) Intellectual property law, (8) Competition policy, (9) Financial services, (10) Information society and media, (11) Agriculture and rural development, (12) Food safety, veterinary and phytosanitary policy, (13) Fisheries, (14) Transport policy, (15) Energy, (16) Taxation, (17) Economic and Monetary policy, (18) Statistics, (19) Social policy and employment, (20) Enterprise and industrial policy, (21) Trans-European networks, (22) Regional policy and coordination of structural instruments, (23) Judiciary and fundamental rights, (24) Justice, freedom and security, (25) Science and research, (26) Education and culture, (27) Environment, (28) Consumer and health protection, (29) Customs union, (30) External relations, (31) Foreign, security and defence policy, (32) Financial control, (33) Financial and budgetary provisions, (34) Institutions, (35) Other issues (for further information see https://ec.europa.eu/neighbourhood-enlargement/policy/conditions-membership/chapters-of-the-acquis_en). The *acquis* requirements tend to constitute a serious challenge for Candidate Countries' administrative capacities (interview Member State B civil servant who worked in COELA in 2009; 08-12-2016). Some Member State, especially those who have experienced EU accession themselves recently, provide assistance to Candidate Countries, as was the case with Slovakia advising Croatia as from 2005 (interview Eduard Kukan, 27-09-2017).

[26]For previous EU enlargement rounds see e.g. Emmert and Petrović (2014) or Preston (1995).

- *Economic criteria*: a functioning market economy and the capacity to cope with competition and market forces;
- *Administrative and institutional capacity* to effectively implement the EU *acquis* and the ability to take on the obligations of EU membership (Presidency Conclusions European Council Copenhagen, 22 June 1993: 13; emphasis added).

(ii) There have been a number of crucial additional requirements for the accession criteria introduced more recently:

- Priority is given to the rule-of-law Chap. 23 (judiciary and fundamental rights) and 24 (justice, freedom and security). These Chapters are to be tackled at an early stage of the accession negotiations (European Commission Enlargement Strategy, 12 October 2011: 23). In addition to the usual opening benchmarks and closing benchmarks to go with every Chapter, there are *interim* benchmarks as a new feature with Chaps. 23 and 24. The interim benchmarks are part of the EU Common Position (CP) on a Chapter, drafted by the Commission and discussed and finalised by the Member States by unanimity (see e.g. EU Information Centre Belgrade 2014: 38);
- No target date for accession is set until the negotiations move close to completion. This marks a new phase as the timetable no longer appears to be a dominant political factor (see e.g. European Commission presentation paper Belgrade, 18 July 2013: 6);
- Regional cooperation and reconciliation in terms of past conflicts play an important role. In the same vein, bilateral issues are expressly to be tackled by the parties "in a good neighbourly spirit and [...] [should] not hold up the accession process" (European Commission Enlargement Strategy, 12 October 2011: 24).

It must be noted that this new Commission strategy, known as the *new approach*, reflects the experience with Croatia's accession negotiations and may be seen as (i) marking a sea-change in terms of Chapter re-prioritization, and (ii) putting more focus on "monitor[ing] progress with increased attention" (European Commission Enlargement Strategy, 12 October 2011: 23; interview Member State E COELA civil servant, 21-10-2016; interview Member State H COELA civil servant, 07-03-2018). The new approach, more recently and colloquially termed "*fundamentals first*" (e.g. European Commission Enlargement Strategy, 9 November 2016: 2), became operational at the beginning of the EU accession negotiations with Montenegro on 29 June 2012. It has since been applied in the same vein also to the negotiations with Serbia, which started on 21 January 2014.[27]

The focus of attention has since been on implementation of the rule-of-law Chapters on the ground, i.e. the so-called *track record*. "We have recently started to focus on the actual output of judicial systems. And that output is indeed quantifiable. In

[27]For Montenegro see https://ec.europa.eu/neighbourhood-enlargement/countries/detailed-country-information/montenegro_en; for Serbia see https://ec.europa.eu/neighbourhood-enlargement/countries/detailed-country-information/serbia_en.

fact, one can look at the ratio between the number of investigations, the number of actual charges resulting from them, and whether the court handed down a judgement." To that end, expert groups are selected by the Commission and composed of practitioners who work alongside their full-time occupation and gather information on the ground. Some of the expert groups' findings ("case-based peer reviews") tend to be incorporated into the interim benchmarks proposed by the Commission later on (interview European Commission civil servant, 10-01-2018). However, it is the view of this author that there is a shortcoming with the track-record approach: Quantifiable as one selected item may be, there is no definition of track record in terms of what kind of performance in what areas exactly is going to be measured over what time period.

Miščević and Mrak (2017: 196–7) argue that the new emphasis on Chaps. 23 and 24, not least by the introduction of the interim benchmarks, renders these two Chapters "the role of 'controller' of the negotiations". As a result, Member States increasingly shaped these negotiations by setting benchmarks and deciding whether they "have been met or not". In fact, this analysis appears to neatly correspond to contemporary State practice in the Council Working Group on Enlargement (COELA). A practitioner's view is that "interim benchmarks actually tend to be worded in a way that they can never be met" (interview Member State H COELA civil servant, 07-03-2018).

(iii) In its Enlargement Strategy from February 2018, the European Commission crafted some further fine-tuning of the *new approach* introducing a few new features:

- A strong emphasis on the rule of law, in particular the "independence, quality and efficiency of the judicial system", and the fight against corruption and organised crime (European Commission Enlargement Strategy, 6 February 2018: 4);
- Narrower provisions on *bilateral disputes*. These are supposed to be "solved as a matter of urgency". Where this proves impossible on a bilateral level, "parties should submit them *unconditionally to binding, final international arbitration*" (European Commission Enlargement Strategy, 6 February 2018: 7). Notably, there was a diplomatic battle on the above wording between the Croatian and the Slovenian Commissioner during the late drafting stage. At some stage of the drafting, the International Court of Justice was also mentioned in brackets, and that issue was hotly debated (information obtained from several Commissioner's Cabinet members in March 2018; draft version of the 2018 Enlargement Strategy from November 2017 this author has seen). The final wording, however, is unusually and unnecessarily fuzzy and confusing, and clearly indicates that it is a compromise formula[28];

[28] Arbitration is always "binding" and thus also "final". Perhaps it was to make up for the deletion of the ICJ in the wording. Then again, why leave out the ICJ as an option in case parties would be willing to agree to submit to the ICJ rather than to an arbitral tribunal?

- An indicative EU accession target date of 2025 has been set for Serbia and for Montenegro. Whilst the Commission hastens to add that such date "is purely indicative and based on the best-case scenario" (European Commission Enlargement Strategy, 6 February 2018: 7), it is there nevertheless and thus goes against the grain of a purely *merits-based* approach, the Commission's very mantra from recent years;
- More emphasis on "soft" ("socio-economic") issues (European Commission Enlargement Strategy, 6 February 2018: 12). To that end, the funds for the "Erasmus+" programme should be "doubled to help even more young citizens of the Western Balkans to study and gain experience in the EU" (European Commission Enlargement Strategy, 6 February 2018: 13). For pre-accession funds generally, the Commission announced a boost in Pre-Accession Assistance for the period close to accession (European Commission Enlargement Strategy, 6 February 2018: 16).

The overall spirit of the 2018 Enlargement Strategy takes up the new emphasis on the Western Balkans highlighted by European Commission President Jean-Claude Juncker in his preceding State of the Union address before the European Parliament in September 2017. It had not gone unnoticed when the Commission President made the following remark:

> [I]f we want more stability in our neighbourhood, then we must also maintain a credible enlargement perspective for the Western Balkans. It is clear that there will be no further enlargement during the mandate of this Commission [ending 31 October 2019] and this Parliament [end of term beginning of July 2019]. No candidate is ready. But thereafter the European Union will be greater than 27 in number. Accession candidates must give the rule of law, justice and fundamental rights utmost priority in the negotiations. (State of the Union address, 13 September 2017)

It was not lost on connaisseurs of EU enlargement either that there was a new *momentum* in the European Commission's enlargement approach. That new dynamism appears to have been taken up subsequently by the European Commission's Candidate Country *status* reports (formerly known as *progress* reports) from April 2018. The Commission's reports actually include the recommendation to start accession negotiations with Albania and Macedonia. However, there was an intense debate in the college of Commissioners on 17 April 2018 as to whether to actually recommend such a start (information obtained from several Commissioners' Cabinet members, 17-04-2018) as the President of France had mentioned a little earlier during his plenary speech in the European Parliament on the morning of the same day, that EU reform had to take precedence over EU enlargement (author's field notes, 17-04-2018).

As reservations with regard to EU enlargement on Member State level were, and in fact are, not limited to France, a (temporarily) face-saving solution had to be found. The General Affairs Council (EU foreign ministers) on 26 June 2018 did in principle endorse the positive recommendation from the European Commission. Yet, it postponed the actual beginning of accession negotiations for Albania and

Montenegro to June 2019 subject to domestic implementation of reform and subsequent Council approval. In return, the technical screening process carried out by the European Commission, somewhat opaquely termed "necessary preparatory work" in the Council Conclusions, was to start immediately which it did (General Affairs Council Conclusions, 26 June 2018: 16, para 44 [FYR Macedonia]; 19–20, para 54 [Albania]; interview European Commission civil servant DG NEAR, 28-08-2018).

However, resistance remained resilient and the June 2019 General Affairs Council (GAC) was unable to live up to its promise from one year ago to give the green light. Even the GAC of 15 October 2019 was not able to produce a text. A few days later, the European Council of 17/18 October 2019 hotly debated the issue. Enlargement-critical Member States such as Denmark or the Netherlands would have been ready to decouple the starting dates, i.e. to give the green light to North Macedonia and to postpone Albania with a reference to the existing merits-based approach. France, however, would block any opening of negotiations altogether regardless of North Macedonia fully meeting the EU criterion of settling the name dispute with Greece by means of the historic Prespa Agreement[29] (author's field notes, 17-10-2019). As a result, the Conclusions of the European Council constitute the shortest-ever wording on enlargement in the history of the EU to date and are worth quoting:

> The European Council will revert to the issue of enlargement before the EU-Western Balkans summit in Zagreb in May 2020. (European Council Conclusions 17/18 October 2019: 2)

(iv) In the light of the French reform demand and proposal[30] for a new methodology for EU accession negotiations, the European Commission presented a revised Enlargement Strategy labelled "A credible EU perspective for the Western Balkans" on 5 February 2020.[31] Building on the merits-based approach, the new "reinvigorating" elements are:

- Regaining and increasing credibility through "Western Balkans leaders [...] deliver[ing] more credibility on their commitment" with regard to fundamental reforms, whilst at the same time the "European Union delivers on its unwavering commitment to a merits-based process" which, notably, includes

[29] For the Prespa Agreement see Sect. 6.4.1.

[30] In November 2019, France submitted a non-paper on "Reforming the European Union accession process" calling for (i) gradual accession to the EU including the reversibility of negotiations, and (ii) stronger political governance. The main novelty was to introduce "several successive stages" along "coherent policy blocks" (stage 1: rule of law, fundamental rights, justice and security, comprising Chaps. 23 and 24; stage 2: education, research and space, youth, culture, sports, environment, transport, telecommunications and energy, relating to Chaps. 14, 15, 21, 22, 26, 25, 27; stage 3: employment, social policy, health and consumer protection, competitiveness, based on Chaps. 19, 28, 5, 7, 8, 20; stage 4: economic and financial affairs, subject to Chaps. 4, 9, 16, 17, 18, 32; stage 5: internal market, agriculture and fisheries, comprising Chaps. 29, 1, 2, 3, 6, 10, 11, 12, 13; stage 6: foreign affairs, relating to Chaps. 30, 31; stage 7: other matters, subject to Chaps. 33, 34, 35; for the contents of the individual Chapters see last footnote in Sect. 4.2.1.

[31] The competent services in the European Commission for the drafting of the new methodology was the General Secretariat and the Directorate General for Enlargement and Neighbourhood (NEAR).

that "all parties must *abstain from misusing outstanding issues* in the accession process"[32] (European Commission Enlargement Strategy, 5 February 2020: 2);

- "Stronger political steer" through, for instance, Member States contributing through monitoring on the ground as for the situation in Candidate Countries and by means of feeding in observations to the European Commission annual reports, and the European Commission "including *proposals for corrective measures* [...] for approval by Member States" in the annual reporting (European Commission Enlargement Strategy, 5 February 2020: 3; emphasis added);
- "A more dynamic process" with the novelty of grouping negotiating chapter in *clusters*.[33] The chapters are subdivided into six clusters. Notably, all chapters of a cluster will be opened as a whole (as opposed to the individual-chapter basis applied previously). Candidates for which negotiations are already ongoing, i.e. Serbia and Montenegro, may adopt the new methodology or stick to the previous approach (European Commission Enlargement Strategy, 5 February 2020: 4–5)[34]; and
- More emphasis on *conditionality, positive or negative*, and predictability. Conditions and incentives are supposed to be defined more clearly. On positive reform performance, Candidate Countries can expect (i) "phasing-in" to exiting EU policies, and (ii) increased funding through a reform-oriented Instrument for Pre-Accession Assistance (IPA). On negative reform performance or back-sliding, Members States can—based on the Commission's annual reports, or, in serious cases, on Commission proposals at any time, decide[35] to (i) put negotiations on hold or suspend them altogether, or to re-open chapters already closed, (ii) decrease EU-funding except for support for civil society, and (iii) suspend or withdraw access to EU programmes

[32]There is no specific reference, however, to bilateral issues involving a Member State and a Candidate Country.

[33]"Fundamentals" comprising Chaps. 23, 24, 5, 18 and 32; "Internal Market" relating to Chaps. 1, 2, 3, 4, 6, 7, 8, 9 and 28; "Competitiveness and inclusive growth" with regard to Chaps. 10, 16, 17, 19, 20, 25, 26 and 29; "Green agenda and sustainable connectivity" with Chaps. 14, 15, 21 and 27; "Resources, agriculture and cohesion" comprising Chaps. 11, 12, 13, 22 and 33; and "External relations" relating to Chaps. 30 and 31 (European Commission Enlargement Strategy 2020: 7; see https://ec.europa.eu/neighbourhood-enlargement/sites/near/files/enlargement-methodology_en.pdf).

[34]There will be no new negotiating frameworks for Serbia and for Montenegro, however. Much of the 2020 approach can be accommodated in the rule-of-law Chapters anyway. Moreover, the cluster approach is hardly relevant for Montenegro and for Serbia, as most Chapters haven been opened (interview European Commission DG NEAR civil servant, 15-04-2020).

[35]So-called reverse qualified-majority voting (QMV) applies, i.e. Member States need a qualified majority to reject Commission proposals on negative sanctioning. This provision was inserted last minute at the College meeting on 5 February 2020. The post-Cabinet version (on file with this author) did not contain a specific provision on voting arrangements in Council. The reverse QMV provision was inserted at the request of France and the Commissioner for Enlargement (interview European Commission DG NEAR civil servant, 15-04-2020).

or market access (European Commission Enlargement Strategy, 5 February 2020: 5–6).

Whilst the 2020 Enlargement Strategy maintains the merits-based approach, the main innovation appears to be the clustering of negotiating chapters and an increased emphasis on positive and negative conditionality. Despite the fact that, at the time of writing, it was as yet impossible to make a preliminary assessment of the operational workings of the new methodology, there nevertheless is some obscurity with the following issues: First, whilst there is the provision of reverse qualified-majority voting on Commission proposals executing the response to a negative reform performance, no provisions exist as of yet on proposals for accelerated phasing-in to EU policies or increased pre-accession funding.[36] Second, there is no clear mention of the fact that, as all parties are supposed to abstain "from misusing outstanding issues", bilateral disputes between a Member State and a Candidate Country must be solved *ahead of* accession, a key provision in the 2018 Enlargement Strategy (see above).

The dynamics with regard to opening accession negotiations with North Macedonia and Albania changed in the aftermath of the new European Commission methodology. In fact, France withdrew its reservations and the General Affairs Council (GAC) of 24 March 2020 endorsed the new methodology and reached a political agreement to open negotiations with Albania and North Macedonia.[37] The relatively swift decision may, however, also be related to a certain sense of urgency and the desire to send a signal of political solidarity and moral support during the emerging coronavirus pandemic[38] where some Western Balkan countries, in particular Serbia and Montenegro, had received some substantial, badly-needed medical equipment support from China (author's field notes March and April 2020; see also Stjepčević, 4 April 2020; Vuksanović, 8 April 2020) in a "humanitarian aid blitz" (Myers and Rubin, 18 March 2020) whilst some EU national governments were discussing or even executing domestic export bans for medical equipment (see e.g. Gostyńska-Jakubowska and Scazzieri, 23 March 2020).

4.2.1.2 Opening and Closure of Chapters

The substantive issues are dealt with at the operational level of the accession negotiations, i.e. when the question of opening and/or closing of negotiation Chapters arises.

---

[36]The European Parliament expressed its concern about a lack of clarity with regard to the reversibility of the accession process calling for "objective criteria when deciding whether negotiations should be put on hold or suspended" (European Parliament Resolution 19 June 2020: 6).

[37]The GAC invited the Commission to draft the negotiation frameworks (GAC Conclusions 24 March 2020: 3-5). The Commission presented the drafts on 1 July 2020 scheduled for adoption by Council before the end of the year.

[38]Council and other meetings switched from physical gatherings to video-conferencing in mid-March 2020.

In a nutshell, the process is as follows (fundamentals-first version as operational since 29 June 2012):

- The European Commission, after screening the Candidate Country's existing legislation and practical implementation on the ground, drafts an *Opening Benchmark Assessment Report* (*OBAR*). Member States, in the format of the Council Working Group on Enlargement (*COELA*), adopt the OBAR;
- The Council Presidency invites the Candidate Country to submit their negotiating position. The Candidate Country will usually have learnt informally about the date of the upcoming request prior to the Council decision;
- The European Commission subsequently drafts the EU *Draft Common Position* (*DCP*) which is then negotiated in COELA, i.e. Member States may request changes subject to unanimity. The final *EU Common Position* (*CP*) is endorsed at the ambassador level (*COREPER*) and then officially adopted at ministerial level (General Affairs Council), the latter usually at the occasion of an *Intergovernmental Conference* (*IGC*). The procedure for closing benchmarks follows the same logic (interview Member State E COELA civil servant, 21-10-2016; interview Member State D COELA civil servant, 15-11-2016; European Commission presentation paper Belgrade, 18-06-2013: 10–11); see Fig. 4.3.

It is useful to note that for rule-of-law issues (Chaps. 23 and 24) the Commission operates a biannual non-paper reporting system to inform the Member States on progress in the field. In addition, the Commission proposes interim benchmarks (including updated ones) for Chaps. 23 and 24 matters if they consider it necessary (see e.g. Council of the European Union, DCP on Chap. 24, accession negotiations with Serbia, 5 July 2016: 22–32).

As both the opening and interim benchmarks are proposed by the Commission and are not debated in COELA, it is up to Member States to individually lobby the Commission on the need and potential content of such benchmarks. The Commission's DCP, however, is more or less openly debated and amended inside COELA

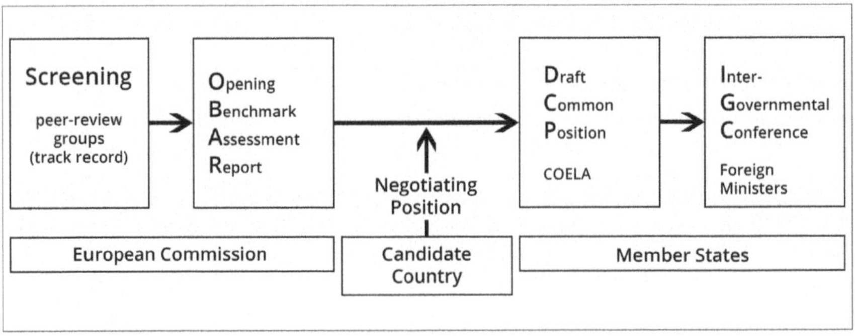

Fig. 4.3 EU accession negotiations: procedure for opening and closure of Chaps. 23 and 24, tentatively applying to all "fundamentals" cluster chapters for newly started accession negotiations since June 2020 (*Source* Author)

depending on the style of the Presidency in office (interview Member State E COELA civil servant, 21-10-2016; interview Member State H COELA civil servant, 16-07-2018). Furthermore, it is understood that Member States may turn to one another bilaterally or pluri-laterally to seek support for their individual points of interest. Thus, it may be said that there is a three-tier opportunity for Member States to influence the EU Common Position vis-à-vis a Candidate Country. The European Commission, nonetheless, has a strong role as guardian of the *acquis* and accession negotiating executive.

A Candidate Country is also free to lobby its interest with the Commission and the Member States. As a third country, however, the Candidate Country is forced to lobby individually with Member States if such communication is meant to take place at an early stage. Still, there is an official body where Member States and individual Candidate Countries meet: the Stabilisation and Association Council, usually referred to as the SA Council.[39] It is a Council forum for broad debate on an equal footing with the Candidate Country about the stage of preparation for EU membership, and usually takes place once a year (interview Member State I COELA civil servant, 12-07-2018; interview Member State E COELA civil servant, 21-10-2016; see e.g. SA Council meeting EU-Montenegro, 25-06-2018[40]).

4.2.2 Early Efforts to Defuse the Conflict

The border dispute with Slovenia was by no means new in the context of Croatia's EU accession process. It had already featured prominently, albeit somewhat in the subtext perhaps, during the introduction and adaptation of the Croatian ecological protection zone in the Adriatic (ZERP) between 2003 and the spring of 2008 (see Sect. 3.1.4.4). However, the border issue only fully impacted the ongoing accession negotiations with Croatia after the Slovenian EU Presidency (which the country held during the first half of 2008) and after the Bled Agreement of August 2007 had begun to run dry due to the once again diverging views on what type of third-party judicial body should be entrusted with the management of the border issue, a dispute that was meant to be overcome by the very Bled Agreement itself in the first place (see Sect. 4.1.5).

[39]The Stabilisation and Association Process was launched in 1999 as a tool of support particularly designed for the so-called Western Balkans countries. It contains (i) a bilateral (EU and applicant country) Stabilisation and Association Agreement (SAA) which usually marks the beginning of the EU accession process, (ii) free trade agreements with the EU, (iii) financial assistance, and (iv) the promotion of regional cooperation and good neighbourly relations. For a comprehensive overview of the SAA process see e.g. https://ec.europa.eu/neighbourhood-enlargement/policy/glossary/terms/sap_en.

[40]https://www.consilium.europa.eu/en/meetings/international-ministerial-meetings/2017/06/20/.

4.2.2.1 Slovenia's Reservations

During October 2008, the Slovenian approach of blocking the ongoing EU accession negotiations with Croatia in a number of areas fully materialized (interview Member State B civil servant working in COELA at the time, 08-12-2016). The actual decision to bring the matter of the prejudging documents to the negotiating table had been taken by the Slovenian government in June 2008 just before the end of the Slovenian EU Council Presidency.[41] The decision was implemented in October of that year, very close to polling day in Slovenia (interview senior Slovenian civil servant, 24-01-2017). The Slovenian "reservations" concerned eleven negotiating chapters on the grounds that the documents submitted by Croatia "prejudice[d] the definition of the border between Slovenia and Croatia" (Information on prejudices in certain negotiating chapters of accession negotiations for Croatia's membership of the EU, Slovenian non-paper, 18 December 2008: 1; see also PCA Partial Award 2016: 3).

In fact, the Slovenian veto was grouped into three categories and applied to

(i) the *opening* of five Chapters (11 Agriculture and rural development; 12 Food safety, veterinary and phytosanitary policy; 16 Taxation; 22 Regional policy and coordination of structural instruments; and 24 Justice, freedom and security);
(ii) the provisional *closing* of two Chapters (21 Trans-European networks; and 29 Customs union); and, due to "additional substantive reservations";
(iii) the *opening* of Chaps. 4 (Free movement of capital), 13 (Fisheries), 27 (Environment), and 31 (Foreign, security and defence policy; Slovenian non-paper, 18 December 2008: 1).

The reservations in the Slovenian paper can be outlined as follows: In Chap. 4 (Free movement of capital), Slovenia does not accept the total area of land under the Croatian Programme of management of State-owned agricultural land, as had already been protested bilaterally (Slovenian non-paper, 18 December 2008: 1–2). As for Chap. 11 (Agriculture and rural development), Slovenia protests against the Territories of Counties, Cities and Municipalities Act, a separate Croatian law to the Local and Regional Self-Management Act mentioned in the Croatian negotiating position, for incorporating the Three Hamlets on the left bank of the Dragonja River (Slovenian non-paper, 18 December 2008: 2; see also Sect. 4.1.2.2 and PCA Final Award 2017: 240–241, paras 767–770). On Food safety, veterinary and phytosanitary policy (Chap. 12), Ljubljana objected since the Croatian rules on veterinary checks and control of animal products in cross-border trade are related to the Croatian

[41] It is established custom and practice on the diplomatic scene in the EU that the rotating Council Presidency refrains from actively advancing matters considered an own national interest. Council Presidencies naturally take on a facilitating role in whatever EU decision-making is due during their Presidency.

Customs Act containing a reference to the Croatian Maritime Code[42] (Slovenian non-paper, 18 December 2008: 2).

In the Fisheries Chapter (13), Slovenia protests against a number of laws and implementing regulations expressly mentioning the Croatian ZERP, the equidistance line in Piran Bay, and the CS boundary with Italy (Slovenian non-paper, 18 December 2008: 2–3; see also Sects. 3.1.4.4 and 3.1.5). With regard to Taxation (Chap. 16), Ljubljana objects to the Croatian Public Roads Act as, in its recent implementing Decree, the Plovanija-Sečovlje border crossing was not listed as "provisional" (as had been agreed on in a 1994 bilateral act; see also Sect. 4.1.2.2) thus predetermining the common State border. In the Trans-European Networks Chapter (21), Slovenia criticises Zagreb's National Programme for the Development of Railway Infrastructure as it contained maps of the Croatian view of the maritime boundary with Slovenia. As for regional policy and coordination of structural instruments (Chap. 22), Slovenia objects to the Croatian Contingency Plan for Accidental Marine Pollution, referring to the maritime border in the annexed map (Slovenian non-paper, 18 December 2008: 3). With regard to Chap. 24 on Justice, freedom, and security, analogous to the Croatian Decree in Chap. 16, the Sečovlje-Plovanija border crossing is listed as a permanent installation (Slovenian non-paper, 18 December 2008: 3–4; see also Sect. 4.1.2.2).

In relation to Environment (Chap. 27), the Contingency Plan for Accidental Marine Pollution is mentioned as is its annexed map (as with Chap. 22). Further, Zagreb's Decree on air quality in inhabited regions, the National Air Quality Protection and Improvement Plan, and the National Strategy on Water Management, contained several maps with the sea border. Lastly and with regard to Chap. 29 (Customs union), there is a protest against the Customs Act since it contained a reference to the Croatian CS "den[ying] Slovenia the possibility of [a] continental shelf" (Slovenian non-paper, 18 December 2008: 4; see also Sects. 3.1.4.4 and 3.1.5).

Nevertheless, the Slovenian reservations did not lead to a complete standstill in the Chapters concerned, as the screening of the Croatian legislation by the European Commission continued at expert level, so that the overall delay was marginal. Further, other Chapters were opened or provisionally closed as foreseen. The tactics of Slovenia were widely considered strategically and skilfully deployed, ranging from debates at ministerial level to behind-the-scenes action such as removing points from the agenda of the Council Working Group COELA. However, the Slovenian case was "a novelty of a country using its status of Member State to enforce its position vis-à-vis a Candidate Country" (interview European Commission civil servant involved in the accession negotiations with Croatia, 07-01-2016) although it was a purely bilateral issue. As a Member State diplomat put it: "The border dispute

[42]That Code *inter alia* defines Croatia's Continental Shelf (CS) claim in the Adriatic which overlaps with Slovenia's own CS claim (see also Sects. 3.1.4.4 and 3.1.5). It must be noted, however, that the Arbitral Tribunal rejected the Slovenian continental shelf claim altogether (PCA Final Award 2017: 354, para 1103).

between Slovenia and Croatia was deeply political, but it is not a part of the accession process" (interview Member State J civil servant who worked in COELA in 2009, 19-10-2016).

The reaction amongst EU Member States was predominantly unenthusiastic in the Council Working Group (interview Member State A civil servant, 23-06-2016). Behind the scenes, "a lot of good-will was lost as the Slovenes had played it rather clumsily by not putting much effort into explaining the situation. The issue got on the nerves of a large number of Member States despite the fact that the spirit in COELA remained professional and no national position was taken personally" (interview Member State B civil servant, 08-12-2016; both civil servants worked in COELA in 2008/09). There was very little support for the Slovenian position, and, accordingly, the French EU Presidency initially took a firmly critical stance towards Ljubljana's position (interview European Commission civil servant involved in the accession negotiations with Croatia, 07-01-2016; interview Member State C civil servant who worked in COELA 2008/2009, 27-01-2017). The very few Member States who tacitly supported the Slovenian move saw Ljubljana's call for access to the high seas as being somewhat justified in a wider historical context of the north-eastern Adriatic where full maritime access for the area of present-day Slovenia was natural under the pre-1918 Habsburg rule and during post-World-War-II Yugoslavia (interview Karel Schwarzenberg,[43] 26-09-2017).

Croatia considered the Slovenian approach unfair and out of proportion as most of the implementing regulations were not part of the Croatian accession documents. The Slovenian reservations had therefore had to be largely based on additional Slovenian screening of Croatian implementing legislation including legal acts three levels down with regard to the legislation referred to in the original Croatian negotiating position. Furthermore, the Slovenian position was perceived as being shared by the other Member States. "There was no outrage, and this appeared to us as a sign of solidarity amongst the members of a club. We felt all this was a manipulation of the Croatian accession negotiation process" (interview member of the then Croatian negotiating team, 30-11-2015). On a lighter note, "Slovenia was not fully supportive of Croatia during our accession negotiations, although they had a great knowledge, expertise, and understanding of Croatia" (interview Vesna Pusić, 24-02-2017).

4.2.2.2 French Presidency Proposal

France had taken over the EU Council Presidency from Slovenia on 1 July 2008. In the later stages of its Presidency, France actively pursued defusing the conflict at ambassador level, i.e. to work out a solution in trilateral meetings (interview civil servant involved in the trilateral meetings, 27-01-2017; Internal note Ministry of Foreign Affairs Croatia 2012: 2). The situation proved fairly tense, first of all for the

[43] Karel Schwarzenberg MP was Minister for Foreign and European Affairs of the Czech Republic 2007–2009 (including the period of the Czech EU Council Presidency in the first half of 2009) and 2010–2013.

accession negotiations as such as the Slovenian reservations had a "systemic effect" on the preparation of the DCPs (see Sect. 4.2.1.2), and secondly "there was a real and open confrontation" between Croatia and Slovenia (interview civil servant involved in the trilateral meetings, 27-01-2017).

The idea of the French diplomacy was to have an exchange of letters between the Council Presidency and Croatia to defuse the prejudging nature of some of the Croatian accession documents towards the common State border. This approach was to address the Slovenian concerns and was supposed to remove the blockade. There was a series of trilateral meetings at the French Permanent Representation, the Slovenian Permanent Representation, and the Croatian Mission in Brussels respectively in which drafts were discussed. They culminated in a non-official "Presidency's proposal" from 15 December 2008 which is worth quoting:

> 1. Letter from the Presidency of the EU Council to Croatia:
>
> The Presidency of the EU Council underlines that the purpose of this exchange is to address the question of any border prejudice, by confirming that the accession negotiations between the EU and Croatia will not in any way prejudice the final resolution of the border issue between Slovenia and Croatia and the positions of both sides, in any procedure relating to the resolution of the border issue.
>
> On this basis, the Presidency [...] confirms that no statement made by Croatia in the context of its accession negotiations to the EU, when related to the border between Slovenia and Croatia, may be relied upon by Croatia in any procedure relating to the settlement of the border issue between Slovenia and Croatia in such a way as to imply acceptance or recognition of such statement by any Member State of the EU. In addition, the fact that Slovenia agrees, following its internal procedures, the EU documents and positions which refer to or summarize Croatian documents and positions, related to the border issue between Slovenia and Croatia, cannot be interpreted, in any procedure relating to the settlement of the border issue, as committing Slovenia and its position regarding this issue.
>
> The above applies to all documents and positions either written or submitted orally, including, *inter alia*, maps, negotiating positions, legal acts and other documents in whatever form, produced, presented or referred to by Croatia in the framework of the EU accession negotiations. It also applies to all EU documents and positions which refer to or summarize the above-mentioned Croatian documents and positions [...].
>
> The Presidency [...] notes that Slovenia and Croatia remain committed to the EU principle of good neighbourly relations [and] recalls the position of the EU related to the Croatian Ecological and Fisheries Protection Zone [ZERP] and that, according to the decision of the Croatian Parliament on 13 March 2008, no aspect of this Zone applies to the EU Member States until a common agreement in EU spirit is reached [see Sect. 3.1.4.4].
>
> [...] The Presidency proposes that this letter and the reply of the Republic of Croatia form an integral part of the accession documents (AD) of the Conference on the Accession to the European Union with Croatia.
>
> 2. Reply from Croatia to the Presidency of the EU Council:
>
> With regard to the letter of the Presidency [...] of xx December 2008, I hereby confirm that the government of [...] Croatia fully agrees to the contents of the said letter and acknowledges its principles.
>
> This is on the understanding that the accession negotiations between the EU and Croatia will not in any way have any affect upon the final resolution of the border issue between Slovenia and Croatia and the position of both sides, in any procedure relating to the resolution of the border issue.

> Croatia further notes that the second and third paragraph of the above-mentioned letter may not be interpreted, in the context of any procedure relating to the settlement of the border issue between Slovenia and Croatia, as implying on the part of any Member State of the EU any acceptance or rejection of Croatian statements and documents related to the border issue when made, produced or referred to in a context other than the accession negotiations between the EU and Croatia.
>
> Croatia remains committed to resolving any border dispute in conformity with the principle of peaceful settlement of disputes in accordance with the United Nations Charter and in the spirit of good neighbourly relations [and] agrees to your proposal that your letter and this reply form an integral part of the accession documents (AD) of the Conference on the Accession to the European Union with Croatia. (Presidency Proposal, 15 December 2008: 1–2)

The above letter and the positive reply of Croatia were supposed to function "as a disclaimer" and be part of the accession documents. The rationale behind this exercise was that the border dispute was a bilateral issue which was in no way related to the *acquis*, i.e. the substantive pieces of EU legislation touched upon in the actual negotiating Chapters, and that the EU was not going to enter into solving the border problem. However, substantial pressure from the Slovenian capital to start the solving of the border dispute was felt in the trilateral meetings, since (i) it was a very sensitive issue for the country anyway, and (ii) polling day in Slovenia was very close (interview civil servant involved in the trilateral meetings, 27-01-2017).

The Slovenian side was dissatisfied with the time-pressure as the French Presidency appeared to "rush it through" before the end of their term (31 December 2008). A solution may perhaps have been in the pipeline had more time been allocated to the drafting of the letters (interview senior Slovenian civil servant, 24-01-2017). On a more fundamental note, Croatia should even have had its accession documents modified to meet Slovenia's concerns (interview senior Slovenian civil servant 17-10-2016). In the end, Slovenia would not accept the Presidency proposal, and it was already becoming apparent that EU Enlargement Commissioner Olli Rehn was aiming at decontaminating the Croatian accession negotiations from the veto before the end of his own term which was to expire on 31 October 2009.

4.2.2.3 Rehn's Expert Group Proposal

As things had developed into a real deadlock, the European Commission started assuming a mediating role in January 2009. Olli Rehn, the then European Commissioner for Enlargement, was determined to "avoid a major new frozen conflict in the Western Balkans" and went on a sentiment-finding mission to Ljubljana and Zagreb on 28 January 2009. He met Prime Minister Borut Pahor and President Danilo Turk in Ljubljana over lunch, and Prime Minister Ivo Sanader and President Stipe Mesić in Zagreb for dinner. Whilst Rehn was facing a mix of rational concern and a very emotional stance towards the other country respectively, there was no enthusiasm for his idea of mediation (interview Olli Rehn, 09-10-2015; interview Rehn Cabinet member who was with him on that trip, 13-11-2015).[44]

Still, a subsequent first confidential draft dated 26 January 2009 was circulated to the parties outlining the basic elements of a mediation exercise by a Senior Experts Group (SEG):

- The SEG would be set up to resolve the bilateral border (at sea and at land) based on international law; it would consist of three personalities, one of them the chair;
- The Expert Group would, after "consult[ing] the authorities in both countries" issue recommendations that Croatia and Slovenia were supposed to respect;
- The SEG would make its recommendations before the end of 2009;
- No document presented in the accession negotiations with Croatia would "commit any of the negotiating States on the border issue";
- The Slovenian reservations were supposed to be lifted as soon as the countries made a declaration on mandating the SEG (Basic elements for a joint statement on European facilitation on the border issue between Slovenia and Croatia, European Commission note, 26 January 2009).

The draft declaration as such went through at least three drafting stages between the end of January and mid-March 2009 (Bickl 2017: 18; see also Draft Joint Declaration, 20 February 2009). A Croatian proposal contained a specific reference to "the work of the two commissions established under the Bled Agreement [2007]" and that the "International Court of Justice was [...] the forum to which the border dispute was to be submitted". There was also talk of both parties acknowledging "the rights and obligations that derive [...] from the UN Convention on the Law of the Sea". Further, bilateral negotiations were foreseen "on granting each other concessions with regard to the navigation regime and fisheries, once the border is decided by [...] the International Court of Justice" (Draft Joint Declaration, undated). The last European Commission draft from 10 March 2009 mentioned, for the first time, the date of 25 June 1991 (the day of the declarations of independence of both Slovenia and Croatia) "as the basis for a solution". Furthermore, the consent of both parliaments was mentioned in the context of both countries respecting the Senior Experts Group's recommendations (Draft Declaration on the border issue between the Republic of Slovenia and the Republic of Croatia, 10 March 2009).

A first fully fledged European Commission "Draft Agreement on Arbitration", albeit still with the Senior Experts Group as the third-party mediator, surfaced towards the end of March 2009. The Commission neatly describes the approach as "contain[ing] elements from mediation and conciliation" (European Commission, note to the file, 12 March 2009; see also Sect. 1.3.1.4) highlighting the fact that what the two parties were supposed to enter into was a legally binding international agreement subject to parliamentary ratification (European Commission, Further reflections on a formalized document, fax dated 24 March 2009).

The "Draft Agreement on Arbitration" contained the following core elements:

---

[44] As for potential mediators, Rehn dropped the names of Martti Arthisaari, Robert Badinter, and Donald Tusk (interview Olli Rehn, 09-10-2015).

- Composition and appointing procedure of the Senior Expert Group
  ("The European Commission will appoint the President [...] on the grounds of his/her experience in international dispute settlement and international reputation within 15 days after signature [...]. The President [...] will appoint two additional members of recognized competence in international dispute settlement and international law [...]. Each side will appoint one member [of the SEG] within 15 days after signature. If either side has not appointed its member within the deadline, [the appointment will be made] by the President of the International Court of Justice.")
- Task of the Senior Expert Group
  ("The [SEG] shall use the submissions of the parties for the determination of the legal scope of the maritime and territorial dispute between the parties [and] shall render an award on the dispute." Further, the SEG was to have "the power to interpret the present Agreement on Arbitration.")
- Applicable Law
  ("The [SEG] shall apply the principles and rules of international law, in particular the UN-Charter." In addition, "[n]o document or action undertaken unilaterally by either side after 25 June 1991 shall be accorded legal significance for the tasks of the Senior Expert Group or commit either side on the border dispute.")
- Procedure
  ("Each side shall prepare a submission to the [SEG] within two months [...]. Each side has the right to comment on the submission of the other side within a fixed deadline [...]. The [SEG] shall seek expert advice and organise oral hearings.")
- The award of the Senior Expert Group
  ("The [SEG] shall strive to issue its award by the end of 2009 [and] adopt the award by majority of its members. [...] The award [...] shall be binding on the parties and constitute a definitive settlement of the dispute. The Parties shall take all necessary steps to implement the award, including by revising national legislation, as necessary, within six months after the adoption of the award.")
- Croatia's accession negotiations
  ("Upon signature of this agreement, [...] Slovenia will lift its reservations as regards opening and closing of negotiation chapters where the obstacle is related to the border dispute. The EU accession negotiations with Croatia will continue according to the negotiating framework." With regard to accession negotiation documents, "no documents presented in the EU accession negotiations will prejudice the [SEG] [...] or commit either side on the border dispute.")
- Ratification
  (The Agreement on Arbitration "shall be ratified by either side" according to the respective constitutional provisions; Draft Agreement on Arbitration, 24 March 2009: 1–4).

The above Draft Agreement already contained distinct features of arbitration such as a five-member body including two party-appointed members, provisions on the task of the third-party dispute resolution body and the applicable law, the submission of documents and counter-documents (albeit not referred to as memorials), oral hearings, and a binding award. Further, the nexus between an arbitration agreement and the lifting of the Slovenian reservations thus unblocking the Croatian accession negotiations was already there, too.

Nevertheless, both Slovenia and Croatia were not fully warming to the idea of the Senior Expert Group mainly because both the task of the Group and the applicable law were not yet sufficiently outlined.[45] As a consequence, the phase for setting up a specific arbitral tribunal began (interview Olli Rehn, 09-10-2015). The Commission had learnt that "a proper judicial procedure was indispensable for the Croats[46]", whereas taking on board some kind of discretionary powers for the tribunal would be vital for the Slovenes. In the following weeks, the Commission drafted a proposal for an arbitration agreement modelled on established arbitral rules and practice and based on the specific definitions needed for the peculiarities of the Croatia–Slovenia case (interview Frank Hoffmeister, then European Commission Legal Service, 03-06-2016; see also PCA Final Award 2017: 33, para 107–8).

4.2.3 Rehn I

The first draft proposal for the later Arbitration Agreement, known as Rehn I, aiming at establishing and mandating an Arbitral Tribunal, was circulated to the parties on 23 April 2009. The gist of the core issues from the preceding proposal based on the Senior Expert Group (see Sect. 4.2.2.3) was retained, whereas the provisions on the task of the Tribunal and the applicable law were revised and defined in greater detail.

To do justice to the evolution of the core provisions of the Arbitration Agreement drafts it is worth quoting the main elements of Rehn I:

> [Preamble]
>
> The Government of the Republic of Slovenia and the Republic of Croatia (hereinafter referred to as "the Parties"),
>
> Whereas through numerous attempts the Parties have not resolved their territorial and maritime border dispute in the course of the past years,
>
> Recalling the peaceful means for the settlement of disputes enumerated in Article 33 of the UN-Charter,
>
> Affirming their commitment to a peaceful settlement of disputes, in the spirit of good-neighbourly relations,
>
> Welcoming the facilitation offered by the European Commission,
>
> Have agreed as follows:

---

[45] Slovenia later expressly suggested that whilst agreeing "to settle this predominantly political dispute through adjudication" it had "consented to the primary proposal by Commissioner Rehn [for] the process of mediation" (Information on the amendments proposed by the Republic of Slovenia, 25 May 2009: 5).

[46] In retrospect, Croatia referred to the Draft SEG Agreement from 24 March 2009 as "political arbitration" as opposed to "judicial settlement" in relation to the final Arbitration Agreement (Croatian Ministry of Foreign Affairs paper, September 2011: 8).

[…]

Article 2: Composition of the Arbitral Tribunal

(1) Both parties shall appoint by common agreement the President of the Arbitral Tribunal and two members recognized for their competence in international law within fifteen days. In case that they cannot agree within this delay, the President and the two members of the Arbitral Tribunal shall be appointed by the President of the International Court of Justice.

(2) Each side shall appoint a further member of the Arbitral Tribunal within fifteen days after the appointments referred to in paragraph 1 have been finalised. In case that no appointment has been made within this delay, the respective member shall be appointed by the President of the Arbitral Tribunal.

(3) If, whether before or after the proceedings have begun, a vacancy should occur on account of death, incapacity or resignation of a member, it shall be filled in accordance with the procedure prescribed for the original appointment.

Article 3: Task of the Arbitral Tribunal

(1) The Arbitral Tribunal shall determine

(a) the course of the maritime and land boundary between the Republic of Croatia and the Republic of Slovenia; and

(b) the regime for the use of the relevant maritime areas and Slovenia's *contact* to the High Sea [emphasis added].

(2) The Parties shall specify the details of the subject-matter of the dispute within one month after entry into force of this Agreement. If they fail to do so, the Arbitral Tribunal shall use submissions of the parties for the determination of the exact scope of the maritime and territorial disputes and claims between the parties.

(3) The Arbitral Tribunal shall render an award on the dispute.

(4) The Arbitral Award has the power to interpret the present Agreement.

Article 4: Applicable Law

(1) The Arbitral Tribunal shall apply

(a) the rules and principles of *international law* for the determination referred to in Article 3 (1) (a) [emphasis added];

(b) international law, *equity* and the principle of *good neighbourly relations* in order to achieve a *fair and just result* for the determination referred to in Article 3 (1) (b) [emphasis added].

Article 5: Critical date

No document or action undertaken unilaterally by either side after 25 June 1991 shall be accorded legal significance for the tasks of the Arbitral Tribunal or commit either side on the dispute and cannot, in any way, prejudge the award.

Article 6: Procedure

(1) Each side shall submit a memorial to the Arbitral Tribunal within two months after entry into force. Each side has the right to comment on the memorial of the other side within a deadline fixed by the Arbitral Tribunal.

(2) Unless envisaged otherwise, the Arbitral Tribunal shall conduct the proceedings according to the Permanent Court of Arbitration Optional Rules for Arbitrating Disputes between Two States.

(3) The Arbitral Tribunal may seek expert advice and organize oral hearings.

[…]

Article 7: The award of the Arbitral Tribunal

(1) The Arbitral Tribunal shall strive to issue its award within one year after its establishment. The Arbitral Tribunal adopts the award by majority of its members […].

(2) The award shall be binding on the Parties and shall constitute a definitive settlement of the dispute.

(3) The Parties shall take all necessary steps to implement the award, including by revising national legislation, as necessary, within six months after the adoption of the award.

Article 8: EU accession negotiation documents

No document presented in the EU accession negotiations shall prejudice the Arbitral Tribunal when performing its tasks or commit either side on the dispute.

The above applies to all documents and positions either written or submitted orally, including, *inter alia*, maps, negotiating positions, legal acts and other documents in whatever form, produced, presented or referred to in the framework of the EU accession negotiations. It also applies to all EU documents and positions which refer to or summarize the above-mentioned documents and positions.[47]

Article 9: The continuation of the EU accession negotiations according to the negotiating framework

(1) The Republic of Slovenia shall lift its reservations as regards opening and closing of negotiation chapters where the obstacle is related to the dispute.

(2) Both parties shall refrain from any action or statement which might negatively affect the accession negotiations.

[…]

Article 11

(1) The present Agreement on Arbitration shall be ratified expeditiously by both sides in accordance with their respective constitutional requirements.

(2) It shall enter into force on the first day of the week following the exchange of diplomatic notes with which the parties express their consent to be bound.

[…]. (Draft Agreement on Dispute Settlement, 24 April 2009: 1–4)

When looking at the revised core provisions of Rehn I (and its evolution in the subsequent proposals) with regard to (i) the task of the Tribunal (Article 3) and (ii) the applicable law (Article 4), it is crucial to recall that the difference between *international law* and *equity*, generally, is such that the judicial body possesses substantially wider discretionary powers under equity than if it exclusively applied international law (see Sect. 3.2.1). This distinction was the *core legal issue of dispute* during the negotiations around the Arbitration Agreement.

The practical implications of the two distinctive legal concepts may be seen as follows: the more leeway there is for the legal deliberations of the Tribunal, the greater the potential for maritime territorial decisions in favour of Slovenia compared to what it could expect under the strict application of international law, the latter obviously favouring Croatia's position. If we look at Articles 3 and 4 of Rehn I, it is apparent that both for the delimitation of the waters inside Piran Bay and for the territorial sea border outside the Bay, the provisions of the United Nations Convention on the Law

[47]This paragraph is identical with the 3rd paragraph of the (draft) "Letter from the Presidency of the EU Council to Croatia"; see Sect. 4.2.2.2.

of the Sea (UNCLOS[48]) apply, whereas for the access of Slovenia to the high seas and the regime for the use of that access a wider set of legal and extra-legal (*praeter legem*) deliberations is available to the Tribunal.

4.2.3.1 Croatia's Response

Croatia approved of Rehn I on the understanding that it was presented to the parties on a "take-it-or-leave-it" basis (interview senior Croatian civil servant, 25-01-2017; see also Preamble[49] of the Sabor Decision on the Acceptance of the Draft Agreement on Dispute Settlement [...] between Croatia and Slovenia, 8 May 2009). Zagreb's view was that it was of paramount importance that the delimitation of the land and maritime border between the two countries as referred to in Article 3(1)(a) was subject to international law exclusively. To that end, the additional equity and provisions relating to good-neighbourly relations for the regime of the maritime areas and the Slovenian access as in Article 3(1)(b) could, according to the Ministry of Foreign Affairs note, be tolerated, like it or not.

Notably, Croatia's green light did include the above-mentioned Sabor endorsement of the Draft Agreement signalling cross-party support. Rehn I was subsequently hailed by the domestic media as a national victory (internal note Ministry of Foreign Affairs Croatia 2012: 4) notwithstanding the fact that 3(1)(b) talked of territorial *contact* for Slovenia.

4.2.3.2 Slovenia's Amendments

There was no vote in the Slovenian parliament. Instead, the government decided to send several amendments to Rehn I to the European Commission in mid-May 2009. Its main elements[50] are worth quoting and deserve a brief discussion.

---

[48] Art. 15 UNCLOS stipulates that "where the coasts of two States are opposite or adjacent to each other, neither of the two States is entitled, failing agreement between them to the contrary, to extend its territorial sea beyond the median line every point of which is equidistant from the nearest points on the baselines from which the breadth of the territorial seas of each of the two States is measured. The above provision does not apply, however, where it is necessary by reason of historic title or other special circumstances to delimit the territorial seas of the two States in a way which is at variance therewith." This provision has, through case law, come to be referred to as the equidistance/special circumstances method (Tanaka 2015: 225–7; Rothwell and Stephens 2016: 427–36). For a discussion on maritime delimitation, the provisions of UNCLOS, and the development of case law see Sect. 3.2.

[49] "Taking into account that the proposed texts of the [arbitration] agreement [...] were offered to the Republic of Croatia and the Republic of Slovenia on a take-it-or-leave-it-basis.".

[50] Slovenia also introduced amendments to Article 2 (Composition of the Tribunal) asking to streamline the provisions on the appointment procedure with the PCA Optional Rules, and to Article 6 (Procedure) proposing to insert the possibility for the Tribunal to assist the parties in reaching an amicable bilateral settlement at any stage (Information on the amendments proposed by the Republic of Slovenia, 25 May 2009: 1–2; 5–6).

As for Article 3 (Task of the Arbitral Tribunal), Slovenia proposed:

(1) The Arbitral Tribunal shall determine

(a) the course of the maritime and land boundary between the Republic of Croatia and the Republic of Slovenia including Slovenia's territorial contact with the High Seas[51]; and

(b) the regime for the use of the relevant maritime areas.~~ and Slovenia's contact to the High Sea.~~

In the Slovenian explanatory note, the amendment is labelled "crucial and […] therefore the most important point" suggesting that if the original wording of Rehn I was kept it would deny Slovenia the territorial contact ("the absolute red line") it had before 25 June 1991, i.e. in SFRY times.[52] It must be noted in that context that the access to the high seas, politically and historically, "is a symbol of freedom [for Slovenia] and carries the notion of real independence for the State" (interview senior Slovenian civil servant, 17-10-2016; see also Petrič 2017: 362). Further, mere "contact" would carry the meaning of access to the High Seas which all States were entitled to anyway under UNCLOS (Information on the amendments proposed by the Republic of Slovenia, 25 May 2009: 3). The note goes on to cite examples from maritime delimitation case law and treaties in support of the term "territorial contact"[53] and concludes that, on Article 3, the incorporation of "territorial contact" with the High Seas was necessary "to ensure that [Slovenia's] vital interest is decided upon by the Arbitral Tribunal" (Information on the amendments proposed by the Republic of Slovenia, 25 May 2009: 4).

With regard to Article 4 (Applicable Law) the amendment reads:

(1) The Arbitral Tribunal shall apply

(a) the rules and principles of international law ~~for the determination referred to in Article 3 (1) (a)~~;

(b) ~~international law, ~~equity and the principle of good neighbourly relations, taking into account also vital interests of both Parties and all relevant circumstances, in order to achieve a fair and just result; ~~for the determination referred to in Article 3 (1) (b).~~

and should therefore decide ex aequo et bono.

In the explanatory note, the original wording of Rehn I in relation to Article 4 ("international law" for the determination of the *land border*; "international law, equity and good-neighbourly relations to achieve a fair and just result" for the regime and the *contact to the high seas*) is critiqued for following "the Croatian demand that the border is settled through the strict application of international law" and for the

[51] *NOTA BENE: Track-changes are deliberately used hereafter for illustration purposes.*

[52] "Slovenia […] succeeded to the 1968 Agreement between [the] former SFRY and Italy on the Delimitation of the Continental Shelf. Since Slovenia has a continental shelf, it also has territorial contact to the High Seas" (Information on the amendments proposed by the Republic of Slovenia, 25 May 2009: 3). For the Slovenian continental shelf claim see Sect. 3.1.4.4 and "Continental Shelf".

[53] Such as the corridor approaches in the 1992 St. Pierre and Miquelon case (Canada v. France; see Sect. 3.2.2.1) and the delimitation agreement between Monaco and France (see Sect. 3.1.1.1).

approach that "the resolution of the border issue would [...] be distinguished from the resolution of the issue of [the] Slovenian more liberal regime through, presumably, Croatian territorial waters". The Tribunal should instead apply "the same principles to the entire dispute" (Information on the amendments proposed by the Republic of Slovenia, 25 May 2009: 4).

The application of the principle *ex aequo et bono* was "crucial due to the very special circumstances of the dissolution of the former SFRY", and "the true meaning of the *ex aequo et bono* principle is in fact to offer the parties a possibility to widen the margin for decision-making and to give the Arbitral Tribunal a discretionary power to find, *outside* the strict legal prescription, the basis for a satisfactory solution, when it considers that strict law would lead to unjust decisions (*summum ius, summa inuria*)". It would be clear, however, that *ex aequo et bono* was meant as an add-on tool for the Tribunal "if it finds the law to be either defective or incomplete, [so] that it could base itself on extra-legal consideration[s]" (Information on the amendments proposed by the Republic of Slovenia, 25 May 2009: 5).[54]

The Slovenian note goes on to highlight the reference to "vital interests" and "relevant circumstances" as "draw[ing the Tribunal's] attention to the need to evaluate the effect of the important economic role of the Port of Koper, historic facts, exercise of fishing rights and other circumstances" (Information on the amendments proposed by the Republic of Slovenia, 25 May 2009: 5).

In relation to Article 9 (continuation of the EU accession negotiations according to the negotiating framework) Slovenia proposed the following:

> Article 9: The continuation of the EU accession negotiations according to the negotiating framework
>
> (1) The Republic of Slovenia shall lift its reservations as regards opening and closing of negotiation chapters where the obstacle is related to the dispute after the entry into force of the present Agreement.
>
> ~~(2) Both parties shall refrain from any action or statement which might negatively affect the accession negotiations.~~

Slovenia argues that since the Agreement would only be legally binding after its ratification by both parliaments and the exchange of diplomatic notes confirming the accomplishment of that task [Article 11(2)], it would only be logical that the provisions of Article 9 could only apply as from the entry into force of the Agreement as a whole. "Consequently, Slovenia can properly protect its vital interests against Croatia's prejudices only with a valid agreement establishing a mechanism which would start the resolution of the border issue as well as annul the legal effect of the prejudices which were introduced into the EU accession negotiations by the Republic of Croatia". The deletion of the second paragraph was necessary because it implied that "the parties do not act in good faith", and that the provision could be interpreted as acting as an impediment "to participate constructively during Croatian

[54]Bantekas (2015: 49) notes that, with international arbitration, "equity is only available through party consent and cannot therefore be imposed as default law by the tribunal".

accession negotiations" (Information on the amendments proposed by the Republic of Slovenia, 25 May 2009: 7–8).

In summary, the Slovenian amendments to Rehn I touch on core elements of the Commission draft, such as the task of the tribunal, the applicable law, and the timeline for the lifting of the Slovenian veto of the Croatian accession negotiations. With regard to the substantive points, the amendments seek to (i) safeguard a *territorial link* between Slovenian territorial waters and the high seas, (ii) enshrine such contact as the country's vital interest listing the special historic circumstances (*inter alia* the territorial contact Slovenia enjoyed during SFRY times), (iii) considerably widen the scope of the deliberations of the Tribunal by adding the principle of *ex aequo et bono* providing a set of extra-legal considerations (political, historic and economic), and (iv) reserve the right to maintain the reservations vis-à-vis Croatia until the entry into force of the Arbitration Agreement.

4.2.4 Rehn II

The European Commission presented a new proposal on 15 June 2009. The changes concern the Preamble, Article 2 (Composition of the Arbitral Tribunal), Article 3 (Task of the Tribunal), Article 4 on the Applicable Law, Article 6 (Procedure), and Article 8 on EU accession negotiation documents, which read as follows and are discussed straight after the respective article.

> [Preamble]
>
> The Government of [...] Slovenia and [...] Croatia (hereinafter referred to as "the Parties"),
>
> Whereas through numerous attempts the parties have not resolved their territorial and maritime border dispute in the course of the past years,
>
> Recalling the peaceful means for the settlement of disputes enumerated in Article 33 of the UN-Charter,
>
> Affirming their commitment to a peaceful settlement of disputes, in the spirit of good neighbourly relations, reflecting their vital interests,
>
> Welcoming the facilitation offered by the European Commission,
>
> Have agreed as follows. (Draft Agreement on Dispute Settlement, 15 June 2009: 1)

This change incorporates "vital interests" as one substantive point of the Slovenian amendment to Article 4, albeit in a new and very different environment. The Commission deliberately inserted "vital interests" in the Preamble to politicise it and render it a joint positive meaning for both Croatia and Slovenia. "It seemed appropriate to insert a 'diplomatic bow' of the EU vis-à-vis both parties" (interview Frank Hoffmeister, then European Commission Legal Service, 03-06-2016). This move may be seen as in contrast to the original meaning intended by Slovenia in the context of Article 4.

On a different note, one needs to see a Slovenian leitmotif during the processing of the border dispute in the context of the EU accession negotiations of Croatia: it is the notion of "*quid pro quo*" in the sense that Croatia receives EU membership in return for a link to the high seas for Slovenia. "There is clearly a double dimension here" (interview senior Slovenian civil servant, 17-10-2016; for *quid pro quo* in relation to the arbitration procedure as such see PCA Partial Award 2016: 28, para 115). The actual Arbitral Tribunal at a later stage noted, in more general terms and, for obvious reasons, without reference to the issue of contact to the high seas, that "a nexus was established between the settlement of the territorial and maritime dispute and the accession of Croatia to the European Union" (PCA Partial Award 2016: 55, para 220). Croatia, however, has never expressly accepted the notion of *quid pro quo*, but the fact appears to have been sinking in during the negotiations over the Arbitration Agreement that the arbitration procedure as such "was the price to pay" for EU membership (interview European Commission civil servant involved in the accession negotiations with Croatia, 07-01-2016).

> Article 2: Composition of the Arbitral Tribunal
>
> (1) Both parties shall appoint by common agreement the President of the Arbitral Tribunal and two members recognized for their competence in international law within fifteen days drawn from a list of candidates established by the President of / by the Member responsible for enlargement of the European Commission. In case that they cannot agree within this delay, the President and the two members of the Arbitral Tribunal shall be appointed by the President of the International Court of Justice from the list.
>
> (2) Each side shall appoint a further member of the Arbitral Tribunal within fifteen days after the appointments referred to in paragraph 1 have been finalised. In case that no appointment has been made within this delay, the respective member shall be appointed by the President of the Arbitral Tribunal.
>
> (3) If, whether before or after the proceedings have begun, a vacancy should occur on account of death, incapacity or resignation of a member, it shall be filled in accordance with the procedure prescribed for the original appointment. (Draft Agreement on Dispute Settlement, 15 June 2009: 1)

The above provision newly inserted by the Commission does not relate to any of the Slovenian amendments. It leaves the pre-selection of candidates for the Tribunal entirely to the Commission. This must be seen as an effort to retain some authority for the Commission over the selection process. "This provision limits the autonomy of the parties, and it was plain to see that they may perceive this as a tough move. It is crucial, however, that the Arbitration Agreement was more than a purely legal affair, and that it was something special after all" (interview Frank Hoffmeister, then European Commission Legal Service, 03-06-2016).

> Article 3: Task of the Arbitral Tribunal
>
> (1) The Arbitral Tribunal shall determine
>
> (a) the course of the maritime and land boundary between the Republic of Croatia and the Republic of Slovenia; and
>
> (b) Slovenia's *junction* to the High Seas;
>
> (c) the regime for the use of the relevant maritime areas ~~and Slovenia's contact to the High Sea~~.
>
> […] (Draft Agreement on Dispute Settlement, 15 June 2009: 2; emphasis added)

There are two new elements in this core article here. First, the link between Slovenia's territorial waters and the high seas has become a separate point. This is of relevance for two reasons, (i) since a separate point carries more weight as compared to being included as the second item of another point (as was the case in Rehn I), and (ii) inserting an additional point establishes a clear *sequence* which the Tribunal has to follow in determining the border. Second, there is a new term ("*junction*") for the link between the Slovenian territorial waters and the high seas. Obviously, "junction" moves away from the previous term "contact" in Rehn I in so far as it denounces the physical connection between two marine areas whilst keeping the notion of them being interconnected in a certain way.

"Junction" appeared to be the right term to the Commission as "it is sufficiently neutral and unclear" to be acceptable to both sides. This view entails the notion that either side can interpret "junction" in a different way, i.e. as a normative term (Slovenia) or rather as a purely factual meaning (Croatia) of some kind of link (interview Frank Hoffmeister, then European Commission Legal Service, 03-06-2016). As to "junction", Slovenia holds that it was taken from the English translation of the 2001 Draft Agreement (see Sect. 4.1.4) and submitted to the Commission during the negotiations of the Arbitration Agreement (interview senior Slovenian civil servant, 17-10-2016; see also PCA Final Award 2017: 342–344, paras 1071–1077).

On balance, it may be said with some accuracy that the Rehn II version of Article 3, whilst retaining its remarkable spirit of compromise, has shifted somewhat in favour of the Croatian position since the increased weight of the link between the Slovenian territorial waters and the high seas (through making it a separate point) appears to have been over-compensated by replacing "contact" (with a clear physical connotation) by the more neutral term "junction".

> Article 4: Applicable Law
>
> (1) The Arbitral Tribunal shall apply
>
> (a) the rules and principles of international law for the determination referred to in Article 3 (1) (a);
>
> (b) international law, equity and the principle of good neighbourly relations in order to achieve a fair and just result by taking into account all relevant circumstances for the determination referred to in Article 3 (1) (b) and (c) (Draft Agreement on Dispute Settlement, 15 June 2009: 2)

The second core article now *prima facie* features an additional criterion of flexibility for the legal framework mandating the Tribunal. Point (b) clearly takes on board the second part of the Slovenian amendment to Article 4 of Rehn I. One could, however, see the "taking into account [of] all relevant circumstances" as a mere paraphrasing of, rather than a supplement to, the preceding provisions of (b) defining the applicable law for the Tribunal as "international law, equity and the principle of good neighbourly relations in order to achieve a fair and just result" as already implying the "taking into account [of] all relevant circumstances".

It is useful to look at the underlying approach of the Commission's wording of Article 3. When drafting the provisions on the applicable law, different legal frameworks (international law, equity[55]) were twinned with more political considerations (good neighbourly relations). "With respect to the first issue [the maritime and land border; Art. 3(1)(a)], the applicable law would be restricted to international law, whereas the two other issues [Slovenia's junction (Art. 3(1)(b)), and the regime for the maritime areas (Art. 3(1)(c))] are to be decided in line with broader considerations" (European Commission internal note, undated). This approach was to "reflect the EU dimension and its political spirit" and the peculiarities of the bilateral case (interview Frank Hoffmeister, then European Commission Legal Service, 03-06-2016).

> Article 6: Procedure
>
> (1) Each side shall submit a memorial to the Arbitral Tribunal within two months after entry into force. Each side has the right to comment on the memorial of the other side within a deadline fixed by the Arbitral Tribunal.
>
> (2) Unless envisaged otherwise, the Arbitral Tribunal shall conduct the proceedings according to the Permanent Court of Arbitration Optional Rules for Arbitrating Disputes between Two States.
>
> (3) The Arbitral Tribunal may seek expert advice and organize oral hearings […].
>
> (8) The Arbitration Tribunal may at any stage of the procedure with the consent of both parties assist them in reaching a friendly settlement (Draft Agreement on Dispute Settlement, 15 June 2009: 2–3)

This additional provision reflects the Slovenian amendment to Article 6 stating that, if the parties so wish, the Tribunal stands ready to facilitate a bilateral settlement of the dispute. This enables a bilaterally negotiated agreement ahead of the conclusion of the arbitration procedure, should both parties really wish to go back to that level. The wording of Art. 6(8) does not constitute any bias vis-à-vis any of the parties. Generally, going back into the bilateral mode opens up endless opportunities for any of the parties to delay the negotiations and/or to finally not sign or ratify a bilateral deal whereas the final award of an arbitral tribunal is considered binding.

> Article 8: EU accession negotiation documents
>
> No document presented in the EU accession negotiations unilaterally shall prejudice the Arbitral Tribunal when performing its tasks or commit either side on the dispute.
>
> The above applies to all documents and positions either written or submitted orally, including, *inter alia*, maps, negotiating positions, legal acts and other documents in whatever form, produced, presented or referred to unilaterally in the framework of the EU accession negotiations. It also applies to all EU documents and positions which refer to or summarize the above-mentioned documents and positions (Draft Agreement on Dispute Settlement, 15 June 2009: 4)

The above insertion can be seen as mere clarification. The Commission made no further changes to the draft arbitration agreement.

Despite the fact that some of the amendments of the Commission could be seen as in favour of the Croatian position, in particular the new wording "junction" in

[55] For the nature of equity and its role in maritime delimitation see Sect. 3.2.1.

Article 3(1)(b), but perhaps also the "vital interests" in the Preamble, Zagreb rejected Rehn II for reasons of principle. The Sabor had already accepted Rehn I which was considered a "grand step forward" as it had moved away from the SEG approach largely based on political criteria to a proper judicial procedure mainly based on international law (internal note Ministry of Foreign Affairs Croatia 2012: 3–4). "It was impossible for the Croatian Government to ignore the vote in the [...] Sabor and re-open the Pandora box of a new wave of amendments" (internal note Ministry of Foreign Affairs Croatia 2012: 5).

Zagreb rejected Rehn II at short notice ahead of a planned trilateral meeting on Rehn II in Brussels (PCA Final Award 2017: 38, para 118). As a result, the European Commission suspended further discussions on the draft arbitration agreement on 16 June 2009 (European Commission internal note, undated). There are, however, different interpretations as to under what circumstances exactly the negotiations broke down. Slovenia argued that Croatia had informed Slovenia and the Commission that it was not going to continue negotiations facilitated by the Commission, whilst Croatia held that, in view of negative replies to Rehn II from both parties, the Commission itself suspended further efforts (PCA Final Award 2017: 38, para 118, footnote 240).

4.2.5 Final Phase

The Croatian Prime Minister Ivo Sanader unexpectedly resigned on 1 July 2009, largely on the grounds that he had not managed to lift the Slovenian veto and that, after all, the EU accession of Croatia had always meant a "life-time project" to him (interview Ivo Sanader, 19-05-2016). Jadranka Kosor became the new Croatian Prime Minister. Bilateral relations appeared to have entered a new phase, mainly for two reasons:

First, the working atmosphere between Pahor and Sanader had always been perceived as difficult by both sides (interview Ivo Sanader, 02-11-2017; interview Borut Pahor, 20-06-2017) and there had been a fundamental disagreement between the two prime ministers on the nexus between EU enlargement and the resolution of the bilateral border dispute. Whilst Slovenia insisted on the *quid pro quo* approach. i.e. Croatia receives EU membership in return for the Slovenian junction to the high seas (interview senior Slovenian civil servant, 17-10-2016), Sanader had always fiercely rejected that package deal. Sanader's position was that the solution of the bilateral border dispute cannot be a precondition for Croatia as it was not one for Slovenia either by the time they joined the EU in the first place (interview Ivo Sanader, 02-11-2017). This clash of positions had become evident at a bilateral meeting at Mokrice Castle on 24 February 2009 when Pahor and Sanader were discussing an early mediation effort by EU Commissioner Rehn (see Sect. 4.2.2.3; interview senior Slovenian civil servant, 24-01-2017; internal note Ministry of Foreign Affairs Croatia 2012: 3).

Second, there appears to have been a mutual sense of having to restore bilateral relations. Both parties felt they were damaging their reputation on the international stage and doing harm to their economies. Croatia was increasingly worried about "losing its European perspective" (internal note Ministry of Foreign Affairs Croatia 2012: 5), whereas Slovenia "felt awkward with the stalemate" over the border dispute (interview Frank Belfrage, State Secretary in the Foreign Ministry of Sweden in charge of the file at the time, 26-04-2017). What contributed to a renewed spirit of bilateralism was the fact that the Swedish Presidency holding office in the second half of 2009 made it clear that it was now up to Croatia and Slovenia to find a solution (internal note Ministry of Foreign Affairs Croatia 2012: 5). However, the Swedish Presidency was happy to facilitate not least because it was in favour of EU enlargement anyway (interview Frank Belfrage, 26-04-2017).

4.2.5.1 Unblocking the Veto

In early July 2009, Pahor phoned his counterpart Kosor expressing his readiness to meet soon. During a subsequent exploratory visit of Kosor's advisor to Ljubljana, it became clear that Pahor was worried about a potential escalation of bilateral tensions on the face of the arrest of a Croatian war veteran by the Slovenian police at the Dobava rail border crossing on 11 July 2009. It turned out that the man was going to attempt to assassinate Pahor. The Slovenian Prime Minister assured Kosor's advisor that he had a friendly attitude towards Croatia, whilst Kosor let it be known that she was aiming to build bilateral relations based on mutual respect and a search for a win-win situation rather than continuing the win-lose approach (internal note Ministry of Foreign Affairs Croatia 2012: 6). Pahor's feeling was that the fact that Kosor was at the head of the Croatian government was a "golden opportunity" to finish off the Croatian accession negotiations (interview senior Slovenian civil servant, 24-01-2017).

It is vital to note that the essential point of the new bilateral approach was to aim at a *reversal* of the previous order of tackling the two main issues. Instead of solving the border issue first and subsequently lifting the veto, the new approach now was to remove the Slovenian reservations by clearing the potentially pre-judging aspects of the Croatian accession documents first to subsequently be able to agree on the terms of the arbitration agreement in a less heated atmosphere. "The timing and the sequencing proved very sensitive, but there emerged a common understanding that the eventual arbitral award had to be de-coupled from Croatia's accession negotiations, and that all this ought to be beneficially face-saving for both sides" (interview Frank Belfrage, 26-04-2017).

The meeting between Kosor and Pahor took place on 31 July 2009 at Trakošćan Castle. There was a solid tête-à-tête where it became clear that Pahor and Kosor were on good terms. A joint understanding was developing that the issue of the border had to be solved at the prime minister level and that arbitration, whilst it would have been unimaginable to agree on it bilaterally in 2008, was now the best way forward (interview Borut Pahor, 20-06-2017), and that "we were courageous enough to do it" (interview Jadranka Kosor, 07-06-2016).[56]

At the Trakošćan meeting, the following points were agreed on:

- the Slovenian reservations would be lifted as soon as the Croatian Prime Minister sent a letter to the Swedish Presidency clearing the issue of the allegedly pre-judging Croatian accession documents;
- the letter would be jointly drafted by a Silent Diplomacy Group[57];
- negotiations on the Arbitration Agreement would resume on the basis of Rehn II as soon as the Slovenian veto was lifted;
- Croatia insisted on a statement on the Arbitration Agreement not pre-judging "territorial contact" of Slovenia with the high seas; and
- the Arbitral Tribunal's award should be rendered *after* Croatia's accession to the EU (interview senior Slovenian civil servant, 24-01-2017; internal note Ministry of Foreign Affairs Croatia 2012: 5).

The drafting of the letter was supposed to be finished by the end of August. Against initial expectations, however, it was by no means a walk in the park given the still existing level of suspicion and sensitivities on either side. Nevertheless, the level of personal trust between the negotiators was constantly growing and it was crucial for the Swedish Presidency to feed the notion of "joint ownership" of an agreement on both the letter and the final Arbitration Agreement (interview Frank Belfrage, 26-04-2017).

The basic challenge with the letter was that "we knew that Pahor was committed to the Trakošćan process, but would seek our assurances that Croatia will not walk away from the negotiations [on the Arbitration Agreement] once the blockage was lifted" (internal note Ministry of Foreign Affairs Croatia 2012: 8). What added to this difficulty of principle caused by the new sequence of tackling the two major issues was that Pahor was also under pressure domestically. Janez Janša, Pahor's predecessor and leader of the main opposition party SDS, wanted the border issue to be solved ahead of Croatian EU accession (interview senior Slovenian civil servant, 24-01-2017).

At the end of the day, the Slovenian Prime Minister consented to holding a meeting in Ljubljana on 11 September 2009 where the lifting of the Slovenian reservations and the re-start of the negotiations over the Arbitration Agreement should be made public. Subsequently, representatives of Pahor and Kosor went to see the Swedish Prime Minister Fredrik Reinfeldt in Stockholm to inform him of the upcoming Ljubljana meeting and the announcement about the veto being lifted and the resumption of the *travaux préparatoires* on the arbitration agreement. The texts of both (i) the

[56]Jadranka Kosor did, however, share her predecessor Ivo Sanader's view to consider it "unfair that the border dispute was not an issue when Slovenia joined the EU" (interview Jadranka Kosor, 07-06-2016).

[57]The Group was composed of State Secretary Iztok Mirošič and foreign policy advisor Marko Makovec for Slovenia, and for the Croatian side of State Secretary Davor Božinović and foreign policy advisor Davor Stier.

Kosor letter clarifying the non-prejudging nature of the Croatian accession documents and the continuation of the negotiations on the Arbitration Agreement and (ii) Reinfeldt's reply were presented to him, including the new timetable for obtaining the arbitral tribunal's award after Croatia's accession to the EU. Reinfeldt welcomed the agreement, which turned into a major achievement of the Swedish Presidency (internal note Ministry of Foreign Affairs Croatia 2012: 8).

The letter was finally sent to Reinfeldt from Pahor's office minutes before the meeting of Pahor and Kosor in Ljubljana on 11 September 2009, which was considered "a major break-through" (interview senior Slovenian civil servant, 24-01-2017). The letter is worth quoting:

> [W]ith the aim of addressing Slovenia's reservations on several negotiating chapters, on behalf of the Croatian Government, I would like to declare that no document in our accession negotiations with the European Union can prejudge the final resolution of the border dispute between Croatia and Slovenia. The above applies to all documents and positions either written or submitted orally, including, *inter alia*, maps, negotiating positions, legal acts and other documents in whatever form, produced, presented or referred to by the Republic of Croatia in the framework of the EU accession negotiations. It also applies to all EU documents and positions which refer to or summarize the above-mentioned documents and positions.[58]
>
> The resolution, or the way of resolution of the border dispute will be pursued through the continuation of the talks between Croatia and Slovenia facilitated by the European Union. It was also agreed that both sides will continue [the] negotiations on [the] border dispute settlement with the understanding either to submit the border dispute to the Arbitral Tribunal or to conclude [a] bilateral agreement on [the] common State border [...]. Both sides also agreed that 25 June 1991 presents the basis for the resolution of the border dispute and that no document or action undertaken unilaterally by either side after that date shall be accorded legal significance for the tasks of any arbitral tribunal, or any other procedure relating to the settlement of the border dispute between Croatia and Slovenia, which will be entitled by Croatia and Slovenia to resolve the border dispute, and cannot, in any way, prejudge the outcome of the process.
>
> Having in mind that we have properly addressed Slovenia's concerns related to the prejudices on the border between Croatia and Slovenia, we kindly invite the Swedish Presidency to convene an Inter-Governmental Conference in order to immediately resume Croatia's accession negotiations with the European Union. (Letter from Kosor to Reinfeldt, 11 September 2009)

Reinfeldt's reply, sent three days later, was as follows:

> The Swedish Presidency welcomes your letter, which properly addressed Slovenia's reservations on prejudices on the border between Croatia and Slovenia in negotiating chapters.
>
> Having consulted the Republic of Slovenia and with the understanding that the guarantees given by the Republic of Croatia are sufficient for lifting its reservations on the opening and closing of the negotiating chapters related to Slovenia's reservations on prejudices on the border between Croatia and Slovenia, the Swedish Presidency will therefore convene on 2 October 2009 an Inter-Governmental Conference to resume Croatia's accession negotiations with the EU.

---

[58]The wording on the non-prejudging nature of the documents and positions is very similar to the 3rd paragraph of the (draft) "Letter from the Presidency of the EU Council to Croatia" in 4.2.2.2.

> The Swedish Presidency takes note that both sides agreed to continue negotiations on the border dispute settlement, under the facilitation of the Presidency of the EU with the understanding either to submit the border dispute to the Arbitral Tribunal or to conclude [a] bilateral agreement on [the] common State border [...]. The continuation of the negotiations between Croatia and Slovenia on the border dispute shall be convened simultaneously with the IGC.
>
> It is understood that both letters present integral part of the accession documents of the IGC on Croatia's accession to the European Union. (Letter from Reinfeldt to Kosor, 15 September 2009)

At the actual Ljubljana meeting on 11 September 2009, Kosor and Pahor managed to sustain their good terms despite the fierce respective domestic opposition to the compromise. They announced that the Slovenian reservations would now be officially lifted and that the talks over the Arbitration Agreement would resume.

4.2.5.2 Road to Stockholm

Both issues materialised on 2 October 2009 when the respective negotiating Chapters with Croatia were opened or closed at an Intergovernmental Conference (IGC) in Brussels. On the sidelines of that IGC, a first trilateral meeting of the Croatian and Slovenian delegations with the Swedish foreign minister Carl Bildt plus Commissioner Rehn took place where Rehn II was on the table again. Participants did discuss a number of items based on a slightly amended Commission draft from 30 September 2009.

As for Article 2 (Composition of the Arbitral Tribunal), it was debated whether it should be the President of the European Commission or rather the Commissioner for Enlargement who would be in charge of drawing up the list of candidates. No agreement was reached. In the same vein, it was discussed whether the President of the International Court of Justice (ICJ) should be attributed the role of last instance in the appointment procedure, as set out in Rehn II. Again, no mutual consent could be reached. However, in relation to Article 6 (Procedure), the parties' preparation period for the memorials to be submitted to the Tribunal was extended from two to twelve months.[59] With regard to the timelines for the Tribunal (Article 7), the initial angle of the discussion centred around the deadline within which the Tribunal was to issue its award. To that end, the Commission had revised Rehn II as follows:

> Article 7: The award of the Arbitral Tribunal
>
> (1) The Arbitral Tribunal shall strive to issue its award expeditiously after due consideration of all relevant facts pertinent to the case ~~within one year after its establishment~~. The Arbitral. Tribunal adopts the award by majority of its members [...]
> (Internal note European Commission, undated)

This point was discussed in more detail at the 2 October 2009 meeting. There was a joint understanding that the aim of Article 7 was for the arbitral award to be delivered

[59] It had become evident that the files could not possibly be prepared within a few weeks. Memorials tend to comprise not only the legal *argumentaire*, but also some detailed documentation of the history of the subject matter including archive material, such as maps or documents many of which had to be translated into English.

after the accession of Croatia to the EU. No agreement could be reached, however, on the wording. Croatia favoured "expeditiously" to be replaced by "within three years", Slovenia would accept a maximum of two years.[60] The issue was referred to a subsequent technical meeting the following week (European Commission internal note, undated). At the end of the day, it proved impossible to meet the ambitions expectations on the part of the Swedish foreign minister to arrive at a mutual consent on the full text of the Arbitration Agreement already during the 2 October meeting (internal note Ministry of Foreign Affairs Croatia 2012: 9).

As for the main facilitating third party in the final phase of the negotiations over the Arbitration Agreement, it must be noted that the subsequent phase was predominantly conducted on the bilateral level with the Swedish Presidency in a facilitating role.

Both parties considered the Swedish EU Presidency as a remarkably valuable facilitator in that respect. The Swedish diplomacy appeared well aware of the sensitivities of both Slovenia and Croatia and of the challenges ahead, played a very objective role, and was unanimously appreciated by both sides (interview senior Slovenian civil servant, 24-01-2017; interview senior Croatian civil servant, 25-01-2017). So was the effort and the role of Olli Rehn in the preceding months, who was perceived as acting with a sense of fairness and tact and with no secret agenda (interview Borut Pahor, 20-06-2017; interview Ivo Sanader, 19-05-2016).

The European Commission obviously played a less active role after the breakdown of the talks over Rehn II (see Sect. 4.2.4), but was kept in the loop at all times (e.g. Swedish Ministry for Foreign Affairs fax to Olli Rehn, 25 September 2009; internal e-mail European Commission, 29 October 2009; interview Frank Belfrage, 26-04-2017). As a new feature, Croatia and Slovenia, at the request of Zagreb, introduced the practice of also keeping the US diplomacy in the loop as a neutral witness (interview senior Slovenian civil servant, 24-01-2017; internal note Ministry of Foreign Affairs Croatia 2012: 10).[61]

As for the remainder of the negotiations, there was mutual consent to start out from Rehn II as the basis (see Sect. 4.2.4), but not to touch on the previously hotly disputed Articles 3 (task of the Tribunal) and 4 (applicable law) any more (European Commission internal note, undated), and to finalise the Arbitration Agreement by November (interview senior Slovenian civil servant, 24-01-2017).

There were three outstanding issues to be tackled at a number of meetings taking place in turn in official residences in Croatia and Slovenia:

(i) the composition of the Arbitral Tribunal (Article 2);
(ii) the non-prejudging issue of the Slovenian territorial contact; and

---

[60] One must bear in mind that, in the autumn of 2009, the EU accession date for Croatia was not yet clear. In addition, the expectation at the time was that the Arbitration Agreement was going to be ratified and enter into force swiftly after its signature, i.e. by the end of 2009.

[61] For the *notes verbales* between the Croatian Ministry of Foreign and European Affairs and the Embassies of the Kingdom of Sweden and the United States of America, the diplomatic cables between the Croatian Ministry of Foreign and European Affairs and the US Embassy in Zagreb, and the diplomatic cables between the US Embassies in Ljubljana and Zagreb to the US State Department see PCA Final Award 2017: 41, footnote 254.

(iii) the timelines for the Tribunal (Article 7).

It turned out that whereas the issue of non-prejudgement could only be resolved by a unilateral declaration[62] by the Sabor on the occasion of the Croatian ratification of the Arbitration Agreement, the two other issues had to be resolved in the text of the Agreement itself.

As for the composition of the Tribunal (Article 2), the question of who in the European Commission would be in charge of drawing up a list of candidates was solved through a compromise. Both the President and the Enlargement Commissioner were entrusted with that task. The President of the International Court of Justice (ICJ) was confirmed as the last instance of the appointment procedure to secure qualified judges as members for the Tribunal (internal e-mail European Commission, 29 October 2009).

With regard to the timelines, a new approach was chosen to safeguard the aim of delivering the award only *after* the accession of Croatia to the EU. Article 7(1) was left as it read in the most recent Commission draft ("The Arbitral Tribunal shall strive to issue its award *expeditiously* after due consideration of all relevant facts [...]"; emphasis added). Instead, a new provision was inserted into Article 11. Croatia's initial position was that the Arbitration Agreement should enter into force on the day of Croatia's EU accession. Slovenia's initial stance was that the Arbitration Agreement should enter into force right after its ratification. The compromise formula agreed on in the end was that all timelines relating to the arbitration procedure would start on the day of signing Croatia's EU Accession Treaty (internal note Ministry of Foreign Affairs Croatia 2012: 11; interview senior Slovenian civil servant, 24-01-2017).

It must be noted, that the (technical) decoupling of the Croatian EU accession from the arbitration procedure as such was largely seen as the main "face-saving opportunity" for both parties (interview senior Croatian civil servant, 25-01-2017; interview senior Slovenian civil servant, 24-01-2017; interview Frank Belfrage, 26-04-2017). On the one hand, Slovenia was lifted of the burden of the role of holding Croatian EU accession hostage to the solution of the bilateral border issue, whilst at the same time receiving a binding Arbitration Agreement that incorporated the gist of Slovenia's vital interest in terms of mandating the Tribunal to create some form of link between the Slovenian territorial sea and the high seas. On the other hand, the obstacle for Croatia's EU accession was removed, Croatia's EU membership was virtually guaranteed, and the Arbitration Agreement provided for a proper judicial procedure where international law and the territorial integrity of Croatia played a strong role.

---

[62]Croatia initially aimed at including the declaration on the non-predetermining issue of the Slovenian territorial contact in the actual Arbitration Agreement in some form. This was not acceptable to Slovenia, however, as it was regarded as a matter for the domestic Croatian ratification process. The US and Sweden were to witness the unilateral declaration (internal note Ministry of Foreign Affairs Croatia 2012: 7; European Commission internal note, undated; interview senior Slovenian civil servant, 24-01-2017).

The concluding agreement was reached on 26 October 2009 at a meeting between Kosor and Pahor in Zagreb (Hoffmeister 2012: 103). The Arbitration Agreement (see Appendix A) was signed by the two prime ministers and witnessed by Reinfeldt on 4 November 2009 in Stockholm. It must be noted, however, that regardless of the high level of mutual personal trust within the bilateral Silent Diplomacy Group, the two parties were still somewhat "suspicious of one another" at the political level which manifested itself in last-minute phone-calls by the foreign ministers to the Swedish Presidency on the morning of 4 November, the day the Arbitration Agreement was to be signed (interview Frank Belfrage, 26-04-2017). Croatia ratified the Arbitration Agreement together with the unilateral Declaration on 20 November 2009,[63] the Slovenian parliament ratified on 19 April 2010 together with a Declaration in disagreement with Croatia's Declaration.[64] After the legislative referendum in Slovenia on 6 June 2010,[65] the Arbitration Agreement entered into force on 29 November 2010. On 25 May 2011, the Agreement was jointly submitted to the Secretary General of the United Nations (PCA Final Award 2017: 43–6, paras 132–143). Table 4.1 provides an overview of the drafting stages of the Arbitration Agreement.

4.2.6 Setting up the Arbitral Tribunal

The signature of the Treaty of Accession of Croatia to the EU on 9 December 2011[66] triggered the timelines laid down in Article 11 of the Arbitration Agreement.

The first task to be accomplished was the composition of the Arbitral Tribunal pursuant to Article 2. To that end, the two Foreign Ministers, Samuel Žbogar (Slovenia) and Vesna Pusić (Croatia), came to Brussels for a trilateral meeting with the sitting EU Commissioner for Enlargement, Štefan Füle, in early January 2012.

[63]The core element of the declaration reads: "Nothing in the Arbitration Agreement between the Government of the Republic of Croatia and the Government of the Republic of Slovenia shall be understood as Croatia's consent to Slovenia's claim to its territorial contact with the high seas" (*Note verbale* Ministry of Foreign and European Affairs of Croatia to the Embassy of Slovenia in Zagreb, No. 6257/09, 9 November 2009).

[64]In relation to the above declaration of Croatia, Slovenia insisted that "in accordance with international law the unilateral statement given with respect to the [...] Arbitration Agreement cannot affect its substance and considers the Statement of the Republic of Croatia from 9 November 2009 as unacceptable and without any effect for the arbitral proceedings" (*Note verbale* of the Ministry of Foreign Affairs of Slovenia to the Embassy of Croatia in Ljubljana, No. ZMP 170/09, 21 November 2009; see also Petrič 2017: 365).

[65]The result was 51.5% in favour and 48.5% against with a turnout of 42.7% (Electoral Commission of Slovenia, 6 October 2010, see https://www.dvk-rs.si/index.php/si/arhiv-referendumi/referendum-o-zakonu-o-arbitraznem-sporazumu-6-junij-2010).

[66]The Croatian accession treaty was signed by the EU Heads of State and Government, by the Croatian President and the Croatian Prime Minister at the European Council in Brussels (European Commission press release 9-12-2011; see https://europa.eu/rapid/press-release_MEMO-11-883_de.htm). The European Parliament had consented on 1 December 2011: https://www.europarl.europa.eu/sides/getDoc.do?pubRef=-//EP//TEXT+TA+P7-TA-2011-0538+0+DOC+XML+V0//EN&language=EN).

Table 4.1 Overview drafting stages Croatia–Slovenia arbitration agreement

Rehn I (First draft 23 April 2009)	**Rehn II** (Second draft 15 June 2009)	**Arbitration Agreement** (Final version 4 November 2009)
Draft Agreement on Dispute Settlement	**Draft Agreement on Dispute Settlement**	**Arbitration Agreement between the Government of the Republic of Croatia and the Government of the Republic of Slovenia***
The Governments of the Republic of Croatia and the Republic of Slovenia (hereinafter referred to as "the Parties")	The Governments of the Republic of Croatia and the Republic of Slovenia (hereinafter referred to as "the Parties")	The Governments of the Republic of Croatia and the Republic of Slovenia (hereinafter referred to as "the Parties")
Whereas through numerous attempts the parties have not resolved their territorial and maritime border dispute in the course of the past years	Whereas through numerous attempts the parties have not resolved their territorial and maritime border dispute in the course of the past years	Whereas through numerous attempts the parties have not resolved their territorial and maritime border dispute in the course of the past years
Recalling the peaceful means for the settlement of disputes enumerated in Article 33 of the UN-Charter, Affirming their commitment to a peaceful settlement of disputes, in the spirit of good neighbourly relations	Recalling the peaceful means for the settlement of disputes enumerated in Article 33 of the UN-Charter, Affirming their commitment to a peaceful settlement of disputes, in the spirit of good neighbourly relations, reflecting their vital interests	Recalling the peaceful means for the settlement of disputes enumerated in Article 33 of the UN-Charter, Affirming their commitment to a peaceful settlement of disputes, in the spirit of good neighbourly relations, reflecting their vital interests
Welcoming the facilitation offered by the European Commission	Welcoming the facilitation offered by the European Commission	Welcoming the facilitation offered by the European Commission
Have agreed as follows:	Have agreed as follows:	Have agreed as follows:
Article 1: Establishment of the Arbitral Tribunal	Article 1: Establishment of the Arbitral Tribunal	Article 1: Establishment of the Arbitral Tribunal

(continued)

Table 4.1 (continued)

The parties hereby set up an Arbitral Tribunal	The parties hereby set up an Arbitral Tribunal	The parties hereby set up an Arbitral Tribunal
Article 2: Composition of the Arbitral Tribunal	Article 2: Composition of the Arbitral Tribunal	Article 2: Composition of the Arbitral Tribunal
(1) Both parties shall appoint by common agreement the President of the Arbitral Tribunal and two members recognised for their competence in international law within fifteen days. In case that they cannot agree within this delay, the President and the two members of the Arbitral Tribunal shall be appointed by the President of the International Court of Justice	(1) Both parties shall appoint by common agreement the President of the Arbitral Tribunal and two members recognized for their competence in international law within fifteen days drawn from a list of candidates established by the President of/by the Member responsible for enlargement of the European Commission. In case that they cannot agree within this delay, the President and the two members of the Arbitral Tribunal shall be appointed by the President of the International Court of Justice from the list	(1) Both parties shall appoint by common agreement the President of the Arbitral Tribunal and two members recognized for their competence in international law within fifteen days drawn from a list of candidates established by the President of the European Commission and the Member responsible for the enlargement of the European Commission. In case that they cannot agree within this delay, the President and the two members of the Arbitral Tribunal shall be appointed by the President of the International Court of Justice from the list
(2) Each side shall appoint a further member of the Arbitral Tribunal within fifteen days after the appointments referred to in paragraph 1 have been finalised. In case that no appointment has been made within this delay, the respective member shall be appointed by the President of the Arbitral Tribunal	(2) Each side shall appoint a further member of the Arbitral Tribunal within fifteen days after the appointments referred to in paragraph 1 have been finalised. In case that no appointment has been made within this delay, the respective member shall be appointed by the President of the Arbitral Tribunal	(2) Each side shall appoint a further member of the Arbitral Tribunal within fifteen days after the appointments referred to in paragraph 1 have been finalised. In case that no appointment has been made within this delay, the respective member shall be appointed by the President of the Arbitral Tribunal

(continued)

Table 4.1 (continued)

(3) If, whether before or after the proceedings have begun, a vacancy should occur on account of the death, incapacity or resignation of a member, it shall be filled in accordance with the procedure prescribed for the original appointment	(3) If, whether before or after the proceedings have begun, a vacancy should occur on account of the death, incapacity or resignation of a member, it shall be filled in accordance with the procedure prescribed for the original appointment	(3) If, whether before or after the proceedings have begun, a vacancy should occur on account of the death, incapacity or resignation of a member, it shall be filled in accordance with the procedure prescribed for the original appointment
Article 3: Task of the Arbitral Tribunal	Article 3: Task of the Arbitral Tribunal	Article 3: Task of the Arbitral Tribunal
(1) The Arbitral Tribunal shall determine	(1) The Arbitral Tribunal shall determine	(1) The Arbitral Tribunal shall determine
(a) the course of the maritime and land boundary between the Republic of Croatia and the Republic of Slovenia; and	(a) the course of the maritime and land boundary between the Republic of Croatia and the Republic of Slovenia	(a) the course of the maritime and land boundary between the Republic of Slovenia and the Republic of Croatia
(b) the regime for the use of the relevant maritime areas and Slovenia's contact to the High Sea	(b) Slovenia's junction to the High Sea	(b) Slovenia's junction to the High Sea
	(c) the regime for the use of the relevant maritime areas	(c) the regime for the use of the relevant maritime areas
(2) The Parties shall specify the details of the subject-matter of the dispute within one month after entry into force of this Agreement. If they fail to do so, the Arbitral Tribunal shall use the submissions of the parties for the determination of the exact scope of the maritime and territorial disputes and claims between the parties	(2) The Parties shall specify the details of the subject-matter of the dispute within one month after entry into force of this Agreement. If they fail to do so, the Arbitral Tribunal shall use the submissions of the parties for the determination of the exact scope of the maritime and territorial disputes and claims between the parties	(2) The Parties shall specify the details of the subject-matter of the dispute within one month. If they fail to do so, the Arbitral Tribunal shall use the submissions of the parties for the determination of the exact scope of the maritime and territorial disputes and claims between the parties

(continued)

Table 4.1 (continued)

(3) The Arbitral Tribunal shall render an award on the dispute	(3) The Arbitral Tribunal shall render an award on the dispute	(3) The Arbitral Tribunal shall render an award on the dispute
(4) The Arbitral Tribunal has the power to interpret the present Agreement	(4) The Arbitral Tribunal has the power to interpret the present Agreement	(4) The Arbitral Tribunal has the power to interpret the present Agreement
Article 4: Applicable Law	Article 4: Applicable Law	Article 4: Applicable Law
(1) The Arbitral Tribunal shall apply	(1) The Arbitral Tribunal shall apply	(1) The Arbitral Tribunal shall apply
(a) the rules and principles of international law for the determinations referred to in Article 3 (1)(a)	(a) the rules and principles of international law for the determinations referred to in Article 3 (1)(a)	(a) the rules and principles of international law for the determinations referred to in Article 3 (1)(a)
(b) international law, equity and the principle of good neighbourly relations in order to achieve a fair and just result for the determination referred to in Article 3 (1)(b)	(b) international law, equity and the principle of good neighbourly relations in order to achieve a fair and just result by taking into account all relevant circumstances for the determinations referred to in Article 3 (1)(b) and (c)	(b) international law, equity and the principle of good neighbourly relations in order to achieve a fair and just result by taking into account all relevant circumstances for the determinations referred to in Article 3 (1)(b) and (c)
Article 5: Critical date	Article 5: Critical date	Article 5: Critical date
No document or action undertaken unilaterally by either side after 25 June 1991 shall be accorded legal significance for the tasks of the Arbitral Tribunal or commit either side on the dispute and cannot, in any way, prejudge the award	No document or action undertaken unilaterally by either side after 25 June 1991 shall be accorded legal significance for the tasks of the Arbitral Tribunal or commit either side on the dispute and cannot, in any way, prejudge the award	No document or action undertaken unilaterally by either side after 25 June 1991 shall be accorded legal significance for the tasks of the Arbitral Tribunal or commit either side on the dispute and cannot, in any way, prejudge the award

(continued)

Table 4.1 (continued)

Article 6: Procedure	Article 6: Procedure	Article 6: Procedure
(1) Each side shall submit a memorial to the Arbitral Tribunal within two months after entry into force. Each side has the right to comment on the memorial of the other side within a deadline fixed by the Arbitral Tribunal	(1) Each side shall submit a memorial to the Arbitral Tribunal within two months after entry into force. Each side has the right to comment on the memorial of the other side within a deadline fixed by the Arbitral Tribunal	(1) Each side shall submit a memorial to the Arbitral Tribunal within twelve months. Each Party has the right to comment on the memorial of the other Party within a deadline fixed by the Arbitral Tribunal
(2) Unless envisaged otherwise, the Arbitral Tribunal shall conduct the proceedings according to the Permanent Court of Arbitration Optional Rules for Arbitrating Disputes between Two States	(2) Unless envisaged otherwise, the Arbitral Tribunal shall conduct the proceedings according to the Permanent Court of Arbitration Optional Rules for Arbitrating Disputes between Two States	(2) Unless envisaged otherwise, the Arbitral Tribunal shall conduct the proceedings according to the Permanent Court of Arbitration Optional Rules for Arbitrating Disputes between Two States
(3) The Arbitral Tribunal may seek expert advice and organize oral hearings	(3) The Arbitral Tribunal may seek expert advice and organize oral hearings	(3) The Arbitral Tribunal may seek expert advice and organize oral hearings
(4) The Arbitral Tribunal shall, after consultation of the parties, decide expeditiously on all procedural matters by majority of its members	(4) The Arbitral Tribunal shall, after consultation of the parties, decide expeditiously on all procedural matters by majority of its members	(4) The Arbitral Tribunal shall, after consultation of the parties, decide expeditiously on all procedural matters by majority of its members
(5) The proceedings are confidential and shall be conducted in English	(5) The proceedings are confidential and shall be conducted in English	(5) The proceedings are confidential and shall be conducted in English
(6) The parties shall appoint representatives to act as intermediary between them and the Arbitral Tribunal. They may retain counsel to support their representative	(6) The parties shall appoint representatives to act as intermediary between them and the Arbitral Tribunal. They may retain counsel to support their representative	(6) The parties shall appoint representatives to act as intermediary between them and the Arbitral Tribunal. They may retain counsel to support their representative

(continued)

Table 4.1 (continued)

(7) The Arbitral Tribunal shall be supported by a Secretariat. The costs of the Arbitral Tribunal shall be borne in equal terms by the two parties. The parties invite the European Commission to provide secretarial support to the Arbitral Tribunal. The place of arbitration shall be Brussels, Belgium	(7) The Arbitral Tribunal shall be supported by a Secretariat. The costs of the Arbitral Tribunal shall be borne in equal terms by the two parties. The parties invite the European Commission to provide secretarial support to the Arbitral Tribunal. The place of arbitration shall be Brussels, Belgium	(7) The Arbitral Tribunal shall be supported by a Secretariat. The costs of the Arbitral Tribunal shall be borne in equal terms by the two parties. The parties invite the European Commission to provide secretarial support to the Arbitral Tribunal. The place of arbitration shall be Brussels, Belgium
	(8) The Arbitral Tribunal may at any stage of the procedure with the consent of both parties assist them in reaching a friendly settlement	(8) The Arbitral Tribunal may at any stage of the procedure with the consent of both parties assist them in reaching a friendly settlement
Article 7: The award of the Arbitral Tribunal	Article 7: The award of the Arbitral Tribunal	Article 7: The award of the Arbitral Tribunal
(1) The Arbitral Tribunal shall strive to issue its award within one year after its establishment. The Arbitral Tribunal adopts the award by majority of its members. The award shall state the reasons on which it is based. No individual or dissenting opinions shall be attached to the award	(1) The Arbitral Tribunal shall strive to issue its award within one year after its establishment. The Arbitral Tribunal adopts the award by majority of its members. The award shall state the reasons on which it is based. No individual or dissenting opinions shall be attached to the award	(1) The Arbitral Tribunal shall issue its award expeditiously after due consideration of all relevant facts pertinent to the case. The Arbitral Tribunal adopts the award by majority of its members. The award shall state the reasons on which it is based. No individual or dissenting opinions shall be attached to the award
(2) The award of the Arbitral Tribunal shall be binding on the parties and shall constitute a definitive settlement of the dispute	(2) The award of the Arbitral Tribunal shall be binding on the parties and shall constitute a definitive settlement of the dispute	(2) The award of the Arbitral Tribunal shall be binding on the parties and shall constitute a definitive settlement of the dispute

(continued)

Table 4.1 (continued)

(3) The Parties shall take all necessary steps to implement the award, including by revising national legislation, as necessary, within six months after the adoption of the award	(3) The Parties shall take all necessary steps to implement the award, including by revising national legislation, as necessary, within six months after the adoption of the award	(3) The Parties shall take all necessary steps to implement the award, including by revising national legislation, as necessary, within six months after the adoption of the award
Article 8: EU accession negotiation documents	Article 8: EU accession negotiation documents	Article 8: EU accession negotiation documents
(1) No document presented in the EU accession negotiations shall prejudice the Arbitral Tribunal when performing its tasks or commit either side on the dispute	(1) No document presented in the EU accession negotiations unilaterally shall prejudice the Arbitral Tribunal when performing its tasks or commit either side on the dispute	(1) No document presented in the EU accession negotiations shall prejudice the Arbitral Tribunal when performing its tasks or commit either side on the dispute
(2) The above applies to all documents and positions either written or submitted orally, including, *inter alia*, maps, negotiating positions, legal acts and other documents in whatever form, produced, presented or referred to in the framework of the EU accession negotiations. It also applies to all EU documents and positions which refer to or summarize the above-mentioned documents and positions	(2) The above applies to all documents and positions either written or submitted orally, including, *inter alia*, maps, negotiating positions, legal acts and other documents in whatever form, produced, presented or referred to unilaterally in the framework of the EU accession negotiations. It also applies to all EU documents and positions which refer to or summarize the above-mentioned documents and positions	(2) The above applies to all documents and positions either written or submitted orally, including, *inter alia*, maps, negotiating positions, legal acts and other documents in whatever form, produced, presented or referred to unilaterally in the framework of the EU accession negotiations. It also applies to all EU documents and positions which refer to or summarize the above-mentioned documents and positions
Article 9: The continuation of the EU accession negotiations according to the negotiating framework	Article 9: The continuation of the EU accession negotiations according to the negotiating framework	Article 9: The continuation of the EU accession negotiations according to the negotiating framework

(continued)

Table 4.1 (continued)

(1) The Republic of Slovenia shall lift its reservations as regards opening and closing of negotiation chapters where the obstacle is related to the dispute	(1) The Republic of Slovenia shall lift its reservations as regards opening and closing of negotiation chapters where the obstacle is related to the dispute	(1) The Republic of Slovenia shall lift its reservations as regards opening and closing of negotiation chapters where the obstacle is related to the dispute
(2) Both parties shall refrain from any action or statement which might negatively affect the accession negotiations	(2) Both parties shall refrain from any action or statement which might negatively affect the accession negotiations	(2) Both parties shall refrain from any action or statement which might negatively affect the accession negotiations
Article 10: Stand-still	Article 10: Stand-still	Article 10: Stand-still
(1) Both parties refrain from any action or statement which might intensify the dispute or jeopardize the work of the Arbitral Tribunal	(1) Both parties refrain from any action or statement which might intensify the dispute or jeopardize the work of the Arbitral Tribunal	(1) Both parties refrain from any action or statement which might intensify the dispute or jeopardize the work of the Arbitral Tribunal
(2) The Arbitral Tribunal has the power to order, if it considers that circumstances so require, any provisional measures it deems necessary to preserve the stand-still	(2) The Arbitral Tribunal has the power to order, if it considers that circumstances so require, any provisional measures it deems necessary to preserve the stand-still	(2) The Arbitral Tribunal has the power to order, if it considers that circumstances so require, any provisional measures it deems necessary to preserve the stand-still
Article 11	Article 11	Article 11
(1) The present Agreement on Arbitration shall be ratified expeditiously by both sides in accordance with their respective constitutional requirements	(1) The present Agreement on Arbitration shall be ratified expeditiously by both sides in accordance with their respective constitutional requirements	(1) The Agreement shall be ratified expeditiously by both sides in accordance with their respective constitutional requirements
(2) It shall enter into force on the first day of the week following the exchange of diplomatic notes with which the parties express their consent to be bound	(2) It shall enter into force on the first day of the week following the exchange of diplomatic notes with which the parties express their consent to be bound	(2) The Agreement shall enter into force on the first day of the week following the exchange of diplomatic notes with which the parties express their consent to be bound

(continued)

Table 4.1 (continued)

(3) It shall be registered with the Secretariat of the United Nations in accordance with Article 102 of the Charter of the United Nations	(3) It shall be registered with the Secretariat of the United Nations in accordance with Article 102 of the Charter of the United Nations	(3) All procedural timelines expressed in this Agreement shall start to apply from the date of the signature of Croatia's EU Accession Treaty
		(4) The Agreement shall be registered with the Secretariat of the United Nations in accordance with Article 102 of the Charter of the United Nations
Article 12	Article 12	
The Agreement on Arbitration is drawn up in three originals in the English, Croatian and Slovenian language, the texts in each of these languages being equally authentic. In case of any divergence the English version shall prevail	The Agreement on Arbitration is drawn up in three originals in the English, Croatian and Slovenian language, the texts in each of these languages being equally authentic. In case of any divergence the English version shall prevail	
Done at Brussels on []	Done at Brussels on []	Done at Stockholm on 4 November 2009 in three originals in English language
Signed by	Signed by	Signed by
For Croatia For Slovenia	For Croatia For Slovenia	For Croatia *Jadranka Kosor* For Slovenia *Borut Pahor*
Witnessed by For the European Commission For the French Republic For the Czech Republic For the Kingdom of Sweden	Witnessed by For the European Commission For the French Republic For the Czech Republic For the Kingdom of Sweden	Witnessed by For the Presidency of the Council of the European Union, *Frederik Reinfeldt*

*Parties in alphabetical order. The Arbitration Agreement was signed in three originals in English. In fact, the order of the Parties in the headline of the Agreement alternated in the respective Parties' copy; see Appendix A (Annexes HRLA-75 and SI-395 of the 2017 Final Award)

Source Author

The two parties had made their choice as for the composition of the President of the Tribunal and the two further members according to Article 2(1) of the Arbitration Agreement and submitted—by means of sealed envelopes—the names chosen from a list set up by the European Commission.[67] Croatia and Slovenia happened to agree on Gilbert Guillaume, a former President of the International Court of Justice (ICJ) 2000–2003 and a judge at the Court 1987–2005, as President of the Tribunal, and on Bruno Simma, who was an ICJ judge 2003–2012, as members of the Arbitral Tribunal (interview senior Croatian civil servant, 25-01-2017; interview senior Slovenian civil servant, 24-01-2017; interview European Commission civil servant, 05-07-2017).

Nevertheless, there appeared to be some disagreement as to the way forward in relation to identifying the remaining Tribunal member alongside President Guillaume and Simma. Commissioner Füle insisted on coming forward with a proposal, whilst Foreign Minister Pusić clearly favoured a bilateral agreement with her Slovenian counterpart Žbogar. Both ministers agreed to meet shortly, to bring along their lists, and to agree on the third tribunal member. The meeting which took place in Otočec, Slovenia, a little later in January 2012, was described as very constructive and positive by both sides. After a brief discussion both ministers agreed on Vaughan Lowe, who is a Professor Emeritus of Public International Law, as the third member of the arbitral tribunal (interview Vesna Pusić, 24-02-2017; interview senior Slovenian civil servant 24-01-2017; see also PCA Final Award 2017: 47, para 146).

Both governments subsequently nominated one party-appointed arbitrator each according to Article 2(2) of the Arbitration Agreement. Slovenia appointed Jernej Sekolec, an independent arbitrator of Slovene nationality, on 26 January 2012; Croatia appointed Budislav Vukas, Member of the International Tribunal of the Law of the Sea (ITLOS) 1996–2005 and a Croat national, on 31 January 2012 (see also PCA Final Award 2017: 47, para 147).

4.3 Arbitral Proceedings Before the Permanent Court of Arbitration

At this moment, it is worth briefly recalling a few basic general features of arbitration and the origins of the Permanent Court of Arbitration (PCA).

[67] Olli Rehn had previously provided a list of eight names in a letter to both foreign ministers on 11 June 2009. The list contained Marie Gotton Jacobson (Sweden), Georg Nolte (Germany), Sir Michael Wood (UK), Rolf Einar Fife (Norway), Johan Gerrit Lammers (Netherlands), Erik Franckx (Belgium), Robert Badinter (France), and Nicolas Michel of Switzerland (speaking note European Commission civil servant for a meeting in the European Parliament, 10 November 2009). The European Commission consulted the ICJ when drawing up the list (interview European Commission civil servant, 05-07-2017).

4.3.1 Features of Arbitration

Arbitration can be seen as a most mature means of dispute settlement, and it dates back to 1794 when the UK and the USA, by means of the Jay Treaty, first formed panels of national experts appointed by the two States. The aim was to resolve a number of outstanding disputes between the two countries with regard to the border with Canada and claims of USA and UK citizens (Indlekofer 2013: 24–7; Bantekas 2015: 1–4).

Generally, arbitration tends to be used for subject matters that are of a legal nature, but need to be solved through a binding decision by a third-party judicial body, in this case an arbitral tribunal. The political aim often is to settle a dispute in order to improve or restore bilateral relations (Merrills 2014: 4; 2010: 568)[68] notwithstanding the fact that there are considerably more cases that are resolved by bilateral negotiations and diplomacy than through litigation by international courts or tribunals (Scott 2014: 24).

One distinctive feature of arbitration is that the parties define the mandate of the arbitral tribunal, i.e. the questions the parties want the tribunal to answer and the criteria to be used to arrive at the final verdict. Thus, the mandate for the judicial body establishes both the scope of the arbitrators' jurisdiction and the applicable law (Tanaka 2018b: 116–118; Merrills 2014: 4–5). It is vital to note that the parties can require that the arbitral tribunal apply specific rules on wider considerations other than international law (Tanaka 2018b: 106). Scope and applicable law are one aspect of the parties exercising control over the process of arbitration.

Another feature of control over the process is that the parties nominate the arbitrators. This is usually done in two ways. First, the parties jointly agree on several members of the tribunal. Second, each party nominates one party-appointed arbitrator. It is of fundamental importance that, in so proceeding, the subject matter in question is considered to be going to be dealt with by a tribunal that commands the parties' trust (Tanaka 2018b: 106; Mourre 2010; Merrills 2010: 568). It has become standard practice in State-to-State arbitration to have a Tribunal composed of three arbitrators and two party-appointed arbitrators, although three- or seven-member tribunals have also recently been in operation.[69]

[68]For territorial issues in particular, Brilmayer and Faure (2014: 195–6) posit three basic assumptions: (i) the uniqueness of territory (territory has a strong emotional component as people care about their homeland, and once territory is lost the grievance can last for several generations), (ii) judicial dispute settlement as a maximization strategy (if diplomacy is difficult and war is not on the cards, the acquisition of territory through third-party adjudication may be a viable alternative), (iii) avoidance of jurisdiction (territorial disputes are zero-sum by nature, so if one State can expect to gain, the other State will try to avoid adjudication).

[69]Inter-State cases recently administered by or ongoing at the PCA at the time of writing include six five-member tribunals (Ukraine v. Russia, Italy v. India, Croatia v. Slovenia, Mauritius v. United Kingdom, Netherlands v. Russia, and Bangladesh v. India), two three-member tribunals (Malta v. São Tomé and Príncipe, Ecuador v. United States), and one seven-member tribunals (Pakistan v. India); see https://pca-cpa.org/en/cases/.

Fundamentally, arbitration plays a solid role in the dispute resolution toolbox of the United Nations Convention on the Law of the Sea (UNCLOS; see Sect. 3.2.2.1).[70]

State-to-State arbitration does have its limitations, however. Negotiations in the diplomatic field account for a maximum degree of control over the process by the parties, whereas once the process of setting up an arbitral tribunal is over, so is direct control by the parties. A further weakness is that regardless of the task of arbitration to produce a binding settlement of a case, and unlike in commercial arbitration where the recognition and enforcement of foreign arbitral awards is considered truly global (Bantekas 2015: 223–7),[71] enforcement in State-to-State arbitration cannot be guaranteed (Merrills 2010: 569).[72] In a world of sovereign States, arbitration must rely "for its effectiveness on responsible behaviour from the parties" (Merrills 2014: 7).

The Permanent Court of Arbitration (PCA) is the oldest existing dispute settlement body in the world. It was established in 1899 following the Hague Peace Conference the same year, which had adopted a Convention for the Peaceful Settlement of International Disputes. The Convention created the PCA, which subsequently enjoyed a first "Golden Age" until the creation of the Permanent Court of International Justice (PCIJ), the judicial institution of the League of Nations, in 1922 (Indlekofer 2013: 42–69), and precursor to the International Court of Justice (ICJ) founded in 1945. Several reforms were carried out in the 1990s to render the PCA more attractive. The adoption of a number of optional rules and guidelines facilitated the use of arbitration (Tanaka 2018b: 109) and rendered arbitration a popular means of contemporary judicial dispute settlement.

4.3.2 *Written Memorials 2013 and Hearing 2014*

Following the appointment of the members of the arbitral tribunal at the end of January 2012, the Tribunal held a first procedural meeting with the Parties on 13 April 2012. After a brief discussion of the procedural framework, the Arbitral Tribunal endorsed a proposal from the Parties for the following calendar for the pleadings: The Parties' first written memorials would be simultaneously submitted on 11 February 2013, and the Parties' counter-memorials were going to be submitted simultaneously

[70] Inter-State-arbitration must be distinguished from investor-State (or mixed) arbitration between a State and an individual or a company, and, closely related, commercial arbitration between individual corporations. There are countless examples in the world of politics and business. For a contemporary and comprehensive survey see Moses (2017).

[71] Recognition and enforcement of awards in commercial arbitration are governed by the 1958 New York Convention which has been ratified by 157 States (as of 30 September 2018). For the Convention see https://www.uncitral.org/uncitral/de/uncitral_texts/arbitration/NYConvention.html.

[72] Judgements of the International Court of Justice (ICJ), however, may be enforced by the UN Security Council (Scott 2014: 28). Yet, such enforcement decision requires unanimity amongst its permanent members.

on 11 November 2013. A hearing was scheduled for the spring of 2014 (PCA press release 13 April 2012; see also Article 6(1) of the Arbitration Agreement), and the Tribunal reserved the period from 26 May to 13 June 2014 for a hearing (PCA Final Award 2017: 48, para 153).

It must be noted that, pursuant to Article 6(5) of the Arbitration Agreement, the proceedings of the arbitration were confidential, so none of the submissions by the Parties are in the public domain except for the maps both Parties submitted for the purposes of the determination of the land border.[73] Therefore, any insight into the actual proceedings is somewhat limited to the official communication by the PCA and the Parties, and to pieces of information provided to the author by the Parties. In addition, some of the contents of the Parties' submissions is disclosed *ex-post* by "The Parties' Legal Arguments" in the Partial Award (PCA Partial Award 2016: 20–36, paras 87–140) and from "The Parties' Positions"/"Croatia's Position"/Slovenia's Position" throughout large parts of the Final Award (see PCA Final Award 2017: 69–359).

4.3.2.1 Written Memorials and Counter-Memorials

In the submissions of a judicial procedure, each of the Parties usually starts out with its so-called Requests where they state what they wish the Tribunal to adjudge and declare. In the following, the Requests of Croatia and Slovenia shall be summarised as for the *maritime* border. The *land* border requests will be neglected here as the corresponding maps were made public by the Tribunal with the consent of the Parties (see previous footnote).

Croatia's Requests

With regard to maritime delimitation, Croatia, in its Memorial and Counter-Memorial, requested the Tribunal to adjudge and declare that

(i) the delimitation in the Bay and of the territorial sea outside the Bay followed a simplified equidistance line starting from the mouth of the Dragonja (St. Odoric's Canal) to the sea border with Italy;
(ii) the "Junction to the High Seas" under Article 3(1)(b) of the Arbitration Agreement did "not imply or allow any territorial contact between Slovenia and the High Seas";
(iii) pursuant to Article 3(1)(b) and (c) the Junction and the regime for the relevant maritime areas "shall be, *mutatis mutandis*, […] the regime of innocent passage

[73]Slovenia submitted a document of 46 maps (numbered from the tri-point with Hungary to Piran Bay) as a part of the requests of the Slovenian memorial from 11 February 2013. Croatia submitted a document of 45 maps (numbered from Piran Bay to the tri-point with Hungary) as a part of the requests of the Croatian counter-memorial from 11 November 2013. Both documents are accessible on https://pca-cpa.org/en/cases/3/.

through international straits, as […] in Article 45 [UNCLOS], and subject to the […] IMO traffic separation scheme[74] […]" (PCA Final Award 2017: 60, para 210).

Slovenia's Requests

As for the maritime border, Slovenia requested the Tribunal to adjudge and declare that

(i) the Bay "has the status of Slovenian internal waters and is closed by a straight baseline connecting the most prominent points on the coasts of the Madona and Savudrija promontories";
(ii) with regard to the territorial sea boundary, the border runs from Cape Savudrija in a west-southwest direction up to a point three miles from the Treaty of Osimo line and then, in a three-mile-distance parallel to the Osimo line further south west to a point 12 nautical miles off the Croatian coast south of Poreč [sic];
(iii) Slovenia's Junction to the high seas goes from the southern limits of its territorial sea to the Osimo line between Italy and the former SFRY;
(iv) the regime for the use of the relevant maritime areas enables Slovenian fishermen to "enjoy their historical fishing rights in Croatia's territorial waters, which are also guaranteed by [Croatia's EU Accession Treaty] and the 1997 [SOPS] Agreement […]"; the corridor between Slovenia's territorial sea and the high seas constitutes high seas "within which Slovenia possesses sovereign rights over the continental shelf (sea bed and sub-soil)" (PCA Final Award 2017: 65–6, para 216).

Corresponding to (i) above, one Slovenian *land* border request needs to be mentioned here, namely the one running along the Croatian shores of Piran Bay, as Slovenia claims the Bay in its entirety. As a result, the land border, according to the Slovenian request, after reaching the Bay, "follows the coast of the Savudrija peninsula to the most prominent point of the Savudrija promontory […]" (PCA Final Award 2017: 63, para 214).

4.3.2.2 Hearing 2014

The hearing took place from 2 to 13 June 2014 at the PCA in The Hague, the Netherlands, where the Tribunal members put questions to the Parties to which they

[74] A Traffic Separation Scheme (TSS) in the Northern Adriatic which was confirmed by the International Maritime Organisation (IMO) on 28 May 2004 has been in force since 1 December 2004. The TSS regulates navigation for maritime vessels to and from the ports of Trieste and Monfalcone (Italy) and Koper (Slovenia). There are designated sea lanes crossing the respective territorial sea of Croatia, Italy and Slovenia (see Fig. 6.1. and Sect. 6.1.1.1). The separation scheme originates from a trilateral Memorandum of Understanding concluded by Croatia, Italy and Slovenia on 19 October 2000. See IMO Report of the Maritime Safety Committee on its Seventy-Eight Session, MSC 78/26 of 28 May 2004, cited in Grbec (2015: 227) and Vidas (2009: 33).

replied orally; certain technical questions were answered in writing. The Tribunal issued a summary of the Parties' positions by means of a press release on 17 June 2014 the contents of which was consented by the Parties (PCA Final Award 2017: 50–2, paras 171–3).

Croatia's Position

The Deputy Prime Minister and Minister of Foreign Affairs, Vesna Pusić, started off her country's pleadings by expressing the government's confidence in the arbitral proceedings and the importance the country and its people attached to the procedure (PCA press release, 17 June 2014: 1).

As for the applicable law, Croatia put an emphasis on Articles 3(1) and 4 of the Arbitration Agreement stressing that both the maritime and land border had to be determined first strictly applying the rules and principles of international law. Only after that boundary had so been determined could the Tribunal turn to items (b) and (c) of Article 3 regarding Slovenia's "junction to the high seas" and the "regime for the use of the relevant maritime areas". The determination of the two latter issues involved two further elements, equity and the principle of good-neighbourly relations. Croatia stressed that the two elements were to serve as a supplement to international law, not as a means to act in opposition to it. With regard to the *land* boundary, on the day of the critical date mentioned in the Arbitration Agreement, 25 June 1991, the republican boundary became the new international border between Croatia and Slovenia following the principle of *uti possidetis juris*. In practical terms, that meant that the outer limits of the respective cadastral units would define the border. To that end, Croatia urged Slovenia to give up the military post at Croatian Sveta Gera and to allow for unhindered travel between Sveti Martin na Muri and Murišće (PCA press release, 17 June 2014: 2).

In relation to maritime delimitation in particular, Croatia insisted that Article 15 of UNCLOS was the relevant rule of international law. It followed that the sea boundary, starting at the mouth of the Dragonja, had to follow the equidistance line through the Bay (which was not internal waters) and further up to the Osimo line, the sea border with Italy. According to Croatia, there were no special circumstances warranting a departure from the equidistance line (PCA press release, 17 June 2014: 2; see also Sect. 3.2.1).

With regard to the foreseen "junction", Croatia repeated its view that "junction" did *not* include the notion of territorial contact. As to the interpretation of "vital interests" mentioned in the Preamble of the Arbitration Agreement, they related to the Parties' commitment to the peaceful settlement of disputes. With regard to Croatia's vital interests in the negotiation of the Arbitration Agreement, they concerned (i) the country's territorial integrity, including its territorial sea, first of all, and (ii) EU membership (PCA Final Award 2017: 288, para 933; for maritime delimitation and Article 15 UNCLOS see also Sect. 3.2.1).

Further on the terms "junction", and "regime" (for the use of the maritime areas) referred to in Article 3(1)(b) and (c) of the Arbitration Agreement, Croatia stressed its position that they could not affect the course of the territorial sea boundary. Rather, these terms would be "limited exclusively to matters of maritime access and communications", i.e. the existing IMO Traffic Separation Scheme in the Northern Adriatic [PCA press release, 17 June 2014: 2–3; see also Section "Croatia's Requests" (iii)]. Croatia also noted that it had "legitimate interests" with regard to "security and defence concerns" and that the area south of the point where the Croatian territorial waters meet the sea border with Italy was not a relevant area in terms of the Arbitration Agreement and thus "excluded from any determinations by the Tribunal" (PCA press release, 17 June 2014: 3).

Slovenia's Position

Slovenia's Agents introduced their country's pleadings referring to the Arbitration Agreement as a compromise respecting "the vital interests of both Slovenia and Croatia". The vital interest of Slovenia was the junction in terms of "direct geographical contact" to the high seas. That link was to be determined "by applying equity and the principle of good neighbourly relations in addition to international law" as stipulated in Article 4(b) of the Arbitration Agreement. The task of establishing such direct geographical contact was the *conditio sine qua non* for Slovenia's signing and ratifying of the Arbitration Agreement. Croatia's vital interest, according to Slovenia, was to become an EU member, a condition met by the time the Arbitration Agreement was adopted. Foreign Minister Karl Erjavec said the junction to the high seas was a "*quid pro quo* for the conclusion of the Arbitration Agreement", whilst the Slovenian Agent drew on the country's wider considerations in terms of security, navigation, historic and fishing rights, environmental protection, and the notion of the Slovenian identity of a European sea-faring nation (PCA press release, 17 June 2014: 3).

As for the land boundary, Slovenia called for the delimitation of the whole land border on the basis of legal title as of the critical date 25 June 1991. In the Mura River sector and the Central sector, delimitation based on existing historic legal title should be the rule, whereas in the Istria sector (including Snežnik and the lower Dragonja) the boundary should follow the cadastre as there was "no historic root of title". The Croatian reference to Slovenian activities on Trdinov Vrh/Sveta Gera and Sveti Martin na Muri was beyond the Tribunal's task, i.e. *ultra vires* (PCA press release, 17 June 2014: 4; for the history of Istria see also Sects. 2.2–2.4).

In relation to Piran Bay, Slovenia argued it was entirely internal waters of Slovenia as during SFRY times the Bay had been both a juridical and a historic bay. The status of the Bay "did not change after the dissolution of [...] Yugoslavia" and therefore the principle of *uti possidetis juris* applied meaning it belonged to Slovenia which had "administered" the Bay from Piran for centuries (PCA press release, 17 June 2014: 4; see also Cataldi 2013: 7–8; for juridical bays see Sect. 3.1.1.2).

With regard to maritime delimitation, Slovenia addressed Article 15 UNCLOS (just as Croatia did) with an emphasis on the Article's second sentence covering special circumstances warranting a departure from the equidistance line. To that end, the Slovenia mentioned the "coastal concavity and the cut-off effect of the Istrian peninsula and Cape Savudrija", and the Slovenian continental shelf claim (PCA press release, 17 June 2014: 4).

The terms "maritime delimitation", "junction" and "regime", according to Slovenia, mentioned in Article 3(1)(a), (b) and (c) of the Arbitration Agreement, were three separate issues of one joint task the Tribunal was bound to fully comply with. As for the meaning of "junction" in particular, Slovenia argued that it would have to be "a line joining Slovenia's territorial sea to the high seas" which was an interpretation that covered both the term's ordinary meaning and "the drafting history of the Arbitration Agreement" whilst it was in line with "international law, equity and the principle of good neighbourly relations". Further, the existence of such junction would entail Slovenia not being separated from the high seas or any future economic zone.

Regarding to the regime for the use of the relevant maritime areas, Slovenia posited that the area south of the junction proposed by Slovenia, which was in line with UNCLOS, would remain high seas. That matter would go in line with Slovenia's continental shelf claim. Further, Slovenia stressed its "historic fishing rights in Croatia's territorial sea off the coast of Istria would be preserved" (PCA press release, 17 June 2014: 4).

4.3.3 *Summer of Disruption 2015*

The first time the Tribunal learnt of the fact that breaches of the confidentiality requirements of the arbitral proceedings[75] had possibly occurred was on 30 April 2015, by means of a Croatian letter including a *note verbale* (diplomatic note) to Slovenia dated 24 April 2015 (PCA Partial Award 2016: 12, para 67).[76] Foreign Minister Vesna Pusić expressed her government's concern vis-à-vis the Tribunal about two public statements of Slovenia's Foreign Minister from 7 January 2015 and 22 April 2015. The Croatian Foreign Minister also informed the President and the First Vice-President of the European Commission[77] as the Commission had facilitated the Arbitration Agreement in the first place.

[75] Article 6(5) of the Arbitration Agreement reads: "The proceedings are confidential [...]." Section 9.1 of the Terms of Appointment for the members of the arbitral tribunal stipulates that "[t]he Parties shall not engage in any oral or written communication with any member of the Arbitral Tribunal *ex parte* in connection with the subject matter of the arbitration or any procedural issues that are related to the proceedings" (Letter of the Tribunal to the Parties' Agents, 5 May 2015: 1).

[76] Another letter from the Croatian Minister for Foreign and European Affairs to the Registrar of the Arbitral Tribunal reiterating the contents was sent on 30 May 2015.

[77] Letter from the Minister of Foreign and European Affairs of Croatia to Frans Timmermans, 7 May 2015.

4.3.3.1 Statements of the Slovenian Foreign Minister

The Croatian Minister's letter to the Tribunal quotes the Foreign Minister of Slovenia saying on the TV channel SLO 3 that he

> had talks in The Hague last year. And I made it very clear to the Arbitral Tribunal[78] that if they do not fulfil this task - we in Slovenia shall consider that the Arbitral Tribunal has not executed its mandate. Because the contact with the high seas has not been determined. (Letter from the Ministry of Foreign and European Affairs of the Republic of Croatia to the Registrar of the Tribunal, 30 May 2015: 2)

With regard to another interview with the Slovenian TV on 22 April 2015, the Slovenian Foreign Minister is quoted as saying:

> According to the information that I have, which is very much unofficial, as well as on the basis of a feeling that our legal team has, being composed of the world's best renowned scholars of the law of the sea, we are somehow optimistic in a way that the Arbitral Tribunal will determine that contact with the high seas. (letter from the Ministry of Foreign and European Affairs of the Republic of Croatia to the Registrar of the Tribunal, 30 May 2015: 1)

Croatia was "deeply troubled by the language of both statements" suggesting they could be seen as "implying that one of the Parties to the proceedings may have an informal channel of communication with the Tribunal that may compromise the arbitration procedure" (letter from the Ministry of Foreign and European Affairs of the Republic of Croatia to the Registrar of the Tribunal, 30 May 2015: 2). The Croatian Foreign Minister's suspicion appears to have been triggered at an early stage already in September 2014 when she noted that the Secretary General of the Permanent Court of Arbitration (PCA) was a guest of the Slovenian government at the occasion of the annual Bled Forum (interview Vesna Pusić, 24-02-2017). Slovenia, in a reply from 1 May 2015, submitted that it "ha[d] no information whatsoever concerning the outcome of the arbitration, nor any 'informal channel' of communication with the Tribunal" (PCA Final Award 2017: 52, para 175).

The Tribunal itself sent a letter to the Parties' Agents on 5 May 2015[79] stating that

> [t]he Tribunal is seriously concerned by the suggestion that one Party would have been privy to confidential information related to the Tribunal's deliberations. The Tribunal considers that such a meaning could be attributed to statements by the Slovenian Foreign Minister, and takes the view that such statements are unhelpful for the resolution of the present dispute [...].
>
> In this regard, the Tribunal [...] recalls the duty, incumbent on the arbitrators and the Parties' representatives alike [...] that '[t]he Parties shall not engage in any oral or written communication with any member of the Arbitral Tribunal *ex parte* in connection with the subject

[78]The Arbitral Tribunal asserts that "no private meeting between the Tribunal and Minister Erjavec occurred. The only occasions on which the Minister addressed the Tribunal were the hearings [...] held at the Peace Palace in The Hague" (PCA Partial Award 2016: 12, footnote 8).

[79]The letter was published on the PCA website on 20 June 2015 after the consent of both Parties. The official disclosure of any information relating to confidential arbitral proceedings can be regarded as exceptional.

> matter of the arbitration or any procedural issues that are related to the proceedings'. To the Tribunal, safeguarding the confidentiality of the deliberations until the issuance of an award is a matter of highest priority [...].
>
> The Tribunal has also requested the PCA [...] to review the processes that it has put in place to protect confidential information and has found these to be satisfactory [...] The Tribunal is therefore confident that no information about the likely outcome of any aspect of the arbitration has been disclosed. (Letter of the Tribunal to the Parties' Agents, 5 May 2015: 1–2)

4.3.3.2 *Ex Parte* Communication

On 10 July 2015, the Tribunal informed the Parties that it "contemplates rendering the award in mid-December 2015" (PCA press release, 10 July 2015).

On 22 July 2015, a Croatian daily newspaper (*Večernji list*) and a Serbian weekly newspaper (*Newsweek Srbija*) published transcripts and audio files of "two telephone conversations reportedly involving the arbitrator appointed by Slovenia [...] and one of Slovenia's Agents [...]" occurring on 15 November 2014 and 11 January 2015 (PCA Partial Award 2016: 13, para 74; see also Ministry of Foreign and European Affairs of the Republic of Croatia, Termination of the Arbitration Process between Croatia and Slovenia: Causes and Consequences[80]).

It is worth noting that no explanation had been provided as to the relation between the reported dates of the recordings and their publication, the source of the intercepted phone conversations, and how the recordings were handed on to the media (see PCA Partial Award 2016: 13–4, para 74).

Yet, at the beginning of April 2019, the Slovenian Prime Minister publicly announced that he had learnt from his intelligence service (SOVA) that the Croatian intelligence service (SOA) crafted the recordings (STA news, 4 April 2019). Further, it was revealed that a SOA operative was trying to prevent the Slovenian commercial TV station POP from breaking the news (STA news, 9 April 2019). The Foreign Ministry of Slovenia subsequently withdrew its Ambassador from Croatia for consultations (Foreign Affairs Ministry of Slovenia press release, 9 April 2019).

The matters touched upon in the recorded conversations mainly relate to (i) the arbitrators' preliminary views on contested issues, (ii) attempts to identify opportunities to influence Tribunal members, and (iii) documents received from the Slovenian Agent which the arbitrator appointed by Slovenia would submit to the arbitrators as his own.

---

[80] https://www.mvep.hr/en/other/termination-of-the-arbitration-process; The website lists events between 30 April 2015, when the Tribunal was made aware of the statements of the foreign minister of Slovenia, and 25 June 2017, four days before the PCA Final Award. With regard to 22 July 2015, the Croatian Ministry has produced excerpts (translations from Slovene into English) of the published recorded conversations, see https://www.mvep.hr/files/file/dokumenti/arbitraza/en/150820-excerpts-from-recordings-between-dr-sekolec-and-mr-drenik-14082015.pdf.

The following excerpts are taken from the PCA Partial Award and constitute certified translations commisioned by the PCA Registry.[81]

(i) Arbitrators views on contested issues:

Drenik: Maybe Vaughan Lowe.[82] Vaughan Lowe is more interested in these ecological issues, I think. Maybe he could…

Sekolec: But he, he was quiet.

[…]

Drenik: This is typically French, if you ask me.… This is the same, the exact same mentality as Pellet,[83] he said to me 'knowing Guillaume'[84] he said to me. We will get the major part of the Gulf of Piran, we'll get the junction, but we will loss on Dragonja. We will lose on Dragonja [the speaker corrects herself].

Sekolec: Yes, yes. It seems … from the way he looks at things …. (Recording dated 05-11-2014; PCA Partial Award 2016: 14, para 76)

(ii) Identifying opportunities to influence Tribunal members:

Drenik: What if you … I'm thinking … what if you … a day before, I don't know … or whenever … meet with Bruno, for example, with Simma?[85]

Sekolec: I have a dinner appointment with Bruno at his place anyway. Just the two of us.

Drenik: Excellent! You see, and you could just give him … 'I'm fine with that, I understand', you see, take-it-easy attitude … 'but look, I've checked this and here, I think that …' The point is not to give him 500 arguments, but just to say 'I still think it wasn't quite like this here.' Maybe he would then bring it up …

Sekolec: Yes, yes.

Drenik: … because if it's you who does it [brings it up], Guillaume will wonder, but if Simma says 'I think we should nevertheless look into it a bit more …'.

Sekolec: I understand. I will …

Drenik: Simma is certainly the one who knows best and the one who will delve into it.

Sekolec: Yes, I will work on Simma. This has been agreed already. The dinner. (Recording dated 11-01-2015; PCA Partial Award 2016: 14–5, para 77)

(iii) Documents from the Slovenian Agent which the arbitrator appointed by Slovenia would submit as his own:

Drenik: Well, you see, I could prepare all this for you, but there is something else. It would be a good thing to forward all these documents …. if you are going to forward them …. in such a way …. that you would bring your computer …

Sekolec: Yes, so that I have the file.

Drenik: … and that we open a file in your computer and just transfer the documents, you know, the text.

[81] For translated excerpts of the recordings in their entirety, see the Croatian Foreign Ministry website referred to in the last but one footnote above. Those transcripts, however, do not constitute certified translations commissioned by the PCA Registry.

[82] Professor Vaughan Lowe was a Member of the Arbitral Tribunal.

[83] Professor Alain Pellet worked as special advisor for Slovenia in the arbitral proceedings.

[84] Judge Gilbert Guillaume was the President of the Arbitral Tribunal.

[85] Judge Bruno Simma was a Member of the Arbitral Tribunal.

Sekolec: Yes.

Drenik: This is very simple to do, you see, so that you are registered as the author of the file.

Sekolec: I understand, I understand yes, yes.

Drenik: Because otherwise, the text doesn't have an author and that would look strange and also, someone may break in and find it ... if I am the author of the file.

Sekolec: Yes, yes.

Drenik: But if I only open it on a [USB] key on my computer and transfer it to a new file ... So, for each *effectivité*[86] we open a new file on your computer and save it, this is the most safe, [...] this would be a good thing to do. (Recording dated 05-11-2014; PCA Partial Award 2016: 15–6, para 78)

On 24 July, the day after the arbitrator appointed by Slovenia had resigned (PCA press release, 23 July 2015), the Croatian Foreign Minister sent a letter to the Tribunal indicating her government's "serious doubt [about] the integrity and fairness of the entire arbitration proceedings" in the light of the "shocking developments" (Letter from the Minister for Foreign and European Affairs to the Registrar of the Tribunal, 24 July 2015: 1). The letter went on to state that

The conversations [...] reveal that the most fundamental principles of procedural fairness, due process, impartiality and integrity of the arbitral process have been systematically and gravely violated, to the prejudice of Croatia. As you will be aware, the Terms of Appointment provide in Section 9.1 that 'the Parties shall not engage in any oral or written communication with any member of the Arbitral Tribunal *ex parte* in connection with the subject matter of the arbitration or any procedural issues that are related to the proceedings.'

[...]

[...] The communications appear to reveal that Arbitrator Sekolec *inter alia* disclosed critical elements of the Arbitral Tribunal's deliberations to Slovenia's Agent; advised her on the issues on which he believed the Tribunal was inclined to rule in Slovenia's favour, and on which issues it was not so inclined; requested [...] arguments and 'facts' not already in the record so that he could use them in his discussions with other members of the Arbitral Tribunal as his own; conspired with Ms. Drenik to assure that the other members of the Tribunal would not know their true source; communicated these arguments and 'facts' to the other members of the Tribunal on the basis that they were his own.

[...]

[...] Croatia considers that the entire arbitral process has been tainted by the actions of Arbitrator Sekolec and Ms. Drenik [...] Croatia has difficulty understanding how it would be possible, at this juncture, for the other Members of the Tribunal, or the PCA staff, to distinguish between the arguments and 'facts' presented by Slovenia through Arbitrator Sekolec, and those developed solely by Arbitrator Sekolec on his own. The official records appear to have been corrupted by improper argument and 'facts' submitted by one of the Parties after the close of the written proceedings and the hearings.

In these circumstances, Croatia asks the Tribunal to suspend the proceedings with immediate effect [and] to review the totality of the materials presented, and reflect on the grave damage that has been done to the integrity of the entire proceedings [...]. (letter from the Minister for Foreign and European Affairs to the Registrar of the Tribunal, 24 July 2015: 1–2; emphasis added)

[86] An *effectivité* is a territorial claim based on the factual and administrative control of an area (as opposed to legal title).

In a reply to a letter from the Tribunal from 25 July 2015 to Slovenia asking to provide any feedback on Croatia's letter, Slovenia, on 26 July 2015, responded informing the Tribunal of the resignation of Ms. Drenik, and conceded that "the conduct of one of the arbitrators and Slovenia's former Agent" had been "entirely inappropriate and intolerable" (PCA Partial Award 2016: 17, para 82; 42, paras 170–1; letter from the Republic of Slovenia to the Registrar of the Tribunal, 26 July 2015). Further, Slovenia opposed Croatia's view that the arbitral proceedings should be suspended (PCA Partial Award 2016: 17, para 83) positing that the Tribunal was still charged with fulfilling the task of settling the dispute that had been submitted to it (letter from the Republic of Slovenia to the Registrar of the Tribunal, 26 July 2015). On 28 July 2015, Slovenia appointed Ronny Abraham, President of the International Court of Justice (ICJ), as the new arbitrator to replace Jernej Sekolec (PCA Final Award 2017: 53, para 181).

4.3.3.3 Croatia's Termination Request

In an extraordinary session on 29 July 2015, the Croatian Parliament (Sabor) unanimously "[put] the Government of the Republic of Croatia under an obligation to begin the procedure of termination of the Arbitration Agreement […] for reasons of material breach of its provisions by the Republic of Slovenia" (Sabor Resolution 29 July 2015). In a diplomatic note (*note verbale*) the following day, Croatia notified Slovenia that, pursuant to the Sabor Resolution,

> [t]he Republic of Croatia considers it is entitled to terminate the Arbitration Agreement […] In accordance with Article 60, paragraph 1 of the Vienna Convention on the Law of the Treaties, the Republic of Croatia considers that the Republic of Slovenia has engaged in one or more material breaches of the Arbitration Agreement. The Republic of Croatia hereby provides the notification pursuant to Article 65, paragraph 1 of the Vienna Convention that it proposes to terminate forthwith the Arbitration Agreement.
>
> […] As a result of the actions of […] Slovenia, the impartiality and integrity of the arbitral proceedings have been irrevocably damaged, giving rise to a manifest violation of the rights of Croatia.
>
> The actions for which Slovenia is internationally responsible have violated *inter alia* Article 6 of the Arbitration Agreement, by violating the agreed procedure and rules of confidentiality and Article 10 of the Arbitration Agreement, which obliges the parties to 'refrain from any action or statement which might […] jeopardize the work of the Arbitral Tribunal'.
>
> […]
>
> The principles of fairness and integrity have been violated, irreparable harm has been done to the legitimacy and prospects of the process. In the absence of any possibility that the arbitral process will now be seen to be fair and proper, and to meet all applicable standards, the object and purpose of the Arbitration Agreement cannot be accomplished.
>
> Taking all this into account, […] *Croatia has the honour to notify its entitlement to propose the termination of the Arbitration Agreement between […] Croatia and […] Slovenia [and] also notifies […] Slovenia that from the date of this note […] Croatia ceases to apply the Arbitration Agreement*. (*Note verbale* from the Ministry of Foreign and European Affairs of Croatia to the Ministry of Foreign Affairs of Slovenia, No. 3303/2015, 30 July 2015; emphasis added)

Croatia also informed the European Commission of the Sabor Ruling and the government's termination request (letter from the Minister for Foreign and European Affairs of Croatia to Frans Timmermans, Vice-President of the European Commission, 30 July 2015), and subsequently sent a letter to the Tribunal notifying the arbitration body that, as of 31 July 2015, Croatia terminates the Arbitration Agreement (and the arbitral proceedings as such) relieving Croatia's Agent, Co-Agent, Counsels and assistants "from their engagement in the case" (letter from the Ministry of Foreign and European Affairs of the Republic of Croatia to the Registrar of the Tribunal, 31 July 2015: 2).

The Croatian government took the view that "*the Tribunal is without competence* to express any views as to the requirements for the termination of the Arbitration Agreement" (letter from the Ministry of Foreign and European Affairs of the Republic of Croatia to the Registrar of the Tribunal, 31 July 2015: 2; emphasis added). For the Tribunal's deliberations on the legality of the Croatian termination request see "Legality of the Croatian Termination Request" in Sect. 4.3.4.3). To that end, however, it must be mentioned that it is a well-established principle that an International Court or Tribunal can decide itself in matters of jurisdiction (*compétence de la compétence* or *Kompetenz-Kompetenz*); see e.g. Bantekas 2015: 109–112, or the ICJ Nottebohm Case (ICJ Reports 1953: 111, para 119). In other words, "procedurally, Croatia was not on a strong footing with withdrawal" (interview Damir Arnaut, 25-01-2018).

The Croatian move was not free of controversy in EU circles either. As the then chairman of the Foreign Affairs Committee in the European Parliament put it: "The Croats have organised their withdrawal from the arbitration procedure within a couple of hours, and they did it in the most brutal way possible. One has to acknowledge at the same time that they politically capitalised on the events in a professional way." (interview Elmar Brok, 15-11-2015).

4.3.3.4 Reconstitution of the Tribunal

The arbitrator appointed by Croatia had resigned on 30 July 2015 on the grounds of the "gravity [of the] wrongful behaviour" of the former arbitrator appointed by Slovenia and the former Slovenian Agent (letter of resignation of Budislav Vukas, 30 July 2015). The arbitrator newly appointed by Slovenia on 28 July 2015, the President of the ICJ, stepped down on 3 August 2015 on the grounds that "the current situation cannot meet [the] expectation […] to help restore confidence between the Parties and the Arbitral Tribunal and to allow the process to continue normally […]" (PCA press release, 5 August 2015).[87]

[87] Sands (2016: 897–8) argues that the quick resignation simply mirrors the fact that the appointment of the President of the ICJ was an "error" in the first place as the ICJ President acts as (last-resort) appointing authority in Article 2(1) of the Arbitration Agreement. For that reason, the appointing authority itself cannot possibly be appointed to the Tribunal. Philippe Sands was a member of the Croatian delegation in the arbitration procedure.

The two vacancies for the respective posts of party-appointed arbitrators remained unfilled by the Parties for the time being (Slovenia refrained from making a re-appointment in order to "preserve the integrity [of the] ongoing proceedings", and Croatia had not made an appointment for reasons of principle due to its *de facto* withdrawal). On 25 September 2015, the President of the Tribunal appointed Rolf Einar Fife of Norway and Professor Nicolas Michel of Switzerland as new Members thus reconstituting the Tribunal (PCA press release, 25 September 2015; see also PCA Partial Award 2016: 7, para 49).[88]

On the same occasion, the Tribunal already indicated that it would now consider the Parties' position with regard to "Croatia's stated intention to terminate the Arbitration Agreement and in respect of the possible implications for the present proceedings of the events reportedly underlying Croatia's decision", and that it "may invite further submissions from the Parties" (PCA press release, 25 September 2015).

The European Commission actively supported the Tribunal's decision to continue the proceedings. In a letter to Prime Minister Cerar and Prime Minister Milanović, Commission President Juncker and the First Vice-President Timmermans wrote:

> We are pleased […] that the Panel […] has appointed two new members and is now again operational. While the setting of borders between Member States does not fall directly within the competences of the Union, the European Commission reiterates that open border conflicts between Member States shall be resolved promptly, not least because these *can have an impact on the application of EU law*. We, therefore, are confident that both Member States act in the spirit of sincere cooperation.
>
> The Commission supports the continuation of the work of the Arbitration Tribunal. We trust that the arbitration process will provide for the appropriate mechanisms to deal with all issues that have arisen in full respect of the Arbitration Agreement, and that the parties will respect the decisions of the Tribunal. (letter from the European Commission President and the First Vice-President to the Prime Minister of Slovenia and to the Prime Minister of Croatia, 30 September 2015; emphasis added)

The Croatian government, however, noting the Tribunal persisted, made it clear that it had no intention whatsoever to come back to the arbitral proceedings, and it dismissed any relevance of the case with regard to the application of EU law. Prime Minister Zoran Milanović stated:

> We are convinced that the Commission has no legal basis and thus should not be actively involved in this and a number of similar border disputes among numerous Member States. In this respect, I do not believe that any of these disputes has 'an impact on the application of EU law'.
>
> The Croatian Government has initiated the procedure of withdrawal from the Arbitration Agreement following an unanimous vote in the Croatian Parliament. Thus, consequently, it has withdrawn from [the] arbitration proceedings, it shall not comment the possible intentions of the Tribunal, shall not participate in its work, and shall not consider itself obliged to receive and act upon any decisions the Tribunal may or may not reach.
>
> We remain convinced that the only decision this *ad-hoc* Tribunal can reach to address the consequences of the actions of one of the Parties, while acting in accordance with the highest

[88] Both Rolf Einar Fife and Professor Nicholas Michel were on the list initially proposed to the Parties by the then EU Commissioner for Enlargement Olli Rehn on 11 June 2009 (see also Sect. 4.2.6).

legal, moral and ethical standards [...] - is to dissolve itself. (Letter from Prime Minister Zoran Milanović to the President of the European Commission, Jean-Claude Juncker, 1 October 2015)

The real motifs of the Croatian government will be difficult to explore. Still, one cannot neglect a general sense amongst the political elite in Croatia that arbitration was just another issue of external pressure. Fundamentally, during its first years after independence, Croatia had consumed territorial sovereignty largely on paper only. The UNPROFOR troops in the country from 1991–1998 are one issue, another being the EU requirement to collaborate with the ICTY (interview Dejan Jović, 02-11-2017).

In a letter to the Parties from 1 December 2015, the Tribunal announced to hold a hearing on the legality of the Croatian termination request on 17 March 2016 setting deadlines for submissions. Annexed to the letter were two internal documents from Jernej Sekolec, the initial arbitrator appointed by Slovenia, on (i) "notes regarding the border on and around Dragonja", and (ii) "Mura River Sector: Various effectivités[89] by Slovenia". Whilst Croatia did not make any submission, Slovenia filed its written submission on 26 February 2016 (PCA Partial Award 2016: 8–9, paras 52–54; 57).

4.3.4 Written Submissions, Hearing, and Partial Award 2016[90]

On the eve of the hearing, Croatia sent a *note verbale* to all Permanent Missions and Permanent Observer Missions at the United Nations confirming it was not going to participate in the actual hearing on 17 March 2016 (*note verbale* 55/2016 from the Permanent Mission of the Republic of Croatia to the U.N. to Permanent Missions and Permanent Observer Missions to the U.N., 16 March 2016; see Appendix B).[91]

The Parties took opposing views on whether the proceedings should continue. Their legal arguments centre around three items:

(i) the jurisdiction of the Tribunal,
(ii) the obligation and/or ability to continue the proceedings, and
(iii) the legality of the Croatian termination of the Arbitration Agreement.

[89] An *effectivité* is a territorial claim based on the factual and administrative control of an area (as opposed to legal title).

[90] No distinction is made here in terms of sub-paragraphs between written submissions and the hearing as (i) Croatia did not make any submission anyway, and (ii) the Tribunal, in its account of the Parties' arguments in the Partial Award, has not separated the written submission from the oral hearing.

[91] This *note verbale*, of which the Tribunal only learnt because it had been forwarded by Slovenia, in fact sets out the Croatian account of the arbitral proceedings in a comprehensive way and is perhaps the single most concise and insightful document shedding light on the rationale of the Croatian approach.

4.3.4.1 Croatia's Legal Arguments

Croatia did not appear at the hearing on 17 March 2016, nor had it filed any additional submissions prior to that hearing. The Tribunal, however, for the purpose of their deliberations, did take on board the positions from two Croatian letters to the Tribunal from 24 and 30 July 2015 (see Sect. 4.3.3.2).

On (i) jurisdiction, Croatia contended that the Arbitration Agreement contained no provision as for disputes on the validity of the Arbitration Agreement, and that the Tribunal therefore had no competence on the matter of termination (PCA Partial Award 2016: 20, para 89).

With regard to (ii) the Tribunal's duty and ability to continue the proceedings, Croatia held that "essential procedural rules have been violated [and that] such violations cannot be remedied by the Tribunal" concluding that the arbitral proceedings had been "totally and irreversibly compromised" (PCA Partial Award 2016: 21–2, paras 90–94).

As for (iii) the legality of the termination request, Croatia claimed it was entitled to terminate the Arbitration Agreement as the *ex parte* communication on the part of Slovenia constituted a material breach of the Arbitration Agreement in such a way that the violations threatened the *object and purpose*[92] of the Arbitration Agreement in relation to Article 60(3) of the Vienna Convention on the Law of Treaties (PCA Partial Award 2016: 22–3, paras 95–101).[93]

---

[92]For the object and purpose of the Arbitration Agreement see "Legality of the Croatian Termination Request" in Sect. 4.3.4.3.

[93]The Vienna Convention, signed on 23 May 1969, entered into force on 27 January 1980; for the Convention see https://legal.un.org/ilc/texts/instruments/english/conventions/1_1_1969.pdf.

Article 60 Vienna Convention on the Law of Treaties (VCLT):
Termination or suspension of the operation of a treaty as a consequence of its breach

1. A material breach of a bilateral treaty by one of the parties entitles the other to invoke the breach as a ground for terminating the treaty or suspending its operation in whole or in part.
2. A material breach of a multilateral treaty by one of the parties entitles:
   (a) the other parties by unanimous agreement to suspend the operation of the treaty in whole or in part or to terminate it either:
      (i) in the relations between themselves and the defaulting State; or
      (ii) as between all the parties;
   (b) a party specially affected by the breach to invoke it as a ground for suspending the operation of the treaty in whole or in part in the relations between itself and the defaulting State;
   (c) any party other than the defaulting State to invoke the breach as a ground for suspending the operation of the treaty in whole or in part with respect to itself if the treaty is of such a character that a material breach of its provisions by one party radically changes the position of every party with respect to the further performance of its obligations under the treaty.
3. A material breach of a treaty, for the purposes of this article, consists in:
   (a) a repudiation of the treaty not sanctioned by the present Convention; or
   (b) the violation of a provision essential to the accomplishment of the object or purpose of the treaty.
4. The foregoing paragraphs are without prejudice to any provision in the treaty applicable in the event of a breach.

4.3.4.2 Slovenia's Legal Arguments

In relation to (i) jurisdiction, Slovenia held that the Tribunal was competent to decide on the Croatian termination request referring to the well-established principle in international law named *compétence de la compétence/Kompetenz-Kompetenz* stipulating that an International Court or Tribunal can decide by itself in matters of jurisdiction (PCA Partial Award 2016: 24–27, paras 102–110; for the *Kompetenz-Kompetenz* power of arbitral tribunals see also e.g. Bantekas 2015: 109–112).

On (ii) the Tribunal's duty and ability to continue the proceedings, Slovenia noted that the general duty and competence of the Tribunal had been set out in the Arbitration Agreement, and that the duty to settle the submitted dispute had been confirmed by many decisions of international courts and tribunals. Further, Croatia, having achieved its vital interest of becoming an EU member, was not to "be released from its commitment to arbitrate". Moreover, the Tribunal had "the possibility to redress the breach of confidentiality"[94] and that it had done so by replacing the party-appointed arbitrators, and by the *de novo* deliberations (PCA Partial Award 2016: 27–31, paras 111–123).

With regard to (iii) the legality of the Croatian termination request, Slovenia argued that only "a gross infringement of an essential provision" of the Arbitration Agreement merited triggering Article 60(3)(b) of the Vienna Convention, i.e. entitling a party to terminating the obligation to arbitrate, which was not the case in the present circumstances. Therefore, according to Slovenia, the Tribunal did have "the means to accomplish the object and purpose of the Arbitration Agreement" (PCA Partial Award 2016: 34–36, paras 133–140).

4.3.4.3 Partial Award

On 30 June 2016, the Tribunal issued its Partial Award on the contested issue of whether the arbitral proceedings will continue. The Tribunal members unanimously decided that

- Slovenia had been in violation of the Arbitration Agreement, but the Arbitration Agreement as such remained in force.
- Thus, the arbitration procedure would continue (Partial Award 2016: 57, para 231).

---

5. Paragraphs 1–3 do not apply to provisions relating to the protection of the human person contained in treaties of a humanitarian character, in particular to provisions prohibiting any form of reprisals against persons protected by such treaties

[94] Slovenia recalled (i) the ICJ *Nuclear Tests* case *(Australia v. France)*, I.C.J. Reports 1974: paras 259–260, and (ii) the *Victor Pey Casado et al. v. Chile ICSID* case (No. ARB/98/2, Award 08 May 2008, paras 34–43) where both judicial bodies continued the proceedings under similar circumstances.

Yet, it is worth looking at the Tribunal's analysis in more detail: The Tribunal noted that Croatia did not make any formal submissions prior to the hearing on 17 March 2016, nor did Croatia participate in the hearing. However, Croatia had made its views clear by means of the letters to the Tribunal from July 2015 (see Sects. 4.3.3.2 and 4.3.4.1) and via the *note verbale* from 16 March 2016 (see Sect. 4.3.4 and Appendix B). Further, the Tribunal noted that Croatia was provided with the Slovenian submissions and the transcripts of the 17 March 2016 hearing. In procedural terms, the Tribunal referred to the "well-established principle of international procedural law that a unilateral decision to withdraw from dispute settlement proceedings cannot bring such proceedings to a halt" and that this principle was also set out in the PCA Optional Rules.[95] Therefore, the Tribunal was in a position and under an obligation to carry on with the arbitral proceedings (PCA Partial Award 2016: 36, paras 141–143).

Jurisdiction

The Tribunal cited various court and arbitral decisions,[96] *inter alia* the ICTY *Tadić* case:

> This power, known as the principle of '*Kompetenz-Kompetenz*' in German, or '*compétence de la compétence*' in French, is [...] indeed a major part of the incidental or inherent jurisdiction of any judicial or arbitral tribunal, consisting of its 'jurisdiction to determine its own jurisdiction'. It is a necessary component in the exercise of the judicial function and does not need to be expressly provided for in the constitutive documents of those tribunals. (Prosecutor v. Duško Tadić a/k/a "Dule", ICTY Case No. IT-94-1, Decision on the Defence Motion for Interlocutory Appeal on Jurisdiction, 2 October 1995, para 18)

The Tribunal concluded that, under general international law, an arbitral tribunal or judicial body had "the jurisdiction to determine its own jurisdiction" (PCA Partial Award 2016: 39, para 157).

As for the Arbitration Agreement and the Tribunal's jurisdiction to decide on the validity of the Croatian termination request, the Tribunal, amongst other things, quoted from the *ICAO Council* case of the ICJ:

> [A] merely unilateral suspension per se [cannot] render jurisdictional clauses inoperative, since, one of their purposes [might be] to enable the validity of the suspension to be tested. If a mere allegation, as yet unestablished, that a treaty was no longer operative could be used to defeat its jurisdictional clauses, all such clauses would become potentially a dead letter, even in cases like the present, where one of the very questions at issue on the merits, and as yet undecided, is whether or not the treaty is operative - i.e. whether it has been validly

[95] Article 28(2) and (3) of the PCA Optional Rules read: "2. If one of the parties, duly notified under these Rules, fails to appear at a hearing, without showing sufficient cause for such failure, the arbitral tribunal may proceed with the arbitration. 3. If one of the parties, duly invited to produce documentary evidence, fails to do so within the established period of time, without showing sufficient cause for such failure, the arbitral tribunal may make the award on the evidence before it".

[96] Such as the *Guano* case (Chile v. France) from 1900, the *Walfish Bay Boundary* case (Germany v. Great Britain) from 1911, or the *Rio Grande Irrigation and Land Company* case (Great Britain v. United States) from 1928, see Partial Award (2016: 38–9, paras 150–153).

terminated or suspended. The result would be that means of defeating jurisdictional clauses would never be wanting. (I.C.J. Reports 1972: 53–4, para 16)

In conclusion, there was "no doubt that the Tribunal also has inherent jurisdiction to decide" whether the arbitral proceedings can continue (PCA Final Award 2016: 58, para 168).

Continuation of the Arbitration Procedure

The Tribunal noted that, by means of the *ex parte* communication (see Sect. 4.3.3.2), the Agent of Slovenia and the arbitrator appointed by Slovenia "acted in blatant violation of [the confidentiality] provisions" (PCA Partial Award 2016: 43–4, para 175).

As for cases comparable to the present one, the Tribunal looked into *Victor Pey Casado* et al. *v. Chile* where one of the party-appointed arbitrators had provided that party with a draft decision from the Tribunal's deliberations. That arbitrator and a second one who had been challenged on different grounds resigned. Two new arbitrators were appointed, and, to ensure a level playing-field, the draft decision was communicated to the other party.[97] After a new hearing the then Tribunal rendered an award (PCA Partial Award 2016: 45–6, para 182).

The Tribunal subsequently explored whether the integrity of the proceedings in the Croatia–Slovenia case can be preserved, and, if so, in what way. It recalled that the Tribunal was recomposed properly with two new and independent Members following the resignation of the two party-appointed arbitrators (PCA Partial Award 2016: 46–7, para 183–6; see also Sect. 4.3.3.4). In relation to the two documents the arbitrator appointed by Slovenia had introduced into the proceedings after the *ex parte* communication with Slovenia's Agent, the Tribunal found that the arbitrator had not presented any new arguments or facts that were not already in the official record of the Tribunal.[98] Besides, the views expressed by both party-appointed arbitrators vis-à-vis the arguments and facts on the Tribunal's record were of no relevance for the work of the Tribunal as they both had resigned, so procedural imbalance could not be observed, either. In conclusion, the Tribunal noted no obstacles as to the continuation of the arbitral proceedings (PCA Partial Award 2016: 48–9, paras 187–196).

Legality of the Croatian Termination Request

The Tribunal examined whether the actions of the arbitrator appointed by Slovenia and Slovenia's Agent constituted a material breach of the Arbitration Agreement by Slovenia which would entitle Croatia to terminate the Arbitration Agreement under Article 60(1) of the Vienna Convention (see Sect. 4.3.4.1). It is important to note,

---

[97] ICSID Case No. ARB/98/2, Award 08 May 2008, paras 34–43.

[98] By late 2014, the Tribunal's Registry had prepared a list of both Parties' evidence of (i) legal title and (ii) *effectivités* of 142 pages (PCA Partial Award 2016: 47–8, para 190).

that the breach of the provisions under Article 60(3)(b) cannot be measured in terms of gravity or intensity, but that the crucial issue here is whether a breach is essential for the accomplishment of the treaty's, i.e. the Arbitration Agreement's *object and purpose* (see PCA Partial Award 2016: 53, para 215).

According to the Tribunal, the first object and purpose of the Arbitration Agreement was to secure Croatia's access to the EU, and that therefore "a nexus was established between the settlement of the territorial and maritime dispute and the [EU] accession of Croatia" (PCA Partial Award 2016: 54–5, para 220). The second object and purpose was "the settlement of the maritime and territorial dispute between the Parties", so that the "decisive question" was whether the breaches of the Arbitration Agreement's provisions by Slovenia rendered the very settlement of the border dispute unattainable (PCA Partial Award 2016: 55, para 222).

The Tribunal found that, by (i) communicating to the Parties the two documents that had been submitted by the arbitrator appointed by Slovenia in collaboration with Slovenia's Agent, (ii) demonstrating that the documents contained no new arguments or facts not already presented in the written or oral pleadings, and through (iii) recomposing the Tribunal to safeguard its independence and impartiality,[99] "the procedural balance between the Parties is secured" (PCA Partial Award 2016: 55, para 224). In conclusion, the Tribunal held that remedial action was taken so that breaches of the Arbitration Agreement by Slovenia did "*not* defeat the object and purpose of the Agreement" with regard to Article 60(1) of the Vienna Convention, and that therefore the Arbitration Agreement remained in force and the arbitration proceedings could continue (PCA Partial Award 2016: 55, para 225; emphasis added).

4.3.4.4 Alternative Views

Whilst it would be difficult to challenge the jurisdiction of the Arbitral Tribunal arising from the well-established *Kompetenz-Kompetenz* principle (see Sect. 4.3.3 and Section "Jurisdiction"; interview Vladmir-Đuro Degan, 21-11-2019), there have been alternative views as to both the continuation of the arbitral proceedings and the legality of the Croatian termination request.

In the aftermath of the publication of the *ex parte* communication, Sands (2016) felt that, notwithstanding the fact that he had acted as counsel for Croatia in the proceedings, "the centrality of the independence of the adjudicator" was at stake, and that the affair was going to cause "tremendous harm to the system of international arbitration both within and outside the PCA system" (2016: 898). On the way ahead, Savarian and Baker (2015) argued that it was legally and politically impossible to continue the arbitral proceedings since (i) it would be very difficult to enforce a final award under the circumstances of one party determined to withdraw from both the Arbitration Agreement and the arbitration process, and (ii) that, given the *ex parte*

[99]The Tribunal "has found no reason to consider that any aspect of its future decision on the merits would be affected by past events, for which none of its current members was responsible" (PCA Partial Award 2016: 56, para 227).

communication, there would be doubts about the award as such irrespective of its contents. Thus, the Tribunal itself should "terminate the proceedings citing grave procedural misconduct" to avoid "an unenforced and discredited award". Savarian (2016), ahead of the Partial Award, however, opined that Croatia was not entitled to terminate the Arbitration Agreement (as opposed to the arbitral proceedings as such), i.e. the *quid-pro-quo* nexus remained and "Croatia would either have to accept a re-start of the arbitration [...] or [...] have to agree with Slovenia on alternative means [such as ICJ or ITLOS] to settle the dispute".

With regard to the PCA Partial Award, Ilić (2017) contends, *inter alia*, that the object or purpose of the Arbitration Agreement was to be found in (i) Article 4(b) of the Agreement mandating the Tribunal to apply "international law, equity, and the principle of good neighbourly relations",[100] and in (ii) the PCA Optional Rules' provisions on arbitrator impartiality.[101] Therefore, according to Ilić, the Tribunal had "placed too much weight on finality as the main goal of arbitration" (2017: 373), and the nexus between the arbitration procedure and Croatian EU accession (see "Legality of the Croatian Termination Request" in Sect. 4.3.4.3) was "not as strong as the Tribunal described it" (2017: 374). In his view, the *quid-pro-quo* aspect of arbitration in terms of EU accession of Croatia could not contradict the purpose "to settle all disputes in an impartial and procedurally fair manner" which was why the *ex parte* communication could well be seen as a material breach under Article 60 of the Vienna Convention (2017: 375) thus entitling Croatia to terminate the proceedings. As to the replacement of the party-appointed arbitrators, Ilić holds that what was impossible to remedy is that the Slovenian side had learnt about the other arbitrators' viewpoints on certain facts or arguments (2017: 377) providing Slovenia with some "strategic insight [...] as to how the Tribunal might in the future react to particular arguments" (2017: 382). In conclusion, the arbitral proceedings had been affected unfairly to the detriment of Croatia rendering the task of the Tribunal "impossible to fulfil" (2017: 382).

4.3.5 *Final Award 2017*

On 29 June 2017, one year after the Partial Award, the Tribunal issued the Final Award. The following sections will focus on the Tribunal's decision on the *maritime*

---

[100]The author of this book, however, considers the provision in Article 4(b) of minor relevance in terms of *object* or *purpose* of the Arbitration Agreement, since the above article defines the Tribunal's toolbox of applicable law for the actual maritime delimitation *stricto sensu* (in particular the high seas corridor and the regime for the maritime areas in relation to Article 3 of the Arbitration Agreement labelled "task of the arbitral tribunal"; see also Sect. 4.2.4).

[101]Article 15(1) PCA Optional Rules: "Subject to these Rules, the arbitral tribunal may conduct the arbitration in such manner as it considers appropriate, provided that the parties are treated with equality and that at any stage of the proceedings each party is given a full opportunity of presenting its case".

border and areas. Nevertheless, the *land* border decision will be briefly addressed whilst a full land-border survey regrettably is beyond the scope of this study.[102]

4.3.5.1 Land Border

In its analysis with regard to the land border (as well as the maritime border), the Tribunal was bound to strictly apply *international law* as stipulated in Articles 3(1)(a) and 4(a) of the Arbitration Agreement (see Sect. 4.2.4). It is worth noting in this context that, therefore, "the Tribunal is required to decide the matter from the legal, and not from the historical or political or sociological perspective. This is what the two [g]overnments have chosen and mandated" (PCA Final Award 2017: 108, para 335).

The *approach* of the Tribunal as for the delimitation of the land border was as follows:

(i) The Tribunal's starting point was to check whether the cadastral limits of Croatia and Slovenia were aligned at the time of the independence in 1991 in the respective disputed spots;
(ii) Disputed land border spots were cleared starting with the principle of legal title (*uti possidetis juris*) including historic evidence or agreements between the Parties;
(iii) Where no title could be established, the factual administrative control of the area (*uti possidetis effectivités*) served as a basis for the Tribunal's decision (PCA Final Award 2017: 109–110, paras 340–343).[103]

---

[102] For the Final Award see https://pcacases.com/web/sendAttach/2172; for the read-out video of the press conference (01:55) see https://files.pca-cpa.org/hr-sl/2017-06-29_VOD_V4.mp4.

[103] It may be useful to note that the Tribunal approached the handling of *effectivités* with great caution: "[The] evaluation of effectivités is not a matter of counting or comparing instances of the exercise or display of authority *à titre de souverain*. Each instance—and the number of relevant instances put before an international tribunal in cases such as this tends to be low—must be examined in order to identify precisely what can properly be inferred from it. For example, a payment of taxes to an authority of State A and not of State B may evidence a belief that State A and no other State has authority over a particular place, or it may evidence no more than the fact that although both State A and State B maintained claims to the location in question, it was decided that the tax-payer should not (at least on that occasion) be required to pay twice. To take another example, the referral of a dispute to a particular court may be based upon the presence of the property in question or one or both of the litigating parties, or the making of a relevant legal instrument such as a will, within the jurisdiction of the court, or upon an agreement between the litigating parties. An exercise of sovereign authority with respect to facts or things at a particular location should not be assessed in isolation: it does not necessarily evidence the existence of exclusive sovereign authority at that location. The Tribunal has accordingly taken particular care to look for evidence that points clearly to the assertion of the public power of the State at the location in question, to the exclusion of the public power of other States. In doing so, it has been mindful of the fact that some activities, such as the levying of taxes, the organization of elections, conscription for military service, and law enforcement, are more likely to demonstrate the exercise of authority *à titre de souverain* than others, such as the delivery of mail or the provision of telephone or other services" (PCA Final Award 2017: 110–111, paras 342–3).

Further, it is important to note that there are "limits to the degree of detail" of any delimitation decision as for the later *demarcation* on the ground (PCA Final Award 2017: 113, para 354) for a number of reasons:

(i) The Tribunal had to work with the maps and verbal descriptions provided by the parties, so the precision of the decision may be seen as "inherently limited". As this makes it impossible to determine "every metre" of the land boundary, the parties will in any event need to deal with minor adjustments at the stage of demarcation (PCA Final Award 2017: 113, para 355);
(ii) In its analysis, the Tribunal was limited to the submissions of the parties. It had been agreed on that the Tribunal would *not* carry out any independent on-site investigation themselves (PCA Final Award 2017: 114, para 356);
(iii) There are cases where matters of convenience or practicality (such as avoiding meanders or enclaves) could *not* be considered, since the Tribunal was strictly bound to international law. This meant the parties may reach diverging practical arrangements for the course of the border on the ground (PCA Final Award 2017: 109, paras 337–9; 114, para 357; see also Petrič 2017: 367).

With regard to the course of the land border, the Tribunal divided the boundary up into three sections: (I) Mura River Region, (II) Central Region, and (III) Istria Region. For illustration purposes, a tiny few prominent or noteworthy particular land border spots in the afore-mentioned regions must be addressed, such as

(i) in the Mura river region (starting at the border tripoint Croatia-Slovenia-Hungary following the river downstream for about 25 km) where the border crosses the river many times—with all the impracticalities that entails for agriculture or river ferries, for example—a number of delimitations were made,[104] such as the Brezovec-del/Murišće hamlet which was determined to be Slovenian (PCA Final Award 2017: 131–6, paras 405–414);
(ii) in the Haloze/Macelj area of the Central Region, a tiny forest strip of 0.5 ha which was *not* recorded in either of the border municipalities (sic) was delimitated according to a historic map from 1914 (PCA Final Award 2017: 163–4, paras 502–5);
(iii) the peak of Sveta Gera/Trdinov Vrh, also in the Central Region, owing its significance to a television tower and a military facility constructed by the former Yugoslav Army and staffed by the Slovenian Army since October 1991 was delimitated to the effect that the border runs between the television tower (Slovenia) and the military facility (Croatia; PCA Final Award 2017: 189–190, paras 586–590);
(iv) the Three Hamlets (Istria Region) south of the Dragonja river (see Sect. 4.1.2.2) were allocated to Croatia as the river was the boundary (PCA Final Award 2017:

[104]The Tribunal would not rely on the bilateral Expert Group Report findings from 1996 (see Sect. 3.1.1), but base its decisions on the many *effectivités* invoked by the Parties by means of the written and oral submissions (PCA Final Award 2017: 133, para 411).

241, para 769).[105] For the entire land boundary decision see PCA Final Award 2017: 114–241, paras 359–770.[106]

4.3.5.2 Sea Border/Maritime Areas

It is useful to bear in mind that the Arbitral Tribunal was mandated to delimitate the maritime boundary and to decide on the maritime areas according to the Arbitration Agreement, i.e.

(i) the (land and) maritime border by applying *international law* [Art. 3(1)(a)];
(ii) Slovenia's junction to the high seas and the regime for the maritime areas by applying "*international law, equity and [...] good-neighbourly relations [...] to achieve a fair and just result by taking into account all relevant circumstances [...]*" (Art. 4(b); emphases added).

The decisions will be outlined below followed by a brief discussion of scholarly views on the maritime aspects of the Final Award.

The Bay

The Tribunal first determined the status of Piran Bay and concluded that, prior to the dissolution of the SFRY, the Bay had the status of juridical bay (see Sect. 3.1.1.2) and had been declared internal waters by Yugoslavia through the Coast Sea Acts from 1963 and 1987, and that the latter Act also defined the closing line of the Bay. That closing line was also included in a negotiating document from 1964 leading to the bilateral Osimo Treaty 1975 between Italy and Yugoslavia on the territorial sea border. The Tribunal thus decided that on 25 June 1991 the Bay was internal waters of Yugoslavia[107] closed by a line between the low-water marks of Cape Madona and Cape Savudrija (PCA Final Award 2017: 267–272, paras 862–885).

As there are no UNCLOS provisions on the delimitation of internal waters, the Tribunal took the view that the delimitation in the Bay had to follow the same principles as the delimitation of a *land* boundary, notably the principle of *uti possidetis* (*juris* and *effectivités*). As there was no division of the Bay in SFRY times, neither a legal title inherited by any of the Parties, nor a *condominium* arrangement, delimitation was thus to be made on the basis of *effectivités*, i.e. claims of sovereignty based

[105] The Tribunal gives express mention to the fact that its decision "may present some practical inconvenience" to the inhabitants of the settlements as they "are economically tied to the Slovenian town of Sečovlje" and appeals "to the Parties to cooperate in order to ensure that inhabitants in the hamlets on the Croatian side of the border have adequate facilities and access rights to Slovenia" (PCA Final Award 2017: 241, para 770).

[106] For a summary see PCA press release 29 June 2017 available at https://pcacases.com/web/sendAttach/2175.

[107] Slovenia had claimed the status of internal waters, Croatia had repudiated it calling for territorial sea delimitation inside the Bay (PCA Final Award 2017: 247–8, para 790).

on factual control or administration of the area in question (PCA Final Award 2017: 273, paras 886–8).

The Tribunal mainly looked at fishing activities and police patrolling in the Bay at the date of independence (25 June 1991). The arbitrators noted that the Slovenian fishing reserve was established in 1962 and managed throughout up until 1991, whereas the Croatian fishing reserve was created in 1976 without any follow-up management activity. The municipalities of Buje (Croatia) and Piran (Slovenia) did, however, get in touch in 1975 to co-ordinate the limits of the fishing reserves and reciprocal consent was sought and given in 1976 and 1978 respectively. This led the Tribunal to conclude that the fishing reserves covered the entire Bay eastward of the closing line, but that there was no express mutual recognition of the respective territorial extent of each of them (PCA Final Award 2017: 274–6, paras 891–901).

As for policing, the Tribunal noted that whilst the coast was controlled by the Yugoslav Navy stationed in Pula operating a radar facility at the Savudrija promontory,[108] at Republican level it was the police stations in Koper and Umag exercising the patrols to enforce safety regulations and the fight against illegal fishing and smuggling. The arbitrators found that Koper police station patrolled the Bay with two vessels supported by a radio link with the Savudrija Navy observatory, and that Umag police station was active mostly in the immediate vicinity of the Bay's Croatian shores (PCA Final Award 2017: 276–9, paras 902–913).

In view of the above *effectivités*, the Tribunal decided that the delimitation line in the Bay was to be between the lines claimed by Croatia (equidistance) and Slovenia (entire Bay) expressly adopting the line from the bilateral Initialled Draft Agreement 2001 (Drnovšek-Račan Agreement; see Sect. 4.1.4). The said delimitation line meets the closing line of the Bay at a point "which is at a distance from Cape Madona that is three times the distance from that same point to Cape Savudrija" (PCA Final Award 2017: 279, para 912). As a result and in terms of surface, the Tribunal apportioned roughly four fifths of the Bay to Slovenia and one fifth to Croatia.[109]

Territorial Sea Boundary

Ahead of its analysis of the Parties' arguments, the Tribunal started out by clarifying that it was bound to conduct a *sequential* analysis of the tasks it was mandated in Article 3(1) of the Arbitration Agreement, i.e. the Tribunal needed to determine the course of the land and maritime boundary first, followed by the determination of the Slovenian junction to the high seas, and lastly by a decision on the regime for the maritime areas. Practically, the Tribunal outlined to look at (i) the delimitation of the territorial sea between Croatia and Slovenia, (ii) the determination of the junction to the high seas, Slovenia's claim to a continental shelf, and to the regime for the maritime areas (PCA Final Award 2017: 292, paras 947–8).

---

[108] Today, the Savudrija radar facility is used by the Croatian Navy (author's field notes, 26-07-2020).

[109] According to Petrič (2017: 370), the allocation is 82% to Slovenia and 18% to Croatia.

It must be noted that the Parties had taken different views on the question of whether the Arbitration Agreement did foresee distinct steps of analysis. Croatia argued that the drafting history of the Arbitration Agreement (see Sects. 4.2.3–4.2.5) clearly mirrored the fact that the issues territorial sea boundary, junction to the high seas, and regime for the maritime areas had been carefully kept apart on purpose. Slovenia, however, contended that the Tribunal had discretionary powers to decide the issues under Article 3(1) separately or together to arrive at a workable result (PCA Final Award 2017: 285–6, paras 922–5).

Referring to the three-stage approach,[110] but in fact applying the two-stage approach for the delimitation of the territorial sea, the arbitral tribunal first drew a provisional equidistance line between the point where the delimitation line established in the Bay met the closing line at the mouth of the Bay and the maritime boundary between Italy and Yugoslavia inherited by the 1975 Treaty of Osimo (see Sect. 2.4.3) which delimitated the territorial sea in the Gulf of Trieste (PCA Final Award 2017: 312–313, paras 1002–3).

Considering special circumstances which would warrant a departure from the provisional equidistance line, the Tribunal dismissed several of Slovenia's arguments notably the concave nature of the coast along the Gulf of Trieste, and the (short) length of the Slovenian coast in relation to the (very long) overall Croatian coastline. Slovenia had also claimed maritime entitlements it considers to have inherited from the SFRY. The Tribunal noted that the Yugoslav Republic of Slovenia enjoyed these maritime entitlements "as a matter of the SFRY law to share and participate in the uses of the maritime zones of the SFRY" and went on to state that

> [a]s a sovereign coastal State, Slovenia's entitlement is to the maritime zones generated by its own coastline alone, limited as that might be. It is very well established that international law cannot refashion nature by allocating to a State a maritime entitlement other than that generated by its own coastline. (PCA Final Award 2017: 315, para 1006)

The length of the coastal fronts of Slovenia and Croatia the Tribunal did not consider a special circumstance. No historic titles[111] had been established on the part of Slovenia either. The arbitrators did, however, consider the *coastal configuration* a special circumstance:

> [T]he coastline of Croatia turns sharply southwards around Cape Savudrija, so that the Croatian basepoints [controlling] the equidistance line are located on a very small stretch of coast whose general (*north*-facing) direction is markedly different from the general (*southwest*-facing) direction of much the greater part of the Croatian coastline [...], and deflect the equidistance line very significantly towards the north, *greatly exaggerating the 'boxed-in' nature of Slovenia's maritime zone.* (PCA Final Award 2017: 319, para 1011; emphasis added)

---

[110] Drawing of provisional equidistance line, consideration of special circumstances warranting a departure from the provisional line, and proportionality test to check for alignment with ratio of relevant coastal lengths and maritime areas (with EEZ and continental shelf); see Sect. 3.2.2.3. For the UNCLOS provisions on territorial sea delimitation (Article 15) see Sect. 3.2.1.

[111] Both historic title and special circumstances warrant a departure from the equidistance line; see Sect. 3.2.1.

The arbitrators thus modified the provisional equidistance line in a way to make sure that the delimitation line does "not disproportionately exacerbate Slovenia's boxed-in condition". This resulted in the final delimitation line of the territorial sea border between Slovenia and Croatia pointing slightly further southwest being approximately parallel to the first seaward stretch of the Slovenian–Italian territorial sea border starting out at San Bartolomeo Bay (PCA Final Award 2017: 321–2, para 1014; emphasis added).

Junction Area

The Tribunal first interpreted the term "junction" which was highly disputed between the Parties (see Sect. 4.2.4; see also PCA Final Award 2017: 324–331, paras 1016–1033). The arbitrators took the view that "the term 'junction' has an essentially spatial meaning and connotation" (PCA Final Award 2017: 342, para 1073) and determined that "'junction' signifies the physical location of a connection between two or more areas. In the present case, the Tribunal defined the term 'junction' as the connection between the territorial sea of Slovenia and an area beyond the territorial seas of Croatia and Italy" (PCA Final Award 2017: 344, para 1076).

As for the location of the Junction Area, the Tribunal decided that it be along the sea border between Croatia and Italy (Osimo border) inside Croatia's territorial sea with a width of 2.5 nm[112] running from Slovenia's territorial sea border with Croatia to the point where Croatian territorial sea meets the high seas (see Fig. 4.4).

Continental Shelf

Slovenia had made a continental shelf (CS) claim overlapping with the Croatian CS and asked the Tribunal to delimitate the Parties' continental shelves on the grounds that a CS was to be subsumed under "relevant maritime areas" in article 3(1)(c) of the Arbitration Agreement.

The Tribunal determined in one single paragraph that the territorial sea boundary between Slovenia and Croatia established between the point on the closing line of Piran Bay and the Osimo border was an all-purpose boundary and that Slovenia thus "has no maritime zones extending west beyond that maritime boundary". Further, "Slovenia's claim to continental shelf rights is therefore incompatible with the Tribunal's determination of the entitlements of the two States in this area, and no question of continental shelf determination arises" (PCA Final Award 2017: 354, para 1103).

[112] Slovenia had requested 3 nm (PCA Final Award 2017: 340, para 1060).

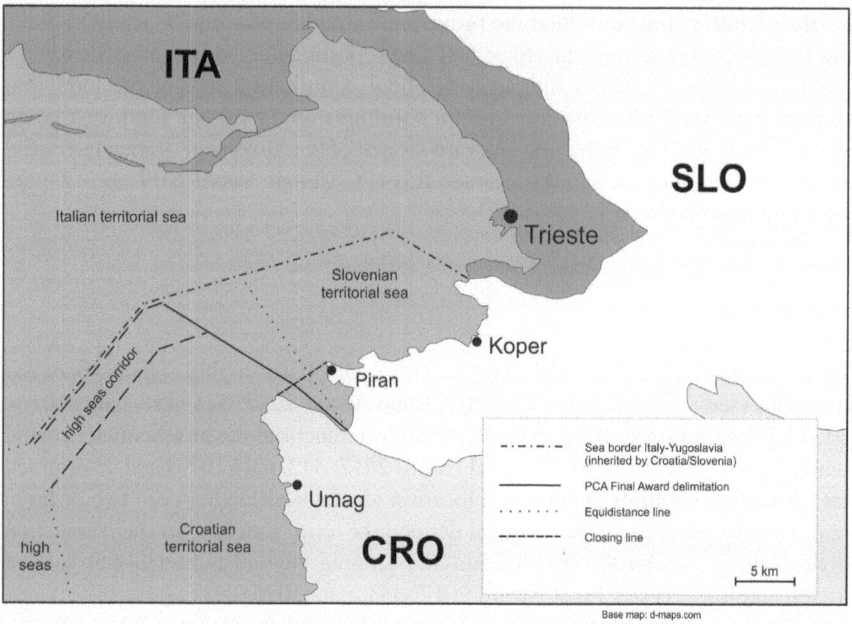

Fig. 4.4 Delimitation in Piran Bay, territorial sea border and junction area according to the 2017 Final Award (schematic view; *Source* Author; base map: d-maps.com)

Regime for the Use of the Maritime Areas

Applying the mandate of Article 4(b) of the Arbitration Agreement ("international law, equity and the principle of good-neighbourly relations in order to achieve a fair and just result") as the applicable law, the Tribunal determined a regime which "is intended to guarantee both the integrity of Croatia's territorial sea and Slovenia's freedoms of communication between its territory and the high seas" (PCA Final Award 2017: 360, para 1123).

The *freedoms of communication* in the Junction Area are characterised as follows:

- Uninterrupted and uninterruptable access to and from Slovenia including its airspace;
- Freedom of navigation and overflight, and the lying of submarine cables and pipelines;
- All ships and aircraft of all States enjoy these freedoms irrespective of their nationality;
- Passage is unconditional and cannot be suspended under any circumstances;
- Submarine vessels have no duty to navigate on the surface[113];

[113]Non-suspendible transit passage (Art. 39 1(b) UNCLOS) applying to international straits used for international navigation (such as the Strait of Gibraltar, The Sound/Öresund, or the Strait of

- No exploring or exploiting of natural resources, i.e. no fishing or oil/gas exploitation.

The *guarantees and limitations* of the freedoms of communication in the Junction Area are:

- No boarding, arrest, detention or other interference of ships or aircraft by Croatia;
- Croatia cannot enforce its laws and regulations for ships and aircraft in the Junction Area[114];
- Croatia may provide assistance to vessels when called upon including emergency situations (PCA Final Award 2017: 360–3, paras 1123–1136).

With regard to the "*Duty of Cooperation and Other Agreements between the Parties*" (emphasis added), the Tribunal, *inter alia*, raises the following main issues:

The Junction Area regime must be exercised with due regard also to the rights and obligations of other States. The Tribunal noted that "given the small size of the Junction Area and its *proximity to adjacent States*, this obligation is a particularly important element of the legal regime of the Junction Area" (PCA Final Award 2017: 362, para 1134; emphasis added).

Further, the arbitrators noted that the Award does not affect any existing or future agreements (on implementation, for example) between Croatia and Slovenia. In the same vein, the *IMO Traffic Separation Scheme in the North Adriatic* (with designated sea lanes for vessels going to and from the Gulf of Trieste and to/from the ports of Koper and Trieste) and international rules for air navigation, i.e. those of the International Civil Aviation Organization (ICAO), shall not be affected either. Similarly, the rights and obligations of Slovenia under *EU law* are not touched upon (PCA Final Award 2017: 363, paras 1136–7).

4.3.5.3 Scholarly Response

The maritime determinations of the Final Award have received a variety of scholarly responses which merits a brief discussion.

The Bay

Bankes (2017: 3) notes that the Tribunal's decision stipulating that the legal status of Piran Bay remains internal waters, and is thus inherited from SFRY times, is consistent with the ICJ's 1992 judgement in the *Gulf of Fonseca* case (El Salvador/Honduras/Nicaragua) where the status of internal waters was confirmed for

Otranto) does *not* include the freedom for submarine vessels to navigate under the surface (see e.g. Tanaka 2015: 109).

[114] Ships and aircraft, however, must comply with Croatian laws and regulations, and Croatia can take enforcement action *outside* the Junction Area in accordance with international law.

a pluri-national bay following decolonisation. Grbec (interview 10-07-2018) highlights that it was "a balanced and sound Award" and by confirming the Bay of Fonseca judgement the Tribunal had set a precedent for maritime issues in the post-Yugoslav region in the Adriatic. Further, this decision confirmed the principle of *uti possidetis* and that there was no automatic switch to territorial waters after independence. By delimitating using *uti possidetis effectivités* the Tribunal did not apply maritime law, but a principle otherwise used for delimitation on land. The 80–20 partition of the Bay, according to Grbec, pretty much reflected an informal agreement from February 1991 by the authorities on the ground for policing purposes which was applied at least up until the date of independence.[115]

Insolia (2019: 228–229) notes that the Tribunal's reference to the *Gulf of Fonseca* case omitted a vital aspect for determining the status of the Bay, namely an agreement of the coastal States in terms of a consistent joint claim of the status of internal waters which the ICJ had emphasised in its 1992 judgement. This is to say that the ICJ focused most on the attitude of the successor States rather than merely assessing the status of the Bay at a time when it belonged to a single State. However, the Tribunal may have been restricted in their analysis by Article 5 of the Arbitration Agreement stipulating 25 June 1991 as the critical date meaning documents or actions after that date could not be considered. Degan (interview 21-11-2019) objects to the notion of internal waters: The Bay's status should have been determined as territorial sea and delimitated by means of the equidistance/special circumstances method.

There has been some criticism of the fact that the Tribunal made no determinations with regard to the use of Piran Bay. Cataldi (interview 18-07-2018) argues that a *condominium* approach would be a win–win situation with a particular regard to fisheries, as one would not have to worry about borders, referring to the 1983 agreement between Italy and Yugoslavia on a joint fishing zone in the Gulf of Trieste, whereby borders played a useful role when delimiting communities but not for the exploitation of resources. The Italy-Yugoslavia agreement is also mentioned by Insolia (2019: 231) who contends that, contemplating the 1992 *Gulf of Fonseca* judgement of the ICJ, State succession could well create *condominium* where a single undivided maritime area passes to successor States. The States were not bound to such regime indefinitely, as they may well agree on a delimitation bilaterally if they so wish. Further, *condominium* was a solution perfectly in line with Art. 123 UNCLOS stipulating that riparian States to a semi-enclosed sea are under an obligation to cooperate.

[115] Slovenia holds that there were two meetings between the police authorities of both countries on 29 January and 26 February 1991 in Pula where that agreement had been reached. Croatia denies that such agreement was arrived at. The arbitral tribunal, however, could not take on board any of these arguments as there are no agreed records of the Pula meetings (PCA Final Award 2017: 278, para 909).

Maritime Boundary

As for the Tribunal's decision to modify the provisional equidistance line for the maritime boundary recognizing the coastal configuration around Cape Savudrija as a special circumstance, Solomou (2017: 5) opines that the half-effect[116] given to the Cape and its coast was predictable and "in line with *jurisprudence constante* [...] as established by a series of cases handled by the ICJ, ITLOS and arbitral tribunals alike". In the same vain, Grbec (interview 10-07-2018) takes the view that, generally, the Tribunal did not depart from settled jurisprudence.

Oude Elferink (2017), however is critical of the Tribunal's determinations, notably as for its treatment of Cape Savudrija as a special circumstance. First, in looking at the seaward projection of the southwest-facing part of the Croatian coastline south of Cape Savudrija, the Tribunal took "into account a part of the coast of Croatia that is *not* part of the *relevant* coast for the territorial sea delimitation" (2017: 6; emphasis added). According to Oude Elferink, "the limited maritime zone of Slovenia is not due to a notional cut-off effect resulting from the equidistance line [...], but the result of the limited dimensions of the Gulf of Trieste" with Slovenia being in a different geographical situation than Croatia "which faces the Adriatic proper beyond the Gulf of Trieste" (2017: 5–6). The treatment of the shape of Cape Savudrija in relation to the south-west facing direction of the remainder of the Croatian coast is also taken up by Insolia (2019: 233). Whilst he acknowledges that the coast south-west of Cape Savudrija did not account for any base points for the construction of the equidistance line, this feature had been the only way for the Tribunal to take into consideration the unique geographical situation of Slovenia with its concave coast.

Junction Area

On the Junction Area and its regime, a task for the Arbitral Tribunal that required a "creative, innovative approach" (Petrič 2017: 371), Grbec (interview 10-07-2018) posits that it was clear that the Tribunal could not take away any territorial sea from Croatia. With the solution of the Junction Area still being Croatian territorial sea, but with high-seas freedoms and absolute passage, the Tribunal had "reconciled the battle of principles in maritime delimitation" which constituted a highly interesting precedent. Bankes (2017: 4) considers the solution of the Tribunal "certainly elegant" in terms of offering Slovenia *de facto* high seas access, albeit without resource-related rights such as fishing or seabed exploitation, and keeping the limitation of Croatia's sovereignty in the Junction Area to a minimum. Much in the same vein, Insolia (2019: 233–234) considers the determinations of the Tribunal in respect of the Junction Area "creative and balanced" subjecting a part of the Croatian territorial sea to a functional regime guaranteeing the freedom of uninterrupted communication with

[116]"Half-effect" refers to islands or coastal configurations being identified by a court or tribunal as to leading to distorting effects in maritime boundary delimitation, such as in the present case, and thus recognized as special circumstance (see e.g. Beazley 1979: 154).

an *erga omnes* character as in an EEZ whilst preserving the territorial sovereignty of Croatia.

Comparing the Junction Area with traditional instruments of transit passage or high-seas corridors, Ferri (2018) notes that the *sui generis* regime in the Junction Area provides for a number of novelties, in particular the complete exclusion of enforcement of domestic legislation on the part of Croatia in the Junction Area. In her view, an international straits regime with some corrective elements would have made for a fairer balance. In terms of precedent-setting value, the judgement constituted a strengthening of the claims of geographically disadvantaged States with regard to access to the high seas (2018: 671).

Cataldi (interview 18-07-2018) posits that the Junction Area and its location are not free of controversy, mainly because it was not clear yet how Italy as the adjacent State should react. Italy was affected by that corridor solution, but not a party to the conflict. He goes on to question the need for a *sui generis* corridor for Slovenia altogether as innocent passage was a far-reaching principle where the riparian State hardly had any means to stop a ship in its territorial sea anyway. Scovazzi (interview 03-08-2018) holds that the Tribunal's decision on the Junction Area was well explained, and that the Junction Area was the crucial point for Slovenia outweighing by far the territorial sea delimitation. Yet, with regard to the regime inside the Junction Area, the fact that Croatia retained the right to adopt legislation, but was not going to be able to enforce domestic legislation in the Junction Area, was "strange".

This author submits that the Tribunal's decision on the Junction Area appears to be very much in line with the mandate from the Arbitration Agreement. Further, there is some precedent-setting value in terms of, first, interpreting the term "junction", notably a novel term in the jurisprudence of maritime delimitation, and, second, developing a regime for a junction corridor in the territorial sea of a State having to marry the principle of territorial sovereignty with the principle of freedom of navigation under the delicate circumstances arising from the Arbitration Agreement. Notwithstanding the Tribunal's express mention that the Final Award shall not affect other agreements, the Junction Area provisions nevertheless do have practical implications not least on the existing Traffic Separation Scheme in the Northern Adriatic; see Sect. 6.1.1.1.

It is not difficult to agree with Bankes (2017) that the Tribunal, on the whole, acted rather elegantly on the Junction Area. The precedent-setting value of the junction regime must not be underestimated in the post-Yugoslav context. There are pending maritime disputes, or provisional arrangements calling for a permanent solution, between Croatia and Montenegro, and between Croatia and Bosnia-Herzegovina, both in the context of the two countries' EU accession process. This issue will be addressed in more detail in Sects. 6.3.1 and 6.3.5.

With regard to the delimitation method for the territorial sea border (see Sect. 3.2.2.3), it may be observed that the Tribunal suggested that there is a uniform delimitation method for all maritime zones (territorial sea, EEZ, and continental shelf; PCA Final Award 2017: 311–312, paras 999–1000), whilst in *Croatia v. Slovenia* the Tribunal applied the two-stage approach. This calls for two comments: First, the Tribunal's express mention of the three-stage approach referring to its application by the ICJ's recent 2014 *Peru v. Chile* case (PCA Final Award 2017: 311, para 999) in contrast with the effective non-use of the test by the Tribunal itself in *Croatia v. Slovenia* creates some confusion as to the universal application of the three-stage approach and the need of the proportionality test generally. Second, this leaves the (dis)proportionality test—where no court or tribunal has ever managed to produce objective criteria in a scientific manner—ever more contested (see also Tanaka 2018a). When every allowance is made for the fact that the proportionality test remains a sensitive issue, it would have been a good idea, for the sake of transparency, for the Tribunal to explain why it was not in a position to apply the test under the specific circumstances of *Croatia v. Slovenia*. It appears that, as regards delimitation of the territorial sea, simply no mathematical calculation is possible as no coastal lengths or other features in terms of relevant areas can be identified in the first place where a ratio with the maritime areas apportioned can be established.

4.3.6 Follow-up to the Final Award

There were a number of responses to the Final Award. For the analytical purposes of this study, it is useful to distinguish between the bilateral and the third-party level.

4.3.6.1 Bilateral

On the day the PCA Final Award was handed down, the Slovenian Prime Minister Miro Cerar said at a press conference in Ljubljana:

> In accordance with the arbitration ruling we will first call on the Republic of Croatia to pursue joint implementation. To this end, [...] we will shortly [...] be sending the Croatian side a formal call for dialogue regarding fulfillment and implementation of the ruling within a reasonable time frame [...].
>
> I expect Croatia to respond to this and for us to be able to agree on joint further steps regarding implementation. We have six months to prepare for implementation of the ruling. And we will resolve any possible complications with our neighbouring country in an amicable and responsible manner, in accordance with the principle of observing good neighbourly relations. (Slovenian Prime Minister's Office press release, 29 June 2017)

At a press conference in Zagreb on the same day, the Croatian prime minister Andrej Plenković said:

> The first and most important message [...] is that today's arbitration decision does not bind us in any way, nor are we thinking about applying its contents. The second message is that Croatia adopted its position on the arbitration very clearly and unambiguously in parliament two years ago today [...].
>
> For us, this arbitration has no legal effect, but we remain willing for talks with Slovenia on resolving the outstanding border issue and we don't expect Slovenia to take any unilateral

> steps [...]. Croatia, too, believes in peaceful ways of resolving disputes, including in arbitration, but only when it is clean, fair and in line with agreed rules. (Croatian Prime Minister's press release, 29 June 2017)

Ljubljana Meeting

On 12 July 2017, Cerar and Plenković discussed the way forward in a 40-min tête-à-tête meeting in Ljubljana, agreed to keep in touch on the border issue, not to raise tensions, refrain from any unilateral acts, and to continue the dialogue at their next meeting agreed to be held in Zagreb in September. In the second part of the meeting, the delegations were tasked with preparatory work for the Zagreb meeting on the border issue and all other open bilateral issues (interview Miro Cerar, 15-10-2018, interview Andrej Plenković 28-06-2018). There were also several other informal meetings of representatives of both sides. The intention was to create a bilateral document, which would outline the entire border and entail the provisions of the arbitration award (land, sea, maritime areas) without specifically citing the Final Award. The bilateral document would serve as the base document for the demarcation of the border. Ljubljana indicated some flexibility for necessary adjustments of the course of the land border whilst insisting on the Tribunal's decision regarding the maritime border and the Junction Area (interview senior Slovenian civil servant, 17-04-2020).

Whilst there appears to have been some sense of de-escalation at the above bilateral Ljubljana meeting, things soon re-escalated, however. At a Council meeting of the Organization for Economic Co-operation and Development (OECD) in Paris on 8 September, Slovenia and Hungary objected to Croatia's bid for OECD membership. Slovenia opposed the Croatian bid on the grounds that Zagreb was not implementing the arbitral award on the border (STA News, 8 September 2017).[117] Further, on 15 September 2017, Slovenia filed a lawsuit against the European Commission for granting Croatia the derogation right to use "Teran" on wine labels of Croatian Istrian origin, "Teran" originally being a Slovenian Protected Designation of Origin (STA News, 15 September 2017; European Commission news, 19 May 2017). The General Court of the EU dismissed the Slovenian action on 9 September 2020 (Judgement T-626/17).

New York Incident

On the sidelines of the UN General Assembly in New York on 19 September 2017, Plenković and Cerar agreed to hold the bilateral follow-up meeting in Zagreb on 27 September. Two days later, however, Plenković, in his speech before the UN referring to Slovenia's *ex parte* communication during the arbitration procedure, publicly accused Slovenia of "undermining the rule of law" (Address at the 72nd

[117] Hungary's objection related to Croatia's arrest warrant vis-à-vis the CEO of Hungary's energy company MOL (MTI news, 11 September 2017).

Session of the General Assembly, 21 September 2017: 6).[118] That statement came only a few hours after a bilateral meeting in a very good atmosphere. Cerar was "shocked" at Plenković's "impolite and unacceptable" wording, so that he cancelled his visit to Zagreb foreseen later that month (interview Miro Cerar, 15-10-2018).

Zagreb Meeting

The atmosphere proved tense for some time, and after an exchange of letters in October, Cerar finally came to Zagreb on 19 December 2017. The border issue was the main topic, and Plenković had presented a draft paper to Cerar which aimed at the bilateral *de facto* implementation of main elements of the Final Award, but with a few adjustments.

It is worth quoting from the press conference with questions and answers. Miro Cerar, the Prime Minister of Slovenia, said:

> I came to Zagreb today primarily with the intention of discussing this issue that is important for both countries, given that the deadline for the preparation of the arbitral award implementation expires very soon, on 29 December.[119] I understand the standpoint presented by my colleague, Mr Plenković that the arbitral award is not binding for Croatia, although I cannot agree with it, personally and as the Prime Minister of the Republic of Slovenia […].
>
> The only way forward for Slovenia is to respect the arbitral award and to implement it together […] The arbitral award is an indivisible whole and must be respected as such. It covers two different dimensions, one being the sea which the Arbitral Tribunal delineated by a very clear line that does not require any particular implementation arrangements. Naturally, the situation is different on the land border, which calls for a formation of a joint mixed committee that will carry out the demarcation, naturally within the framework of the arbitral award, considering that there are still some minor adjustments to be made […] Slovenia insists on the application of the arbitral award, to which we are obliged by international law, as well as European law, because we are also aware of the European aspect of the award. (Government of the Republic of Croatia News press conference notes, 19 December 2017)

Andrej Plenković, the Prime Minister of Croatia, said:

---

[118]The Croatian prime minister said the following: "We believe that disputes should be resolved through peaceful means and in conformity with international law. It is of the utmost importance that all international adjudications meet the highest legal standards and fully respect their relevant rules. Compromising the impartiality or independence of international adjudicators and tribunals, as was the case in the *terminated* Arbitration Process between Croatia and Slovenia, *makes their decisions legally void* and left Croatia with no choice other than to withdraw from the arbitration process. We consider that this example of *undermining the rule of law* is a discouragement for States considering third-party dispute settlement" (Address UN General Assembly Session, 21 September 2017: 5–6; emphasis added). One must keep in mind that the Tribunal, in its Partial Award, found that (i) Slovenia did violate the Arbitration Agreement, but not to such extent that a termination would be justified, (ii) the files introduced by the arbitrator appointed by Slovenia contained no new facts which were not already there at the record of the written or oral pleadings, (iii) the Arbitration Agreement remained in force, and (iv) that the recomposed Tribunal's ability to render a Final Award impartially was unaffected (PCA Partial Award 2016: 36–58, paras 157–225; see also Sect. 4.3.4.3).

[119]There is an implementation deadline for the Final Award of six months laid down in Article 7(3) of the Arbitration Agreement. Thus, the expiry date for implementation was 29 December 2017; see Sect. 4.2.3.

> As far as 29 December [2017] is concerned, for Croatia it is a date like any other in terms of international law [...] In order for us to reach agreement from these two positions, we need to maintain discussions, reach an understanding on elements that are dividing us [...] Our message is: the border, regardless of what it will look like in the end, needs to be set in a way that is acceptable to both countries and that it can be internally approved by both parliaments with the appropriate majority vote [...] This requires a certain flexibility from both sides. (Government of the Republic of Croatia News press conference notes, 19 December 2017)

Plenković referred to the draft legal framework he had handed over to his Slovenian counterpart on how to proceed with a bilateral solution. Croatia's aim was to

> agree on a *protocol*[120] regarding the state border which would include several key elements. One of them would concern the land border, another one the sea border, the third would concentrate on the navigation regime in Croatian waters [Junction Area] beyond the Bay of Savudrija, the fourth on forming a mixed [bilateral] committee which would address aspects of the identification and demarcation of the border, while the fifth would concern the manner in which such a document would be submitted to the parliaments of both countries and ratified in the end. (Government of the Republic of Croatia News press conference notes, 19 December 2017; emphasis and footnote added)

Both sides apparently had a different understanding of where flexibility should apply. Fundamentally, however, it must be noted that whilst it is clear that any implementation of the decision of any judicial body on the course of the *land* border requires minor adjustments and demarcation on the ground,[121] sea border delimitations usually are absolute, fixed by the coordinates from the court/tribunal decision and require no fine-tuning, unless the parties agree to negotiate an alternative solution.

At the actual tête-à-tête part of the 19 December Zagreb meeting, Plenković had proposed to negotiate a bilateral agreement that would take the arbitration award as a starting point. His approach for the *land* border was that minor adjustments of the course of the land border could indeed be achieved during the demarcation stage. Yet, as regards the *sea* border, he mentioned to Cerar that he needed an adjustment of the delimitation line inside Piran Bay. "We wanted to see something closer to the equidistance line" than the partition determined by the Final Award, and that due to domestic pressure "I have no room for manoeuvre here" (interview Andrej Plenković, 28-06-2018).

Cerar, however, firmly rejected the proposal to put aside the arbitration award and negotiate a bilateral agreement. "That approach was unacceptable to us. With the arbitration award we have something binding in our hands. Moreover, the border was in its entirety—on land and at sea—defined for the first time in the history of the two countries. Going down the bilateral path again, we would have the incalculable

---

[120] A protocol is a bilateral agreement between governments which they undertake to apply, but which, unlike a treaty, is not subject to mandatory ratification. The Croatian prime minister later explained that the idea was that each government could decide whether it wishes to ratify the protocol (interview Andrej Plenković, 18-02-2018).

[121] It is standard practise to have a bilateral identification and demarcation body to remove impracticable features of the course of the border determined by an international court or tribunal, so that the border does not run through buildings, installations, or farmlands, for example (see also PCA Final Award 2017: 109, paras 337–9; 114, para 357).

hurdle of ratification in Sabor." There had been not-so-fond memories in Slovenia of the 2001 Drnovšek-Račan deal the ratification of which failed in Croatia. "Why should we try that option again? You can have the most brilliant bilateral agreement on paper, but we would have no guarantees that it is actually going to be implemented" (interview Miro Cerar, 15-10-2018).

4.3.6.2 Third Party

The European Commission already made it clear at their meeting on 4 July 2017 that the arbitration ruling had some direct effect on the implementation of EU law, and that infringement proceedings may well be on the cards.

According to the minutes of the meeting, European Commission Vice President Timmermans said that

> although the Commission was not a party to the arbitration agreement, it *had played a facilitating role in the process which led to the creation of an arbitration panel between Slovenia and Croatia*. The Commission had unequivocally supported this arbitration process which should provide legal certainty in the interests of both parties and ensure the *effective implementation of EU law* [...]. The Commission had clearly expressed the hope that both parties would respect the decision taken by the Arbitral Tribunal, thereby putting a definitive end to the border dispute between them. Although the award of the Arbitral Tribunal would not be directly binding on the Union as it was not a party to the agreement or the arbitral procedure [...] it was likely that, in future, the European Court of Justice would be asked for a preliminary ruling on *the award's effects on EU law*.
>
> Regardless of the substance of the award, the principle of international law that the decisions of an arbitral tribunal must be complied with and implemented was all the more important because it continued to be relevant in the context of territorial claims and border disputes [...]. (minutes of the 2219th meeting of the Commission held in Strasburg, 4 July 2017: 20–1; emphasis added)

The Director-General of the European Commission's Legal Service reported that

> the *arbitral award was the result of a valid international agreement entered into by Croatia and Slovenia* and supported by the Union. The Commission had witnessed this agreement in the context of the accession negotiations with Croatia and had *played a facilitating role* in the appointment of arbitrators of the Arbitral Tribunal. In particular, the Accession Treaty of Croatia referred explicitly to the use of an arbitration procedure to settle the border dispute.
>
> While the border between the two countries was a bilateral issue, it nonetheless had a *direct effect on EU law, and therefore the Union had jurisdiction in respect of this matter*. Pursuant to Article 17 of the Treaty on European Union, the Commission oversees the implementation of EU law under the control of the Court of Justice of the European Union. Lastly, *EU case-law left no room for doubt as to the obligation of the Union and the Member States to implement public international law*, which it would be bound to demonstrate in this case. In conclusion, the Union could be requested to clarify the effects of the award on EU law in the event of infringement proceedings. (minutes of the 2219th meeting of the Commission held in Strasburg, 4 July 2017: 22–3; emphasis added)

European Commission Vice President Timmermans said the day after that he "expects both parties to implement [the ruling]" (EC Daily News, 5 July 2017).

Several EU Member States and the US issued statements. The Benelux Prime Ministers stressed "the importance of the rule of law as the foundation upon which the EU is built [...]" calling "on both sides to respect the arbitration award in a constructive spirit" (Joint Benelux Statement on Croatia-Slovenia arbitration award, 4 July 2017). A German Foreign Ministry statement had said that "[...] preserving the integrity of international courts and tribunals is in the common interest of all States. EU Member States must play an exemplary role in this" (German Foreign Ministry press release, 30 June 2017). The British Embassy in Zagreb, upon request, gave a statement to the Croatian media saying that the UK "support[ed] the Tribunal process [and] the lawful resolution of disputes", but that "the bilateral dispute was a matter for the Croatian and Slovenian Governments, which the UK wishes to see solved" and that "it is for the two parties to decide themselves how that is achieved" (UK Embassy Zagreb statement, 30 June 2017). The US Embassies in Ljubljana and Zagreb issued a statement saying "we are not taking sides in this dispute. It is up to [the] two countries, both EU members and NATO allies, to resolve this bilateral issue, and we are hopeful they can do so" (US Embassy in Slovenia Statement, 29 June 2017).[122] It is worth noting in this context that the entire Slovenian political and diplomatic elite had been engaged in "silent diplomacy" over the preceding months to highlight the importance of the arbitration ruling (interview Tanja Fajon, 22-11-2016; interview senior Slovenian civil servant, 10-07-2017).

4.4 Lawsuit Before the CJEU

The Slovenian government subsequently finalised preparations for a lawsuit before the Court of Justice of the European Union (CJEU) against Croatia for violations of EU law due to non-implementation of the 2017 Final Award.

It is useful to recall that there are two types of infringement procedures in the EU institutional set-up: proceedings (i) initiated by the European Commission against a Member State mostly on the grounds of insufficient or non-implementation of existing EU legislation (Article 258 TFEU), or those (ii) launched by a Member State against another Member State for not respecting norms in EU legislation or the Treaties (Article 259 TFEU).

Whilst the Commission, as Guardian of the Treaties, has launched hundreds of infringement procedures against Member States, legal proceedings of one Member State against another one are indeed very rare. So far and excluding the *Slovenia v. Croatia* case, there have only been five judgements handed down in the history of the EC/EU.[123]

---

[122] An identical text featured in the statement of the US Embassy in Zagreb on 30 June 2017.

[123] France v United Kingdom [on the designation of protection zones in fisheries, judgement 4 October 1979 C-141/78 (http://curia.europa.eu/juris/liste.jsf?language=en&jur=C,T,F&num=C-141/78&td=ALL)], Belgium v. Spain [on the labelling of the designation of origin on bottled wines, judgement 16 May 2000 C-388/95 (http://curia.europa.eu/juris/liste.jsf?language=en&jur=C,T,F&num=C-388/95&td=ALL)], Spain v. United Kingdom [on the right to vote for Commonwealth

Art. 259 TFEU provides that an EU Member State must bring the complaint against another EU Member State before the Commission first. The Commission may or may not, within three months after the submission of the complaint, and after each of the parties concerned have submitted their position, issue an opinion and bring the matter before the CJEU. If the Commission does not produce an opinion, the Member State lodging the complaint may bring the matter before the Court directly after the expiry of the three-months deadline.[124]

Slovenia's complaint was sent to the Commission on 16 March 2018 (STA News, 16 March 2018) following a consultation of the Foreign Affairs Committee of the Slovenian Parliament. The Foreign Affairs Committee mandated both the filing of the complaint with the European Commission and, in case of non-opinion by the Commission, the subsequent filing with the CJEU (STA News, 13 July 2018). Processing the complaint, an in-camera hearing with government representatives of Slovenia and Croatia was held at the European Commission on 2 May 2018. The three-months deadline for a Commission opinion expired on 17 June 2018. To that end, the Commission refrained from issuing an opinion on the Slovenian complaint[125] in order to stay neutral (information obtained from several European Commission Cabinet members; the decision was taken at a meeting of Cabinets' representatives on 15 June 2018) despite the Commission's principle view on the merits expressed in the College meeting on 4 July 2017 which could be read as questioning Croatia's non-implementation of the Final Award.

It is useful to note in that context, that, following the 2 May hearing, the Commission's Legal Service produced a note in mid-May 2018 which, in its rationale on

---

citizens in Gibraltar, judgement 12 September 2006 C-145/04 (http://curia.europa.eu/juris/liste.jsf?language=en&jur=C,T,F&num=C-145/04&td=ALL)], Hungary v. Slovakia [on the prohibition of the President of Hungary from entering Slovakia, judgement 16 October 2012 C-364/10 (http://curia.europa.eu/juris/liste.jsf?language=en&jur=C,T,F&num=C-364/10&td=ALL)], and Austria v. Germany [on the planned German road-toll scheme for car holders C-591-17 (http://curia.europa.eu/juris/fiche.jsf?pro=&lgrec=de&nat=or&oqp=&lg=&dates=&language=en&id=C%3B591%3B17%3BRD%3B1%3BP%3B1%3BC2017%2F0591%2FP&jur=C%2CT%2CF&cit=none%252CC%252CCJ%252CR%252C2008E%252C%252C%252C%252C%252C%252C%252C%252C%252C%252Ctrue%252Cfalse%252Cfalse&td=%3BALL&pcs=Oor&avg=&mat=or&etat=pend&parties=%25C3%2596sterreich&jge=&for=&cid=178887)].

[124] Article 259 TFEU: A Member State which considers that another Member State has failed to fulfil an obligation under the Treaties may bring the matter before the Court of Justice of the European Union. Before a Member State brings an action against another Member State for an alleged infringement of an obligation under the Treaties, it shall bring the matter before the Commission.

The Commission shall deliver a reasoned opinion after each of the States concerned has been given the opportunity to submit its own case and its observations on the other party's case both orally and in writing.

If the Commission has not delivered an opinion within three months of the date on which the matter was brought before it, the absence of such opinion shall not prevent the matter from being brought before the Court.

[125] In the event of proceedings before the CJEU at a later stage, the Commission may well present an opinion—and did so, on the Court's request regarding the issue of Croatian inadmissibility motion. Any Member State interested in making a submission to a CJEU file can do so, too. See Art. 196 Rules of Procedure CJEU.

the binding nature of the Final Award, corresponds to the findings presented during the Commission College meeting of 4 July 2017 (see Sect. 4.3.6.2) confirming that the border dispute was solved by means of the Final Award which was now part of international law the EU had to respect (Internal note European Commission, 14 May 2018: 3–4).

The Slovenian caretaker government[126] subsequently launched the Art. 259 lawsuit directly before the Court on 13 July 2018 (C-457/18). The government had consulted the Foreign Affairs Committee of the newly elected domestic Parliament on 9 July 2018. Acting Prime Minister Cerar publicly explained the official rationale of the lawsuit after the meeting:

> The lawsuit is not an obstacle to the continued search for an implementation agreement that we want in Slovenia. [However, any] delay could send a completely wrong message, as if we either renounce legal remedies or we do not believe in our own arguments.
>
> We will relieve politics of further tensions and thus transfer the matter to the *legal*-professional level. Let the competent court decide on this matter, which means that at the *political* level we can develop relations with Croatia, and keep on looking for [a] solution for implementation. If we succeed [at the political level], then the [legal] action will be withdrawn. (STA News, 9 July 2018; emphasis added)

4.4.1 Slovenia's Claims and Croatia's Inadmissibility Motion

The original Slovenian complaint from 16 March 2018 of approximately one hundred pages (including supporting documents and media documentation) is confidential, so a detailed account of the legal and political reasoning appears impossible.

4.4.1.1 Slovenia's Pleas

The lawsuit filed with the CJEU directly on 13 July 2018 contains the following elements, as summarised by the Court (Official Journal of the EU, C 399, 19–21, 5 November 2018; emphases added):

> First plea in law:
>
> By unilaterally falling short of the commitment, which it made during the EU accession process, to comply with the arbitration award and thus with the boundary delimited by that award and the other obligations imposed thereby, the Republic of *Croatia refuses to respect the rule of law,* which is a fundamental value of the European Union (Article 2 TEU).
>
> Second plea in law:
>
> By [...] unilaterally refus[ing] to fulfil its obligations under the arbitration award, while at the same time preventing Slovenia from fully exercising its sovereignty over certain parts of its territory under the Treaty, the Republic of *Croatia is in breach of its duty of sincere cooperation with the European Union and with the Republic of Slovenia* as laid down in Article 4(3) TEU.[...] The *Republic of Croatia is making it impossible for the Republic of*

[126] The (early) general election in Slovenia took place on 3 June 2018.

Slovenia to implement EU law throughout its mainland and marine territory and to act in accordance with that law, and in particular in compliance with the secondary Union rules relating to the territory of the Member States (first subparagraph of Article 4(3) TEU).

Third plea in law:

The Republic of *Croatia is infringing* Regulation (EU) No 1380/2013 of the European Parliament and of the Council of 11 December 2013 on *the Common Fisheries Policy, and in particular the mutual access regime* laid down in Article 5 thereof and Annex I thereto. The regime, which applies to Croatia and Slovenia since 30 December 2017, grants 25 fishing vessels from each country free access to the other country's territorial sea, as determined [...] under the arbitration award. The Republic of Croatia is not permitting the Republic of Slovenia to exercise its rights under that regime and is thus infringing Article 5 of that regulation due to the fact that: (i) it is refusing to implement the mutual access regime; (ii) it is refusing to recognise the validity of the legislation adopted by the Republic of Slovenia for that purpose; and (iii) by systematically applying fines, it is denying Slovenian fishing vessels free access to the marine waters which the arbitration award of 2017 has defined as Slovene, and, a fortiori, free access to Croatian waters falling within the scope of the mutual access regime.

Fourth plea in law:

The Republic of *Croatia is infringing* Council Regulation (EC) No 1224/2009 of 20 November 2009 establishing a *Community control system for ensuring compliance with the rules of the common fisheries policy* and Implementing Regulation (EU) No 404/2011 of 8 April 2011. Croatian police patrol boats [...] are accompanying Croatian fishing vessels when they fish in Slovenian waters, thereby preventing Slovenian fishing inspectors from carrying out controls. At the same time, the Croatian authorities are imposing fines on Slovenian fishing vessels for unlawful boundary crossing and illegal fishing when they fish in Slovenian waters which Croatia claims for itself.[127] In addition, Croatia is not sending Slovenia the data regarding the activities of Croatian vessels in Slovenian waters, as is required by those two regulations. Thus, *the Republic of Croatia is not permitting the Republic of Slovenia to carry out controls in waters under its sovereignty and jurisdiction and is not respecting Slovenia's exclusive jurisdiction as a coastal State in its territorial sea*, thereby infringing Regulation (EC) No 1224/2009 and Regulation (EU) No 404/2011.

Fifth plea in law:

The Republic of *Croatia has infringed and continues to infringe* Regulation (EU) 2016/399 of the European Parliament and of the Council of 9 March 2016 on a Union Code on the rules governing the movement of persons across borders (*Schengen Borders Code*). Croatia does not recognise the boundaries established by the arbitration award as a common boundary with Slovenia, is not cooperating with Slovenia to protect that 'external border', and is not in a position to guarantee adequate protection of that border, so that it is infringing Articles 13 and 17 of that regulation, and Article 4 thereof, which requires borders to be established in accordance with international law.

[127] [Footnote inserted by the author of this book.] The Slovenian police dealt with 737 incidents in Slovenian waters in Piran Bay between 30 December 2017 (after the expiry of the implementation period; see Art. 7(1) Arbitration Agreement and e.g. 4.3.6.1) and 30 August 2018 involving 1151 Croatian vessels (622 fishing boats and 529 police boats; STA News, 8 September 2018; no news from HINA or Croatian authorities available). The Croatian police also inspected and fined Slovenian vessels fishing in the area claimed by Croatia, but attributed to Slovenia by the arbitral award (information obtained from a civil servant involved in the 2 May 2018 European Commission hearing with the Parties). A graver incident happened on 24 March 2019 when a Croatian police boat went 1.3 km across the (theoretical) equidistance line in the Bay coming very close to the town of Piran. According to Croatian police authorities, there was a problem with the vessel's navigation device (HINA News, 27 March 2019; STA News, 27 March 2019).

> Sixth plea in law:
>
> The Republic of *Croatia has infringed and continues to infringe* Directive 2014/89/EU of the European Parliament and of the Council of 23 July 2014 establishing a *framework for maritime spatial planning*, which is to apply to 'marine waters' of Member States, as defined in accordance with the relevant provisions of the United Nations Convention on the Law of the Sea of 1982 ('Unclos') (Article 2(4) of the Directive). The Republic of Croatia rejects the arbitration award which has established that delimitation of the boundaries and - on the contrary - includes Slovenian waters in its own maritime spatial planning: consequently, it does not allow for harmonisation with the geographical maps of the Republic of Slovenia, thereby infringing that Directive, in particular Articles 8 and 11 thereof.

4.4.1.2 Croatia's Inadmissibility Claim

On 21 December 2018, Croatia filed a motion with the CJEU with regard to Slovenia's Article 259 lawsuit. The Ministry of Foreign and European Affairs communication focused on the aspect of the bilateral dispute being a matter of international law rather than EU law:

> [...] Croatia is asking the ECJ to dismiss Slovenia's lawsuit as inadmissible, since the ECJ is not competent to decide on Slovenia's demands in proceedings envisaged under Article 259 of the Treaty on the Functioning of the European Union given that the dispute between Croatia and Slovenia should be settled by applying international law and that the settlement of the dispute does not depend on the application of the EU law or its interpretation. (Press release Ministry of Foreign and European Affairs of the Republic of Croatia, 21 December 2018)

Croatia appeared to primarily uphold its position that the border issue is *not* settled under international law as Zagreb does not recognize the Final Award of the arbitral tribunal for the reasons outlined earlier (see e.g. Sect. 4.3.6.1). Following that logic, one could indeed take the view that the CJEU would not be competent since a (prospective) settlement of the border dispute as such under international law has *prima facie* nothing to do with the application of EU law.[128]

In fact, Croatia's motion of inadmissibility was more comprehensive and based on three pillars altogether:

(i) The claims of Slovenia were only ancillary to the settlement of the bilateral dispute about the validity of the arbitration agreement and the arbitration award;
(ii) the above dispute had to be settled according to the rules of international law which were not related to the application of EU law;

---

[128] Nevertheless, even if the Final Award did *not* constitute a binding settlement under international law, there is a pertinent provision of EU legislation in so far as the mutual access to the territorial sea for fisheries purposes stipulated in Art. 5(2) of Annex I of Regulation 1380/2013 expressly refers to the decision of the arbitration procedure (the proceedings were ongoing by the time the Regulation was adopted). It would appear, therefore, that the above provision in Annex I constitutes a link to EU law rendering the settlement of the border mandatory for the application of the EU Regulation. This issue was broadly discussed at the CJEU hearing on inadmissibility on 8 July 2019 (author's field notes, 8-07-2019); see, however, Sect. 4.4.2 (ii)–(v).

(iii) the Court had no jurisdiction to rule on the validity or legal effects of either the arbitration agreement or the arbitration award both of which were not an integral part of EU law as the arbitration agreement was the real basis of the infringements of EU law pleaded by the Republic of Slovenia (Judgement C-457/18, 31 January 2020, paras 75–77).

The Court subsequently decided to separate the issues of admissibility and, should the necessity arise, the merits of the Case. A hearing on the issue of admissibility and jurisdiction was held before the Grand Chamber on 8 July 2019. The Advocate General presented its Opinion on 11 December 2019 recommending the Court had no jurisdiction.[129]

4.4.2 *CJEU Judgement*

The Court has examined whether it has jurisdiction, i.e. whether the arbitration agreement and the arbitration award are a matter of EU law and thus create obligations under EU competence. In its judgement of 31 January 2020, the Grand Chamber, *inter alia*, found:

(i) It was *not* competent to interpret an international agreement concluded by the Member States in an area outside EU competence, quoting from existing jurisprudence (C-132/09, *Commission v Belgium*), in particular when the pleaded failure to fulfil obligations is ancillary to the obligations from the very international agreement at issue (Judgement C-457/18, paras 91–92; 104);
(ii) The Final Award handed down by the Arbitral Tribunal was governed by international law which was not within the EU competence, and that the EU was not a party to the subject matter despite its mediating role. Nevertheless, there was a clear link between the arbitration agreement and the arbitral proceedings on the one hand and the accession of Croatia to the EU on the other hand. However, those circumstances were insufficient to be seen as an integral part of EU law (Judgement C-457/18, para 102);
(iii) The provisions in Annex II of the Act of Accession of Croatia to the EU referring to the Fisheries Regulation with regard to mutual access to the territorial waters of Croatia and Slovenia to be determined by the arbitration award did not mean that the commitments from the arbitration agreement were incorporated into EU law (Judgement C-457/18, para 103);
(iv) It is within the competence of the Member States to determine the limits of its territories in accordance with international law, quoting C-111/05 (*Aktiebolaget NN*), that this principle was enshrined in Articles 52 TEU and 355 TFEU, and that the Member States have the competence for the geographical demarcation of their borders in accordance with international law (Judgement C-457/18, para 105);

[129] For an analysis of the General Advocate's Opinion see Bickl (2020).

(v) There was a clear obligation for the parties, i.e. the Republic of Croatia and the Republic of Slovenia, in Article 7(3) of the arbitration agreement, to take all necessary steps, including revising national legislation where necessary, to implement the arbitration award, within six months after its adoption, for the purposes of the mutual access regime provided for in the Fisheries Regulation 1380/2013, and that there was no doubt that implementation is pending (Judgement C-457/18, para 106);

(vi) It is beyond the jurisdiction of the Court to examine the respective extent and the limits of the territories of the Republic of Croatia and the Republic of Slovenia by applying directly the border determined by the arbitration award (Judgement C-457/18, para 107); and

(vii) Nevertheless, both the Republic of Croatia and the Republic of Slovenia have an obligation to "strive sincerely to bring about a definitive legal solution consistent with international law, as suggested in the Act of Accession [of the Republic of Croatia]" that ensures the application of EU law, and that an option to settle their dispute could be a submission "to the Court under a special agreement pursuant to Article 273 TFEU" (Judgement C-457/18, para 109).

4.4.3 Discussion

The judgement on *Slovenia v Croatia* has some substantial precedent-setting characteristics since (i) it is the first Art. 259 TFEU Case Member State against a Member State on a territorial issue with a focus on the issue of jurisdiction of the CJEU, (ii) the territorial dispute was subject to third-party judicial dispute resolution under international law where the EU played a strong role in the drafting stages for the mandate for the arbitral tribunal, and (iii) the territorial dispute surfaced during EU accession negotiations. The following analysis of the judgement will tackle these issues in turn.

4.4.3.1 Jurisdiction and the Concept of Ancillary

Slovenia v Croatia is a *sui generis* Art. 259 TFEU dispute Member State v Member State. In fact, it is the first Case where the territorial application of EU law is at issue in Art. 259 TFEU infringement proceedings. The Court had to examine whether obligations arise under EU competence from an international agreement, i.e. the arbitration agreement, entered into by two Member States (Croatia was still a third country by the time the arbitration agreement was signed in 2009) under international law, and its subsequent binding settlement through an arbitration award. The deliberations of the Court were governed by the issue of admissibility or jurisdiction.

Let us look at the judgement's key paragraphs with regard to existing jurisprudence:

> It should [...] be noted that the Court, in the context of an action for failure to fulfil obligations, has already held that it lacks jurisdiction to rule on the *interpretation* [emphasis added] of an international agreement concluded by Member States whose subject matter falls outside the areas of EU competence and on the obligations arising under it for them (see, to that effect [...] *Commission* v *Belgium*, C-132/09 [...], paragraph 44). (Judgement C-457/18, para 91).
>
> It is clear from that case-law that the Court lacks jurisdiction to rule on an action for failure to fulfil obligations, whether it is brought under Article 258 TFEU or under Article 259 TFEU, where the infringement of provisions of EU law that is pleaded in support of the action is *ancillary* to the alleged failure to comply with obligations arising from such an agreement. (Judgement C-457/18, para 92; emphasis added)

With reference to a previous judgement, the Court draws on the concept of *ancillary*, i.e. a legal argument used in an auxiliary or subordinate manner to seek the fulfilment of obligations stemming from a different area of law (international law, in this instance) than the one an Art. 258/259 TFEU claim is based on (EU law). The Court notes that, if infringement proceedings for failure to fulfil obligations relate to an international agreement which is outside EU competence, it has no jurisdiction on the interpretation of that agreement.

The concept of ancillary the Court subsequently employs with regard to the pleas of the Republic of Slovenia when stating that

> the infringements of EU law pleaded are ancillary to the alleged failure by the Republic of Croatia to comply with the obligations arising from a bilateral international agreement to which the European Union is not a party and whose subject matter falls outside the areas of EU competence. Since the subject matter of an action for failure to fulfil obligations brought under Article 259 TFEU can only be non-compliance with obligations arising from EU law, the Court, in accordance with what has been stated in paragraphs 91 and 92 of the present judgment, lacks jurisdiction to rule in the present action on an alleged failure to comply with the obligations arising from the arbitration agreement and the arbitration award, which are the source of the Republic of Slovenia's complaints regarding alleged infringements of EU law. (Judgement C-457/18, para 104)

4.4.3.2 Third-Party Judicial Dispute Settlement: International Law and the Role of the EU

The Court, by examining the relationship between the arbitration agreement and the arbitration award on the one hand, and the issue of the level of incorporation into EU law on the other hand, noted that

> it must be stated that the arbitration award was made by an international tribunal established under a bilateral arbitration agreement governed by international law, the subject matter of which does not fall within the areas of EU competence referred to in Articles 3 to 6 TFEU and to which the European Union is not a party. It is true that the *European Union offered its good offices to both parties* to the border dispute with a view to its resolution and that the *Presidency of the Council signed the arbitration agreement on behalf of the European Union, as a witness*. Furthermore, there are links between, on the one hand, the conclusion of the arbitration agreement, and the arbitration proceedings conducted on the basis of that agreement, and on the other, the process of negotiation and accession by the Republic of Croatia to the European Union. Such circumstances are not, however, sufficient for the arbitration agreement and the arbitration award to be considered an integral part of EU law. (Judgement C-457/18, para 102; emphases added)

The Court rightly acknowledges the (political and legal) link between the conclusion of the arbitration agreement and the accession of Croatia to the EU and also the role of the EU in the settlement of the border dispute. Nevertheless, the Grand Chamber falls short of recognising the true performance of the EU institutions in that process. Regrettably, "good offices" inadequately and insufficiently describes the undertakings of the European Commission and the Council Presidency. In established third-party conflict resolution, *good offices* equals allowing for the parties to communicate directly with one another but with almost zero intrusion by the third party, with little active control over the process and the substantive issues, and without the third party making any proposals (see e.g. Sects. 1.3.1.1 and 1.3.1.4).

As a matter of fact, however, the European Commission did play an active role as a *mediator/facilitator* in the *travaux préparatoires* of the Arbitration Agreement. This was not least expressly acknowledged in the Agreement's Preamble ("Welcoming the facilitation offered by the European Commission"). Precisely, as this author has demonstrated, the Commission prepared two drafts of the Arbitration Agreement (Rehn I and Rehn II)—following an initial draft for a mandate for a Senior Experts Group—and discussed them with the parties in various meetings and through written correspondence including amendments to the drafts by the parties. That phase, where the European Commission brokered the lion's share of the later Agreement, lasted from January to June 2009 (see Sects. 4.2.2.3–4.2.4).

In addition, from July to November 2009, the Swedish EU Presidency assisted the parties in their bilateral finalising of the Arbitration Agreement. The Swedish Presidency's positive facilitating role, which included the country's Foreign Minister and State Secretary, has been expressly acknowledged to this author by both parties. During the Swedish Presidency, a remaining obstacle ahead of concluding the Agreement was removed: the issue of the potentially prejudging Croatian documents from the accession negotiations with reference to the common State border. An exchange of letters between the Croatian Prime Minister and the Swedish Prime Minister in his role as EU Council President defused the issue. The drafting of that letter had taken several weeks and involved members of the bilateral Croatian-Slovenian Silent Diplomacy Group, the Swedish State Secretary and the Swedish Prime Minister (see Sect. 4.2.5). The role of the Swedish Presidency was officially recognised by signing the Arbitration Agreement as a witness together with the parties on 4 November 2009, as the Court correctly finds.

4.4.3.3 Arbitration Procedure, Croatia's Act of Accession and Issues of Competence

As the Court observed in para 102 (see Sect. 4.4.3.2), the resolution of the border dispute (by means of the arbitration agreement) is linked to the accession of the Republic of Croatia to the European Union. This link materialises in EU law in the Act of Accession of the Republic of Croatia and subsequently in pertinent EU legislation. As the Court notes,

> Point 5 of Annex III to the Act of Accession, headed 'Fisheries', adapted Council Regulation (EC) No 2371/2002 of 20 December 2002 on the conservation and sustainable exploitation of fisheries resources under the Common Fisheries Policy (OJ 2002 L 358, p. 59) by adding points 11 and 12, respectively headed 'Coastal waters of Croatia' and 'Coastal waters of Slovenia', to Annex I to that regulation. The footnotes to points 11 and 12 state, in identical terms, that '*[the] regime [governing access to the coastal waters of Croatia and Slovenia under neighbourhood relations] shall apply from the full implementation of the arbitration award resulting from the [arbitration agreement]*'. Those points and footnotes were, in essence, reproduced in Regulation No 1380/2013, which repealed Regulation No 2371/2002. (Judgement C-457/18, para 14; emphasis added)

With regard to the obligations under international law arising from the arbitration agreement and the arbitration award in the context of EU legislation, the Court further observes that

> [i]n the case in point, Article 7(3) of the arbitration agreement provides that the parties are to take all necessary steps to implement the arbitration award, including by revising national legislation, as necessary, within six months after the adoption of that award. Furthermore, the footnotes relating to points 8 and 10 of Annex I to Regulation No 1380/2013 state that, as regards the Republic of Croatia and the Republic of Slovenia, the regime, laid down in that annex, governing access to the coastal waters of those Member States under neighbourhood relations 'shall apply from the *full implementation* of the arbitration award'. It is not in dispute, as the Advocate General has also observed in essence in point 164 of his Opinion, that effect has not been given to the arbitration award. (Judgement C-457/18, para 106; emphasis added)

Whilst the Court expressly states the implementation obligations of the parties arising from the arbitration agreement, it also observes that the application of the fisheries regime for the territorial waters of Slovenia and Croatia respectively is subject to the full *implementation* of the arbitration award. What the Court appears to have avoided, however, is to interpret the *Act of Accession* of the Republic of Croatia. Such interpretation would have had to include a broader taking into account of the arbitration award as part of the link between Croatia's accession to the EU and the resolution of the border dispute. A true interpretation of the Act of Accession could have gone beyond a mechanistic reading of the footnotes in the Act of Accession and the Fisheries regulation.

In relation to the competence for territorial issues, including the delimitation and demarcation of borders, the Court notes that

> it is for each Member State to determine the extent and limits of its own territory, in accordance with the rules of public international law (see, to that effect, judgment of 29 March 2007, *Aktiebolaget NN*, C-111/05 [...], paragraph 54). Indeed, it is by reference to national territories that the territorial scope of the Treaties is established, for the purposes of Article 52 TEU and Article 355 TFEU. Moreover, Article 77(4) TFEU points out that the Member States have competence concerning the geographical demarcation of their borders, in accordance with international law. (Judgement C-457/18, para 105)

As a result, it appears that the fact that (i) the arbitration award has not yet been implemented, (ii) there nevertheless is an implementation obligation from international law, however not from EU law, and (iii) the Member State competence for territorial issues, has led the Court to the finding that

> [i]n those circumstances, it is not for the Court — if it is not to step beyond the powers conferred upon it by the Treaties and encroach upon the powers reserved for the Member States regarding geographical determination of their borders — to examine, in the present action brought under Article 259 TFEU, the question of the extent and limits of the respective territories of the Republic of Croatia and the Republic of Slovenia, by applying directly the border determined by the arbitration award in order to verify the existence of the infringements of EU law at issue. (Judgement C-457/18, para 107)

and that therefore

> it must be held that the Court lacks jurisdiction to rule on the present action for failure to fulfil obligations. (Judgement C-457/18, para 108)

It must be noted, that, in conclusion, the Court nevertheless explicitly states that Art. 4(3) TEU, enshrining the principle of "sincere cooperation", creates an obligation to bring about a definite settlement of the dispute in practice:

> This conclusion is without prejudice to any obligation arising — for both of the Member States concerned, in their reciprocal relations but also vis-à-vis the European Union and the other Member States — from Article 4(3) TEU to strive sincerely to bring about a definitive legal solution consistent with international law, as suggested in the Act of Accession, that ensures the effective and unhindered application of EU law in the areas concerned, and to bring their dispute to an end by using one or other means of settling it, including, as the case may be, by submitting it to the Court under a special agreement pursuant to Article 273 TFEU. (Judgement C-457/18, para 109)

The above concluding paragraph, however, leaves the observer somewhat puzzled. First, the Court refers to the Art. 4(3) TEU principle of sincere cooperation implying a real effort from both parties to bring about a definitive legal solution, as stipulated in Croatia's Act of Accession to ensure the territorial application of EU law. This appears to be a clear reference to the fact that implementation of the arbitration award is indeed pending. Second, the Court calls on the parties "to bring their dispute to an end". Here, the Court appears to refer not to the initial dispute over the common State border which is *res judicata,* but to the fact that one party, the Republic of Slovenia, insists on the implementation of the arbitration award, a binding settlement under international law, whereas the other party, the Republic of Croatia, does not recognise the arbitration award.

Third, as for the settlement of that dispute, the Court suggests "using one or other means of settling it", including a joint submission to the Court under Art. 273 TFEU. However, it is difficult to see the motivation of either party to settle their difference of opinion about the obligations arising from the Final Award. Slovenia can rely on the well-established fact that the award is a binding settlement under international law (see Art. 7(3) arbitration agreement which the Court quoted in para 106; see also e.g. Bantekas 2015: 109–112; Tanaka 2018b: 106; 109; Degan 2019). Croatia, for its part, may be expected to want to avoid its position of non-recognition of the award being repudiated by a judicial body. Nevertheless and in theory, the two parties could bring the matter before the ICJ (under Article 36(1) of the Model Rules on Arbitral Procedure) or indeed before the CJEU under Art. 273 TFEU. In practice, however, it would appear unlikely for obvious reasons that the two parties could reach agreement on a joint submission under the present circumstances.

4.4.4 *Reactions of the Parties*

Not unexpectedly, the decision of the EU Court of Justice was received differently in Croatia and in Slovenia.

The Slovenian Foreign Minister, Miro Cerar, said:

> This is a clear message that the course of the border between the two countries has been determined […]. Today, the Court explicitly confirmed what Slovenia has claimed all along and what no country has denied: the Arbitral Award is applicable and binding, both countries must implement it. This is yet another proof – and that from the top legal institution of the EU – that Slovenia was right in arguing that Croatia, too, must implement the Arbitral Award. (Slovenian Ministry of Foreign Affairs news 31 January 2020)

The Croatian Prime Minister, Andrej Plenković, said:

> Croatia [is] neither called upon in this ruling to implement the arbitration agreement, nor can Slovenia resolve this matter on its own. That's the key, the gist of today's message. Croatia is taking this opportunity to reiterate its invitation to Slovenia to resume bilateral talks in search of a final solution to the border issue which objectively is not far away, but which is challenging because both parties need the support of their respective parliaments to ratify an agreement. (HINA news 31 January 2020)

The impact of the Court's judgement on the immediate obligation to start implementing the arbitration award is obviously being interpreted in a different manner by both sides. Nevertheless, there appears to be some kind of common understanding that the issue is now at the bilateral level and that there is no solution but in the bilateral sphere.

For the time being, however, any bilateral follow-up to the CJEU judgement seems absent due to the overriding preoccupation with the coronavirus crisis management. Still, the decisive question for a final bilateral agreement indeed is the threshold of parliamentary ratification, in particular the two-third requirement in the Croatian Sabor, a fact that the Slovenian side is well aware of (interview senior Slovenian civil servant, 17-04-2020).

In the words of the current Foreign Minister of Slovenia:

> […] The ruling of the Court of Justice of the EU should be seen as a call on Slovenia and Croatia to resolve the issue in accordance with international law, as stipulated in the Act of Accession of Croatia to the EU […]. Slovenia will continue to seek dialogue with Croatia in view to resolve the open issues and enhance bilateral cooperation. There is, of course, no timeline; it would only raise false expectations. (Letter Anže Logar to the author, 17 April 2020)

4.5 Concluding Considerations

The concluding analysis of this core Chapter will sum-up developments within each of the four phases. Corresponding to the research questions that this study is based on, the analysis of the developments employs the process-tracing toolbox of *conflict issues*, *conflict dynamics*, *conflict management*, *actors in the conflict*, and *EU power issues* (see Sect. 1.3). For a comprehensive feedback as to the individual theory strands of the analytical framework see Chap. 5.

I. ***Bilateral phase***

The early phase: post-independence bilateral stock-tacking

The *conflict issues*: As to the origins of the conflict, the (conflictual) dismemberment of Yugoslavia created a new conflict. Fundamentally, the independence of both countries in 1991, i.e. the visible beginning of the territorial end of the Socialist Federal Republic of Yugoslavia (SFRY), is the new conflict's starting point. Internal SFRY republican borders were going to become international borders. All of a sudden, what used to be administrative or cadastral borders became distinct territorial and, thus, also political borders. Perhaps largely unnoticed, the location of the new Slovenian border-crossing at Sečovlje-Plovanija was the first territorial point of contention between the two countries as early as June 1991, on the eve of the declarations of independence. This is an example of the situation on land. At sea, no formal partition by Republics whatsoever existed in the Yugoslav maritime space. Still, it was only in the spring of 1993 when sovereignty over Piran Bay and access to the high seas became a salient issue in the Slovenian parliament. The response of the Croatian parliament followed six months later, a matter for which allowance must be made for the fact that the country was busy with the fully-blown Homeland War over territory in large parts of its hinterland where Croatian State-building was yet to be completed. Nevertheless, the issues at stake in the border conflict with Slovenia were now plain to see. By the autumn of 1993, the dispute over Piran Bay and the maritime border as regards access to the high seas for Slovenia was fully established. Furthermore, the interests of the parties had been put on the table, too, and there was no doubt about the competing sovereignty claims of either side.

With regard to *conflict dynamics*, one can clearly talk of a stable initial phase where positions evolved, and a low level of intensity as positions were exchanged below the political level. The *conflict management* mode was purely bilateral, and the main setting was the technical level. A rich body of bilateral expert groups, the *actors in the conflict*, was up and running by then and going through a screening phase. The expert groups were able to identify the strips and spots along the border where the cadastral limits were not aligned. As a result, there was a solid account of the disputed sections of the common State border outlined in the Expert Group Report from December 1996. One may therefore posit a pragmatic stance taken by both sides towards the border issue in the early phase. After all, cross-border life is what matters to citizens on the ground where relations had been very close for many decades during Yugoslav times and thereafter. However, the maritime border was not yet part of the bilateral talks. Still, any progress in terms of clearing up the substantive dispute over the land border proved difficult. This is why the expert group talks stalled in mid-1998. Croatia and Slovenia subsequently launched an attempt at third-party mediation by a former senior US politician in the early summer of 1999. That move proved fruitless, however.

The Agreement that never was: a fully negotiated bilateral settlement

A fresh start on the bilateral level was made in early 2001. In fact, it was an effort to find a comprehensive bilateral settlement at the highest political level. In terms of *actors in the conflict*, therefore, it was a clear shift from the technical to the political level accompanied by a novel behavioural conduct of good-neighbourly spirit and a sense of de-escalation on both sides. Likewise, there was a new momentum of *conflict dynamics*, as fully fledged negotiations between the heads of government must be seen as a very real opportunity to resolve the dispute. Indeed, in a remarkable move, by-passing traditional diplomatic channels of communication, the two prime ministers Drnovšek and Račan were sitting together determined to arrive at a fully negotiated settlement. It must be noted that political will and a special level of mutual respect and trust were indispensable prerequisites for that to happen. It remains a "chicken and egg" question, however, whether Račan should have taken the opposition and the law-of-the-sea establishment on board much earlier to secure domestic support in Croatia for a bilateral deal, or whether the secrecy of the talks was the only way to arrive at an agreement at all in the first place. As for *conflict issues*, the maritime border, however, became even more contentious in the end. One may argue that the sea-border solution foreseen in the Draft Agreement was perhaps too far away from what the political elite in Croatia considered or perceived as legitimate at the time (and certainly would today), a notion of great sensitivity only three years after the full re-integration of the territories in Slavonia and the Krajina. In any case, the fact that both a novel and contentious solution of the maritime border failed, hardened the positions, and rendered the conflict an intractable one, also leading to a new dead-lock in terms of *conflict dynamics*.

Too good to be true: the failed effort to submit the dispute to the ICJ

Over the following years there were no efforts whatsoever at finding a resolution. Thus, the *conflict dynamics* were in cooling-off mode. Only in 2007, the *actors in the conflict* being the heads of government (i.e. the highest political level), was the new (bilateral) effort to submit the dispute to the International Court of Justice (ICJ) made. Somewhat ironically perhaps, after the *ex-post* burial of the Drnovšek-Račan Draft Agreement in Croatia, one could witness a similar turn of events in Slovenia after the Bled Agreement. The 2007 accord between Janša and Sanader at first appeared to be a pragmatic and workable agreement. After all, it would have been very difficult to go down the path of bilateral negotiations again, where there was hardly any room for face-saving manoeuvres bearing in mind the failure of the 2001 Draft Agreement. So, for a moment at least, the new *conflict management* mode was a bilaterally and voluntarily agreed submission to third-party resolution. However, the new *conflict issue* now was the terms of submission to third-party resolution. It turned out, during the technical-level drafting stage of the mandate for the Court, that a submission to the ICJ which—in its deliberations on the merits—would be restricted to international law rather than equitable principles, was apparently an untenable approach for the Slovenian government. This was because it seems Slovenia considered it necessary to have room for equity in order to achieve access to the high seas. At the end of the day, the task of agreeing on a mandate for a court does require bilateral agreement and that is where the process yet again stalled. As a result, the *conflict dynamics* mode yet again levelled up. It remains obscure, however, to what degree the focus of attention of the Slovenian side may have already shifted to the 'golden opportunity' of using the leverage of veto power (that decision being taken in June 2008) in Croatia's EU accession negotiations, which were going on in parallel, a vital *EU power issue* indeed.

II. ***Croatia's EU Accession Negotiations***

Now or never: forced delegation of conflict management in a hybrid line-up

It was in the autumn of 2008 that Slovenia transferred the bilateral border dispute onto the EU stage through Ljubljana's veto during Croatia's accession negotiations. With regard to *conflict actors*, the technical level (the Council Working Group on Enlargement COELA) was in the driving seat. As for the new *conflict issue*, the prejudging maps in the Croatian accession negotiations documents were the official reason. The real interest of Slovenia, however, was to solve the border dispute ahead of Croatian EU accession. It appears fair to say that this is the first instance in the history of the border dispute that the official claims and the real interests of a party to the dispute diverge. In terms of *EU power issues*, also the first time that they appear, inserting a bilateral issue into EU accession negotiations amounted to nothing less than linking the border dispute to the EU *acquis* despite the fact that it had nothing to do with the *acquis*. As a result, a bilateral (territorial) issue with a Member State became an add-on to the (political) conditionality of EU accession for the first time ever. Such was the new *conflict issue* likewise. With regard to *conflict management*, the third-party role entered the scene. Within the remit of the intergovernmental level, the French EU Council Presidency was facing, at first hand, the unique circumstances of a Member State using its status as a Member State vis-à-vis a Candidate Country, i.e. blunt blackmailing, and this proved to be an unsurmountable task at the technical level. From a *conflict-dynamics* point of view, the level of escalation may be seen on a new all-time high as it was no longer a bilateral conflict, but also one that had directly affected the EU level.

The following phase marks a completely new line-up in terms of *conflict management*. The EU's Enlargement Commissioner Olli Rehn took over by the beginning of 2009, stepping into what was *terra incognita* in the history of EU accession negotiations: clearing the accession process of a bilateral issue by means of third-party dispute resolution. To be sure, it was a hybrid set-up of third-party mediation and bilateral negotiating. The Commission itself took on the role of mediating third party in the first place. After an unsuccessful attempt at soft mediation, Rehn and his legal team managed to produce drafts of the later Arbitration Agreement seeking to take on board the vital interests of both Slovenia and Croatia. The *conflict issue*, very much like in the post-Bled phase around 2008, was the terms of the mandate for the third-party judicial body. The first of two crucial issues, the *task of the arbitral tribunal*, i.e. to secure access for Slovenia to the high seas whilst preserving classical approaches of international law for the maritime border and for the land border, the

Commission managed to hammer out with great expertise in the first half of 2009. To that end and in terms of *actors in the conflict*, one can say with some accuracy that it was the European Commission who was running the management of the conflict and that it was running it at its own initiative. As for *conflict dynamics*, one may posit that the conflict was on a stable level whilst it was, by and large, being treated constructively also by Croatia and Slovenia over the first half of 2009.

After a brief stalling of the process at the beginning of July 2009, the finalising phase, with regard to *conflict management*, saw a re-bilateralisation of the negotiations skilfully facilitated by the Swedish EU Council Presidency. The second crucial development, widely perceived as a game-changer in terms of a great face-saving and de-escalating opportunity of *conflict dynamics*, was the *new sequencing* of (i) Croatian accession and (ii) the start of the arbitration procedure. It appears fair to say that it was the reversal of the original order, i.e. the lifting of the Slovenian veto and the idea to have the Croatian Accession Treaty signed first before starting the actual arbitration procedure, which rendered the finalisation of the Arbitration Agreement possible. In other words, the new sequence solved the *conflict issue* (delaying Croatian EU accession until the end of a future arbitration procedure) of the second drafting stage of the Arbitration Agreement. It is important to note that this was predominantly achieved in a bilateral manner, so the *conflict actors* were the two parties to the conflict. Indispensable prerequisites were the high level of mutual trust both between Kosor and Pahor and between the prime ministers' negotiator-advisors. Nevertheless, one must recall that the unilateral declaration upon Croatian ratification of the Arbitration Agreement was a sign of the asymmetry in the power relationship between Croatia as a Candidate Country and Slovenia as a Member State at the time, in particular in the context of the great unease with and enormous conflictual potential of territorial issues in Croatia. *EU power issues*, on their part, were successfully dampened, and it seemed that the conflict was finally going to be contained by the conclusion of the Arbitration Agreement.

III. ***Arbitration Procedure and Follow-up***

To hell and back: the arbitration procedure heavily bruised but alive

With regard to *conflict dynamics*, it is easily forgotten that the arbitration procedure had a smooth start indeed. The arbitral tribunal was formed in a constructive and timely manner on the bilateral political level at the beginning of 2012. The subsequent written submissions for the judicial procedure were comprehensive, also containing replies to the counter-memorials. Equally, an extensive two-week hearing provided the parties with ample opportunity to raise any point that they wished to raise. In terms of *conflict issues* and the result, not only the Tribunal but also the parties themselves were fully in the picture of all arguments and real interests of the parties presented for the Tribunal's deliberations on the merits. One can say with some accuracy, too, that the *conflict management* was firmly in the hands of the Arbitral Tribunal as the third-party judicial body with the parties submitting their claims in written form and during an extensive hearing.

The summer of disruption saw the arbitration procedure implode at the end of July 2015, which left the actual proceedings heavily tainted politically and moved the *conflict dynamics* to yet another peak. As collateral damage, the events affected the reputation of international arbitration as such, still a major and successful dispute settlement tool, at least temporarily. It may be morally questionable and perhaps unethical, and certainly unlawful vis-à-vis domestic Slovenian law, to tap into the communication of government actors, all the more so from a State that one is supposed to enjoy good-neighbourly relations with. Then again, it simply goes against the express confidentiality provisions of the arbitration procedure, and is therefore unlawful, to engage in *ex parte* communication (the new *conflict issue*) with a Tribunal member in the first place. This piece of illegal communication resulted in unprecedented outrage among the political elite in Croatia, leading to the unanimously adopted Sabor resolution asking the government to leave the arbitration procedure, which it did. As regards *actors in the conflict*, the entire political level in Croatia was one dominating player (the government being in the driving seat, of course) in late July 2015, another one being the arbitrator appointed by Slovenia and the Slovenian Agent and their revealed pieces of communication from November 2014 and January 2015 (*ex ante*, as it were). The third actor was the Arbitral Tribunal which had to assess the implications of the Croatian *de facto* withdrawal from the arbitral proceedings.

The legal arguments of the Croatian side, however, were not very strong. The weakest of them was to challenge the jurisdiction of the Arbitral Tribunal to look into the termination request. It is a well-established fact that international courts and tribunals do possess the *compétence de la compétence* to decide themselves not only about the merits of a case, but also on procedural matters. The fact that Croatia no longer participated in the arbitral proceedings followed the political logic—and indeed the express request—of the Sabor vote, but not the legal reality. In addition, the reconstituted Tribunal, which no longer had party-appointed arbitrators but five neutral members, had increased the Tribunal's independence and legitimacy. In terms of *conflict issues*, the new point of contention now was the gravity of Slovenia's violation of the Arbitration Agreement. Croatia (notwithstanding its legal *argumentaire*) considered the violation as fundamental and absolute thus legitimising Zagreb's move to terminate the Arbitration Agreement and the arbitral proceedings, whereas the Tribunal, in its Partial Award in June 2016, had to assess and did assess the impact of Slovenia's *ex parte* communication from a strictly legal-procedural point of view for which it had jurisdiction. From a *conflict-dynamics* point of view, the stance had hardened further by the time the Final Award was handed down in June 2017. Croatia had boxed itself into a corner where no face-saving move was possible despite the fact that the substantive contents of the Award was not unfavourable to Croatia. The military installation at Sveta Gera was going to "come home", the status of the Dragonja strip on the left bank of the river was confirmed to be Croatian, and the maritime border departure from the equidistance line in favour of Slovenia must be seen as modest. The partition inside Piran Bay appears to properly reflect its use in 1991, and even the corridor regime inside the Croatian territorial waters for the purposes of providing unhindered communication between the high seas and the Slovenian territorial sea can be regarded as very close to the Croatian position set out in the written submission of the arbitration proceedings. Nevertheless, the sobering news was that, after the arbitration procedure that was supposed to settle the matter, the border conflict was more intractable than ever before.

Lifting it up: bilateral conflict hits EU implementation

It is difficult to say whether any of the parties seriously believed that efforts to achieve bilateral implementation of the Final Award would bear fruit. In terms of *conflict issues*, the largely contradicting real interests of the parties were as follows: the Slovenian government had an internationally binding Final Award at hand, which in its substantive points was not much more than the access to the high seas which had been *de facto* secured by the Arbitration Agreement in the first place. The Croatian government, for its part, needed to avoid at all costs any one-to-one implementation of the (not so unfavourable) Award for the principle reason that it could not recognise the arbitral award as such due to the unanimous 2015 Sabor vote. In the period between July 2017 and March 2018, the *actors-in-the-conflict* line-up was bilateral, again searching for implementation of different kinds. The parties were in touch, although the road was rather rocky. Nevertheless, it is fair to say that the *conflict dynamics* were somewhat dampened during that period.

Fundamentally and further to the real interests of the parties, the consideration of the political costs of direct implementation apparently carried more weight in Zagreb than the benefits of a once-and-for-all settlement of the border with the EU neighbour Slovenia. This decision must be seen against the background of Croatia's application to join the Schengen area and the Eurozone for both of which Slovenia's support is needed due to the unanimity requirement in Council for those areas. In a similar vein, the political costs for any Slovenian government to sustain bilateral talks with Croatia on implementation that were likely to lead nowhere seem to have been calculated as too high. It does not take a deterministic view, therefore, to suggest that there was no alternative for Slovenia other than going to the European Court of Justice to seek implementation of the arbitration award—which it did not receive.

IV. ***Case before EU Court of Justice***

Competent or not? The issue of jurisdiction sends the conflict back to square one

Slovenia's decision to go to the EU Court of Justice rendered the matter a fully fledged *EU power issue*. In fact, the Slovenia-Croatia border dispute had now become a question of application of EU law, an issue perhaps unthinkable when it first appeared on the EU stage in autumn 2008. With regard to *conflict management*, the CJEU as a third-party judicial body became involved at the request of one of the parties. It is crucial to note, however, that the European Court of Justice is not an international court of appeal, i.e. it could not look into the substantive decision of the Arbitral Tribunal (which is a definite settlement of the case under international law), but was invited to assess the Slovenian claims of failure to fulfil obligations of EU law on the part of Croatia. To that end, the *conflict issue* here (between Croatia and

Slovenia) in very fundamental terms was whether the implementation of the Final Award is mandatory to fulfil the obligations of applying EU law.

The Court, as the competent body to interpret EU law, decided to investigate the issue of admissibility first. To that end, the *conflict issue* was narrowed down to the question of how strong the link between the arbitration procedure and the reference to its implementation in the EU Fisheries Regulation was. This issue was extensively discussed during the hearing at the Court in July 2019. With regard to *conflict dynamics*, the "battle-field", as it were, was now one of jurisdiction. The level of conflict was high again, albeit confined to the argumentation before the Court. In addition, one can contend that the conflict had escalated by the decision of the Court, now the sole *actor* in the conflict, to address the issue of admissibility first. With regard to the *management of the conflict*, this decision presented two clear-cut alternatives. The Court would either manage the conflict—if it decided in favour of admissibility, or it would not—if it decided it had no jurisdiction. At the same time, this juncture virtually killed off any face-saving options. The parties and the wider public alike were confronted with a clear win-lose scenario: If the Court declared the Slovenian claim admissible, Slovenia would be the clear winner with well-founded expectations that the Court would largely endorse the country's claims on the merits later on. If the Court decided that it had no jurisdiction, Croatia would be the clear winner.

With the judgement of the Court handed down, the conflict is clearly back at the bilateral level. The *actors* in the conflict are now the governments of Croatia and Slovenia. They are in charge of the *management* of the dispute again. In view of the fact that the conflict about the validity of the arbitration award remains, it appears that, for the foreseeable future, it is impossible to make any prediction, neither in terms of the conflict *dynamics* nor as for the possibility of an agreement at all.

Interviews

Arnaut, Dr. Damir. MP for Bosnia-Herzegovina. Member of the Parliamentary Assembly of the Council of Europe. Ambassador of Bosnia-Herzegovina to Australia and New Zealand 2010–2014. Strasburg, 25 January 2018.

Belfrage, Frank. State Secretary in the Ministry of Foreign Affairs of Sweden 2005–2014. Phone interview, 26 April 2017.

Brok, Elmar. MEP. Chair of the Foreign Affairs Committee 1999–2007 and 2012–2017. Strasburg, 15 November 2015.

Cabinet member of Olli Rehn 2009. Brussels, 13 November 2015.

Cataldi, Dr. Giuseppe. Professor for International Law, Naples University. President of the International Association of the Law of the Sea. Phone interview, 18 July 2018.

Cerar, Dr. Miro. MP. Minister for Foreign Affairs of Slovenia. Prime Minister of Slovenia 2014–2018. Luxemburg, 16 October 2018.

Civil servant involved in the trilateral meetings during the French EU Council Presidency in 2008. Phone interview, 27 January 2017.

Degan, Dr. Vladimir-Đuro. Professor emeritus. Director Adriatic Institute, Zagreb. Zagreb, 21 November 2019.

European Commission civil servant. Strasburg, 05 July 2017.
European Commission civil servant in charge of the accession negotiations with Croatia 2008/2009. Brussels, 07 January 2016.
European Commission civil servant involved in the Enlargement Strategy 2018. Brussels, 10 January 2018.
European Commission DG NEAR senior civil servant. Phone interview, 15 April 2020.
European Commission DG NEAR senior civil servant. Brussels, 28 August 2018.
Fajon, Tanja. MEP. Chair European Parliament Delegation with Serbia. Rapporteur for EU visa liberalisation with Serbia, Bosnia-Herzegovina, Montenegro, North Macedonia, Albania, and Kosovo 2014–2019. Strasburg, 22 November 2016.
Grbec, Dr. Mitja. Vice-President of the Maritime Law Association of Slovenia (MLAS). Koper, 10 July 2018.
Hoffmeister, Dr. Frank. European Commission Legal Service 2008/2009. Brussels, 03 June 2016.
Jović, Dr. Dejan. Professor for International Relations, Zagreb University. Zagreb, 02 November 2017.
Kosor, Jadranka. Prime Minister of Croatia 2009–2011. Minister of Family, Veterans' Affairs and Inter-Generational Solidarity 2003–2009. Strasburg, 07 June 2016.
Kukan, Eduard. MEP. Chair of the European Parliament Delegation with Serbia. Foreign Minister of Slovakia 1998–2006. Strasburg, 27 September 2017.
Member of the Croatian negotiating team for EU accession 2008/2009. Brussels, 30 November 2015.
Member State A civil servant. COELA member 2008/2009. Phone interview, 23 June 2016.
Member State B civil servant. COELA member 2008/2009. Phone interview, 08 December 2016.
Member State C civil servant. COELA member 2008/2009. Phone interview, 27 January 2017.
Member State D civil servant. COELA member 2016/2017. Brussels, 15 November 2016.
Member State E civil servant. COELA member 2016. Brussels, 21 October 2016.
Member State H civil servant. COELA member 2017/2018. Brussels, 07 March 2018; 16 July 2018.
Member State I civil servant. COELA member 2017/2018. Brussels, 12 July 2018.
Member State J civil servant. COELA member 2010–2014. Phone interview, 19 October 2016.
Pahor, Borut. President of Slovenia. Prime Minister of Slovenia 2008–2012. Brussels, 26 June 2018; Ljubljana, 20 June 2017.
Peterle, Alojz. MEP 2004–2019. Prime Minister of Slovenia 1990–1992, Foreign Minister of Slovenia 1993–1994 and 2000. Brussels, 28 June 2017; 16 September 2015.
Plenković, Andrej. MP. Prime Minister of Croatia. MEP 2011–2016. State Secretary for European Integration 2010–2011. Brussels, 28 June and 06 February 2018.
Pusić, Dr. Vesna. MP. Minister for Foreign and European Affairs of Croatia 2011–2016. Chair of the European Integration Committee of the Sabor 2008–2011. Zagreb, 24 February 2017.
Rehn, Dr. Olli. Governor of the Bank of Finland. European Commissioner for Economic and Monetary Affairs 2009–2014. European Commissioner for Enlargement 2004–2009. Brussels, 09 October 2015.
Sanader, Dr. Ivo. Prime Minister of Croatia 2003–2009. Deputy Foreign Minister 1993–2000. Zagreb, 02 November 2017; Velika Gorica, 19 May 2016.
Schwarzenberg, Karel. MP. Foreign Minister of the Czech Republic 2007–2009 including the Czech EU Council Presidency in the first half of 2009, and 2010–2013. Phone interview, 26 September 2017.
Scovazzi, Dr. Tullio. Professor for International Law, University of Milano-Bicocca. Law-of-the-sea expert. Elected Member of the *Institut du Droit International*. Phone interview, 03 August 2018.
Senior Croatian civil servant. Zagreb, 25 January 2017 and 19 August 2016.
Senior Slovenian civil servant. Brussels, 10 July 2017; Ljubljana, 24 January 2017.
Senior Slovenian civil servant. Phone interview, 17 April 2020.
Senior Slovenian civil servant. Member of the Slovenian negotiating team with Croatia 2001. Brussels, 02 December 2016.
Senior Slovenian civil servant. Brnik, 17 October 2016.
Stier, Davor. MP. Foreign Minister of Croatia October 2016 to June 2017. MEP July 2013 to October 2016. Brussels, 23 September 2015.

References

Agreement between the Republic of Slovenia and the Republic of Croatia on border traffic and cooperation. (1997, April 25).

Arnaut, D. (2002). Stormy waters on the way to the high seas: The case of the territorial sea delimitation between Croatia and Slovenia. *Ocean and Coastal Law Journal, 8*(1), 21–70.

Arnaut, D. (2014). Adriatic blues: Delimiting the former Yugoslavia's final frontier. In C. Schofield, S. Lee, & M. S. Kwon (Eds.), *The limits of maritime jurisdiction* (pp. 145–173). Leiden and Boston: Martinus Nijhoff.

Bangert, K. (1997). Denmark and the law of the sea. In T. Treves (Ed.), *The law of the sea. The European Union and its member states* (pp. 97–126). The Hague: Martinus Nijhoff.

Bankes, N. (2017, July 19). The maritime aspects of the award in the arbitration between Croatia and Slovenia. *NCLOS Blog*. Available at: https://site.uit.no/nclos/2017/07/19/the-maritime-aspects-of-the-award-in-the-arbitration-between-croatia-and-slovenia/. Accessed April 23, 2020.

Bantekas, I. (2015). *An introduction to international arbitration*. Cambridge: Cambridge University Press.

Beazley, P. (1979). Half-effect applied to equidistance lines. *International Hydrographic Review, 56*(1), 153–160.

Bickl, T. (2017). Reconstructing the intractable. The Croatia-Slovenia border dispute and its implications for EU enlargement. *Politička Misao, 54*(4), 7–39.

Bickl, T. (2020). The advocate general's opinion on Slovenia v Croatia: A proper reflection of international law and the EU's role in the arbitration agreement? *NCLOS Blog*. https://site.uit.no/nclos/2020/01/07/the-advocate-generals-opinion-on-slovenia-v-croatia-a-proper-reflection-of-international-law-and-the-eus-role-in-the-arbitration-agreement/. Accessed April 21, 2020.

Brilmayer, L., & Faure, A. (2014). Initiating territorial adjudication: The who, how, when, and why of litigating contested sovereignty. In N. Klein (Ed.), *Litigating international law disputes: Weighing the options* (pp. 193–229). Cambridge: Cambridge University Press.

Cataldi, G. (2013). Prospects for the judicial settlement of the dispute between Croatia and Slovenia over Piran Bay. In N. Boschiero, T. Scovazzi, C. Pitea, & C. Ragni (Eds.), *International courts and the development of international law* (pp. 257–268). The Hague: T.M.C. Asser Press.

Council of the European Union. (2005, March 16). Press release on postponement of start accession negotiations with Croatia. 2649th Council Meeting.

Council of the European Union. (2016, July 5). Draft common position on chapter 24, accession negotiations with Serbia.

Council of the European Union. (2016, June 28). Conclusions on enlargement and stabilisation and association process. General Affairs Council. https://www.consilium.europa.eu/media/35863/st10555-en18.pdf. Accessed March 27, 2020.

Council of the European Union. (2018, June 25). Joint press statement Stabilisation and Association Council ministerial meeting EU-Montenegro. https://www.consilium.europa.eu/en/press/press-releases/2018/06/25/joint-statement-following-the-ninth-meeting-of-the-stabilisation-and-association-council-between-the-eu-and-montenegro/. Accessed March 27, 2020.

Council of the European Union. (2020, March 25). Council conclusions on enlargement and stabilisation and association process. General Affairs Council. The Republic of North Macedonia and the Republic of Albania. https://data.consilium.europa.eu/doc/document/ST-7002-2020-INIT/en/pdf. Accessed April 10, 2020.

Court of Justice of the European Union. (2019, December 11). Opinion advocate general. Case C-457/18 Republic of Slovenia v Republic of Croatia. https://curia.europa.eu/juris/document/document.jsf?docid=223861&mode=req&pageIndex=1&dir=&occ=first&part=1&text=&doclang=FR&cid=5389808 [French-language version]. Accessed April 13, 2020.

Court of Justice of the European Union. (2020). Rules of procedure. https://curia.europa.eu/jcms/upload/docs/application/pdf/2012-10/rp_en.pdf. Accessed April 04, 2020.

Court of Justice of the European Union. (2020, January 31). Judgement of the court (Grand Chamber). Case C-457/18 Republic of Slovenia v Republic of Croatia. https://curia.europa.eu/juris/document/document.jsf?text=&docid=223863&pageIndex=0&doclang=EN&mode=req&dir=&occ=first&part=1&cid=5389808. Accessed April 13, 2020.

Croatian Parliament. (1993, November 18). Resolution regarding the determination of the state border in Piran Bay and the Dragonja river area.

Croatian Parliament. (2009, May 8). Decision on the acceptance of the Draft Agreement on dispute settlement [Rehn I].

Croatian Parliament. (2015, July 29). Ruling on the obligation of the Government of the Republic of Croatia to begin the procedure of termination of the Arbitration Agreement between the Government of the Republic of Croatia and the Government of the Republic of Slovenia. https://www.mvep.hr/files/file/dokumenti/arbitraza/en/150820-ruling-of-the-croatian-parliament-29072015.pdf. Accessed March 30, 2020.

Cvrtila, V. (1993). The boundaries of the Republic of Croatia. *Politička Misao, 30*(2), 35–43.

Degan, V. (2019). Spor o granicama između Hrvatske i Slovenije. *Poredbeno Pomorsko Pravo, 58*(173), 11–66. https://hrcak.srce.hr/file/324286. Accessed April 13, 2020.

Dolenec, D. (2013). *Democratic institutions and authoritarian rule in southeast Europe*. Colchester: ECPR Press.

Emmert, F., & Petrović, S. (2014). The past, present, and future of EU enlargement. *Fordham International Law Journal, 37*(5), 1349–1419.

European Commission. (2000, November 8). Progress report Slovenia.

European Commission. (2009, March 10). Draft declaration on the border issue between the Republic of Slovenia and the Republic of Croatia.

European Commission. (2009, March 12). Note to the file [background on dispute settlement and arbitration].

European Commission. (2009, March 24). Draft agreement on [Senior Expert Group] arbitration.

European Commission. (2009, March 24). Further reflections on a formalized document [on an arbitration agreement].

European Commission. (2009, April 24). Draft agreement on dispute settlement [Rehn I].

European Commission. (2009, June 15). Draft agreement on dispute settlement [Rehn II].

European Commission. (2009, October 29). Internal e-mail [on the state of play of the Draft Arbitration Agreement].

European Commission. (2009, November). Internal note [on the state of play of the Draft Arbitration Agreement].

European Commission. (2011, October 12). Enlargement strategy. https://ec.europa.eu/neighbourhood-enlargement/sites/near/files/pdf/key_documents/2011/package/mk_rapport_2011_en.pdf. Accessed March 27, 2020.

European Commission. (2011, December 7). Signature of the accession treaty of the European Union (EU) with Croatia: Background note. https://ec.europa.eu/commission/presscorner/detail/de/MEMO_11_883. Accessed March 28, 2020.

European Commission. (2013, July 18). EU accession negotiations [presentation paper Belgrade].

European Commission. (2015, September 30). Letter from the President and the First Vice-President to the Prime Minister of Slovenia and the Prime Minister of Croatia [on the reconstitution of the Arbitral Tribunal].

European Commission. (2016, November 9). Enlargement strategy. https://ec.europa.eu/neighbourhood-enlargement/sites/near/files/20161109_strategy_paper_en.pdf. Accessed March 27, 2020.

European Commission. (2017, July 4). Minutes of the 2219th meeting of the European Commission in Strasburg.

European Commission. (2017, September 13). State of the union address [of the President of the Commission]. Available at: https://ec.europa.eu/commission/news/president-juncker-delivers-state-union-address-2017-2017-sep-13_en. Accessed March 27, 2020.

European Commission. (2017, November). [Draft] Enlargement strategy.
European Commission. (2018, February 6). Enlargement strategy. https://ec.europa.eu/commission/sites/beta-political/files/communication-credible-enlargement-perspective-western-balkans_en.pdf. Accessed March 27, 2020.
European Commission. (2020, undated). Enhancing the accession process—A credible EU perspective for the Western Balkans. COM (2020) 57/2 ["SENSITIVE: Cabinets UNTIL ADOPTION"].
European Commission. (2020, February 5). Enhancing the accession process—A credible EU perspective for the Western Balkans. https://ec.europa.eu/neighbourhood-enlargement/sites/near/files/enlargement-methodology_en.pdf. Accessed April 10, 2020.
European Commission Daily News. (2017, May 19). Commission adopts delegated act to amend regulation on wine labels ["Teran" can be used in the labelling of Hrvatska Istra wines under the Protected Designation of Origin (PDO)]. https://ec.europa.eu/commission/presscorner/detail/en/MEX_17_1403. Accessed March 31, 2020.
European Commission Daily News. (2017, July 5). Statement by First Vice-President Timmermans on the final award made on 29 June by the Arbitration Tribunal of the Permanent Court of Arbitration in the arbitration between Croatia and Slovenia. https://ec.europa.eu/commission/presscorner/detail/en/STATEMENT_17_1911. Accessed April 04, 2020.
European Commission EU Information Centre Belgrade. (2014, January). Negotiation chapters. 35 steps towards the European Union.
European Commission Legal Service. (2018, May 14). Note for the attention of [the] Chef de Cabinet of the President. Follow-up to the hearing on the dispute between Slovenia and Croatia.
European Council. (2019, October 18). Conclusions. https://www.consilium.europa.eu/media/41123/17-18-euco-final-conclusions-en.pdf. Accessed April 10, 2020.
European Council Copenhagen. (1993, June 22). Conclusions of the presidency. https://www.consilium.europa.eu/media/21225/72921.pdf. Accessed March 27, 2020.
European Court of Human Rights. (2014, July 16). Judgement. Case of Ališić and others v. Bosnia and Herzegovina, Croatia, Serbia, Slovenia, and the Former Yugoslav Republic of Macedonia [on reimbursement of Ljubljanska Banka foreign-currency account holders]. https://hudoc.echr.coe.int/eng#{"itemid":["001-114243"]}. Accessed April 24, 2020.
European Parliament. (2020, June 19). Western Balkans, following the 2020 summit. https://www.europarl.europa.eu/doceo/document/TA-9-2020-0168_EN.pdf. Accessed June 21, 2020.
Ferri, M. (2018). A new (and questionable) institute to guarantee the right of access to the high seas: The junction area established in Croatian sea. *DPCE Online, 3*, 639–671. https://publicatt.unicatt.it/retrieve/handle/10807/132187/217759/A_new_and_questionable_institute_to_guar%20%282%29.pdf. Accessed April 05, 2020.
Foreign Affairs Committee of the Slovenian Parliament. (1993, April 7). Memorandum on the Bay of Piran.
Foreign and Commonwealth Office United Kingdom Embassy Zagreb. (2017, June 30). Statement on the arbitration award Croatia-Slovenia.
General Court of the European Union (2020, September 9). Judgement Case T-626/17 Slovenia v Commission. http://curia.europa.eu/juris/document/document.jsf?text=&docid=230824&pageIndex=0&doclang=en&mode=req&dir=&occ=first&part=1&cid=2443266. Accessed September 17, 2020.
General Affairs and External Relations. https://ec.europa.eu/commission/presscorner/detail/en/PRES_05_44. Accessed March 27, 2020.
Gostyńska-Jakubowska, A., & Scazzieri, L. (2020, March 23). The EU needs to step up its response to the COVID-19 outbreak. Centre for European Reform. https://www.cer.eu/insights/eu-needs-step-its-response-covid-19-outbreak. Accessed April 10, 2020.
Gouvernement luxembourgeois. (2017, July 4). Joint Benelux statement on Croatia-Slovenia border arbitration award. https://gouvernement.lu/fr/actualites/toutes_actualites/communiques/2017/07-juillet/04-benelux-craotia-slovenia.html. Accessed April 04, 2020.

Government of the Republic of Croatia News. (2017, December 19). Prime Minister Plenković: I believe we are close to reaching a solution for the border issue. Acceptable to both sides. Available at: https://vlada.gov.hr/news/prime-minister-plenkovic-i-believe-we-are-close-to-reaching-a-solution-for-the-border-issue-acceptable-to-both-sides/23086. Accessed March 31, 2020.

Grbec, M. (2015). *Extension of coastal state jurisdiction in enclosed and semi-enclosed seas—A Mediterranean and Adriatic perspective*. London and New York: Routledge.

HINA News. (2019, March 27). Cerar najavio prosvjednu notu Hrvatskoj 'zbog provokacije visokog intenziteta.

HINA News. (2020, January 31). Croatian Prime Minister Andrej Plenkovic on Friday dismissed the claim by Slovenian Foreign Minister Miro Cerar that the Court of Justice of the European Union urged the two countries to implement the border arbitration ruling. https://vlada.gov.hr/news/plenkovic-court-ruling-doesn-t-call-for-implementation-of-border-arbitration-award/28693. Accessed April 28, 2020.

Hoffmeister, F. (2012). The European Union and the peaceful settlement of international disputes. *Chinese Journal of International Law, 11*(1), 77–105.

Hojnik, J., & Mevel, M. (2016). Obligation juridique directe des États pour les dettes contractées par les banques situées à l'exterieur de leur territoire national: l'approche de la Cour EDH dans l'affaire de la dissolution de la Yugoslavie. *Revue de Droit Bancaire et Financier, 17*(2), 10–13.

Ilić, M. (2017). Croatia v. Slovenia: The defiled proceedings. *Arbitration Law Review, 9*(1), 347–382.

Indlekofer, M. (2013). *International arbitration and the permanent court of arbitration*. Alphen aan den Rijn: Kluwer Law International.

Information on prejudices in certain negotiating chapters of accession negotiations for Croatia's membership of the EU. Non-paper Ministry of Foreign Affairs Slovenia. 18 December 2008.

[Initialled Draft] Treaty between the Republic of Slovenia and the Republic of Croatia on the Common State Border. (2001, July 17). [English translation by the Slovenian Ministry of Foreign Affairs of the original initialled by the two heads of the negotiating delegations; "Drnovšek-Račan Agreement"]. Reprinted in Appendix C.

Insolia, A. (2019). The law of maritime delimitation in the Croatia/Slovenia final award. In A. Del Vecchio & R. Virzo (Eds.), *Interpretations of the United Nations convention on the law of the sea by international courts and tribunals* (pp. 225–265). Cham: Springer.

International Centre for Settlement of Investment Disputes. (2008, May 8). Victor Pey Casado and President Allende Foundation v. Chile. Award. https://icsid.worldbank.org/en/Pages/cases/casedetail.aspx?CaseNo=ARB/98/2. Accessed April 24, 2020.

International Centre for Settlement of Investment Disputes. (2015, December 17). HEP vs. Slovenia. Award. https://icsidfiles.worldbank.org/icsid/ICSIDBLOBS/OnlineAwards/C69/DC7132_En.pdf. Accessed April 24, 2020.

International Court of Justice (1953, November 18). Nottebohm case (Liechtenstein/Guatemala). Judgement. https://www.icj-cij.org/files/case-related/18/018-19531118-JUD-01-00-EN.pdf. Accessed April 24, 2020.

International Court of Justice. (1972, August 18). ICAO Council case (India/Pakistan). Appeal relating to the jurisdiction of the ICAO Council. Judgement. https://www.icj-cij.org/files/case-related/54/054-19720818-JUD-01-00-EN.pdf. Accessed April 24, 2020.

International Court of Justice. (1974, December 20). Nuclear tests (Australia/France). Judgement. https://www.icj-cij.org/files/case-related/58/058-19741220-JUD-01-00-EN.pdf. Accessed April 24, 2020.

Jović, D. (2011). Turning nationalists into EU supporters: The case of Croatia. In J. Rupnik (Ed.), *The Western Balkans and the EU: 'The hour of Europe'* (pp. 33–45). Chaillot Paper 126. Paris: European Union Institute for Security Studies (EUISS).

Keohane, R., Moravcsik, A., & Slaughter, A. M. (2000). Legalized dispute resolution: Interstate and transnational. *International Organization, 54*(3), 457–488.

Klemenčić, M., & Schofield, C. (1995). Croatia and Slovenia: The "four hamlets" case. *IBRU Boundary and Security Bulletin, 2*(4), 65–77.

Klemenčić, M., & Topalović, D. (2009). The maritime boundaries of the Adriatic Sea. *Geoadria, 14*(2), 311–324.
Koska, V., & Matan, A. (2017). Croatian citizenship regime and traumatized categories of Croatian Citizens: Serb minority and Croatian defenders of the homeland war. *Politička Misao, 54*(1–2), 119–149.
Lamont, C. (2015). Contested histories of Croatia's homeland war. *Groniek, 45*(194), 69–80.
Lando, M. (2017). The Croatia/Slovenia arbitral award of 29 June 2017: Is there a common method for delimiting all maritime zones under international law? *Rivista di diritto internazionale, 100*(4), 1184–1190. https://dialnet.unirioja.es/servlet/articulo?codigo=6356301. Accessed April 05, 2020.
Meier, V. (1995). *Wie Jugoslawien verspielt wurde.* München: C.H. Beck.
Merrills, J. (2010). The means of dispute settlement. In M. Evans (Ed.), *International law* (pp. 559–585). Oxford: Oxford University Press.
Merrills, J. (2014). The place of international litigation in international law. In N. Klein (Ed.), *Litigating international law disputes: Weighing the options* (pp. 3–23). Cambridge: Cambridge University Press.
Ministry of Foreign Affairs France. (2008, December 15). [Draft] EU Council Presidency proposal [on an exchange of letters between Croatia and the Council Presidency].
Ministry of Foreign Affairs Germany. (2017, June 30). Embassies in Ljubljana and Zagreb. Statement on the arbitration award Croatia-Slovenia.
Ministry of Foreign Affairs Slovenia. (2006). Task force on the border with Croatia. White paper on the border between Slovenia and Croatia.
Ministry of Foreign Affairs Slovenia. (2008, September). [Draft] Special Agreement [follow-up to Bled Agreement].
Ministry of Foreign Affairs Slovenia. (2009, May 15). Amendments to the Draft Agreement on Dispute Settlement of 24 April 2009 [Rehn I].
Ministry of Foreign Affairs Slovenia. (2009, May 25). Information on the amendments [to Rehn I] proposed by the Republic of Slovenia.
Ministry of Foreign Affairs Slovenia. (2009, November 21). Note verbale to the Embassy of Croatia in Ljubljana [notification of ratification of Arbitration Agreement], No. ZMP 170/09.
Ministry of Foreign Affairs Slovenia. (2015, July 26). Letter from the Republic of Slovenia to the Registrar of the [Arbitral] Tribunal [on the regret of the ex parte communication, the resignation of Jernej Sekolec and the Slovenian Agent, and on the commitment to the continuation of the arbitration procedure].
Ministry of Foreign Affairs Slovenia. (2019, April 9). Press release [on attempts to influence Slovenian media outlet reporting].
Ministry of Foreign Affairs Slovenia. (2020, April 17). Letter from the Foreign Minister to the author.
Ministry of Foreign Affairs Slovenia News. (2020, January 31). The Arbitral Award is applicable and binding, both countries must implement it. https://www.gov.si/en/news/2020-01-31-the-arbitral-award-is-applicable-and-binding-both-countries-must-implement-it/. Accessed April 28, 2020.
Ministry of Foreign Affairs Sweden. (2009, September 15). Letter from Prime Minister Reinfeldt [as EU Council President] to Prime Minister Kosor [on acknowledgement of the non-prejudging nature of the Croatian accession negotiation documents].
Ministry of Foreign Affairs Sweden. (2009, September 25). Fax to EU Enlargement Commissioner Olli Rehn [on the latest draft of the Arbitration Agreement].
Ministry of Foreign and European Affairs Croatia. (Undated). Termination of the arbitration process between Croatia and Slovenia: Causes and consequences. https://www.mvep.hr/en/other/termination-of-the-arbitration-process. Accessed March 29, 2020.
Ministry of Foreign and European Affairs Croatia. (2006, May 12). Press release on the Plovanija border checkpoint and Slovenian territorial claims.
Ministry of Foreign and European Affairs Croatia. (2008, September). [Draft] Special Agreement between the government of the Republic of Croatia and the government of the Republic of

Slovenia on the submission of the boundary dispute between the two States to the International Court of Justice [follow-up to Bled Agreement].

Ministry of Foreign and European Affairs Croatia. (2009, November 9). Note verbale to the Embassy of Slovenia in Zagreb [notification of ratification of Arbitration Agreement], No. 6257/09.

Ministry of Foreign and European Affairs Croatia. (2011, September). Non-paper [on the arbitration procedure].

Ministry of Foreign and European Affairs Croatia. (2012). Note [on the genesis of the Arbitration Agreement].

Ministry of Foreign and European Affairs Croatia. (2015, May 7). Letter of the Minister to the European Commission First Vice President [on the statements of the Slovenian Foreign Minister].

Ministry of Foreign and European Affairs Croatia. (2015, May 30). Letter of the Minister to the Registrar of the [Arbitral] Tribunal [on presumed informal channels of communication between Slovenia and the Tribunal].

Ministry of Foreign and European Affairs Croatia. (2015, July 24). Letter of the Minister for Foreign and European Affairs of the Republic of Croatia to the Registrar of the [Arbitral] Tribunal [on media reports on ex parte communication between Slovenia and the Tribunal].

Ministry of Foreign and European Affairs Croatia. (2015, July 30). Letter of the Minister for Foreign and European Affairs of the Republic of Croatia to the Registrar of the [Arbitral] Tribunal [on Croatia's withdrawal from the arbitration procedure].

Ministry of Foreign and European Affairs Croatia. (2015, July 30). Note verbale to the Ministry of Foreign Affairs Slovenia [on Croatia's withdrawal from the arbitration procedure], No. 3303/2015.

Ministry of Foreign and European Affairs Croatia. (2016, March 16). Note verbale Permanent Mission of the Republic of Croatia to the U.N. to Permanent Missions and Permanent Observer Missions to the U.N. [on the reasons for non-participation in the 17 March 2016 hearing of the Arbitral Tribunal ahead of the Partial Award and explaining the Croatian government's withdrawal decision from 30 July 2015], No. 55/2016. http://www.mvep.hr/files/file/dokumenti/arbitraza/en/160330-nv-pm-croatia-no-55-2016.pdf. Accessed 30 March 2020. Reprinted in Appendix B.

Ministry of Foreign and European Affairs Croatia. (2018, December 21). Croatia files motion with ECJ regarding Slovenia's lawsuit. https://www.mvep.hr/en/info-servis/press-releases/,31882.html. Accessed April 04, 2020.

Miščević, T., & Mrak, M. (2017). The EU accession process: Western Balkans vs EU-10. *Politička Misao, 54*(4), 185–204.

Moses, M. (2017). *The principles and practice of international commercial arbitration*. Cambridge: Cambridge University Press.

Mourre, A. (2010). Are unilateral appointments defensible? On Jan Paulsson's moral hazard in international arbitration. *Kluwer Arbitration Blog*. https://arbitrationblog.kluwerarbitration.com/2010/10/05/are-unilateral-appointments-defensible-on-jan-paulssons-moral-hazard-in-international-arbitration/. Accessed February 10, 2019.

MTI News. (2017, September 11). Hungary blocks OECD membership for Romania, Croatia.

Myers, S., & Rubin., A. (2020, March 18). Its coronavirus cases dwindling, China turns focus outward. *New York Times*. https://www.nytimes.com/2020/03/18/world/asia/coronavirus-china-aid.html. Accessed April 10, 2020.

Office of the Prime Minister of the Republic of Slovenia. (2007, August 26). Tape-recording transcript of the [Janša] statement at the [Bled Agreement] press conference.

Official Gazette of the Republic of Croatia. (1994). [Sabor repudiation of the inclusion of the Three Hamlets in the municipality of Piran]. No. 71/1994.

Official Gazette of the Republic of Slovenia. (1994). [Suspension of inclusion of Dragonja strip]. No. 69/1994.

Official Gazette of the Republic of Slovenia. (1994). [Inclusion of Dragonja strip in municipality of Piran]. No. 60/1994.

Official Gazette of the Republic of Croatia. (2000). [Sabor Declaration on the Homeland War]. No. 102/2000.

Official Journal of the European Union. (2018, November 5). C-399. 19-21. https://eur-lex.europa.eu/legal-content/EN/TXT/PDF/?uri=OJ:C:2018:399:FULL&from=EN. Accessed April 04, 2020.

Opassi, E. (1991, June 23). Grade se prijelazi. *Večernji list* (p. 3).

Oude Elferink, A. (2017). Slovenia/Croatia arbitration—Is the territorial sea delimitation inconsistent with the case law on maritime delimitation? *NCLOS Blog*. Available at: https://site.uit.no/nclos/2017/08/16/sloveniacroatia-arbitration-is-the-territorial-sea-delimitation-inconsistent-with-the-case-law-on-maritime-delimitation/. Accessed March 30, 2020.

Permanent Court of Arbitration. (2012, April 13). Press release. Arbitration between the Republic of Croatia and the Republic of Slovenia. Arbitral tribunal holds first procedural meeting with the parties. https://pcacases.com/web/sendAttach/238. Accessed March 28, 2020.

Permanent Court of Arbitration. (2014, June 17). Press release. Conclusion of hearing in the arbitration between the Republic of Croatia and the Republic of Slovenia. 17 June 2014. Available at: https://pcacases.com/web/sendAttach/241. Last accessed March 29, 2020.

Permanent Court of Arbitration. (2015, May 5). Arbitration between the Republic of Croatia and the Republic of Slovenia. Letter of the tribunal to the parties' agents. https://pcacases.com/web/sendAttach/1307. Accessed March 29, 2020.

Permanent Court of Arbitration. (2015, July 10). Press release. Arbitration between the Republic of Croatia and the Republic of Slovenia. Arbitral tribunal schedules award. https://pcacases.com/web/sendAttach/1308. Accessed March 29, 2020.

Permanent Court of Arbitration. (2015, August 5). Press release. Arbitration between the Republic of Croatia and the Republic of Slovenia. Republic of Croatia notifies its intention to terminate the arbitration agreement—Judge Ronny Abraham resigns from the arbitral tribunal. https://pcacases.com/web/sendAttach/1389. Accessed March 30, 2020.

Permanent Court of Arbitration. (2015, September 25). Press release. Arbitration between the Republic of Croatia and the Republic of Slovenia. Tribunal reconstituted by appointment of Norwegian and Swiss arbitrators, H.E. Mr. Rolf Fife and Professor Nicolas Michel. https://pcacases.com/web/sendAttach/1468. Accessed March 30, 2020.

Permanent Court of Arbitration. (2016, June 30). Croatia v Slovenia. PCA Case No. 2012-04. Partial Award. https://pcacases.com/web/sendAttach/1787. Accessed March 27, 2020.

Permanent Court of Arbitration. (2017, June 29). Croatia v Slovenia. PCA Case No. 2012-04. Final Award. https://pcacases.com/web/sendAttach/2172. Accessed March 20, 2020.

Permanent Court of Arbitration. (2017, June 29). Press release. Arbitration between the Republic of Croatia and the Republic of Slovenia. Tribunal determines land and maritime boundaries in final award. https://pcacases.com/web/sendAttach/2175. Accessed March 30, 2020.

Petrič, E. (2017). "Junction Area"—A new legal regime. Permanent Court of Arbitration (PCA) Case No. 2012-04 (Slovenia v. Croatia). *Czech Yearbook of Public and Private International Law, 8*, 361–378. https://rozkotova.cld.bz/CYIL-vol-8-2017/381/#zoom=z. Accessed April 05, 2020.

Pipan, P. (2008). Border dispute between Croatia and Slovenia along the lower reaches of the Dragonja river. *Acta Geographica Slovenica, 48*(2), 331–356.

Preston, C. (1995). Obstacles to EU enlargement: The classical community method and the prospects for a wider Europe. *Journal of Common Market Studies, 33*(3), 451–463.

Prime Minister of the Republic of Croatia. (2002, September 3). Letter from Prime Minister Račan to Prime Minister Drnovšek [on non-ratification of the bilateral Draft Agreement of 17 July 2001].

Prime Minister of the Republic of Croatia. (2015, October 1). Letter from Prime Minister Milanović to European Commission President Jean-Claude Juncker [on non-recognition of the reconstitution of the Arbitral Tribunal].

Prime Minister of the Republic of Croatia. (2017, June 29). Press release [non-recognition of the final award]. https://vlada.gov.hr/news/pm-plenkovic-croatia-doesn-t-intend-to-apply-border-arbitration-ruling/21947. Accessed March 31, 2020.

Prime Minister of the Republic of Croatia. (2017, September 21). Address at the 72nd session of the UN General Assembly.

Prime Minister of the Republic of Croatia. (2017, December 19). Government News press conference notes [bilateral Plenković-Cerar meeting].
Prime Minister of the Republic of Slovenia. (2017, June 29). Press release [on the Final Award].
Regulation (EU). (2013, December 11). No 1380/2013 of the European Parliament and of the Council on the Common Fisheries Policy. https://eur-lex.europa.eu/legal-content/EN/TXT/?uri=CELEX%3A32013R1380. Accessed March 27, 2020.
Rothwell, D., & Stephens, T. (2016). *The international law of the sea*. Oxford and Portland: Hart Publishing.
Sancin, V. (2010). Slovenia-Croatia border dispute: From 'Drnovšek-Račan' to 'Pahor-Kosor' agreement. *European Perspectives, 2*(2), 93–111.
Sands, P. (2016). Reflections on international judicialization. *European Journal of International Law, 27*(4), 885–900.
Sarvarian, A. (2016, May 3). Arbitration between Croatia and Slovenia: Leaks, wiretaps, scandal (Part 4). *EJIL Blog*. https://www.ejiltalk.org/author/asarvarian/. Accessed April 24, 2020.
Sarvarian, A., & Baker, R. (2015, August 7). Arbitration between Croatia and Slovenia: Leaks, wiretaps, scandal (Part 2). *EJIL Blog*. https://www.ejiltalk.org/arbitration-between-croatia-and-slovenia-leaks-wiretaps-scandal-part-2/. Accessed April 24, 2020.
Scott, S. (2014). Litigation versus dispute resolution through political processes. In N. Klein (Ed.), *Litigating international law disputes: Weighing the options* (pp. 24–41). Cambridge: Cambridge University Press.
Solomou, A. (2017, September 15). A commentary on the maritime delimitation issues in the Croatia v. Slovenia final award. *EJIL Blog*. https://www.ejiltalk.org/a-commentary-on-the-maritime-delimitation-issues-in-the-croatia-v-slovenia-final-award/. Accessed April 24, 2020.
STA News. (2017, September 8). Slovenia opposes Croatian bid for OECD membership.
STA News. (2017, September 15). Slovenia takes EU Commission to court over Teran.
STA News. (2018, March 16). Slovenia hands Croatia letter to EU Commission.
STA News. (2018, July 9). Government to take final decision on Croatia border arbitration suit this week.
STA News. (2018, July 13). Government takes Croatia to EU Court of Justice over border arbitration.
STA News. (2018, September 08). Business as usual for fishermen in Piran Bay.
STA News. (2019, March 27). Slovenia protests as Croatian police boat crosses deep into Slovenian waters.
STA News. (2019, April 5). Šarec concerned by arbitration scandal revelations. 05 April 2019.
STA News. (2019, April 9). Plot thickens on wiretapping story.
Stjepčević, A. (2020, April 4). COVID-19 in Montenegro: 201 cases, two deaths. Update April 4, 2020. *Total Montenegro News*. https://www.total-montenegro-news.com/news/5477-covid-19-in-montenegro-201-cases-two-deaths-update-april-4-2020. Accessed April 10, 2020.
Tanaka, Y. (2015). *The international law of the sea*. Cambridge: Cambridge University Press.
Tanaka, Y. (2018a). The disproportionality test in the law of maritime delimitation. In A. Oude Elferink, T. Henriksen, & S. Busch (Eds.), *Maritime boundary delimitation: The case law. Is it consistent and predictable?* (pp. 291–318). Cambridge: Cambridge University Press.
Tanaka, Y. (2018b). *The peaceful settlement of international disputes*. Cambridge: Cambridge University Press.
Telegram.hr. (2018, January 12). Njemački znanstvenik hvali sporazum Račan-Drnovšek, ali u SDP-u ne misle tako. Ima li ljevica rješenje za slovensku granicu? Za Telegram govore Thomas Bickl, Tonino Picula i Joško Klisović. https://www.telegram.hr/politika-kriminal/njemacki-znanstvenik-hvali-sporazum-racan-drnovsek-ali-u-sdp-u-ne-misle-tako-ima-li-ljevica-rjesenje-za-granicu-sa-slovenijom/. Accessed April 24, 2020.
United Nations. (1958). Convention on the recognition and enforcement of Foreign Arbitral Awards. New York, 1958 [The New York Convention]. https://uncitral.un.org/sites/uncitral.un.org/files/media-documents/uncitral/en/new-york-convention-e.pdf. Accessed April 24, 2020.
United Nations. (1969, May 23). Vienna Convention on the Law of Treaties. https://legal.un.org/ilc/texts/instruments/english/conventions/1_1_1969.pdf. Accessed April 24, 2020.

United Nations. (1982, December 10). United Nations Convention on the Law of the Sea. https://www.un.org/Depts/los/convention_agreements/texts/unclos/unclos_e.pdf. Accessed April 24, 2020.

United Nations. (2005). Model rules on arbitral procedure. 1958. https://legal.un.org/ilc/texts/instruments/english/draft_articles/10_1_1958.pdf. Accessed April 28, 2020.

United States Department of State (2017, June 30). Embassies in Ljubljana and Zagreb. Statement on the arbitration award Croatia-Slovenia.

Vidas, D. (2009). The UN Convention on the Law of the Sea, the European Union and the Rule of Law: What is going on in the Adriatic Sea? *The International Journal of Marine and Coastal Law, 24*(1), 1–66.

Vukas, B. (2015, July 30). Letter of resignation from the Arbitral Tribunal.

Vuksanović, V. (2020, April 8). China has its eyes on Serbia. *Foreign Policy*. https://foreignpolicy.com/2020/04/08/china-serbia-aleksander-vucic-xi-jinping-coronavirus/. Accessed April 10, 2020.

Chapter 5
Analytical Framework Findings

Abstract This Chapter draws on the empirical findings of Chap. 4 on the border dispute between Slovenia and Croatia. The aim is (i) to identify critical junctures in the conflictual process, and (ii) to see whether the findings allow for some fine-tuning of the analytical framework that have informed the process-tracing of this study. In fact, the analytical toolbox and the research questions developed in Chap. 1 constitute a guide to the researcher and the reader alike in the exploration of the causal mechanisms throughout the management of the bilateral dispute. Looking ahead, the analytical toolbox should be practitioner-proof to allow for a proper analysis of similar bilateral disputes in the context of EU enlargement.

Keywords Conditionality · National identity · Compliance · Mediation · Arbitration · Conflict

5.1 Conflict Analysis and Management

As posited in many framework strands, the role of third parties is crucial in the management of a conflict. We shall look at the feedback of the research findings to the individual frameworks in turn. It may be useful to note, that the issue under scrutiny here, the border dispute between Croatia and Slovenia, is a qualitative within-case or single-case study. Any analysis in terms of theory-building, therefore, is *hypothesis-generating* within the remit of a *single-case* study. Nevertheless, there are conclusions that can be drawn for the application of the analytical toolbox to bilateral disputes in a similar context.

T. Bickl, *The Border Dispute Between Croatia and Slovenia*,
Contributions to Political Science,
https://doi.org/10.1007/978-3-030-53333-5_5

5.1.1 Participation and Communication Aspects of Third-Party Involvement

Recalling John Burton's three-component model

- *participation* by the parties,
- *communication* between the parties, and
- *third-party involvement* in terms of decision-making power,

there are three quasi-default types of relevance here (Burton 1990: 188–192).

First, the *bilateral* approach of direct *negotiations* is categorised as follows:

Full participation of the parties and a high level of interaction with third-party involvement being close to zero.

Participation:	---------------
Communication:	---------
Third Party:	-

Second, for *mediation* Burton posits some substantial participation of the parties and a leading role for the third party. Communication can be assumed to take place more between the parties and the third party, but also between the parties:

Participation:	------
Communication:	---
Third Party:	---------

Third, quasi-judicial *arbitration* Burton defines as communication between the parties being very low, and participation being substantial through involvement in the nomination of the panel members. The third-party role is "decisive".

Participation:	------
Communication:	-
Third Party:	------------

For the purposes of third-party conflict management of the Croatia–Slovenia border dispute, we must distinguish between three phases: (i) the drafting of the Arbitration Agreement; (ii) the arbitral proceedings as such, and (iii) the post-arbitration phase, at times all of the periods intersected by direct bilateral negotiations.

5.1.1.1 Genesis of Arbitration Agreement

When Croatia's EU accessions negotiations were held hostage by the Slovenian veto as from October 2008, the French EU Council Presidency took on the third-party role of a mediator (Sect. 4.2.2.2). They were trying to defuse the conflict at ambassador level which is to say there was no externalisation of the conflict management. The participation of the parties can be assumed as being solid, and the same can be said of the level of communication, whilst it is worth noting that the communication was mostly trilateral, i.e. meetings of the two conflicting parties Slovenia and Croatia with the French Presidency who would subsequently draft an exchange of letters. The Presidency would explore possibilities with each of the parties in turn, come back with a new draft in a trilateral meeting, discuss it there, then contacting the parties again in turn.

The Burton model may thus be differentiated one step further in so far as the feature "communication" must distinguish between communication (i) *between the parties* to the conflict themselves and (ii) *between the parties and the third-party*, whilst communication between the parties bilaterally was virtually at zero.

Participation:	-------
Communication between conflicting parties:	-
Communication with third party:	-------
Third Party:	---------

This observation largely holds also for the drafting stage of the Arbitration Agreement. In the first phase after the European Commission had taken over in January 2009, Rehn explored his initial idea of mediation by an Expert Group (see Sect. 4.2.2.3). His role was that of a classical mediator talking to the parties in turn before presenting a (new) proposal. When Rehn, after two more drafts, learnt that an Expert Group the first core elements of which he had proposed by the end of January 2009 was not far-reaching enough compared to a judicial procedure, he presented his first proposal for an arbitration procedure proper at the end of March 2009.

The role of the European Commission as a third party intensified with the drafts for a full Arbitration Agreement aiming at establishing a judicial *ad-hoc* arbitral tribunal (Rehn I April 2009, Rehn II June 2009). The Commission, drawing on the expertise of its Legal Service, was in the driving seat. The parties came back with replies to the Commission but were not in touch directly with each other bilaterally. The feedback to the Commission drafts was side-lined by trilateral meetings (Sects. 4.2.3 and 4.2.4).

After the temporary deadlock in July 2009, the line-up changed. The Commission had largely withdrawn from the mediating third-party role, and the *travaux préparatoires* on the finalisation of the Arbitration Agreement were actively carried on by the parties to the conflict bilaterally with the Swedish EU Council Presidency skilfully facilitating in the background. The Commission was constantly kept in the loop by the Presidency, however. There were a number of bilateral meetings, two on the level of the prime ministers and many at expert level (see Sect. 4.2.5). The revised component model for the phase between July and early November 2009, when the Arbitration Agreement was signed, may therefore be seen as follows:

Participation:	----------
Communication between conflicting parties:	-------
Communication with third party:	----
Third Party:	----

5.1.1.2 Arbitration Procedure

The Commission continued its role of a third party for a little whilst when the timelines for the arbitration procedure started triggered by the signing of the Croatian EU Accession Treaty in December 2011. The Commission, entrusted with establishing a list of candidates for the three jointly appointed members of the arbitral tribunal, hosted a meeting with the two foreign ministers in January 2012. Whilst two of the candidates were appointed by identical preferences of the parties right away, the parties agreed on the third tribunal member purely bilaterally (see Sect. 4.2.6) and subsequently notified their choice to the Commission. This is what the modified Burton model for that stage would look like:

Participation:	---------
Communication between conflicting parties:	------
Communication with third party:	-
Third Party:	--

With regard to the arbitral proceedings proper in the first phase between April 2012 and July 2015, it can be observed that the parties not only jointly appointed three members and one party-appointed member each, a factor perhaps somewhat overrated by Burton in his determination of participation of the parties, but actively engaged in the written submissions and the oral hearing. In fact, the parties submitted their memorials, counter-memorials, and replies, followed by oral pleadings in an enormous two-week hearing (see Sect. 4.3.2). It is suggested here that the two-fold opportunity of replying to the other party's arguments may be seen as both communication between the parties and communication with the third party. It is not difficult, therefore, to adjust Burton's model on arbitration as follows:

Participation:	--------
Communication:	--------
Third Party:	---------

The phase between the major perturbation of the arbitration procedure through the *ex parte* communication by Slovenia (see Sect. 4.3.3) and the Final Award took on a notably different shape, however. Croatia left the arbitral proceedings, and the Tribunal arranged for a new round of submissions and an additional hearing in March 2016 to assess the legal consequences of the Croatian termination request. Only Slovenia took part in that hearing (see Sect. 4.3.4). The Tribunal issued its Partial Award establishing that Slovenia had violated the Arbitration Agreement, but not to the extent that a termination of the proceedings was justified, and that the reconstituted Tribunal would look at the merits of the case *de novo*. The Final Award was issued in June 2017 (see Sect. 4.3.5). This is the amended Burton model for the second phase of the arbitration procedure:

Participation Slovenia:	--------
Participation Croatia:	.
Communication Slovenia:	----
Communication Croatia:	.
Third Party:	-----------

5.1.1.3 Post-arbitration

From the immediate aftermath of the Final Award (July 2017) until the end of that year, the parties were in touch again bilaterally exploring ways of implementing the gist of the Final Award (Sect. 4.3.6.1) which translates into the following model:

Participation:	--------
Communication between conflicting parties:	-----
Third Party:	-

The subsequent filing of the lawsuit considerably changed the constellation. After it had become apparent that any further bilateral attempts would hardly be successful, the Slovenian government took the decision to initiate Article 259 TFEU proceedings against Croatia. In procedural terms, the complaint had to be filed with the Commission first who held a hearing on the legal aspects of the Slovenian claim. It is worth noting that Slovenia *and* Croatia took part in the hearing which related to EU aspects only. As the Commission stayed neutral in not issuing an opinion itself, Slovenia filed the lawsuit before the CJEU directly. This leads to the below '*Burton plus*' model:

Participation:	---------
Communication between conflicting parties:	-
Communication with third party (Commission):	----
Third Party:	--

5.1.1.4 CJEU Proceedings

For the judicial proceedings before the CJEU, written submissions were filed followed by a hearing on admissibility outlining the parties' positions. The "*Burton plus*" *model* for the proceedings before the EU Court of Justice would thus be the following:

Participation:	---------
Communication between conflicting parties:	--
Communication with third party (CJEU):	-----
Third Party (CJEU):	----------

In summary, there are some new or more fine-grained elements as to the communication and participation aspects which merit an adjustment of the Burton (1990) model (see above). Whilst the classical three-component model as such is an appropriate toolkit for any conflict line-up as it neatly catches the vital elements of conflict management, it appears that the following considerations for the present case study need to be taken into account:

(i) The Slovenia–Croatia case goes beyond a classical bilateral issue and can thus not be seen in an isolated fashion. The two parties to the conflict are presently both members in the same international organisation (in this case the regional organisation EU). However, at the time the Arbitration Agreement was drafted (see Sect. 5.1.1.1), one of the parties was already a member, whilst the other party aspired to the club. That context made for a hybrid conflict management environment: the classical nation State line-up plus the international/regional organisation (which in itself is a blend of inter-governmental and supranational elements[1]) with its particular customs and social norms. This is to say that the circumstances in 2008/2009 considerably differ from the Croatian-Slovenian bilateral constellation between 1991 and 2007. The third party from the regional organisation renders the line-up trilateral, a completely new experience for any of the parties. As a result, a more multi-facetted pattern of communication develops, bilateral (Croatia/Slovenia amongst themselves, or one of them respectively with the third-party European Commission or Council Presidency), or trilateral (all three parties are in touch), and there are no fixed rules as to who communicates with whom at what time. Both communication and participation develop and flow organically and are at the same time very volatile.

(ii) The level and types of communication during a judicial procedure (see Sects. 5.1.1.2 and 5.1.1.4) tend to be underrated in the original Burton model. In an arbitration procedure, there is a robust level of formal and informal communication during the appointment phase for the tribunal members. The Croatian-Slovenian bilateral approach during that (short) phase appears to have been very positive with agreements reached in a good-neighbourly spirit and in a timely fashion. During the phase of the written submissions, communication was substantial. If every allowance is made for the formal nature of the channels of communication during judicial proceedings, the parties' memorials were not only sent to the judicial third party, but also to the other party to the conflict, and they produced counter-memorials and replies to the counter-memorials. Those documents usually are confidential in arbitral proceedings, and so it was in the Slovenia–Croatia case. Nevertheless, in a judicial procedure before the International Court of Justice (ICJ), the memorials and replies are made public after the final judgement, so one could posit an additional layer of communication vis-à-vis the public domain. During a hearing—the Croatia–Slovenia one before the Arbitral Tribunal lasted for ten days—the level of communication and also participation is very high and comprehensive,

[1]This holds not only holds for the EU, but also for other regional organizations, such as the OAU or ASEAN, or for multilateral organizations such as the WTO or ICAO.

particularly with regard to the third party at which the pleadings are directed and which can ask questions to the conflicting parties. The same holds for a hearing before the CJEU, notwithstanding the fact that the one on admissibility in Slovenia v Croatia only lasted for a few hours.

In the framework of conflict management, both the communication aspect in its type or intensity and the role of the third party, are closely related to another aspect of the processing of conflict, the issue of conflict dynamics.

5.1.2 *Conflict Dynamics*

The main idea of the *dynamic* aspect of conflict is that every conflict has its own life cycle and that (re)solutions are never final, but only a more or less stable equilibrium in the life cycle of a conflict (Galtung 1978, 1996, 2000). According to the *conflict triangle*, dynamic flows can be traced in all of the possible six directions (see Sect. 1.3.1.4).

5.1.2.1 Latent and Manifest Stages (Protraction/Relaxation)

The border dispute between Croatia and Slovenia can be assessed against the background of the notion of the potential dynamics with regard to protraction or relaxation. The distinction between the *latent* and *manifest* level of conflict may serve as a further criterion.

Bilateral

An early stage of the conflict back in 1993 was the Memorandum on Piran Bay by the Foreign Affairs Committee of the Slovenian Parliament, when it asserted the maritime claims for the first time. It expressed the claim of full sovereignty over the Bay plus access to the high seas. Together with the response of the Croatian Parliament renouncing the Slovenian claim and advancing the equidistance line in the Bay and in the territorial sea instead, this was a moment when the contradiction of goals became apparent for the first time. However, the declaratory nature did have no practical effect for the time being. Clearly, contradiction and attitude were present, but not behaviour which would have made for a *manifest* or full conflict in Galtung's terms.

It may be argued that the major undertaking of negotiating a bilateral agreement in 2001 ("Drnovšek-Račan" Draft Agreement; see Sect. 4.1.4) has shifted the conflict from the *latent* to the *manifest* level. The two parties were ready to face non-attainment of their mutual goals. At such point, according to Galtung, the parties can either go for anger, hatred, or "verbal or physical violence" (2000: 13) or, positively, resort to dialogue and cooperation (1996: 71). The parties chose the latter option, and in a spirit of collaboration and good-neighbourly relations arrived at a fully negotiated solution which, however, failed due to unsurmountable opposition in Croatia. As a result, one may upgrade the conflict from "solved" to "manifest".

From a general point of view, as there was never any use of force, let alone warfare, it appears fair to say that in the border dispute between Slovenia and Croatia every time there were direct negotiations between the parties, the conflict became a manifest conflict in its positive fashion, i.e. a real problem-solving phase emerged. This can be said of the 2007 Bled Agreement with the principle aim of referring the dispute to third-party dispute resolution, the International Court of Justice (ICJ). That exercise failed a little later when the task was to negotiate the terms of the mandate. Slovenia put alternative options for third-party resolution on the table (see Sect. 4.1.5) that move itself being a matter of shifting the conflict from a latent to a manifest level.

As for the second half of 2009, the parties were back in the bilateral mode (with soft facilitation by the Swedish EU Presidency) finalising the drafting of the Arbitration Agreement. It is observed that the conflict level shifted down to perhaps "latent minus" after the implosion of Rehn II in early July when everything had been on fully manifest (see below).

A certain degree of cooling-off can also be pinpointed for the phase between July and December 2017 when the two parties were in bilateral touch on whether and how to implement the Final Award (see Sect. 4.3.6.1). When every allowance is made for the apparent non-feasibility of reconciling the positions of "full implementation is what it takes" (Slovenia) and "no recognition of the Award, but let's explore ways of agreeing on something" (Croatia), that phase may qualify for shifting from manifest to close to latent. It appears useful in this regard to coin a new subcategory "*manifest relaxed*".

Third-Party Involvement

Looking at the drafting stage of the Arbitration Agreement 2009, the third-party role of the Commission was strong in the first half of the year when, after a first phase of exploring the possibility of "soft mediation", the Rehn I and Rehn II drafts were developed and discussed with the parties. Although the Commission had a firm grip on the management of the conflict as such, one may still opt for "manifest" when describing it in terms of the Galtung levels. Whilst there was a fierce battle over the terms of the Arbitration Agreement in the spheres of diplomacy, it would still appear that there was a half-stable "equilibrium" in Galtung's terms except for the situation in July 2009 when there was a stalemate after the presentation of Rehn II, and the Commission suspended its efforts for the time being (see Sect. 4.2.4) resulting in a high degree of protraction. In terms of another new subcategory, "*manifest protracted*" appears to be a workable term here.

The subsequent phase (from the Kosor–Pahor meeting at the end of July to the signing of the Agreement in early November 2009) may qualify as "*manifest relaxed*" as a sense of relaxation was coming back to the scene due to the bilateral political will to resolve the crisis and a build-up of mutual trust, not least skilfully supported by the Swedish EU Council Presidency (see Sects. 4.2.5.1 and 4.2.5.2).

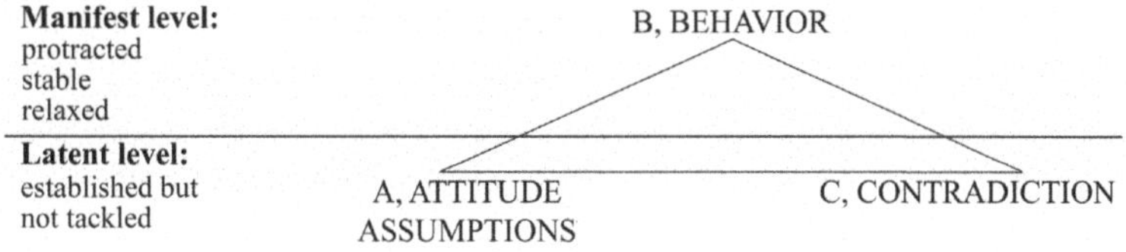

Fig. 5.1 Diplomacy conflict management (*Source* Author; base figure: Galtung 1996: 72)

In retrospect, it is worth noting that towards the beginning of the arbitral proceedings when the parties had agreed on the three neutral members of the Tribunal members in a remarkably smooth manner in mid-January 2012 (see Sect. 4.2.6), the degree of relaxation seems to have been the most advanced ever in the conflict at the time of writing. The subsequent phase of the written submissions and the hearing may have increased the parties' awareness that there is quite some gap to bridge with regard to their positions, and the arbitration environment provided for a civilised conduct using the power of the argument. That level may be newly termed "*manifest stable*".

It will not be difficult to posit that the implosion of the arbitration procedure in the summer of 2015 (see Sect. 4.3.3) may be designated "manifest protracted". The same holds for the entire second phase of the arbitration procedure including the March 2016 hearing on the implications of the Croatian termination request (Croatia did not take part in the hearing), the Partial Award in June 2016 (see Sect. 4.3.4), and the Final Award in June 2017 which Croatia did not recognize (see Sect. 4.3.5).

For the phase of the proceedings before the EU Court of Justice (see Sect. 4.4) one can posit "*manifest stable*": Whilst Slovenia was seeking quasi-enforcement of the implementation of the Final Award through EU law, Croatia was aiming at keeping any EU infringement proceedings at bay to be able to remain at the bilateral level. The hearing at the CJEU was a civilised competition for the better argument, and there was no doubt that both parties would accept the judgement of the Court. Nevertheless, positions were stable and there were no informal side talks on reaching a bilateral agreement.

In the light of the above deliberations, Galtung's Conflict Triangle, whilst still exemplary (i) in its assumptions on *contradiction*, *attitude*, and *behaviour*, and (ii) through the distinction between *latent* and *manifest* conflict, requires adaptation for the purposes of what could be termed "diplomacy conflict management", i.e. in a context where there is *no* armed conflict, but where the conflict at issue has been long-standing; see Fig. 5.1.

5.1.3 Voluntary Versus Coercive Dispute Settlement

Burton (1990) who developed the useful three-component model as for communication, participation and the role of the third party (see Sect. 5.1.1), also takes issue of the distinction between *coercive* and *voluntary* problem-solving approaches (for his original idea on "analytical problem-solving" see Sect. 1.3.1.1).

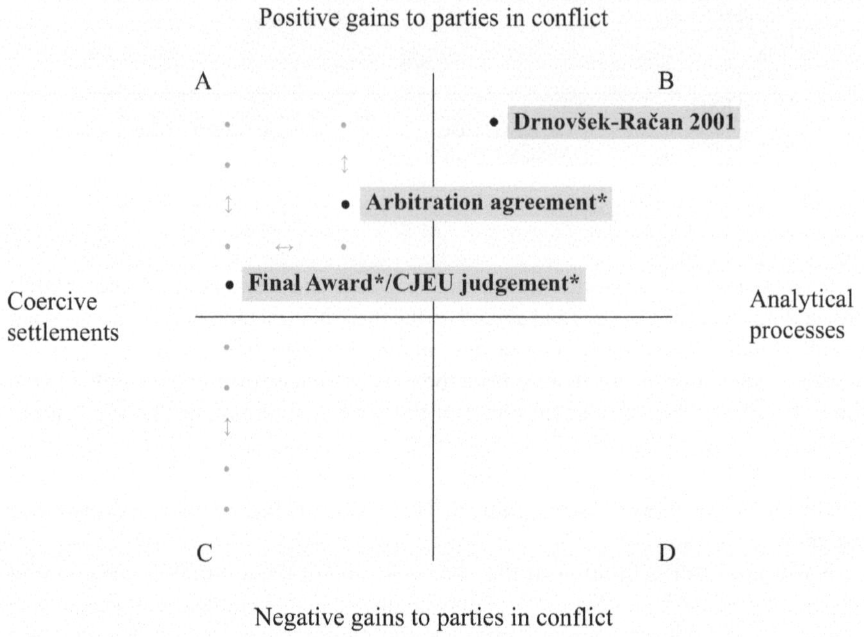

Fig. 5.2 Resolution attempts and coercive versus problem-solving approaches (*Source* Author; base figure: Burton 1990: 197). *—Positive or negative depending on parties' and observers' individual perceptions

To illustrate the differences between coercive and voluntary elements: segment A contains imposed settlements supposed to be favourable to the parties to the conflict (historically the Dayton Peace Accord for Bosnia-Herzegovina in 1995 may be mentioned[2]). Segment D diagonally across represents a win-lose scenario, where the rules are accepted (for example a change of government after elections). Segment C stands for "classical" authoritative-power settlements (e.g. the Berlin Congress of 1878), and segment B is the prototype result of a voluntary problem-solving approach (see Burton 1990; 192–7), for which, to the best knowledge of this author, no successful examples that meet Burton's conditions exist yet.

As analysed in Chap. 4, there have been a number of resolution attempts to the border conflict between Slovenia and Croatia thus far: on a bilateral basis (the 2001 Draft Agreement), involving a mediating third party (the Arbitration Agreement 2009), or involving a judicial third party (the Final Award 2017 and the CJEU judgement 2020).

These attempts can be neatly pointed out along Burton's terms of coercion or voluntariness and the gains related to the parties (see Fig. 5.2). It must be noted, however, that the overleaf model does *not* address the question of implementation or enforcement (such as ratification and subsequent amendment of national legislation).

[2]One would obviously have had to agree that Dayton was indeed "favourable" to the parties.

The Initialled Draft Agreement from 2001 ("Drnovšek-Račan") was negotiated bilaterally in a non-coercive environment. Both Croatia and Slovenia were not yet EU members. The positive gains to both parties would have been a full settlement of the border dispute as such, an agreed maritime and land border, and the removal of the major bilateral conflict ahead of EU accession. Negative gains can only be stipulated vis-à-vis an interpretation of the respective *claims* and can thus not be measured since there was no agreed border in the first place which was being re-negotiated. This is why this author holds that the solution of the border issue is a gain as such, the degree of which may of course be debatable.

The Arbitration Agreement from 2009 was negotiated in an asymmetric bilateral relationship. Slovenia as an EU member had vetoed Croatia as a Candidate Country on the single issue of forcing a solution to the border problem. Still, the terms of the Arbitration Agreement were negotiated bilaterally, but under (firm) mediation of the Commission and (soft) facilitation by the Swedish Presidency, so one has to acknowledge some degree of coercion. The immediate gain for Croatia was the lifting of the Slovenian veto and thus the very real prospect of EU accession. The medium-term gain for Slovenia was the very real prospect of access to the high seas it would perhaps not have achieved in a settlement *after* Croatia's EU accession.

The Final Award from 2017 was delivered in a context where Croatia had de facto withdrawn from the arbitration procedure notwithstanding the fact that the award is a binding decision under international law. Therefore, the coercive nature is fairly clear. The gain for Slovenia is access to the high seas, albeit at the cost of some sobering decisions (from Ljubljana's point of view) here and there along the land border, and the reputational damage caused by the *ex parte* communication. The gain for Croatia may (from Zagreb's point of view) be perceived as negative since the political costs of and the reputational damage to its legal standing for upholding the non-recognition of an internationally binding award cannot be dismissed.

With regard to the CJEU judgement, the proceedings were triggered by Slovenia. The Court is the ultimate EU judicial authority for Croatia and Slovenia as Member States, and it is not difficult to recognise the coercive nature of the Court judgement. With the Court's decision that it has no jurisdiction, it is difficult to posit any gains for anyone *prima facie*, as the only legal certainty that can be derived from that decision is that EU law is not a means to enforce implementation of the Final Award. There may be perceived or real gains of different kinds for the parties involved in the CJEU Case. Whilst Croatia may perceive a positive gain in terms of non-coercion from EU law with regard to the implementation of the arbitral award, Slovenia may perceive a negative gain as the question of implementation of the Final Award is now back at the (non-coercive, i.e. voluntary) bilateral level. Nevertheless, there is one positive gain for Slovenia in that the Court has confirmed that the Final Award was a settlement both parties had an obligation to implement.

5.1.4 Timing of Conflict Management Initiatives

Drawing on the *timing* of third-party involvement in dispute resolution one has to recall:

> If it is to succeed, a mediation initiative cannot be launched at just any time; the conflict must be ripe for the initiation of negotiation. Parties resolve their conflict only when they have to do so - when each party's efforts to achieve a unilaterally satisfactory result are blocked and the parties feel trapped in an uncomfortable and costly predicament. (Zartman and de Soto 2010: 5)

Further, ripeness can be traced, and there are two conditions: First, the parties to a conflict must perceive a situation as a stalemate, and second, there must be a sense that a solution through negotiations is possible (Zartman and de Soto 2010: 6). The following observations can be made in that context:

When the Slovenian blockade surfaced in October 2008, the French Presidency was in a difficult position. One could argue, that intra-Council mediating efforts should have started a bit earlier, but the benefit of hindsight suggests that no solution by means of an exchange of letters to renounce the allegedly prejudging nature of the Croatian accession would have been enough to accommodate the Slovenian concerns (see Sects. 4.2.2.1 and 4.2.2.2), and perhaps a sense of urgency for the need of third-party mediation was not there yet. It must be acknowledged, too, that the French Presidency was facing a completely new situation of a Member State veto, and having to unblock the situation in a trilateral line-up with the affected Candidate Country was, in reality, more serious than Ljubljana's reservations on paper. It is not difficult to posit, therefore, that there was nothing "wrong" with the timing of the French Presidency, but the underlying conflict (Slovenia actually wanted an arbitration procedure on the border issue before accepting Croatia's EU accession) simply was not solvable with an exchange of letters on the diplomatic level.

The first moves by EU Enlargement Commissioner Rehn in January 2009 (see Sect. 4.2.2.3) did probably meet the preconditions outlined by Zartman and de Soto. It is difficult, however, to assess parties' real sense of a need for negotiations, as such attitudes tend to include sensitive political-tactical deliberations which are not disclosed. The timing of the Commission's further steps, and its quick adaptation to the apparent need for a third-party judicial procedure must be acknowledged. Early efforts of Rehn who proposed mediation to the parties at the beginning of 2009 did not bear fruit as there was probably not a sufficient enough grasp of procedural certainty for the parties, and their perception perhaps was that they would not have enough control of the process under mediation. Rehn and his legal team were fast in drafting and discussing a first proposal for an arbitration agreement (Rehn I; see Sect. 4.2.3) with the parties, and discussed and developed it further (Rehn II; see Sect. 4.2.4) accommodating what where truly tricky legal and political issues.

In the same vein, the soft mediation by the Swedish Presidency in the second half of 2009 can be seen as carefully timed. After the process had stalled in July (see Sect. 4.2.5), the Swedes took over the mediating role from the Commission. Whilst the lion share of the finalisation of the Arbitration Agreement had shifted to the bilateral level, i.e. there was no drafting input by the mediating third party, the Swedish Presidency had a tuned ear and sharp eye and was of great assistance to the parties checking their perception and the need for assistance, and delivered soft mediation in an impeccable manner when behind-the-scenes evidence suggests that it was indeed hanging by a thread whether the conflicting parties would arrive at an agreement at all (see Sect. 4.2.5.2).

On balance, it appears that in the absence of hostilities and war—the classical context most of the mediation concepts were developed for—the perfect timing for mediation initiatives on the level of diplomacy in a non-violent environment is not easy to determine. It seems that many of the circumstances are *sui generis* and therefore difficult to grasp, let alone categorise. Only fuzzy assumptions can be made of what makes for successful timing. One such assumption perhaps is a sound knowledge of the parties and the issue in question, and another one is a genuine interest of the mediator to actually solve the crisis. In the Croatia–Slovenia case, it is fair to say that both mediating parties in the pre-arbitration phase, the Commission and the Swedish Council Presidency, were in favour of EU enlargement: the Commission *ex officio* (the Commission is the institutional driver of EU accession negotiations and thus interested in successful accession of Candidates Countries; see Sect. 4.2.1), and the Swedish Presidency with a long-standing pro-enlargement policy commitment. As a result, it is not difficult to contend that anything that would help getting the process of the Croatian EU accession process back on track was an intrinsic motivation for both mediating third parties.

5.1.5 Positions and Real Interests

A major assumption in the theory of conflict resolution originates from the concept of *principled* or *collaborative negotiation* (Fischer et al. 2012). The hypothesis is that in many instances the real obstacle to a solution is *positional bargaining*. Fisher et al. contend that arguing over positions "produces unwise outcomes" the main difficulty being that "the more you clarify your position and defend it against attack, the more committed you become to it [...]. Your ego becomes identified with your position. You now have an interest in 'saving face' [...] making it less and less likely that any agreement will wisely reconcile the parties' original interests" (Fischer et al. 2012: xxvi; see Sect. 1.3.1.2).

An enlightening example is the breakdown of the talks about a ban on nuclear testing from 1961. One of the issues was how many on-site inspections per year should the USA and the USSR be allowed to carry out on the other party's territory. Whilst the Soviet Union favoured three, the USA insisted on no less than ten. The talks actually broke down over this disagreement whilst the nature of the "inspection" had never been discussed, so that it was not at all clear whether there would be "one person looking around for one day, or hundred people [...] for a month". In fact, little attempt had been made to reconcile verification with the mutual aim of minimal intrusion (Fischer et al. 2012: 5).

In relation to the 2001 Draft Agreement between Croatia and Slovenia on the maritime and land border, not a great deal can be said about whether there was positional bargaining or not during the negotiations as, sadly, both former prime ministers who had conducted most of the negotiations face to face passed away well before the research of this book commenced, so no personal account from them could be had. However, there are several empirical findings on the circumstances back then. First, the border issue was mentioned as an outstanding bilateral issue for Slovenia in the 2000 European Commission Progress Report for the country, so one can assume a sense of urgency on the part of Drnovšek. Second, also Račan apparently knew that EU and NATO accession was only possible for Croatia with the support of Slovenia. And third, there was a link with two other bilateral issues, Ljubljanska Banka (where Croatia had an interest that foreign currency depositors of the former Ljubljanska Banka in Yugoslav times, of which there were many in Croatia, will be reimbursed) and Krško (the joint nuclear power station where Slovenia had temporarily cut-off Croatia from electricity supply for some time); see Sect. 4.1.4. So, there must have been a mutual interest in good-neighbourly relations and a spirit of collaboration between Drnovšek and Račan, and thus a genuine interest in solving the border issue as such rather than defending particular positions and underlying interests.

As for the negotiations on the Arbitration Agreement 2009, it is worth tracing what positions were taken to defend what interest. It is established here that some substantial positional bargaining took place, mainly on the two issues of (i) the maritime border in Piran Bay and (ii) the link between the Slovenian territorial sea and the high seas. Whilst the main interest of Slovenia was the access to the high seas, Croatia's main interest was to have the blockade lifted and become EU member, but ideally without any territorial concessions neither in the Croatian territorial sea nor in Piran Bay. It is useful to note that there is a reference to "vital interests" in the preamble to the Arbitration Agreement (see Sect. 4.2.4). It turned out that, during the hearing, Croatia emphasised its *territorial integrity* as the main interest apart from EU membership in suggesting that there was actually no need to devise a corridor through the Croatian territorial sea. According to Croatia, the existing law-of-the-sea concept of innocent passage secured navigation from Slovenia to the high seas and vice versa. Further, the agreed sea lanes to and from the Slovenian port of Koper proved that a link between Slovenia and the high seas was sufficiently in place already (see "Croatia's Position" in Sect. 4.3.2.2). Slovenia, on its part, did make it clear that the access to the high seas was the quid pro quo for accepting the Arbitration Agreement. The vital issue for Ljubljana was not to depend on the goodwill of Croatia in relation to innocent passage through their territorial waters and to secure full and unrestricted freedom of navigation between the Slovenian territorial sea and the high seas (see "Slovenia's Position" in Sect. 4.3.2.2).

To avoid territorial concessions, Croatia aimed at insisting on *international law* as the applicable law wherever possible since international law is bound to codified law such as UNCLOS where the principle "the land dominates the sea" leaves little room for compensating for coastal configurations of geographically disadvantaged States such as Slovenia, for example. With its tiny coastline and the huge coastlines of Italy and Croatia, Slovenia has very little maritime space under its full sovereignty as the Croatian and Italian waters meet in the proximity of the Slovenian coast. In addition, the concave coast in the Gulf of Trieste geographically aggravates the boxed-in situation of the Slovenian maritime entitlements under UNCLOS (see "Territorial Sea Boundary" in Sect. 4.3.5.2). Slovenia, on its part, aimed at widening the discretionary powers of the Tribunal to a maximum extent to exactly trigger the infringements on the Croatian territorial sea to enable the creation of a corridor link. The corridor, or junction, would have to entail the right to absolute (rather than innocent) passage, so that any stopping of vessels (which is possible under innocent passage, albeit in very particular and rare circumstances) would be impossible. Thus, Ljubljana insisted on factors other than international law to be taken into account, such as *equity* and a "fair and just result" drawing on considerations beyond the Law of the Sea (*ex aequo et bono*). The aim was to have some sort of bargain to make up for the fact that Slovenia is a geographically disadvantaged State and that a solution for legally unhindered access to the high seas could be found that took into account a spirit of good-neighbourly relations with Croatia (see Sect. 4.2.3.2).

It is not easy to make an assessment of the Croatian withdrawal from the arbitral proceedings in mid-2015 in terms of real interest, as the circumstances of both the intercepted telephone conversations (*ex parte* communication) and its making into the media are highly obscure. Nevertheless, assuming that the Croatian foremost interest still was to ensure its territorial integrity, a termination of the arbitration procedure would certainly have met that goal for the time being. Slovenia, on its part, had to insist on the continuation of the proceedings as this was the only way to achieve legally guaranteed uninterruptable access to the high seas given that the Arbitration Agreement had actually mandated the Tribunal to find a solution for that very access.

The aftermath of the Final Award is also subject to some obscurity in terms of interest. This is mainly due to the fact that the Croatian government was still locked in by the unanimous Sabor vote from July 2015 which had called on the then government to leave the arbitration procedure (see Sect. 4.3.3.3). On the other hand, the contents of the Final Award Croatia refused to recognise appears to be rather positive for Zagreb, a fact that cannot have been lost on the government, and was indeed not. The Tribunal's decisions on the land border were predominantly in favour of Croatia's claims (e.g. the military installation at Sveta Gera would "come home", and the contested Dragonja strip on the left bank of the river was confirmed to be Croatian), the equidistance line in the territorial sea was only modestly deflected in favour of Slovenia (the Tribunal did in fact not take into account the very short coastline of Slovenia), and even the delimitation inside Piran Bay, from Zagreb's point of view, must have seemed to half-fairly reflect the *effectivités* invoked by both parties (the Bay was predominantly used by Slovenia, and there was no active fishing management in the Bay nor was there any other considerable economic activity by Croatia).

Besides, the Tribunal's determination of the high-seas corridor through Croatian territorial waters may be seen as in line with the actual predetermination in the Arbitration Agreement, so one cannot say that the Tribunal's decision exceeded the mandate of the Arbitration Agreement (see Junction Area in Sect. 4.3.5.2).

To that end, Croatia, on the one hand, had to continue distancing itself from the arbitration award per se as it regarded the arbitration procedure contaminated because of Slovenia's earlier illegal pieces of communication, and was bound by the 2015 Sabor resolution. On the other hand, Zagreb had some interest in implementing at least the gist of the Tribunal's decisions perhaps with some additional, mainly symbolic, fine-tuning inside the Bay. It appears that Croatia's stance that *all* open bilateral issues should be discussed, may be seen as an effort to deflect public attention somewhat away from the arbitration award as the latter included some territorial infringements on the maritime side of affairs, in particular the Junction Area in the Croatian territorial sea (see also Sect. 4.3.6.1).

Slovenia's interest was to timely implement the Final Award as it provided for the sought-after direct access to the high seas. To achieve that it was bound to go down the path of bilateral meetings discussing implementation with Croatia. The assumption here is that showing one's own good-neighbourly credentials and perhaps developing some de-escalating and face-saving momentum would make it easier for Croatia to agree on implementation. It appears, however, that the fall-back position for Slovenia was the road to the CJEU in Luxemburg, and that preparations for the lawsuit had to go in parallel (see Sect. 4.4).

In a nutshell, to distinguish between the interests of the parties to a conflict and their positions, and to work with the former, is a worthwhile point in successful conflict resolution. It avoids unnecessary prolongations and debates over superficial issues. With regard to the Croatia–Slovenia case, it appears fair to say that it is established that the interests of the parties have been long-standing, not least due to the joint history of the border dispute, and therefore as good as fully transparent to the opposite party. If a third-party mediator is involved, however, it is crucial for the mediator to be fully familiar with these interests and its historic foundations.

5.1.6 Judicial Dispute Resolution

There are two issues with relevant findings from the Croatia–Slovenia border dispute, (i) legal discretion, i.e. the contents of the mandate submitted to the judicial body by the parties to the dispute, and (ii) legal embeddedness, i.e. the enforcement of judgements and whether the judicial body depends on international or domestic actors (see Sect. 1.3.1.5).

With regard to (i) legal discretion, it is useful to recall that the fiercest negotiating between the parties to a conflict takes place over the terms of the mandate for third-party judicial dispute resolution (Keohane et al. 2000: 470). The empirical findings from the Slovenia–Croatia border issue appear to confirm the above proposition in two instances:

At their meeting in Bled in August 2007, Prime Ministers Janša and Sanader agreed to submit the border dispute to the International Court of Justice (ICJ). That apparently was the easy part of the agreement. What was supposed to be a matter of a few months, however, turned out to be a lengthy process. The joint Croatian–Slovenian team of legal experts tasked with drafting the mandate for the Court could not reach agreement. Whilst a Croatian draft from September 2008 was based on the ICJ as the judicial third party, a Slovenian draft mentioned three options, one of them the ICJ, and the other two the Permanent Court of Arbitration (PCA) and *Ad-hoc* Arbitration. The process stalled, as the ICJ had been a *sine qua non* for Croatia, and Slovenia withdrew its members from the joint expert group in March 2009, so that the agreement of submitting the dispute to the ICJ was as a matter of fact extinct. Despite the principle agreement to submit the dispute it proved impossible to agree on the mandate in three meetings over a period of 18 months (see Sect. 4.1.5), not least because of the "golden opportunity" to solve the border issue through a veto in the ongoing EU accession negotiations with Croatia.

The negotiations on the actual Arbitration Agreement in 2009 are another case in point. They did prove successful in the end, but it is submitted here that this was only possible because of the pressure exerted by the vital interests of both parties: Croatia wanted to secure EU accession, and Slovenia was keen to secure unhindered access to the high seas and feeling increasingly uncomfortable with blocking the accession negotiations of Croatia. Still, the drafting of the Arbitration Agreement required the firm mediation and drafting input from a mediating third party (European Commission) and some skilful soft mediation at the final negotiating stage (Swedish Presidency). That intense process with many meetings (bilateral and trilateral), which even stalled for a moment, lasted from the beginning of January to the beginning of November 2009 (see Sects. 4.2.2.3–4.2.5).

In respect of (ii) legal embeddedness, the proposition is that in cases where a judgement is not enforceable, such as State-to-State arbitration, governments may face pressure from the domestic opposition or from the public domain arguing that non-implementation damaged the legitimacy of a government (Keohane et al. 2000: 466–467).

However, the non-implementation of the 2017 Final Award by the Croatian government (for the reason of its own prior withdrawal from the arbitration process altogether due to the Slovenian *ex parte* communication) appears to disconfirm the above proposition. In fact, there was no blaming of the Croatian government by the domestic opposition at all. Rather, such a move would be surprising in view of the unanimous Sabor vote from July 2015 calling on the government to leave the arbitration process (see Sect. 4.3.3.3). When a (real or perceived) nationalist interest is at stake, it is naturally very difficult for any opposition to accuse the government of putting at stake the international reputation of the country. All the more so, when the government did not show any readiness to "give in" to widespread calls for implementation on the part of the European Commission and some Member States (see Sect. 4.3.6.2). Also, the Arbitral Tribunal's 2016 Partial Award stipulating that the Slovenian illegal communication was not as grave as to give rise to the cancellation of the Arbitration Agreement, and that the arbitral proceedings as such were going to continue (see Sect. 4.3.4.3), had not caused a split between the government and the opposition.

It unquestionably remains a shortcoming of State-to-State arbitration, however, when compared to a judicial procedure at the ICJ, that a judgement cannot be enforced, irrespective of a prior commitment of the parties to that end (as was the case in Article 7(2) of the Arbitration Agreement between Croatia and Slovenia; see Appendix A). There are two instances of non-compliance with an arbitration award in the recent history of State-to-State arbitration: the first one was China in 2016 (when it refused to acknowledge the arbitral tribunal's jurisdiction; see Table 3.1 in Sect. 3.2.2.3), and Croatia 2017 (refusing to recognise the Final Award after dropping out of the proceedings due to illegal communication on the part of Slovenia; see Sects. 4.3.3.2 and 4.3.3.3). Whilst the China case constitutes a blatant repudiation of the UNCLOS provisions on dispute settlement altogether (the Philippines had initiated proceedings unilaterally; for the UNCLOS provisions see Sect. 3.2.1.1), the Croatia case is a refusal of recognition of the Final (and Partial) Award. Yet, Croatia is a party to the original Arbitration Agreement with Slovenia (for the legal aspects see Sects. 4.3.4.1–4.3.4.3; for the EU enlargement explanatory mode see Sect. 5.2). Still, arbitration has its particular strengths, especially with regard to bilateral disputes in a *sui generis* line-up of conflictual heritage in the context of State succession and EU accession. The flexibility to accommodate those historical and political circumstances is of utmost value (see Sect. 6.2 which includes recommendations on reform of State-to-State arbitration).

Article 259 TFEU infringement proceedings brought before the EU Court of Justice by Slovenia do not provide for new findings for the analytical framework with regard to "access" to a judicial body, i.e. the hurdles for the submission of a dispute (Keohane et al. 2000: 462–464). The difference between the arbitration case and the Member-State-against-Member-State CJEU case is that the former required an agreement by the parties through joint submission of the mandate, whereas the latter was initiated unilaterally by a claim of one party against the other one (see Sect. 4.4). The Court's decision of non-jurisdiction appears to confirm the above-mentioned structural shortcoming of State-to-State arbitration, namely the lack of enforcement. It must be noted, however, that (i) the EU Court is free to decide differently in similar cases in the future, and that (ii) there may be cases in other international–regional organisations, such as the Organisation for African Union (OAU), where the question of enforcement of State-to-State arbitration through the law of the international–regional organisation arises and may be answered in the positive.

5.2 EU Enlargement Approaches

The issue here is under which circumstances Candidate Countries for EU membership are able or ready to meet the EU's political or *acquis* requirements, and how the interplay between domestic actors and the EU unfolds from both a rationalist and constructivist angle (see Sect. 1.3.2).

5.2.1 Conditionality (Rationalist Approach)

Starting out on the general proposition that the constituent logic of EU conditionality is "a bargaining strategy of reinforcement by reward, under which the EU provides external incentives for a target government to comply with [the EU's] conditions" (Schimmelfennig and Sedelmeier 2004: 661), Candidate Countries are assumed to comply with conditionality if EU membership is seen by the domestic actors as a credible incentive which, as a minimum, compensates the compliance costs for the domestic government (see Sect. 1.3.2.1).

In the light of the findings from the Slovenia–Croatia border dispute, this calls for three comments:

First, regardless of the distinction between political and legal-technical (EU legislation) criteria (*acquis*), it can be observed that the issue of Slovenia's reservations vis-à-vis the alleged prejudging nature of the Croatian EU accession negotiations documents on the border made the solution of the border dispute imperative. In other words, the solution of the boundary issue became a political criterion on top of the existing criteria. Each Candidate Country is supposed to fulfil the *acquis* criteria laid down in the 35 negotiating Chapters. Bilateral issues are not part of the *acquis*. As any opening of negotiating Chapters is subject to unanimity, this gives any of the Member States a right of veto. Slovenia framed the unresolved border with Croatia in terms of maps from the Croatian accession documents as an obstacle for several Chapters (such as transport or environment, see Sect. 4.2.2.1). This may be defined as an *add-on* of political conditionality, as it had nothing to do with EU legislation (*acquis*). As a result, the compliance costs or the price for EU membership for Croatia went up considerably. The solution of the border issue came on top of the domestic political costs and, at first sight, also meant a potential delay of EU accession. In any case, it may be seen as additional political costs.

Second, not only is it an additional criterion. In the Croatian-Slovenian border dispute, the add-on conditionality originated "on the spot", as it were, when the accession negotiations were in midstream. As a result, such *ad-hoc* add-on of (political) conditionality during the accession negotiations has raised the compliance costs without prior notice. In other words, the price for membership has gone up *unexpectedly*. After a rocky start of the Croatian EU accession negotiations (the beginning of the negotiations was postponed from March 2005 to the end of the same year as General Gotovina had not been extradited to the ICTY yet, a delay which Croatia could see coming and for which it was responsible itself), Zagreb was now facing a potential delay as the preparations for opening Chapters were frozen for several months (see Sect. 4.2.2.2).

Third, the additional political criterion or condition is not related to an agreed EU set of rules, let alone through joint decision-making, whatever short term it may be. Notably, the add-on conditionality was induced unilaterally by one Member State as a bilateral issue. In conditionality terms, therefore, it may be referred to as *ad-hoc* add-on political conditionality *induced by national veto*. This is an entirely new type of conditionality which *stricto sensu* has nothing to do with either political or *acquis* aspects of EU conditionality. However, it is (ab)used in the very EU institutional line-up it does not belong to. To that end, it is not lost on the observer that this model has, regrettably, already been imitated by other parties, ironically by Croatia itself in the EU accession negotiations with Serbia in the first half of 2016 where Zagreb vetoed the opening of Chaps. 23 and 24 on the grounds that the Serbian regional war crime jurisdiction infringed the sovereignty of other States (i.e. Croatia), the question of minority seats for ethnic Croats in the Serbian Parliament, and insufficient collaboration with the ICTY (see Sect. 6.3.3).

All in all, it is suggested here that there is a need to introduce a new type of conditionality: *ad-hoc add-on* political conditionality.

The implications of the empirical findings from the Croatia–Slovenia border dispute on the conditionality model are such that *ad-hoc* and off-*acquis* add-on political conditionality may considerably affect the domestic costs of complying with EU conditionality. If a Candidate Country does not know what to expect around the corner other than the scheduled EU criteria, and if that add-on conditionality is from a neighbouring State irresponsibly loading the accession process by blackmailing on purely bilateral issues, the motivation for EU accession and thus the motivation for domestic reform, is heavily affected. In cost-benefit considerations, the price for membership becomes somewhat incalculable, and the domestic weighing-up between costs and benefits less predictable. In addition, the level of credibility of the EU incentive is lowered when there is an unexpected (political) price-increase of EU membership. Taking everything into consideration, the abuse of the national veto in the accession process has hugely detrimental effects on EU conditionality vis-à-vis Candidate Countries in many respects.

5.2.2 *National-Identity and Legitimacy Considerations (Constructivist Approach)*

With regard to the *effectiveness* of conditionality, both the identity-filter model and the compliance behaviour model play a role here.

5.2.2.1 National-Identity Filter

The basic assumption here is that government decisions about external incentives, such as EU membership conditionality, have to pass the "identity test" first of all. If an EU incentive turns out, to some degree or fully, as at odds with what is perceived as the national identity, the appropriateness reasoning may lead to non-compliance. In turn, if a requirement is filtered as non-problematic, its further consideration can go down the consequentialist cost-benefit path. In essence, the *identity filter* comes ahead of the compliance-costs deliberations (Freyburg and Richter 2010: 265–6; see Sect. 1.3.2.2).

In terms of the border dispute with Slovenia, the additional requirement of having to accept a binding third-party settlement of the border issue was facing the identity test in Croatia. It appears fair to say that given the high level of sensitivity in Croatia with regard to territorial issues, mainly due to the traumatic experience during the Homeland War 1991–95 with a huge death-toll, the political cost of having to agree to a real or perceived loss of territory by means of an arbitration procedure was, at least at some point, considered too high. As a result, (i) the EU Commission, in its role as third-party mediator, saw no way out of suspending the negotiations on the Arbitration Agreement at least temporarily, and (ii) the impasse also appears to have forwarded a change in the leadership of the Croatian government (see Sects. 4.2.4 and 4.2.5).

In the same vein, when every allowance is made for the fact that EU membership was seen in the Croatian political elite as indeed a very desirable incentive despite the blackmailing on the part of Slovenia, the sense of loss of territory was so strong that the Croatian Parliament adopted a declaration stating that no provision in the Arbitration Agreement could be regarded as Croatia's consent to Slovenia's demand for territorial contact to the high seas at the expense of the Croatian territorial sea. The Croatian side had even aimed at annexing such declaration to the Arbitration Agreement itself in the first place (see Sect. 4.2.5.2). Still, the Arbitration Agreement was ratified along with the down-toning declaration, as the crucial cost-benefit calculation at the time was that EU membership as the ultimate policy goal outweighed a certain (foreseeable) degree of infringement of Croatia's territorial sea (see Fig. 5.3).

On a different note, that declaration may also be seen as a face-saving move in order to highlight that any decision on the territorial integrity of Croatia, notably the country's foremost vital interest above EU membership, at least officially (see "Croatia's Position" in Sect. 4.3.2.2), was a solution imposed on the country rather than freely arrived at. In other words, the commitment to a foreseeable infringement of the Croatian territorial sea had to be down-toned. In addition, the responsibility for such infringement had to be assigned to actors outside the domestic political domain.

The preservation of Croatia's territorial integrity as a distinctive national-identity feature also surfaced at the arbitral proceeding's 2013 written submissions and the 2014 hearing. Regardless of the fact that a corridor solution inside the Croatian territorial sea was very much predictable due to the agreed provisions in the

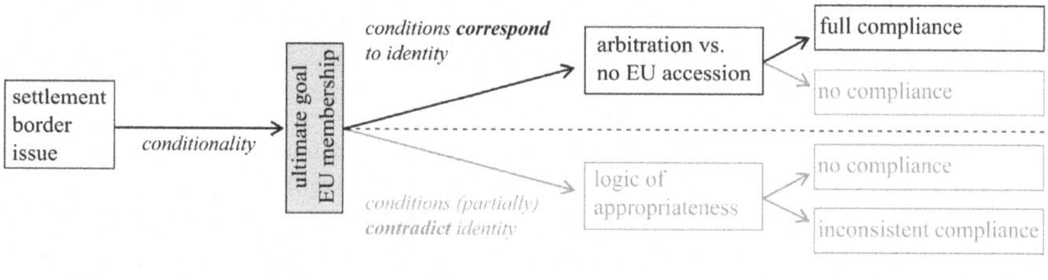

Fig. 5.3 Croatian national-identity filter (EU membership) for acceptance of Arbitration Agreement (*Source* Author; base figure: Freyburg and Richter 2010: 266)

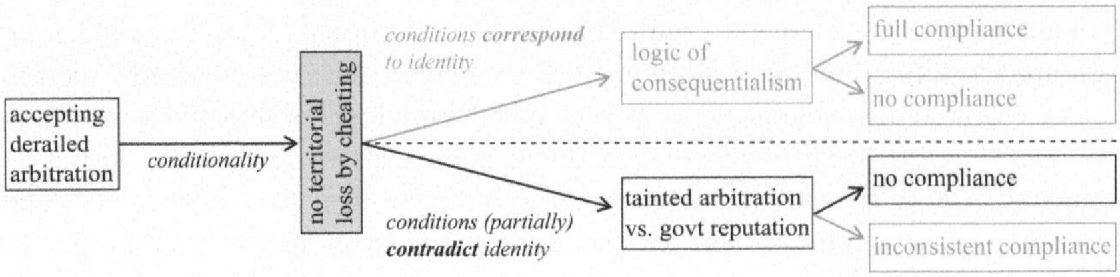

Fig. 5.4 Croatian national-identity filter (no unfounded loss of territory) for withdrawal from arbitration procedure (*Source* Author; base figure: Freyburg and Richter 2010: 266)

Arbitration Agreement (see Sect. 4.2.4), Croatia's position was that existing law-of-the-sea provisions (innocent passage or passage through international straits) and the IMO Traffic Separation Scheme in the Northern Adriatic were sufficient to secure access between the Slovenian territorial sea and the high seas (see "Croatia's Requests" in Sect. 4.3.2.1).

In retrospect, it may be argued that the border issue is on a comparable level of national identity in relation to the Croatian government's decision back in 2005 to arrest and extradite General Gotovina to the ICTY, an express conditionality item on the part of the EU, in return for finally opening Croatia's accession negotiations. The two conflicting identities back then were Croatia as the innocent, heroic nation on the one hand (see Sect. 2.5.2), and the desire to join the EU. The face-saving solution at the time was to have Gotovina arrested abroad in Spain which avoided a humiliating extradition from Croatia.

Croatia's exiting of the arbitration procedure following the Slovenian *ex parte* communication marks a turn of compliance events. The Croatian Parliament (Sabor) unanimously called on the government to leave the arbitration proceedings. The notification of the Croatian withdrawal contains express reference to fairness and legitimacy considerations[3] (see Sect. 4.3.3.3).[4] It appears that Croatia left the arbitration procedure on the grounds that illegal communication was morally inacceptable, destructive to the trustworthiness of the arbitral proceedings, and fundamentally disqualifying the proceedings altogether (regardless of whether the legal-procedural conditions for withdrawal were met). The calculations appear to have been whether leaving a politically (not legally) tainted arbitration is less costly than accepting a potential reputational damage of the government and the country (caused by the disrespect for the jurisdiction of the Tribunal); see Fig. 5.4.

The compliance pattern with regard to the Final Award did not change during the proceedings at the EU Court of Justice. On the contrary, the Slovenian Art. 259

[3]"The principles of fairness and integrity have been violated, irreparable harm has been done to the legitimacy and prospects of the process [...]" (*Note verbale* from the Ministry of Foreign and European Affairs of Croatia to the Ministry of Foreign Affairs of Slovenia, No. 3303/2015, 30 July 2015).

[4]Apart from the legal arguments which not least neglected the Tribunal's factual and firmly established jurisdiction to decide whether a withdrawal is possible at all; see Sects. 4.3.4.2 and "Jurisdiction" in Sect. 4.3.4.3.

TFEU infringement proceedings against Croatia were an opportunity for Zagreb to insist on its position that the real dispute was about the validity of the Arbitration Agreement and the Final Award which was outside the realm of EU law. Therefore, it may be said that, in a way, the CJEU proceedings and its judgement reinforced the Croatian *argumentaire* regardless of the fact that the Court expressly noted that both parties have an obligation under international law to implement the arbitration award (see Sect. 4.4.2).

5.2.2.2 Compliance Behaviour

Similarly, the basic assumption on the compliance behaviour in Candidate Countries is that compliance depends on "rational calculations and/or normative considerations of political leaders in power" which drive the compliance behaviour of candidate countries' governments vis-à vis EU conditionality (Noutcheva 2012: 17).

First, there is *non-compliance* if both the costs outweigh the benefits and the legitimacy is low. Second, if an actor complies in a case which is against their interests, i.e. costs exceed benefits, but the perceived level of legitimacy is high, the result is *legitimacy-based* compliance. Third, if an actor sees their interests in line with the EU demands for reform, e.g. benefits exceed costs, but are not convinced of its legitimacy, what follows is *rationality-based* compliance. Fourth, when the benefits exceed the costs and the EU conditionality is perceived as appropriate and high, there is *genuine compliance.* However, if the rational cost-benefit ratio is very positive whilst at the same time the level of legitimacy is very low, we will see *non-compliance*, very well a possibility with intensely popular issues of national identity (see Sect. 1.3.2.3). It is defined here that the conclusion of the Arbitration Agreement and the following arbitration procedure constitutes EU conditionality (for the particular type of conditionality, see Sect. 5.2.1).

By the time it became clear, in the spring of 2009, that an arbitration agreement was due (see Sect. 4.2.2.3), it may be said that (i) for Slovenia we can assume the benefits of arbitration (the prospective access to the high seas) considerably outweighed the costs (duration of arbitration process, no immediate result), so that the result is genuine compliance. On the part of (ii) Croatia, it appears fair to say that the political costs of accepting an arbitration procedure were considerable, but weighed up against the huge benefit of EU membership in political, economic, and reputational terms, the behaviour was rationality-based compliance (see Fig. 5.5).

The deadlock in June 2009, when Croatia rejected Rehn II as the Sabor had already approved of Rehn I (see Sect. 4.2.4), may be seen as a temporary non-compliance on the part of Croatia, as the political costs of accepting a revised draft after having obtained the support of the domestic Parliament would have been too high. For Slovenia, the continuation of the drafting stage was of utmost importance, notwithstanding the fact that Rehn II constituted a step back in terms of territorial contact to the high seas and represents substantial costs. As a result, one can posit legitimacy-based compliance for Slovenia.

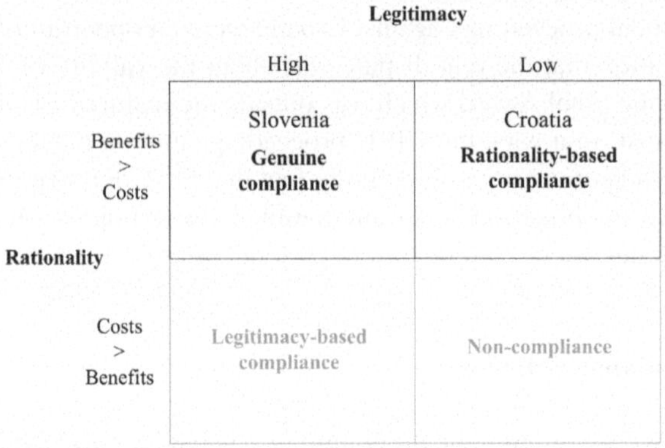

Fig. 5.5 Compliance behaviour when arbitration procedure was in sight in the spring of 2009 (*Source* Author; base figure: Noutcheva 2012: 29)

A rare phase of a compliance quasi-equilibrium can be assumed for the phase between the end of July 2009 and the signature of the Arbitration Agreement in early November of that year. Two issues are of relevance here: (i) the reversal of the order in which the main items were tackled, i.e. unblocking the accession negotiations prior to finalising the Arbitration Agreement (see Sect. 4.2.5.1), and (ii) postponing the start of the time-lines of the arbitration procedure to the date of signing of the Croatian Treaty of Accession (Sect. 4.2.5.2). Whilst Croatia gained the assurance of becoming an EU member, Slovenia had to rely both on the continuation of the drafting stage and the finalising of the Arbitration Agreement plus the fact that the arbitration procedure would only start once Croatian membership was already a safe pair of hands. Therefore, the compliance behaviour of Slovenia is downgraded from genuine compliance to rationality-based compliance equalling the level of Croatia's compliance behaviour.

The quasi-equilibrium phase of compliance can be said to have continued into 2012 when, at the beginning of the year, the selection procedure for the members of the Arbitral Tribunal unfolded. For a start, it went relatively quickly and in a collaborative spirit (there was agreement on two of the three jointly appointed members straight away, and it took only one bilateral meeting to agree on the third member; see Sect. 4.2.6), so one can perhaps assume a level of compliance between rationality-based and genuine for both parties. Slovenia was pleased that the timelines were finally running, and Croatia was ready to start (and get done) a process it had not been able to avoid anyway; see Fig. 5.6.

For the first phase of the arbitration procedure, the submissions and the hearing, one may posit genuine compliance for Slovenia and rationality-based compliance for Croatia. The solution of the border dispute including the creation of a legally binding access to the high seas was what Slovenia had always considered a legitimate national interest, whereas Croatia knew that the arbitration procedure was the price to pay for EU membership, and one could argue that the provisions of the Arbitration Agreement amount to "damage limitation" for Croatia, and that the real or perceived

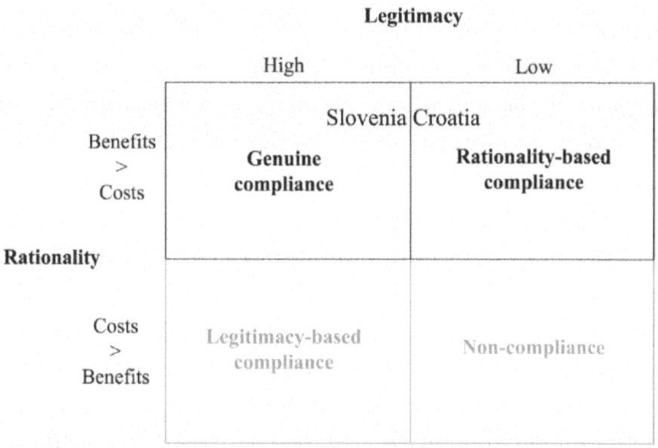

Fig. 5.6 Compliance behaviour in the quasi-equilibrium phase between July 2009 and July 2015 (*Source* Author; base figure: Noutcheva 2012: 29)

"territorial loss" was neatly defined and restricted to a minimum in the Arbitration Agreement.

The publication of the intercepted *ex parte* communication changed that quasi-equilibrium of compliance drastically, however. Although it has never become transparent what the real interest of Croatia behind the withdrawal from the arbitration procedure was apart from the legal arguments, one can make the general assumption that the domestic political costs of withdrawal must have been reckoned lower than those of a continuation of the procedure (see Sect. 4.3.3.3). Further, EU membership, one of Croatia's vital interests, had already been achieved. Territorial integrity as the other genuine if not paramount national interest (see "Croatia's Position" in Sect. 4.3.2.2), however, was to some degree questioned with regard to the high-seas-access provisions in the Arbitration Agreement (see Sect. 4.2.4). As legitimacy remained low, the result therefore was non-compliance *ex-post* (see Fig. 5.7). Such

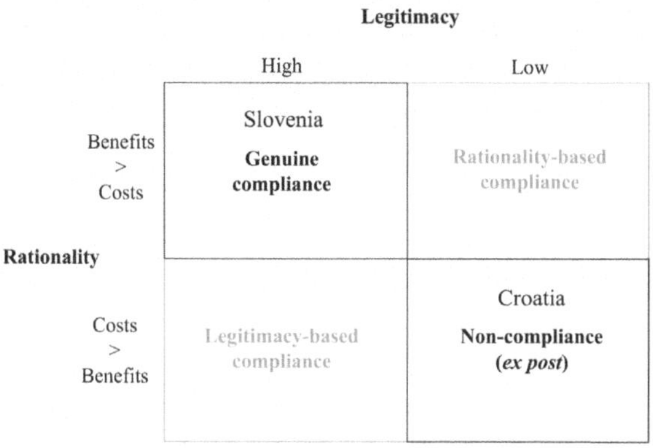

Fig. 5.7 Compliance behaviour as from August 2015 after Croatia exiting the arbitration procedure (*Source* Author; base figure: Noutcheva 2012: 29)

remained the default compliance level of Croatia for the rest of the arbitration procedure and during the follow-up phase. Slovenia, conversely, retained the level of genuine compliance as it had a vital interest in a Final Award and its implementation to accomplish its aim of guaranteed access to the high seas.

After the implementation deadline of the Final Award expired on 29 December 2017, domestic compliance costs in Croatia for implementation continued to be reckoned higher than non-recognition of the Award. Whilst it remains obscure whether an effort to have a bilateral agreement on implementation of *all* delimitation decisions from the Award was ever on the cards for Zagreb, the approach did not change after Slovenia had launched the infringement complaint before the European Commission on 16 March 2018 and before the CJEU on 12 July 2018. Slovenia's compliance mode remained at genuine as the lawsuit was seen as the most promising avenue of securing implementation of the Award's provisions on the high-seas corridor (see Sect. 4.4).

During the CJEU procedure (which turned out to be deliberations solely on the issue of admissibility), there were no changes to the compliance patterns of both parties. Slovenia was firmly committed to the implementation of the Final Award through EU law (see Sect. 4.4.1.1), whereas Croatia held that the real dispute was about the validity of the Final Award for which question the EU Court of Justice had no jurisdiction anyway (see Sect. 4.4.1.2).

5.3 Concluding Considerations

For an overall assessment of the three phases of the border dispute dynamics between Croatia and Slovenia, it is useful to look for *critical junctures* in the process. Relevant landmark events in that context can be found in the timeline in Fig. 5.8.

- The bilateral *Draft Agreement from 2001*, to start with, was an agreement reached at the highest political level and without any third-party impact. Building on the negotiations at expert level in the 1990s, the two prime ministers sat together negotiating face to face in what appeared to be a true spirit of good-neighbourly relations, mutual trust, and a European perspective. It was a unique line-up in

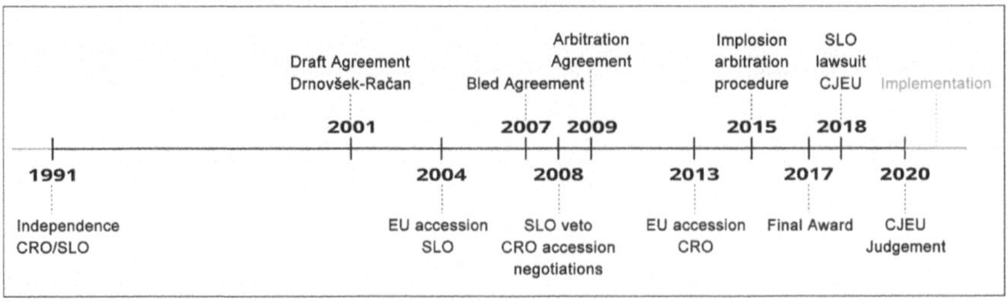

Fig. 5.8 Timeline of Croatia–Slovenia border conflict (*Source* Author)

many ways and perhaps a laboratory experiment in post-Yugoslav bilateral dispute resolution.[5] What went wrong apparently was that Račan had not kept the domestic opposition in the loop, and even within his multi-party coalition, the first one in post-independence Croatia, there was not enough support for his deal with Drnovšek. At a time when Croatia's territories in Eastern Slavonia had only been reintegrated three years ago after the painful and traumatic Homeland War, the sensitivity towards territorial issues was very solid. The fact that virtually the entire Croatian law-of-the-sea establishment was not consulted, catered for a maximum reach of their criticism in the public domain and the media, and the fat was in the fire. As a result, ratification in Sabor did not even reach the voting stage in Committee.

One is always wiser after the event, and some might say the deal on the table was too far-reaching and even adventurous for the Croatian political elite anyway. Still, if one does believe in the power of political leadership and persuasion, it is indeed vital to keep high-level talks on a sensitive issue secret until a relatively late stage. However, the critical moment to secure domestic support *ahead* of concluding the negotiations must not be missed. Drumming up support for an agreement which includes territorial concessions is not a walk in the park. After all, the lack of support in Croatia is why the agreement with Slovenia on the resolution of the border dispute collapsed. As a result of the stalling right at the beginning of the Croatian ratification process, the bilateral avenue was scorched earth.

- The 2001 experience must be borne in mind when drawing conclusions from the *Bled Agreement 2007 and its aftermath.* "Bilateralism 2.0" it was only at first sight. In fact, the talks took place under very different circumstances. Slovenia had joined the EU in the meantime, and Croatia's EU accession negotiations were already in full swing. The submission of the bilateral dispute to the International Court of Justice (ICJ) looked like a common-sense move and an easy task. And it perhaps could have been just that. Yet, the critical juncture here was *Slovenia jumping ship from the bilateral negotiations on the mandate for the ICJ to blocking the EU accession negotiations with Croatia.* It was before the summer break of 2008 when the government in Ljubljana took the decision to raise the veto in the accession negotiations with Croatia to secure a solution of the border dispute. The bilateral expert group with Croatia on the ICJ mandate was still up and running at the time, and Slovenia withdrew its members from that group in the spring of 2009 when the negotiations on the later Arbitration Agreement had already started. Notwithstanding the fact that the border with Croatia was a bilateral issue and had nothing to do with the EU acquis, Slovenia changed course from the "soft" voluntary submission-to-ICJ approach to a "hard" blackmailing strategy using its veto as EU member vis-à-vis Croatia as an EU applicant. The collateral damage

[5]The recent Prespa Agreement between Greece and (North) Macedonia from June 2018 also counts as bilateral. It must be noted, however, that there has been strong third-party mediation on the part of Matthew Nimetz, Personal Envoy of the United Nations Secretary-General since 1999 (see https://dppa.un.org/en/mission/personal-envoy-greece-former-yugoslav-republic-of-macedonia; for the Prespa Agreement see Sect. 6.4.1).

was the holding hostage of the EU as a whole and the damaging of Ljubljana's own reputation as a young EU Member State. What is more, the Slovenian move marked a precedent of a Member State (ab)using its position vis-à-vis a Candidate Country to enforce a bilateral policy goal during EU accession negotiations.

- The constructive role of the European Commission must be mentioned. Had Olli Rehn not started to assume a mediating role at the beginning of 2009, immediately after the attempt of the French EU Council Presidency in December 2008 had failed, the blockade situation could have persisted for much longer. The *process of drafting an agreement to submit the dispute to international arbitration* already started in the spring of 2009. It was by no means a given to be able to level off the vital interests of Slovenia and Croatia and to accommodate tricky legal issues in a highly political context. What is more, the *sui generis* situation was *terra incognita* for everyone, and so was the communication during the drafting stage. The firm grip of the European Commission on the Arbitration Agreement paid off, as Rehn II proved solid enough to survive the temporary disruption at the beginning of July 2009.
- In a rare moment of mutual bilateral face-saving, with the help of the skilful soft mediation by the Swedish EU Council Presidency, a compromise could be found in the *final phase of the negotiations on the Arbitration Agreement* in the summer of 2009. The (procedural) de-coupling of (i) the lifting of the Slovenian blockade of Zagreb's EU accession negotiations and (ii) the beginning of the arbitration procedure for the resolution of the border dispute as such did do the trick: Slovenia was no longer the bad guy who vetoed Croatia, and Croatia could secure EU membership without any delay caused by a lengthy dispute resolution procedure for a start. Both parties were stripped off the escalating conflict dynamics there had been since the beginning of the Slovenian veto in the autumn of 2008. An intense phase of drafting the mandate for third-party judicial dispute resolution was finally on the right track after a very critical phase in June and July 2009.
- The most visible critical juncture is the *Slovenian ex parte communication and Croatia's withdrawal from the arbitration procedure.* The illegal pieces of communication were revealed in the summer of 2015, at a moment following the announcement by the Arbitral Tribunal that the Final Award was going to be handed down by the end of the year. The publication of the intercepted communication (in a Serbian and a Croatian newspaper) caused sheer outrage amongst the political elite in Croatia, and led to un unanimous Sabor resolution calling on the government to leave the arbitration procedure. There was full unity across the political spectrum which is rare not only in Croatia. Yet, the critical aspect here is that regardless of the fact that *ex parte* communication constitutes a violation of both the Arbitration Agreement and the terms of appointment for the members of an arbitral tribunal, only the Tribunal itself, like it or not, has the jurisdiction to assess the implications of a violation and whether the arbitration procedure must be terminated or continue. In retrospect, the political answer from Zagreb, however, was virtually immediate and predominantly based on legitimacy

considerations irrespective of the (not entirely convincing) legal arguments put forward. It did not come as a surprise, therefore, that the Croatian governments disregarded both the Tribunal's Partial Award (assessing the implications of the Slovenian violation and the legality of the Croatian termination request) in June 2016 and the Final Award in June 2017.

It is suggested here that the *legitimacy perceptions in Croatia were so strong that no turning back from leaving the arbitration procedure regardless of any legality considerations was even thinkable.* In other words, legitimacy and appropriateness consideration outweighed a full rule-of-law approach. It appears that a strong sense of injustice due to the Slovenian blackmailing in 2008/09 in the first place was heavily amplified by the pieces of *ex parte* communication, undoubtedly an unlawful act and a violation of the Arbitration Agreement as the Tribunal emphasised, which was seen in Zagreb as a fundamental breach of the fairness and impartiality rules of the game. For reasons of principle and consistency, the continuation of the arbitral proceedings and even a prior assessment of events by the Tribunal (which has the well-established jurisdiction to do so) had to be ignored. An escape from recognising the Final Award must have seemed a feasible way forward in Zagreb, all the more so as the terms of the arbitration decision were quite favourable to Croatia, so that the prospects of a bilateral implementation of the gist of the Final Award seemed not entirely unrealistic. Yet, the readiness of Ljubljana to consider departures from the provisions in the Final Award was apparently overestimated in Zagreb. In fact, as the contents of the arbitration decision, from a Slovenian point of view, were not a great deal more than the vital national interest in terms of a special regime for the access to the high seas, there was no room for manoeuvre in Ljubljana to embark on bilateralism again having in mind the painful experience from 2001. Nor was there any room for manoeuvre in Zagreb to depart from the unanimous Sabor vote from July 2015. As full implementation of the Final Award was the only way forward for Slovenia, the lawsuit before the European Court of Justice was in fact the only option.

- Ljubljana's high hopes with respect to the Court in Luxemburg were not met, however. Compelling as it seemed *prima facie* to have identified a hopefully sufficiently strong link between the Final Award and the EU law, the Court did not assume jurisdiction. In fact, it applied a fairly mechanistic approach and appears not to have fully considered the strong mediating role the European Commission and the EU Council Presidency had played in the drafting stages of the Arbitration Agreement. Nevertheless, the Court noted the parties' obligations under international law to implement the arbitration award, and indeed it sent the conflict management back to the bilateral level.

Where does all that leave us?

- A bilateral conflict the management of which is undertaken in an environment of coercion and power asymmetry can have a hard life. In an EU context in particular, (i) using the Member State veto vis-à vis a Candidate Country is a sledgehammer approach, even if there may be a "legitimate" national interest to do so, and (ii) the veto approach constitutes an abuse of the EU institutional line-up and the accession process as a whole if the matter has nothing to do with the EU *acquis*. That course of action by Slovenia poisoned the good-neighbourly relations with Croatia (that do indeed exist safe for the border issue) and damaged the country's international standing.

- The *ex parte* communication of Slovenia tainted the arbitration procedure politically and questioned the rule of law. Notwithstanding legitimacy considerations, the Final Award is nevertheless a lawful and binding settlement of the border between Slovenia and Croatia under international law. The unilateral withdrawal of Croatia from the arbitration process poisoned the otherwise good-neighbourly relations with Slovenia, too, and likewise disrespects the rule of law and damaged the country's international reputation. In essence, the result is a lose-lose situation with regard to the arbitral proceedings. It is important to note, however, that this finding does *not* disqualify arbitration from being a valuable and efficient means of third-party dispute settlement (see Sect. 6.2.2).

- After the CJEU's judgement of non-jurisdiction, which one may like or not, the conflict is back to where it was after the arbitration procedure. It is not difficult to predict a longer time-span for the achievement of a robust bilateral settlement of the border dispute. For a stable solution to be achieved, the threshold for parliamentary ratification—a *conditio sine qua non* for Ljubljana—would have to be met, by no means a walk in the park given the two-third requirement in Sabor and the sensitivities for territorial questions in Croatia. The challenge is to frame a future agreement in a positive way. Zagreb's aspiration to join both the Euro and Schengen (for both of which Slovenia's support is needed) might help. However, it appears that any reference to the implementation obligations of the arbitration award ought to be avoided. In any case, a final settlement will require the true leadership of the two prime ministers and an atmosphere of responsibility, shared purpose and mutual trust.

- At the end of the day, the moral of the story seems to be that it is impossible to solve a deeply political dispute by legal means without the free will of both parties. A skilled third party can help form that will, but not replace it. The treatment of the Croatia–Slovenia border conflict is not a role-model for the resolution of bilateral disputes in an EU context. It was crisis management all over, yet the third-party roles of the European Commission and the Swedish EU Presidency were played professionally and successfully. Also, the bilateral collaboration between Ljubljana and Zagreb was, during some phases, pragmatic and constructive. There are lessons to be learnt from that case, and they will be discussed in Chap. 6.

References

Burton, J. (1990). *Conflict: Human needs theory*. Houndmills and London: Macmillan Press.

Fischer, R., Ury, W., & Patton, B. (2012). *Getting to yes: Negotiating an agreement without giving in*. London: Random House.

Freyburg, T., & Richter, S. (2010). National identity matters: The limited impact of EU political conditionality in the Western Balkans. *Journal of European Public Policy, 17*(2), 263–281.

Galtung, J. (1978). *The theory of conflict and the concept of probability*. Oslo: University of Oslo.

Galtung, J. (1996). *Peace by peaceful means*. International Peace Research Institute Oslo: SAGE Publications.

Galtung, J. (2000). Conflict transformation by peaceful means. The transcend method. Participants'/Trainers' Manual. United Nations. https://www.transcend.org/pctrcluj2004/TRANSCEND_manual.pdf. Accessed February 02, 2019.

Keohane, R., Moravcsik, A., & Slaughter, A. M. (2000). Legalized dispute resolution: Interstate and transnational. *International Organization, 54*(3), 457–488.

Noutcheva, G. (2012). *European foreign policy and the challenges of Balkan accession*. London and New York: Routledge.

Schimmelfennig, F., & Sedelmeier, U. (2004). Governance by conditionality: EU rule transfer to the candidate countries of Central and Eastern Europe. *Journal of European Public Policy, 11*(4), 661–679.

Zartman, W., & de Soto, A. (2010). *Timing mediation initiatives: The peacemaker's toolkit*. Washington, D.C.: United States Institute of Peace.

References

Chapter 6
Policy Recommendations

Abstract The recommendations below are based on this book's research findings and are subdivided into four categories. To start with, they will pinpoint the way ahead with regard to *implementation issues of the arbitration award* on the Croatian–Slovenian border. Implementation not only depends on the political will of both parties, but also on the ability to amend existing agreements in the Northern Adriatic involving Italy as a third party. Secondly, the recommendations touch on the area of *strengthening dispute settlement processes*, both in an EU context and with regard to reform of international arbitration. There are a few lessons to be learnt from the Croatia–Slovenia case which must be translated into a more robust dispute resolution infrastructure, both internally within the EU and in view of future arbitration procedures. Third, the recommendations address outstanding *bilateral issues* relevant to the EU enlargement process in the post-Yugoslav space. Proposals will be outlined as to how to tackle them to steer clear of the risk of Candidate Countries being vetoed by Member States. Lastly, EU accession negotiations must become more credible and predictable, including the operational level. Member States will need to become more responsive by implementing positive and negative rewards based on clear conditionality. Interviewees include Damir Arnaut, Jean Asselborn, Vladimir-Đuro Degan, Tanja Fajon, Dejan Jović, Tanja Miščević, and Aleksandra Tomanić.

Keywords EU enlargement · Serbia · Kosovo · Montenegro · Arbitration · Dispute resolution

6.1 Way Forward with Final Award Implementation

Much has been written about and recommended as to what the EU and the countries from the former Yugoslavia and Albania could or should (not) do to make EU enlargement for the so-called Western Balkans work. Most of it is either based on

T. Bickl, *The Border Dispute Between Croatia and Slovenia*, Contributions to Political Science,
https://doi.org/10.1007/978-3-030-53333-5_6

a grand design or limited to the technicalities of existing EU institutional accession process structures.

This set of recommendations goes down a different avenue. The undertaking is, first, to try to think out of the box, and, second, to present suggestions that have not been elaborated in an ivory tower, but are precise steps that are practitioner-proof and feasible without any institutional or treaty reform whatsoever. As far as feasibility and implementation go, however, there is one prerequisite common to them all: political will.

With the CJEU's decision of non-jurisdiction of 31 January 2020, the *Slovenia v Croatia* Case has been formally closed. What remains pending, however, is the issue of (non-) implementation of the arbitration award and its delimitation decision on the course of the terrestrial and maritime State border between the two countries. As discussed in Sect. 4.4.3.3, it is unlikely that the two parties will reach agreement to submit the issue of the validity of the arbitration award to either the ICJ or the CJEU. After all, the award is a binding settlement under international law, and the CJEU has confirmed that in various paragraphs of its judgement. Thus, it may be said with some accuracy that, irrespective of the non-existence of any enforcement means through EU law, there is no doubt that an obligation to implement does exist under international law.

It would appear, therefore, that it is now for the parties to sit down bilaterally to negotiate on implementation and demarcation. However, this would require the political will and a spirit of good-neighbourly relations of *both* parties to do so and an agreement at the highest political level. Once a settlement is reached and ratified, the existing bilateral joint Commission of the Republic of Croatia and the Republic of Slovenia on the identification and marking of the common State border could be entrusted with that task. For the time being, it could be an opportune moment for silent diplomacy by a third-party State actor or an individual commanding the respect of both parties. At the time of writing, the fight against the coronavirus pandemic and its economic impact after the lockdown of the spring of 2020 is clearly dominating the political scene. In the medium term, however, Croatia's ambitions to join the Euro and the Schengen Area may indirectly open the door for a package-deal solution. It is useful to note in that context, that accession to both clubs requires the unanimous consent of the Member of the Eurozone and the Schengen Area. Slovenia is a member of both clubs.

No swift moves are to be expected, however. A decision on Schengen membership may be a considerable way off, after all, as security aspects of the external Schengen border and border controls tend to be sensitive matters for Member States generally. This comes regardless of the positive recommendation of the European Commission on the *technical* readiness of Croatia issued in October 2019.[1] By way of example, Bulgaria and Romania received a positive recommendation as early as in 2011, and a decision on accession to the Schengen Area on the part of the EU Member States is still pending.

[1]See European Commission press release 22 October 2019; https://ec.europa.eu/commission/presscorner/detail/en/IP_19_6140.

All in all, there is a wider political context in which the implementation of a final settlement of the common State border between Slovenia and Croatia is situated. However, and *sine dubio*, there is clearly an opportunity for a win-win scenario for both sides. The opportunity for a more relaxed phase allowing for a real effort could perhaps arise once the burden of managing the post-coronavirus recovery has eased off and after the conclusion of the Slovenian EU Presidency, i.e. as from the beginning of 2022. Whilst the parties are free to jointly agree on a bilateral settlement that departs, in one way or another, from the provisions of the Final Award, there are matters touching on existing agreements also involving other parties that need to be taken care of.

6.1.1 Implementation Needs to Consider Existing Agreements

As set out in the Final Award, the implementation of the Croatian–Slovenian sea border and the regime for the use of the maritime areas is not an isolated undertaking and must respect existing agreements (PCA Final Award 2017: 362, para 1134). With regard to Croatia, another border issue which is similar in nature is arising in the south with Montenegro. In this context of border bays, an alternative approach to tiny border bays is going to be presented.

As for Croatia-Slovenia, two agreements are of particular salience here, (i) the IMO Traffic Separation Scheme in the Northern Adriatic from 2004 and (ii) the 1983 Italy–Yugoslavia Fisheries Zone.

6.1.1.1 Revision of IMO Traffic Separation Scheme in the Northern Adriatic

The Traffic Separation Scheme (TSS) in the Northern Adriatic confirmed by the International Maritime Organisation (IMO) on 28 May 2004 has been in force since 1 December 2004. The TSS regulates navigation for maritime vessels to and from the ports of Trieste and Monfalcone (Italy) and Koper (Slovenia). There are designated sea lanes for both directions crossing the respective territorial sea of Croatia, Italy, and Slovenia. The separation scheme originates from a trilateral Memorandum of Understanding concluded by Croatia, Italy, and Slovenia on 19 October 2000 (see "Croatia's Requests" (iii) in Sect. 4.3.2.1; Fig. 6.1).

There is a clear need to bring the planned high-seas corridor (Junction Area) in the Croatian territorial sea from the Final Award (see "Regime for the Use of the Maritime Areas" in Sect. 4.3.5.2) into line with the designated sea lanes of the Traffic Separation Scheme. Firstly and generally, the Junction Area may overlap with one or more of the TSS sea lanes. Secondly and more specifically as for the navigation

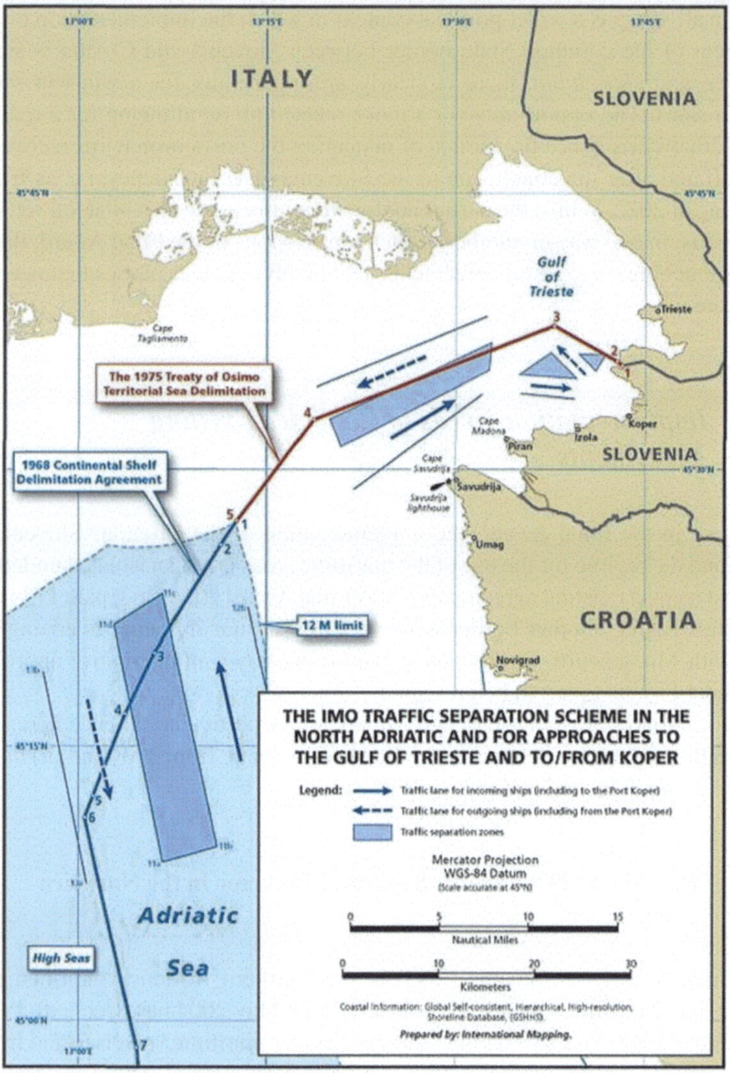

Fig. 6.1 IMO Traffic Separation Scheme 2004 with designated sea lanes to and from Koper (PCA Final Award 2017: 334, para 1040). ©Permanent Court of Arbitration

to and from Koper, the current outbound lane cuts across the Italian territorial sea, whilst the current inbound lane cuts across the Croatian territorial sea.

Presuming that the Junction Area (see "Junction Area" in Sect. 4.3.5.2) is to accommodate both inbound and outbound traffic to secure the foreseen high-seas freedoms of navigation (and not just innocent passage), the existing outbound TSS sea lane obviously has to be brought within the Junction Area, i.e. within the Croatian territorial sea. However, the width of the overall inbound/outbound lanes including the separation buffer would decrease from currently 5 nm or more to the 2.5 nm of the Junction Area bringing the inbound/outbound vessels very close to one another with only a very tight buffer zone. However, the parties are of course free to negotiate a departure from the width stipulated in the Final Award.

In view of the above, it is vital to note that the implementation of the arbitration award is no longer a bilateral affair between Slovenia and Croatia, but a trilateral one also including Italy. Safety of navigation not least in terms of the environmental impact is of utmost importance in the Upper Adriatic with its vulnerable ecosystem and shallow waters.

- It is a matter of urgency, therefore, to amend the 2000 Memorandum of Understanding between Croatia, Italy, and Slovenia with regard to traffic separation and sea-lanes by taking into account the Junction Area (high-seas corridor) from the Final Award. Only in this framework is the implementation/adaptation of a corridor to and from the Slovenian territorial sea feasible. Notwithstanding the positions of the three riparian States, it is suggested here that some flexibility from all sides is required to arrive at a workable solution to meet both navigational and environmental concerns.

6.1.1.2 Italy–Yugoslavia Fisheries Zone

In February 1983, Italy and Yugoslavia signed an agreement on a joint cross-border Fishing Zone in the Gulf of Trieste.[2] The Zone is located in the territorial sea of Italy and Slovenia and appears also to touch on the territorial sea of Croatia (see Fig. 6.2).

The Fishing Zone has neither been renounced nor confirmed—unlike the Italian–Yugoslav sea border, the succession to which was declared by Croatia and Slovenia and not objected to by Italy (see, e.g. Klemenčić and Topalović 2009: 313–314). Legally, it is established that successor States, by the time they become independent, inherit existing international borders (see "Self-determination and Internal Borders as International Ones (Opinions 2 and 3)" in Sect. 2.5.1.1). As for the status of bilateral treaties (such as the one on the Fishing Zone), the situation is governed by the 1978 Vienna Convention on succession of States in respect of treaties (UNTS).[3] The Convention indeed stipulates that, in the event of secession or dissolution, there is automatic continuity to the effect that the successor State is bound *ipso facto*

[2]Exchange of letters signed by the Foreign Ministers Emilio Colombo (Italy) and Lazar Mojsov (Yugoslavia) in Rome on 18 February 1983. The Fishing Zone entered into force in February 1987. The letters are reprinted in the Parliamentary Act of Italy's *Camera dei Deputati* No. 3289 from 18 November 1985.

[3]The Convention entered into force on 6 November 1996 and only 37 States currently participate; see https://treaties.un.org/Pages/ViewDetails.aspx?src=IND&mtdsg_no=XXIII-2&chapter=23&clang=_en. Strikingly, the Convention applies different rules for Newly Independent States emerging in the context of decolonisation. For those States, the concept of *tabula rasa* holds, i.e. the new States are not bound by the treaties entered into by the predecessor (colonial) State (Article 16). Dumberry (2015) argues that the *tabula rasa* principle should apply to all new States as it is unjustifiable why a new State should not be able to decide whether or not they want to continue the relationship governed by the original treaty.

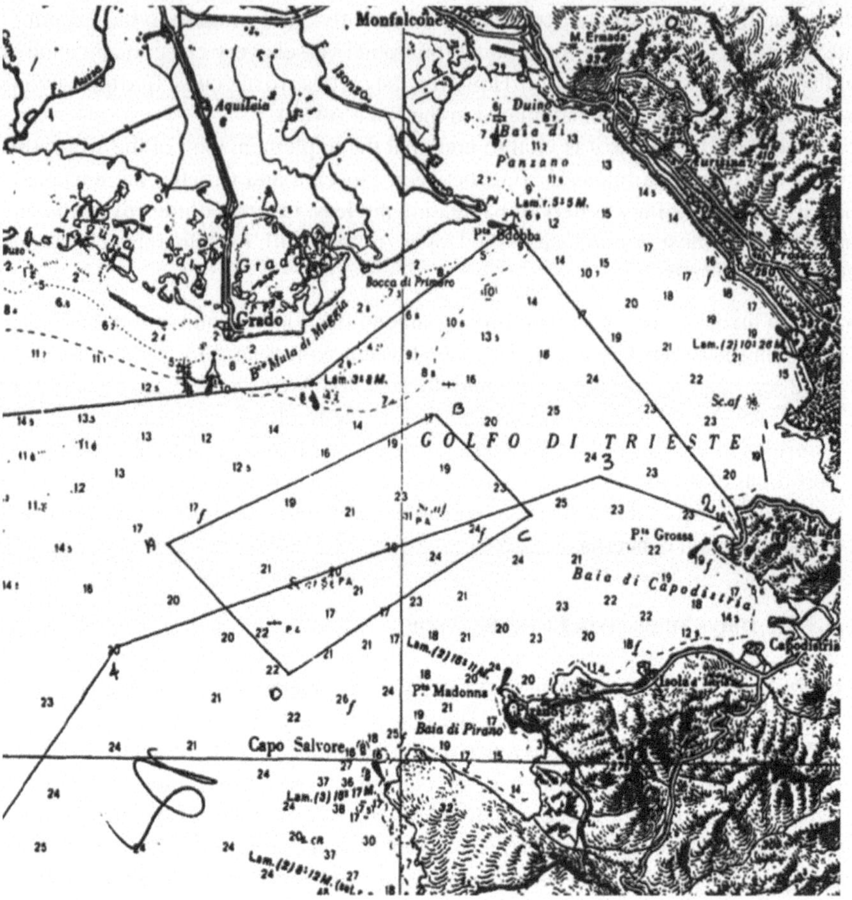

Fig. 6.2 Fisheries zone Italy–Yugoslavia (the equidistance line through the Zone marks the Italian–Yugoslav sea border (Treaty of Osimo 1975). The lines along the Italian coast constitute the straight baselines of Italy.) (taken from the 18 February 1983 exchange of letters) ©Camera dei deputati, Parlamento Italiano

by bilateral (and multilateral) treaties entered into by the predecessor State (Art. 34 UNTS).[4] Croatia and Slovenia are Parties to UNTS. Italy, however, is not. It follows that it is unclear whether the Fishing Zone is still in force since, to the best knowledge of this author, there has been no agreement or declaration in that regard by Italy, Croatia, or Slovenia.

As for the implementation of the Final Award, a contradiction arises between the Fishing Zone and the Junction Area. With regard to the actual fishing aspect,

[4]With regard to the UNTS Convention, Slovenia and Croatia are successor States in two ways: (i) succession to any bilateral (and multilateral) treaties entered into by the SFRY and (ii) succession to the SFRY as a signatory State of the UNTS as such (Slovenia declared succession on 6 July 1992, Croatia did so on 22 October 1992).

the arbitration decision's regime for the high-seas corridor stipulates that there be no fishing or other exploration or exploitation activities in the Junction Area (PCA Final Award 2017: 361, para 1126). As a result, in view of the considerable overlap between the Fishing Zone and the Junction Area, an amendment to the Italian–Yugoslav Fishing Zone with regard to its territorial application is definitely necessary. Alternatively, the Zone could be declared extinct. As with the Traffic Separation Scheme above (see Sect. 6.1.1.1), any decision would require trilateral agreement between Croatia, Italy, and Slovenia.

- Therefore, the Fishing Zone issue must be tackled together with the trilateral exercise of implementing the Final Award and adapting the Traffic Separation Scheme sea lanes accordingly (see above). Data on marine casualties in relation to traffic monitoring systems provided from maritime authorities from Italy, Slovenia, Croatia, and Montenegro for the period 2006–2015 strongly suggest that collisions between freight vessels and fishing boats are by far the most common type of accident.[5]

6.1.1.3 New Approach for Small Border Bays

Sovereignty over territory is a distinctive feature of States. And it also touches on notions of independence, autonomy, identity, and being an equal member of the community of States. In addition, territorial sovereignty over land or maritime areas matters most when there has been a dispute over the respective territory—at the negotiating table or through an armed conflict. All of that renders territorial issues remarkably salient, irrespective of economic or environmental considerations.

The fight over Piran Bay between Slovenia and Croatia is an impressive case in point in many ways. Where there are "red lines" in terms of its delimitation and in terms of the national narrative, it becomes very difficult to look at a dispute for what it often is: a symbolic issue over real, perceived, or alleged identity with very little real-world impact. The political elites become (self-)boxed into a corner of patriotic (and nationalist) sentiments where there are only winners and losers, and where saving face becomes unthinkable. Under such circumstances, it is very difficult to take a step back and consider alternative options.

They do exist, however, and are even being applied in the region. The Italy–Yugoslavia Fisheries Zone from 1983 is a perfect example of a special-purpose *condominium* notwithstanding its unclear post-succession present-day legal status (see Sect. 6.1.1.2). The Protocol in operation with regard to the Croatian–Montenegrin sea border at Prevlaka, provisional as it may be and reflecting the historic demilitarisation background of 2002, provides for a *condominium* approach in one maritime area in which there is joint policing by mixed-crew vessels. Further, there is

[5]See Guardia Costiera (2016). Analysis of Traffic Monitoring Systems—the marine casualties. https://www.guardiacostiera.gov.it/mezzi-e-tecnologie/Documents/MRS%20Adriatic%20Traffic/Easyconnecting_4.4_Marine%20casualties%20v1.1.pdf.

no equidistance line of demarcation in Prevlaka Bay, but special regimes for different maritime areas (see Sect. 6.3.1).

Joint management instead of focus on sovereignty

In tiny maritime areas along the Adriatic, irrespective of the question as to whether they constitute border bays or single-State bays, the main issues on the ground are usually tourism, fishing, and the preservation of the environment. A strong sense of sustainability and environmental protection tends to be linked to economic well-being. For border bays, therefore, and provided there is (i) no economic activity in terms of natural resources in the seabed and (ii) no security or defence issue in the bay as such, shared sovereignty could be the key to an amicable and good-neighbourly solution for the management of bays.

The more focus there is on sustainable tourism and the protection of the marine environment to the mutual benefit of both riparian States, the less important becomes the sovereignty issue.[6] However, in the territorial sea outside of bays, *condominium* approaches are unrealistic as fishing is more relevant there, and, what is more, existing or potential offshore or seabed exploitation activities require clear jurisdictions not least to attract and secure investment.

- With regard to Piran Bay, to focus on the delimitation line in the Bay seems increasingly flawed. Slovenia wanted sovereignty over the entire Bay, Croatia wanted a partition by the median line. Neither party will ever be happy with the 80-20 division stipulated by the Final Award and the initialled 2001 Draft Agreement. Then again, it will be very difficult to seek departures that can be face-saving when there is so much focus on a given blueprint. Therefore, the proposal submitted here is to bilaterally agree on making the entire Bay a joint fishing zone and to include it in the wider Croatian–Slovenian SOPS zone referred to in EU Regulation 1380/2013 (see Sects. 4.1.3 and "Slovenia's Requests" (iv) in Sect. 4.3.2.1).

After all, Piran Bay constitutes internal waters, there is no major economic activity in the Bay except for the Sečovlje salt pans which are land-based anyway, and the fish stock outside the Bay is far more substantial than inside the Bay. Recreational activities such as diving, swimming, and yachting constitute the main activities during the holiday season, the most profitable business along the Slovenian and Croatian shores of the Bay. In addition, patrolling and policing of the Bay could be carried

[6] A long-standing example in this regard is the bilateral treaty between the Netherlands and Germany on the Dollard-Ems border bay on the North Sea (concluded in 1960 and amended in 2014) contains no provisions on the delimitation line inside the bay. Instead it provides for jurisdiction for the safety of navigation, the maintenance and demarcation of the navigation channel (affected by a substantial tidal range) and environmental issues. The territorial delimitation only starts at the outer edge of the Bay which is subject to the continental shelf agreement of both States from 1973. For the bilingual 2014 Treaty, see Official Journal of the Federal Republic of Germany (Bundesgesetzblatt) 2016/II No. 15.

out by mixed-crew vessels. This would not only foster the solid collaborative cross-border spirit on the ground, but it would help bring that spirit back to the political level of the border issue where it is badly needed. The delimitation line could still be maintained legally and it would certainly help for the ratification of the Final Award, but practically its salience could gradually fade away.

6.2 Strengthening Dispute Resolution

It is one thing to have bilateral disputes resolved before EU accession, and it is another thing to narrow down what this entails in practice to actively support that process and to manage bilateral conflict in the context of EU enlargement more efficiently. There are two operational levels here: dispute resolution in the framework of EU accession negotiations, and third-party dispute resolution by means of international arbitration.

6.2.1 Strong EU Framework

Dispute resolution in the context of EU enlargement must become a priority for the European Commission whose term ends in late 2024.

A vital step was the fundamentals-first principle applied to the operational stage of EU accession negotiations since 2011, which stipulates that rule-of-law issues and the resolution of bilateral disputes are key priorities, not least in the order in which the chapters are negotiated (see Sect. 4.2.1.1). The latest update from February 2020 strongly confirmed that approach regardless of the prospective new cluster approach. There has been no effort, however, under the fundamentals-first approach to actively support dispute resolution and provide a *framework*. It is none of the European Commission's or the Member States' business to tell Candidate Countries *how* to settle bilateral issues. Bilateral negotiations can be a very good means to do it, especially amongst neighbouring States from the region which have spent 70 years in the same political unit. Arbitration may be an equally appropriate avenue, as can be a submission to the International Court of Justice (ICJ), or to the International Tribunal for the Law of the Sea (ITLOS) if it is an entirely maritime dispute.

However, there must be a clear framework which includes transparent procedures to *identify* the issues at dispute, the *timetable* for their resolution, and a range of *facilitation* services by the European Commission and the Member States.

6.2.1.1 Clear Identification and Timetable

A realistic but hard-and-fast timetable must be set. No dispute is equal, of course, but there is some experience as to how long the settlement may take procedurally.

Depending on the nature of the conflict, 12 months appear a reasonable deadline to conclude an Arbitration Agreement or a mandate for the ICJ. The judicial procedure itself would potentially take up another 24 months on average. For bilateral negotiations, a maximum of 24 months seems reasonable, too.

It is important to note that the incentive is there for both the Candidate Country and the Member State in question. The popular argument goes that the Member State is always in a superior position because of its veto power. This is true from a strictly legal–political or procedural perspective. The new identification and timetable approach, however, must also be seen as a form of peer pressure on any Member State tempted to use its veto. In an environment where dispute resolution is a priority in EU enlargement, no Member State can easily accept to damage its own reputation.

- In practice, the Commission should start to include clear identifications of the respective bilateral conflicts in its annual country reports, starting in 2021. Through the vast network of Delegations (offices of the European External Action Service on the ground) and Member State embassies monitoring developments, there is a crystal clear picture about disputed bilateral issues. They must be addressed very clearly in the country reports. In the past, much of the wording in Commission country reports would be obscure and unnecessarily filtered through the nebulous language of diplomacy and EU speak, although there has been some progress in that respect over the recent years.

6.2.1.2 Dispute Resolution Infrastructure

The EU Commissioners in charge of external relations and enlargement must bring a fresh start to the EU enlargement policy. A functioning dispute resolution mechanism is just as vital as the classical incentive of financial support. The EU needs both to operate a proactive and successful enlargement and accession policy.

To that end, the European Commission and the Council Presidency *must* offer assistance and facilitation. There is great expertise in the Commission Services and in the national civil service of many Member States on how to deal with brokering agreements on dispute resolution and on drafting mandates for a judicial procedure, not least through the (occasionally painful) experience in the Slovenia–Croatia case.

- As a priority with EU Enlargement, the European Commission and the Member States must make sure that there is a new special standing Dispute Resolution Task Force (DRTF) takes shape. Some of the Candidate Countries are likely to enter the decisive stage to accession negotiations in the next few years. The Task Force must be composed of trained and experienced experts from the Directorates-General NEAR (Neighbourhood and Enlargement), JUST (Justice and Consumers), and the Legal Service, plus Member States experts from the trio Council Presidency (current, predecessor, and successor Council Presidency) and from wherever there is recognised facilitation expertise from previous cases.

6.2.1.3 Strengthening the EU Institutional Role and Legal Certainty

In the event of unforeseen issues surfacing *during* EU accession negotiations, dispute resolution must be bulletproof in a legal sense. Dispute resolution in an emergency situation must still be reliable and robust and provide legal certainty. Two aspects merit particular attention.

(i) A crucial element in strengthening the EU's role in a legal sense would be to appropriately highlight the role of EU bodies in bilateral dispute resolution. In retrospect, the very strong mediating role in the Slovenia–Croatia instance, where the European Commission drafted the Arbitration Agreement and discussed it with the parties and the Council Presidency skilfully assisted the parties in the finalising stage (see Sects. 4.2.2.3–4.2.5) could or should have been reflected somewhat more prominently. On the one hand, the role of the Council Presidency could have been added to the one of the European Commission in the Arbitration Agreement's preamble. Secondly, the European Commission who undoubtedly drafted the lion's share of the Arbitration Agreement could have signed the agreement as a witness together with the Council Presidency.

(ii) A second issue is the question of enforcement of an arbitral award. In State-to-State arbitration, more often than not the need for a tailor-made mandate for judicial third-party resolution arises. This was indeed the case with Slovenia v Croatia, where, as for the applicable law, *equity* and *good-neighbourly relations* had to be employed as additional criteria to international law to create the junction between the territorial sea of Slovenia and the high seas in the Adriatic (see Art. 4 Arbitration Agreement in Appendix A). Generally, an arbitral award may well be indirectly enforced if there is a sufficiently strong link to EU law. A lesson to be learnt from Croatia v Slovenia and the Court's finding, however, is that wherever there is a link between an arbitral award and an EU legal act, as was the case in Croatia's Treaty of Accession with regard to the Fisheries Regulation, the EU legal act ought to draw *directly* on the (upcoming) *decision* of the arbitral tribunal. If reference is made to *implementation*, let alone its completion, as was the case with the footnotes in the Act of Accession of Croatia and the related Fisheries Regulation, the link is less strong. The Court indeed found it was not strong enough, so it decided against admissibility of the Slovenian Art. 259 TFEU lawsuit (see Sect. 4.4.3.3). Therefore, it would appear that, in order to provide for enforcement jurisdiction of the CJEU in the event of infringement proceedings, the link between an arbitral award and EU law must be sufficiently strong in avoiding the issue of implementation.

6.2.2 Arbitration Must Become More Robust

It may be popular to draw the conclusion that arbitration is not a suitable means of dispute resolution any more because of the "bad experience" which was had in the Slovenia–Croatia case. But was it that arbitration *as such* failed operationally and politically? Not really. The confidentiality and independence provisions were violated by one of the party-appointed arbitrators, so it clearly is unjustified to dismiss the framework of arbitration as such altogether. The record of arbitral proceedings in border disputes is entirely positive, and it constitutes an established and popular means of judicial dispute settlement (see Sect. 4.3.1). Arbitration also commands widespread support at the political level in the EU (e.g. interview Jean Asselborn,[7] 28-09-2016) and worldwide (see Table 3.1 in Sect. 3.2.2.3).

Notwithstanding the fact that the ICJ or ITLOS are still viable alternatives, arbitration has indeed two distinct features which make it particularly suitable for bilateral dispute resolution in a highly politicised context:

First, both parties can define the mandate for the judicial body in a tailor-made fashion according to the (political–legal) needs of the dispute in question. As was demonstrated in the case of the Arbitration Agreement between Croatia and Slovenia, there is a wide range of applicable law available, from the strict application of international law to equity including novel criteria such as good-neighbourly relations, a crucial notion in the EU enlargement context in Southeast Europe, and also allowing for separating and sequencing particular issues, so as to arrive at a clear-cut roadmap for the arbitral tribunal.

Second, the parties to the dispute can choose (together) whom they feel like appointing as arbitrators by taking into account the qualifications for a particular kind of dispute, i.e. parties do not depend on a fixed pool of judges as is the case at the ICJ (which is, *nota bene*, by no means meant to question the expertise of any of the ICJ judges, the Court's workings, or its impressive record on boundary or other items of dispute settlement).

Nevertheless, international arbitration must become more resilient in relation to mishaps or breaches of confidentiality. To achieve that, it appears appropriate to reconsider the role of party-appointed arbitrators. It is worth recalling the special role of party-appointed arbitrators, namely to increase the parties' acceptance of and the trust in the arbitral procedure. Then again, party-appointed arbitrators potentially raise the expectations of the parties in terms of "our expert" influencing the proceedings in their interest. This, in turn, carries an implicit temptation to engage in unlawful *ex parte* communication with the party-appointed arbitrator. The sobering news in this respect is that massive intelligence operations by both parties and even third parties to avoid or prove illegal communication appear to have become State practice (see Sect. 4.3.3.2).

- The way out of that dilemma is to scrap party-appointed arbitrators altogether. The benefits would be manifold and groundbreaking: first, the temptation to engage in *ex parte* communication would be reduced drastically. Even if a party to the dispute was to contact a member of the arbitral tribunal, the member could be assumed to refuse communication (and perhaps treat the party unfavourably in the further proceedings in the light of such a blatant effort to compromise the independence of the tribunal). After all, an arbitrator that has engaged in unlawful

[7] Jean Asselborn is the Foreign Minister of Luxemburg. He has been in office since 2004 and is the longest-serving of all EU Member State foreign ministers.

communication would lose their most valuable assets, namely credibility and standing, indispensable prerequisites for (re-)appointments in arbitral proceedings in future cases.

- Second, a team of independent arbitrators chosen by the parties by way of mutual agreement fosters both the internal cohesion and the independence of a tribunal. The members of a judicial body who know that they command the parties' joint trust are likely to go about their work in a different spirit compared to a situation where two party-appointed members may be perceived as "persuaders" by the other tribunal members. Third, tribunals comprising just three members, for instance, would reduce the costs of arbitration proceedings—of which there may be the need for many—amongst and between the successor States of Yugoslavia (see Sect. 6.3). Three-member tribunals have worked perfectly well in the past, and there is no reason why that set-up without party-appointed members could not become the default format for State-to-State arbitration on bilateral disputes.

6.3 Pressing Bilateral Issues Ahead of EU Accession

It has been a mantra of the EU hemisphere for quite a while that Candidate Countries from Southeast Europe, the so-called Western Balkans Six (Serbia, Montenegro, Bosnia-Herzegovina, Macedonia, Kosovo, and Albania), must resolve bilateral disputes with one another or with neighbouring States before they can join the EU.

It is worth illustrating, therefore, what the major bilateral disputes are and how they could be tackled. Open bilateral issues include (i) the Croatia–Montenegro sea border, (ii) the land border between Croatia and Serbia along the Danube, (ii) war crime jurisdiction between Serbia and Croatia, (iii) the normalisation of relations between Serbia and Kosovo, and (iv) maritime access for Bosnia and Herzegovina.

6.3.1 Croatia–Montenegro Sea Border

The border dispute between Croatia and Slovenia has come a fairly long way since 1991. As this book has demonstrated, there have been several efforts to resolve the conflict, bilaterally and by different types of third-party management. As it happened, each failed resolution effort in a single-issue dispute, however, tends to diminish the room for a face-saving solution at a future stage.

In Croatia, domestic opposition to implementation of the arbitration award continues to be robust across the political spectrum. The unanimous Sabor vote from 2015 to leave the arbitration procedure is a rock solid benchmark against which any prospect of ratification must be measured, regardless of the fact that it was the last-but-two Croatian Parliament that adopted the resolution, not the current one.

It appears fair to see the level of salience of the arbitration award's implementation on an equal footing with the one of General Gotovina's extradition to the ICTY back in 2005. Both issues are highly sensitive and greatly touch upon Croatia's national identity and legitimacy considerations. Looking at both matters in a purely domestic context, no Croatian government would ever find a majority in Sabor to endorse them. If, however, a measure was going to serve "the greater good" of the EU, the prestigious club confirming Croatia's return to Europe (the extradition of Gotovina marked the beginning of the accession negotiations for Croatia in October 2005), or the country's solid situatedness in the EU the country would stick to the narrative of the political elite: to belong to Central Europe rather than the "Balkans".

On the one hand, when every allowance is made for the positive contents of the Final Award for Croatia in respect of the land border, the high-seas corridor may be seen as an infringement of Croatian territorial waters, and therefore of Croatian territory altogether. Such a notion is very difficult to swallow for historical reasons (see Sect. 2.5.2), even for the sake of being a respected EU Member State. On the other hand, whilst there may be a negative territorial balance sheet at Croatia's northern sea border, there may be something to gain on its southern sea border.

The provisional sea border arrangement of Croatia with Montenegro, the 2002 Protocol, was concluded soon after Yugoslav troops had withdrawn from the (Croatian) peninsula of Prevlaka (from where Dubrovnik was shelled in November/December 1991).[8] As the Yugoslav Navy was stationed in Kotor back then, unhindered access to Kotor Bay was of utmost importance for Montenegro. The Protocol, which has since been applied in good faith (interview Vladimir Radulović,[9] 20-04-2018; interview senior Croatian civil servant, 25-01-2017; see also Huszka 2020; Orlandić 2019: 88–89; Šelo Šabić and Borić 2016: 9), deprives Croatia of full sovereignty along its inner shores at Prevlaka and stipulates joint Croatian–Montenegrin policing in the Zone (*condominium*) west of the line between Cape Konfin and a point near Cape Oštro (Article 7). At the same time, naval activity on the Montenegrin side is restricted including the provision for submarines to navigate on the surface (Article 15; see Fig. 6.3).

EU accession negotiations with Montenegro have been ongoing for a number of years, and it is time to prioritise the finalisation of a permanent border agreement with Croatia. There were, for instance, no meetings of the bilateral commission in 2016 and 2017 to agree on the mandate for submission to the International Court of Justice (interview Vladimir Radulović, 20-04-2018).[10] However, leaving the matter to a late stage would make it vulnerable to domestic pressure in Croatia potentially triggering a veto situation in the accession negotiations.

A transformation of the Protocol into a final agreement would entail the opportunity to reflect the current situation of fundamentally different security interests (the Montenegrin Navy is no longer stationed in Kotor, and both Croatia and Montenegro

[8]The Protocol contains provisions on the de-militarisation of the Prevlaka peninsula and a strip along the Croatian–Montenegrin land border in the proximity of Prevlaka (Article 7).

[9]Vladimir Radulović is the Ambassador of Montenegro to the Benelux countries. He used to be involved in the 2002 Protocol in the Ministry for Foreign Affairs of Montenegro.

[10]The original idea to submit the issue to the ICJ was born at a meeting between Croatian Prime Minister Ivo Sanader and Montenegrin Prime Minister Milo Đukanović in March 2008 (interview Ivo Sanader, 02-11-2017; BETA News, 22-03-2008).

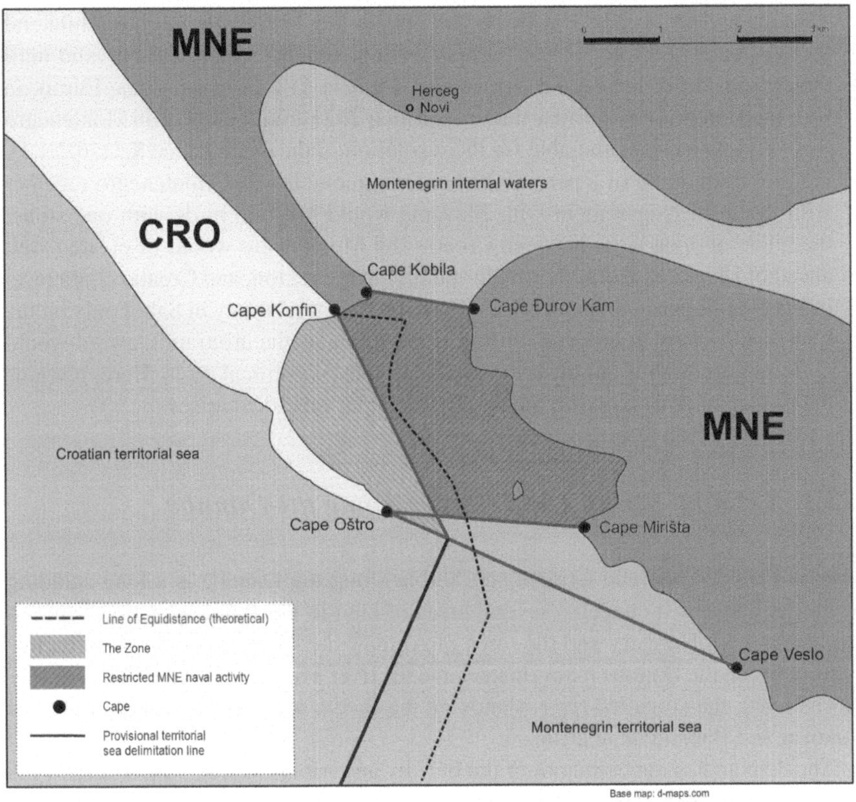

Fig. 6.3 Delimitation around Prevlaka and entrance to Herceg Novi Bay according to 2002 protocol (schematic view; *Source* Author; base map: d-maps.com)

are now NATO members). The outer Bay could be delimitated with an equidistance line apportioning full sovereignty for either side accordingly. Alternatively, the *condominium* regime in the Zone could be extended to the whole area east of the Zone perhaps except for a corridor securing unhindered access from the internal waters of Herceg Novi/Kotor Bay to the Montenegrin territorial sea south of the line from Cape Oštro to Cape Veslo and vice versa. However, the territorial sea would appear to be in more urgent need of final delimitation due to the economic interests involved. Natural resources are presumed to be located in the seabed in front of the coast where exploratory drillings have severely affected bilateral Croatia–Montenegro relations.[11]

[11]Montenegro protested exploratory drillings off the Croatian coast south of Prevlaka in 2013 on the grounds that Croatia did not consult prior to contracting drillings in an area where no final delimitation existed (see *note verbale* 09/16-167/35 of the Ministry of Foreign Affairs of Montenegro from 2 July 2014 to the UN Secretary-General; *note verbale* 09/16-167/121 of the Ministry of Foreign Affairs of Montenegro from 1 December 2014 to the UN Division for Ocean Affairs and the Law of the Sea). Likewise, Croatia criticised Montenegro for exploring resources in the seabed in the area of the preliminary territorial sea delimitation (Orlandić 2019: 89).

- There is a clear need to transform and amend the 2002 Protocol into a bilateral treaty soon. The Protocol is a "temporary [agreement] which will be valid until the conclusion of the border agreement" (Article 1)[12] anyway, so the European Commission should prioritise the issue in their 2021 country report on Montenegro by including a clear timetable for the resolution of the dispute (see Sect. 6.2.1.1).
- Parallel ratification of a permanent border agreement with Montenegro together with the border agreement with Slovenia would kill two birds with one stone: the bilateral open issue between Croatia and Montenegro would be cleared well ahead of EU accession and provide stability in the region, and Croatia could level off its overall border balance sheet. To ratify a bilateral treaty in Sabor only on the Croatian–Slovenian order according to the terms of the arbitration award would come at very high if not unsurmountable domestic political costs. Here, it seems the golden opportunity of a bilateral borders package-deal arises.

6.3.2 Croatia–Serbia Land Border Along the Danube

The land border between Croatia and Serbia along the Danube is a long-standing territorial dispute. It concerns several areas of land in the Baranja section between the border with Hungary and the town of Aljmaš, the so-called pockets, and a few spots between the Danube main channel and the river's tributaries or branches further downstream, the so-called river islands, in the Bačka section between the towns of Vukovar and Bačka Palanka/Ilok.

The dispute has not come out of the blue by any means. Rather, the course of the river has changed due to natural meandering and regulation works where channels were cut out between 1890 and 1894 in the Baranja section, and, in 1922, in the Bačka section. As a result, the course of the river is no longer aligned with the cadastral limit of the commune of Beli Manastir (Croatia). That cadastre dates back to the Austrian–Hungarian administration in the nineteenth century. Some sections of the cadastral border run along tributaries/branches of the Danube's present-day main channel (see Fig. 6.4).

In fact, the old cadastral border, the cutting out of channels, and the natural river meandering over time created the pockets, six on the left bank and two on the right bank of the river. Further downstream in the Bačka section between Vukovar and Ilok/Bačka Palanka, there are a few river islands on the left bank of the main river course. The dispute actually centres around the following arguments: Croatia claims the pockets on the left bank and the river islands based on the cadastral limits of Beli Manastir. Serbia holds that the navigable channel of the river (Thalweg) constitutes the border all along the Danube as this is not least the international standard on navigable rivers (Dimitrijević 2012: 13–19; Klemenčić and Schofield 2001: 16–25).

[12]Protocol on the interim regime along the southern border between the Republic of Croatia and the Federal Republic of Yugoslavia (Serbia and Montenegro), signed on 10 December 2002. The Preamble suggests that "the provisional regime established by this Protocol will make it easier to find a final solution [...]".

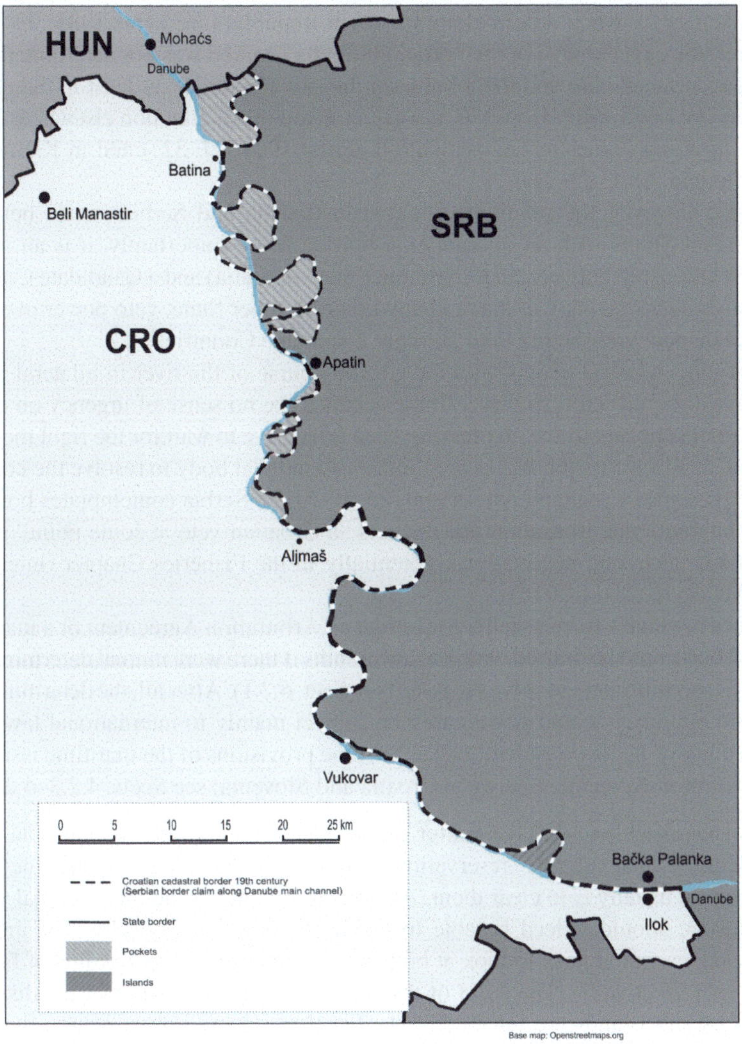

Fig. 6.4 Disputed spots of State border Croatia–Serbia along Danube (schematic view; *Source* Author; base map: openstreetmaps.org)

The dispute covers roughly 110 km^2 of land on the left bank and around 10 km^2 of land on the right bank of the Danube (Šelo Šabić and Borić 2016: 10).

Unlike the land border dispute between Croatia and Slovenia along the Dragonja, Sava or Mura, the Danube border dispute between Croatia and Serbia is *not* a post-1991 one. It goes back to the time right after the re-establishment of Yugoslavia at the end of World War II. Back then, the Đilas Commission was looking at the boundary between the Yugoslav Republics of Croatia and Serbia. Several decisions were taken as to which areas belong to which Republic (see Đilas 1985: 99–100). However, the exact course of the border along the Danube was not determined. The dispute resurfaced here and there between the two Republics, at least in the period between 1947 and 1965. However, it was not given much attention elsewhere at the time as it was a domestic Yugoslav affair (Reba 1999: 27–32; cited in Klemenčić and Schofield 2001: 22–24).

Today, however, the relationship between Croatia and Serbia is one between independent States with an international border. More importantly, it is an asymmetric relationship between an EU Member State (Croatia) and a Candidate Country (Serbia) *de facto* giving Croatia, and any other Member State, veto power over any bilateral dispute with Serbia (and all other Candidate Countries).

Marrying cadastral claims with the current course of the river in bilateral negotiations will be difficult. However, there seems to be no sense of urgency on either side. Croatia appears to see no pressing need ("we have to wait for the right moment to agree") and favours the ICJ as the third-party judicial body to resolve the conflict (interview senior Croatian civil servant, 25-01-2017). Serbia contemplates both the ICJ or international arbitration and expects "a Croatian veto at some point" in the current EU accession negotiations, potentially in the Fisheries Chapter (interview Tanja Miščević, 28-11-2016).

It does not take a fortune-teller to see that an Arbitration Agreement or a mandate for the Court could be drafted within a few months if there were mutual determination and an EU commitment to solve the issue (see Sect. 6.2.1). After all, the determination of a land boundary would presumably be subject mainly to international law (and not to equity or wider considerations as in some provisions of the maritime issues of the Arbitration Agreement between Croatia and Slovenia; see Sects. 4.2.3–4.2.5).

- It is suggested here that the matter cannot wait for too long. The later the stage a Member State submits "reservations" vis-à-vis a Candidate Country, the more difficult it usually is to clear them. An arbitral tribunal or the International Court of Justice should indeed be able to tackle the issue successfully. The arbitrators/judges would have to look at both the cadastral record and claims of factual control (*effectivités*). The court or tribunal would examine whether the disputed pockets and islands are inhabited, whether there is any infrastructure, the land is used for farming, or whether there is any kind of economic or other activity. Negotiations on the mandate for international arbitration or the ICJ should start any time soon. It must be noted that the subsequent proceedings before a court or tribunal including hearings may take approximately two years.

6.3.3 *Universal/Regional Jurisdiction for War Crimes (Serbia–Croatia)*

In the EU accession negotiation with Serbia, a major point of contention appeared in the first half of 2016 when Croatia took issue with the Serbian Law on Organisation and Competences of State Authorities in War Crime Proceedings (ZORZ; Official Gazette of the Republic of Serbia, No. 67/2003). Croatia raised its reservations in the context of opening Chaps. 23 (Judiciary and fundamental rights) and 24 (Justice, freedom and security), in particular with regard to the opening benchmarks (for procedural aspects see Sects. 4.2.1.1 and 4.2.1.2).[13]

It is useful to recall that the jurisdiction of national courts is usually confined to the national territory and to domestic legislation. *Universal jurisdiction*, however, "an essential tool of international justice, is the ability of the court of any State to try persons for crimes committed *outside its territory* that are not linked to the State by the nationality of the suspect or the victims [...]". Universal jurisdiction plays a crucial role in "the need to punish perpetrators of [...] *war crimes*" (Amnesty International 2012: 1; emphasis added). It is understood that "universal jurisdiction, by its nature, does not operate within the parameters of an existing, bounded or defined jurisdictional community" (Hovell 2018: 3).

The Serbian ZORZ contains provisions on the material and territorial scope of war crime jurisdiction. Article 2(2) has the following definition on the scope of the legislation:

> [S]erious violations of international humanitarian law *committed in the territory of the former Yugoslavia since 1 January 1991* specified in the Statute of the International Criminal Tribunal for the Former Yugoslavia. (emphasis added)

Article 3 reads:

> The government authorities of the Republic of Serbia specified in this Law shall have the competent jurisdiction for conducting the proceedings for criminal offences referred to in Article 2 of the present Law which were *committed in the territory of the former Socialist Federal Republic of Yugoslavia, regardless of the nationality of the perpetrator or victim.* (emphasis added)

Serbia contends that jurisdiction "over the whole territory of the former Yugoslavia" regardless of the citizenship of the perpetrators or victims was necessary because "Serbia was not the scene of the armed conflict 1991-1995" and that amongst the refugees looking for shelter in Serbia "there were a number of those who had perpetrated [...] war crimes". Further, the ICTY had appreciated that kind of universal jurisdiction of the Serbian judiciary, and Croatia had not objected to the 2003 ZORZ until the beginning of 2015 (Comments on the request for abolition of

[13]Zagreb also had reservations vis-à-vis the non-implementation of a guaranteed seat for the Croatian minority in the Serbian Parliament and with regard to Serbia's cooperation with the ICTY. In addition, Croatia introduced a reservation with regard to victims' rights/compensation from the dissolution wars as a last-minute add-on in June 2016 (interview Member State E COELA civil servant, 21-10-2016; interview Member State D COELA civil servant, 15-11-2016).

universal jurisdiction of Serbian authorities with regard to war crimes, note of the Government of Serbia, March 2015: 2).

Conversely, Croatia held that ZORZ interfered with the sovereignty of other States as "such territorially limited 'universal jurisdiction' [was] without any basis in international law, precisely because of this limitation [implying the] inability or unwillingness of strictly defined States to undertake such prosecution" which amounted to "legal aggression" (The problems of Serbia's regional jurisdiction, note of the Ministry of Foreign and European Affairs of Croatia, April 2016: 1). As a result, Article 3 of ZORZ was "incompatible with the political criteria related to individual chapters [...] and in particular Chapter 23" (note MFEA Croatia 2016: 3). Even if universal jurisdiction was not part of the EU *acquis*, Serbia's approach was "an attempt to turn [universal jurisdiction] into a regional criminal law dictatorship" and was thus "by no means a bilateral issue between Croatia and Serbia, but a matter of defence and full respect for the values and fundamental legal principles [of] the EU". Consequently, ZORZ was going to have to be amended including a deletion of Article 3 "as an important prerequisite for the Chapter 23 within the accession negotiations between the EU and Serbia" (note MFEA Croatia 2016: 4).

The European Commission noted that the assertion of universal jurisdiction over war crimes is rooted in treaty law and customary international law,[14] and that many EU Member States had actually implemented universal jurisdiction over war crimes.[15] The ZORZ provisions, therefore, "could not be considered as a violation of the principle of non-intervention and of the sovereignty of the Croatian State" (Non-paper on Croatian argumentaire for repealing relevant articles of the Serbian ZORZ, European Commission, February 2016: 6). Further, even if Article 3 of ZORZ was deleted, it would have no effect on the (post-Yugoslavia) regional jurisdiction issue as the undisputed universal jurisdiction principle would still apply (Non-paper, European Commission, February 2016: 7). The Commission had already made it clear in 2015, that it "cannot take issue as such with the principle of Serbia claiming universal jurisdiction" (letter European Commission to Marijana Petir MEP, 29-01-2015). However, the Commission took the view that exchange of information and views between the Prosecutor's Offices of Croatia and Serbia had to be intensified (Non-paper, European Commission, February 2016: 8).[16]

The Croatian veto lasted from April to the beginning of July 2016 and could only be resolved through high-level talks involving the EU Commissioner for Enlargement,

[14]The Geneva Conventions of 1949, the 1984 UN Convention against torture, and other cruel, inhuman, or degrading treatment or punishment, and the Preamble of the Statute of the International Criminal Court (ICC) from 1998.

[15]Such as Belgium, the Czech Republic, Denmark, Finland, France, Germany, Luxemburg, the Netherlands, Spain, Sweden, and the UK. Amnesty International (2012: 12) holds that 136 (approximately 70.5%) UN Member States have universal jurisdiction over war crimes in place.

[16]As of 2016, Serbia had conducted 347 exchanges of information and evidence related to domestic war crime trials. 173 exchanges were with Croatia, 56 with Bosnia and Herzegovina, 14 with Montenegro, and 104 with EULEX and UNMIK in Kosovo (Negotiating position of the Republic of Serbia for Inter-Governmental Conference on accession of the Republic of Serbia to the European Union for Chapter 23 Judiciary and Fundamental Rights 2016: 20).

the Foreign Minister of Croatia, and the Dutch Foreign Minister representing the EU Council Presidency (interview Member State E COELA civil servant, 21-10-2016; interview Member State F COELA civil servant, 15-11-2016). No other Member State shared Croatia's reservations on the war crime jurisdiction issue (interview senior European Commission civil servant, 29-11-2018). In the European Parliament, many perceived Zagreb's blockade as a "blatant example of irresponsibility" (interview Eduard Kukan,[17] 27-09-2017). In the view of the European Commission, the Croatian position proved untenable not least due to Zagreb's view that, on principle, the prosecution of war crimes should be carried out in the country where the crime was perpetrated. That position ran counter to the universal jurisdiction approach not least supported by the ICTY (interview senior European Commission civil servant, 29-11-2018). The issue with Serbia's regional jurisdiction approach appears to be that "Croatia has legitimate fears of Serbia judging Croats. And fundamentally, both Croatia and Serbia had always regarded the ICTY as biased and have never accepted the Criminal Tribunal's legitimacy" (interview war crime prosecution expert at the ICTY, 31-03-2017). One likely reason for Belgrade's position and Zagreb's position may be the issue of infringed sovereignty. Croatia and Serbia were or have been subject to the EU conditionality issue of collaboration with the ICTY for a long time considerably reducing the countries' *de facto* sovereignty (interview Dejan Jović, 02-11-2017).[18]

Coming back to the operational level of EU accession negotiations, Chaps. 23 and 24 with Serbia were eventually opened at the EU-Serbia IGC on 18 July 2016. The final wording in the EU Common Position (CP) on Chap. 23 for Serbia with regard to the domestic handling of war crimes reads:

> The EU underlines the need for *meaningful regional cooperation and good-neighbourly relations in the handling of war crimes*, including the aim to *avoid conflicts in jurisdiction*. Accordingly, as called for by the relevant February 2016 European Parliament Resolution,[19] all outstanding issues in that regard must be fully resolved. War crimes must be prosecuted without any discrimination. (EU Common Position on Serbia for Chapter 23, 5 July 2016: 8; emphasis added; the wording of the respective *interim benchmark* is virtually identical.)

There was no subsequent deletion of Article 3 of ZORZ (interview senior European Commission civil servant, 29-11-2018). Nevertheless, the above wording as a compromise formula is open to different interpretations, so that the issue of war crime jurisdiction in Serbia does retain considerable potential for bilateral conflict for the next steps in the EU accession process of Serbia.

---

[17] Eduard Kukan was an MEP and Chair of the European Parliament Delegation with Serbia and was Foreign Minister of Slovakia 1998–2009.

[18] "The conditionality of collaboration with the ICTY was tough for us. Our negotiations on Chapter 23 were held hostage by the Homeland War." (Jadranka Kosor at the ALDE Group event "Five years of Croatian EU membership", European Parliament, 28-06-2018).

[19] "[The European Parliament] reiterates its call on Serbia to re-examine its legislation on jurisdiction in war crime proceedings in the spirit of reconciliation and good-neighbourly relations together with the Commission and with its neighbours." (European Parliament Resolution on the 2015 [European Commission] report on Serbia, 4 February 2016, para 26).

Procedurally, there are at least three further stages where Croatia (or other Member States) may be tempted to use the veto: the assessment of the interim benchmark attainment, the drafting of the closing benchmarks, and the closing of Chap. 23 altogether.

- Thus, irrespective of the fact that it is a matter of years before the rule-of-law Chapters can be closed, it is an urgent issue to clear the dispute between Croatia and Serbia on war crime jurisdiction once and for all. It must not be left to the final stages of the accession negotiations, as the political risk of veto tends to become incalculable. The European Commission should prioritise the issue at the latest in the 2021 country report on Serbia by including a clear timetable for the resolution of the dispute (see also Sect. 6.2.1.1). A bilateral approach should naturally take precedence, but options must include facilitation by the European Commission, another third party, or judicial dispute settlement (arbitration or ICJ).

6.3.4 Normalisation of Serbia–Kosovo Relations

A major EU conditionality issue vis-à-vis Serbia (and Kosovo) is what is diplomatically termed "the normalisation of relations with Kosovo". This entails a "legally binding [bilateral] agreement". Bilateral talks have been facilitated by the EU High Representative for Foreign Affairs and External Relations Commissioner, who has hosted numerous meetings between the Presidents of Serbia and Kosovo, Vučić and Thaçi, to that end, the so-called Brussels Dialogue (Demjaha 2020: 29–36; European Commission Serbia 2018c report: 51–2).

It is understood that the EU accession of Serbia and (potentially) Kosovo is hard to see as being possible without the mutual recognition of the two countries, although such a precondition is not expressly mentioned. It must be noted, that there are five EU Member States (Cyprus, Greece, Romania, Slovakia, Spain) who have not recognised Kosovo (see e.g. Kerr-Lindsay and Armakolas 2020: 2).[20] This is mainly to do with reservations towards domestic separatist trends (in the case of Spain and Catalonia), the position of a principle that unilateral independence is not in accordance with international law (Romania), or with a territorial issue in relation to disputed statehood (Cyprus and the Turkish-Cypriot entity; interview Member State H COELA member, 16-07-2018; interview Member State I COELA member, 12-07-2018; for EU Member States' relations with Kosovo see Armakolas and Ker-Lindsay 2020).

Towards the end of the summer of 2018, high-level relations between the President of Serbia, Aleksandar Vučić, and the President of Kosovo, Hashim Thaçi, appeared to be improving, and there was even talk of a limited and mutually agreed land swap of

[20]As for EU Member State relations with Kosovo, Ker-Lindsay and Armakolas (2020: 3–5) differentiate between "strong recognisers" (Germany and the UK*), "weak recognisers" (the Czech Republic, Poland), "soft non-recognisers" (Greece, Slovakia, Romania), and "hard non-recognisers" (Spain, Cyprus). *The UK left the EU on 31 January 2020.

areas in South Serbia and North Kosovo. At the end of the day, a *tête-à-tête* between the two scheduled for a regular meeting on 7 September 2018 in Brussels did not take place, however. A few days later, when Vučić visited Northern Kosovo, he named Slobodan Milošević "a great leader of Serbia". As a result, relations appeared to be back in conflict mode (AP News, 10 September 2018). A subsequent meeting in Brussels in October 2018 did not yield any results. On the contrary, Kosovo raising the tariff for imports of goods from Serbia from 10 to 100% as a retaliation for Serbia blocking Kosovo's accession to Interpol seemed to aggravate the situation (Reuters News, 21 November 2018). The ban was lifted, however, at the beginning of April 2020 "as a sign of goodwill" according to caretaker prime minister Albin Kurti.

It appears fair to argue that the EU bears some responsibility, too, for the lack of progress. Denying Kosovo visa liberalisation may have been a decisive factor. In fact, Kosovo has fulfilled all EU conditionality items (such as ratification of the border demarcation agreement with neighbouring Montenegro in 2018). Instead, hesitant EU Member States are "not honouring their own pledges and thus running the risk of further destabilising a fragile region" (interview Tanja Fajon,[21] 23-01-2019).

As for the eventual prospect of EU accession for Serbia, the recognition question is indeed a thorny issue, both for Serbia and the five critical EU Member States. This author submits to consider a solution short of full recognition, but subject to special relations which would be established in a bilateral treaty. A similar treaty established the relations between the Federal Republic of Germany (FRG) and the German Democratic Republic (GDR) between 1973 and 1990, albeit admittedly under very different circumstances. The FRG belonged to NATO and the GDR to the Warsaw Pact, two opposite military and political blocs in the Cold War era. What is pertinent, however, is the recognition issue: The then FRG and GDR had so-called permanent representations instead of embassies in the respective territory. The two Germanies had proper diplomatic relations in place without full recognition. However, the bilateral treaty enabled both countries to become full members of the United Nations in September 1973. It goes without saying that no model, wherever it originates, is a one-to-one blueprint for a transplant into a different environment. The political leaders in Belgrade and Pristina, the European Commission, and the Member States ought to take the historic peculiarities in Serbia and Kosovo into account and strive for a pragmatic solution to achieve the sough-after "normalisation of relations".

Somewhat by surprise, a draft version of a future bilateral "Comprehensive Agreement between the Republic of Kosovo and the Republic of Serbia" (hereafter "Draft Comprehensive Agreement") emerged to that end from non-EU quarters in late December 2018. It contains several elements worth quoting:

The Preamble stipulates, *inter alia*, that "newly formed sovereign States should have the same borders as the preceding dependent area before independence" (uti possidetis), and the recognition of the fact that "the Agreement on Succession

[21] Tanja Fajon MEP was the European Parliament Rapporteur on visa liberalisation with Kosovo 2014–2019.

Issues[22] […] provides a framework for assisting in the resolution of […] analogous issues for the Parties".

Chapter 1 (The Political Agreement) stipulates that "the normalisation of relations between the Republic of Kosovo and the Republic of Serbia requires a *sui generis* approach and structures that reflect their shared interests as well as the cultural identities of their citizens" (Art. I.1.1). Further, there is talk of both Parties supporting each other in aspiring international and supranational organisations, "including in the case of *Kosovo in the United Nations*" (Art. I.1.4; emphasis added). In addition, "the Parties commit to […] the resolution of all outstanding issues deriving from the war of 1998–1999 including […] reparations […] and war-crimes" (Art. I.1.9). Lastly, "the Parties agree that the principle of *Parity of Esteem* shall govern their future relations" (Art. I.1.10; emphasis added).

With regard to diplomatic relations, the "Parties agree to establish permanent diplomatic missions in the other Parties' State […] ensuring compliance with international norms establishing diplomatic missions" (Chap. 11, Establishment of Permanent Diplomatic Missions, Art. 1). Further, the Parties are going to "accept that the Republic of Kosovo will become member of the International Telecommunications Union (ITU)" which would include an international country code for Kosovo (Chap. 11, Telecommunications, Art. 1), and that Kosovo "will become member of the Universal Postal Union (UPU)" which would include an internationally recognised postcode for Kosovo (Chap. 11, Telecommunications, Art. 2).

In Chap. 2 (Confidence Building Measures), the Parties engage in establishing "joint university degree programs" (Art. 2.3), "cross-border cooperation programs within the framework of existing Western Balkans programs supported by the European Union" (Art. 2.6), and "inter-municipal cooperation programs and twinning projects" (Art. 2.7). There are fairly detailed provisions under the heading "Participation of the Serb community in the public life of Kosovo" in Chap. 3, such as "the right of the Serbian community to have personal names registered in their original form and script of their language […]" (Participation in […] public life, Art. 1.), and "the right to maintain and use its own media, including […] in its language" (Participation in […] public life, Art. 5), and provisions on the participation of the Kosovo Serb Community in government and in courts (Participation […] at central level, Arts. 1–12).

The provisions on economic matters (Chap. 4) include reciprocal access to the labour market, the "free movement of goods, services, people and capital" (Trade, Art. 3). As for foreign debts, a "Joint Commission to negotiate Kosovo's share of the international debt inherited from the former [SFRY]" (Foreign Debts, Art. 1)[23] is foreseen, as well as "Compensation of Kosovo Citizens' Foreign Currency Damages

[22] Footnote inserted by the author. For the Agreement on Succession Issues see Sect. 2.5.3.

[23] There is express reference to the Agreement on Succession Issues and the allocation of foreign debt between the SFRY successor States (see also Sect. 2.5.3). The provisions in the Draft Comprehensive Agreement actually suggest an opt-in of Kosovo to Serbia's share of the SFRY's foreign debt based on the result of bilateral negotiations.

in the Banking System of the Former [SFRY]" (Outstanding Financial Damages, Art. 1.3).

Chapter 5 addresses "Transitional Justice and Reconciliation", *inter alia* through facilitating "exchange of information on suspects of war crimes" (War crimes, Art. 3), agreeing "in good faith to take all measures necessary to determine and exchange information regarding identities, whereabouts, and fates of missing persons from each Party" (Missing Persons, Art. 1). Further, "Parties undertake to establish a joint commission for assessing the material damage and establishing criteria and procedures for financial compensation schemes" (War reparations, Art. 2).

The Draft Comprehensive Agreement foresees as "Guarantors for the implementation of this Agreement […] The Unites States of America, The United Kingdom, Germany, France and Italy and the European Union" (Chap. 12, Art. 12.1).

There are dispute resolution provisions in Chap. 14 stipulating that any dispute arising between the Parties "as to the interpretation, application or performance of this Agreement, either Party may submit the dispute to final and binding arbitration" aligned to the Permanent Court of Arbitration (PCA) Optional Rules for Arbitrating Disputes between Two States (Art. 14.1). The Tribunal is to comprise five arbitrators (Art. 14.2), and the appointing authority is to be the Secretary-General of the PCA (Art. 14.4).

The recognition issue is addressed in Chap. 15 stating that with the entry into force of the Comprehensive Agreement, the "*Parties and Guarantors agree to initiate the procedure for adoption of a United Nations Security Council Resolution recognising this Agreement and admitting Kosovo to be a full member of the United Nations*" (Art. 15.1; emphasis added). There are also provisions on ruling out blocking Kosovo in international organisations, such as the EU, the Council of Europe, and the OSCE (Art. 15.2).

A brief analysis of the above Draft Comprehensive Agreement must start from the basis that it is a draft on which Serbia's and Kosovo's position is unknown at the time of writing. One must also bear in mind that the normalisation of the relations between Serbia and Kosovo is the *sine qua non* for the EU accession of Serbia:

> If progress in the normalisation of relations with Kosovo significantly lags behind progress in the negotiations overall, due to Serbia failing to act in good faith, in particular in the implementation of agreements reached between Serbia and Kosovo, the [European] Commission will on its own initiative or on the request of one third of the Member States […] propose to withhold its recommendations to open and/or close other negotiating chapters, and adapt the associated preparatory work, as appropriate, until this imbalance is addressed. (EU Common Position on Serbia, Chapter 35, item 1, Normalisation of Relations between Serbia and Kosovo, 25 November 2015: 3).

In this regard, the Draft Comprehensive Agreement provides an opportunity to solve the sensitive issue of enabling the membership of Kosovo in international organisations, first and foremost the United Nations, whilst at the same time enabling Serbia to avoid direct recognition of Kosovo. The mutual agreement on both States being "sovereign and lawfully constituted States" (Art. 1.1.3) is a way of achieving indirect recognition, and the provision of not blocking each other with the express mention of the UN (Art. 1.1.4) is one part of securing UN membership of Kosovo.

The much bigger part, however, is to initiate the process of UN accession by means of the UN Security Council. To this end, the provisions in Article 15.1 on initiating the procedure of Kosovo's accession to the UN upon entry into force of the Comprehensive Agreement appear convincing *prima facie*. Nevertheless, the shortcoming is that Russia (which traditionally enjoys friendly relations with Serbia) is also a member of the UN Security Council, but not foreseen as a Guarantor of the Comprehensive Agreement. The same holds for China which has manifest economic and political interests in the region. Thus, unanimity in the Security Council to go ahead with Kosovo's membership would by no means be guaranteed. And even if it was, the initiating of the procedure to UN accession "upon *entry into force*" (Art. 15.1) of the Comprehensive Agreement bears some considerable uncertainty for Kosovo. To that end, "upon *signature*" would be more promising, as one would want to achieve reciprocity in terms of concluding the agreement and UN membership.

From the point of view of EU diplomacy and the EU facilitated dialogue for the normalisation of relations between Belgrade and Pristina hosted by the EU High Representative,[24] the above Draft Comprehensive Agreement must be bad news since the active input does not originate from the EU. The Trump administration has indeed tried hard to achieve a Serbia-Kosovo settlement, but only managed to strike a deal on normalising economic ties thus far (Reuters news, 4 September 2020). When this book went to print, the EU had resumed its facilitation efforts and talks were being held at political and technical level (BETA news, 17 September 2020).

It is (very) early days still, and it appears impossible to predict at the time of writing whether a comprehensive bilateral settlement between Serbia and Kosovo is within reach in the foreseeable future. There is some solid opposition from the Orthodox Church of Serbia against any agreement with Kosovo, so the odds perhaps are that the matter may well be frozen "*ad calendas graecas*", i.e. for quite some time (interview Thomas Brey, 11-01-2019). In any case, as to the essentials of a Serbia–Kosovo settlement, one needs to consider that any bilateral treaty establishing diplomatic relations with Kosovo requires amending the Serbian constitution accordingly. On the whole, it would seem that there are no simple solutions. "An agreement is possible, but only under circumstances where there are clear gains for either side, such as special assurances from the European Union for Serbia, and UN membership for Kosovo" (interview David McAllister,[25] 15-01-2019). Reflecting the thorniest issues in the EU-sponsored dialogue, it seems that both sides have pledged to suspend provocative action until September 2021: Serbia has temporarily put on ice its de-recognition (of Kosovo) policy towards third countries, and Kosovo refrains from applying for the membership in international organisations (Stojanović 2020).

The stakes are perhaps still too high historically and emotionally—the atrocious Kosovo War (March–June 1999) raged only twenty years ago. Hence, it may still take

[24]For the EU facilitated dialogue between Serbia and Kosovo, see the European External Action Service (EEAS) at https://eeas.europa.eu/diplomatic-network/eu-facilitated-dialogue-belgrade-pristina-relations_en.

[25]David McAllister MEP was the European Parliament Rapporteur on Serbia 2015–2019.

time to prepare the ground for an agreement supplemented by a spirit of reconciliation, whilst it may be true that "it takes genuinely future-oriented leaders who will be able to solve the issue and who are ready to take the risk of not being re-elected" (interview Tanja Fajon, 23-01-2019). On a more sobering note, it appears that the "EU tactics to foster stabilocracies" has led to even "stronger nationalistic rhetoric, destructed institutions, a marginalised opposition, and an impoverished population - with none of the issues solved" (interview Aleksandra Tomanić, 05-05-2020).

- A Serbia–Kosovo Agreement only stands a chance of implementation/ratification, if it represents (i) the final hurdle for Serbia before completing the accession negotiations and therefore securing EU accession, and if it equals (ii) a guarantee of UN membership for Kosovo, perhaps topped up by a (merits-based) start of EU accession negotiations. Although there is a lot to gain, both sides will have to make what is going to be perceived as "concessions" from a legitimacy point of view (see Sects. 1.3.2.2 and 1.3.2.3). It is submitted here, therefore, that it is worth considering, in the case of Serbia, to have a combined referendum on an agreement with Kosovo and on EU accession, and, in the case of Kosovo, to link ratification of the treaty with Serbia to the prospect of EU accession negotiations.

Yet, it must be a worrying signal for the EU that the first draft of a bilateral Serbia–Kosovo treaty has materialised with active support from the USA. It is suggested here, therefore, that the EU step up its efforts from facilitation to mediation. The simple hosting of meetings between the two parties is insufficient. Rather, it appears that it will take some robust drafting input also from the EU to arrive at a settlement in the foreseeable future. It is a good idea for the EU to stand ready to skilfully assist with expertise and input and not to leave the actual third-party mediation of the bilateral negotiations solely to the USA.

After all, it would be a humiliation for the EU's foreign policy, if the USA alone rather than in collaboration with the EU managed to strike a bilateral deal in a region that is aspiring to EU membership in its immediate vicinity.

6.3.5 *Maritime Access for Bosnia-Herzegovina*

The boundary at land and at sea between Croatia and Bosnia-Herzegovina was settled at a relatively early stage through a bilateral treaty in 1999.[26] As a matter of fact, the treaty has not been ratified yet. However, it is being applied in good faith by both

[26] Treaty on the State Border between the Republic of Croatia and Bosnia and Herzegovina, 30 July 1999. The Preamble cites, *inter alia*, Opinion No. 3 of the Badinter Commission stating that the former (internal) boundaries between the SFRY Republics were to become international boundaries protected by international law. Article 2(1) expressly confirms that "the State border [...] is determined on the basis of the state of the borders at the time of the end of the Socialist Federal Republic of Yugoslavia in 1991" (see also "Self-determination and Internal Borders as International Ones (Opinions 2 and 3)" in Sect. 2.5.1.1).

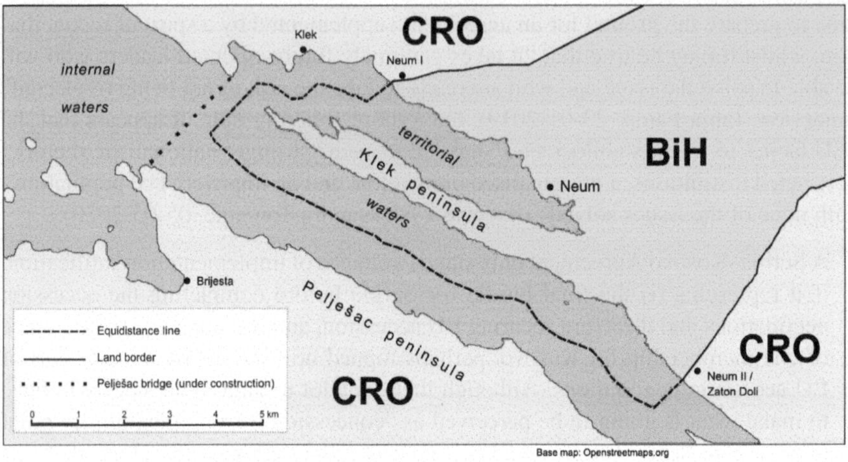

Fig. 6.5 Territorial sea delimitation between Croatia and Bosnia-Herzegovina according to 1999 Border Treaty (schematic view; *Source* Author; base map: openstreetmaps.org)

sides (interview Damir Arnaut, 07-05-2019; interview senior Croatian civil servant, 25-01-2017; see also European Commission Analytical Report on BiH 2019a: 84).[27]

The territorial sea border around Neum and Klek peninsula is delimitated by way of an equidistance line (see Fig. 6.5) in remarkable brevity. Article 4(3) states:

> The State border on the sea stretches along the central line of the sea between the territories of the Republic of Croatia and Bosnia and Herzegovina […].

Regardless of the fact that Bosnia and Herzegovina hardly has any relevant maritime transport activities since the country currently relies on the nearby Croatian port of Ploče for the sea-bound import and export of goods (European Commission Analytical Report on BiH, 2019a: 120; interview European Commission DG REGIO senior civil servant; author's field notes, 10-08-2020), there is a point of contention as to the maritime areas for vessels going from Bosnia and Herzegovina to the high seas in the Adriatic and vice versa. The straight baselines of Croatia run across the outer ends of the Dalmatian islands thus creating internal waters (of Croatia) landwards of the baselines (see also Sect. 3.1.1.1). As a result, vessels going from the high seas or the Croatian territorial sea to the territorial sea of Bosnia-Herzegovina to reach Neum or vice versa have to go through Croatian internal waters (see Fig. 6.6).

It is useful to recall that there is no innocent passage in internal waters. The law of the sea scholarship irrespective of the nationality of the author questions the legality of the Croatian straight baselines on the grounds that they violate Art. 7(6) of the United Nations Convention of the Law of the Sea (UNCLOS). That provision rules out the enclosure of the territorial waters of a State by the straight baselines of another State (see Grbec 2015: 155–7; Arnaut 2014: 165–7; Vukas 2008: 187–8). At the same

[27] There are differences of opinion on a few tiny sections of the land border, however, such as the delimitation line at Kostajnica or along the river Una (Bickl 2020: 54).

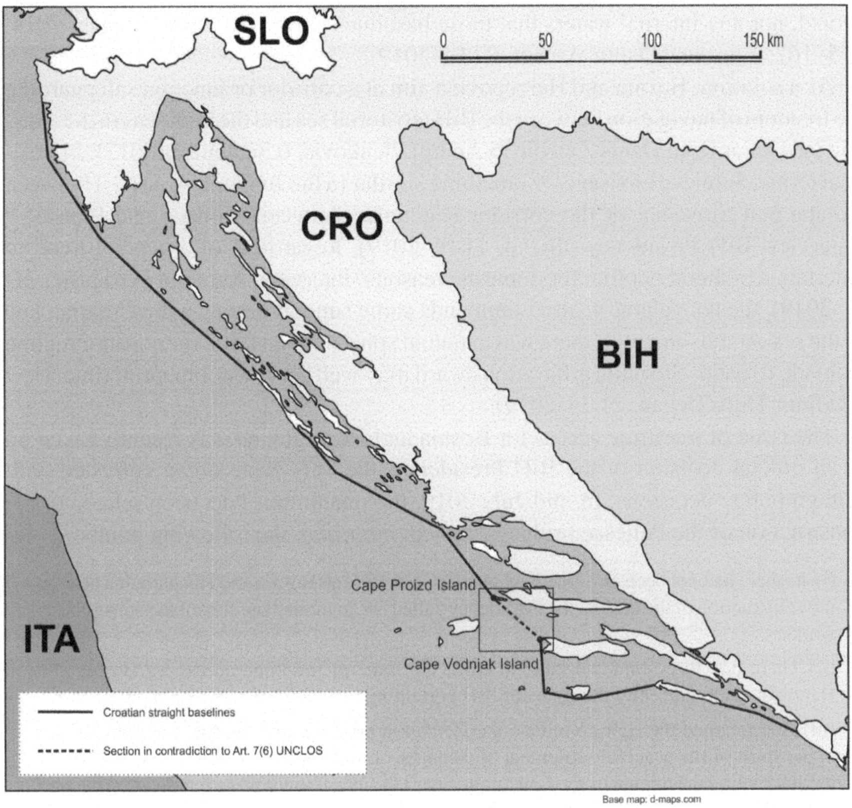

Fig. 6.6 Croatian straight baselines cutting off the territorial waters of Bosnia and Herzegovina (*Source* Author; base map: d-maps.com)

time, Art. 8(2) UNCLOS stipulates that innocent passage does exist when baselines with a cut-off effect have been newly drawn.[28]

From a legal point of view, therefore, innocent passage for vessels to and from Neum does exist. Still, politically, the Croatian straight baselines may be seen as disregarding the existence of Bosnia-Herzegovina as a riparian State to the Adriatic altogether. BiH has informed Croatia on several occasions between 2007 and 2010[29] that it does not recognise Croatia's baselines between the Vodnjak island and Cape

[28] Art. 8(2) UNCLOS: "Where the establishment of a straight baseline [...] has the effect of enclosing as internal waters areas which had not previously been considered as such, a right of innocent passage [...] shall exist in those waters". In its 1994 Maritime Code, Croatia took over the straight baseline system of the former SFRY. Legally, one can argue that these baselines were created *de novo* after the dissolution of the former Yugoslavia.

[29] *Inter alia* at a meeting of the Presidency of Bosnia-Herzegovina and the Prime Minister of Croatia on 29 March 2007 in Sarajevo and through a diplomatic note from Bosnia and Herzegovina to Croatia from 23 April 2009.

Proizd, nor any internal waters that those baselines purport to create (Arnaut 2014: 165–167; interview Damir Arnaut, 07-05-2019).

As a solution, Bosnia and Herzegovina aim at a corridor or junction safeguarding the freedom of navigation between the BiH territorial sea and the high seas in the Adriatic (see letter from Denis Zvizdić to Andrej Plenković, 6 September 2017). In practical terms, Sarajevo envisages "something similar to the Junction Area [...] between Croatia and Slovenia, or the corridor negotiated between Monaco and France"[30] (interview BiH Presidency official, 11-05-2019). Regardless of a general trend to entertain a bilateral conflict for domestic reasons (interview Antonija Petričušić, 21-11-2019), the above notion also commands some support amongst the Croatian law of the sea establishment: If there was a mutual spirit of good faith, the corridor regime from the Croatia–Slovenia arbitration award may well serve as a blueprint (interview Vladimir-Đuro Degan, 21-11-2019).

The issue of maritime access for Bosnia and Herzegovina was recently taken up in an official decision of the BiH Presidency, the only State organ entrusted with foreign policy decisions. In mid-July 2019, the unanimous "decision related to the construction of the Pelješac bridge"[31] raised, *inter alia*, the following points:

> (i) As there had not been an agreement between Croatia and Bosnia and Herzegovina prior to the construction of the bridge, the Presidency called for an immediate stop of the construction works;
>
> (ii) There had to be bilateral talks to solve the issue of maritime access for Bosnia and Herzegovina as currently the rights of BiH pertaining to UNCLOS were violated;
>
> (iii) BiH retained the right to initiate a conciliation procedure under Art. 284 UNCLOS[32] in the spirit of the peaceful settlement of disputes, or ultimately a judicial procedure before the International Tribunal of the Law of the Sea (ITLOS), if there was no answer on the part of Croatia within 30 days. (Decision of the Presidency of Bosnia and Herzegovina, 16 July 2019a).

The following day, however, the President of the Republika Srpska (RS) withdrew its consent on the grounds that the Presidency decision was hazardous to the interest of RS, and thereby annulled the decision. The reasons of the *ex-post* refusal included that

> (i) The Presidency decision damaged the reputation of Bosnia and Herzegovina as one would have had to react *before* the start of the construction of the bridge and not whilst the works were already underway;

---

[30]In a bilaterally negotiated maritime delimitation agreement between France and Monaco from 1984, Monaco was granted a corridor of territorial sea in order not to be cut-off the high seas. The delimitation method was *sui generis* and did not follow any established method of delimitation (Arnaut 2002: 50). A similar solution had been applied by Gambia and Senegal in 1975 (Khan 2019).

[31]For the Pelješac Bridge project, its implications on good-neighbourly relations, EU public procurement, and the role of China in the Western Balkans see Bickl (2020).

[32]The provisions of Art. 284 UNCLOS triggers a conciliation procedure where a commission draws up a report including recommendations within 12 months. The parties can accept or reject the recommendations.

(ii) The Presidency decision only focused on the maritime border with Croatia neglecting the open issue of the *land* border at Kostajnica, a fact that damaged the relations with Croatia;

(iii) There were no benefits for neither the RS nor BiH as a whole in blocking the completion of Pelješac bridge, not least because completion of the cross-border bridge at Gradiska ought not to be put at risk (Statement of the President of Republika Srpska, 17 July 2019).

Nevertheless, it must be noted, that with the annulled decision due to the unanimity requirement and the two-thirds vote in the RS Parliament backing the move of the RS President (Sarajevo Times, 24 July 2019), there is, as a result, neither an official call of the BiH Presidency on Croatia to enter into bilateral talks, nor the possibility to unilaterally initiate a dispute settlement procedure under UNCLOS or a judicial procedure before ITLOS. However, it remains to be seen whether and at what point in time unanimity in the BiH Presidency can be reached which would open up the opportunity to reach a final (presumably judicial) settlement of the issue of maritime access for Bosnia and Herzegovina. Nevertheless, there is a considerable lack of clarity that persists with regard to the freedom of navigation to and from Neum, and the issue of maritime access of Bosnia-Herzegovina ought to be tackled.

- It is recommended, therefore, that both parties addressed the issue by sitting down together bilaterally and seeking a solution in a good-neighbourly manner which would ensure that access to and from the territorial sea of Bosnia-Herzegovina is regarded unhindered in terms of Art. 8(2) UNCLOS.
- The issue of maritime access could be an opportunity also to resolve the minor differences on the exact course of the land border between Croatia and Bosnia-Herzegovina. As a result, this could lead to the eventual ratification of the 1999 State Border Treaty and thus provide for a more stable path to EU accession for Sarajevo.

6.4 EU Accession Must Become Truly Credible and Predictable

The 2020 Enlargement Strategy ("Enhancing the accession process – a credible EU perspective for the Western Balkans") may have been born out of a desire of some Member States to draw on the reversibility of the accession process (*negative* conditionality). However, the new methodology also incorporates *positive* conditionality in terms of a possibility of a phasing-in to EU policies or increased pre-accession funding if Candidate Countries are well on track with reforms (see Sect. 4.2.1.1).

6.4.1 *Credibility Through Real Stick-and-Carrot Responsiveness*

It is the joint responsibility of both the EU Commission and the Member States to provide for positive rewards wherever there is positive performance and to provide for negative rewards for negative performance by countries aspiring to membership. Candidate Countries must be assured that the enlargement process is credible. And the EU must take care of its own reliability and credibility.

(i) Positive rewards for positive reform achievements are a key factor. The EU must never repeat its conduct vis-à vis North Macedonia with regard to the opening of accession negotiations which was delayed by almost two years despite the fact that the country had successfully concluded and ratified a bilateral agreement with Greece over the change of the State's name, a dispute that had lasted for 25 years (see also Sect. 4.2.1.1).[33] Even in a best case scenario where all bilateral disputes can be overcome, there is still the huge task of meeting the EU *acquis*

[33]Macedonia and Greece have been at odds over the former Yugoslav Republic of Macedonia's State name since Skopje's independence in 1992 in the process of the dissolution of Yugoslavia. Essentially, the dispute is about ownership of Macedonia's "historic" cultural heritage, the land of Alexander the Great, and to what geographical extent the term "historic Macedonia" can be accurately applied (see e.g. Messineo 2012: 170–2). Greece, suspecting that the State name "Macedonia" implicitly carried a territorial claim to the Northern Greek province of Macedonia, vetoed the newly independent State's tentative name, so that Skopje could only join the UN under its provisional name Former Yugoslav Republic of Macedonia (FYROM) in 1993.
25 years of blockade included vetoing the start of EU accession negotiations with FYR Macedonia on the part of Greece since October 2009 when the European Commission had recommended the opening of accession negotiations for the first time (see, e.g. European Commission, Former Yugoslav Republic of Macedonia 2018 Report, 17 April 2018a: 4). In early 2018, however, rumours were spreading that bilateral talks had gathered fresh momentum and that the hitherto unthinkable, a bilateral agreement on Macedonia's State name, was within reach. On 17 June 2018, Prime Ministers Zaev (Macedonia) and Tsipras (Greece) indeed signed a bilateral agreement (New York Times, 17 June 2018). In the Preamble, there is talk of "underlining [the] strong will for mutual friendship, good neighbourliness and co-operative partnership", and also of "strengthening an atmosphere of trust and good-neighbourly relations [...] to put to rest permanently [...] irredentism and revisionism in any form". With regard to the future State name of FYR Macedonia, it was agreed to be "Republic of North Macedonia" (Art. 1(3)(a)). The nationality is referred to as "Macedonian/citizen of the Republic of North Macedonia" in all travel documents (Art. 1(3)(b)). Macedonia will ratify the Agreement and may decide to hold a referendum (Art. 4(a) and (c)). The name "North Macedonia" was already in the pipeline in 2008. Then Prime Minister Nikola Gruevski (VRMO) had offered that solution, but it was rejected by the Greek government on the grounds it still entailed "Macedonia" (interview Doris Pack, 03-12-2018).
The consultative referendum on 30 September 2018 did bring a very high percentage of approval. Yet, the quorum of 50% was clearly missed. During the referendum campaign, Prime Minister Zaev was strongly in favour, whereas President Ivanov had called the State name change "historical suicide" and campaigned for non-participation (Washington Post, 2 October 2018). Still, the government announced to go ahead with ratification of the referendum result regardless of the fact that at least 12 opposition MPs would be needed to reach the required two-thirds majority as the main opposition party VMRO abstained. At the end of a number of simple majority votes on the contents, the final implementation vote on the amendments to the constitution again required a two-third majority. Ratification did take place and was successfully concluded on 10 January 2019

and the political criteria. This means hard work for the Candidate Country, but also hard work for the European Commission and the Member States in being supportive in practice rather than just paying lip service.

(ii) In the same vein, the EU must not shy away from rewarding negative sanctions, either, when developments on the grounds clearly indicate backsliding, as is the case with Serbia and with Montenegro in the area of the rule of law, in particular freedom of expression and the media. The issue has become a major point of concern with both countries (European Commission report Serbia, 29 May 2019c: 29; European Commission report Serbia, 17 April 2018c: 25[34]; European Commission report Montenegro, 29 May 2019b: 27; European Commission report Montenegro, 17 April 2018b: 25–6[35]). Further, some Member States have pointed out a clear backtracking with regard to media freedom in Serbia and in Montenegro over the last few years (interview Member State H COELA civil servant, 16-07-2018; interview Member State I COELA civil servant, 12-07-2018).

The 2020 and 2019 Freedom House Reports for Serbia confirm these alarming findings. In 2019, for the first time, the country was no longer rated "free", but "partly free" due to a "deterioration in the conduct of elections [and] continued attempts by the government and allied media outlets to undermine independent journalists through legal harassment and smear campaigns [...]"[36] (Freedom in the World 2019 Serbia Report, Status Change Explanation). The 2020 Freedom House Report for

(New York Times, 11 January 2019). On 25 January 2019, the Greek parliament adopted the Prespa Agreement by 153 to 146 votes with the main opposition party ND voting against (ekathimerini.com, 25 January 2019). On 6 February 2019, North Macedonia signed the Accession Protocol to NATO and became member on 27 March 2020 (NATO, Relations with the Republic of North Macedonia, 30 March 2020).

[34]"Intimidation and violence against journalists remain a concern. There are numerous credible reports of verbal, physical attacks and attacks against property of journalists. In this respect, Serbia needs to [classify such attacks] as criminal or other type of offences and closely monitor their follow-up by the law enforcement authorities. Whilst several cases have been solved and some criminal charges have been filed, convictions are still rare. Serious efforts are needed to identify and prosecute those suspected of violating internet freedoms.".

[35]"Progress on addressing violence against journalists and media remains very limited, especially in dealing with old unsolved cases. Seven cases of attacks on journalists took place in 2017. Three of these cases resulted in misdemeanour proceedings, whilst in one case the authorities found no elements of criminal or minor offences. Criminal investigations into old cases, including the 2004 murder of an editor-in-chief, continue to be ineffective and the authorities have so far failed to step up and prioritise efforts to solve these cases. In October 2017, a first-instance court awarded compensation to a journalist for lack of effective investigation into an attempt on his life in 2007. In the same case, in November 2017 the Constitutional Court awarded the journalist additional compensation. Protection offered to the same journalist was withdrawn based on the assessment that the threat was no longer imminent. There have also been reports of undue pressure on journalists by law enforcement to disclose their sources.".

[36]The Freedom House 2019 assessment of Serbia on the issue of "free and independent media": "Despite a constitution that guarantees freedom of the press and a penal code that does not treat libel as a criminal offence, media freedom is undermined by the threat of lawsuits or criminal charges against journalists for other offences, lack of transparency in media ownership, editorial pressure from politicians and politically connected media owners, and high rates of self-censorship. The

Serbia maintains the status of "partly free" with the overall freedom rating at 66/100 slightly down compared to 67/100 in 2019. As for Montenegro, Freedom House has rated the country "partly free" already since 2017 (69/100). The overall freedom rating for Montenegro has been decreasing since and is at 62/100 in 2020.

- The EU must be consistent and regain credibility by treating all Candidate Countries on their real individual merits, positive or negative. As a consequence, conditional increase or cuts in pre-accession funds or further action should be considered and implemented with immediate effect. The new 2020 Enlargement Strategy must be taken at face value, and the European Commission and the Member States have to find an operational modus vivendi to implement this new approach in a credible manner. The EU has lost a fair amount of its credibility in the Western Balkans. It has to regain it. If Europe fails, it will lose the countries in the region to other international players, such as China, Russia, Turkey, the USA, and the Gulf States, all of whom have pursued their interests more vigorously in recent years.

6.4.2 *Unanimity Cannot Be Scrapped*

It is one thing to consider introducing qualified majority voting (QMV) at the operational level of EU foreign policy, and proposals have indeed been presented to that end (see European Commission, Qualified majority voting: a tool to make Europe's Foreign and Security Policy more effective, 12 September 2018d). One could even argue, in theory, that majority voting when deciding on the start of accession negotiations or on the final take-in of new EU members would abolish the "nasty" veto power of individual Member States.

However, EU accession must rely on unanimity simply because majority voting in the area of club membership would not only destroy the internal cohesion of the EU, but it would also take away any incentive to overcome bilateral disputes prior to accession and would thus result in chaos. Scrapping unanimity at the operational level of accession negotiations (COELA or even the IGCs) would not make sense either given that at the end of the process the ratification of accession treaties in the Member States would become an incalculable risk—and may have the potential to destroy the process of EU enlargement altogether.

state and ruling party exercise influence over private media in part through advertising contracts and other indirect subsidies. Whilst many outlets take a pro-government line or avoid criticism of the leadership, some continue to produce independent coverage. A number of critical journalists and outlets faced smear campaigns, punitive tax inspections, and other forms of pressure in 2018. According to NUNS, there were 102 media freedom violations against journalists during the year. They included physical assaults, though most incidents involved aggressive rhetoric and other forms of pressure or intimidation. In December 2018, investigative reporter Milan Jovanović, who has reported extensively on corruption, was the victim of an arson attack in which unknown assailants threw a Molotov cocktail into his home.".

Interviews

Arnaut, Dr. Damir. MP for Bosnia-Herzegovina. Member of the Parliamentary Assembly of the Council of Europe. Ambassador of Bosnia-Herzegovina to Australia and New Zealand 2010–2014. E-mail interview, 07 May 2019.
Asselborn, Jean. Minister for Foreign Affairs of Luxemburg since 2004. E-mail interview. 28 September 2016.
Brey, Dr. Thomas. Former dpa correspondent Southeast Europe. Head of dpa Southeast Europe 2004–2018. E-mail interview, 10 January 2019.
Degan, Dr. Vladimir-Đuro. Professor emeritus. Director Adriatic Institute, Zagreb. Zagreb, 21 November 2019.
European Commission DG REGIO senior civil servant. Brussels, 04 May 2018.
European Commission senior civil servant. Brussels, 29 November 2018.
Fajon, Tanja. MEP. Chair European Parliament Delegation with Serbia. European Parliament Rapporteur for EU visa liberalisation with Serbia, Kosovo, Bosnia-Herzegovina, Montenegro, North Macedonia and Albania 2014–2019. Brussels, 23 January 2019.
ICTY war crime prosecution expert. The Hague, 31 March 2017.
Jović, Dr. Dejan. Professor for International Relations, Zagreb University. Zagreb, 02 November 2017.
Kukan, Eduard. MEP 2009–2019. Chair European Parliament Delegation with Serbia 2014–2019. Foreign Minister of Slovakia 1998–2006. Strasburg, 27 September 2017.
McAllister, David. MEP. Chair of the Foreign Affairs Committee of the European Parliament. European Parliament Rapporteur for Serbia 2014–2019. Brussels, 15 January 2019.
Member State D civil servant. COELA member 2016/2017. Brussels, 15 November 2016.
Member State E civil servant. COELA member 2016. Brussels, 21 October 2016.
Member State F civil servant. COELA member 2016. Brussels, 15 November 2016.
Member State H civil servant. COELA member 2017/2018. Brussels, 16 July 2018.
Member State I civil servant. COELA member 2017/2018. Brussels, 12 July 2018.
Miščević, Dr. Tanja. Chief Negotiator of Serbia for EU accession 2013–2019. Professor for International Relations and European Integration, Belgrade University. Brussels, 28 November 2016.
Pack, Doris. MEP 1989–2014, MP 1974–1989. European Parliament Rapporteur *inter alia* on Bosnia-Herzegovina, Macedonia, and Kosovo. Chair of the European Parliament Delegation with Southeast Europe 2004–2009. Brussels, 03 December 2018.
Petričušić, Dr. Antonija. Assistant professor at the Chair of Sociology, Faculty of Law, Zagreb University. Zagreb, 21 November 2019.
Presidency of Bosnia and Herzegovina official. Phone interview, 11 May 2019.
Radulović, Vladimir. Ambassador of Montenegro to the Benelux States. Brussels, 20 April 2018.
Sanader, Dr. Ivo. Prime Minister of Croatia 2003–2009. Deputy Foreign Minister 1993–2000. Zagreb, 02 November 2017.
Senior Croatian civil servant. Zagreb, 25 January 2017.
Tomanić, Aleksandra. Executive Director European Fund for the Balkans, Belgrade. E-mail interview, 05 May 2020.

References

Amnesty International. (2012). *Universal jurisdiction. A preliminary survey of legislation around the world—2012 update.* London: Amnesty International.
Arnaut, D. (2002). Stormy waters on the way to the high seas: The case of the territorial sea delimitation between Croatia and Slovenia. *Ocean and Coastal Law Journal, 8*(1), 21–70.

Arnaut, D. (2014). Adriatic Blues: Delimiting the former Yugoslavia's final frontier. In C. Schofield, S. Lee, & M.-S. Kwon (Eds.), *The limits of maritime jurisdiction* (pp. 145–173). Leiden and Boston: Martinus Nijhoff.

BETA news. (2020, September 17). Lajčak: New round of expert talks complete, to be continued.

BETA News. (2008, March 22). Đukanović: Montenegro owes Croatia nothing.

Bickl, T. (2020). Bridge over troubled waters: The Pelješac Project, China, and the implications for good-neighbourly relations and the EU. *Politička Misao, 56*(3–4), 50–78. https://doi.org/10.20901/pm.56.3-4.03. Accessed April 20, 2020.

Bundesrepublik Deutschland. Bundesgesetzblatt. (2016, June 3). Gesetz zu dem Vertrag vom 24. Oktober 2014 zwischen der Bundesrepublik Deutschland und dem Königreich der Niederlande über die Nutzung und Verwaltung des Küstenmeers zwischen 3 und 12 Seemeilen. https://www.bgbl.de/xaver/bgbl/start.xav?start=%2F%2F%5B%40attr-id%3D%27bgbl216015.pdf%27%5D-bgbl-%2F%2F%5B%40attr-id%3D%27bgbl216s0602.pdf%27%5D-1550320509585. Accessed April 18, 2020.

Council of Ministers of Bosnia and Herzegovina. (2017, September 6). Letter from the chairman of the council of ministers of Bosnia and Herzegovina to the prime minister of Croatia.

Council of the European Union. (2015, November 25). EU common position on Serbia, Chapter 35, item 1. Normalisation of Relations between Serbia and Kosovo.

Council of the European Union. (2016, July 5). EU common position on Serbia for Chapter 23.

Demjaha, A. (2020). Kosovo's strategy for recognition and engagement. In J. Armakolas & J. Ker-Lindsay (Eds.), *The politics of recognition and engagement* (pp. 19–40). Cham: Springer.

Đilas, M. (1985). *Rise and fall*. San Diego: Harcourt Brace Jovanovich.

Dimitrijević, D. (2012). A review of the issue of the border between Serbia and Croatia on the Danube. *Megatrend Review, 9*(3), 1–22.

Dimishkovski, A., & Santora, M. (2019, January 11). Macedonia votes to change its name, taking step to end dispute with Greece. *New York Times*. https://www.nytimes.com/2019/01/11/world/europe/macedonia-greece-name-change.html. Accessed April 18, 2020.

Draft Comprehensive Agreement between Republic of Kosovo and Republic of Serbia. (2018, December). https://www.peacefare.net/wp-content/uploads/2018/12/DRAFT-Comprehensive-Agreement-between-Republic-of-Kosovo-and-Republic-of-Serbia-2018-12-12-v7.pdf. Accessed April 29, 2020.

Dumberry, P. (2015). State succession to bilateral treaties: A few observations on the incoherent and unjustifiable solution adopted for secession and dissolution of states under the 1978 Vienna convention. *Leiden Journal of International Law, 28*(1), 13–30.

European Commission. (2015, January 29). Letter to Marijana Petir MEP.

European Commission. (2016, February). Non-paper on Croatian argumentaire for repealing relevant articles of the Serbian ZORZ.

European Commission. (2018a, April 17). Former Yugoslav Republic of Macedonia 2018 report. https://ec.europa.eu/neighbourhood-enlargement/sites/near/files/20180417-the-former-yugoslav-republic-of-macedonia-report.pdf. Accessed April 18, 2020.

European Commission. (2018b, April 17). Montenegro 2018 report. https://ec.europa.eu/neighbourhood-enlargement/sites/near/files/20180417-montenegro-report.pdf. Accessed April 19, 2020.

European Commission. (2018c, April 17). Serbia 2018 report. https://ec.europa.eu/neighbourhood-enlargement/sites/near/files/20180417-serbia-report.pdf. Accessed April 19, 2020.

European Commission. (2018d, September 12). Qualified majority voting: A tool to make Europe's Foreign and Security Policy more effective. https://ec.europa.eu/commission/publications/qualified-majority-voting-tool-make-europes-foreign-and-security-policy-more-effective_en. Accessed April 20, 2020.

European Commission. (2019a, May). Analytical report accompanying the document communication from the commission to the European Parliament and the council: Commission opinion on Bosnia and Herzegovina's application for membership of the European Union. https://ec.europa.eu/neighbourhood-enlargement/sites/near/files/20190529-bosnia-and-herzegovina-analytical-report.pdf. Accessed April 20, 2020.

European Commission. (2019b, May 29). Montenegro 2019 report. https://ec.europa.eu/neighbourhood-enlargement/sites/near/files/20190529-montenegro-report.pdf. Accessed April 19, 2020.

European Commission. (2019c, May 29). Serbia 2019 report. https://ec.europa.eu/neighbourhood-enlargement/sites/near/files/20190529-serbia-report.pdf; https://ec.europa.eu/neighbourhood-enlargement/sites/near/files/20190529-serbia-report.pdf. Accessed April 19, 2020.

European Commission. (2020, February 5). Enhancing the accession process—A credible EU perspective for the Western Balkans. COM 57. https://ec.europa.eu/neighbourhood-enlargement/sites/near/files/enlargement-methodology_en.pdf. Accessed April 10, 2020.

European Parliament. (2016, February 4). Resolution on the 2015 [European Commission] report on Serbia. https://www.europarl.europa.eu/sides/getDoc.do?pubRef=-//EP//TEXT+TA+P8-TA-2016-0046+0+DOC+XML+V0//EN. Accessed April 19, 2020.

Ekathimerini. (2019, January 25). Greek PM hails ratification of Prespes deal. https://www.ekathimerini.com/237003/article/ekathimerini/news/greek-pm-hails-ratification-of-prespes-deal. Accessed April 18, 2020.

Freedom House. (2019a). 2019 Montenegro country report. https://freedomhouse.org/country/montenegro/freedom-world/2019. Accessed April 20, 2020.

Freedom House. (2019b). 2019 Serbia country report. https://freedomhouse.org/report/freedom-world/2019/serbia. Accessed April 18, 2020.

Freedom House. (2020a). 2020 Montenegro country report. https://freedomhouse.org/country/montenegro/freedom-world/2020. Accessed May 07, 2020.

Freedom House. (2020b). 2020 Serbia country report. https://freedomhouse.org/country/serbia/freedom-world/2020. Accessed May 07, 2020.

Government of the Republic of Serbia. (2015). *Comments on the request for abolition of universal jurisdiction of Serbian authorities with regard to war crimes* (unpublished).

Government of the Republic of Serbia. (2016). Negotiating Position of the Republic of Serbia for Inter-Governmental Conference on Accession of the Republic of Serbia to the European Union for Chapter 23 Judiciary and Fundamental Rights.

Grbec, M. (2015). *Extension of coastal state jurisdiction in enclosed and semi-enclosed seas—A Mediterranean and Adriatic perspective.* London and New York: Routledge.

Guardia Costiera. (2016). Analysis of traffic monitoring systems—The marine casualties. https://www.guardiacostiera.gov.it/mezzi-e-tecnologie/Documents/MRS%20Adriatic%20Traffic/Easyconnecting_4.4_Marine%20casualties%20v1.1.pdf. Accessed April 18, 2020.

Hovell, D. (2018). The authority of universal jurisdiction. *European Journal of International Law, 29*(2), 427–456.

Huszka, B. (2020, January 7). The power of perspective: Why EU membership still matters in the Western Balkans. European Council on Foreign Relations Policy Brief. https://www.ecfr.eu/publications/summary/the_power_of_perspective_why_eu_membership_still_matters_in_western_balkans. Accessed April 19, 2020.

International Maritime Organisation. (2004, May 28). Traffic separation scheme Northern Adriatic. COLREG.2/Circ.54, Annex III.

Ker-Lindsay, J., & Armakolas, I. (2020). Kosovo, EU member states and the recognition-engagement nexus. In J. Armakolas & J. Ker-Lindsay (Eds.), *The politics of recognition and engagement* (pp. 1–18). Cham: Springer.

Kitsanonis, N. (2018, June 17). Macedonia and Greece sign historic deal on name change. *New York Times*. https://www.nytimes.com/2018/06/17/world/europe/greece-macedonia-name-dispute.html. Accessed April 20, 2020.

Khan, M. (2019). *The Gambia-Senegal border. Issues in regional integration.* New York: Routledge.

Klemenčić, M., & Schofield, C. (2001). War and peace on the Danube: The evolution of the Croatia-Serbia boundary. *Boundary and Territory Briefing, 3*(3), 1–65.

Klemenčić, M., & Topalović, D. (2009). The maritime boundaries of the Adriatic Sea. *Geoadria, 14*(2), 311–324.

Messineo, F. (2012). Maps of Ephemeral Empires. The ICJ and the Macedonian name dispute. *Cambridge Journal of International and Comparative Law, 1*(1), 169–190.

Ministry of Foreign and European Affairs Croatia. (2016, April). The problems of Serbia's regional jurisdiction.
North Atlantic Treaty Organisation. (2020). Relations with the Republic of North Macedonia. https://www.nato.int/cps/en/natohq/topics_48830.htm. Accessed April 18, 2020.
Official Gazette of the Republic of Serbia, No. 67/2003. Law on the universal and regional war-crime jurisdiction. ZORZ. https://www.mpravde.gov.rs/files/Law%20on%20the%20Organisation%20and%20Competences%20of%20the%20Government%20Authorities%20in%20War%20Crimes%20Proceedings_180411.doc. Accessed April 19, 2020.
Orlandić, S. (2019). The EU's paternalistic approach to the integration of the Western Balkans—Border disputes as a new conditionality: Case of Prevlaka. *Romanian Journal of European Affairs, 19*(1), 79–96.
Permanent Court of Arbitration. (2017, June 29). *Croatia v Slovenia.* PCA Case No. 2012-04. Final Award. https://pcacases.com/web/sendAttach/2172. Accessed March 20, 2020.
Presidency of Bosnia and Herzegovina. (2019a, July 16). Decision on the Komarna-Pelješac bridge. 01-50-1-2685-4/19.
Presidency of Bosnia and Herzegovina. (2019b, July 2017). Statement of the President of Republika Srpska. 04-52-2753-1/19.
Protocol between the Federal Government of the Federal Republic of Yugoslavia and the Government of the Republic of Croatia on the Interim Regime along the Southern Border between the two States (2002, December 10).
Reba, M. (1999). *Croatia-Yugoslavia boundary on the River Danube* (M.A thesis). Durham: Institute for Geography, University of Durham.
Republic of Italy. Camera dei deputati (1985, November 18). No. 3289. Testo delle lettere. https://www.camera.it/_dati/leg09/lavori/stampati/pdf/32890001.pdf. Accessed April 18, 2020.
Republic of Montenegro. (2014a, December 1). Note verbale Ministry of Foreign Affairs to the UN Division for Ocean Affairs and the Law of the Sea, No. 09/16-167/121 [on Croatia's exploratory drillings in the preliminary territorial sea border area with Montenegro].
Republic of Montenegro. (2014b, July 2). Note verbale Ministry of Foreign Affairs to the UN Secretary General, No. 09/16-167/35 [on Croatia's exploratory drillings in the preliminary territorial sea border area with Montenegro].
Reuters News. (2018, November 21). Kosovo hits Serbia, Bosnia with 100 percent customs fees after Interpol snub.
Reuters News. (2020, September 4). Serbia, Kosovo agreed to normalize economic ties.
Sarajevo Times. (2019, July 24). BiH's Presidency to examine the question of the Peljesac Bridge and Croatia's plans for a nuclear waste site. https://www.sarajevotimes.com/bihs-presidency-to-examine-the-question-of-the-peljesac-bridge-and-croatias-plans-for-a-nuclear-waste-site/. Accessed April 20, 2020.
Šelo Šabić, S., & Borić, S. (2016). *Crossing over. A perspective on Croatian open border issues.* Zagreb: Friedrich-Ebert-Foundation.
Stojanović, D. (2018, September 10). Serbian president's praise of Milosevic triggers outrage. *Associated Press.*
Stojanović, M. (2020, September 7). Serbia, Kosovo 'Make Progress' on Wartime Missing Persons: Vučić. *Balkan Insight.* https://balkaninsight.com/2020/09/07/serbia-kosovo-make-progress-on-wartime-missing-persons-vucic/. Accessed September 19, 2020.
Thaaror, I. (2018, October 2). Macedonia's referendum makes things awkward for the West. *Washington Post.* https://www.washingtonpost.com/world/2018/10/02/macedonias-referendum-makes-things-awkward-west/?utm_term=.cac4b5848744. Accessed April 18, 2020.

Treaty on the State Border between the Republic of Croatia and Bosnia and Herzegovina. (1999, July 30). https://www.un.org/Depts/los/LEGISLATIONANDTREATIES/PDFFILES/TREATIES/HRV-BIH1999SB.PDF. Accessed April 19, 2020.

United Nations. (1978, August 23). Vienna convention on succession of states in respect of treaties. https://treaties.un.org/Pages/ViewDetails.aspx?src=IND&mtdsg_no=XXIII-2&chapter=23&clang=_en. Accessed April 20, 2020.

Vukas, B. (2008). Pomorski zakonik Republike Hrvatske i međunarodno pravo mora. *Zbornik Pravnog Fakulteta u Zagrebu, 58*(1–2), 181–204.

Appendix A

PCA CASE NO. 2012-04

IN THE MATTER OF AN ARBITRATION UNDER THE ARBITRATION AGREEMENT BETWEEN THE GOVERNMENT OF THE REPUBLIC OF CROATIA AND THE GOVERNMENT OF THE REPUBLIC OF SLOVENIA, SIGNED ON 4 NOVEMBER 2009

- between -

THE REPUBLIC OF CROATIA

- and -

THE REPUBLIC OF SLOVENIA

(together, the "Parties")

T. Bickl, *The Border Dispute Between Croatia and Slovenia*,
Contributions to Political Science,
https://doi.org/10.1007/978-3-030-53333-5

ANNEX TO THE FINAL AWARD

29 June 2017

ARBITRAL TRIBUNAL:
Judge Gilbert Guillaume (President)
Ambassador Rolf Einar Fife
Professor Vaughan Lowe
Professor Nicolas Michel
Judge Bruno Simma

REGISTRAR:
Dr. Dirk Pulkowski
The Permanent Court of Arbitration

PCA CASE NO. 2012-04

IN THE MATTER OF AN ARBITRATION UNDER THE ARBITRATION AGREEMENT BETWEEN THE GOVERNMENT OF THE REPUBLIC OF CROATIA AND THE GOVERNMENT OF THE REPUBLIC OF SLOVENIA, SIGNED ON 4 NOVEMBER 2009

- between -

THE REPUBLIC OF CROATIA

- and -

THE REPUBLIC OF SLOVENIA

(together, the "Parties")

ANNEX TO THE FINAL AWARD

29 June 2017

ARBITRAL TRIBUNAL:
Judge Gilbert Guillaume (President)
Ambassador Rolf Einar Fife
Professor Vaughan Lowe
Professor Nicolas Michel
Judge Bruno Simma

REGISTRAR:
Dr. Dirk Pulkowski
The Permanent Court of Arbitration

Annex HRLA-75

ARBITRATION AGREEMENT
between the Government of the Republic of Croatia
and the Government of the Republic of Slovenia

The Governments of the Republic of Croatia and the Republic of Slovenia (hereinafter referred to as "the Parties"),

Whereas through numerous attempts the Parties have not resolved their territorial and maritime border dispute in the course of the past years,

Recalling the peaceful means for the settlement of disputes enumerated in Article 33 of the UN-Charter,

Affirming their commitment to a peaceful settlement of disputes, in the spirit of good neighbourly relations, reflecting their vital interests,

Welcoming the facilitation offered by the European Commission,

Have agreed as follows:

Article 1: Establishment of the Arbitral Tribunal

The Parties hereby set up an Arbitral Tribunal.

Article 2: Composition of the Arbitral Tribunal

(1) Both Parties shall appoint by common agreement the President of the Arbitral Tribunal and two members recognized for their competence in international law within fifteen days drawn from a list of candidates established by the President of the European Commission and the Member responsible for the enlargement of the European Commission. In case that they cannot agree within this delay, the President and the two members of the Arbitral Tribunal shall be appointed by the President of the International Court of Justice from the list.

(2) Each Party shall appoint a further member of the Arbitral Tribunal within fifteen days after the appointments referred to in paragraph 1 have been finalised. In case that no appointment has been made within this delay, the respective member shall be appointed by the President of the Arbitral Tribunal.

(3) If, whether before or after the proceedings have begun, a vacancy should occur on account of the death, incapacity or resignation of a member, it shall be filled in accordance with the procedure prescribed for the original appointment.

Annex HRLA-75

Article 3: Task of the Arbitral Tribunal

(1) The Arbitral Tribunal shall determine

(a) the course of the maritime and land boundary between the Republic of Croatia and the Republic of Slovenia;

(b) Slovenia's junction to the High Sea;

(c) the regime for the use of the relevant maritime areas.

(2) The Parties shall specify the details of the subject-matter of the dispute within one month. If they fail to do so, the Arbitral Tribunal shall use the submissions of the Parties for the determination of the exact scope of the maritime and territorial disputes and claims between the Parties.

(3) The Arbitral Tribunal shall render an award on the dispute.

(4) The Arbitral Tribunal has the power to interpret the present Agreement.

Article 4: Applicable Law

The Arbitral Tribunal shall apply

(a) the rules and principles of international law for the determinations referred to in Article 3 (1) (a);

(b) international law, equity and the principle of good neighbourly relations in order to achieve a fair and just result by taking into account all relevant circumstances for the determinations referred to in Article 3 (1) (b) and (c).

Article 5: Critical date

No document or action undertaken unilaterally by either side after 25 June 1991 shall be accorded legal significance for the tasks of the Arbitral Tribunal or commit either side of the dispute and cannot, in any way, prejudge the award.

Article 6: Procedure

(1) Each Party shall submit a memorial to the Arbitral Tribunal within twelve months. Each Party has the right to comment on the memorial of the other Party within a deadline fixed by the Arbitral Tribunal.

(2) Unless envisaged otherwise, the Arbitral Tribunal shall conduct the proceedings according to the Permanent Court of Arbitration Optional Rules for Arbitrating Disputes between Two States.

Annex HRLA-75

(3) The Arbitral Tribunal may seek expert advice and organize oral hearings.

(4) The Arbitral Tribunal shall, after consultation of the Parties, decide expeditiously on all procedural matters by majority of its members.

(5) The proceedings are confidential and shall be conducted in English.

(6) The Parties shall appoint representatives to act as intermediary between them and the Arbitral Tribunal. They may retain counsels to support their representative.

(7) The Arbitral Tribunal shall be supported by a Secretariat. The costs of the Arbitral Tribunal shall be borne in equal terms by the two Parties. The Parties invite the European Commission to provide secretarial support to the Arbitral Tribunal. The place of arbitration shall be Brussels, Belgium.

(8) The Arbitration Tribunal may at any stage of the procedure with the consent of both Parties assist them in reaching a friendly settlement.

Article 7: The award of the Arbitral Tribunal

(1) The Arbitral Tribunal shall issue its award expeditiously after due consideration of all relevant facts pertinent to the case. The Arbitral Tribunal adopts the award by majority of its members. The award shall state the reasons on which it is based. No individual or dissenting opinions shall be attached to the award.

(2) The award of the Arbitral Tribunal shall be binding on the Parties and shall constitute a definitive settlement of the dispute.

(3) The Parties shall take all necessary steps to implement the award, including by revising national legislation, as necessary, within six months after the adoption of the award.

Article 8: EU accession negotiation documents

(1) No document presented in the EU accession negotiations unilaterally shall prejudice the Arbitral Tribunal when performing its tasks or commit either side on the dispute.

(2) The above applies to all documents and positions either written or submitted orally, including, *inter alia*, maps, negotiating positions, legal acts and other documents in whatever form, produced, presented or referred to unilaterally in the framework of the EU accession negptiations. It also applies to all EU documents and positions which refer to or summarize the above-mentioned documents and positions.

Annex HRLA-75

Article 9: The continuation of the EU accession negotiations according to the negotiating framework

(1) The Republic of Slovenia shall lift its reservations as regards opening and closing of negotiation chapters where the obstacle is related to the dispute.

(2) Both Parties shall refrain from any action or statement which might negatively affect the accession negotiations.

Article 10: Stand-still

(1) Both Parties refrain from any action or statement which might intensify the dispute or jeopardize the work of the Arbitral Tribunal.

(2) The Arbitral Tribunal has the power to order, if it considers that circumstances so require, any provisional measures it deems necessary to preserve the stand-still.

Article 11

(1) The Agreement shall be ratified expeditiously by both sides in accordance with their respective constitutional requirements.

(2) The Agreement shall enter into force on the first day of the week following the exchange of diplomatic notes with which the Parties express their consent to be bound.

(3) All procedural timelines expressed in this Agreement shall start to apply from the date of the signature of Croatia's EU Accession Treaty.

(4) The Agreement shall be registered with the Secretariat of the United Nations in accordance with Article 102 of the Charter of the United Nations.

Done at Stockholm, on 4 November 2009 in three originals in English language.

Signed by

For the Government of the Republic of Croatia

For the Government of the Republic of Slovenia

Witnessed by

For the Presidency of the Council of the European Union

SI-395

ARBITRATION AGREEMENT
between the Government of the Republic of Slovenia and the Government of the Republic of Croatia

The Governments of the Republic of Slovenia and the Republic of Croatia (hereinafter referred to as "the Parties"),

Whereas through numerous attempts the Parties have not resolved their territorial and maritime border dispute in the course of the past years,

Recalling the peaceful means for the settlement of disputes enumerated in Article 33 of the UN-Charter,

Affirming their commitment to a peaceful settlement of disputes, in the spirit of good neighbourly relations, reflecting their vital interests,

Welcoming the facilitation offered by the European Commission,

Have agreed as follows:

Article 1: Establishment of the Arbitral Tribunal

The Parties hereby set up an Arbitral Tribunal.

Article 2: Composition of the Arbitral Tribunal

(1) Both Parties shall appoint by common agreement the President of the Arbitral Tribunal and two members recognized for their competence in international law within fifteen days drawn from a list of candidates established by the President of the European Commission and the Member responsible for the enlargement of the European Commission. In case that they cannot agree within this delay, the President and the two members of the Arbitral Tribunal shall be appointed by the President of the International Court of Justice from the list.

(2) Each Party shall appoint a further member of the Arbitral Tribunal within fifteen days after the appointments referred to in paragraph 1 have been finalised. In case that no appointment has been made within this delay, the respective member shall be appointed by the President of the Arbitral Tribunal.

(3) If, whether before or after the proceedings have begun, a vacancy should occur on account of the death, incapacity or resignation of a member, it shall be filled in accordance with the procedure prescribed for the original appointment.

Article 3: Task of the Arbitral Tribunal

(1) The Arbitral Tribunal shall determine

(a) the course of the maritime and land boundary between the Republic of Slovenia and the Republic of Croatia;

(b) Slovenia's junction to the High Sea;

(c) the regime for the use of the relevant maritime areas.

(2) The Parties shall specify the details of the subject-matter of the dispute within one month. If they fail to do so, the Arbitral Tribunal shall use the submissions of the Parties for the determination of the exact scope of the maritime and territorial disputes and claims between the Parties.

(3) The Arbitral Tribunal shall render an award on the dispute.

(4) The Arbitral Tribunal has the power to interpret the present Agreement.

Article 4: Applicable Law

The Arbitral Tribunal shall apply

(a) the rules and principles of international law for the determinations referred to in Article 3 (1) (a);

(b) international law, equity and the principle of good neighbourly relations in order to achieve a fair and just result by taking into account all relevant circumstances for the determinations referred to in Article 3 (1) (b) and (c).

Article 5: Critical date

No document or action undertaken unilaterally by either side after 25 June 1991 shall be accorded legal significance for the tasks of the Arbitral Tribunal or commit either side of the dispute and cannot, in any way, prejudge the award.

Article 6: Procedure

(1) Each Party shall submit a memorial to the Arbitral Tribunal within twelve months. Each Party has the right to comment on the memorial of the other Party within a deadline fixed by the Arbitral Tribunal.

(2) Unless envisaged otherwise, the Arbitral Tribunal shall conduct the proceedings according to the Permanent Court of Arbitration Optional Rules for Arbitrating Disputes between Two States.

(3) The Arbitral Tribunal may seek expert advice and organize oral hearings. **SI-395**

(4) The Arbitral Tribunal shall, after consultation of the Parties, decide expeditiously on all procedural matters by majority of its members.

(5) The proceedings are confidential and shall be conducted in English.

(6) The Parties shall appoint representatives to act as intermediary between them and the Arbitral Tribunal. They may retain counsels to support their representative.

(7) The Arbitral Tribunal shall be supported by a Secretariat. The costs of the Arbitral Tribunal shall be borne in equal terms by the two Parties. The Parties invite the European Commission to provide secretarial support to the Arbitral Tribunal. The place of arbitration shall be Brussels, Belgium.

(8) The Arbitration Tribunal may at any stage of the procedure with the consent of both Parties assist them in reaching a friendly settlement.

Article 7: The award of the Arbitral Tribunal

(1) The Arbitral Tribunal shall issue its award expeditiously after due consideration of all relevant facts pertinent to the case. The Arbitral Tribunal adopts the award by majority of its members. The award shall state the reasons on which it is based. No individual or dissenting opinions shall be attached to the award.

(2) The award of the Arbitral Tribunal shall be binding on the Parties and shall constitute a definitive settlement of the dispute.

(3) The Parties shall take all necessary steps to implement the award, including by revising national legislation, as necessary, within six months after the adoption of the award.

Article 8: EU accession negotiation documents

(1) No document presented in the EU accession negotiations unilaterally shall prejudice the Arbitral Tribunal when performing its tasks or commit either side on the dispute.

(2) The above applies to all documents and positions either written or submitted orally, including, *inter alia*, maps, negotiating positions, legal acts and other documents in whatever form, produced, presented or referred to unilaterally in the framework of the EU accession negotiations. It also applies to all EU documents and positions which refer to or summarize the above-mentioned documents and positions.

Article 9: The continuation of the EU accession negotiations according to the negotiating framework

(1) The Republic of Slovenia shall lift its reservations as regards opening and closing of negotiation chapters where the obstacle is related to the dispute.

(2) Both Parties shall refrain from any action or statement which might negatively affect the accession negotiations.

Article 10: Stand-still

(1) Both Parties refrain from any action or statement which might intensify the dispute or jeopardize the work of the Arbitral Tribunal.

(2) The Arbitral Tribunal has the power to order, if it considers that circumstances so require, any provisional measures it deems necessary to preserve the stand-still.

Article 11

(1) The Agreement shall be ratified expeditiously by both sides in accordance with their respective constitutional requirements.

(2) The Agreement shall enter into force on the first day of the week following the exchange of diplomatic notes with which the Parties express their consent to be bound.

(3) All procedural timelines expressed in this Agreement shall start to apply from the date of the signature of Croatia's EU Accession Treaty.

(4) The Agreement shall be registered with the Secretariat of the United Nations in accordance with Article 102 of the Charter of the United Nations.

Done at Stockholm, on 4 November 2009 in three originals in English language.

Signed by

For the Government of the Republic of Slovenia

For the Government of the Republic of Croatia

Witnessed by

For the Presidency of the Council of the European Union

Appendix B

©Ministry of Foreign and European Affairs Republic of Croatia

PERMANENT MISSION OF THE REPUBLIC OF CROATIA TO THE UNITED NATIONS

820 Second Avenue, 19th Floor
New York, N.Y. 10017 USA

Tel: (212) 986-1585
Fax: (212) 986-2011

No. 55/2016

The Permanent Mission of the Republic of Croatia to the United Nations presents its compliments to the Permanent Missions and Permanent Observer Missions accredited to the United Nations and with reference to the arbitration between Croatia and Slovenia to resolve the two states' territorial and maritime border dispute at an *ad hoc* Arbitral Tribunal, has the honour to state the following position of the Croatian Government:

By its actions, the Republic of Slovenia has caused irreparable harm to the arbitration process and the work of the Arbitral Tribunal, committing at the same time material breach of the Arbitration Agreement. The Republic of Croatia, in order to protect its legitimate interests and rights, reacted to the breach by ceasing to apply the Arbitration Agreement and initiating its termination. The Republic of Croatia expects that the Arbitral Tribunal terminates its work without delay and expresses its willingness to work with the Republic of Slovenia in the spirit of good neighbourly relations to resolve the matter in accordance with international law.

The Arbitration Agreement between the Government of the Republic of Croatia and the Government of the Republic of Slovenia was signed on 4 November 2009. It entered into force on 29 November 2010. Following the appointment of the President of the Arbitral Tribunal and its members, the two States submitted three rounds of written pleadings – on 11 February 2013, 11 November 2013 and on 26 March 2014. Oral hearings were held in The Hague from 2 to 13 June 2014.

T. Bickl, *The Border Dispute Between Croatia and Slovenia*, Contributions to Political Science, https://doi.org/10.1007/978-3-030-53333-5

Throughout the proceedings Croatia has acted in good faith in carrying out and respecting all obligations under the Arbitration Agreement. Croatia invested significant resources to ensure that the proceedings would succeed and bring about a final determination of the state border between the two States. On the other hand, Slovenia has clearly breached the provisions of the Arbitration Agreement and undermined the role, the trustworthiness and the authority of the Arbitral Tribunal. Slovenia has irrevocably corrupted the proceedings and the sound administration of justice. As a result, the process has been fundamentally tainted and no award issued under these legally and ethically completely compromised proceedings could be considered as effective, authoritative or credible.

Permanent Missions and Permanent Observer Missions
to the United Nations
New York

This first indication of Slovenia's regrettable actions came as early as in February 2013, when the Slovenian Parliament, in authorising Slovenia's first written submission in the arbitration, adopted a public decision with the effect that Slovenia would not recognize an award that did not meet its expectations. (In express terms, Slovenia's parliamentary decision stated that Slovenia "will consider any decision of the (...) Tribunal that would not ensure [its] territorial contact (...) with the High Seas (...) as a decision ultra vires (in violation of the mandate of the Arbitral Tribunal).") This decision, while indicative of Slovenia's further intentions, was for all intents and purposes a negation of the Arbitration Agreement.

In April 2015, following reports throughout the Slovenian media that Slovenia had "unofficial" information about the Tribunal's award and that it had communicated certain messages to the Tribunal, which were not found in the official verbatim of the proceedings, Croatia approached the Arbitral Tribunal and informed it of its concerns that Slovenia might have a "separate channel" of communication with the Tribunal. The Tribunal investigated the matter and assured Croatia that there were no reasons for concern.

In July 2015, in manifest contradiction with those assurances, recordings of telephone conversations between a member of the Arbitral Tribunal and the Agent of Slovenia were made public. Transcripts of recordings plainly revealed that confidential information about the Tribunal's deliberations had been disclosed to Slovenia and that Slovenia had been continuously and meticulously informed about internal deliberations of the Arbitral Tribunal. Further, the transcripts and recordings demonstrated that the Member of the Tribunal had requested the production of additional arguments and evidence from the Agent of Slovenia, that Slovenia had provided such arguments and evidence, and that these were then made available to the Tribunal. In this way, the factual record of the case was changed well after the closing of the oral hearings. The Member of the Tribunal and the Agent of Slovenia also colluded to conceal the true source of these documents and the Member of the Tribunal presented to the Arbitral Tribunal these documents, prepared by the Slovenian side, as being produced by himself, thus including them into the official records of the proceedings.

Slovenia has neither denied, nor challenged acts revealed by these recordings.

These actions have irrevocably tainted and irreparably damaged the entire process. It is impossible to conclude that the arbitrators have not been influenced by Slovenia's actions and by materials made available to them through the actions of the arbitrator serving as a conduit for Slovenia. The grave wrong that has occurred cannot be repaired by tinkering with the procedure, or merely replacing one or two arbitrators. The entire process has been profoundly and irreversibly corrupted and stripped of basic credibility and integrity required for third party dispute settlement.

Such conduct amounts to a repudiation of the Arbitration Agreement, and a rejection of the most fundamental principles that govern the integrity of international proceedings such as this. Under international law, these acts, including those of the Agent of Slovenia, are directly attributable to Slovenia. In accordance with the Vienna Convention on the Law of Treaties, they constitute material breach of a treaty, entitling Croatia to seek its termination and suspend its operation.

Accordingly, and to protect its rights under international law, subsequent to a unanimous decision of the Croatian Parliament, on 30 July 2015 Croatia initiated the procedure to terminate the Arbitration Agreement, ceased to apply it and withdrew from the arbitration process. Slovenia objected and the question of termination of the Arbitration Agreement is to be resolved bilaterally "through the means indicated in article 33 of the Charter of the United Nations", as foreseen by the Vienna Convention on the Law of Treaties. The Convention also avails Croatia of another mechanism, i.e. conciliation, to resolve the question of termination of the Arbitration Agreement. Nevertheless, the Vienna Convention on the Law of Treaties does not provide a role for the Arbitral Tribunal in this process.

As for the arbitration process itself, Croatia submits that – to assure the sound administration of justice, and for legal and ethical reasons – the Arbitral Tribunal should terminate its work with immediate effect. An international adjudicatory process as tainted and compromised as this cannot reasonably continue in any form. Any award it might give would lack essential authority, and propel the parties to an interminable dispute. Such an award could never be implemented, or enforced. Consequently, any effort to continue this arbitration would be futile and counterproductive.

Immediate termination of these compromised proceedings is of paramount importance for peaceful settlement of disputes between states and the system of international adjudication as a whole, as it is for the bilateral relations between Croatia and Slovenia. It also has the potential of reassuring the many states with unresolved bilateral issues – in Southeast Europe and elsewhere – that their disputes shall indeed be resolved competently, independently and impartially, thus reaffirming their confidence in international adjudication that meets all appropriate legal and ethical standards. The adverse consequences of Slovenia's actions are widely recognised. In this context, Croatia notes that the prompt resignation of the President of the International Court of Justice (ICJ) from this Arbitral Tribunal confirms its concerns. The President of the ICJ, after initially accepting appointment by Slovenia to replace the Member of the Tribunal directly involved in the wrongdoing with the Agent of Slovenia – resigned on 3 August 2015, having served on the Tribunal for just six days. In resigning, he stated that he "agreed to be appointed to the Arbitral Tribunal (...) in the hope that this appointment would help restore confidence between the Parties and the Arbitral Tribunal and to allow the process to continue normally, with the consent of both Parties", but decided to resign when he came to appreciate that "the current situation cannot meet that expectation".

In December 2015, the Arbitral Tribunal requested further written submissions from the two States on the most recent developments and scheduled an additional oral hearing for 17 March 2016. Since Croatia withdrew from the proceedings, it did not formally react to these communiqués: it will not do so, and will not participate in the oral hearing. The Arbitral Tribunal is aware of Croatia's position. At the time when it initiated the termination of the Arbitration Agreement and ceased to apply it, Croatia provided the Tribunal with all the relevant information on the recent events, allowing it to decide on the termination of its work.

This arbitration cannot resolve the outstanding border issue between the two States. Croatia has invited Slovenia to discuss other modalities to settle the outstanding border issues in accordance with international law and in the spirit of good neighbourly relations stands ready to resolve the matter bilaterally, as many states have done so far, or refer it to a different international judicial body.

In the meantime, the border between the two States has existed as an international border for twenty-five years and normal everyday life of people living on both sides of the border functions well, with full local border cooperation. At sea, pursuant to the International Maritime Organization's navigational routes in the Northern Adriatic, all vessels enjoy unimpeded access to and from Slovenian ports, which register continuous rise in passenger and cargo throughput. The two States are members of the European Union and NATO. Therefore, there exist no pressing obstacles which should prevent the two States from creating conditions for a constructive exchange on the way forward, leaving behind a failed arbitration process which endangers their bilateral relations and the confidence of States in international adjudication.

The Permanent Mission of the Republic of Croatia to the United Nations avails itself of this opportunity to renew to the Permanent Missions and Permanent Observer Missions accredited to the United Nations the assurances of its highest consideration.

New York, 16 March 2016

Appendix C

TREATY BETWEEN THE REPUBLIC OF SLOVENIA AND THE REPUBLIC OF CROATIA ON THE COMMON STATE BORDER

The Republic of Slovenia and the Republic of Croatia (hereinafter referred to as "the Contracting Parties");

Convinced that peaceful cooperation and good neighbourly relations between the two states and their citizens are in the vital interest of both states, and that the agreements concluded thus far provide favourable conditions for the further development and strengthening of their mutual relations;

Respecting the principles of international law, in particular the inviolability of international borders and the protection of fundamental human rights and freedoms;

Proceeding from the Basic Constitutional Charter on the Sovereignty and Independence of the Republic of Slovenia of 25 June 1991 and the Constitutional Decision on Sovereignty and Independence of the Republic of Croatia of 25 June 1991;

Considering that the two states have no territorial claims towards each other;

Respecting the existing state borders;

T. Bickl, *The Border Dispute Between Croatia and Slovenia*, Contributions to Political Science,
https://doi.org/10.1007/978-3-030-53333-5

Have agreed as follows:

I SUBJECT OF THE TREATY

Article 1

SUBJECT OF THE TREATY

The subject of this Treaty is the determination of the maritime boundary and the establishment of the course of the land border between the Contracting Parties, as well as the principles of demarcation, maintenance and restoration of the state border.

Article 2

DEFINITION OF THE STATE BORDER

The state border between the Republic of Slovenia and the Republic of Croatia (hereinafter referred to as the "state border") is the surface perpendicular to the line of the border on the surface of the Earth dividing the territory of the two states, their air space, subsoil, and any above and underground structures and installations.

Article 3

LATERAL BORDER

1. The state border at sea between the Contracting Parties shall be determined as follows: The border shall run from the middle of the outfall of the Dragonja River into the sea from point A (Y 5.389.794, X 5.038.097; φ 45°28'43.3", λ 13°35'25.7")[*] and in a straight line to point B (Y 5.385.011, X 5.041.869; φ 45°30'42.7", λ 13°31'41.3"), representing one fourth of the distance between the northernmost points of the Savudrija and the Madona promontories measured from the northernmost point of the Savudrija promontory. The border shall run from point B along the parallel in the straight line through point B westwards to point C (Y 5.365.527, X 5.042.258; φ 45°30'42.7", λ 13°16'43.4"), located on the border determined in the Treaty between the Socialist Federal Republic of Yugoslavia and the Italian Republic, signed in Osimo (Ancona) on 10 November 1975, except at the point of junction of the territorial sea of the Republic of Slovenia with the high seas, as defined in Article 4 of this Treaty.

2. The map at a scale of 1:25,000, to which this description refers, is contained in Annex I.

3. Where the description of the state border does not correspond to the map, the verbal description shall prevail.

Article 4

JUNCTION OF THE TERRTTORIAL SEA OF THE REPUBLIC OF SLOVENIA WITH THE HIGH SEAS

1. The Contracting Parties agree that the sea surface limited with points Cl (Y 5.372.959, X 5.042.102; φ 45°30'42.7", λ 13°22'25.9"), C2 (Y 5.367.526, X 5.042.215; φ 45°30'42.7", λ13°18'15.5"), T5 (Y 5.360.404, X 5.035.862; φ 45°27'12.0", λ 13°12'54.0") and T6 (Y 5.361.377, X 5.031.764; φ 45°25'00.0", λ 13°13'42.9") shall be the high seas.

2. The width of the junction of the territorial sea of the Republic of Slovenia with the high seas shall equal the distance from point B referred to in Article 3, paragraph 1, of this Treaty, to the Madona promontory.

3. The map at a scale of 1:25,000, to which this description refers, is contained in Annex I.

4. Where the description of the state border does not correspond to the map, the verbal description shall prevail.

---

* The points are given in rectangular coordinates of Zone 5 of the Gauss-Krueger projection rounded off to 1 metre and in geographic coordinates based on the Bessel ellipsoid rounded off to 0.1".
The accuracy of the definition of the position of the points is 10 metres.

5. No sovereign rights may be acquired in relation to the water column under the sea surface referred to in paragraph 1 hereof. The Contracting Parties shall, in their mutual relations, refrain from exercising sovereign rights in the seabed and the relevant subsoil under the sea surface referred to in paragraph 1 hereof.

Article 5

JUNCTION BETWEEN THE TERRITORIAL SEA OF THE REPUBLIC OF CROATIA AND THE ITALIAN REPUBLIC

1. The Contracting Parties agree that the sea surface limited with points C (Y 5.365.527, X 5.042.258; φ 45°30'42.7", λ 13°16'43.4"), C2 (Y 5.367.526, X 5.042.215; φ 45°30'42.7", λ 13°18'15.5") and T5 (Y 5.360.404, X 5.035.862; φ 45°27'12.0", λ 13° 12'54.0") shall be the territorial sea of the Republic of Croatia.

2. The map at a scale of 1:25,000, to which this description refers, is contained in Annex I.

3. Where the description of the state border does not correspond to the map, the verbal description shall prevail.

III STATE BORDER ON LAND

Article 6

ESTABLISHMENT OF THE COURSE OF THE STATE BORDER

1. The state border on land between the Republic of Slovenia and the Republic of Croatia shall be the border between the Republic of Slovenia and the Republic of Croatia within the former Socialist Federal Republic of Yugoslavia, running from the tripoint between the Contracting Parties and the Republic of Hungary to the Adriatic Sea.

2. The state border on land between the Contracting Parties has been established as presented in the verbal description with coordinates contained in Annex II.

3. Maps nos. 1-47 at a scale of 1:25,000, referred to in the verbal description with coordinates under the foregoing paragraph are contained in Annex III.

4. Where the description of the state border does not correspond to the map, the map shall prevail.

Article 7

EXCHANGE OF AREAS

1. The Contracting Parties confirm that the exchange of areas, which occurred on the occasion of the consensual establishment of the course of the state border, is balanced.

2. The exchange of areas shall have no effect on any rights of natural or legal entities under the law of property and law of obligations with regard to land and other immovable property included in such an exchange. Holders of rights under the law of property and law of obligations shall use such property in accordance with a special agreement between the Contracting Parties.

Article 8

DEMARCATION OF THE COURSE OF THE STATE BORDER

1. The course of the state border on land shall be demarcated by joint bodies, as established by this Treaty, and in the manner defined in the instructions for the work of mixed technical groups.

2. The Contracting Parties shall, within the period of five years after the date of entry into force of this Treaty, measure, demarcate and mark the state border on the ground.

Article 9

PRINCIPLES OF DEMARCATION OF THE COURSE OF THE STATE BORDER

1. The demarcation of the state border on the ground shall be carried out with border markers directly on the border line or indirectly in the following ways:

(a) Single — directly on the border line or alternately on both sides of roads, channels and watercourses on the common state border;

(b) Double — at the beginnings and ends of roads, channels and watercourses on the common state border and in locations where the terrain does not allow placing markers directly on the border line;

(c) Triple — in cases where double border markers are not sufficient for a clear demarcation of the course of the state border.

2. Detailed provisions on demarcation shall be defined in accordance with the instructions referred to in Article 8, paragraph 1, of this Treaty.

Article 10

MAINTENANCE AND RESTORATION OF THE STATE BORDER

1. After the demarcation of the state border on the ground, the Contracting Parties undertake to regularly inspect, maintain and restore border markers in accordance with the instructions referred to in Article 8, paragraph 1, of this Treaty.

2. The Contracting Parties shall, in intervals not longer than five years, jointly inspect the condition of the border line and border markers, and, if necessary, restore the demarcation of the state border or additionally mark it. The five-year interval shall be calculated as of the date of the beginning of the last joint restoration.

Article 11

INALTERABILITY OF THE COURSE OF THE STATE BORDER

The established border line shall not change even in the case of changed courses of roads, channels or watercourses on the common state border.

Article 12

UNIFORMITY OF BORDER MARKERS

The course of the state border shall always be demarcated in a uniform and unequivocal manner. The border line and the belt along it shall be regularly maintained and restored. Any replacements of border markers and any activity undertaken shall be entered into documents relating to the border immediately.

Article 13

BELT ALONG THE BORDER LINE

1. The belt along the border line shall mean the area along the border line extending not more than 1.5 meters to both sides of the border line.

2. The Contracting Parties shall regularly clear and maintain the belt along the border line in accordance with the instructions referred to in Article 8, paragraph 1, of this Treaty.

Article 14

COSTS

The Contracting Parties shall ensure financial resources for demarcation, maintenance and restoration of the state border. The Contracting Parties shall adhere to the principle that each side shall carry out a comparable amount of work and bear an equal amount of costs.

Article 15

OBLIGATIONS OF OWNERS, USERS, ADMINISTRATORS AND OTHER HOLDERS OF RIGHTS UNDER THE LAW OF PROPERTY AND THE LAW OF OBLIGATIONS

1. Owners, users, administrators and other holders of rights under the law of property and the law of obligations on land, facilities and instillations situated on or in the vicinity of the state border must allow any works and measures that are necessary for the demarcation, measuring, maintenance, clearing and restoration of the state border, as well as grant access to any person carrying out these works. In performing such works the legitimate interests of owners, users, administrators and other holders of rights under the law of property and the law of obligations must be taken into account; they must be notified in advance about the beginning of these works.

2. In performing the works referred to in paragraph 1 hereof as well as in accessing or driving onto such land and towards such facilities and installations, the national legislation of the Contracting Party on whose territory these works are being carried out shall be respected.

Article 16

COMPENSATION FOR DAMAGE

Any damage resulting from the works referred to in Article 15, paragraph 1, of this Treaty shall be compensated for by the Contracting Party on whose territory such damage occurred. In filing claims for damages, the national legislation of the Contracting Party on whose territory such damage occurred shall be applied.

Article 17

TRIPOINT

Works relating to the demarcation, maintenance, clearing and restoration of the tripoint can only be carried out by mutual agreement of the three states.

Article 18

PROTECTION OF MARKERS

The Contracting Parties shall ensure the protection of border and geodetic markers and other equipment used in demarcation of the state border against damage, destruction, illicit displacement and any use that is inconsistent with their purpose.

IV JOINT REGIMES

Article 19

SPECIAL REGIMES AND MEASURES IN THE BORDER AREA

1. The Contracting Parties shall conclude special agreements on special regimes and measures in the border area, such as the use of transport connections for the needs of population and authorities of the Contracting Parties, and any other issues resulting from the established course of the state border.

2. The Contracting Parties engage to retain at least the present level of the protection of nature along the entire course of the state border and particularly in the protected areas, such as the nature reserves *Krajinski park Sečovlje* and *Park prirode Žumberak — Samoborsko gorje*, and to continue to develop mutual cooperation. The Contracting Parties shall ensure environmental regime complying with the highest environmental standards of the European Union along the entire course of the state border, particularly in the areas intended for the development of tourism.

3. The Contracting Parties engage to guarantee to each other the use of water sources in the border area at least to the present extent for a period of 30 years as of the date of the entry into force of this Treaty. The Contracting Parties shall conclude a special agreement on this issue within one year after the entry into force of this Treaty.

Article 20

BENEFITS OF THE INHABITANTS OF THE HAMLETS MLINI-ŠKRILE, BUŽINI AND ŠKODELIN

In addition to benefits provided for in the concluded agreements between the Contracting Parties for the border population, persons with permanent residence in the hamlets Mlini-Škrile, Bužini and Škodelin as at the date of the signing of this Treaty, shall have:

(a) The right, when returning from the neighbouring state, to bring with them, free of customs duties and import charges, goods of such type and in such quantity as appropriate for their personal use and for the use by the members of their households: the Contracting Parties shall conclude in this respect a separate implementing agreement within six months from the date of the entry into force of this Treaty;

(b) The right to acquire citizenship of the Republic of Slovenia.

V JOINT BODIES

Article 21

PERMANENT SLOVENIAN-CROATIAN COMMISSION FOR THE STATE BORDER

1. The Contracting Parties shall set up a Permanent Slovenian-Croatian Commission for the State Border (hereinafter referred to as "the Commission"), responsible for the implementation of the present Treaty.

2. The Commission shall be composed of the delegation of the Republic of Slovenia and the delegation of the Republic of Croatia. Each Contracting Party shall appoint a chairperson and five members to its part of the Commission. The Contracting Parties shall notify each other of the appointment and discharge from office of the chairperson and members of the Commission through diplomatic channels. The chairpersons shall notify each other in writing of any changes in the composition of the delegations.

3. Each delegation may engage experts and auxiliary staff in its work, if necessary.

4. The Contracting Parties shall cover the costs incurred by their respective delegations in the Commission.

Article 22

TASKS AND WORKING METHOD OF THE COMMISSION

1. The tasks of the Commission shall be:

(a) To decide on the manner of demarcation of the border line on the ground and to adopt instructions for the work of mixed technical groups;

(b) To organise and supervise the demarcation, maintenance, clearing and restoration of the entire border line on the ground;

(c) To draw up new and supplementary documents relating to the border and to enter new data in the applicable documents relating to the border;

(d) To propose changes to the state border, if necessary.

2. The Commission shall decide unanimously. If the Commission fails to adopt a decision, the matter shall be submitted to the governments of the Contracting Parties for settlement.

3. The working method of the Commission shall be defined in detail in its rules of procedure.

Article 23

MIXED TECHNICAL GROUPS

The Commission shall set up mixed technical groups to carry out certain works on the state border. Their number and composition shall be determined according to the scope and type of the work to be performed.

Article 24

DEVIATIONS

With the aim of the final demarcation of the course of the state border on the spot, the Commission may deviate for not more than 50 metres from the line determined by this Treaty, in order to adjust the state border to the local geographic and economic circumstances. However, no important road or railway track, important water or power supply facility, or property of historical or cultural significance may be placed under the jurisdiction of the state whose jurisdiction does not derive from the delimitation determined and established by this Treaty.

VI SETTLEMENT OF DISPUTES BETWEEN THE CONTRACTING PARTIES

Article 25

1. Any potential disputes between the Contracting Parties arising from the interpretation and application of this Treaty shall be settled through negotiations in accordance with the principle of good neighbourly relations.

2. Should the Contracting Parties be unable to reach an agreement within six months from the date of receiving the initiative for negotiations, the dispute shall be submitted for arbitration at the request of either Contracting Party.

3. The arbitral tribunal shall be set up on a case-by-case basis in the following manner. Each Contracting Party shall appoint two arbitrators two months after receiving the request for arbitration. The appointed four arbitrators shall then select a national of a third country who shall be appointed president of the arbitral tribunal after he/she has been approved by both Contracting Parties. The president shall be appointed within two months after the date of appointment of the other four arbitrators.

4. Should these appointments not be made within the deadlines set in paragraph 3 hereof, either Contracting Party may, unless otherwise agreed, request the President of the International Court of Justice to make the necessary appointments. If the President is a national of one or the other Contracting Party or if he/she cannot perform this task for any other reason, the Vice-President of the International Court of Justice shall be requested to make the necessary appointments. If the Vice-President is a national of one or the other Contracting Party or cannot performed this task for any other reason, the senior member of the International Court of Justice who is not a national of either Contracting Party shall be requested to make the necessary appointments.

5. The arbitral tribunal shall decide by the majority of votes. The decisions of the arbitral tribunal shall be final and binding on the Contracting Parties. Each Contracting Party shall cover the costs of its arbitrators and its representation in the arbitral procedure. The remaining costs shall be covered by both Contracting Parties in equal shares.

6. The arbitral tribunal shall define the rules of procedure, taking into consideration the provisions of this Article and the Model Rules on Arbitral Procedure drawn up by the United Nations International Law Commission.

VII TRANSITIONAL PROVISIONS

Article 26

TRANSFER OF THE ENTRY IN THE LAND REGISTER

The transfer of the entry of the rights under the law of property and the law of obligations in the land register relating to the areas exchanged under Article 7 of this Treaty, shall be carried out *ex officio* no later than one year after the final demarcation of the state border.

Article 27

EXEMPTION FROM ADMINISTRATIVE FEES

1. The dealings of natural and legal entities relating to regulating the property relations in the areas exchanged under Article 7 of this Treaty shall be exempt from administrative fees. The scope, method and duration of this exemption shall be regulated by the Contracting Parties in a special agreement.

2. The Contracting Parties shall ensure, free of charge, the exchange of all data, documents and other documentation relating to the areas exchanged under Article 7 of this Treaty no later than one year after the entry into force of this Treaty.

Article 28

CARTOGRAPHIC DOCUMENTATION

Within one year after the entry into force of this Treaty, the Contracting Parties shall make a digital orthophoto map of the state border depiction contained in Annexes II and III, which shall be applied in the event referred to in Article 6, paragraph 4, of this Treaty.

VIII FINAL PROVISIONS

Article 29

ANNEXES

Annex I (a map of the state border at sea at a scale of 1:25,000), Annex II (a verbal description of the course of the state border on land with coordinates), and Annex III (maps nos. 1- 47 at a scale of 1:25,000) shall be integral parts of this Treaty.

Article 30

ENTRY INTO FORCE

1. This Treaty shall be subject to ratification in accordance with the national legislations of the Contracting Parties.

2. This Treaty shall enter into force on the date of the receipt of the last of the notifications by which the Contracting Parties notify each other through diplomatic channels that the internal legal requirements for the entry into force of this Treaty have been fulfilled.

Done at .... on .... in two originals in the Slovenian and Croatian languages, both texts being equally authentic.

FOR THE REPUBLIC OF SLOVENIA FOR THE REPUBLIC OF CROATIA

ANNEX II

The border runs from the confluence of the Krka and the Ledava (point 1) southward for 250 meters (point 2). It then turns westward to the former Mura channel, crosses the Margitmajor–Podturen road (point 3) and continues westward across benchmark 152 (point 4) up to the middle of the course of the Mura (point 5). It continues along the middle of the riverbed to the middle of the railway bridge of the Lendava–Mursko Središče railway line, turning north along the west side of the railway line up to the middle of the spillway, continuing 200 meters and than turning westward at the middle of the road spillway on the Lendava–Mursko Središče road. Midway from the western edge of the road and the left bank of the Mura's tributary (point 6), it turns north and continues to the heel of the Mura dyke.

The border then runs along the heel of the dyke along the Mura up to the tributary of the Mura beneath the Gaberje settlement (point 7). It continues along the south side of the Mura tributary towards benchm.3 (point 8), turns westward along the track to the point that is a t 230 meters from the benchmark (point 9) and turns north-westward again to the heel of the dyke. It then continues its course under the dyke to the Hotiza–Sv. Martin na Muri road, crosses it and turns towards the river at point 10, continuing up to the middle of the course of the Mura. From there, it runs along the middle of the riverbed to point 11 beneath the Gibina settlement, then turning southward to the Gibina–Mursko Središče road. It runs along the north side of the road for approximately 300 meters westward (point 12). It turns south to the first hillsides of the Slovenske Gorice hills through Šafarsko (point 13), then westward, thereby circumventing the Cmager estate, leaving it on the north side of the border (point 14). West of the estate, it turns uphill across the Razkrižje–Banfi road. After 105 meters, it turns north (point 15), continuing west and than again north, circumventing from the north side the Bedekovič estate (point 16). From there, it continues mainly south-westward up to point 17. It then continues across Slovenske Gorice, past Šprinc and Globoka towards the valley of the Presika stream. It runs on the stream, along the east side of the Presika–Štrigova road and the eastern edge of the Madgič-bound track (point 18).

The border then continues southward across benchmark 226 on the Šantavec stream, past the Kocijan estate to the Trnava stream. At point 19, it turns south-westward to the valley of the Zelen stream and then southward. Near benchmark 179.4 it crosses the Mursko Središče–Čakovec railway track. It then runs southward; after 1125 meters (point 20), it turns westward through Trnovščak. It continues southward from Sekelj to the former riverbed of the Drava beneath Majerček (point 21). It then runs along the middle of the former riverbed of the Drava to point 22, Mehika, and from there westward beneath Jurkovec to the heel of the dyke of Lake Ormož (point 23). It continues beneath the northern heel of the dyke to the garden of the lake house (point 24), then to the middle of the lake and, along the middle, to the middle of the Ormož–Virje bridge. On the west side of the bridge, it turns to the right side of the penstock of the Drava, continuing along it up to Meka (point 25) and past benchmark 195.8 (Brezji Otok) westward to point 26, where it turns south and passes Dubrava Križovljanska, running along the hillside above Goričak up to Drenovec (point 27) and past benchmark 319 towards Sv. Mohor (benchmark 365) and from there along the hill crest towards Sv. Florjan (benchmark 349). There, it turns southward and runs westward across Vranika past benchmarks 334, 401, 424, 459, 481 up to Sv. Avguštin (benchmark 503). It continues along Vučje (benchmark 459) and Brezova Gora (benchmark 567) to the valley of the Lipnica stream. It runs on the stream to the Gruškovje settlement (point 28), turningthward beneath the settlement and running on the east side of the Ptuj –Macelj regional road through the underpass of the local road up to the Lipnica stream to point 29, where it turns westward to Maceljska Gora across Debeli Vrh (benchmarks 628, 623, 614, 718) to point 30 at 150 meters from benchmark 714. There, it turns south to the Sotla valley.

The border then runs on the middle of the Sotla River to the Rigonci settlement, except in the area of Rajnkovec, where it turns from the riverbed and continues for some 300 meters along the former riverbed of the Sotla (points 31 and 32). In the area of Lake Vonarsko, the border runs along the south-eastern lake shore, leaving both barriers on the west side of the border. Before the confluence with the Sava beneath the Spodnji Rigonci settlement at benchmark 137.0, the border turns off the riverbed to the right bank of the Sotla and across Nego and Potfrenk entering the middle of the Sava riverbed (point 33). It then continues on the middle of the Sava riverbed to point 34 at 500 meters upstream from benchmark 133.0.

The border then runs westward across Panovje (points 35 and 36) past the Obrežje border crossing point through the Bregana and Obrežje settlements up to the bridge across the Bregana River (point 37) on the Bregana–Obrežje road.

From the west side of the bridge, the border continues on the Bregana River, past Gabrovice, on the streams of Usklopec, Sklednik and Gramski Jarek above the Čedenj village up to point 38, which is at 200 meters from benchmark 648. There, it turns north to point 39, Blatnica, and continues westward across Sinja Reber to the valley of the Piroški stream. It runs across the valley of the stream up to point 40 and across Planinska Gora (benchmark 844) under Goli Vrh (benchmark 707) to Tršljikovina (benchmark 567) to the valley of the Laznica stream and across benchmark 647 to the valley of the

Sušica River (point 41). Here, it turns south to the Strašni Jarek valley up to Luka (point 42) and then westward across Stričanica, benchmark 844 on Opatova Gora and benchmark 955, reaching Japetova Košenica at benchmark 978, leaving the forest road Petričko Selo–Sopotske Planine on the south. It continues along the crest of the Gorjanci hills across benchmark 946 to Trdinov Vrh by crossing the road towards the TV tower above the junction of the Vahta–Trdinov Vrh road, turning across the peak of Trdinov Vrh (1178 metres). It continues westward along the railing of the TV tower between the churches of Sv. Jera and Sv. Ilija. In the Gorjansko ravine it turns south-westward and then southward at Mišino Brdo (point 43) across benchmark 830. At point 44, it turns south-eastward (point 45). From thereon, it runs to the east (point 46) and above Garjevec and beneath Štula across benchmarks 549, 518 and 389, reaching the Bušinja Vas–Radovica road (point 47). It then runs along the north side of the road for 200 meters (point 48), then turning northward and north-eastward above vineyards (point 49) and again northward to Tatinska Draga (point 50). There, it turns to the east and between the Malo Lešče and Goleši Žumberački settlements (points 51, 52) south across the Bušinja Vas–Radovica road (point 53). It continues south-eastward to Smolanovec (benchmark 358). At point 54, it turns north to point 55, then north-eastward (point 56) and finally eastward (point 57). From there, it runs southward to Mrzla Draga (point 58) and along the east side of the settlement Brašljevica northward to point 59 (Kamenica). It runs on the Kamenica stream up to the confluence of the Kolpa and the Kamenica (point 60).

From the confluence, the border runs upstream on the middle of the riverbed of the Kolpa to the confluence of the Kolpa and the Čabranka.

From the confluence of the Kolpa and the Čabranka, the border runs on the middle of the riverbed of the Čabranka to the confluence with its left tributary above Čabar and from there along the ravine beneath Kapišče up to the Pužeti settlement (point 61). There, it turns north across the Novi Kot–Prezid road, runs next to benchmark 882 up to point 62, which is at 100 meters to the west from benchmark 997. It then runs westward across benchmark 934 to point 63. It turns to the south and crosses Vražji Vrtec (benchmark 904) towards Solnički Vrh. It then runs across Beriščkova Draga to the south-west up to point 64, where it turns south along the road towards the Škodovnik hunting lodge and continues through Praprotna Draga (benchmarks 783, 849 and 1028) up to Paravičeva Miza. Then it runs through Jelenja Draga to the south-west to Klana Plateau and across Gomanci (point 65), Gumanška Gora hill up to Boršt (point 66), where it turns south to Vela voda (point 67). It continues across Oštarija (benchmark 712) and Prvonoh to point 68 beneath Liskovec. There, it turns northward to Visoč (benchmark 756) across the Novokračine–Rupa road (benchmark 547) and benchmark 657 to point 69. From there, it runs south-westward to point 70 and then north-westward to Velika reber (benchmark 519), and then again south-westward, across benchmark 619 towards Kališče and to Buričini (benchmark 825). There, it turns to the west across Kovnica (benchmark 901) and Strahovica (benchmark 771) up to Mala Vrata (benchmark 695). It then continues through Jelovščina beneath M. Grižan to point 71, where it turns to the west (point 72) and then south-west across benchmark 603 to Kosmačič (benchmark 736). There, it turns to the south across benchmark 904 up to point 73, where it turns south-westward across point 74 to the Buzet–Vodice road, where it runs to the north or the west of the road up to point 75. Then it runs westward across Stražnica (benchmark 493) and past Mlini beneath Goričica south-westward to Dugo brdo (point 76). From there, the border runs westward across Vele Njive to Klenovica (point 77) and further across benchmarks 363 and 438 up to point 78. There, it turns to the north past point 79 to the Hrvoji settlement (point 80) and along the valley of the Pasjok stream to the Dragonja River (benchmark 118). It then runs for approximately 1,500 meters on the Dragonja to Ferm's mill (point 81), where it turns to the south to the ravine towards Novi Brič. At point 82, it crosses the Brič–Koštabona road and continues westward to point 83. It runs southward for 400 meters to the crest, then turns to the west and after 1,400 meters continues north again to the Dragonja (point 84). It then runs on the middle of the riverbed of the Dragonja to Mlini at the Kaštel border crossing point (point 85).

From there it runs on the middle of the Dragonja up to its outfall into the Adriatic Sea at point A.

COORDINATES – LAND AND ~~SEA~~*

POINT	Y	X	
...			

The points are given in rectangular coordinates of Zone 5 of the Gauss-Krueger projection rounded off to 1 metre

The accuracy of the definition of the position of the points is 10 metres.

---

* Translator's note: crossed out in the original by hand.

Appendix D

©Ministry of Foreign Affairs Republic of Slovenia

POGODBA

MED REPUBLIKO SLOVENIJO IN

REPUBLIKO HRVAŠKO

O SKUPNI DRŽAVNI MEJI

T. Bickl, *The Border Dispute Between Croatia and Slovenia*, Contributions to Political Science,
https://doi.org/10.1007/978-3-030-53333-5

Republika Slovenija in Republika Hrvaška (v nadaljnjem besedilu: pogodbenici) se

v prepričanju, da miroljubno sodelovanje in dobri sosedski odnosi med državama ter njunimi državljani ustrezajo bistvenim interesom obeh držav in da doslej sklenjeni sporazumi ustvarjajo ugodne pogoje za nadaljnji razvoj in krepitev njunih medsebojnih odnosov,

ob spoštovanju načel mednarodnega prava, predvsem nedotakljivosti mednarodnih meja in varstva temeljnih človekovih pravic in svoboščin,

izhajajoč iz Temeljne ustavne listine o samostojnosti in neodvisnosti Republike Slovenije z dne 25. junija 1991 in Ustavne odluke o suverenosti i samostalnosti Republike Hrvatske z dne 25. junija 1991,

ob upoštevanju, da državi nimata ozemeljskih zahtev druga proti drugi,

ob spoštovanju obstoječih državnih meja,

sporazumeta o naslednjem:

I. PREDMET POGODBE

1. člen
PREDMET POGODBE

Predmet te pogodbe je določitev meje na morju in ugotovitev poteka meje na kopnem med pogodbenicama ter načela označevanja, vzdrževanja in obnavljanja državne meje.

2. člen
DEFINICIJA DRŽAVNE MEJE

Državna meja med Republiko Slovenijo in Republiko Hrvaško (v nadaljnjem besedilu: državna meja) je ploskev, ki poteka navpično skozi mejno črto na površini Zemlje in deli ozemlje dveh držav, njun zračni prostor, prostor pod zemeljsko površino, nadzemne in podzemne gradnje in naprave vseh vrst.

Lunina delin ...

II. DOLOČITEV DRŽAVNE MEJE NA MORJU

3. člen
BOČNA MEJA

(1) Državna meja med pogodbenicama na morju se določi kot sledi:
Meja poteka od sredine izliva reke Dragonje v morje od točke A (Y 5.389.794, X 5.038.097; φ 45°28'43,3", λ 13°35'25,7")* in nato v ravni črti do točke B (Y 5.385.011, X 5.041.869; φ 45°30'42,7", λ 13°31'41,3"), ki predstavlja eno četrtino razdalje med najsevernejšo točko Rta Savudrija in Rtom Madona, merjeno od najsevernejše točke Rta Savudrija. Od točke B poteka meja po vzporedniku, ki poteka v ravni črti skozi točko B proti zahodu do točke C (Y 5.365.527, X 5.042.258; φ 45°30'42,7", λ 13°16'43,4"), ki leži na meji, določeni v Pogodbi med Socialistično federativno republiko Jugoslavijo in Republiko Italijo, podpisani v Osimu (Ancona) 10. novembra 1975, razen v predelu stika teritorialnega morja Republike Slovenije z odprtim morjem, ki je opredeljen v 4. členu te pogodbe.

(2) Zemljevid v merilu 1:25000, na katerega se nanaša ta opis, je v prilogi I.

(3) Če se opis državne meje in zemljevid ne ujemata, je odločilen besedni opis.

4. člen
STIK TERITORIALNEGA MORJA REPUBLIKE SLOVENIJE Z ODPRTIM MORJEM

(1) Pogodbenici soglašata, da je morska površina, ki je zamejena s točkami C1 (Y 5.372.959, X 5.042.102; φ 45°30'42,7", λ 13°22'25,9"), C2 (Y 5.367.526, X 5.042.215; φ 45°30'42,7", λ 13°18'15,5"), T5 (Y 5.360.404, X 5.035.862; φ 45°27'12,0", λ 13°12'54,0") in T6 (Y 5.361.377, X 5.031.764; φ 45°25'00,0", λ 13°13'42,9"), odprto morje.

(2) Širina stika teritorialnega morja Republike Slovenije z odprtim morjem je enaka razdalji od točke B iz prvega odstavka 3. člena te pogodbe do Rta Madona.

(3) Zemljevid v merilu 1:25000, na katerega se nanaša ta opis, je v prilogi I.

(4) Če se opis državne meje in zemljevid ne ujemata, je odločilen besedni opis.

(5) Vodni steber pod morsko površino iz prvega odstavka tega člena ne more biti predmet pridobitve suverenih pravic. Pogodbenici se v medsebojnih odnosih vzdržita izvrševanja suverenih pravic na morskem dnu in pripadajočem podzemlju pod morsko površino iz prvega odstavka tega člena.

* Točke so podane v pravokotnih koordinatah 5. cone Gauss-Kruegerjeve projekcije, zaokrožene na 1 meter in v geografskih koordinatah na Besslovem elipsoidu, zaokrožene na 0,1".
Natančnost določitve lege točk je 10 metrov.

5. člen

STIK TERITORIALNEGA MORJA REPUBLIKE HRVAŠKE Z ITALIJANSKO REPUBLIKO

(1) Pogodbenici soglašata, da je morska površina, ki je zamejena s točkami C (Y 5.365.527, X 5.042.258; φ 45°30'42,7", λ 13°16'43,4"), C2 (Y 5.367.526, X 5.042.215; φ 45°30'42,7", λ 13°18'15,5") in T5 (Y 5.360.404, X 5.035.862; φ 45°27'12,0", λ 13°12'54,0"), teritorialno morje Republike Hrvaške.

(2) Zemljevid v merilu 1:25000, na katerega se nanaša ta opis, je v prilogi I.

(3) Če se opis državne meje in zemljevid ne ujemata, je odločilen besedni opis.

III. DRŽAVNA MEJA NA KOPNEM

6. člen

UGOTOVITEV POTEKA DRŽAVNE MEJE

(1) Državna meja na kopnem med Republiko Slovenijo in Republiko Hrvaško je meja med Republiko Slovenijo in Republiko Hrvaško v okviru nekdanje Socialistične federativne republike Jugoslavije in poteka od tromeje državne meje pogodbenic in Republike Madžarske do Jadranskega morja.

(2) Državna meja na kopnem med pogodbenicama je ugotovljena, kot je razvidno iz besednega opisa s koordinatami v prilogi II.

(3) Zemljevidi od št. 1 do št. 47 v merilu 1: 25000, na katere se nanaša besedni opis s koordinatami iz prejšnjega odstavka, so v prilogi III.

(4) Če se opis državne meje in zemljevid ne ujemata, je odločilen zemljevid.

7. člen

ZAMENJAVA POVRŠIN

(1) Pogodbenici potrjujeta, da je zamenjava površin, do katere je prišlo pri sporazumni ugotovitvi poteka državne meje, uravnotežena.

(2) Zamenjava površin ne vpliva na stvarnopravne in obligacijskopravne pravice fizičnih in pravnih oseb nad zemljišči in drugim nepremičnim premoženjem, ki je vključeno v zamenjave. Imetniki stvarnopravnih in obligacijskopravnih pravic to premoženje uporabljajo v skladu s posebnim sporazumom med pogodbenicama.

8. člen
OZNAČITEV POTEKA DRŽAVNE MEJE

(1) Potek državne meje na kopnem označijo skupni organi, ustanovljeni s to pogodbo, in na način, definiran z navodili za delo mešanih tehničnih skupin.

(2) Pogodbenici v roku petih let od dneva uveljavitve te pogodbe opravita izmero, označevanje in zaznamovanje državne meje.

9. člen
NAČELA OZNAČEVANJA POTEKA DRŽAVNE MEJE

(1) Označevanje državne meje v naravi se opravi z mejnimi oznakami neposredno na mejni črti ali posredno na naslednji način:
a) enkratno – neposredno na mejni črti ali izmenično na obeh straneh ob cestah, kanalih in vodotokih na skupni državni meji;
b) dvakratno – na začetku in na koncu cest, kanalov in vodotokov na skupni državni meji ter na mestih, na katerih zaradi konfiguracije terena ni mogoče postaviti oznak neposredno na mejni črti;
c) trikratno – v primerih, ko dvakratne oznake meje ne zadoščajo za jasno označitev poteka mejne črte.

(2) Podrobnejše določbe o označevanju so določene v skladu z navodili iz prvega odstavka 8. člena te pogodbe.

10. člen
VZDRŽEVANJE IN OBNAVLJANJE DRŽAVNE MEJE

(1) Pogodbenici se zavezujeta, da bosta po označitvi državne meje v naravi redno opravljali pregled, vzdrževanje in obnavljanje mejnih oznak v skladu z navodili iz prvega odstavka 8. člena te pogodbe.

(2) Pogodbenici najmanj vsakih pet let skupaj opraviti pregled stanja mejne črte in mejnih oznak ter po potrebi obnoviti ali dopolniti označitev državne meje. Doba petih let se računa od dneva začetka zadnjega skupnega obnavljanja.

11. člen
NESPREMENLJIVOST POTEKA DRŽAVNE MEJE

Ugotovljena mejna črta se ne spremeni, tudi če pride do sprememb v poteku poti, kanalov ali vodotokov na skupni državni meji.

12. člen
ENOTNOST MEJNIH OZNAK

Potek državne meje bo vedno označen enotno in nedvoumno. Mejna črta in pas ob njej se redno vzdržuje in obnavlja. Vse izvršene zamenjave mejnih oznak in opravljena dela se takoj vnesejo v dokumentacijo o meji.

13. člen
PAS OB MEJNI ČRTI

(1) Pas ob mejni črti je območje ob mejni črti v širini največ 1,5 metra na vsaki strani mejne črte.

(2) Pogodbenici pas ob mejni črti redno čistita in vzdržujeta v skladu z navodili iz prvega odstavka 8. člena te pogodbe.

14. člen
STROŠKI

Pogodbenici zagotovita finančna sredstva za označevanje, vzdrževanje in obnavljanje državne meje. Pri tem pogodbenici izhajata iz načela, da vsaka stran opravi približno enako delo in da vsaka pogodbenica nosi enake stroške.

15. člen
OBVEZNOSTI LASTNIKOV, UPORABNIKOV, UPRAVLJALCEV IN DRUGIH IMETNIKOV STVARNOPRAVNIH IN OBLIGACIJSKOPRAVNIH PRAVIC

(1) Lastniki, uporabniki in upravljavci ter drugi imetniki stvarnopravnih in obligacijskopravnih pravic na zemljiščih, objektih in napravah, ki se nahajajo na državni meji ali v njeni bližini, so dolžni dopustiti vsa dela in ukrepe, ki so potrebni za označitev, izmero, vzdrževanje, čiščenje in obnavljanje državne meje, kot tudi dostop oseb, ki opravljajo ta dela. Pri opravljanju teh del je treba upoštevati upravičene interese lastnikov, uporabnikov in upravljavcev ter drugih imetnikov stvarnopravnih in obligacijskopravnih pravic, ki morajo biti o začetku del vnaprej obveščeni.

(2) Pri opravljanju del iz prvega odstavka tega člena, kot tudi pri dostopu ali dovozu na zemljišče, k objektom in napravam, je treba spoštovati notranjo zakonodajo tiste pogodbenice, na ozemlju katere se opravljajo dela.

16. člen
POVRAČILO ŠKODE

Škodo, ki nastane pri opravljanju del iz prvega odstavka 15. člena te pogodbe, povrne tista pogodbenica, na ozemlju katere se je zgodila. Pri uveljavljanju zahtevkov za odškodnino se uporablja notranja zakonodaja tiste pogodbenice, na ozemlju katere je nastala škoda.

17. člen
TROMEJNA TOČKA

Dela v zvezi označevanjem, vzdrževanjem, čiščenjem in obnavljanjem tromejne točke se lahko opravijo le z medsebojnim sporazumom vseh treh držav.

18. člen
VARSTVO OZNAK

Pogodbenici zagotavljata varstvo mejnih oznak, geodetskih oznak in drugih naprav, ki služijo za označitev državne meje, pred poškodovanjem, uničenjem, neupravičeno premestitvijo in uporabo, ki ni v skladu z njihovim namenom.

IV. POVEZANI REŽIMI

19. člen
POSEBNI REŽIMI IN UKREPI NA OBMEJNEM OBMOČJU

(1) O posebnih režimih in ukrepih na obmejnem območju, kot so na primer uporaba prometnih povezav za potrebe prebivalcev in organov obeh pogodbenic in druga vprašanja, ki se pojavijo kot posledica ugotovljenega poteka državne meje, pogodbenici skleneta posebne sporazume.

(2) Pogodbenici se zavezujeta, da bosta vzdolž cele državne meje, še posebej pa na zaščitenih območjih, kot sta na primer Krajinski park Sečovlje, Park prirode Žumberak – Samoborsko gorje in drugi, ohranili vsaj dosedanji nivo varstva narave in nadalje razvijali medsebojno sodelovanje. Vzdolž cele državne meje, še posebej pa na območjih, predvidenih za razvoj turizma, pogodbenici zagotovita okoljevarstveni režim v skladu z najvišjimi standardi varstva okolja Evropske unije.

(3) Pogodbenici se zavezujeta, da bosta druga drugi zagotovili izkoriščanje vodnih virov na obmejnem območju vsaj v dosedanjem obsegu za 30 let od dneva uveljavitve te pogodbe. O tem pogodbenici skleneta poseben sporazum v roku enega leta od dneva uveljavitve te pogodbe.

20. člen
UGODNOSTI PREBIVALCEV ZASELKOV MLINI-ŠKRILE, BUŽINI IN ŠKODELIN

Poleg ugodnosti, ki jih za obmejno prebivalstvo predvidevajo že sklenjeni sporazumi med pogodbenicama, imajo osebe, ki imajo na dan podpisa te pogodbe stalno bivališče v zaselkih Mlini-Škrile, Bužini in Škodelin, tudi:

a) pravico pri vrnitvi z območja sosednje države brez plačila carine in drugih uvoznih dajatev vnesti blago take vrste in količine, ki je primerno za osebno uporabo in za uporabo članov njihovega gospodinjstva. O tem pogodbenici skleneta poseben izvedbeni sporazum v roku šestih mesecev od dneva uveljavitve te pogodbe;

b) pravico do pridobitve državljanstva Republike Slovenije.

V. SKUPNI ORGANI

21. člen
STALNA SLOVENSKO-HRVAŠKA KOMISIJA ZA DRŽAVNO MEJO

(1) Za izvajanje te pogodbe pogodbenici ustanovita Stalno slovensko-hrvaško komisijo za državno mejo (v nadaljnjem besedilu: komisija).

(2) Komisija je sestavljena iz delegacije Republike Slovenije in delegacije Republike Hrvaške. Vsaka pogodbenica imenuje v svoj del komisije predsednika in pet članov. O imenovanju in razrešitvi predsednikov in članov komisije se pogodbenici obvestita po diplomatski poti. O spremembah v sestavi delegacij se predsednika pisno obvestita.

(3) Vsaka delegacija lahko v svoje delo po potrebi vključi eksperte in pomožno osebje.

(4) Pogodbenici krijeta stroške svoje delegacije v komisiji.

22. člen
NALOGE IN NAČIN DELA KOMISIJE

(1) Komisija ima naslednje naloge:

a) odloča o načinu označevanja mejne črte v naravi in sprejema navodila za delo mešanih tehničnih skupin;
b) organizira in nadzira označevanje, vzdrževanje, čiščenje in obnavljanje celotne mejne črte v naravi;
c) izdeluje nove in dopolnilne dokumente o meji ter vnaša nove podatke v veljavne dokumente o meji;
d) če smatra za potrebno, predlaga popravek državne meje.

(2) Komisija odloča soglasno. Če komisija ne more sprejeti odločitve, se vprašanje predloži v reševanje vladama pogodbenic.

(3) Način dela komisije se podrobneje določi s poslovnikom.

23. člen
MEŠANE TEHNIČNE SKUPINE

Za opravljanje določenih del na državni meji komisija ustanovi mešane tehnične skupine. Njihovo število in sestava se določi glede na obseg in vrsto dela, ki ga je treba opraviti.

24. člen
ODSTOPANJA

Z namenom končne označitve poteka državne meje na kraju samem se komisija lahko oddalji do 50 metrov od črte, določene s to pogodbo, z namenom prilagoditve državne meje krajevnim geografskim in gospodarskim razmeram. Pri tem ne sme uvrstiti pod jurisdikcijo države, katere jurisdikcija ne izhaja iz razmejitve, določene in ugotovljene s to pogodbo, nobene pomembne ceste ali železniške proge, pomembnega oskrbovalnega objekta za vodo ali električno energijo in objektov zgodovinskega ali kulturnega pomena.

VI. REŠEVANJE SPOROV MED POGODBENICAMA

25. člen

(1) Vsi spori, ki lahko nastanejo med pogodbenicama v zvezi z razlago in uporabo te pogodbe, se rešujejo s pogajanji v skladu z načelom dobrih sosedskih odnosov.

(2) Če pogodbenici ne moreta doseči dogovora v šestih mesecih od dneva prejema pobude za pogajanja, se spor na zahtevo ene od pogodbenic predloži v arbitražno reševanje.

(3) Arbitražni tribunal se ustanovi za vsak primer posebej na naslednji način. V dveh mesecih od prejema zahteve za arbitražo imenuje vsaka pogodbenica dva arbitra. Imenovani štirje arbitri nato izberejo državljana tretje države, ki se po odobritvi obeh pogodbenic imenuje za predsednika arbitražnega tribunala. Predsednik se imenuje v dveh mesecih od dneva, ko so bili imenovani ostali štirje arbitri.

(4) Če potrebna imenovanja niso opravljena v rokih, določenih v tretjem odstavku tega člena, lahko ena od pogodbenic, če ni dogovorjeno drugače, zaprosi predsednika Meddržavnega sodišča, da opravi potrebna imenovanja. Če je predsednik državljan ene ali druge pogodbenice ali če iz kakršnega koli drugega razloga ne more opraviti omenjene naloge, se zaprosi podpredsednika Meddržavnega sodišča, da opravi potrebna imenovanja. Če je podpredsednik državljan ene ali druge pogodbenice ali če zaradi kakršnega koli drugega razloga ne more opraviti omenjene naloge, se zaprosi najstarejšega člana Meddržavnega

sodišča, ki ni državljan ene ali druge pogodbenice, da opravi potrebna imenovanja.

(5) Arbitražni tribunal odloča z večino glasov. Odločitve arbitražnega tribunala so za pogodbenici dokončne in zavezujoče. Vsaka pogodbenica krije stroške svojih arbitrov in svojega zastopanja v arbitražnem postopku. Preostale stroške krijeta pogodbenici v enakih delih.

(6) Arbitražni tribunal določi pravila postopka ob upoštevanju določb tega člena in Modelnih pravil arbitražnega postopka, ki jih je izdelala Komisija za mednarodno pravo Organizacije Združenih narodov.

VII. PREHODNE DOLOČBE

26. člen
PRENOS VPISA V ZEMLJIŠKO KNJIGO

Prenos vpisa stvarnopravnih in obligacijskopravnih pravic v zemljiško knjigo v zvezi s površinami, zamenjanimi po 7. členu te pogodbe, se opravi po uradni dolžnosti najkasneje v enem letu od dokončne označitve državne meje.

27. člen
OPROSTITEV UPRAVNIH TAKS

(1) Opravila fizičnih in pravnih oseb v zvezi z ureditvijo premoženjskopravnih odnosov na površinah, zamenjanih po 7. členu te pogodbe, so prosta upravnih taks. Obseg, način in čas trajanja te oprostitve pogodbenici uredita s posebnim sporazumom.

(2) Pogodbenici najkasneje v enem letu od začetka veljavnosti te pogodbe zagotovita brezplačno izmenjavo vseh podatkov, dokumentov in ostale dokumentacije, ki se nanaša na površine, zamenjane po 7. členu te pogodbe.

28. člen
KARTOGRAFSKA DOKUMENTACIJA

Pogodbenici v enem letu po začetku veljavnosti te pogodbe izdelata prikaz državne meje, vsebovan v prilogah II in III, v digitalnem orto foto načrtu, ki se uporablja v primeru iz četrtega odstavka 6. člena tega pogodbe.

VIII. KONČNE DOLOČBE

29. člen
PRILOGE

Priloga I (zemljevid državne meje na morju v merilu 1: 25000), priloga II (besedni opis poteka državne meje na kopnem s koordinatami) in priloga III (zemljevidi od št. 1 do št. 47 v merilu 1: 25000) so sestavni del te pogodbe.

30. člen
ZAČETEK VELJAVNOSTI

(1) To pogodbo je treba ratificirati v skladu z notranjo zakonodajo pogodbenic.

(2) Ta pogodba začne veljati z dnem prejema zadnjega obvestila, s katerim pogodbenici po diplomatski poti obvestita druga drugo, da so izpolnjeni notranjepravni pogoji za začetek veljavnosti te pogodbe.

Sestavljeno v .... dne .... v dveh izvirnikih v slovenskem in hrvaškem jeziku, pri čemer sta obe besedili enako verodostojni.

ZA REPUBLIKO SLOVENIJO ZA REPUBLIKO HRVAŠKO

The manufacturer's authorised representative in the EU is Springer
Nature Customer Service Centre GmbH, Europaplatz 3, 69115 Heidelberg,
Germany. If you have any concerns regarding our products, please
contact ProductSafety@springernature.com

Printed and bound by CPI Group (UK) Ltd, Croydon, CR0 4YY
30/09/2026
02225689-0015